RAOUL WALLENBERG

Ingrid Carlberg

RAOUL WALLENBERG
The Biography

With an Introduction by Kofi A. Annan

Translated from the Swedish by
Ebba Segerberg

MACLEHOSE PRESS
QUERCUS · LONDON

First published in the Swedish language as *Det står ett rum här och väntar på dig . . . : Berättelsen om Raoul Wallenberg* by Norstedts, Stockholm in 2012
First published in Great Britain in 2016 by Editions Limited

MacLehose Press
an imprint of Quercus Editions Limited
Carmelite House
50 Victoria Embankment
London EC4Y 0DZ

AN HACHETTE UK COMPANY

Part of the cost of this translation has been defrayed by a subsidy from the Swedish Arts Council, gratefully acknowledged.

ISBN (HB) 978 085705 328 2
ISBN (TPB) 978 085705 329 9
ISBN (Ebook) 978 184866 595 8

10 9 8 7 6 5 4 3 2 1

Designed and typeset in Minion by Libanus Press Ltd, Marlborough
Printed and bound in Great Britain by Clays Ltd, St Ives plc

To my parents, Sonja and Per Carlberg

In this narrative of Raoul Wallenberg's life and destiny I have taken great care to adhere with absolute fidelity to the facts. There are no invented dialogues, and I have neither added fabricated scenes and details nor made any ungrounded assumptions about individuals' motives or emotions.

The Swedish edition of this book was accompanied by 1,705 footnotes. In this shortened English-language edition those detailed references have been published online at www.maclehosepress.com/wallenbergnotes. Any reader who is interested in locating specific information or references for any passages in this book is welcome to consult the website, or to contact me directly at www.ingridcarlberg.se

INGRID CARLBERG

Be a door half-open
That leads to a place for all

– TOMAS TRANSTRÖMER

CONTENTS

PART III: WHAT DETERMINES A PERSON'S FATE?

LIST OF ILLUSTRATIONS

INTRODUCTION BY KOFI A. ANNAN

*Chair of the Kofi Annan Foundation, Nobel Peace Laureate and
Former Secretary-General of the United Nations (1997–2006)*

Then they came for the Jews, and I did not speak out –
Because I was not a Jew

Then they came for me – and there was no-one left to speak for me.

These are the last lines of a famous poem by Michael Niemöller, which has
moved many of us to ask the most searching questions of ourselves.

Some individuals, however, not only spoke out but acted on their beliefs.

When Raoul Wallenberg left his native country of Sweden in July 1944 to
pursue a temporary diplomatic assignment in Budapest, he was thirty-two
years old and a relatively unknown Stockholm businessman. Those who knew
him appreciated his creativity, his sense of humour, his unceasing energy and
his superb organisational abilities. However, none surely imagined that he
would become an international hero.

Today he is honoured around the world for his courage and his historic
deeds, because his actions in Budapest in the autumn of 1944 saved the lives
of thousands of Hungarian Jews.

This is why Wallenberg is such an important figure for us all, not least
today, when intolerance is once again casting its long shadow across the
world. He demonstrated that everyone – regardless of position and ability –
can make a difference. He showed us that the struggle for human equality
cannot be left to governments alone, or political theory. He understood that it
is an individual responsibility and acted accordingly.

Unsatisfied with beautiful words or gestures, he sought concrete results, achieved by organisation and cunning. Where others retreated before the impossible, he saw a challenge and sprang into action. He responded to the Nazi bureaucratic killing machine by forming one of the Second World War's most effective rescue organisations.

By the end of 1944, when the bloody anarchy of terror had paralysed Budapest, Raoul Wallenberg was employing hundreds of people in various office locations, delivering a wide range of services, from shelter, daily food rations and medical care to protective documents and security patrols. Raoul Wallenberg's title and position as a Swedish diplomat were clearly important, but it was his personal authority, energy and initiative that made the difference. He was not always successful in his rescue efforts, but he never stopped trying.

In January 1945, the Red Army reached Budapest and Raoul Wallenberg voluntarily sought contact with the Soviet leadership. He wanted to suggest a collaborative approach to saving the Budapest Jews and providing post-war aid. They responded by arresting and imprisoning him in the Lubyanka prison in Moscow.

He would never see his homeland again. The man who challenged one of the worst regimes in history, the German Nazi state, fell victim to another, Stalin's Soviet Union. At the end, when he needed help there was no-one to speak out and act to free him.

This award-winning biography presents for the first time the complete story of Raoul Wallenberg – his life leading up to 1944, his activities in Budapest, and the tragic mystery of his fate that remains unresolved to this day. It is absorbing reading. Ingrid Carlberg's meticulous research brings the period to life and deepens our understanding of the man and his achievements.

In 1981, the United States named Raoul Wallenberg its second honorary citizen, after Sir Winston Churchill. He is also an honorary citizen of Israel, Canada and Australia. Named "Righteous Among Nations" by the state of Israel, in the summer of 2014 he was awarded the U.S. Congressional Gold Medal for his heroic conduct during the Holocaust.

Raoul Wallenberg has deservedly received his share of international recognition. But it is imperative not to reduce him to the abstract glory of awards and honours. He himself would never have felt comfortable in the role of a hero. The best way to honour him is to remember him as a fellow human being who, in one of the darkest periods of history, found the inner strength and courage to act and save others, oblivious to the risk to his own life. Raoul's example should continue to inspire us and future generations.

Although the Universal Declaration of Human Rights was born out of the horror of the war, Raoul already acted in the spirit of its first article: "All human beings are born free and equal in dignity . . . and shall act towards one another in a spirit of brotherhood."

We must remember that genocide begins with the humiliation of one man, not because of what he has done, but because of who he is. Let Raoul's example also guide us in our daily lives and help us to stand up against injustice in all its forms. Wherever individuals are shunned, humiliated or hurt because they are different, scapegoated at work, bullied at school, or vilified in cyberspace, let us never be passive by-standers.

Raoul Wallenberg was one of the most inspiring figures of the twentieth century. This is his story.

KOFI A. ANNAN
December 2015

PROLOGUE

Djursholm, autumn 2009

We have spoken about the tin soldiers several times and now the boxes have arrived. Raoul Wallenberg's half-sister Nina Lagergren sounds excited when I call. Assisted by a great-grandchild, she has arranged them on a shelf in her basement: the hand-painted soldiers, standard bearers and musicians from the toy manufacturer E. Heinrichsen in Nuremberg.

Nina remembers the delicate tin figures from Raoul's boyhood room on Riddargatan in Stockholm in the 1920s. Her brother, older by nine years, had inherited them from his father who died before Raoul was born. The two thousand pieces were packed in eighty-five oval wooden boxes. They took up almost an entire cupboard.

"You have to come out here and have a look," Nina says.

A few days later I drive over to Djursholm. Nina Lagergren opens the door wearing her bluest jacket and sunniest smile. I take off my coat and cast a glance at the collection of paintings on the wall. There are many framed postage stamps with her brother's portrait. There is the certificate from 1981 when Raoul Wallenberg was granted honorary United States citizenship, the first person to be so honoured since Winston Churchill. And there, of course, is one of the thousands of "protective passports", known as Schutzpässe, from Budapest in the autumn of 1944.

This particular passport is dated August 20, 1944. It was a Sunday and Raoul Wallenberg was at his office on Gellért Hill in Budapest, sifting through piles of applications from desperate Hungarian Jews. That day he took yet another pre-printed cream-coloured document and had it issued to the fourteen-year-old

Judith Kopstein. The girl looks grim in the black-and-white photograph that has been stamped by the Swedish legation. This passport probably saved Judith Kopstein's life. I have found her name among lists of Holocaust survivors. But unfortunately nothing since.*

Nina says she does not know what happened to her.

The stairs to the basement are narrow and winding. We have to steady ourselves against the walls in order to get down in one piece. I automatically head towards the boiler room. This is where Nina keeps her Raoul chest as well as placards from countless protests outside the Soviet Embassy in Stockholm. The chest stirs up deep emotions. It was there that she placed the wooden box with Raoul's possessions that Nina and her siblings were given during their disturbing visit to Moscow in 1989.

After a forty-five-year silence, officials in the Soviet Union, clearly affected by glasnost giddiness, invited Nina and her brother Guy von Dardel† to attend a historic meeting with the K.G.B. Among other things, they were shown Raoul's registration card, which was issued after his arrival in the Lubyanka prison in Moscow on February 6, 1945. In the middle of the meeting, the vice chairman of the K.G.B. stood up and, to their shock, gave them the box. There was their elder brother's diplomatic passport, his pocket diary from 1944, his address book and a relatively large amount of cash in Swiss francs and the Hungarian war currency, pengő. So, a collection of his possessions, just no credible answer as to what had really happened.

Nina Lagergren is almost ninety years old. She is still waiting, just like the rest of the family. Now she turns the key to a storage space. She waves me over.

There is not space for all of Raoul's tin soldiers, but the military array is nonetheless impressive. Colourful miniature warriors ready for attack. There are feather hats and antique muskets, cannons, drums and trumpets.

Some time during the 1970s, Raoul's mother, Maj von Dardel, packed his tin soldiers into two large boxes and deposited them at the Nordic Museum in Stockholm. But the '70s were a time when questions about Raoul Wallenberg

* We eventually tracked down Judith – now Weiszmann by marriage – in Winnipeg, Canada in 2013. She died in 2014.

† The half-brother of Raoul Wallenberg, who died on August 28, 2009, two days after his ninetieth birthday.

were mostly met with silence in Soviet-cowed Sweden. The boxes were carried down to the storage area in the museum's so-called garden level. And there they remained. Decades went by and no-one knew what had happened to the toy soldiers. Until now.

Staff at the museum contacted Nina Lagergren a couple of months ago. They were sorting through old items left in storage and came across Maj von Dardel's boxes. Now they wanted to get rid of them, unless the family was interested in donating them.

Nina lifts a little soldier in a red coat, his rifle raised to his shoulder. She looks lovingly at him and I suspect that she feels the same way I do, that it was a little sad that the museum did not care about the collection. But she would never say anything like this.

"So you did not want to give them the tin soldiers?" I ask, tentatively.

Nina Lagergren looks at me with dismay.

"But how could I do that? They aren't mine. They are Raoul's."

PART I

WHAT MAKES A PERSON?

CHAPTER 1

A Fragile Happiness

Sorrow and joy walk hand in hand, or so is the claim of a melancholy seventeenth-century Nordic hymn. In the spring and autumn of 1912, the truth behind these words would become painfully evident to the newly married Maj Wallenberg.

She had recently experienced what, to that point, had been the happiest day of her life: her wedding to the 23-year-old sub-lieutenant of the navy, Raoul Oscar Wallenberg.* The wedding in Jacobs kyrka on September 27, 1911 had been celebrated with the appropriate pomp and circumstance: Mendelssohn's "Wedding March" and the bridal chorus from Wagner's "Lohengrin". Afterwards the guests were served a nine-course dinner at Stockholm's Grand Hôtel. They dined on Sole Walewska, partridge, and the Russian tsar's favourite champagne, Charles Heidsieck. The wine list was more or less identical with that of the Nobel banquet dinner held several months later.

Raoul Oscar Wallenberg and Maj Wising had become acquainted two years earlier. Maj was a school friend of Sonja Wallenberg, Raoul Oscar's cousin, and all three were members of the same sports club, which organised Sunday afternoon hikes in the area around Stockholm. After a few months of increasingly frequent meetings with Maj, Raoul Oscar was unable to conceal his feelings. "To my chagrin, I must admit that I have gone and fallen in love," he wrote to his father, Gustaf Wallenberg, from the ship *H.M. Göta* in the spring of 1910.

So strong were his feelings that Raoul Oscar felt compelled to propose first and ask his father's permission later. He agonised over this, especially as his

---

* Raoul Wallenberg shared his name with his father. For the purposes of clarity here our subject's father is referred to as Raoul Oscar Wallenberg throughout.

father had lately called him in for a talk on the topic of women. Gustaf warned his son about "the sly sirens who seek to snare young men in their traps".

Raoul Oscar's unusual course of action did, however, also have a practical explanation. For the past few years, his parents had lived in Japan, where Gustaf was Sweden's diplomatic envoy. In the letter to his father, Raoul Oscar revealed that he had proposed in March 1910, two days before he left with the navy on the *H.M. Göta*. To his great relief, the answer was yes. He could now proudly write to his parents that his fiancée, Maj Wising, was from a good family, the youngest daughter of the famous neurologist, Per Wising, and his wife Sophie.

Raoul described Maj as a "strong and healthy and sturdy girl who does not hesitate to walk some thirty kilometres in an afternoon". His father was informed that she was slender and shapely and had dainty feet but that her hands were not quite as well formed as those of Raoul Oscar's own mother, Annie Wallenberg. Maj Wising, Raoul Oscar wrote, was often gay and bubbly but at the same time also a serious and unusually ambitious young woman. For example, she had recently graduated from Sofie Almqvist's private school. This was a singular achievement at the beginning of the twentieth century: the public grammar schools did not admit girls until 1927.

For his part, Raoul Oscar had sailed through the officer's examination at the Naval Academy – an obligatory part of the education of men in the Wallenberg family – with impressive grades. He now progressed in his career, although the intention had never been that he would remain in the navy.

His father Gustaf was the son of the late André Oscar Wallenberg, a well-known naval officer, politician and banker who, in 1856, founded the Stockholms Enskilda Bank. André Oscar had been a demanding father who liked to entertain his children (twenty by three different mothers) with stories of his own and his ancestors' achievements. Duty and renunciation were the guiding principles of the life philosophy that he strove to pass on to his progeny. André Oscar had therefore created a tough educational programme for his sons, which included foreign boarding schools from a young age, capped with a degree from the Naval Academy. This tradition was now passed down to the next generation.

The young Raoul Oscar was one of the top students of his year. He had already far surpassed his father. In the Wallenberg clan "Rulle", as he was called, was held in high regard. He was the eldest of André Oscar's grand-children, and seen as amiable, wise and expressive. He was the subject of great expectations.

But fate had something different in store.

*

At the time of Raoul Oscar and Maj's wedding in September 1911, the Wallen-bergs were already on their way to becoming the most influential dynasty in the Swedish business world. The industrial revolution had given significant momentum to the Swedish banking industry. Demand for business credit was great and around the turn of the century new banks were springing up like mushrooms.

Within this general banking boom, it was the success story of Stockholms Enskilda Bank (S.E.B.) that was seen as the most impressive. Its transform-ation from threatened upstart in the 1870s and '80s to one of Sweden's three most dominant commercial banks twenty years later demanded respect.

After André Oscar's death in 1886, responsibility for the family business and fortune naturally fell to the older Wallenberg sons – Knut, Gustaf and Marcus. André Oscar had indicated that he saw Knut and then Marcus – Knut's junior by eleven years – as the natural leaders. Perhaps it was this atti-tude towards Gustaf that determined the fate that would befall the branch of the family into which Raoul Wallenberg would be born.

As befitted his age and authority, Knut Wallenberg assumed the position of bank president. But very soon the enterprising Marcus was knocking on his door, eager to take the place at Knut's side that he felt suited him more than it did the the middle brother Gustaf. In contrast to Gustaf, Marcus had left the navy almost immediately after graduation to study law in Uppsala. Marcus was ambitious and stubborn and barely concealed that he was only biding his time before he received a prominent position at the bank.

Knut Wallenberg had shown himself to be both an imposing and an outward-looking leader, but he lacked a financial and legal education. Accordingly, in 1890 he recruited Marcus to the bank as legal ombudsman, despite the fact that his younger brother had not yet completed the usual judicial training. Two years later, Marcus Wallenberg was named vice president and second in command at Enskilda Bank.

By this point Marcus, who had long felt that Gustaf lacked the necessary ability, decided that he should be kept at arm's length from the day-to-day management of the bank.

The relationship between Marcus and Gustaf had never been good, even though they had spent much of their childhood in each other's company. Gustaf and Marcus were twelve and eleven when – in accordance with André Oscar's programme – they were sent to a German boarding school for several years in order to gain a Lutheran, character-building education. André Oscar wanted his sons to speak German, English and French fluently, to learn to obey the dictates of duty and to become emotionally toughened. The boys' parents only answered each fourth letter so as not to spoil them. Homesickness was held to be a sign of weakness.

And yet, even in this difficult context, the brothers appear not to have grown close. In his biography of Marcus Wallenberg, Torsten Gårdlund describes the relationship between the brothers as friendly, but "not exactly warm", during their boyhood.

When Gustaf – around the time of his father's death – failed miserably in a bold business venture in the United States, Marcus judged him harshly. In his eyes, Gustaf lacked both common sense and financial judgement, which for Marcus Wallenberg were serious character flaws. Knut partly shared this critical view, but wanted to make Gustaf a managing director at the bank anyway. Marcus was unable to accept this. He wrote a memorandum detailing Gustaf's failings and convinced Knut to abandon his plans.

As a result, Gustaf never rose further than to a mid-level management position at the family bank and eventually, in 1902, he chose to leave and find his own way. In announcing his decision to leave the board of Enskilda Bank, Gustaf wrote, "My entire being goes in another direction than that of a banker."

In Sweden at the time it was not a big step to go from business to the Foreign Ministry. Since the turn of the century, Gustaf Wallenberg had had a seat in the second chamber of the parliament as a representative for Stockholm and the Liberal Party. After the dissolution of the union with Norway, he was appointed Sweden's first envoy to East Asia, resident in Tokyo. He moved to Japan in 1906 with his wife and two children. His eighteen-year-old son Raoul

Oscar remained in Stockholm with his grandmother.

When the family came together for Raoul Oscar's wedding in September 1911, Marcus had succeeded Knut as president of Enskilda Bank. Knut was approaching sixty years of age and – in contrast to his brother – was no workhorse. For quite a while he had felt that hunting grouse and making recreational jaunts to the Riviera were more entertaining occupations than toiling away at the bank.

While Marcus Wallenberg had achieved a long-held dream, Gustaf was struggling again. In Japan he was treated like a king but his somewhat too impulsive ideas for increasing Swedish trade with the East had not altogether found favour with the upper levels of the Swedish Foreign Ministry, Utrikes-departementet. There were also mutterings about Gustaf Wallenberg's financial accounts not being in order, and he had just been called in to explain himself.

No doubt he had much on his mind during his son's wedding ceremony.

The newlyweds moved to an apartment on the corner of Grev Turegatan and Linnégatan in the same building as Maj's parents. Per Wising had opened a doctor's clinic there after resigning from his professorship at the Karolinska Institute a couple of years earlier.

The new family began to build a life in a Stockholm that was enjoying a period of economic growth and cultural optimism. Sweden had been one of the world's poorer agrarian societies during the 1800s. Now, in the 1900s, it was in a state of significant change, on its way towards becoming one of the world's most successful industrial nations. The part of the city where Raoul Oscar and his bride settled had undergone a transformation from a quarter of rundown wooden shacks and grazing cows to one of elegant apartment buildings with marble vestibules.

Raoul Oscar and Maj furnished their apartment with large rugs and an ample collection of art nouveau furniture. Raoul Oscar, who had a strong interest in interior design, commissioned a skilled carpenter to construct a dozen rococo chairs for the dining room, and a set of bedroom furniture in Gustavian style, all fashionably lacquered white. On the walls were family portraits and gilded mirrors as well as some of Raoul Oscar's own framed watercolours and oil paintings, among them a large work depicting the

French–British sea battle at Aboukir Bay in 1798.

Raoul Oscar had considerable artistic talent. He kept a sketchbook at hand and often returned from his trips – to Granada, Venice or Västervik – with a painting. In the autumn of 1910 he had been commissioned by Marcus Wallenberg to draw up plans for a mausoleum for the Wallenberg family graveyard at the estate in Malmvik, the family's much-loved summer residence. Malmvik was located on Lovö island outside Stockholm and had just been inherited by Marcus after André Oscar's widow Anna's death. Raoul Oscar took the opportunity to paint some scenes in Malmvik, which he framed and sent to his father in Japan as a Christmas present.

Maj was pregnant. At the same time Raoul Oscar experienced the first symptoms of his disease.

Raoul Oscar had been intending to take Christmas leave from the *H.M.Göta*. But he was instead struck by sudden stomach pains and confined to his sick bed. His fellow crew members had fresh memories of the dysentery epidemic that they had experienced after the fleet had docked in Cherbourg in 1909, but this was to prove more serious.

It was soon clear that the source of Raoul Oscar's troubles was a malignant sarcoma. It was an aggressive form of stomach cancer that the medical establishment of the time was helpless to combat: Maj Wallenberg's young husband had only a few months left to live.

A nurse moved into the apartment at Grev Turegatan but could only partially lessen Raoul Oscar's increasing pain. Day by day the father-to-be became more ill.

Several times during the spring he was visited by his uncle Marcus. They had a good relationship; Raoul Oscar had sometimes visited him during his single years in Stockholm to seek advice about his future plans. The last time they had discussed Raoul Oscar's plans to apply to the Technical Institute, which Marcus had encouraged. He appeared to see a future leader in the young sub lieutenant.

In April 1912, a few days after the sinking of the *Titanic*, Marcus Wallenberg wrote to his brother Gustaf:

Truthfully, you are to be pitied if you lose your excellent boy. It may be a small comfort to you to hear that he has consistently conducted himself as a hero and shown more concern for his nearest than for himself. I have gone to him now and then to distract him with conversation. Sadly one cannot do anything for him. Morphine is now his best friend.

*

Towards the end, Raoul Oscar asked Maj to get him his favourite book, Edmond Rostand's play *Cyrano de Bergerac*. One evening he read the final pages aloud to his wife and wept desperately through Cyrano's farewell to Roxane. He said to Maj: "I will be happy if only little Baby becomes a nice and good and simple person."

On Friday, May 10, 1912, Raoul Oscar Wallenberg died at home. When the pallbearers came they were astonished: "We heard that we were to collect a youth, but this is an old man!" Four days later, on the day that Swedish author August Strindberg died, Raoul Oscar's funeral was held at Skeppsholmen church. His fellow officers accompanied the casket to the Malmvik family estate and carried it in between the Dorian columns of the mausoleum that Raoul Oscar had designed only a few years earlier. The 23-year-old "Rulle" was the first to be laid to rest there.

The concrete steps were covered in wreaths. On the casket itself, his friends laid the Swedish flag and his sabre.

Maj Wallenberg, who was seven months pregnant, turned twenty-one during the final dramatic days of her husband's life. After the funeral she sank into a state of depression. In a desperate letter to her mother-in-law Annie, who had returned to Japan, she wrote that she should have realised that such a "great and complete happiness" as the one she had experienced since she met Raoul Oscar could not last:

> With each passing day life feels harder and this endless emptiness
> and longing grows bigger and bigger. How will this end? [...] Oh,
> Mother, what shall become of our little one? I wonder so if I will
> be up to the challenge of raising the child into a good person. Poor
> thing – to have lost a father.

*

In June 1912, Maj moved to her parents' summer house Kappsta in southern Lidingö just outside Stockholm. The capital city, which was preparing to host the fifth Olympics, was struck by a heatwave, which proved as uncomfortable for heavily pregnant women as it was for athletes.

Maj rented out her apartment. Some of her things were moved over to her new little two-room flat, which connected directly to her parents' home, but had its own entrance. She struggled with the question of what to do with all Raoul Oscar's clothes.

At Kappsta, Maj and the nanny prepared a room on the first floor for "Baby". In the room, they placed a few of the white bedroom chairs from the city and a white wooden bed with pink silk bows. On the walls they hung some of Raoul Oscar's paintings.

Towards the end of July the heat dissipated and was replaced by thunder-showers and a dramatic fall in temperature. After one of her many visits to Malmvik, Maj recorded that a lark family had made their nest at the foot of Raoul Oscar's grave. She articulated her grief in frequent letters to her mother-in-law.

> I find life is so boundlessly difficult at present that I do not know what I can do to forget the horror that has befallen me. Sometimes I imagine that it is impossible for such a thing to happen and I think I hear Raoul's steps as I did last summer when we were so incredibly happy. Oh to be able to conjure forth for one minute what has passed – for ever. How strange life is, composed of such contrasts. One moment there is soaring joy and poetry. The next minute there is the deepest and most intractable sorrow and grief.

Sunday, August 4, was grey, wet, and unseasonably chilly. In the early hours of the morning, in a room on the second floor, Maj Wallenberg gave birth to a little boy: Raoul Gustaf Wallenberg. She managed the birth without chloroform and "heroically chose pain instead ", as her proud father wrote to Gustaf Wallenberg in Japan.

During the birth, the foetal membranes ruptured and formed a caul on the baby's head, which the superstitious claimed was a sign that the newborn would conquer all his future battles. Maj was more pleased that her son was born on a Sunday and not a Friday, for ever a day of sorrow after Raoul Oscar's death. She thought from the start that her son had inherited his father's nose and "rococo" mouth. Although her doctors assured her that this was impossible, Maj would worry for several months that he might also have inherited his disease.

As was the norm in the Wallenberg family, the christening was a grand affair with so many godparents that the clerk did not have room on the four lines reserved for the entry in the registry. Father Gustaf's brothers Knut and Marcus were both named in a long line of godparents, as were Raoul Oscar's cousins: Marcus' oldest children Sonja and Jacob.

Jacob was four years younger than Raoul Oscar and perhaps the cousin who had been closest to him. A few weeks after the christening, he was called in to see his father and Uncle Knut for a serious conversation. They explained that, with Raoul Oscar's death, Jacob was now next in line for a position at the bank. They handed him a prepared letter of resignation and urged him to abandon his naval officer career as soon as he graduated. Instructions that he duly followed.

Maj had decided that no-one else would assume guardianship for her son. She would maintain this role herself until Gustaf Wallenberg returned from Japan. But she asked Marcus to look out for "little Raoul's best interests".

After the christening, calm returned to Kappsta. Maj took on the practical arrangements and was happy to receive a letter from the state informing her that she was entitled to 510 kronor per annum as a widow's pension. She asked Jacob Wallenberg to take Raoul Oscar's clothes and sell them to some of his poorer friends. But other things were harder to be parted from. Among the items she kept was Raoul Oscar's sketchbook from his youth. Alongside the amusing pictures of aunts and uncles and of family apartments there is an impressionistic pencil sketch of some mounted soldiers. The drawing has the title "*La retraite de Moscou*".

*

The dreaded anniversary of their wedding came and went. "Only a year and all this infinite happiness that I experienced at the same time last year is destroyed. But it is true that I must have been too happy with my Raoul. And to think that my beloved joyous and healthy husband now lies cold in his damp and gloomy tomb. Oh terrible and cruel fate," the unhappy Maj wrote to her mother-in-law, or "mother" as she called her. "Mother, forgive me for complaining, but I feel compelled to. It is so very difficult at this time. But do not on this account suppose that I am ungrateful for the little one who is a ray of sunshine in all this misery. When he laughs and looks so incredibly delighted as he does then it is quite contagious."

Back in the city she was still dressed in mourning, but she also wrote to her mother-in-law about delightful walks in Humlegården, about how little Raoul had begun to laugh at his own reflection and about the pretty, well-fed rings of baby fat on his thighs. She told her that the colour of his eyes had now changed and he had become the "only living brown-eyed Wallenberg", just as she had predicted. "Oh mother, how enjoyable it is to care for him," she exclaimed in a letter at the end of October.

But her tribulations were not yet over. One month later, Maj's seventy-year-old father came home from some patient visits feeling unwell. The following day he lay unresponsive with a high fever. The family physician was called in and gave a diagnosis of pneumonia. Within a matter of days Per Wising was dead.

This second loss came as dreadful blow to Maj and she was bedridden for a week. The year 1912 continued as violently as it had begun. The un-imaginable emotional chaos she experienced is articulated in a letter from September 1912: "A thousand hugs from Mother's happy and unhappy Maj."

CHAPTER 2

Two Widows and a Child

The reality to which Maj Wallenberg awakened after her initial period of grief involved practical as well as emotional changes. At this time Sweden was a country where the man was considered both the economic and legal guardian for his wife and children. A married woman was regarded as her husband's subordinate on every level, and married women were not expected to work outside the home unless absolutely necessary. Jobs were regarded as a temporary solution for unmarried women who otherwise had no way to support themselves.

At only twenty-one, Maj Wallenberg was a widow and a single mother, a world away from being the wife of a promising naval officer with a future in one of Sweden's largest commercial banks.

Since she was no longer married she did, however, automatically become the legal guardian of her own child. She could seek employment, enter into contracts and even start a business without a man's co-signature. This is what a widow's "privileges" looked like at the time. But she had her son, whom she wanted to raise herself, not hand over to a nanny. And she had her social position.

The pension that she received after Raoul Oscar's death was the equivalent of just a third of the country's lowest-paid worker's yearly wages. Maj could count on a certain amount of financial support from Raoul's grandfather. But she would need additional revenues.

Maj Wallenberg took an evening course in stenography the year after Raoul Oscar's death, but she abandoned this effort after only a few weeks. She would have needed to achieve a speed of 150 characters a minute to make a living from the role, which in turn demanded a nine-month-long full-time education as well as "exceptionally strong nerves". After twenty hours she complained in a letter to her mother-in-law that she was so tired her entire body was shaking and her heart jumping. She told Annie that Doctor Lamberg had put her on a cream diet and ordered her to rest so that these "symptoms of nerves" did not grow worse.

"No, Mother, I need peaceful work and that is the care of my child (my absolutely primary duty), sewing and reading. For the sake of my little Raoul I cannot run myself down."

Maj moved in with her widowed mother Sophie Wising at Linnégatan 9–11. Little Raoul became the sunshine of their lives. They called him "the comforter".

Maj worried a great deal about his upbringing. She had been lectured on this subject by Raoul Oscar: he wished that she would be strict and demanding towards Baby and teach him the values of "simplicity and hard work". She feared that her child would develop a nervous temperament after all that had occurred. During his tender years, therefore, she tried to maintain a calm environment.

Maj felt it important that her late husband should become a part of Raoul's everyday life from the beginning. She hung a portrait of him above Raoul's bed as well as a painting of two guardian angels, a detail from a watercolour by the nineteenth-century artist Egron Lundgren that Raoul Oscar had copied and given to Maj in 1910. She was successful in her efforts. Every morning the one-year-old Raoul sat up in bed, pointed to the picture of Raoul Oscar and said "Daddy there".

Marcus Wallenberg and his wife Amalia had their hands full with their six children, but they remained attentive towards Maj and their great-nephew. Raoul benefitted from the improvement in his grandfather's relationship with Marcus once Gustaf had left the family bank and resolved his problematic affairs.

Amalia invited Maj and Raoul to Malmvik to mark Raoul Oscar's birthday. For his part, Marcus made sure that the construction of the mausoleum in Malmvik was completed and well maintained, something that meant a great deal to Maj. The child paid regular visits to Marcus. One day in December 1913 Marcus sent his new Fiat "automobile" to fetch Maj and Raoul. He had delayed making this investment longer than most other wealthy

Swedes, so as not to accustom his children to luxury. Marcus had been brought up to value duty and humility and, if he were to have his way, there would be no excesses in the next generation either.

Step by step, Maj started to enjoy being out among other people. She was called in to run a "charity tea" at the Hôtel Royal. At the beginning of 1914 Maj watched Queen Sofia's funeral from the windows of the Royal Court of Justice, with her friend Elsa von Dardel. They had managed to stake out this vantage point with the assistance of Elsa's brother, Fredrik, who worked at the Royal Courts. Perhaps something happened there: several years later, Fredrik von Dardel would assume great importance in Maj Wallenberg's life.

On Raoul's second birthday, August 4, 1914, Germany invaded Belgium after having declared war on France the day before. Sweden immediately declared itself neutral and would maintain this position without much internal political dispute. Nonetheless, the war left its traces on Swedish society. The prices of bread, potatoes and eggs all rose dramatically.

The war brought no significant changes to the lives of Maj and Raoul. They spent their summers at Kappsta, at Malmvik or at the house of Maj's sister Anna, who lived at the Broby estate in Sörmland. Maj's sisters gathered there and Raoul could play with his cousins; above all with Lennart and Anders Hagströmer, who would become his close childhood friends. Another of Maj's sisters was married to the American military attaché in Stockholm, William Colvin. They had two children with whom Raoul could practise English.

Kappsta remained the favoured summer destination. It was an expansive, rocky and forested piece of land with a view of Lilla Värtan strait. Per Wising had built two houses there: a large one of three-hundred square metres and a smaller "Sea Cottage" closer to the water for guests or seasonal employees. Both were built in the Swiss-chalet style with ornately carved verandas and balconies.

Maj and her siblings had stayed at Kappsta from May to September every year since they were little. She continued that tradition now as a single mother. The summer home had everything. There was a sandy croquet and boules court and, down by the smooth cliffs rounding into the water, Wising had built a swimming dock and a bathhouse. But Kappsta also encompassed five hectares of relatively wild terrain – high hilltops and woods filled with lingonberries and blueberries. It was paradise for a little boy.

Maj had decided to make sure Raoul's father's emphasis on "simplicity and hard work" was combined with an independent spirit, so she let her son roam more or less free on the estate. Even as a three-year-old he could play alone wherever he wanted to at Kappsta, climb the hills, ride his wooden horse or "play boat" on the benches. The only thing she forbade him to do was go down to the water, an admonition that, surprisingly enough, he appears to have observed.

Maj sometimes complained that little Raoul was obstinate, even defiant. He could become so angry that he would shake or beat his arms and legs. In these states it was almost impossible to pacify him. It was only when she was back in the city and she could show him Raoul Oscar's guardian angels that Maj could be confident of calming her son.

While Maj's life was dominated by Raoul, she did not lack interest in the drama taking place elsewhere in Europe. The war affected her deeply and, through a friend, she became a member of a chapter of the Red Cross – one focused on providing aid to the war victims. Her first task was to organise bed linens and mattresses. Later, she and her friends were asked to sew various test garments that the Red Cross was planning to use as models for new work clothes.

The Swedish Red Cross also stationed people in regions affected by the war. This group included the teacher and nurse Elsa Brändström who, when her contributions during and after the Great War became known, would become an idol for Maj and her siblings. Maj's sister Sigrid Hagströmer had married into Elsa Brändström's family.

Brändström was living in Saint Petersburg when the war broke out. The 26-year-old obtained papers as a Russian nurse and travelled to Siberia. There, in –40°C temperatures, she battled against typhus, scurvy and frostbite, and saved the lives of many prisoners of war. She was dubbed "The Angel of Siberia" and became a celebrity in Sweden as well as on the continent.

Later on, just before the Second World War broke out, this Swedish nurse started an extensive aid programme for German Jewish refugees in the U.S.A. This time her winning idea was the mass-production of documents that granted immunity. An admiration for Elsa Brändström was inculcated in Raoul and Maj's other children from an early age.

*

In April 1916, when Raoul was almost four years old, he met his grandfather Gustaf for the first time. His grandmother, Annie, had come back from Japan two years earlier, but Gustaf encountered a boy who had developed quickly. Raoul called himself "Wallberg" and often talked about his father with Maj. She would hear him say, "Good night, dear Daddy," before he fell asleep. Raoul also picked flowers for his father and put them in a vase next to his portrait. He dreamed of having his father's sabre when he was older. One day he looked seriously at his mother and said, "Mother, would you be happy if Raoul were to be a little bit like Father when he grew up?"

Maj became more social. There were dances and dinners and, from time to time during the war years, she wrote about evenings at the home of the artist Fritz von Dardel and his family. It was their son, Fredrik, who had captured Maj's interest. The younger brother Nils, who would go on to become one of Sweden's most successful artists, already had connections with Maj's family. Raoul Oscar's sister, Nita, had met Nils von Dardel in Japan during one of the journeys he took to gather inspiration. Nils von Dardel and Nita Wallenberg had fallen passionately in love. But when it became clear to Gustaf Wallenberg that they were thinking of marriage, he promptly put a stop to it. A bohemian artist was not what he had intended for his daughter.

After the end of the war, when Nita had returned home and Gustaf was back in Japan, Marcus Wallenberg had to intervene. Nita Wallenberg and Nils von Dardel were forced apart. "I hope over time that she will learn to forget all about her cubist," Marcus wrote in a letter. She never did.

Increasingly, Raoul began to wonder why, unlike his friends' families, his father was not around. He would sometimes stand beneath his father's photograph and cry, "Raoul doesn't have a father!"

Gustaf Wallenberg began to take a greater interest in Raoul's upbringing. He wrote to Maj and encouraged her to do more to develop his sense of independence. In November 1917 Maj replied with a description of Raoul's day-to-day life that she felt spoke for itself. She told him that Raoul's cousin Anders Hagström came to the house at nine a.m. every day. The boys then went by themselves to Humlegården, where they played until noon, and then they walked home again. Twice each week they went directly from the park to their gymnastics lessons. They had to watch the time themselves and also remember to change into their sporting shoes.

They were five.

Raoul had played with his American cousin Fitz at Kappsta that summer and now Maj decided that he should learn better English. In a letter to her father-in-law she told him that she had hired an English tutor for forty kronor a month to spend two hours a day with him. They went on walks and talked, or she would read him stories in English at home.

That autumn, Marcus Wallenberg asked about plans for Raoul to begin school. He had recommended that Maj allow Raoul to start as early as possible, just as his own sons Jacob and Marcus Jr had. She was not sure. However, Raoul's cousin and playmate Anders Hagströmer, albeit nine months older, was also going to start school the following year.

The winter of 1917–18 was one of the most severe since the 1860s. The harvests had failed and it was difficult to find sufficient food and fuel. At the same time, the Stockholm Stock Exchange reached a historic high. Business from the war made industry boom while common people suffered. It was a time of severe social tensions. The Wallenbergs were among those who had prospered. Before the war, Marcus had quadrupled his fortune in a matter of months, and the years that followed brought an upswing for both the Swedish export industry and for the Swedish banks. In 1915, Enskilda Bank had finally moved their headquarters to new offices at Kungsträdgården 8, in the heart of Stockholm.

Maj Wallenberg stood on the threshold of a significant life change. She had been spending more and more time with Fredrik von Dardel over the past few years and now they had decided to get married. The thirty-year-old Fredrik von Dardel was a clerk at the Svea Court of Appeals and would soon rise to the post of bureau chief at the National Health and Pharmaceutical Board. He belonged to a family of famous artists. His grandfather Fritz von Dardel had been a prominent artist and his younger brother Nils, formerly engaged to Maj's sister-in-law, was already becoming well known. In 1918 he completed "The Dying Dandy", possibly the most famous Swedish painting of the twentieth century.

In his spare time, Fredrik painted too. He saw himself and his wife-to-be as complementary personalities and thought that their differences would ensure their happiness. Where she was extroverted, filled with energy and interested in others, he was somewhat reserved when meeting new people.

The six-year-old Raoul was not entirely delighted at this news. When the banns were read in church for the last time, Fredrik was sick and unable to attend. Maj regretted it, but Raoul said angrily: "What does it matter? He isn't my father and not yours either!"

Maj Wallenberg and Fredrik von Dardel married on Thursday, October 24, 1918. The relationship between Raoul and his stepfather rapidly improved, and in time, Raoul was happy to call him "father".

CHAPTER 3

No Millionaire's Airs

Shortly after their wedding, Fredrik and Maj von Dardel moved into an apartment close to Raoul's cousins Lennart and Anders Hagströmer.

Just as Maj had hoped, Raoul was placed in the same preparatory elementary class as Anders. The two boys were therefore able to continue as before, playing in Humlegården park and walking together to school. In the afternoons they would spend hours poring over their stamp collections.

This friendship with Anders Hagströmer was an additional source of security for Raoul during these years. His home life had changed abruptly. In August 1919, a year after the wedding, Fredrik and Maj von Dardel had a son, Raoul's half-brother Guy von Dardel. And then, in the spring of 1921, Raoul's half-sister Nina was born. Anders Hagströmer would never forget how they would bow down beside her cradle and pretend that she was a princess. But, however delighted Raoul was with his younger siblings, the new family constellation must have presented a challenging transition for the fatherless seven-year-old who, until this point, had been the undisputed centre of attention for his mother Maj and his grandmother Sophie.

Raoul did well in school. In the weeks before he was due to take the entrance exam to Nya Elementarskolan, Maj wrote to her former in-laws and told them that Raoul had good grades – either average or above average in the majority of his subjects. Nya Elementar was the most respected grammar school in Stockholm and seen by parents as ideal preparation for entrance into the social elite. If Raoul was successful, what awaited him were five years of grammar school and then another three years of study for his university entrance examinations.

On May 20, 1921, Anders and Raoul went to the exam together. In the schoolyard they met Anders' friend, Rolf af Klintberg, who was the same age as Raoul. All three of them talked for a while and Rolf liked the new boy. It was the beginning of a friendship that would last all through their school years. More than 120 boys gathered in the school's Great Hall. They would be tested in their abilities to write correctly and neatly, do arithmetic and read aloud with ease. Of these applicants, only half would be admitted.

A week later, the list of successful applicants was posted on a wall at Nya Elementarskolan. All three of the boys were on it and were placed together in one of the two first-year classes. The school year would begin in late August.

The school was a tall four-storey building behind the former market hall at Hötorget. Its situation was the source of unceasing complaints from the teachers. Between the school and the market hall there was an alley that the faculty referred to as "filthy, in both physical and moral terms". From the sheds next to it rose the stench of fish and meat scraps, as well as of rotten vegetables. But all in all, the school was regarded as possibly the most modern of its kind, with a groundbreaking pedagogical approach.

School days began with the principal, Knut Bohlin, leading fifteen minutes of morning prayers in the Great Hall before the first lesson at 8.00 a.m. The days often ended around 2.30 p.m., after five lessons. Before morning recess every day the younger pupils had forty-five minutes of gymnastics. They were divided up according to height and ability, all except those who were felt to be completely lacking in all physical attributes. These were gathered into a separate group for the "weak".

This was typical of the time: the first decades of the twentieth century were a time when racial theories and ideas flourished in Sweden. This was noticeable in the school books that teachers at the Nya Elementar School put in the hands of their students. One can well imagine a nine-year-old reciting aloud the rivers in northern Sweden, followed by the supposed distinguishing characteristics of the Lapps: "of Mongolian origin, short of stature, with wide faces, small, peering eyes and lank, black hair".

Raoul and his classmates learned that the inhabitants of Sudan were called "negroes" and were characterised by a "dark-brown colour, woolly hair, flat noses and thick, jutting lips". According to his schoolbook, these "negroes" were of a "very low educational level" and were "for the most part childlike, cheerful people with a love of decorative objects, but also with a tendency to mendacity and unreliability, and with only extremely basic religious concepts".

Later in life, Raoul Wallenberg would witness at first hand the most sinister manifestation of this mania for racial stereotyping.

Raoul's first years in grammar school coincided with a deep economic crisis in Sweden.

"Stockholm is in the grips of a depression. There is everywhere talk of how all is lost and how one company after another collapses. How will this end?" Maj von Dardel wrote in a letter to Annie Wallenberg in February 1922. "One of the worst years that I have experienced," was how Marcus Wallenberg summed up 1922.

In view of her remarriage it was only natural that relations between Maj von Dardel and Raoul Oscar's family should become more distant. But, throughout Raoul's time at school, Maj was determined to keep the connection alive and to attend all the important celebrations of her late husband's family.

Stockholms Enskilda Bank managed to remain untouched by the financial crisis. The Wallenberg family's reputation rose as it became evident that the bank had not been struck by the devastating credit losses suffered by other Swedish banks.

Now fifty, Marcus Wallenberg had begun to usher the next generation into the bank's senior posts. He had stepped down as president to give himself more time at the League of Nations Finance Committee, which was dealing with the economic aftermath of the Great War. His 27-year-old son Jacob, Raoul's father's favourite cousin, was now appointed managing director. Marcus Sr continued, however, to serve as a particularly active vice chairman for many years to come, at the side of the new chairman Knut Wallenberg.

Gustaf Wallenberg, Raoul's grandfather, had returned in dramatic fashion from his post in Japan. He had been trapped in Siberia after the Russian Revolution and had to turn back and take a route across North America, a journey that took him a year altogether. But his stay in Sweden was fleeting. In the spring of 1920, he was appointed envoy to Constantinople.

Nevertheless, even if he was forced to play his role of guardian and father figure from a distance, Gustaf became increasingly interested in his grandson's upbringing and education. In Raoul's eyes, his grandfather seemed the embodiment of his dead father's will.

His placement also brought an unexpected kind of glory to his grandson in Stockholm: Turkish stamps were highly prized by the passionate stamp collectors at his school.

Raoul's first four years of grammar school were relatively uneventful: his mother conceding that he was not among the very best students. But, she said, what good would come if he instead exerted himself too much? She was still convinced he was one of the most intelligent in his class. In her letters she expresses her high expectations of her son and, at the same time, generous doses of motherly compassion and care. She might complain that he had been lazy in mathematics, German and plant pressing on his summer holiday, but would immediately add that she felt he needed to rest in his time away from school. Raoul often handled these expectations with jokes about himself as a "little lazybones".

Raoul developed new outside interests. He liked to walk around Stockholm, looking at new building works and exchanging a few words with the construction managers. Towards the end of his time at grammar school, he began to exhibit more of an intellectual mindset; collecting annual reports from various large companies and eagerly awaiting the next instalment of the *Nordisk Familjebok* encyclopedia in the mail. Singing was one of his best subjects and sometimes he opened his window to the courtyard and sang loud solos for the neighbours. For a while he also sang in the boys' choir at church. By contrast, he was rarely seen on the soccer field, which some of his classmates viewed as strange.

Anders Hagströmer regarded his cousin as a relatively anxious and sensitive boy. Raoul had been afraid of water when they were little and still had to battle in many situations to overcome his fear. In his early years at the grammar school he sometimes burst into tears. This gradually passed, but his classmates thought it girlish. All his life, Raoul would joke about how cowardly he was at heart.

*

From the start, the pupils at Nya Elementarskolan received marks in all subjects at the end of each term as well as for diligence and behaviour. In the first few years, Raoul was always just a few steps behind the brightest star of the class: his new friend, Rolf af Klintberg.

After this, something happened to Raoul's ambitions at school. In the autumn of 1924 his grades began to slip and, by spring 1925, they were poor. Having failed German and with a question mark beside his grade in the new subject, English, he was not moved up to the next class. Raoul was one of nine in the class in this position. It was a harsh sentence. The struggling students had to come back before the beginning of the term and retake their exams in order not to be held back.

Perhaps significantly, during the same year Raoul discovered that he could not distinguish between all colours. A physician who examined him before Christmas declared him "red-blind", which meant Raoul was not going to be able to follow his father into the naval academy. That spring he was unusually sombre as he visited his father's grave with his mother. "Poor little Raoul, he is so devastated," Maj wrote to Gustaf.

The crisis provoked by Raoul's failure at German prompted his grandfather to intervene. Together with Maj, Gustaf ensured that his grandson – as family tradition demanded – was able to begin his international education. That summer, the twelve-year-old Raoul spent several weeks with a German family who happened to live in a resort town outside Rostock in northern Germany. Once he was home again, he was tutored by a German instructor before finally passing the German exam. The whole family could breathe a sigh of relief.

In 1926, Raoul Wallenberg finished the first stage of grammar school and passed the tests needed to qualify for the first of three years of preparatory study toward his university entrance examinations. Among other things he had been able to raise his grade in Swedish after a year in which he completed an unusually large number of essays. "Write about something you consider to be a heroic deed," was one of the topics that Raoul and his classmates were assigned.

Jacob Wallenberg had begun to take on the role of the family's social coordinator. His siblings married and had children, but Jacob remained a bachelor and for most of the '20s he lived at home with his parents, Marcus and Amalia, at Strandvägen 27. When he finally moved, it was into the apartment directly above them.

With more and more grandchildren, Marcus and Amalia's family circle was so large that important holidays like Christmas were celebrated without the extended family present. Nevertheless, Jacob went on giving presents to his godson Raoul, and Maj von Dardel and her family were regular guests at Marcus and Amalia's annual New Year's buffet. Except for the years that he was abroad, Raoul Wallenberg would continue this tradition all the way to January 1944, the last New Year he spent at home in freedom.

In 1927, Jacob Wallenberg became president of S.E.B. and his younger brother Marcus was made managing director. The brothers were rather different. Jacob, who had been almost like another father to Marcus Jr, who was seven years his junior, was more thoughtful and analytical. Whilst Marcus Jr was the more restless of the two: quick-witted and swift in his decision-making. But they had the same work ethic, sense of duty and admiration for Marcus Sr. Every Thursday morning the bank's directors convened for a fifteen-minute meeting in the boardroom. It began with Jacob and Marcus shaking Uncle Knut's hand and kissing their father on the cheek.

Jacob and Marcus Wallenberg Jr soon flourished in their new roles, as the Swedish economy boomed in the years leading up to the large stock market crash on Wall Street in 1929. The Wallenberg group's influence in Swedish business had grown significantly after some successful acquisitions of Swedish industrial companies, such as Stora Kopparberg and Asea.

But these good times co-existed with increasing public disapproval at the large disparities in income between those at the top and bottom. While some could amass millions, others had to work themselves to the bone as *statare* – agricultural labourers who were paid in kind. Developments in Sweden's large neighbour to its east had not gone unnoticed. In the decade after the Russian Revolution, Bolshevism was never far away from Swedish political discourse – for the right it figured as a threat, but for the left it was a source of inspiration.

The Bolshevik seizure of power had split the Swedish left in two. A conflict over the appropriate method to reach socialist goals broke out in the Social

Democratic Party. Reformists were pitted against revolutionaries. Finally the revolutionaries broke away and formed the Swedish Communist Party (S.K.P.).

But neither of the two left-wing parties enjoyed conspicuous success. In 1928 the Conservatives secured an easy election victory by conjuring up unflattering pictures of brutal Russian Cossacks – invoking amongst the electorate the combined threat posed by Russians and communists to Swedish society.

This pejorative image of Russia was mirrored in the schoolbooks. In the history curriculum of the university entrance preparation, Raoul and his classmates met a depiction of the Great War in which "the Germans' worthy achievements" were compared to the Russians' "brutal power and expansionist desires".

The road to the university entrance examination was not without struggles for Raoul. He had chosen to study Latin and, after some encounters with cases and morphology, Raoul realised that he had little interest in learning a dead language. This disengagement was borne out by his autumn grades.

Luckily, Nya Elementar offered the chance – unusual among schools at the time – of taking Russian instead. Better still, the instructor, Alexander de Roubetz, a Russian aristocrat who had taught at the tsar's court, was widely regarded as an amiable and lively teacher.

In spring 1927, Raoul switched subjects. Maj supported his unusual choice. "Russian is something that may prove very useful in future," she wrote to her mother-in-law, displaying unconscious foresight.

Raoul was energised by this change and after a while his increased motivation spilled over into his performance in other subjects. According to Rolf af Klintberg, Raoul soon became one of Roubetz's favourite students. But, despite this improvement, the first year of his university entrance preparations ended in disappointment: Raoul failed both maths and Swedish. For the second time he had to study over the summer and retake his exams in August in order not to have to repeat the year. After this setback, things went better. But Maj remained worried up until the university entrance examinations, so worried that she would even call and speak with Rolf af Klintberg about it.

Raoul was by now very different to the sensitive little boy he once had been. During these years he liked to engage his teachers in discussion, which not everyone in the class dared to do. He had a sense of humour and his friends appreciated his ability to create an atmosphere of fun around him. At the same time he could sometimes be a bit of a know-all with a streak of preachy morality. For example, he had been known to denounce cheating in class, and loudly proclaim to his classmates that he was going to write an anonymous letter to the principal about it.

To Rolf af Klintberg it seemed as if Raoul needed to assert himself, to show that he was not like everyone else. It was clear from Raoul's manner that those in his family circle expected him to do well. In the background were the glorified stories of his dead father, and Raoul knew that Raoul's grandfather, still Sweden's envoy in Constantinople, had high expectations of him.

In their last years at school, Rolf and Raoul spent more time together. They supported each other and believed themselves to be unusually intelligent young men, destined to do something spectacular. Rolf was planning a career in law like his father, while Raoul dreamed of becoming an international businessman. Rolf found Raoul's strong international engagement exotic and fascinating. Raoul appeared to think it was only natural to want to travel a great deal and get to know people in other countries. He would talk about Sweden's role in the world, while Rolf felt that one "should till one's soil at home".

During his school years, Raoul often travelled abroad during the summer, at his grandfather's expense. In 1928, he spent almost two months in Cambridge, with a language tutor who was also a minister in the Church, without once meeting any Swedes. On this trip, Raoul flew for the first time and stayed for a couple of nights at the famous Hotel Cecil in London. But a simpler standard of living awaited him after this, as well as a return trip by freighter via Amsterdam. "Dear Mama, do not for a moment think that I am raising Raoul to become accustomed to a millionaire's lifestyle. In fact, he is always hearing talk of how important it is to deny oneself frivolities so that there may be enough money for the essentials (but I haven't noticed any spendthrift tendencies)," Maj assured Annie.

The von Dardel family moved again, this time to an apartment on the fourth floor at Riddargatan 43. It was spacious, with six rooms, a balcony, and a space reserved for the dining room set that Raoul Oscar had once ordered. Rolf af Klintberg was a frequent visitor. If Raoul was not at home he would linger and speak with Maj instead. Rolf also appreciated Raoul's stepfather. He thought that Fredrik was solid and down to earth, in many ways an ideal father for as "fanciful a gentleman as Raoul".

As Raoul progressed through school he was allowed to take new and exciting classes such as French and fencing. The fact that Raoul enjoyed fencing, as well as the riding lessons that he had taken up at the military headquarters in Stockholm, delighted his mother.

Much of life for Raoul and his friends centred around the Nye Elementar's student association, which organised evenings of lectures and panel discussions, sometimes with a dance immediately following. Rolf af Klintberg was appointed secretary and engaged his classmate Raoul as "director of advertising". The thinking behind this was clear. Like the rest of his family, Raoul had considerable artistic talent. Drawing was the first subject in which Raoul managed to get a "small a", the second highest grade. The student association took advantage of his talent and had him paint colourful and striking posters that Rolf then hung all over the school in order to draw more people to the evening events.

A year before the entrance examinations Raoul and his family began to give closer consideration to his future. Raoul was interested in attending Stockholm's business school, Handelshögskolan, but he also told his mother and his grandfather that he would not have anything against becoming an architect. Gustaf Wallenberg, still in Constantinople, found this a good and "productive" idea. He was of the opinion that young men should enter a practical profession and only concern themselves with greater life goals thereafter. For Gustaf, the important thing was that Raoul select an American university for the professional education he had chosen.

Maj suggested that Raoul could attend the Handelshögskolan for a couple of years and then continue his education in the United States, perhaps at Harvard Business School. She gently observed that it would do no harm if Raoul managed to get a little past his seventeenth birthday before he shipped off to America.

Maj and Gustaf also had a final summer holiday to plan for him. They agreed that it would be best to send the sixteen-year-old Raoul to France for a couple of months since French was included in his university entrance examinations.

Raoul was placed with a French family for two months in the village of Thonon-les-Bains, which was beside Lake Geneva. He was one of five foreign teenagers that the family had taken in for language studies. The father of the family was a school inspector, but daily instruction was given by the mother, Madame Bourdillon. Raoul soon got to know the other students well, among them two Serbian boys his own age and László Pető, a fourteen-year-old Jewish boy from Hungary.

László became something of a target for the other Bourdillon family summer students that year. He was small, far from robust, and was made to take the blame for an embezzlement scandal involving the Hungarian government. In a clumsy attempt to save the devastated Hungarian economy after the Great War, Hungarian leaders had ordered the printing of false French franc notes. This incident did not pass unnoticed by the summer students in Thonon-les-Bains. Wherever they went, they introduced László as the "descendant of an embezzler nation". But Raoul did not join in, doing what he could to shield László from the bullying.

Almost fifteen years later, Raoul Wallenberg and László Pető met again, by accident – this time in Budapest right after the first major wave of deportation of Hungarian Jews. László would turn out to be the last person to see Raoul Wallenberg before he disappeared from Budapest in January 1945.

During his stint in Thonon-les-Bains, Raoul also probably saved the young Hungarian's life. The summer students had decided to climb the alpine peak Dent d'Oche, 2,300 metres high. The climb took them three and a half hours and involved considerable risk, especially during the steep final ascent. László was close to losing his grip and things might have gone very badly if Raoul had not had his wits about him, stretched out a hand and pulled him up. With Raoul now carrying László's heavy pack in addition to his own they all made their way up and looked admiringly at the lake, and across to the Alps and the snowclad Mont Blanc. They spent the night in a hut at the summit, Raoul lamenting that he had forgotten to bring the sketch pad that he had bought in the village.

The exchange of letters between Raoul in Thonon-les-Bains and Gustaf in Constantinople was unusually intense that summer. Raoul's future hung in the balance and Gustaf, who had already decided what was best for him, wanted his grandson to see things his way. "I wish to see you, my dear boy, raised to be a capable citizen who can stand on his own two feet from the very beginning," Gustaf explained. He wanted Raoul to be able to support himself and become "an independent man who would enter your maturity learning from the experiences of others, able to occupy yourself with the sorts of problems that are best suited to your sensibility". If Raoul could simply settle the matter of supporting himself by deciding on a practical profession, the final decision of selecting a life's work could be postponed into his thirties.

After having read these words, Raoul saw his chance. In his next letter, he observed that he would be only seventeen if he took his university entrance examinations in the spring of 1930. Would he be mature enough to travel to America and compete with the other, older students? He appealed to his grandfather to let him stay longer in Sweden. But Gustaf had already begun to pull strings for the America experience and was not about to give in. He explained in his reply to Raoul that this was not primarily a question of an academic education. "No, there is something very different that I want for you, an insight into the American mentality, the lesson of becoming men who rely on themselves that is given to the young, even with the addition of a feeling of being better than others and that may in fact be the source of the dominant position that America holds today in the world. This is something other than the 'falling in line' we have here at home."

In his letter, Gustaf also wrote pointedly that Raoul should not think that the name Wallenberg would grant him any favours: "Nepotism is not tolerated." What was expected was for him to find his own way and evoke admiration from others for what he managed to accomplish. Gustaf drew parallels to successful Swedish businessmen who had spent time in America. There they had absorbed the right "social spirit", which was the reason for their prosperity. They had gained a "love of life, the true spirit of entrepreneurship and an unshakeable faith in their success", he wrote.

Raoul replied despondently that they would have to revisit these plans at a later stage. He wrote about how hard he was studying and how good the stay at Thonon-les-Bains had been for his French. "I will not forget that this and so much more has been made possible by your generosity."

*

So rigorous was the selection process in the preparatory university entrance class that, of the thirty-one students who began the first year of Latin and modern language studies with Raoul, only twenty remained on the final day of registration in August 1929.

They entered the final phase leading up to the written examinations at the end of April and the oral examinations in May. Raoul's study habits improved significantly now that this crucial stage was drawing nearer. By Christmas he had improved half his grades, with the exception of Russian. But notwithstanding his new dedication to his studies, Raoul also managed to read several novels, attend some Saturday dances and maintain close contact with his relatives. In a Christmas letter, Raoul told his grandfather about his new side-interest in political economy.

Around the New Year, the question of Raoul's future was raised again. After pressure from Maj and Fredrik, Gustaf eventually gave way to the idea of allowing Raoul to postpone his studies in America for a year, and instead undertake his compulsory military service. In a letter, Gustav stated that, in the final analysis, he wished that the most important questions regarding Raoul should be decided by Maj and Fredrik. But it was also clear that Gustaf's preferences continued to play a decisive role. He contributed an allowance for Raoul and he was the one who was going to finance his education abroad.

The plan that now took shape was for Raoul to start at an American university in the autumn of 1931. Gustaf did not conceal that he was worried by the wild night-life of young people in Stockholm, and for this reason also Gustaf liked the idea of Raoul going abroad.

May 13, 1930 was cool and overcast. A great deal was at stake for Raoul on this long day of examinations. After a brilliant performance in the written portion in April, things looked promising. If Raoul was successful in his oral examinations, he would go on to a month-long internship at the Enskilda Bank the very next day. He was also planning to visit the large Stockholm Exhibition that was opening a few days later. After this, on June 16, he was due to begin service at the Royal Lifeguard Regiment of Grenadiers I 3 in Örebro. If he failed the examinations he would have to slip out through the back door and face a period in limbo.

The examinations began at 9.00 a.m. with Swedish, and continued to Biology and Christianity without a break – forty-five minutes devoted to each subject. After lunch the orals resumed at 12.45 for the final four subjects – in Raoul's case, German, Russian, French and Geography. At 3.15 p.m. it was over. The principal, teachers and examination officials then gathered in the teachers' room for a final vote: pass or fail.

Raoul's results were never in doubt. In fact he left the school with one of the best results of students in the Foreign Languages major. He was awarded three "large A's" in English, French and Geography.

His close family and some other relatives were waiting in the schoolyard. Raoul was wearing a bright-white student cap and they hung garlands of flowers around his neck and attached blue and yellow balloons to his coat. There was a reception that afternoon and a dinner at 7.00 p.m at which there were "a great deal of older folk and a few candidates with female companions", according to Rolf af Klintberg.

Fredrik wanted to celebrate this momentous occasion. He told Raoul that hereafter they should address each other informally. Fredrik meant that they should use the informal "du", but Raoul misunderstood. After this day he began to call Fredrik "Daddy". This was immensely gratifying for Fredrik, who had always treated Raoul as his own son.

For Maj the joy was mixed with an undertone of grief, which she had felt for several months whenever she thought about this day. As she had said in February of that year, Raoul's graduation also represented a tragic turning point "for then I am bound to lose sight of him".

Marcus and Amalia Wallenberg happened to be abroad and had conveyed their regrets regarding the graduation dinner. But they had sent a fine watch as a gift. Raoul wrote a letter of thanks:

> I wish to thank you for your kind show of congratulations upon my graduation. Uncle's generosity and interest are a tremendous inspiration for me to do my best in whichever paths lie before me and I hope that I will not become the kind of fellow who would bring dishonour to the family name.

CHAPTER 4

Machine Guns and American Architecture

Gustaf Wallenberg had supposed that Raoul's colourblindness would exempt him from compulsory military service. He was wrong. On June 16, his seventeen-year-old grandson was summoned to his new regiment in Örebro. Raoul could take some pleasure in the fact that his friend Rolf af Klintberg had been called up to the same unit.

Raoul was the youngest in the whole platoon. He was the object of some teasing since, ambitious and driven as he was, Raoul was not the sort to hang back simply because the others were older. "From the start he dedicated himself to becoming the perfect soldier and even managed to influence the rest of us, with the result that we became the most vigorous fellows by far," Rolf af Klintberg wrote later in his reminiscences from this time. But Raoul also became renowned for his ironic witticisms.

Almost from the beginning, Raoul seems to have found military life, with its procedures and strict hierarchies, comical. "I am working with energy and patriotic zeal for the defence of my country, trotting to and fro in the forest to the right and to the left etc. etc. All in all I am quite pleased with my existence, although clearly one could have a bit more fun . . . We have had quite a few marches, but what I like best is the shooting, in particular the kind with what is called a machine gun," he told his Aunt Amalia in a letter dated July 1930.

In a contest in August of that year, Raoul won a silver medal in small arms marksmanship. At this point he was also already, by his own account, the best in his platoon at machine-gun marksmanship. He saw this as welcome compensation for his lack of success at sports.

But Private Raoul Wallenberg had trouble toeing the line. His officers did not always understand his intellectual jokes or respond to his high ambitions. Before too long, Raoul lost respect for his superiors.

He also began to play pranks. On one occasion, two of the unit's "notorious troublemakers" had returned drunk and gone berserk in the barracks. Raoul had tried to help them escape punishment, but without success. According to Rolf af Klintberg, Raoul then organised a "triumphal procession for the sinners, to and from the arrest facilities; they were carried on shoulders with shouts of 'hurrah' and, after having served their time, were raised high and praised by the entire congregation." The incident led his superiors to brand Raoul a communist.

But his comrades in the unit had the impression that his political sympathies lay on the right rather than the left. According to one of them, Raoul sometimes introduced himself as "a Wallenberg and one-eighth Jew". He appears to have been proud of both strands of his heritage, dramatically exaggerating the latter. People found him intense but, despite having a high opinion of his own abilities, not arrogant.

Raoul was discharged in December with a grade that left him somewhere in the middle of his unit.

Around this time, Gustaf Wallenberg was turning his plans for his grandson's studies in the United States into reality. His choice was, somewhat surprisingly, the University of Michigan in the city of Ann Arbor. Gustaf had heard from his colleagues at the American Embassy in Constantinople that the mentality on the East Coast had changed. He felt there was a great risk that the cosmopolitan life in Boston or New York would have the same detrimental effect that he feared Raoul would be exposed to in Stockholm. The American Midwest appeared reassuringly wholesome.

As he explained his decision to Raoul, it was not the "education as such" he was after, but "the everyday life, social interaction with American youth, becoming educated into a well-organised fighter who under all circumstances remains aware that he should continue to make his way forward".

Later he would declare that the entire purpose of Raoul's adventure in America was to "make him into a person", reminding everyone that it was during a similar stay in the United States that his own father, André Oscar Wallenberg, founder of S.E.B., received his "financial impulses". And Gustaf too had been sent to the United States in his youth.

Perhaps Gustaf should have cared a little more about the details. When the idea of the degree in architecture in the United States was first raised, Gustaf's brother, Axel, had pointed out that Swedish architectural institutes were superior to those in America. His brother thought it would be better for Raoul to do his degree at home and then, using his superior education, seek employment in the United States. But Gustaf had vehemently objected. Axel's plan would have resulted in Raoul remaining in the United States and that was not what Gustaf had in mind. He only wanted Raoul to be "better equipped for his future ventures at home", and that he should acquire "a small advantage in the competition he will meet at home among his peers". Gustaf would have done well to reflect more on his brother's proposals: most Swedish architectural firms did not feel that an American degree represented being "better equipped".

Ann Arbor could at this time be regarded as an intellectual and cultural island in the otherwise heavily industrialised American Midwest. This was in large part due to the fact that Ann Arbor had been allowed to become the principal site for the University of Michigan – a kind of consolation prize at the time for not being made the state capital. With its 10,000 students, the university in Ann Arbor was one of the largest in the United States, even if it was regarded as a place to which families who could not afford the elite colleges sent their children. Life in the city was strongly influenced by the university, whose students made up a third of its population.

The first semester began on September 28, only three weeks after Raoul's discharge from his second round of military service. This already felt constrictive, but Raoul was also required to report to Ann Arbor a week earlier for the obligatory entrance exams.

Gustaf came home to Sweden to take care of the practical arrangements. He booked a ticket for Raoul on the Swedish American Line's passenger vessel the *Kungsholm*, which was due to depart Gothenburg on September 12. But the *Kungsholm* was not scheduled to arrive in New York until September 21, the same day that the entrance exams were to begin, some 800 kilometres to the west.

It was an impossible equation.

Gustaf found a solution. He wrote to the famous Swedish sculptor Carl Milles, who happened to have moved to the United States the same year and settled outside Detroit in Michigan. Gustaf did not know Milles personally but still turned to him for assistance. He told him that his grandson was likely to be late and wondered if Carl Milles "who must know several of the professors at Ann Arbor university, might be willing to assist him in connecting with someone who can help him at the door".

Gustaf told Carl Milles that Raoul would call on him when he arrived in Michigan on September 22 or 23.

The *Kungsholm* was the pride of the Swedish American Line, with an interior designed by leading Swedish artists and craftsmen. There was even a swimming pool. Raoul boarded the ship buoyed by the fact that, during his weeks at the Svea Life Guard Regiment, he had managed to lift his grades to the highest available to a conscript. He had now been promoted to *furir*, a rank equivalent to that of sergeant.

Raoul travelled through the U.S.A. at a time when the country was experiencing one of the deepest financial crises in its history. The two years that had passed since the stock market crash on Wall Street in 1929 had seen a downward spiral twisting ever deeper into the darkness of economic depression. In 1929 there were 1.5 million unemployed Americans. Four years later there were 12 million – a shocking 25 per cent of the country's labour force. No-one was buying anything any more. Entire industries stood still, as did construction projects.

Raoul Wallenberg had come to a land of despair.

The development of the city of Ann Arbor was like a model in miniature of the American crash. This was particularly true of the university itself. During the '20s the local automobile industry had boomed and the state of Michigan could scoop money out of a seemingly bottomless well. A significant amount went to the university. The campus area doubled in size, as did the professors' salaries, the number of students and the cheap restaurants. The College of Architecture received funds to erect a magnificent school building, Jazz music played across campus. There were dances everywhere and a boundless sense of optimism.

The turning point came the same autumn that Raoul walked into the College of Architecture to take his entrance exam. In the prospectus he was given, the university still claimed that, "there has never been a more promising outlook for the newly examined architect". By the next year that sentence had been erased. The number of university students decreased as precipitously as the instructors' salaries, and the last thing anyone in Michigan wanted to become, during those dark years of 1931–33, was an architect.

Raoul Wallenberg moved into a room in a house on East Madison Street, a ten-minute walk from the university in the city's centre. He soon adapted to his new routines, but he could not really understand his grand-father's enthusiasm for the United States. Raoul was disappointed. He thought he had landed in a tiny residential backwater that lacked a single trace of the over-whelming "American spirit" found in the big cities.

Nor did the instruction he received in class have an especially American flavour, Raoul observed in a letter to his grandfather in November. "Americanism is not something that is encouraged at the American universities. They think the American youth receive so much of this in their high schools that they prefer to provide them with a little bit of a classical education and European polish when they come to college. There is a very overt propaganda campaign for the European countries here."

He told him that the university he had come to consciously toned down competitiveness in favour of team spirit and fostering a sense of connection between the students. This did not seem particularly American, Raoul thought. "I'm writing all this so that you will understand and excuse me if my 'human education' . . . goes a little more slowly than yours did."

The architectural college had almost 400 students when Raoul was en-rolled. Two years later there were only half as many. Called "Rudy" by the students of the "Class of 1935", he quickly slipped into American college life, going about in sneakers and eating hot dogs. "He seemed as American as could be – in his dress, in his manner and in the slang expressions that he quickly absorbed," wrote Lilian E. Stafford in the Michigan alumnus magazine, May 1985.

Raoul's alarm clock went off at 7.00 a.m. every day. His room had so many windows he could hardly bear to be there once the sun had come up. Raoul would always begin his day with coffee and toast at the student centre, "Michigan Union", before his classes began at 8.00. During his lunch break he would go to a drug store to pick up his copy of the *New York Times*, and every night during the week there was a meeting for the debate club that he had joined in order to practise English. Afterwards he would eat dinner with some of his newfound friends, often at the German-American Restaurant. "My habits are as particular as those of an old man," he told his mother in a letter in November 1931. His Swedish military service had clearly whetted his appetite, because the nineteen-year-old Raoul joined the Reserve Officers' Training Corps, the R.O.T.C., one of the options on his course.

On Saturdays he would sit in the empty college and complete the homework that he had accumulated during the week. He took the opportunity to do this while his classmates went to football games. On Fridays and Sundays he would go to the movies with his friends, when they didn't head into Detroit for a concert or ballet. His classmates later recalled that "Rudy" loved music and was particularly fond of Mozart.

But he did not entirely neglect Sweden. In November 1931 he wrote to his mother, "It would be nice if you could enclose newspaper clippings with your letters. I would like articles on the following: 1) business 2) exploitable Swedish inventions 3) new building and city plans with accompanying drawings 4) election results etc."

In his first semester, the young Raoul Wallenberg surprisingly came top of his class in English Composition. There was a new assignment every week, so he had the opportunity to cover a number of topics. Among other things he wrote about the use of historical styles in nineteenth-century architecture, about the "magic mirror of statistics" as well as the meaning of having an open mind in social debates, not simply automatically supporting already established ideas. Dare to think in new and free ways was his clear message.

Few thought about the fact that he was not American. Raoul "Rudy" Wallenberg had travelled a great deal, but nonetheless his feeling for language must have been in a class of its own. He was analytically inclined and many of his arguments are exciting even eighty years later. For one of the first essays that Raoul wrote in Ann Arbor, entitled "What does the concept 'The United States of Europe' mean?", the instructor gave him high marks and commented: "This is an excellent piece of work." He was not always as clear eyed. At the end of November he devoted an essay to the subject of Sweden's large neighbour to the east, the Soviet Union. Raoul described Stalin's five-year plans as "an enormous financial and commercial revolution".

"A study of the situation in Russia today is perhaps not so encouraging," he wrote, emphasising that Stalin's five-year plans were not about global revolution, but economic development. "It is of course impossible to determine if this was Lenin's plan, but one thing is certain: ideals necessarily had to make way for Stalin's ambitions to give a great people an honest chance to live and prosper," Raoul wrote in the autumn of 1931, still happily unaware that Joseph Stalin's desire to give people the chance to live and prosper was still a long way from being fulfilled.

Meanwhile, in Sweden, the global economic crisis would soon harvest its first significant victim. The businessman Ivar Kreuger's empire had been in jeopardy since the Wall Street crash in 1929, and by February 1932 the situation was truly precarious. His loans were of such magnitude that the Swedish government had to intervene. In March Kreuger committed suicide and the ensuing bankruptcy – the Kreuger Crash – unleashed a deep financial and political crisis in Sweden. Swedish financial institutions fell like ninepins and many individuals were ruined. But the Wallenberg banking family had kept their composure, refused Kreuger's requests for loans and, in this way, contrived to escape the worst of the crisis.

For the freshman Raoul Wallenberg, the Kreuger Crash was his first financial challenge. He had made the mistake of investing some of the travel money from his grandfather in Kreuger shares. Gustaf's reaction was harsh. He demanded that Raoul pay back half of the loss from his future inheritance.

During the Christmas holiday, Raoul took the bus to see his aunt, Elsa Colvin, who lived two hours outside New York City. For several days he wandered around, admiring the – in his view – beautiful, airy and graceful skyscrapers. It was with a heavy heart that he boarded the bus to return to the "monotonous life" at Ann Arbor. "Here I have learned more about the real America in two weeks than in a whole semester at Ann Arbor, because there nothing is ever seriously discussed," he wrote.

He complained about how hard it was at Ann Arbor to find friends who were interested in something. It was a little better with the female students, as they were both more cultured and less conservative. He felt the entire environment was regressive. If he strolled around Ann Arbor he was more likely to find antique columns and copies of old Grecian temples than modern architecture. The newly constructed architectural college building laid claims to be groundbreaking, but in actuality, with its towers and large studio windows, it looked very like an imposing church from the Middle Ages.

"All the cultured people that I know here, especially the ones who study architecture, are horrified at skyscrapers and standardisation and straight walls, which they find ugly, and factories, which they feel lack poetry, and jazz music, which they hate . . . I have also noticed that one does everything here to dig up historical connections in order to feel part of the chain of development," he complained in a letter to Gustaf. Raoul was beginning to wonder if this really was America.

But he enjoyed the history of architecture and wasn't perturbed that the semester began with antiquity and in-depth studies of columns and ornamental details or sketches of the Parthenon. Classmates remember that the teachers lavished praise on Raoul's drawings and paintings. His unusual but beautiful combinations of strong colours evoked both attention and admiration. Fellow students would often gather around his drawing table. A professor even ordered a pastel drawing from Raoul and hung it in his office. "Would you mind telling the others that you are colour blind?" he asked Raoul in front of the entire class.

The more affluent students joined various student organisations, or fraternities. When his classmates asked Raoul why he didn't follow their lead he replied that it was not his way to isolate himself among a certain segment of the student population. Nonetheless he did not pass unnoticed through student life. His appearance was unremarkable, nor was he considered particularly good looking, but, according to his contemporaries, he radiated presence, confidence and charm. "I think it was the result of his seemingly tireless energy, enthusiasm, warmth, esprit and conviviality. His sense of humor that often bubbled up to the surface had a particular quality that in hindsight makes me think of Victor Borge,"* a student in a lower class noted much later.

For a while Raoul dreamed of going home to Sweden during his first summer break. He had half promised his mother that he would return at least occa-

* Victor Borge was a Danish-American pianist and entertainer. In 1956 he was named "The world's funniest man" by the *New York Times*.

sionally during his years in the U.S.A. But Gustaf would not hear of it, not even when his grandson pointed out that tickets to Europe had never been so cheap. For Gustaf, a trip home smacked of entertainment.

As Gustaf saw it there were only two alternatives. Either Raoul had to find a summer job "in order to develop an understanding of what it means to support oneself". Or else he could take the study trip to California that his grandfather had envisioned for at least one of the summers that he would spend abroad. Gustaf's idea was that Raoul should seek out and converse with important individuals in California – Swedes as well as Americans – and absorb "their experience and world view".

It was decided that Raoul would go to California, but without incurring prohibitive costs for his grandfather. "Everyone knows our name. You will easily be able to awaken interest in others. You have seen so much and have a talent for conversation. Employ this in the manner that I have instructed and you will have great benefits from your summer . . . Behave simply and without pretentiousness. Seek out the young. You should not live at luxury hotels but in unassuming quarters . . . It is not your hotel address that should spark their interest but your talents," Gustaf told him.

In particular he urged his grandson to learn about the horticultural industry in California, not in order to admire the machinery but to "come into contact with the individuals who know how to run enormous organisations". At the same time, Gustaf sent a letter to the consul in San Francisco and asked him to help his grandson to locate the appropriate contacts.

Raoul could not do much else except bow his head and obey: "I want to take this opportunity to express the deep gratitude that I owe you not only because of the financial sacrifices that you have undertaken for my sake but because I feel that I am the object of your constant attentions and love." Raoul told Gustaf that it was now common in the United States to catch rides in cars, so-called hitchhiking. "Anyway, it is mostly for Mother's sake that I even consider going home and you should not think that I have some uncontrolled desire to spend money."

He left for California. For a month he hitchhiked his way around the western United States with week-long stays in Los Angeles, San Francisco and Seattle. On the way he admired both the Grand Canyon and Death Valley. He spent his twentieth birthday in Los Angeles where he arrived shortly after the opening of the Olympic Games. "My birthday was spent in relative calm as I had asked the city officials not to take any extraordinary measures," he wrote home in jest.

That summer Raoul did learn life lessons: the difficult art of sleeping in bags on jolting truck beds, to walk long stretches without food and water, and in seemingly impossible situations to win the confidence of strangers and convince them of his good intentions. It was an experience that would serve him well later on. "One comes into intimate connection with many new people every day. It is a training in diplomacy and tact for it is through these connections that one catches new rides."

The following summer, Raoul managed to get himself a job in Chicago. Or, rather, he was accepted as an unpaid intern at the Swedish pavilion at the World's Fair in Chicago, which opened in 1933.

Perhaps Raoul had this idea when he visited the famous Swedish sculptor Carl Milles at the Cranbrook Academy of Art outside Detroit. He had done so on several occasions the previous autumn in the company of a Swedish-American woman named Bernice Ringman, with whom he had been spending time. She worked as a nanny and was two years older than Raoul, had studied in Sweden and could speak a little Swedish. She also had her driving licence and could drive Raoul the sixty miles to Carl Milles.

Modern design and technical innovations were at the centre of the Chicago World's Fair of 1933. Contemporary architecture was now one of Raoul's primary interests and he thought the American-style skyscrapers had a place, even in European cities. As soon as Raoul was summoned by the Swedish Pavilion he left Ann Arbor. Bernice Ringman drove him to the motorway that would take him to Chicago. He then hitchhiked the rest of the way there and checked in to the Y.M.C.A.'s enormous hotel.

At the Swedish Pavilion, Raoul cleaned windows and sold Swedish ice cream. He was also the man behind the Swedish triumph of illumination during the exhibition. Raoul convinced officials to erect spotlights in a high tower so that the Milles statues outside the Swedish Pavilion were bathed in a fine light. The number of visitors exceeded all expectations, prominent Swedes jostling to attend. One day the "very polite and decent" Count Folke Bernadotte turned up with his wife, Raoul noted. Bernadotte would later became famous for his negotiations leading to the release of thousands of Jews from German concentration camps at the end of the Second World War.

The trip home three weeks later went badly. The car that Raoul had hitched a ride with drove straight into another car that had stopped for a train. It skidded off the road and into a fence. No-one was hurt but Raoul had to continue alone on foot.

It was not until it was getting dark that he was able to get another ride, with four young men. He thought they looked unpleasant and, sure enough, the car turned onto a side road and everyone got out "to check the gas tank". They called out to Raoul, who stepped out and had a gun pointed at him. He had to give them all his money and was then thrown into a ditch with his bags on top. He eventually made his way back to Ann Arbor by train.

He had moved a fair amount in the past two years but in the autumn of 1933 Raoul found a more permanent residence in a room on Hill Street, just around the corner from the university. There he stayed for the remainder of his time at Ann Arbor, which he was now liking better and better. He was a regular at both the cinema and concerts, sometimes going several times a week. Among other things he had adopted a tradition from home – every year in December he took Bernice Ringman to the impressive performance of Handel's "Messiah" at the university auditorium. "It is a fantastic piece of music. I don't think there is anything I would rather listen to," as he put it in a letter to his grandfather.

Studies did not dominate his time as much as they had previously. He spent the weekends with his friends, wading through ditches on long, physically demanding hikes. Raoul enjoyed this tremendously and felt it was a little like his military service.

His room on Hill Street was an object of admiration for his friends. Raoul had decorated the walls with large, colourful murals on thick paper. "On two walls I have the Garden of Eden with Adam and Eve, an elephant, a pig, a giraffe, a polyp, a peacock and a lot of trees and hills. On two other walls I have City Hall, a white Atlantic passenger ship, the harbour in New York in allegorical representation. I paint with ordinary pastel crayon on paper and it really isn't particularly artistic."

This was not entirely true. The professor of art in Ann Arbor regarded Raoul as one of the greatest talents he had encountered in all his years of teaching: he even asked Raoul if he had considered pursuing art as a career.

Raoul himself was beginning to doubt his capacity to find gainful employment as an architect in Sweden. He could see that American building styles differed substantially from the Swedish. In the spring he had also dropped a more engineering-oriented course on construction techniques that he had initially selected because he felt it would be of use in Sweden. But he felt so deficient in physics and mathematics that he returned to the purely architectural courses so as to avoid these subjects. "It is better to become a good architect than a bad engineer," he told his mother. "Although I like architecture very much I think it will go better for me the sooner I seek out some branch of business after I finish my degree."

But, aside from his academic doubts, Raoul felt that he was becoming very much attached to his American life. During the spring of 1934 he realised that he did not even need to take any courses over the summer in order to finish his degree – a semester earlier than he had supposed – in February 1935. He was suddenly struck by how sad he would be to leave Ann Arbor and American culture: the positive go-getter attitude that he knew he would miss at home. "The best thing about America is that people are not envious and they are not petty. Just think of how much effort we expend at home doubting everything and everyone! Think how much unpleasantness we make for ourselves andeveryone else by being pessimists by nature instead of optimists."

Raoul had made a list of various interesting areas that he wanted to learn more about before going home: "Air conditioning, restaurants, hot-dog stands, drug stores, hotels, kitchen installations, small newsreel cinemas, cleaning and laundry businesses as well as advertising and newspaper industries."

Raoul's feeling for the United States was probably influenced by the fact that the country was beginning to emerge from the Great Depression. He noticed this in everyday life. In the spring of 1934 the number of cars on the streets of Ann Arbor visibly increased. One by one the banks that had closed re-opened. An increase in advertising made the newspapers thicker and the newly elected president Franklin D. Roosevelt's reform programme, the "New Deal", involved public ventures that created more jobs, even for the architecture students in Ann Arbor.

Raoul had belonged to the minority in Republican-dominated Ann Arbor

who did not despair over the Democrat Roosevelt's victory in the presidential elections of autumn 1932. Raoul, who enjoyed reading Winston Churchill's book *Amid These Storms* in the evenings, regarded President Roosevelt as
America's "strong man". Twelve years later it was this same President Roosevelt
who gave Raoul Wallenberg his Budapest assignment.

The wheels were turning again and the air was becoming easier to breathe.
At the College of Architecture it was decided to reinstate an earlier tradition
and hold a lavish spring masquerade for both students and teachers. The so-
called Architect's Ball had been deemed an "unnecessary extravagance"
during the years of crisis; now it came back with a vengeance. In the spring of
1934 it had an Arabian theme and was called "Ramadan Bayran". Raoul G.
Wallenberg was elected to the event committee and turned up in the tropical
setting as a heavily made-up Ali Baba, turban and all, possibly the most exotic
costume of the ball. It was a striking contrast to his girlfriend, Bernice Ringman, who was wearing a Swedish folk costume.

Afterwards, against all odds, the event committee had money left over.
Raoul and his friends decided that this had to be used up. The local alcohol
restrictions had been revoked some years earlier so the committee decided
to fund a night at a bar. It was so wild that the staff had to call the police. Most
of the party, including Raoul, managed to get away in time but one committee
member had to spend the night in jail.

Ignoring the sharp admonishments she had received from Gustaf in the past,
Maj could no longer resist asking her son to come home. Already during the
summer of 1933 she had written to Knut Wallenberg and asked him to see if
Raoul could have a position at the Enskilda Bank.

Knut Wallenberg's reponse to Maj von Dardel's request was encouraging.
"The boy is quick and it is [unreadable] of undeniable use for a young man of
his age to acquire experience abroad. When I get Father Gustaf in earshot I
shall have discussions with him about the boy's future."

But Gustaf's letters from this time indicate that he wanted to keep his
grandson away from Stockholm for some time to come. His plan was to send
Raoul on a long-term professional assignment very soon after graduation.
Gustaf was of the opinion that Raoul's "theoretical education" should swiftly
be complemented by a practical one somewhere abroad. South America was

one option: Gustaf knew the Swedish business attaché in Colombia and he would probably be able to arrange an unpaid internship in a trading company for a year. Thereafter he wanted Raoul to go to Haifa in Palestine where one of Gustaf's friends, the C.E.O. of the Dutch Bank in Constantinople, was planning to open a new branch. The banker had already stated that he was willing to take on Gustaf's grandson.

The question of where Raoul should spend the next couple of years was clearly emotionally charged for Gustaf. During his grandson's time in Ann Arbor Gustaf had put on the emergency brakes whenever Raoul hinted at a desire to go home for a visit. Gustaf appears to have seen it as his primary task to prolong the foreign experience and minimise Raoul's time in Stockholm. There was considerable back-and-forth on this point, but Gustaf finally relented and gave his consent to a visit home after graduation as long as it was a short one.

Gustaf gave his grandson one reason after another as to why it was so important for him to leave Sweden again as soon as possible. He told him that the Swedish economy was going "from bad to worse" and that it was sheer folly to try to start a career in Sweden at this time. In addition, Gustaf observed, it would be difficult for Raoul to return home and live up to the lofty expectations that his absence had created. An army of jealous Swedes was ready to take him down.

But the real grounds for these concerns appear to have been Stockholm's supposedly treacherous young women and Gustaf's fears of what they might do to his grandson. Gustaf's opinion of the opposite sex could only be described as contemptuous. He regarded young women as insidious parasites with a single purpose: to ensnare a man in order to secure his financial support. He related with disgust how, increasingly, young men in Stockholm's upper classes had sadly "turned out to lack self-discipline", and bound themselves to the very first woman they met without regard for whether or not she belonged to "the same species of human". Gustaf's judgement was harsh: "It will intellectually destroy the ability of your race and class that has cost so many hundreds of years to build up – one must resist the constant attacks from below." He warned Raoul how easily he could be snared. "It can happen in a moment of confusion and under the influence of the unfettered forces of nature."

The longer Raoul stayed away from Stockholm, the greater the chances he could resist the siren song. Or so Gustaf argued. He gave his grandson some additional advice: "Tempted by feminine charms, you should remember that womanly beauty is nothing other than more or less well-distributed fat beneath the skin," he wrote. "Thus, when you do come home and visit the dance halls, you should not neglect to study the older women and reflect on how they appear some twenty years later."

To Maj, Gustaf openly declared that he was afraid of the young women of the day. "Not the ones who run in the streets, but the ones who spin their webs in the dance halls, in the living rooms and in sports." He urged Maj to prevent Raoul from tying himself down too early and to this Maj had no objection.

Raoul fired off additional arguments in defence of a longer stay in Sweden. But under this barrage of opposition from his grandfather, he capitulated. Raoul was all too aware that his studies in America had cost his grandfather a great deal. He knew that he did not have the right to object.

There was an additional reason for Gustaf Wallenberg's actions, perhaps still too raw to acknowledge and perhaps too humiliating for a man of Gustaf's stature.

What Gustaf did not reveal to his grandson was that, during the spring of 1934, he had met with his brother Marcus on the Riviera. There Gustaf had brought up the question of Raoul's future. Gustaf had explored with his brother the prospect of Raoul taking up a position at the bank, or in any of the other firms within the Wallenberg family business. However Marcus informed his shocked brother that he found Raoul to be "too talkative". When Gustaf later heard that Marcus Sr had told other relatives that Raoul "should seek his livelihood in the – to us so distasteful – realm of politics", the rift between the brothers deepened and relations between them remained cold for the rest of their lives.

But Gustaf did not allude to any of this in his letters to Raoul. His fear that their relatives would continue to find fault with his grandson and perhaps crush his dreams drove him instead to further inflate the glorious career he envisioned for Raoul. Gustaf explained that the underlying purpose of Raoul's educational programme had been to make him unique. It would provide

Raoul with a knowledge of the world and an understanding of its "mentality, customs and attitudes" that most of Raoul's generation entirely lacked. As Gustaf – the humiliated grandfather – wrote in a letter at the end of August 1934, "There have to be leaders and innovators. It is the responsibility of the gifted to execute the greater tasks and rise above the average among his generation. It is not presumptuous of me to count on your talent. You have it in your blood, your inherited characteristics and the fortunate ability to think calmly."

Gustaf's chief expectation lay in the potential internship at the newly opened Dutch bank in Haifa. "It is seething with activity, more than any other place on earth," Gustaf wrote, praising the pioneering spirit he felt he had observed. "During your employment you will have the opportunity to make observations in many areas. You will see ideas brought to fruition by immigrating Jews, whose talents and experiences are considerable. Haifa is a community that is very much growing." Gustaf revealed to Raoul that he had plans to start a pioneering "oriental bank" himself, since he did not feel that Swedish banks were sufficiently represented abroad.

Raoul would have time for one more adventurous journey across the American continent before he returned to Sweden. This time his plans were more defined. In the spring of 1934, a friend had excitedly shared the news that he was going to have the use of his family's Ford over the summer. And thus a plan to drive to Mexico was born. Raoul's Aunt Nita lived there with her husband, Carl Axel Söderlund, who worked for a Swedish firm in Mexico City.

The owner of the Ford eventually decided against going on the trip, so in the end it was Raoul's friend Dick Shields from Indiana who accompanied him on his summer adventure. They left in early July and headed directly south toward New Orleans. At night they pitched a tent next to the car and every afternoon they drew pictures that they sold or used as partial payment for a more comfortable bed for the night. "It is excellent training for one's salesmanship . . . I know that at a pinch I could support myself in this way," Raoul told his grandfather in a letter from Texas.

Problems started once they had crossed the Mexican border. Rain storms had destroyed the already poor roads and they had to try to make their way along muddy donkey trails in the elderly Ford. After a couple of days they met two newly married Jewish couples in a similar vehicle and with the same destination. They decided to accompany each other through the desert and to help each other.

The trip from the border took them ten days. Both cars experienced frequent flat tyres. They had to dig each other out of dried-up river beds and wade through sewage-contaminated ditches. Bearded, worn and dirty, they finally arrived in the capital city. Raoul had a high fever and a stomach bug. Most likely dysentery, according to his Aunt Nita. Or traveller's diarrhoea, "Montezuma's Revenge", Raoul confided to his friends later. He was given Mexican herbs and after a couple of days he was back on his feet.

One of Raoul's goals for the trip was to study what was left of the Aztec and Mayan culture. With Nita and Carl Axel, he travelled to Monte Albán, the renowned city of ruins in southern Mexico. Raoul was fascinated by the prehistoric Mexican architecture. "It is remarkable," he wrote, "that although it is several hundreds of years old, the exteriors resemble most modern architecture."

Raoul Wallenberg was bored by his last Christmas in Ann Arbor. A cold front had settled over the university town and dressed both the trees and the empty streets in a thick layer of ice. It was beautiful, but Raoul was persuaded that Ann Arbor at Christmas time was "one of the dreariest places on Earth". He felt alone. All his friends had left as soon as classes were over in order to celebrate the holidays with their families. The town felt as deserted as a graveyard.

Raoul was planning to spend this lonely time on his final thesis on Swedish architecture. In his last course on the subject, which was on the topic of affordable housing, he had received the highest possible grade. The assignment had been to fit housing for 4,500 people into a space of about sixteen blocks. Raoul had chosen to make the whole area into a park in which he then placed four-storey multi-family apartment buildings. He had made sure that there was also a church, a school, day-care facilities and shops. In short, everything that was required for daily life. "Cheap housing" was not wasted training in view of the tasks that awaited him in Budapest's international ghetto ten years later.

He went to the cinema most evenings. He assuaged his loneliness on

Christmas Eve with a comedy he found so funny he chuckled to himself the whole way home. But he still had more than enough time to think. In only another few months his American adventure would draw to an end and Raoul did not really know what was waiting for him next. From his grandfather he heard that feelers for an international internship in Colombia had not yielded anything and that he was trying a contact in Calcutta instead. This did not matter very much. As far as Raoul was concerned, the next international expedition could be put off indefinitely. He was so homesick that he had begun to dream about Sweden. He was extremely excited at the prospect of seeing his younger siblings Nina and Guy again. What would they look like? Was it true that his little brother was taking his university entrance exams already this spring? He felt a sudden craving for Swedish chives and he even felt happy when he thought about the remainder of his military service.

In January he wrote to his mother saying he wanted to send her a long list of all the Swedish dishes he had been longing for, but that he had unfortunately been gone so long that he had forgotten their names. There was not much time left before they would see each other. "Right now they are playing a new song on the radio called 'Nina'. I think it will arrive in Sweden at about the same time that I do."

CHAPTER 5

The Globetrotter

At lunchtime on February 26, 1935, the Norwegian passenger ship S.S. *Bergensfjord* left from Pier 30 in Brooklyn, New York: destination Oslo. The 22-year-old Raoul Wallenberg had managed to reserve a cabin space at the last minute. Just before the ship lifted anchor he received a final greeting by telegram from Bernice Ringman in Ann Arbor: "Smooth passage, my angel . . . Watch baggage. Lock Cabin. Check valuables . . . Write and please be sweet, nice and clean."

After three and a half years on the other side of the Atlantic, Raoul now missed his family terribly. The prospect of not being able to stay at home for very long pained him. As of yet nothing had been finalised with regard to the international internship, but his grandfather was insisting on an imminent departure and, in the worst case scenario, Raoul would only have a couple of weeks in Stockholm. He was planning to do everything in his power to extend this time. He did not want to leave his homeland on any account before May 1. He loved the Swedish spring.

Gustaf had been deeply wounded by Marcus' derogatory comments about Raoul the year before, but Marcus did in fact have some feelings of responsibility toward his brother's fatherless son. In February 1935 he was resting up at the Grand Hôtel in Cannes. When he heard from Gustaf that Raoul was shortly expected in Oslo he penned a letter to his youngest son, Marcus Jr. It happened to be on the very same day that Raoul set sail from New York:

> The purpose of this letter is to impress upon you and Jacob the necessity of reflecting on how you envision Raoul's future career. I am convinced that Raoul's deepest desire is to gain a position at

the bank and to advance there as far as possible. His qualifications in this regard are not too bad.

He told them that Gustaf was grooming Raoul to become a "pioneering bank director" abroad. Maj, however, was still trying to convince Knut Wallenberg to arrange a post in the family bank here at home. He felt that this last point was important for Jacob and Marcus Jr to know.

> Once or twice I have said to your Uncle Knut that it is not we but the two of you who should select your future colleagues. I think it is appropriate for Jacob to have a word with Uncle Knut about this so that he does not rashly promise something with which the two of you are not in agreement. It is so easily done to make lofty promises which one then finds oneself bound to fulfil although one may not want to.

He concluded with some lines about the temperamental weather on the Riviera, but assured them that they were still managing to play golf every day.

The Sweden that Raoul returned to in March 1935 was a country that had managed to recover more rapidly than any other from the effects of the Wall Street Crash of 1929. The crisis had reached its nadir in Sweden in 1933. Thereafter the economy had started to pick up again and the previously dramatic unemployment figures were now decreasing. Everything, of course, was relative. Some segments of the population were still suffering considerably.

The hard times had their political consequences. The Swedish Social Democratic party had won the parliamentary elections of 1932 and the party leader Per Albin Hansson was now the prime minister. No-one could sense it then, but with this victory the Social Democrats had begun an era of historical dominance in Swedish politics. With the exception of a couple of months, the post of prime minister would hereafter remain in Social Democratic hands for forty-four years, from 1932 to 1976.

The Stockholms Enskilda Bank had managed better than most during these difficult years and the Wallenbergs had also stepped up as major shareholders of several large Swedish industrial firms. It was a period of expansion for the Wallenberg family empire, which would in the coming decades become the single most powerful business group in Sweden.

Marcus Jr, who for so long had stood in the shadow of his elder brother Jacob, had begun to advance his career. Jacob, meanwhile, was working harder than ever. He had now to shoulder a part of his father's international activities. Jacob Wallenberg had at first been the Swedish banking organisation's representative in the credit negotiations after the German banking crisis. In the international dealings that followed he was appointed the government's official representative. He thereafter became chairman of the Swedish–German business commission. Germany was at this time one of Sweden's most important trade partners and, during the thirties, would double its share of Swedish exports, a consequence of the growing interest in Swedish iron that came with increased investment in military armament.

Jacob Wallenberg eventually came to shuttle back and forth between Stockholm and Berlin on various government assignments. He soon created a network for himself in Germany, initially in the Weimar Republic. After Adolf Hitler's assumption of power in 1933, Jacob Wallenberg also made connections in the top Nazi circles, but during the war his most important German partners were to be found in the anti-Nazi opposition.

In the spring of 1935, Hitler reintroduced conscription in Germany, a flagrant violation of the terms of the Treaty of Versailles. He now officially declared that he wanted to mobilise half a million Germans. At the beginning of March, the day before Raoul arrived in Oslo, the British government had also openly declared that they were preparing for war.

Raoul was very interested in international politics and followed the events in Europe closely. Before he left the United States, he had read the Nazi sympathiser Ewald Banse's book, *Germany, Prepare for War!*, which he understood to express the Nazis' beliefs. In it, Banse discusses, among other things, Nazi conceptions regarding the German people's need for *Lebensraum* or living space. "But the whole thing seems rather extreme, although at the same time also very earnest and presumably written for an internal audience," Raoul wrote to his mother in January 1935.

This spring, however, his thoughts were predominantly focused on the task of swiftly entering the world of Swedish architecture or business. He knew he didn't have much time. Soon, his grandfather's foreign plans would send him away again, even if it was not yet decided when and where he would go.

Naturally, he would try to fit in a few visits to relatives on his late father's side. In one of his most recent letters, his grandfather had informed him that it was now Jacob and Marcus Jr who were the most important members of the family, not the older generation. It was Jacob and Marcus Jr – called "Dodde" by family – who would determine Raoul's future. In March 1935, Marcus Jr wrote a reply to his father's letter about Raoul:

> Thank you for the letters about Little Rulle. I have shown them to Jacob who is going to talk to Uncle Knut. We do think we should have a look at him after so many years and how he has developed after his years abroad. Kisses from your son, Dodde.

Gustaf did not need to worry. Raoul Wallenberg, the newly graduated architect, was energetic and driven. Almost immediately upon his return to Stockholm, he ventured out with his architectural portfolio, and "ran about town trying to find a job", as his grandfather later put it. But it wasn't easy. Raoul would soon realise that his American architectural studies had an artistic bent that did not impress Swedish employers. Though his task may have been made somewhat easier by the happy news from the College of Architecture that he had been selected for the school's top prize for the graduating class: a medal from the American Institute of Architects.

After a while Raoul was pulled into a debate about the best location for a new central outdoor swimming complex in Stockholm. The old unheated swimming pool at Riddarholmen had been forced to close and now various replacement options were discussed. Only a few weeks after he returned home, Raoul was hired by the director for the commission that managed state-owned property in Stockholm and was assigned the task of coming up with a proposal for a new, smaller swimming facility in the same location.

At the end of April, the newspaper *Svenska Dagbladet* revealed the unknown young architect's sketches in a large front-page feature. The piece made a big impact, but the headline, "Riddarholm Baths With Historical Traditions," was perhaps out of step with the times. Modern functionalism had long since superseded the more backward-looking classicism of the twenties, a change in direction that Raoul did not actually find appealing. "The Funkis style is so revolting that it would almost be better if no-one built anything at all," he stated a few years later.

Raoul envisioned a 50-metre-long swimming pool next to the dock with a lounging area for sunbathing next to it. It would be an outdoor swimming pool with one of Stockholm's most beautiful views "but should be positioned so that it does not detract from the many palaces from the 1600s". Raoul experimented with multi-use partitions between the dressing rooms and lounging areas to make adjustments "in case the relationship regarding the frequency of bathing should change between the two sexes in the future". Nude sunbathing would be available on special floating docks on the water, something he had spent a little extra time on. "With a simple rope and pulley system these could be shifted to ensure full sun exposure during the most important hours for sunbathing."

His proposal was given attention by a number of newspapers and a little bit later Raoul even published a small pamphlet with his sketches. But the mouthpiece of Functionalism, the journal *Byggmästaren*, gave it the thumbs down and called the proposal "theatrical". It was never realised.

Gustaf Wallenberg, who had travelled home from Constantinople that spring in order to see his grandson, was very pleased with Raoul's diligence and the burst of attention it had brought him.

He was so impressed to see Raoul putting his career before leisure that he let him stay in Sweden for another couple of weeks. Raoul used this time for an internship at an architect's office. There he worked on a sketch for a theatre project, among other things.

That spring Raoul's entire family was absorbed in construction projects of various kinds. After the death of her mother, Sophie Wising, Maj had inherited a fairly large sum of money. This she invested in a relatively extensive piece of property by the water in one of Stockholm's northern suburbs. She had poured all her energy and enterprising talents into the project and now some dozen subdivided parcels of land were ready for sale – all with an attractive southern exposure and a view of Ulriksdal Palace. One of the parcels had been set aside for the von Dardels themselves.

But Raoul would not see this project to its conclusion. Halfway through

May, Gustaf felt that enough was enough, it was time for Raoul to go abroad again. Gustaf coined the expression "commerce proficiency" for the internship that now awaited Raoul, which simply meant that he would learn how to make money. Since neither the enquiries in India nor in South America had yielded anything, Gustaf Wallenberg had instead turned to his former colleague at the legation* in Tokyo, Theodor Fevrell. He was the Swedish general consul in South Africa and managed, via another colleague – the consul in Cape Town – to arrange an unpaid internship for Raoul at a local timber company with Norwegian ties.

Gustaf's plan was for Raoul to spend half a year there and then to conclude his education with at least as long a spell at the Dutch bank in Palestinian Haifa. There the intention was that Raoul would work with Gustaf's close friend, Erwin Freund. Freund was a Czech of Jewish heritage whom Gustaf regarded as an extremely talented banker with the right "pioneering qualities". He was secretly hoping that Erwin Freund would become manager of the foreign division of the Swedish oriental bank that he dreamed of. They had known each other for fourteen years and Freund had said that he would be happy to take on Raoul after his adventures in South Africa.

Gustaf was eager for his grandson to do internships in newly settled countries in order to learn the art of making money in its most elemental form, to absorb something of the pioneering mentality. At the same time he was eager to find smaller companies so that Raoul had closer contact with the executive leadership. In larger firms, the risk was that a young intern like Raoul would end up licking stamps and running errands in the city without being able to learn anything about business.

Gustaf booked a cabin on the M.S. *Hammaren*, with a departure from Oslo to Cape Town on June 15. Raoul found it extremely painful to tear himself away from his stimulating and enjoyable life in Stockholm after such a short time, but he knew he had no choice but to comply with his grandfather's wishes.

When M.S. *Hammaren* approached Cape Town on an unusually warm day in July 1935, Raoul was standing on the bridge with the man that he had

* Swedish diplomatic representations abroad were known as "legations". They were not called "embassies" until after the Second World War.

befriended during the trip, Björn Burchardt. They squinted into the sun and haze. Earlier they had spotted Table Mountain like a "jagged cloud over the horizon", if one believes the account that Raoul published in the magazine *Jorden Runt* the following year. His initial impression of Cape Town was overwhelming – the mountains, the white buildings and the hills that in Raoul's words "shifted in various shades of blue, as mild and tender as anything on the French Riviera".

When they finally went ashore, they were enveloped in a multi-racial crowd of dock workers: Raoul watched them with fascination, remembering his geography lessons. "Some looked like Abyssinian warriors, others were light and smooth. I thought I could distinguish Malayan and Chinese racial features here and there in the throng," he wrote in his travel article. The next moment he seems to have had his first eye-opener. "After we docked, we immediately began to unload. The ship's first mate was overseeing the negro boys' efforts with a critical eye, although I could see that they were working so hard that sweat poured down their faces."

During his months in South Africa, Raoul would wrestle a great deal with the race question, which for him was complicated. He disliked what he saw but did not see an easy solution. "We Swedes naturally find it difficult not to get indignant and ask why it is that one cannot – or rather that one must – give the coloureds and the blacks each and every right that we whites have," he wrote in the article. At the same time, he did not find it easy to determine which of the various groups had arrived first. He was also squeamish about the thought of interracial relationships, perhaps because he had been schooled in thinking in typological ways about race.

Raoul would eventually come to the conclusion that South Africa should create a system of equality between blacks and whites but without mixing the races. "Owing to the unfortunate frequent and unrestrained interrelations between the races here in the Cape Province – southwestern South Africa – a mixed race has been created that presents a very difficult problem. It contains the blood of whites, Hottentots, Bushmen, immigrant Malays as well as Indians."

The article ended with a celebration of the white South African who, regardless of what happened, had "created a rich land out of wilderness. He has struggled on behalf of his race, glory and honour and advancement. He has sown the seeds so that his descendants may reap."

*

Raoul's initial infatuation with Cape Town cooled fairly quickly. Seen close up, the city turned out to consist mainly of "dirty cats and dogs". The unexpected summer weather on the first day was followed by a return to normal South African winter temperatures, and the hotel that Raoul and his friend Björn Burchardt had found by the water offered no protection against the frigid weather. Raoul had never been so cold in his life.

Raoul thought that Cape Town was a relatively boring city, old fashioned and a little desolate. The food was dull and expensive, as were clothes and cinema tickets. The nightlife felt muted and stale: "For me, it has so far consisted of visits to the cinema and the occasional beer or whiskey in one of the city's numerous old-fashioned bars."

His work was not much better. Raoul had a half-hour commute to the timber and iron goods company, Thesens Ltd, whose office, in Raoul's eyes, resembled a shed. His duties consisted largely in counting out receipts and, on the whole, he felt ignored.

After a month he gave up and left. Björn Burchardt arranged for him to move over to his company instead, the Swedish African Co. Ltd. The director there was Carl Frykberg and the company dealt with paper, timber and imitation leather. Frykberg was constantly receiving offers of new business opportunities that he never had time to follow up. Raoul's first assignment was to look into these opportunities, and at the top of the list there was an interesting Swedish chemical invention that claimed to extend the life of cinematographic film stock.

Raoul spent the remainder of his time in South Africa as a salesman, mostly on behalf of Carl Fryksberg's company. He developed an impressively varied array of products – sporting goods, travel accessories, tents and chemicals. Two evenings a week he followed his grandfather's advice and did night classes in bookkeeping, typewriting and business English.

Work was not the only thing that concerned Raoul during the first period of his time in South Africa. Letters from his girlfriend in Ann Arbor, Bernice Ringman, were beginning to come more frequently and had begun to express feelings that, unfortunately, Raoul did not share.

Bernice had been one of his closest friends during his time in the United

States and most of his college friends assumed they were an item. He had liked her very much but he had never been in love with her. This was something that he had tactfully tried to explain to her in his letters, even before he left for South Africa. But it seemed as if Bernice had not understood. The issue came to a head when she sent him a telegram on his birthday with the direct question: "Do you love me?"

Raoul was already feeling uncomfortable with the fact that he had made her unhappy. Now he decided after long deliberations that it was best to cut off contact with her, since he simply risked hurting her more, whatever he did. The worst thing he could do would be to give her false hope. He therefore immediately replied in the negative with a telegram as well as a letter that concluded with his saying good-bye and wishing her the very best for the future.

In a letter to his grandfather he vented his feelings and told him how sorry he was to have caused this tragedy. The temperamental Gustaf became panic-stricken. For him, a tragedy in combination with a woman could only mean one thing. He immediately assumed that Raoul had ignored his repeated warnings, had become ensnared by a woman's beauty, and had made Bernice Ringman pregnant. All at once, the world for Gustaf became dark. "If one seduces an American girl then all is lost. Then all of my castles in the air will tumble to the ground," he wrote back in desperation.

For Gustaf, great love only existed in novels. In real life it was an industry. Women wanted to be supported and only had one thing in their heads, to entice suitable young men with erotic temptation that they could not withstand and then put their claws into them. "It is strange, but there is a great deal of the hyena in women," the distraught Gustaf wrote.

Desperately, he began to think of a plan B. It seemed as if he "perhaps had lost what I imagined to be the ideal of all my dreams". As Gustaf saw the matter, it was impossible for Raoul to bring a pregnant Bernice Ringman to Sweden. Tainted by an illegitimate relation, she would never be admitted to Swedish society. "I can not see any alternative but that you make your way in America," Gustaf concluded and his words vibrated with equal parts of self-pity, bitterness and disappointment. Raoul had to send an emergency telegram in order pull his grandfather from his despair. "Please don't worry/no complications/affection her part only . . . Raoul."

*

After switching his internship positions, Raoul began to flourish. He had decided to rent an apartment with Björn Burchardt, with whom he was now close friends.

In November, Björn and Raoul left on a five-week business trip together with Carl Frykberg. It was at the very beginning of the South African summer and the trio travelled over 5,000 kilometres in 30°C heat in Frykberg's car. They drove through the fruit districts around Paarl and Worcester, over the deserts "filled with scorpions and snakes", past the vast gold fields and arrived in Johannesburg, with its frenzy of construction projects, where they stayed for several weeks.

Raoul still found the politics of segregation disturbing and was unsettled by the shanty towns outside Johannesburg where the black population was forced to live in shacks made of old doors, boxes and tin cans. "Tragically, especially in the case of labourers and skilled workers, whites don't seem to think it possible to get ahead without completely excluding the blacks or, in the best case scenario, by relegating them to the bottom layer of society," he wrote in his travel article the following year.

At the same time he was himself trapped in the racially grounded view of human beings that he had learned at school. He had brought along his camera and took photographs of beautiful landscapes and buildings, but also of Zulu rickshaw drivers on the streets of Durban, which he referred to in his article as a "picturesque detail".

They wear feathers in their hair and bells around their ankles. We drove around in the heat with a rickshaw and admired our driver's skill at balancing his small vehicle so that our weight in part lifted him. He hung from the shafts and moved in springy, enormous strides, only touching the ground with the tips of his toes, accopanied by loud singing and the jangling of the bells.

At the end of the year, Raoul Wallenberg had settled in so well in South Africa that he started to consider staying longer than originally planned. A little later, in September 1936, he had a five-week-long refresher course in the Swedish army to look forward to. Before then, grandfather Gustaf wanted to see him in Haifa. Raoul now wrote a long and well-argued letter to Gustaf where he objected to the unnecessary complication of heading to Palestine for only a couple of months, especially as he now had so many deals under way. Among other things, Frykberg had promised him that he would be allowed to sell Swedish boxes and waxed paper if he stayed. For another business contact, the director Albert Florén, he had begun to prepare deals for toilets and sinks. If he was not actually making any money, he was nevertheless learning a great deal about trade and important Swedish exports.

But Gustaf could not be swayed on this point. After a while it emerged that he was simply afraid that his time was beginning to run out and was therefore eager to see Raoul conclude his "commercial education" as soon as possible.

If Raoul was willing to leave relatively quickly, Gustaf was in return willing to travel back to Sweden at the time of Raoul's military service in September. With a couple of months of bank work behind him, Raoul would then be ready to be presented to the elite of the Swedish business world or, as Gustaf put it, prepared to "in my company come into contact with persons in prominent positions who might possibly have use of you". It was not primarily the Wallenberg family that Gustaf was thinking of, but the "heads of banking and business" outside that sphere. He would not tolerate any nepotism: no begging for a position. Raoul would make his case through the force of his own person and his exceptional experience.

On Friday, February 7, 1936, Raoul Wallenberg boarded the Italian liner *Duilio* for his third long intercontinental journey within the space of a year. He wore a flower in his buttonhole and had had his hair cropped closely. The latter was on his doctor's orders. At only twenty-three years of age, Raoul's hair was beginning to recede, and he had been recommended to shave it in order to improve the growth. There is no evidence that this was successful.

In his bag he had two glowing recommendations from Frykberg and Florén in which his personal attributes were praised to the skies. "I have found him to be an excellent organiser and have put his abilities to negotiate to great use. With his boundless energy and vitality, he is an impressive creative force and he has the ability to apply his lucid and original mind to all manner of problems that have appeared," Albert Florén wrote.

However, Raoul felt miserable and dejected. Even his practical arrangements for the trip had been a challenge. Although he had been able to reserve a nice first-class cabin for himself with a bathroom, a window and a sofa, he was – to judge from his letters – sceptical about his travel companions: some two hundred Jews on their way to a Zionist congress in Palestine. The experience he had of "the regular South African Jews" indicated that the trip could be a trial.

But things went relatively well. In two weeks he took himself from heat to winter with interesting stops at Monrovia and Dakar on the west coast of Africa. Once he reached Gibraltar he sent a postcard to his mother depicting the white ship, the largest in service on the route between South Africa and Europe. "The passengers are mostly Zionist Jews who are unexpectedly interesting and enjoyable. The sea has been calm and it has been hot," he reported briskly. On the inside, however, his frustration was nearing boiling point.

It was a far more uncertain world that Raoul Wallenberg now ventured into in the early spring of 1936. In October 1935, Mussolini's Italy had, without declaring war, attacked Ethiopia with an army of a hundred thousand soldiers. The invasion was brutal, with the Italians dropping bombs and releasing mustard gas. Their ruthless attack was denounced by a nearly unanimous League of Nations. The war would, however, continue until 5 May, 1936, when the capital city, Addis Ababa, fell into the hands of the Italians and the League of Nations descended into a crisis from which the organisation never recovered.

Gustaf downplayed the risks to Raoul. He did not believe that the Italian–Ethiopian conflict would spread, and he was appalled that the papers back home in Sweden carried warnings of an impending second world war. He based his reasoning in part on a comparative study of dictators through history he had completed for his own amusement. His conclusion was that, in comparison with an Oliver Cromwell or a Genghis Khan, the modern dictators like Mussolini, Hitler and Stalin were superior, "both as political strategists and field marshals. This is the fact that saves us from a new war."

In Gustaf's eyes, Mussolini's leadership exceeded even Hitler's in strength since the latter's international power was based more on fear and force. "It is self-control in its highest potency," Gustaf had written of Mussolini in a letter to Raoul a year or so earlier.

After the invasion of Ethiopia he was admittedly sceptical of the Italian dictator's judgement, but he still did not understand how Sweden and the other countries could so emphatically denounce the Italians. "Through the taking of sides that has taken place at home, the whole of the Italian market has been completely lost to us," Gustaf complained to Raoul and urged his grandson to choose a more strategic position and always adopt a strict neutrality in political conflicts. "One should keep one's eyes and ears open for observation but refrain from voicing opinion," Gustaf wrote. It was a piece of advice that Raoul Wallenberg appears to have listened to.

The conflict in Abyssinia was not the only source of concern. In the British protectorate of Palestine – which is where Raoul was heading – things were hardly more calm. That same spring, in 1936, the significant tensions between the Palestinian Arabs and the ever-increasing group of immigrant Jews – most of whom came from Germany – would reach their peak.

After Hitler took power in Germany in 1933, Zionist emigration to Palestine had increased dramatically, especially after the Nuremberg laws of 1935, when the Nazis excluded all Jews from German citizenship. The Jewish settlers had grown from 20 to almost 30 per cent of Palestine's population in only three years: from 235,000 to 384,000 individuals.

A month or so after Raoul's arrival in Haifa, the Arab Palestinians went on general strike. They demanded a stop to all further Jewish immigration. Violence broke out and soon the Arab revolt against the Jewish newcomers and the British officials became serious. The revolt was incited by the Arab leader, Haj Amin al-Husseini, Grand Mufti of Jerusalem who, in his efforts to drive Jews and the British out of Palestine, finally resorted to cooperating with the German Nazis.

Raoul Wallenberg was forced to spend a week in Genoa at the end of 1936, in order to arrange his work permit for Palestine. During this time he squeezed in a brief visit to his grandparents Gustaf and Annie who were on holiday in Nice, only a few hours away.

They were, as usual, staying at the Hôtel d'Angleterre, right on the beach. The fond reunion was, however, not without its complications. In seeing his grandfather, Raoul finally could not contain his frustration. During a discussion about plans for the coming year, he became incensed. There were six months to go before the remainder of his military service began in September. Gustaf insisted that Raoul afterwards return immediately to Haifa. Raoul pleaded and asked his grandfather to let him stay home a little longer. When Gustaf questioned his motives, Raoul departed from the usual diplomatic and mild-mannered tone he used with him.

The eruption must have been dramatic. When Raoul returned to Genoa he felt compelled to write a letter that, at least on the surface, resembled an apology. But no-one who read it could mistake Raoul's despondent capitulation in the face of forces stronger than himself:

> As to our final conversation regarding the possibility of interrupting my sejour in Haifa, I would again like to apologise for my outburst. I am all too aware of the debt of gratitude I owe you not to bow to your decision. But I am sorry that you tried to look for motives in my objections that did not exist [. . .] I do not have any particular objection to living abroad and since I haven't earned any money I also do not have a strong longing to come home. Thank you again for your hospitality in Nice.
>
> Your faithful Raoul.

The following day, Raoul boarded a slow passenger and cargo ship headed to Haifa. The martial atmosphere in the region was immediately noticeable. During the approach into Alexandria the ship passed a hundred British warships, and on the way out it met an Italian troop transport in the entrance to the canal. Even Raoul joined in the chorus when the Italian crew began loudly started to sing "*Duce, Duce, Duce*," together with the thousands of Italian soldiers.

One evening towards the end of the voyage, a rumour spread on board that Germany had marched into the demilitarised zone in the Rhineland. This troop movement was in direct violation of the Treaty of Versailles and in consequence the French started to mobilise and the British sent their warships to the North Sea's German coast. There was little information but it created great concern, Raoul later told his grandfather in a letter: "I was sorry to meet such a widespread pessimism in terms of the view of Europe's future. This was particularly true of the Jews but I suppose they had their reasons."

*

Gustaf Wallenberg had made it sound as if the bank director Erwin Freund intended to drop everything he was doing and focus exclusively on Raoul's business education. Instead, Freund looked astonished when Raoul appeared one morning in March at his overflowing office at the Holland Bank Union. Freund had not expected him for at least a year.

During his four months in Haifa, Raoul did not see a great deal of his grandfather's much-lauded friend, nor was he much impressed by him when he did appear. To Raoul, Erwin Freund seemed a nervous and stressed boss, quick to outbursts of temper. But among staff at the Holland Bank Union, Raoul found several Jewish friends that he began to see frequently.

In South Africa, Raoul had been given the name of Gerzon, a young Dutch Jew. He found, to his surprise and delight, that the 21-year-old Gerzon turned out to be Erwin Freund's secretary. Gerzon's family had a boarding house on 17 Arlozorov Street, where many recently relocated German Jews lived. The boarding house was only a couple of streets back from the harbour in Haifa, which at this time was filled with British cruisers. Raoul moved in there and soon began socialising with the Jewish immigrants as well as his peers at the bank, who all turned out to be adept at languages. He adopted some Jewish customs such as, for example, keeping his hat on during the Sabbath.

Raoul heard horror stories about the situation in Germany. A woman who lived in the boarding house told him that her brother had been killed by the Nazis. Raoul, who saw the challenges that the Jews encountered in Palestine, felt a strong sympathy for his new friends. In Palestine they were met by hostility from the Arabs, in Germany from the Nazis. In his first letter from Haifa he wrote:

These poor people apparently have to accept being the minority wherever they go. Here, however, they are filled with a boundless enthusiasm and idealism that immediately strikes one as the common trait for all Zionists. It is a gamble for them to try to relocate a hundred thousand Jews here in a dry little rocky land surrounded by, and already populated with, Arabs.

*

Raoul Wallenberg was fascinated by the work ethic of the immigrant Jews and the almost paradisiacal conceptions they held of their future in Palestine, despite the fact that the country offered them so little. As far as Raoul could tell, there was far too little water and far too many stones in the ground for viable agriculture. In addition, the country had been inhabited by hundreds of thousands of Arabs before the Jewish settlers arrived. Nonetheless, all Jews were confident of success and "it would be a pity if that were not to be the case because Palestine is their home and the realisation of a long-held dream", Raoul observed. "They are accustomed to suffering that is greater than an economic crisis so they do not bother to think about the risks and anyway, they have no other choice but to settle here."

The religious fervour that he met in the immigrant Jews in Haifa was something that Raoul had never encountered before. He marvelled at their conviction that the promised land of Palestine would, in time, be able to accommodate four million Jews as well as the Arabs. To his grandfather he related the fable that his Jewish friends would tell him when anyone wondered how so many people would be able to live there.

> They say that Palestine is like a deer's hide. Once the skin has been removed from the animal and the latter is no longer in the skin to which it once belonged, it shrinks and one wonders how the animal ever fitted inside it. It is the same with Palestine. As long as Palestine contains a Jewish people it will flow with milk and honey and can accommodate a large population, but when the Jews are no longer here it shrinks in value and not even a small Arab population with few needs can get by.

Raoul's life in Haifa came to closely resemble that which he had left behind in Cape Town, even if he only had one free day a week. His friends went to the beach of Bat Galim where the strong south-westerly breezes were sweetly cooling when the heat of the summer was at its worst. On free days they also hiked up Mount Carmel to admire the view of the Mediterranean. After a while, Raoul met a girl in Haifa. Her name was Dora Aronowski, she had a Chinese father and she worked as a nurse alongside her studies. Raoul taught her a few sentences in Swedish, among them *jag älskar dig*, or, "I love you."

For Easter he travelled in a Volvo bus with Gerzon and another friend from work through the city of Nazareth and on to the city of Tiberias by the shores of Lake Galilee. Not long after, new bouts of unrest broke out in the cities they had just left. From Tel Aviv there were reports of some twenty fatalities. The increased tension between Arabs and Jews was also noticeable in Haifa, even though it lay outside the zone with the most violence. Raoul would meet armed British military on the streets, but claimed that he was not concerned since the British fleet was still in its place in the harbour.

Raoul's grandfather followed the events in Palestine but wrote that he too did not feel any great concern over the developments. Gustaf waved away the worst alarmist reports in the press for, according to his view of the matter, it was in the interests of the foreign correspondents to exaggerate. Only when the correspondent for the newspaper *Dagens Nyheter* reported that the situation was in fact far more serious than had emerged in the previous coverage did Gustaf seriously reconsider allowing Raoul to stay on.

Raoul himself was never really alarmed by the political situation. In fact the main reason that he was beginning to feel that he had had enough of Haifa was that he was bored and did not feel professionally challenged.

Raoul began to long for a regular, responsible and paid position. It was frustrating to continue as an unpaid intern in a bank that failed to offer him any kind of intellectual stimulation. Everything followed prescribed rules, which was a stark contrast to the freedom he had experienced in architecture and the sales work in South Africa.

After his confrontation with Gustaf in Nice in February, Raoul had gathered his courage. He had realised that if he did not voice his true feelings and doubts it could jeopardise the entire educational project. He had to be honest.

For the first time, Raoul dared to oppose his grandfather in earnest. He wrote to Gustaf and confessed that he was not certain he should pursue anything to do with banking. Architecture was something that he had shown talent for. Construction projects had interested him since he was a child. But to be a banker, he felt, one had to have a cool and cynical personality, as well as "something judgelike and calm", which he felt he completely lacked. "Freund and Jacob W are probably typical and I feel I am as unlike them as I could possibly be. I think I have the potential to do something more constructive than sit around saying no to people."

And he did not stop there. Raoul also wanted to take the opportunity, at least partially, to remove the halo that surrounded bank director Erwin Freund in his grandfather's glowing descriptions. In mid-May, Freund had sent a letter to Gustaf in which he showered his grandson with compliments. Freund had told him how intelligent and cultivated he found Raoul, how much everyone liked him, and how thoroughly and seriously the grandson went about his work. Freund did not hesitate to call Raoul the very best worker among his contemporaries at the bank. Gustaf soaked up every last punctuation mark in this letter and shared the praise widely, including with Raoul himself. But Raoul simply snorted at this flattery. He explained to Gustaf that Freund had not spent more than four hours with him altogether. According to Raoul the letter in question was nothing but an "insincere fiction".

Confronted with this obviously well-grounded scepticism, Gustaf replied that Raoul should still take advantage of the letter, regardless of how he felt about its contents.

It is not clear whether it was the political instabilities, Raoul's new courage or his grandfather's wavering health that was the determining factor. But, as time passed, Gustaf became more and more accommodating regarding Raoul's future. His former insistence on strict compliance fell away.

Nevertheless, this new accommodating attitude contained a streak of irritation. Gustaf made it clear to Raoul that he could decide what to do after his military service, but if he remained in Sweden he would have to find a way to support himself. Gustaf still did not like the idea of Raoul returning to Sweden in the summer, before his military service began in September. If the political instability in the region grew too serious, it would be better for him to come to Gustaf in Istanbul, he reasoned.

Now that the tone had changed between them, he became more direct with his grandson:

> The only thing that I fear with regard to a visit home is the girls, not the ones on the street, but those in the parlours. It is not advisable to attach oneself, particularly in these uncertain times when it is not yet

clear what the future holds. Nothing fetters a young man's spirit like having to go off to work in an impoverished state. First, one must establish a position of independence, have an annual income of 20,000 kronor [around £40,000 today] and be able to support two maids. Otherwise one has nothing to offer one's wife but to become a maid herself. And this does not taste good in the long run.

In his letters that summer, these sort of sharp warnings were interwoven with Gustaf's grandiose tributes to his grandson's maturity, competence and career prospects. It was as if the 73-year-old former diplomat had overseen the polishing of a diamond whose value was now about to be carefully tested on the market. He could not allow the tiniest scratch to diminish its worth.

Twenty-four years earlier, Gustaf had lost his only son Raoul Oscar in tragic circumstances. At the time of his death, his son had been twenty-three years old, about to turn twenty-four: the same age his grandson Raoul was now. In his eleventh hour of life, Gustaf could now, through young Raoul, finally enjoy the promise of a gilded path into the highest levels of society.

This time absolutely nothing was to be allowed to go wrong. The diamond would be displayed in its very best light as it made the tour of Sweden's business elite, which Gustaf planned to follow Raoul's military service in October.

Gustaf was so nervous that he could not resist beginning to direct Raoul in preparation for these introductory meetings: Raoul must not seem too eager or appear needy for a job. Even if Raoul decided to stay in Sweden now, he should give the impression that he was in demand overseas, in Haifa, for example. Raoul was neither to show off nor display ignorance. Everything was a delicate game, which called for no small amount of acting talent and a feeling for what the particular audience was looking for. He did not conceal from Raoul the fact that he thought a great deal about Raoul Oscar and what might have become of him had he not died so young.

Raoul had no intention of disappointing him. He made it clear to Gustaf that the reason he wanted a paid job was not in order to run away and get married. "However, I do feel a strong longing to make money, preferably a lot of money. I will probably want a wife too, but for now, I'm putting the money first."

Raoul was also moved by the reference to his late father:

When I read the first sentence I immediately wanted to hear more from you regarding my father. Preferably in the form of a letter so I can have it with me always. I have always felt inferior to him in a half-subconscious way. In my photographs he looks so fine and honest and self-sacrificing, and I feel like a poor substitute.

Thus loaded with his grandfather's enormous expectations, Raoul booked a trip home in the middle of August, allowing himself a one-day stop at Gustaf's home in Istanbul. He continued by boat to the Romanian city of Constanţa where he changed to an overcrowded immigrant train that took him up through a frigid Poland. He travelled by way of the cities Katowice and Warsaw to Berlin. There he visited his favourite cousin, Maj Nisser, who had married and now lived with her German husband, Count Enzio von Plauen, in a castle just east of the German capital. After the chaos of Romania, Raoul was impressed with the well-tended forests bordering the estate. "Nazi Germany itself also made a good impression and those I spoke with, except the Jews, said they were well contented," Raoul later wrote to his grandfather.

One year later a German Nazi and Sicherheitsdienst (S.D.) bureaucrat by the name of Adolf Eichmann selected exactly same travel route through Eastern Europe on his way to Haifa. Eichmann was thirty-one years old at the time and a cadet in the S.S., a lower-level official in the Nazi hierarchy. His task was to report on Jewish and Zionist organisations in Germany. In his reports, Eichmann observed the newly adopted principles that established the Jews as the most dangerous enemy of National Socialism. What mattered, therefore, was how to rid Germany entirely of Jews. The favoured solution of the day was emigration. A Zionist mass exodus to Palestine, Eichmann reasoned, would help realise the Nazi dream if one could achieve a steady flow of departures.

In September 1937, Eichmann was travelling to Haifa with a colleague to explore the possibility of expediting the emigration of Jews from Germany to Palestine. In the back of his mind he nurtured a plan to give each emigrating Jew some starter capital in order to tempt others to leave Germany. But his trip was a failure. When he arrived in Haifa, he was only granted a twenty-four-hour visa and did not have time for much more than a hike up Mount Carmel.

Later, when Raoul Wallenberg and Adolf Eichmann met in Budapest in 1944 the German Nazis had for some time been using another, far more malevolent strategic solution to rid not only Germany but all of Europe of their Jewish "enemies". Eichmann was still very much involved with this issue.

Raoul was looking forward to the military refresher course, both because September was unusually beautiful in Sweden that autumn, and also because he was someone who enjoyed physical challenges such as sleeping only a few hours at night, or charging through difficult terrain to the point of exhaustion.

The same day that Raoul reported for duty, his grandfather wrote from Istanbul and told him that the British were going to send an additional ten thousand troops to Palestine and that he therefore no longer wished Raoul to return there.

Raoul completed his military duties on Tuesday, October 6 and moved back in with his family in the newly built house just north of Stockholm. Once there, he eagerly awaited his grandfather's arrival. He had already made some contacts on his own, as well as visiting some of his relatives. When Gustaf's brother Knut Wallenberg had asked him point-blank if he would like to start working at the bank, Raoul remembered his grandfather's warning and answered evasively. He was pleased to note, however, Knut's comment that if this were to be the case, Raoul should go to straight "to the top".

A week later, Raoul began to worry. Gustaf should have been home by now. Raoul had not received any letters about new plans. He felt stuck. He was eager to start building his career but did not dare to look around for a position before his grandfather's planned tour of the Swedish business world.

Not until October 20 did Raoul hear that his grandfather Gustaf had become unwell and had gone to Nice to regain his health. Raoul was very concerned for his grandfather's well-being and, at the same time, anxiously aware that the weeks were going by. As he tried to explain in a letter to Gustaf, he did not want to be a burden to his stepfather. Since he could not take an allowance from Gustaf as long as he remained in Sweden, it was becoming necessary for him to get a job. Yet, he would rather wait, "in order that I not take on any obligations before the planned tour of visits with you have taken place".

Finally Raoul took the train down to Nice. He was reassured when Gustaf met him at the station, looking well, though thirteen kilos lighter. He was even happier when he discovered that his grandfather had the energy to go to the cinema, sit up and play solitaire and, with Raoul, visit his brother Knut Wallenberg, who was staying on the Riviera as well.

Gustaf and Raoul's visit to Knut troubled Marcus Sr back in Sweden. He voiced his concerns to his daughter Gertrud in a letter at the end of November. "It would be interesting to . . . learn if Uncle Gustaf forced some sort of half promise out of Uncle Knut regarding R's employment at the bank. I know that R's mother has already been to see Uncle Knut in this regard."

Perhaps in order to prevent such a development, Marcus Sr had written to Raoul in Nice the week before mentioning a patent, which the Emissionsinstitutet, or Securities Institute, partly owned by the Wallenbergs, had recently acquired. The patent was for some kind of Japanese zip, which they were considering launching in Sweden, possibly through a newly established corporation. Marcus Sr wondered in his letter if this might be a task that interested Raoul. If so, he urged Raoul to travel via Neustadt in Germany on his way home, take a look at a factory and meet with Nachmanson, a director from the Securities Institute.

A few weeks later Raoul Wallenberg took the train to Neustadt.

It was a delicate time for a Scandinavian to travel through Nazi Germany. The Nobel Peace Prize had just been awarded to the German pacifist Carl von Ossietzky, whom the Nazis had arrested in 1933 and sent to a concentration camp. The Nobel committee's decision had caused strong protests from the Nazi regime. Ossietzky was forbidden to leave the camp and was unable to accept the prize at the ceremony in Oslo on December 10, 1936. After this, Hitler went on to forbid all German Nobel Prize winners to accept their awards, regardless of the discipline.

Raoul does not appear to have reflected much on the strained situation in Hitler's Germany at the time, however. He returned home after his visit to Neustadt, enthusiastic about his new project, and spent several weeks around the end of the year on his report to Marcus Sr for the proposed zip factory.

The decision regarding the licensing rights was urgent, so he worked day and night in the new family villa in Kevinge, digging up information from all over the world and writing long calculations about the cost of production, among other things, which he hung on the wall.

He allowed himself a few breaks, such as a family gathering with his Broby cousins. In the evening, he entertained them as usual with his party pieces – terrific parodies of "the German, the French, the American and the Swede". His cousin Lennart Hagströmer remembered these parodies his entire life and often talked about how those present were always doubled over with laughter.

On Tuesday, January 19, 1937, Raoul wrote his very last letter to his grandfather. He updated Gustaf about his work on the zip report. He wrote about a lunch with Knut and Alice Wallenberg and said that he and his parents had been invited to visit "Little Marcus", which is what Raoul preferred to call Marcus Jr. "His new wife is liked by all and looks to suit him well."

It was the first time in several months that Raoul wrote without referring to his grandfather's health or their planned tour of the business elite. Perhaps seeing his grandfather looking better took some pressure off and Raoul could now trust that these introductions would soon take place. Perhaps he did not feel the same urgency now that Marcus Sr had given him a measure of responsibility. When the time was right, his grandfather would lead him into the Swedish business elite. Everything would go according to the plan they had worked on for so many years.

But the light quickly turned to darkness. When his grandfather returned to Sweden a little later, he was again very ill. On March 21, 1937, the 74-year-old Gustaf Wallenberg died at the Red Cross hospital in Stockholm.

Stockholm, February 2010

The attorney Lennart Hagströmer was born three years before Raoul Wallenberg. He has placed his cousin's framed graduation picture on the dining-room table in his apartment in Stockholm. It shows a very serious Raoul, dressed in a suit and standing with his arms firmly crossed. He looks as if he is glaring at us or, possibly, scrutinising the piles of old letters and yellowed photograph envelopes that Lennart Hagströmer has brought out.

This is the interview I have been putting off, paralysed by respect for Hagströmer's advanced age. A couple of months ago, he turned one hundred. Was it appropriate to call a centenarian on the telephone? Could he see well enough to read a letter? I was finally able to reach his nephew, Sven Hagströmer, and was able to ask his advice.

"Lennart?" he said. "Just call him. No problem."

I did as he said. Lennart checked his calendar and suggested a date.

"It will have to be in the morning," he said. "I have a meeting in the afternoon."

We meet in his apartment, up three flights of stairs in a tall Functionalist-style building close to Gärdet in Stockholm. There are those who make pilgrimages here in order to gaze at one of the most clearly articulated expressions of the design philosophy.

Lennart is the second of the three Hagströmer cousins who Raoul Wallenberg spent so much time with. He greets me at the door wearing a white shirt and a grey cardigan. He moves around his apartment with ease, assisted only by a brown walking stick. The apartment is filled with books, both on the shelves and on the tables. Here is the entire second or "Owl" edition of the famous old Swedish encyclopedia, Nordisk familjebok, in twenty-eight volumes, but also Stieg Larsson's successful trilogy about Lisbeth Salander from the first decade of the twenty-first century.

We sit down at the dining-room table. Lennart begins by carefully pulling out a small picture from one of his transparent photograph envelopes. It shows four little boys in laced-up boots outside the entrance to Rådmansgatan 18 where the Hagströmer family lived for many years. The Hagströmer brothers are wearing sailor suits. Raoul wears a shirt and long trousers.

I am told that the warm, adult friendship between Lennart and Raoul only really began in the middle of the 1930s. When Raoul returned from the United States at the age of twenty-two they got to know each other in a new way. And perhaps even more the following year after his sojourns in Cape Town and Haifa. Lennart remembers the zips.

"He was trying to find a position as an architect, but it wasn't very easy because times were tough. Then Raoul wanted to go into the business. My brother Anders and I both found contacts for him. Later, I played a small part in a company he set up with a Jewish refugee who held patents to some interesting products."

By this time Hagströmer had graduated from Stockholm's business school and gained a law degree. When Raoul returned from the United States in February 1935, Lennart was doing his legal internship at the Södra Roslag District Court. In his spare time he was the ombudsman for the life insurance company Thule (later Scandia). He remembers trying to trick Raoul into getting an endowment policy and his friend said, "Yes, perhaps I should get one of those so I don't become a Wallenberg who dies penniless."

"Raoul was very much a salesman. I was with him in Paris once when he was going to visit the department store Galeries Lafayette to try to sell them a cork for soda bottles that he and his partner held the patent to. 'I'm not coming along. You handle that yourself,' I said. But Raoul insisted. 'You are to act as my "technical assistant". When I need time to think during the discussion, I'll just turn to you, my technician, and say some nonsense in Swedish.'"

Lennart laughs at this memory.

"But you were not a technician?"

"No, I wasn't. I was a lawyer."

"How would you describe Raoul Wallenberg as a person?"

"High tempo. He was almost always happy. And funny. He was very good at impersonations. I have never laughed as much as when he performed and imitated Hitler, Churchill and Stalin at my cousin's house in Broby. But perhaps this was later."

"Was he brave?"

"How do you mean?"

"Was he a risk-taker?"

"Well, I don't know about that. I suppose he showed courage in Budapest. I thought he was a helpful and reliable friend, someone you could count on. When we went sailing he always wanted to handle doing the dishes. He explained it like this, 'I am an architect, generally I have to wait many years to see the results of what I do. When I do the dishes, the result is immediate.'"

Lennart takes more photographs out of the envelopes. Many of them are from the years 1935–9, before Lennart Hagströmer got married. They show the cousins on outings on Lennart's sailing boat in the Stockholm archipelago. Raoul sits in a bathrobe in front of a table in the cockpit set with silverware and plates. There are cans of herring and milk bottles, and glasses in a special contraption to prevent sliding. They jump ashore in their swimsuits on beautiful islands with flat rocks. Raoul's hair crinkles into baby curls after swimming, and there are indeed pictures of him doing the dishes in sea water. It is Swedish summer at its finest.

Judging from the pictures, they are almost never alone.

"No, some pretty girl or other would usually come along. I particularly remember one of them as I saw in the paper the other day that she died," Lennart says and takes out the snapshot of a young blonde woman, thoughtfully resting her chin in her hand. Lennart doesn't want to say her name.

"Was she your girlfriend or Raoul's?"

"Well, it was probably, what do you call it, *l'amour à trois*," Lennart Hagströmer answers and gives me a sly wink with his warm blue-grey eye.

From time to time we have to take a break. Lennart has difficulties breathing after a recent cold. But we talk for a long time and a great deal falls into place. I once again look at Raoul's graduation photo that is next to us on the table. I study the nicely ironed suit trousers, the well-combed hair and the almost childishly puffy cheeks. His personality is becoming more clear to me, as if I knew him too.

Just as I am about to pack up, Lennart stops me. There was one more thing, something he had promised himself not to forget.

"Raoul learned Russian. He used to say that he felt Russia had everything that the United States had. It was a large country, rich in both minerals and oil. Therefore, Russia might just as well be the land of the future, Raoul thought. I sometimes think about that."

Lennart Hagströmer died on November 1, 2010. His brothers Anders and Gösta died before him.

CHAPTER 6

On His Own Two Feet

Raoul Wallenberg's siblings, Guy and Nina von Dardel, were thrilled when their big brother returned from his adventures abroad. It had been fairly quiet at the von Dardel dinner table for the past few years, but now their brother filled the void with his humour, his intense discussions, his plans and his pranks. Everything became so much more exciting when he was around.

When he left, he had been their idol, someone who, because of the age difference, they admired from afar. Now Guy was about to turn eighteen and Nina sixteen, and their relationship with their almost 25-year-old brother changed into something else. Something at once more adult and more playful.

Gustaf Wallenberg's death in March 1937 struck the von Dardels' lively family idyll like a bomb going off. Guy and Nina could not help but notice how difficult this loss was for their elder brother. Raoul had not only lost the most significant father figure in his life, someone who seemed to have felt that nothing was more important than guiding Raoul with his boundless, if somewhat harsh, love and attention. Raoul had also lost all the future plans and dreams that his grandfather had methodically been constructing for him since he was a tiny boy. The introduction into Swedish business life that his grandfather had promised him never even had the chance to get under way.

Ten days after Gustaf's death, Raoul met with Gustaf's brother Marcus Wallenberg Sr. The meeting probably concerned the evaluation of the zip factory and what the Wallenberg-owned firm might make of it.

Since no minutes are available, it is not known what was said during the meeting. What we do know is that the Securities Institute (Emissionsinstitutet) did not invest in the zips. The new company that Raoul Wallenberg had dreamed of and made nightly calculations over would never form part of the family empire. Instead, Raoul seems to have left the headquarters of Enskilda Bank with a suggestion to continue with the zips on his own. Because that is what he did.

Raoul was about to turn twenty-five and desperately needed to find a way to make a living. While he had some savings, they were not to be used for day-to-day expenses. Without a job he would not last very long. If it had been up to Raoul he would have had not only his architecture degree by now, but also a degree from the Stockholm School of Economics, something that would certainly have made things easier. Instead he found himself with an education designed by his grandfather that, he was beginning to discover, not everybody in the Swedish business elite found quite as ingenious as had Gustaf.

Not even his successful studies in the United States opened any real doors despite his public breakthrough in 1935 with the Riddarholm public swimming pool. Raoul had left the scene almost immediately and devoted himself to completely different tasks rather than cultivating his architectural talents. His career was hardly aided by his scepticism bordering on contempt for Functionalism, which now completely dominated Swedish architecture. According to his sister, Nina Lagergren, he had at this point realised that his American degree had little value in Sweden, where a more robust technical foundation was required in architectural degrees.

His friends from that time describe Raoul as stressed and restless, without a secure foothold in life. His school friend Rolf af Klintberg was one of them. He had continued his education by studying law, "following the old worn path". Raoul and Rolf did not see each other as often as before. "But when he showed up it was as if a whirlwind went through the room, with new ideas and bold, sometimes puzzling initiatives . . . It wasn't always easy to follow," Rolf remembered later.

Raoul's cousins, Lennart and Anders Hagströmer, were more directly drawn into Raoul's initiatives. It was to his cousin Lennart, three years his senior, that Raoul turned when things grew dire. What he had at hand at that moment was the possibility of importing Japanese zips: Raoul was in a hurry and needed to borrow money quickly, 5,000 Swedish kronor to be exact (approximately £11,000 today). He offered Lennart 10 per cent of the net gains on sales if he was able to deliver the money within a couple of days. Lennart empathised with his cousin and agreed. He decided to open a line of credit for Raoul, with his own assets as security.

Raoul could not know this at the time but San-S Shokai, the Japanese company that he was in negotiations with, was about to change its name to YKK, the name with which it dominated the global zip markets during the twentieth century. The year 1937 would in fact go down in zip history as the great breakthrough, the turning point at which British and French fashion designers capitulated and stopped using buttons in men's trousers.

But for Raoul the project got no further than a single attempt. He filled his home office on the bottom floor of the Kevinge house with Japanese zips but never really managed to get things going. Perhaps he lacked the necessary patience and concentration. When, around the same time, the Hagströmer cousins connected him with a German Jewish refugee who had a bunch of interesting patents in his briefcase, Raoul got caught up with a new set of plans.

The name of the Jewish refugee was Werner Abernau. Abernau was a chemist and a businessman, acquainted with the father of the Hagströmer brothers, County Governor Sven Hagströmer. Abernau had grown up in Berlin and was eleven years older than Raoul Wallenberg. He had arrived in Sweden as early as 1934 but, like so many others in his situation, he had initially had a difficult time.

In the 1930s Sweden was a country where, until recently, immigration had been an almost unknown phenomenon. With its harsh climate, Sweden had traditionally been a country from which people tended to emigrate, not a place one moved to from the outside. Refugees from Germany and other countries were therefore perceived as a foreign element and met with scepticism.

For the multilingual cosmopolitan Raoul Wallenberg, however, people from other countries were a natural part of everyday life and offered potentially stimulating relationships. He knew a great deal about Abernau's situation. After his time in Haifa, Raoul regarded many German Jewish refugees as his closest friends and he was still in touch with some of them. In 1937, for example, he contacted an ex-girlfriend, Dora Aronowski, to ask her for help with a Jewish woman Raoul knew who would possibly need to emigrate from Sweden to Palestine.

Raoul was also very proud of the small drop of Jewish blood in his own veins. To be precise it was not more than one sixteenth. His maternal grand-mother's paternal grandfather was a Jewish jeweller, Mikael Benedicks, who had emigrated to Sweden from northern Germany at the end of the eight-eenth century at the suggestion of the founder of the Mosaic council in Stock-holm, Aaron Isaac. Raoul often pointed out to his friends that he was part Jewish, occasionally exaggerating the extent of this Jewish heritage.

It is not clear whether it was during his days in Haifa, or later, but long before the start of the Second World War Raoul managed to plough through Adolf Hitler's *Mein Kampf* no less than twice, which was more than many Nazis managed to do. There is good reason therefore to assume that he was better informed than most Swedes about what the new Nazi policies in Ger-many meant for the Jewish population of the country.

Raoul Wallenberg was without a doubt an ideal companion for the Jewish businessman and refugee Werner Abernau.

Raoul Wallenberg was unusually well informed but, during these years, even the ordinary Swedish newspaper reader could receive regular updates about the most significant details of the Nazis' accelerating persecution of the Jews in Germany. It was not until after the beginning of the Second World War that the alarming reports started to disappear from the newspapers, a fickle for-eign policy placing new limitations on the freedom of the press.

As long as the news was of persecution and not extermination, the new German policies towards Jews were well received in certain segments of Swedish society. Anti-Semitism had long been simmering beneath the surface, even in the so-called tolerant country of Sweden. As the Swedish historian Henrik Bachner, has shown, "the Jewish question" was a regular topic in public discussion in the 1930s.

After the Nuremberg laws of 1935, when all Jews in Germany lost their citizenship, many Swedes across the political spectrum expressed concern about the possibility of an imminent Jewish refugee invasion.

The altered political situation in Germany also prompted a revision of the Swedish Aliens Act, which had been introduced in 1927 to, among other things, preserve the Swedish population as "an unusually homogeneous and unmixed race". As was so often the case in Sweden, it ended in a watered-down compromise. The new act avoided making binding statements, so that the number of refugees admitted could be adjusted according to current needs. The power to decide who would be allowed into the country went to the administrators at the newly created foreign bureau of the Swedish National Board for Health and Welfare (Socialstyrelsen). At this time refugees from other European countries required no visas for entry into Sweden, but that would change after Germany's annexation of Austria in March of 1938. it was not until after revelations of the Holocaust that this strain of anti-Semitically tinged "understanding" of German policy faded from Swedish discussions.

It was in this highly complex setting that the German Jewish refugee Werner Abernau tried to make a way for himself. On the one hand, there was always this undercurrent of anti-Semitism and hostility towards foreigners, and on the other, there were also strong appeals to the public's conscience and talk of Sweden's humanitarian responsibility towards the persecuted German refugees.

If there was a group with a particularly ingrained antipathy towards Jews it was among the bureaucrats at the National Board for Health and Welfare's foreign bureau. Abernau would not be alone in tasting the bitter brew that the supposedly "apolitical" Swedish officials served up to the Jewish refugees. How were people to obtain an impartial decision when even the bureau chief Robert Paulsson allowed himself to be recruited as a spy for Nazi Germany? Even less tainted administrators fought hard to prevent persecuted Jews from being accepted as political refugees. This stance was almost regarded as an established policy. Preliminary drafts of the new law explicitly excluded offering sanctuary to those who had, for example, fled Germany "on account of their race or limited opportunities to support themselves or feeling ill at ease there".

Werner Abernau was not in a good place when he first became acquainted with Raoul Wallenberg. His residence permit had not been extended and, since the spring of 1936, he had been forced to travel back and forth between the two nations; never allowed to spend more than three months at a time in Sweden. Nonetheless he had been able to run a company with a Swedish attorney, Hans F. Böhme, who had an office on the ninth floor of one of the towers on Kungsgatan.

During the spring of 1937, Raoul Wallenberg moved in to Böhme's office with his zips, his slumbering architectural ambitions and a new part-share in Abernau's venture – Svensk–Schweiziska Industrisyndikatet, or the Swedish–Swiss Industrial Syndicate.

The patent that had tempted Raoul into this partnership was for a nifty removable cork for glass bottles, which Abernau had obtained during a stay in Switzerland. Machines for production had already been purchased and installed in a mechanical shop in western Stockholm. The idea was to sell the "quick" corks both in Sweden and abroad. Negotiations were soon under way with buyers in Austria, Hungary, Czechoslovakia and Switzerland.

A heavy blow came in July 1937. During a trip to Austria, Abernau was arrested by police in Salzburg and locked up in jail. It took a while to sort out the details but the initial information was enough to throw Raoul into a state of panic. His new partner had been arrested in Austria and charged with sexual misconduct with an underage youth. In a letter to his cousin Lennart who was staying at the Hotel Gellért in Budapest, Raoul aired all his anxieties and concerns. Raoul knew that Abernau saw women, but could he be a homosexual? And could this matter spill over onto him?

Finally, Raoul travelled down to Salzburg only to find that his partner had just been freed after three weeks in jail having been completely cleared. He had apparently crossed paths with a young con artist who was known to offer guided tours to foreigners only to report them for unwanted sexual advances and fleece them of money.

Raoul was able to breathe again. On the train journey back to Sweden he was accompanied by Lennart Hagströmer, who had been in Austria and Hungary. The two of them first stopped in Paris for a few days where they went to see the World's Fair as well as the infamous red light district. They also visited a friend of Lennart's who was stationed at the Swedish legation in Paris. Here they were given a courier bag to deliver to the Foreign Minstry back in Stockholm. The friend's name was Ingemar Hägglöf and he was at the very beginning of his diplomatic career.

Later in life, Ingemar Hägglöf would have reason to think often of Raoul Wallenberg. In early 1945, when the Russians arrested Raoul in Budapest,

Ingemar Hägglöf was second in command at the Swedish legation in Moscow. Raoul and Ingemar spent large stretches of that year only a few blocks from each other in Moscow, Raoul Wallenberg at the Lubyanka prison and Hägglöf at the Swedish legation on ulitsa Vorovskogo (Vorovsky Street). Of course, neither had an inkling of this in 1937. Nor, unfortunately, would they know much more in 1945.

Raoul Wallenberg decided to give Werner Abernau and his corks another chance. In August, when two American friends from Ann Arbor came to Stockholm for a visit, he brought them up to his office. There he showed them the view of the city, the zips and the "Quick" corks. One of them, Frederick Graham, was given the assignment to send over some American bottles once he got back home so that Raoul could test the corks on them.

New ideas came and went on the ninth floor of the north tower where Raoul Wallenberg worked. Hans Böhme's office was becoming a multifaceted venture. Werner Abernau and Raoul Wallenberg tried the most varied business ideas. One time it was concrete tiles, another time some remarkable substance that one could clean wallpaper with – a product that Raoul enthusiastically tested at the office at Kungsgatan 30.

In the Swedish–Swiss Industrial Syndicate's final project it seemed as though Raoul was close to getting Marcus Wallenberg involved. Abernau had managed to acquire sole rights to a new Swiss production method for brass armature components. But by that point the German refugee was already living on borrowed time.

During the autumn, the foreign bureau of the National Board for Health and Welfare received a complaint against Abernau. A Swedish firm wanted to tip off the authorities about the "inappropriate" fact that the German citizen Abernau could live in Dalarö and lead a company in Sweden without having so much as a residency or work permit. One thing led to another.

On Friday, January 21, 1938, two police constables were waiting at the bus stop when Werner Abernau turned up to take the afternoon service to his hostel. He was taken to the police station for questioning. Abernau tried to point out that he had not broken any rules, that he had never stayed longer than three months at a time and that he was in the midst of a large international deal in which even the Enskilda Bank might participate.

All of this was true but the police do not appear to have believed him. Three days later, on 24 January, 1938, the National Board for Health and Welfare determined that Abernau should be deported, effective immediately.

The new iteration of the Aliens Act had just taken effect. Now the anti-Semitic clerks at the foreigners' department gained real power over the fates of Jewish refugees. Werner Abernau was one of the first to be deported under the new system. Thus, his fate was sealed.

On 20 March, 1943, Raoul Wallenberg's former business partner died at Sobibor concentration camp in eastern Poland.

During 1938, dark clouds gathered over Europe. Nazi Germany's annexation of Austria in March was only the beginning, as it turned out. In the autumn, Adolf Hitler made even greater power grabs and deceived both Neville Chamberlain, prime minister of Great Britain, and Édouard Daladier of France in the so-called Munich Agreement. France and the United Kingdom believed that they were entering into an undertaking for peace in exchange for Czechoslovakia relinquishing the Sudetenland to Germany. "Peace in our time!" Chamberlain exclaimed after signing the pact. But Hitler had other intentions.

Raoul Wallenberg followed international politics with interest but he had more pressing issues to worry about than German troop movements. However hard he tried, he was not able to achieve any significant progress in the career that had sounded so straightforward when his grandfather had described it.

On the personal front, the summer of 1938 had been good. Almost every weekend he had sailed in the Stockholm archipelago with Lennart Hagströmer and their friends. They would joke that the boat could float simply from the empty bottles generated by all these excursions. But professionally it was a different matter. The Swedish–Swiss Industrial Syndicate was never the same without Werner Abernau. In the end, Raoul and Böhme decided to drop the cork patent and liquidate the company. Raoul still had hopes for the Swiss production method for brass armature components but few others shared his enthusiasm.

Knut Wallenberg had died at home in June. The 74-year-old Marcus Wallenberg Sr assumed the chairmanship at Enskilda Bank, but Jacob Wallenberg remained the bank president and he managed the firm with his brother Marcus Jr as his right-hand man.

After Knut Wallenberg's funeral, Raoul visited Jacob Wallenberg several times and was promised a position as soon as Jacob could find "something appropriate". But all that Jacob came up with were temporary and rather unusual assignments – a market research project about a coffee roasting company, for example.

At home, Raoul's mother Maj returned from a long trip to the United States with Raoul's half-sister Nina. They had visited Maj's sister, who was married to an American.

The high point of the trip had been a meeting with the famous Swedish nurse Elsa Brändström, renowned for her lifesaving efforts among Siberian prisoners of war during the Great War. Elsa Brändström was an international celebrity. After the war she had settled in Germany and, among other things, opened a home for the orphans of dead prisoners of war. But when Hitler assumed power in 1933 she moved to the United States with her husband.

Elsa Brändström received Maj and Nina in her home. Brändström was in the midst of a new life mission. She was trying to save Russian Jews from Hitler's persecution. Her work was focused on procuring the necessary security documents.

For a refugee to be admitted into the country, the United States required documents indicating that the US government would not incur any costs resulting from the travel. The affidavit had to be signed by an American citizen. This person assumed responsibility for the financial support of the refugee. Elsa Brändström told them that she was signing these affadavits on a continual basis for Jewish refugees and that she was organising recruitment campaigns on the streets in order to get more people to do the same. She also travelled around the United States in order to try to arrange work and homes for the arriving refugees. Many had moved into her own home.

When Maj arrived back in Stockholm she talked enthusiastically about Elsa Brändström's new mission of organising the mass production of documents that would give Jewish refugees safe refuge in the United States.

Newly energised by her encounter with the world, Maj von Dardel felt an ever-increasing sense of boredom with her lonely life out in Kevinge.

She made a decision. After only two years in that rural paradise, the family sold the house. In the autumn of 1938, they moved back into Stockholm, to a five-room apartment in the city's centre.

Nina had stopped in London on her way home from the United States for a year of study at a British school. Little brother Guy was in Boden, training to become a reserve officer. Among the siblings, only Raoul was in place to share the new move with his parents. In a letter to Nina in November he bemoaned the situation.

"Mother has finished getting the apartment ready in record time and is now upset that she has nothing to do and nothing to experience while at the same time she turns down invitations by claiming that social life is the curse of the times. I have capitulated and on Friday I will begin bridge lessons with Mrs Fagerberg. In this way I hope to gain two more hours of sleep a day, which I sorely need."

Raoul Wallenberg stood out in contemporary Sweden, with his strong international esprit and his foreign language skills. Owing to the professional direction he had chosen, he came into contact with several German engineers and businessmen who for one reason or another had fled Nazi Germany.

After the Nazis' extensive national pogroms that began with Kristallnacht on November 9, 1938, the stream of refugees to Sweden increased. Even earlier, the numbers had grown to the point that the Swedish authorities started to feel an acute need to staunch the flow. This was no easy task. On the one hand the government did not want to introduce a visa requirement for Germany. On the other hand, the thought of an invasion of persecuted Jews was petrifying to more than one leading Swedish politician.

Once again Sweden lived up to its reputation as the golden land of the political middle way or, rather, political cowardice. Authorities attempted to achieve a compromise that, without being overtly anti-Semitic, would have given German "Aryans" unrestricted entry but stop the majority of Jews. A new policy was dispatched to the border stations. In a clumsy, indirect way it stated that any refugees who appeared to have left their homeland on a permanent basis should be turned away. And this was, of course, the case with most Jews.

But under stressful conditions, it could be difficult for the Swedish border officials to differentiate between a German Jew and a German "Aryan" at the passport control. According to many sources, Sweden and Switzerland were therefore strongly supportive when, at the beginning of October 1938, Germany decided to stamp a large red "J" in the passports that belonged to Jewish German citizens.

It was, in other words, not so easy for a persecuted German Jew to slip through Sweden's eye of a needle that autumn. Much later, final calculations determined that every second Jewish refugee had been rejected at the border.

Someone who at last managed to persuade the anti-Jewish Swedish refugee bureaucracy was Erich Philippi, a 57-year-old engineer and businessman from Berlin. The process would involve Raoul Wallenberg's first emergency intervention, when it became clear that the Jewish engineer needed to be saved from Nazi concentration camps.

Erich Philippi had been the director of purchasing for the large German electronics giant AEG before the anti-Jewish laws forced him to leave this post. He was married to a Swede, spoke Swedish and had travelled a great deal in Sweden for his work. His wife and two children were all Protestants and had been active in the Swedish Victoria congregation in Berlin for many years.

Pressured by the German Jewish harassment, the family now decided to move to Sweden. Since summer 1938, his wife and two children had been in Sweden in order to prepare for the move. Ellen had lost her Swedish citizenship when she married a German, and she now appealed to the Swedish authorities to regain it. In October Erich Philippi, who was alone back in Berlin, had submitted his application for residency in Sweden.

Things looked promising. The priest attached to the Swedish Berlin legation, Birger Forell, who also led the Victoria congregation, had written an extremely positive reference. Several heavyweight Swedish business figures also agreed to vouch for him, among them a senior director in Enskilda Bank, and Raoul Wallenberg's partner in North Kungs Tower, the lawyer Hans F. Böhme, also attached his name to the application.

For a while the situation looked as if it was going to be resolved quickly and easily in Philippi's favour. On November 10, the day after Kristallnacht, he was granted residency for six months. But the celebrations came to an abrupt halt. The very next day the Gestapo apprehended Philippi in his home.

This tragic news was immediately communicated by Birger Forell. He was a man of action who had begun to work on behalf of the persecuted Jews early on and prepared a few rooms in the attic of the church where he could conceal refugees. Forell now made his way to the Gestapo headquarters and forced his way in with his diplomatic passport. The Gestapo officers were surprised by the Swedish priest's interest in a German Jew but relented and let Forell know that Philippi had been taken to Sachsenhausen concentration camp.

When the news reached Stockholm, Böhme came to the desperate family's aid. He read up on the judicial details and arrived at the conclusion that Germany did not have the right to retain a person who had been granted Swedish entry.

What exactly happened next is unclear. But we know that, two weeks after Erich Philippi's arrest, Raoul Wallenberg – who had been spending his time playing squash with Lennart Hagströmer and going to restaurants with a classmate of Nina's, the ballet student Viveca Lindfors (later a successful actress in Hollywood) – travelled to Berlin to assist Birger Forell in his attempts to save the engineer and get him to Sweden. It is not clear if this had a decisive effect on his release, but Philippi never forgot Raoul's swift action.

By this point he had spent two weeks in the concentration camp. His hair and moustache had been shaved and his clothes seized for "sterilisation". Shortly thereafter his wife, who initially had been told that she was not welcome back with her "Jewish children", regained her Swedish citizenship.

Raoul remained in Berlin for a few days and Gustaf would have been proud of the impartial stance his grandson adopted. On the one hand, Raoul's heart beat for the Jews – most recently Erich Philippi and his family. On the other he wanted to try to understand German politics: keeping his "eyes and ears open for observation but refrain from voicing opinion".

Raoul spent the evening of Saturday, November 26 at a restaurant where he met a policeman who was in the S.S. Raoul asked him questions, listened and absorbed impressions to the point that he finally allowed himself some conclusions about the people and actions of the S.S. He wrote these down in a letter to some American friends:

They are very hardy types, large and strong and quick in thought and, I think, very strong-willed. They are, however, not in the least emotional and not unaware that some of their actions involve cruelty to individuals. They say that everything that is done now is essential for achieving national goals and that the suffering of individuals is insignificant in relation to the suffering that will strike the entire nation if these changes are not achieved.

Wallenberg also walked around Berlin and was impressed by the new German architecture. He described it in lyrical terms in the same letter.

It represents a longing for greatness which has been repressed for a long time in Europe . . . The Germans are the first in Europe who are now building in a way that corresponds to their nation's size and mass-production possibilities. I have looked into the new plans for Berlin and they are without a doubt marked by a touch of genius, from whatever perspective they are judged.

In peaceful Stockholm, decorating for Christmas began at the end of November. The contrast to the unrest in Germany was troubling and Raoul could not help but joke about the commercial frivolity and all the dressed pigs' heads in the shop windows.

The political worries lay like a heavy blanket over the glitter of Christmas. At most Swedish tables there were back-and-forth discussions over the possibility of war, and the home of the von Dardel family on Östermalmsgatan was no different. Raoul turned once again to *Mein Kampf.* He tried to interpret Hitler's intentions, but however he twisted and turned the matter he had trouble seeing how the situation might degenerate into armed conflict. To his friends in the United States, Raoul wrote that the only thing that spoke for that eventuality were the Führer's comments about the German need for a final confrontation with France after the humiliations of the Great War. But Raoul felt that these declarations remained fairly general in nature. This was in contrast to Hitler's expositions on "the Jewish problem", which in *Mein Kampf* was singled out as more fundamental.

As Raoul saw it, it was unlikely that Hitler would declare war on France just to retake the mines in Alsace-Lorraine, or in order to reunite with the 3.5 million Germans who lived within the French borders. A war was more likely to be fought to establish German supremacy on the continent and this was something they could achieve by other means, he maintained.

Erich Philippi arrived in Sweden on Christmas Eve, 1938. He and his family moved into an apartment in Stockholm. Erich Philippi was a man of short stature and grey hair. Of late, he had been calling himself a consultant engineer and he arrived in Sweden with some potentially interesting ideas in his luggage. For a refugee with a residency permit of only three months, the task of getting a job in Sweden was even more difficult in 1938 than it had been the year before. Starting a company was out of the question. But Raoul Wallenberg and Hans Böhme were now well versed in these things after their collaborations with Werner Abernau. This time they made sure that Philippi's name was not mentioned in any business documents as they formed the financial venture SpecialMetall in January 1939 with a business plan focused on seeking out new patents and then licensing them in the Swedish market. SpecialMetall was given the address Kungsgatan 30 and smoothly slid into place alongside the other diverse activities already established there. Raoul Wallenberg was the only member of the board and basically fronted the entire initial investment of 10,000 kronor (around £25,000 today). But, fairly quickly, SpecialMetall became a way for Raoul Wallenberg to help Philippi make money on the licences he had acquired. On paper the company looked as if it was Raoul's, but in practical terms SpecialMetall was, even in the first year, Erich Philippi's affair.

Raoul never saw a substantial role for himself in Philippi's business and his thoughts were elsewhere. His father's cousin Jacob Wallenberg had promised him a good position and Raoul wanted to be ready for whenever this opportunity presented itself. So he waited. And waited. Several months went by. From time to time he reminded Jacob Wallenberg of it, only to hear that he should be patient and continue to wait. But nothing ever happened.

Towards the end of April 1939, Raoul Wallenberg had definitely tired of the whole thing. He wrote a letter to Jacob Wallenberg where he did not attempt to conceal his disappointment:

It is quite depressing to go around in this way and wait and therefore I would be grateful to you if you could tell me whether you still, as at the beginning of Feburary, advise me to continue waiting for the post you have in mind or if the situation is such that you instead advise me to try to secure such a post on my own. If the case is the former, I wonder if you possibly have something that I could undertake in the meantime.

The letter had the intended effect. One Thursday two weeks later Raoul was called to a meeting with Jacob Wallenberg. There was still no permanent position on offer, but at least there was a small assignment: Jacob Wallenberg wanted Raoul to review the conditions relating to a potentially significant investment in, and exploitation of, the area of Huvudsta outside Stockholm.

Raoul was hesitant. In the long term, he absolutely believed in a future for even fairly remote Stockholm suburbs. He had seen the development in the United States. But the sticking point was that Sweden had an alarmingly low birth rate. This meant that filling Huvudsta would require a significant immigration from the countryside, a miraculous development in the Swedish economy and substantially elevated demands for additional living area, Raoul reasoned.

Altogether it required rather too much wishful thinking.

When he submitted his report to Jacob Wallenberg on 3 August, 1939 he had worked on the question for more than two months.

Raoul had made no mention of the threat of war in his Huvudsta analysis. This despite the fact that news about the tense situation in Europe was coming thick and fast – the parliament drafted a certain number of state of emergency laws that would come into effect "if war arrived". But it is likely that Raoul's pessimistic conclusion in the report was influenced by his sense of the global changes ahead. It is significant that by this time Raoul Wallenberg no longer automatically believed that life in Sweden would continue on the same calm and secure path as before.

He would soon turn twenty-seven. He was healthy and did not yet have his own family to be responsible for. In the middle of June 1939 he sat down in the office in the Norra Kungstornet and signed a will in the presence of two witnesses.

I, Raoul Gustaf Wallenberg, hereby declare my last will and testament
to be that all my material possessions should pass to my half-siblings
Guy and Nina von Dardel in two equal parts. As executor of my estate
and this testament I name Fredrik von Dardel.

August 1939 has gone down in history as the warmest August in Sweden in
ninety-three years. As Stockholmers woke up on the morning of September 1,
a fog lay over the city. The meteorologists had warned of thunderstorms, but
in reality this Friday was to be "one of summer's last lavishly beautiful days",
as one reporter wrote.

It might have been an idyllic day in Stockholm had it not been for the
events at the German–Polish border at 4.45 a.m. The time for speculation was
over, war had arrived. German forces had stormed over the Polish border and
already that morning the first bombs fell on Warsaw and many other cities.

At 10 a.m., a pale Adolf Hitler stood up in the Reichstag. According to the
correspondent for the newspaper Dagens Nyheter he held forth with a "battle
cry the likes of which I've never heard". Hitler was quoted saying, "I do not
want to be anything other than the German Reich's first soldier and so I have
again donned the field-grey uniform. I shall not take it off until victory has
arrived or else I will not live to see that end."

In Stockholm there was a rush on grocery shops. Everyone wanted to
stockpile what they could: flour, coffee, tea, cleaning supplies, soap, spices
and, not least, sugar. Later in the day there was not a single kilo of sugar to be
had in the entire city. And hardly a drop of petrol.

People flocked to the front of the newspapers' dispatch offices, where the
latest telegrams were displayed in the window. Bus travel suddenly became
dangerous as, according to eye witnesses, drivers looked away from traffic in
order to try to read the latest headlines. The atmosphere was agitated. Those
who cursed Hitler received frosty replies from those who felt that such criticism did not fit comfortably with Swedish neutrality: in return they were
called "Nazi thugs".

A special cabinet meeting was called and decisions were made about
defence preparations. A few hours later yellow bulletins announcing the draft
were pinned up at the Central Train Station. The first conscripts were to report
as early as Sunday, September 3, having read up on current military regula-

tions and equipped themselves with shoes, underwear, knife, fork and spoon.

Raoul Wallenberg belonged to the Svea Life Guards. His regiment bore the responsibility of defending the capital city in the case of a surprise attack. His particular year was not among those in the earliest waves of the draft, but he could count on being called up during the next few months.

During the day, Raoul went to his office in the Norrra Kungstornet. On this first day of the war, Raoul wrote a power of attorney that gave Erich Philippi full freedom to act on behalf of SpecialMetall. As the representative of SpecialMetall, Raoul also wrote an agreement with Erich Philippi in which the latter was guaranteed the profits the company earned from the agencies he had brought with him.

It was as if Raoul wanted to assure himself that he wouldn't put his German friend in jeopardy in the event of his being drafted and sent to war.

CHAPTER 7

A Military Man with Entrepreneurial Ambition

By Tuesday, April 9 1940, the war had been raging for seven months. Early that morning *Radiotjänst*, the Swedish National Radio Service, received a tip-off from a listener. Foreign radio stations were reporting that Germany had just attacked Denmark and Norway. Had Swedish radio missed this?

A few days earlier, Sweden's minister* in Berlin, Arvid Richert, had tried to alert the Foreign Ministry in Stockholm that something was afoot. Other sources on the continent had reported concerns – Germans were amassing suspiciously large numbers of troops by their transport ships in the harbours along the Baltic. But the Swedish government had dismissed these reports. There were absolutely no indications that Germany would attack Sweden under any circumstances.

But shortly after midnight on April 9, Germany attacked Oslo and a number of other Norwegian cities. A few hours later, German soldiers stepped ashore in Copenhagen. By that point German troops had long since crossed the Danish border. Denmark capitulated after only a couple of hours. A few areas of Norway held out for almost two months. One can only speculate how long Sweden would have lasted but, on the day of the German invasion of Norway the entire Swedish border to Norway was unguarded.

The Swedish prime minister Per Albin Hansson was woken at 5 a.m. and informed of the events. "Our state of preparedness is good," he had assured the public in a speech at Skansen shortly before the outbreak of war in 1939. In truth, the condition of the Swedish military was not something to brag about. This was the price paid for the Social Democratic government's

---

* Swedish diplomatic envoys/heads of legation were known as ministers. They were not given the title of ambassador until after the Second World War.

investment in welfare rather than defence, the choice of "butter before cannons". The uniforms from the Great War reeked of mothballs, and the long-necked Mauser rifles that were put into the hands of many brand-new Swedish soldiers were said to be from the nineteenth century. It was claimed that the Swedish soldiers were so surprised by the German invasion of Norway that they had to resort to the unconvincing subterfuge of pointing telegraph poles at the German planes that flew close to the border.

The first bitter winter of the conflict had been dominated by blackout exercises and the war between Finland and the Soviet Union. The Swedish people felt sympathy for the Finns and the volunteer efforts broke all records. But when the question of sending Swedish troops was raised, the Social Democratic prime minister Per Albin Hansson said no.

A couple of months previously, Hansson had formed a broad governing coalition with almost all parties represented in a kind of Swedish war ministry. He had been a pacifist in the past and was perhaps not the wartime leader that the Swedish right wing would have wished for. But Hansson's judicious and pragmatic approach garnered respect. He now grew in earnest into the role of the nation's patriarch.

Out of caution he recruited a completely unpolitical figure to the important and sensitive post of minister of foreign affairs: the Oslo envoy, Christian Günther, who was known as a competent if lazy diplomat, who preferred to spend his time at the races or the bridge table rather than in his office.

It was an unusual coincidence that Sweden was led during the war by a prime minister and a minister of foreign affairs who both confessed to having simulated heart problems in order to escape their military service. Only Christian Günther had been successful.

Sweden declared neutrality and settled on a foreign policy designed to avoid unnecessarily provoking Germany into an attack. Strictly speaking, not all of the concessions that were now granted sat well with a position of neutrality. But this was a price that the government was prepared to pay in their struggle to safeguard Swedish lives and Sweden's independence.

The German transit traffic would become the clearest example of this. When Norway capitulated in the summer of 1940, the Swedish government agreed to let some German trains loaded with equipment and soldiers pass through Sweden on their way to or from Norway. It was believed that otherwise there was a severe risk that Germany would secure this right by force. This initial concession to Germany evoked strong feelings of humiliation among the public, and other blows would follow.

The tiptoeing around Germany was most pronounced in the first few years of the war. Günther, the foreign minister, was initially convinced of an ultimate German victory. This was governed less by any particular sympathy for the Nazis than by a pragmatic assessment of the situation and a greater fear – one shared by many other Swedes – of the Soviet Union. Günther's conclusion was strongly supported by the ministry's political chief, Staffan Söderblom, whose star was in the ascendant during these years. Staffan Söderblom would later play a determining role in Raoul Wallenberg's fate.

The goal for the government was to keep Sweden out of the war, by keeping the Germans in a good mood. It was a strategy that both Söderblom and Günther were determined to maintain, regardless of the cost.

Furir (a Swedish rank between corporal and sergeant) Raoul Wallenberg was called up for the first time in the middle of November 1939, for a month of guard duty at the Svea Life Guard in Stockholm. He was also one of the many who had been mobilised immediately following the German invasions of Norway and Denmark. A few weeks later, on April 26, 1940, he was formally reinstated in the Svea Life Guard.

Raoul began to set his affairs in order. One year earlier he had written his will, so things were settled on the personal front. But now he thought of Special-Metall. If something happened to Raoul then that could put Erich Philippi in a difficult situation, since Raoul owned the majority of the company.

On April 11, the same day that general conscription began, Raoul Wallenberg wrote a letter to Erich Philippi's wife, Ellen, in which he outlined a standing offer to sell them his share of the company for one krona. This meant in practical terms that he gave away what today would be worth around £25,000. This offer was motivated by the fact that it was Philippi who ran the company and who alone had created its profits. Just to be sure, Raoul wrote an additional letter in which he rejected all claims to the company: "in the event of my death . . . My claims in this context will in this case be transferred to Dr. E. Philippi."

At around the same time, Raoul Wallenberg and Hans Böhme proceeded to shut down their shared offices at Kungsgatan 30.

Three years had gone by since Gustaf Wallenberg had died. In the time since then, Raoul had managed ably but without the professional successes that he had been hoping for. When Jacob Wallenberg mentioned to Raoul that the war could possibly bring with it a few problems – similar to the Huvudsta project – that he might be assigned to solve, Raoul summoned his courage and asked if he might be given a permanent position. Jacob had promised to think it over but nothing had as yet come of this.

One can only speculate as to the reasons behind the apparently nonchalant treatment of Raoul by Jacob and Marcus Wallenberg Jr during these years. They held out a finger many times but never the long-awaited handshake. We sense a collision of the family traditions of responsibility and loyalty on the one hand and the brothers' scepticism toward Raoul's unique but perhaps not so Wallenbergian talents on the other.

The brothers had been absorbing the family's attitude towards the matter of succession within the business since they were children. Neither Jacob nor Marcus Jr could therefore ignore the fact that Raoul was the son of their late older cousin Raoul Oscar who, in light of his birth order and evident competence had been thought of as the first of the next generation to enter the bank.

Since then, much had changed. Nowadays at least Marcus Jr had his own children to care for, which could have created a conscious or unconscious desire to keep Raoul Oscar's son at bay. Young Raoul was, despite everything, no closer a relative to Jacob and Marcus than the son of a cousin. Even for Jacob, Marcus' three children would have been much closer.

But it is difficult to avoid the feeling that this behaviour also signalled a certain doubt regarding young Raoul's personal qualifications and character-istics. Both the brothers and Marcus Sr appear to have regarded Raoul as charming, extroverted and creative, but also somewhat impulsive. He was known as a talker, something that may not have sat comfortably with the motto that Marcus Wallenberg Sr had adopted: "*Esse, non videri.*" His intention was that the motto should serve as "a reminder to conscientiously perform one's work without striving for recognition and without making oneself appear to be more than what one actually is".

In an early book about Raoul Wallenberg, a friend described his way of pursuing a business deal as "labyrinthine". He would proceed slowly towards the goal, in a kind of arc. His thoughts never went along the usual tracks as he negotiated and his motivations and arguments often upset and shocked his counterparts.

This was possibly a style that felt foreign to the Wallenberg brothers. Peter Wallenberg, son of Marcus Jr, said that, "In the long run, I think that these gentlemen did not think too much of Raoul . . . They studied all the relatives who wanted to join the bank, assigned them tests over a long period of time and then made the decision – yes or no. You didn't get into the bank just because you had the family name. Those smaller assignments that Raoul was given were typical of their tests, to see how he managed them and what kind of judgement he showed under those circumstances. I think that is the likely explanation."

Raoul Wallenberg was now about to turn twenty-eight and still lived at home with his parents. He had no work to occupy him full time and he was soon to lose his office. There was reason for him to worry about his future. How would he be able to marry and have a family without being remotely close to the kind of yearly income that his grandfather Gustaf had declared a minimum?

But in April 1940 such trivial private troubles paled in comparison to the great threats that loomed on the horizon.

A strong desire to defend the motherland was growing among those adult Swedish men who had not yet been called up. There had been a lot of talk in the thriving rifle associations in Sweden that had doubled their membership after September 1, 1939. Couldn't the old men and youths who were still at home also turn out, gun in hand, at a pinch? As fate would have it, these old and young men would become a significant part of Raoul Wallenberg's daily life over the next few years.

When the Finnish Winter War broke out, interest in establishing a formal organisation grew. More and more voices were raised in support of creating a home guard in Sweden, which was voted into existence by the Swedish parliament in May 1940. One month later, almost 100,000 men had registered, double what had been expected. But two problems looked as if they could stop the entire enterprise in its tracks: the lack of weapons and the lack of instructors.

Raoul Wallenberg happened to belong to a unit of the Svea Life Guards whose main focus was the training of other troops. During his service that summer he was promoted to sergeant and assigned to instruct the first Home Guard enlistees. These courses – which would go under the name of "the War School" – lasted a week, with the trainees housed in empty worker residences just outside Stockholm.

The atmosphere among those who had volunteered for service was quite different from those who had been drafted. As Sweden's first chief of the National Home Guard recalled in his memoirs, "For many instructors it was a completely new experience to get to know a new troop where every man burned with the desire to absorb as much as possible." Raoul Wallenberg liked what he saw and the appreciation appears to have been mutual. Several times the Home Guard requested Sergeant Wallenberg as the instructor for its local training courses.

Raoul was hooked. When he had completed his service with the Svea Life Guard at the end of September, he volunteered to stay and continue with the Home Guard training in his spare time.

"There is a great risk of Sweden becoming involved in armed conflict," a sombre Raoul explained at a meeting for the youth chapter of a rifle association. Many felt inspired and registered for the Home Guard courses. They had to begin with basic weapons training at a specially built firing range under Hötorget that a grocery firm had prepared for them.

Foot marches and street battles became Raoul's areas of expertise. As he saw it, the Home Guard enlistees had all that was required in terms of motivation and enthusiasm – they had volunteered, after all. What they lacked was physical conditioning. A major in the Home Guard related in a memorial article that in 1940 and 1941 Raoul arranged what were then fairly unusual "quick marches" at varying tempos.

In the spring of 1941, Raoul was presented with the task of arranging exercises and foot marches for as many as a thousand men from various units. The "Speed March" of May 7, 1941, became his first trial by fire: an organisational challenge of daunting proportions.

It was a rather chilly evening and a thousand Home Guard enlistees were gathered in Kungsträdgården in Stockholm. Raoul had divided the men into separate groups according to how quickly they were expected to finish their foot march, just as if they were in the gym classes at the Nya Elementarskolan. His instructions were meticulous: "Full gear required. Bag to be worn on the right side, cap to be worn two fingers over the right eyebrow, three fingers over the left ear."

At 7.25 p.m., at the command of "Silence! At ease!" they took off on a route around central Stockholm. Marching at a high tempo was alternated with faster running. The best group went almost twelve kilometres that night.

Afterwards, some of the no doubt breathless participants could be heard praising the exquisite precision of the schedule. The newspaper *Svenska Dagbladet* reported the following day that, "No mishaps occurred during the proceedings and the troops were in such good condition that they even sang as they ran. So Sergeant Wallenberg had reason to be pleased with the evening. As indeed he was, to judge from his expression."

The "Speed March" was above all a logistical challenge, but Raoul also organised more explicitly military exercises, mostly in urban settings. That same spring he had one hundred young men imagine that the enemy had landed at one of Stockholm's piers and established a beachhead in a nearby school.

The men also trained by simulating battles in tougher terrain outside Stockholm, crawling through muddy fens and throwing grenades. Raoul was extremely energetic and placed high demands on the men, and soon he was considered a more skilled and creative instructor than many of the career military.

One of his foremen recalled in a book on Raoul Wallenberg that came out as early as 1946, that: "He took his work so seriously that he always adopted the most correct military form in conversations with his superiors even if these were his personal friends. His subordinates appreciated him but they did not have an easy life." Or, as another friend from the Home Guard put it, "Raoul Wallenberg was not your average kind of person."

When Raoul was interviewed in *Svenska Dagbladet* in the middle of June 1941 he could not conceal how pleased he was with the results of his efforts. The newspaper caught up with him in a square in Stockholm one rainy Thursday evening, several thousands of Home Guard enlistees and spectators around him. They recited the war prayer "God and Motherland" and sang the Swedish National anthem together. "The Home Guard is becoming an elite force," Sergeant Wallenberg explained to the reporter.

In the summer of 1941 Raoul Wallenberg wrote to the local head of the Home Guard requesting a promotion to lieutenant. He promised to continue working for the Home Guard without pay in his spare time whether on foot marches or on propaganda.

Raoul's request was dismissed, but this does not appear to have dismayed him greatly. He upheld his promise to continue working for the Home Guard without pay, doing so in his spare time even though a position as a director would eventually be offered to him.

After the outbreak of war, even Jacob and Marcus Wallenberg were tapped for the good of the country. Marcus Jr was a close friend of Erik Boheman, who was the cabinet secretary of the Foreign Ministry during the entire Second World War. He also had good connections in London's most influential political circles. Jacob Wallenberg, in turn, had shouldered his father Marcus Sr's role and was one of the most important members of the Swedish delegation that handled trade negotiations with Germany. The brothers would maintain this division of labour throughout the war. Marcus was asked to participate in trade negotiations with Great Britain and France, Jacob with Germany.

The first assignments were as early as September 1939. Marcus Jr travelled to London with Erik Boheman. With his humour and charm he tried to convince the British that Swedish neutrality meant that Sweden had no choice but to continue to export iron ore to Germany.

The more muted and thoughtful Jacob Wallenberg had, for his part, to receive the German trade delegation to Stockholm along with the head of the trade division at the Swedish Foreign Ministry. The Germans were already buying 80 per cent of the iron ore that Sweden exported and were to be cajoled into not increasing their demands.

Both Jacob and Marcus Jr spent a great deal of their time during the war years on trade negotiations on behalf of the Foreign Ministry. Boheman noted later in his memoirs that: "The services that the Wallenbergs provided Sweden during the war years can hardly be exaggerated."

Sometimes the tasks from the Foreign Ministry took on a more straightforward political form. The Wallenberg brothers were used as a kind of un-official line of communication on behalf of the Swedish government. In the autumn of 1939, Marcus Wallenberg Jr met, among others, with Winston Churchill who shortly thereafter – in May 1940 – became the new British prime minister.

At the government's behest, Jacob Wallenberg was tasked with visiting Hermann Göring at Carinhall in August 1940. Göring had wanted to speak with the minister of foreign affairs, Christian Günther, or someone close to him, in order to complain about the anti-German attitude of the Swedish press. This someone turned out to be Jacob Wallenberg. Göring began the encounter at Carinhall by railing at the Swedish bank director for twenty-five minutes, but their five-hour-long meeting nonetheless ended with Göring venturing thoughts of a future Swedish–German alliance.

The Wallenberg family was not uniformly negative about Germany. A more robust Germany was seen as a good "democratic" counterweight to the large communist dictatorship to the east. This was not an unusual attitude among those Swedes who were conservatively inclined and it did not mean that they were outright Nazi sympathisers. For example, the 75-year-old Marcus Wallenberg Sr wrote to a friend four months before the beginning of the war, "Hitler is a terrible example of the role of psychological forces in history." And, during negotiations about the war agreements of 1939, Jacob had written to his brother Marcus Jr who was in London and suggested that the British should demand Hitler's removal before they entered into any peace negotiations.

Jacob Wallenberg came to supplement his extensive network in the German industrial and financial worlds with a few key contacts in the German resistance movement. Sometimes these coincided. The most significant was Carl Goerdeler, who was among the conspirators behind the assassination attempt against Hitler in the summer of 1944.

Shortly before Jacob wrote the letter about demanding Hitler's removal to his brother Marcus Jr, he had met Goerdeler for the second time in only a few months. It was to be the first but far from the last time that the Wallenberg brothers would be used as an unofficial intelligence channel between German anti-Nazis and the British government. Jacob would transmit several messages to Marcus who, in turn, passed them on to Western powers through his political contacts in Great Britain.

*

Carl Friedrich Goerdeler was a well-known name in Germany. He had been the mayor of Leipzig, but became increasingly disenchanted after the Nuremberg laws of 1935. The following year he left and took a position as head of the trade division of the German electronics firm Bosch in Stuttgart. He also became a leader, along with a number of the company's other executives, in the anti-Nazi movement.

On September 1, the day before the outbreak of the war, Goerdeler was in Stockholm to see a few people, among them Jacob and Marcus Wallenberg Sr. Jacob Wallenberg later wrote in a memo that: "He gave a very honest account of his extremely critical stance toward Nazism and made it clear that he was very pessimistic regarding the developments in Germany."

Goerdeler had an underlying motive for his trip to Sweden. Bosch produced engine parts for aeroplanes among other things and were now testing the interest among banks in neutral countries in buying the Bosch group's foreign holdings. They wanted to be well prepared for the war, which they now fully expected to arrive before long, and avoid the confiscation of the foreign Bosch companies as hostile property. If these companies were officially owned by a bank in a neutral state the situation would be different and their empire could be kept intact.

The Bosch board had a sophisticated solution in mind. The foreign Bosch companies would be sold, some only for a short period. A supplementary agreement, a so-called pre-emption clause, gave the Bosch group the right – for a period of two years after the end of the war – to buy back the company at the same price at which it had been sold. Compensation for the favour would be awarded in the form of dividends during the period in question, interest on the investment amount and a large one-off fee.

The Wallenbergs bought several European Bosch companies and thereafter also American Bosch, all with separate agreements. The camouflaged purchase of American Bosch was a ticking time bomb. In the United States there were early suspicions that the sale was simply a way to conceal actual German ownership and the Americans eventually confiscated the shares in American Bosch as hostile property. But it was not until after the end of the war that the Bosch scandal – which would haunt Jacob Wallenberg for the remainder of his life – broke.

For the moment he continued his frequent trips to Germany for trade negotiations. In total he made seventeen trips to Berlin during the first four years of the war. Almost every time, he met with the resistance fighter Carl Goerdeler.

In the summer of 1941, Jacob Wallenberg was forty-eight years old and unmarried. He still lived in an apartment above his parents on Strandvägen 27 and spent – as always – a great deal of his spare time racing yachts. He counted the well-known Swedish shipowner Sven Salén among his sailing friends.

Salén became the person who helped Jacob Wallenberg discharge his obligations to his cousin's child, Raoul Wallenberg. As far as Sven Salén was concerned, Raoul Wallenberg had exactly the kind of skills he required at that moment. Salén was planning to launch a new company that would cover shortfalls in Swedish grocery stocks during the war with imports, mainly from Hungary.

Sven Salén owned several shipping companies. He was also chairman and director, with responsibility for steamship traffic, of the successful A.B. Banan-kompaniet (Banana Company). Before the start of the war, Banan-kompaniet had over one hundred employees and five large ships devoted to importing bananas from Jamaica. The so-called "Fyffe's bananas" had been extremely popular in Sweden.

But now this activity had ground to a halt. After the attacks on Denmark and Norway in April 1940, the Germans had laid a string of mines across the Skagerrak and in one blow blocked all Swedish trade to the west. Admittedly there had been a small amount of Swedish foreign trade traffic since February 1941 – a couple of ships a month had been let through after laborious negotiations with the warring parties. Yet it remained severely limited and risky. Luxury goods such as bananas were not prioritised in these infrequent transports, not when the available stock of basic goods was threatened.

The rationing of goods had been increasing over the past year. By 1941 almost everything was rationed – tea and coffee, bread and butter, meat, eggs and cheese. In Stockholm there was both fox and badger on the menu and one could not invite people over for dinner without asking for ration coupons from the guests. Fish and fowl were still freely available, which would come to be significant for Raoul Wallenberg.

*

Sven Salén had foreseen the possibility of a halt of banana imports in the event of war. Banan-kompaniet had started to expand into new areas as early as 1939. Among other things the company had opened a canning factory in Malmö, called Svenska Konservfabriken Globus A.B. This was how the contact with Hungary was established. On the hunt for the best possible foreign partners, Salén and Banan-kompaniet had landed on, as they described themselves, "Europe's largest and most successful company within the food preservation industry, Manfred Weiss A-G in Budapest".

Banan-kompaniet and the Svenska Konservfabriken Globus were given the main trade licence in Sweden for the famous Hungarian Globus products – tomato purée, goose-liver pâté, tinned vegetables and soups. Sven Salén had also seen the potential to extend the import of groceries from Hungary, Europe's grain store. Admittedly Hungary was allied with Germany but in February 1941 a new trade agreement had been made between Sweden and Hungary that promised to supply Sweden with more than had even been hoped for.

A year earlier, Salén had got to know an enterprising Hungarian grocer in his forties, Kálmán Lauer. For many years, Lauer had been the international representative for Hungary's largest food export company, Hangyas. Over the past several years, he had travelled back and forth to Sweden on different kinds of business, and not just regarding tinned goods. After the war broke out, he was behind a campaign to popularise cheap Hungarian goose in relatively goose-sceptic Stockholm. It succeeded beyond all expectation. The sale of Hungarian geese increased fivefold.

During the spring of 1941, Lauer contributed to saving Easter in many Swedish homes: the 3,500 boxes of Hungarian eggs he imported kept the escalating price of eggs in check. And it was at this time that the board of Banan-kompaniet started to talk about forming a Swedish–Hungarian Chamber of Commerce with Lauer.

Kálmán Lauer actually had a law degree but, as was the case with many Hungarian intellectuals, he had been forced to interrupt his career after Hungary's defeat in the Great War. In the peace agreement of 1920, the German-allied Hungary lost more than two-thirds of its territory and 60 per cent of its population. In one fell swoop, available positions in law decreased dramatically, especially for those Hungarians who, like Lauer, found themselves in Romania after the new borders were drawn.

Lauer presented himself as a "Calvinist" or "Protestant" to the Swedish authorities, most likely in an attempt to conceal his own Jewish heritage. Towards the end of the thirties, when Hungary's German-friendly government increasingly turned the screws on its Jewish population, Lauer began to spend more and more time abroad. Now he wanted to remain in Sweden with his wife, Maria, who was also of Jewish extraction. Sven Salén thought that was a good idea. Salén even called the recalcitrant foreign bureau of the Swedish National Board for Health and Welfare.

As time went on, their business plans changed. Instead of a Chamber of Commerce, they formed the Mellaneuropeiska Handels A.B. or the Mid-European Trading Company Inc. in July of 1941. Or, rather, Salén invested the bulk of the capital in the company and gave Lauer half the shares in return for his expert knowledge: the thought was that Lauer would run the company. The only problem was that he was not a Swedish citizen and the application for a residency permit was taking a long time. They needed to hire someone who could be the authorised signatory, sit on the board and make the necessary European trips that were becoming increasingly more challenging for Lauer. Jacob Wallenberg's unemployed cousin Raoul more than fitted the bill.

Raoul Wallenberg duly met with Kálmán Lauer and was offered a position as the foreign director of the Mid-European Trading Company, starting in August 1941. Raoul retained this position until the summer of 1944 when he was – almost by accident – given the assignment to travel to Budapest on a Swedish–American mission to save the Hungarian Jews. Perhaps it was because no-one else dared to do it, or perhaps he was just the right man in the right place at the right time.

By the time of the Midsummer holiday of 1941, Germany had begun its attack on the Soviet Union. A couple of days later, Finland joined the war on the side of Germany. Sweden's foreign policy situation was shakier than ever and officials in the Foreign Ministry later described how Sweden that summer became a precariously isolated island in the German sea. A cabinet minister described it "as living in front of the mouth of a loaded cannon".

When the Germans demanded to be able to transport their Engelbrekt Division of 15,000 soldiers from Norway across Swedish territory to the front in Finland, the anxious Swedish government did not dare to refuse.

The summer of 1941 became an important turning point for Raoul Wallenberg's career. Importing eggs, fowl and tinned goods was perhaps not the kind of job that he had dreamed of. But that did not matter. He had a permanent position, one that allowed him to work in business. It had taken a long time but, in the days before his twenty-ninth birthday, Raoul Wallenberg finally found full-time employment and a steady income – even if it was not quite at the salary level that his grandfather had in mind. It was however enough for him to be able to move out on his own.

He found a vacant one-bedroom apartment close to his parents, on Bragevägen 12. It was only fifty-seven square metres with a living room, a bedroom and a very tiny kitchenette. But it had a ceiling almost three and a half metres high and it was the only one in the building that had a balcony – an ample six-sided space ready made for cocktail parties in the summer.

Bragevägen 12, November 2010, "Farewell Blues"

You can see Raoul Wallenberg's balcony from a long way away. A gate made of black wrought iron separates the building from the pavement on Bragevägen. In the dusk I think I see the hint of a patch of grass and a frostbitten flower bed.

The oak door, not surprisingly, offers some resistance, but I persist. In the entrance hall there is a brown marble floor and walls decoratively painted with National Romantic garlands. There is a remarkable amount of blue and yellow, I note, and continue up the stairs. In Raoul's time there was a porter here and the residences came with maids' quarters. But his one-bedroom apartment was one of the smaller ones and was called a *dubblett*.

I linger outside the door for a while and imagine that it is the same as it was back then – the same light-coloured wood, the same frame and panel construction.

The current tenant has lived here for eighteen years. He has promised to receive me on the condition that I do not reveal his name. Sure enough, the door opens almost at once and out streams soft jazz music. That was probably how it was back then too. I know that Raoul had a gramophone here and I know that he loved music, both jazz and church compositions such as Handel's "Messiah" and Bach's Oratorios.

On a page of Raoul's calendar from 1944 there is a list of jazz songs, which appears to have been jotted down in haste. No-one knows why. Maybe they were his favourites, or perhaps it was his dance card for the evening. Glenn Miller and Benny Goodman are included, of course. Songs like "Minnie the Moocher", "You Are Too Beautiful", "(I've Got a Gal in) Kalamazoo" and the wonderful "At Last" are all listed, if I have interpreted his notes correctly. There is also that treasure from the twenties, "Farewell Blues", which Glenn Miller recorded on the album *On the Alamo* in 1941, the same year that Raoul moved in here.

The apartment's current resident is listening to the American tenor saxophonist Dexter Gordon when I arrive. He tells me that he is an American but the son of a diplomat and has therefore lived in many parts of the world. Apparently it was love that brought him back to Sweden at the beginning of the eighties. He will tell me all about it after we have looked around what became Raoul Wallenberg's final home in Sweden.

My host takes me on a tour. In the hall I see an exercise bike. After that there are two square rooms side by side with a tiny bathroom between them. Red oriental rugs cover the worn parquet floors.

Raoul's sister Nina Lagergren has described for me how things looked when her brother lived here. The first room was the living room. Raoul had a sofa and two large Japanese vases made out of blue-and-white china on either side, which his mother Maj von Dardel had cleverly converted into lamps. They were an inheritance from Gustaf, from his time as an envoy in Japan. Several paintings by his father hung on the walls. Nina Lagergren cannot remember exactly which, since they were later stolen from the storage facility where they had been placed.

The door out to the balcony is in the second room. That was the bedroom in Raoul's day, now it is a sitting area. I look around. I have heard a bit about the kitchenette. Raoul did not cook very often from what I understand. He had quite a few of his dinners at his parents' around the corner, even breakfast sometimes, according to Nina. But he could make himself an omelette and, from time to time, he arranged dinners and parties here, where he often served Hungarian goose-liver pâté.

In his brother Guy von Dardel's archive I have found an impressive collection of invitations and thank-you cards from Raoul's time on Bragevägen 12. I have brought copies with me in my bag but I have no need to pull them out as I almost know them by heart. At a cocktail party in December 1943 I counted over thirty guests, among them Jacob Wallenberg, Sven Salén, Kálmán Lauer, his parents, siblings and the Hungarian minister Antal Ullein-Reviczky.

I walk around the apartment and try to size up the space per person that night, perhaps thirty-five guests between the two main rooms that add up to forty-five square metres at most. It must have been a squeeze, even if Raoul only served cocktails. It was almost a stroke of luck that Marcus Jr and his wife Marianne were on a trip in Bergslagen and had to decline the invitation.

During certain periods, Raoul appears to have put on several dinners or parties per month. To judge from the thank-you notes these were often very special events. "When one is invited to your place one is always guaranteed to have an exceptional time. One meets the most wonderful people in Stockholm and the food and drink are unmatched," someone called Jan wrote after a party at the end of 1942. "You are truly a master host and organiser," a person called Gösta said in thanks, though without a date. An enthusiastic Birgitta Broomé wrote in May 1942 about an enchanting evening in Raoul's home "with its personal and wonderfully artistic atmosphere".

From Sture Petrén, who would go on to become a member of the Swedish Academy, there came a cheerful card with sprawling words written in ink about another party that same month, apparently a very good one: "I only regret one thing – that I was stupid enough to leave as early as 3, which meant that I missed an entertaining account of your latest trip."

I close my eyes and try to imagine these parties, how people moved from the living room through the narrow passage outside the bathroom into the bedroom and then out onto the hexagonal terrace. Crowded and warm. Hustle and bustle and probably a myriad of colours reflected in the almost two-metre-high windows. From time to time, conversations in English since Raoul, according to the thank-you notes, included guests from the British legation. There are no German names but one or two Hungarians. The collection includes the American military attaché's card, and I know from the Security Police's surveillance of the legation that the attaché was invited here once.

Among the thank you's there are a number of aristocratic names, such as Dinkelspiel and Nordenskiöld, von Kantzow and von Platen. But not exclusively. Stig Ahlgren, cultural editor at the social-democratic newspaper *Aftontidningen*, wrote to Raoul in June 1942: "My most heartfelt thanks for a splendid dinner. The red wine was like a note on the violin and the sherry like a cello solo." Ahlgren expressed his regret that he had suddenly become ill and had to leave, adding that: "the Indian wisdom that streams towards your delighted friends, emanating from your curiously Eastern presence, will surely help you to overlook this."

My eyes fall on a bust of the Buddha on top of a bookshelf. Does the oriental inclination get passed down from one tenant to the next?

There is a kerosene lamp on the coffee table as well as an open bottle of white wine, a modern and perfectly chilled Chardonnay, as it turned out. We sit down on the sofa and I say something about Raoul and all his vintage wines. They were apparently characterised by fantastically high peaks and equally low troughs:

some were delicious, others revolting. He had inherited them from his grand-father Gustaf, and most of the bottles were from the end of the nineteenth century. It so happened that Raoul's father, Raoul Oscar, had stored away at least 250 bottles in Gustaf Wallenberg's wine cellar in Saltsjöbaden shortly before Christmas 1908, when Gustaf was still in Japan. There were thirteen bottles of Château Poujeaux, and eight bottles of Château Margaux, according to Raoul Oscar's list.

For the legendary Swedish journalist Gustaf von Platen, who was part of Raoul's circle, Raoul's inheritance was a transcendent experience. "The best wines I have ever sampled . . . the bottles that survived made one reverent," von Platen wrote in a memoir in 1993. And therein lay the rub. The other bottles, the ones that had not kept, Raoul had to pour down the drain in the kitchenette.

The current occupant is also a single man these days, just as Raoul was. He has been divorced for many years. He laughs when I ask what Sweden was for him before he moved here.

"I would sum it up in a few words – the Nobel prize, polar bears on the streets, naked women and Raoul Wallenberg. I absolutely knew who he was. But I had no idea that he had lived in this particular apartment, not until a neighbour told me so a couple of years ago. But not many people know about it."

It's not so strange that he should have been familiar with the name Raoul Wallenberg. In 1981 Raoul was named an honorary citizen of the United States and, at a stroke, became known to many Americans. Perhaps even better known than in Sweden, where most teenagers may have heard the name but rarely know who he was – a soccer player from Örgryte perhaps?

My host lights a cigarette. He has one more Raoul Wallenberg story to tell. For a while his father, a diplomat, worked for the C.I.A. In his old age, after his son had moved to Sweden, his father told him that the Russians had tried to exchange Raoul Wallenberg several times when they were holding him captive in the Lubyanka. But, as the father understood it, the Swedes didn't want to have any-thing to do with it.

"Terrible, isn't it? If it was true," he says and blows smoke out into the historic surroundings.

On the train on the way home I search for some of Raoul's jazz favourites on the Internet. It becomes an entire list on Spotify. I fall asleep with Glenn Miller's "Farewell Blues" in my headphones.

CHAPTER 8

The Grocer

The newly formed Mid-European Trading Company Inc. moved into Sven Salén's new offices in one of the showy buildings along Strandvägen Avenue. They were assigned two rooms connected to the larger office that would hold Salén's overarching business – Salén Shipping.

Strandvägen was Stockholm's finest promenade, with its linden tree-lined allée that stretched all the way to the Djurgården bridge, its wide quay out to Nybroviken bay and all the archipelago boats docked side by side. The street was laid out like an esplanade and edged with genteel palaces in a mixture of baroque and Art Nouveau styles. Here the cream of Stockholm society had their apartments. Number 27, for example was the residence of Marcus Wallenberg Sr and his wife Amalia, and Jacob Wallenberg also had his home there. Strandvägen 7a was by no means a shabby address for a newly established import/export firm.

Number 7 was an Art Nouveau-style building a bit further up the street with its entrance facing an inner courtyard. The family-owned hotel Grand Pensionat Dehn was on the first floor and above that there were two grand floors for the American Embassy, with residences as well as offices for the steadily growing diplomatic corps.

According to Kálmán Lauer's account of the preliminary events leading to the "Wallenberg Operation", the Mid-European Trading Company had its office on the fifth floor. Lauer and Wallenberg would take the elevator up from the marble-clad entrance hall. Its arches were a masterpiece of hand-wrought iron and brass.

Kálmán Lauer's situation had not been improved by Germany's attack on the Soviet Union in June 1941. German-allied Hungary declared war on the U.S.S.R. soon after. The Nazis' grip on Hungary hardened and the country introduced new and more severe race laws aimed at the Jewish population. It became increasingly risky for a Hungarian Jew such as Lauer to travel across Europe in general, and in Germany and Hungary in particular.

By the autumn of 1941, like many other foreigners, Lauer had already been caught in the far-reaching net of the Swedish security police. Truth be told, not much was needed to get one's name in their records. Members of the public were prone to calling the police to report suspected spying as soon as they saw someone at a café reading a Swedish newspaper with the help of a dictionary. Raoul Wallenberg had also been noted in these lists, because of a joke he told loudly in a restaurant.

The "General Security Service" had been formed by the government a couple of years earlier under the greatest secrecy. At its height it employed one thousand people, who listened to telephone calls, read letters and spied on suspicious persons, sometimes in ridiculously amateurish ways. The notes about Kálmán Lauer claimed that he had "shady dealings" in Stockholm, but there was no evidence offered to accompany the accusation.

As time went on, Lauer received his own security police file, with a detailed physical description and regular updates. This did not, however, prevent him from receiving renewals on his residency and work permits. Lauer was generally regarded as trustworthy and his work was seen as being of value to the Swedish people.

Raoul's new boss was, according to the security police records, 174 centimetres tall and corpulent. He had a full, oval face, light brown hair and eyes and pale skin. The report states that he had wide shoulders and a square chin, a high forehead, thin lips and healthy teeth. In the photograph, a pair of bushy eyebrows are in evidence. Lauer was forty-two years old, dressed in "bluish suits" and – again, according to the security police – spoke Swedish with a German accent.

It was said that he had been a communist in his youth, but certain informants described him as "being capable of supporting any government, red or black or of no colour, as long as Lauer can make money from the arrangement". According to co-workers from the time, Kálmán Lauer was a very intense and driven businessman with high expectations. He has been described as having a southern temperament and perhaps could not always be relied upon to be congenial.

*

The first ventures of the Mid-European Trading Company were politically well timed. In the autumn of 1941, everyone was talking about the lack of rubber, and the national rationing of eggs was introduced in September. Suitably enough, Raoul Wallenberg's first period of time in the company was devoted in large part to the import of a substitute egg powder and the export of Swedish horses in exchange for rubber tyres.

Raoul was thrown into the horse trade from the start. The sale of horses had become popular among Swedish farmers after the beginning of the war, since the export of groceries otherwise had slowed to nothing. A special licensing agency had been formed, the National Horse Export Regulatory Commission.

In 1941, Kálmán Lauer, who had worked in the horse trade back in Hungary, applied for permission to export 2,000 Swedish Ardennes horses to the unoccupied part of France. In return, the French would, according to Lauer's plan, supply them with large quantities of hotly coveted truck tyres.

The horse export commission had said yes to this proposition, on condition that the horses did not impinge on the then fairly extensive export of quality horses to Germany. The proposed Mid-European deal was alarmingly large, according to managers at the commission: even when it came to the horse trade, it seemed that the primary Swedish task was to keep the Germans happy.

The export of the Ardennes horses to France turned out to be a long-term operation for the enterprising duo of the Mid-European Trading Company. The French affair required several visits to the regulatory commission. Raoul also had to undertake two lengthy trips abroad, as well as sending countless laboriously dictated business letters.

Since the Mid-European Trading Company was also importing geese, ducks, egg products, dried vegetables and tomato purée, Raoul had his hands full. An equal number of letters, telephone calls and meetings were required to placate the other licensing authorities – the Food and Trade commissions.

During these telephone calls, Raoul would, as later in Budapest, absently doodle architectural sketches of victory arches in his notebook.

Full-time work was a new experience for Raoul Wallenberg, who had never been a nine-to-five person. Not that he had any intention of becoming a sedentary office rat. He often began his days by making his way from Bra-gevägen to the nearby Lill-Jansskogen forest for a walk or run, sometimes as early as six o'clock in the morning. Occasionally he stopped at his parents' home on the way and persuaded his sister Nina to join him.

When the work day was over at five o'clock, Raoul often had an evening session scheduled with the Home Guard. On such occasions he cycled home, had a sandwich and a glass of milk and quickly left again in his uniform, per-haps to train a carpenter's apprentice or a middle-aged dentist in the art of crawling through a ditch with a rifle.

The work at the Mid-European Trading Company cannot have been too sedentary either. At the Swedish Trade Commission, Kálmán Lauer had the reputation of being almost overly energetic and impulsive, at least compared to Swedish norms. They acknowledged that this could be an asset in tough international business negotiations, but the offices on Strandvägen could hardly have been an oasis of calm.

Compared to Lauer, Raoul Wallenberg gave a reserved and almost shy impression, but he rivalled him in both energy and zeal. Soon he was going full steam in his letter writing. The arguments in favour of various import licences were formulated in such detail and at the same time so sharply and precisely that the average Swedish clerk often stood no chance.

These were letters that could address anything from the ridiculously low profit margins on duck imports to the significance of the high percentage of fat in Hungarian geese given the ongoing national shortage of meat and fat.

Raoul quickly acquired an impressive skill in bureaucratic gambling, that he would have so much use of later in Budapest.

The third winter of the war was the coldest so far. Sweden remained a dark and frozen country until the middle of March. The merciless cold claimed several victims and Wednesday, February 26, 1942 would go down in history as the coldest day of the century, with record lows across the country and temperatures approaching −35°C. It was as if the weather itself was mourning the moral freezing point of the war that had just passed.

On January 20, 1942 the head of the German Reich Security Head Office (R.S.H.A.), Reinhard Heydrich, called fourteen top-ranking Nazi officials to a meeting in a villa by Wannsee, a lake south-west of Berlin. His subordinate, Adolf Eichmann, was responsible for the practical arrangements. Eichmann was the man who had been responsible for the evacuation of the Jews when forced emigration was still regarded as the best method to achieve Hitler's goal of a Jew-free Germany and Europe. But, during that autumn, the so-called "relocation" of the Jews had stalled. There was simply not enough room for all the deported Jews at the intended destinations in the east, especially when the Wehrmacht failed to secure as much territory in the Soviet Union as had been anticipated.

More powerful tools were needed. Already during the summer of 1941, Heydrich had been tasked by Hermann Göring with coming up with an alter-native. What the fourteen officials from the related ministries were now going to discuss were the organisational and practical matters concerning "the final solution of the European Jewish question".

Adolf Eichmann had prepared an estimate of the number of European Jews in order to give the assembled V.I.P.s a clear sense of the task that lay before them. He estimated eleven million, including the 8,000 Jews resident in politically neutral Sweden.

At a party meeting in December 1941, the day after Germany's declaration of war on the United States, Hitler had eliminated any doubt about the mean-ing of this next step. According to the diary of Joseph Goebbels, the Führer then explained that, when it came to the Jews, he wanted to "sweep the floor clean . . . World war is upon us; extermination of the Jews is the necessary consequence."

The Wannsee Conference lasted at most one and a half hours. The Nazi officials did not require any more time to agree on the new direction for resolving the "Jewish Problem": it had been decided to exterminate the Jews instead of deporting them as they had done previously. Those assembled in Wannsee apparently never used the word "exterminate", at least not according to the records that Eichmann was responsible for producing. But the minutes were nonetheless sufficiently explicit.

The Wannsee Conference in January 1942 opened the doors to hell. As the historian Christopher Browning observed in the introduction to his famous book about the foot soldiers of the Holocaust, *Ordinary Men*, about 75–80 per cent of the victims of the Holocaust were still alive in the middle of

March 1942. Eleven months later the "percentages were the exact opposite".

The course of the war had just begun to turn. The Americans had entered the fray and Germany's planned final attack on Moscow had met with an unexpected setback. Hitler had not prepared for the Russian winter and now suffered his first significant reverse. This would be followed by more. But these hopeful signs of a break in the darkness of the war meant nothing to the millions of people whose fate had just been determined in Wannsee.

In Sweden, these dark winter months at the beginning of 1942 were the final and perhaps the hardest test before matters began to improve. Few could of course predict it then, but after this there would be both milder winters and less to fear from foreign powers. At the Ministry of Foreign Affairs, the officials would soon be breathing easier, assured that the threat of a German invasion was no longer imminent: the Germans were fully occupied on the Eastern Front.

But it would still take a while before the more extreme manifestations of an anxious willingness to please would disappear from Swedish wartime politics. During 1941 the government continued to allow German rail transports through Sweden. In almost all cases these involved the transportation of unarmed soldiers on leave. The exception to this attracted the most attention – the transportation of the German Army's battle-ready Engelbrekt Division through Sweden in the summer of 1941. The Swedish government thereafter declined requests for the transportation of armed troops, but the passage of soldiers on leave remained frequent. During 1942 some 850,000 German soldiers travelled on Swedish trains.

Foreign Minister Günther's eagerness to maintain good relations with Germany was beginning to worry Prime Minister Per Albin Hansson, who wanted above all to remain on good terms with his coalition government. Günther was moving ever closer to what could be defined as a pro-German attitude. The situation was not improved when Günther's colleague Staffan Söderblom, the head of the political section, pushed even harder at the boundaries of what could be permitted. As expected, German diplomats in Stockholm had a very clear sense that the Swedish foreign minister's sympathies lay with them.

The coalition government also continued to appease the Germans with censorship of the Swedish press. Critical articles about Hitler and Nazism immediately provoked German rage. The cabinet's reaction time and time again had been to confiscate the newspapers, with the rationale that the press could not adopt a position towards either side in the war in a way that affected Sweden's security. Eighty-five per cent of these cases involved negative coverage of Germany.

On one of the last extremely cold days of March 1942, seventeen Swedish papers were recalled in response to the publication of the same article about how Germans were engaged in torture in Norwegian prisons. These accounts were suppressed under the rubric of "cruelty propaganda".

It was in this political climate that the Swedish diplomat Göran von Otter, legation secretary in Berlin, submitted to the Foreign Ministry in Stockholm what is probably the first ever precise report regarding the Nazis' systematic mass murder of Jews. Later in the summer of 1942 von Otter encountered the German S.S. officer Kurt Gerstein on a train. Gerstein asked the diplomat if he could inform him about something important, something that he wished to be conveyed back to the British. The day before Gerstein had witnessed the death of ten thousand Jews and now he wanted to tell everything he knew about the Holocaust. Gerstein related convincing details. He even displayed some documents that contained references to the gas Zyklon B.

This was not the first report of the Holocaust to reach the outside world but nothing with this level of concrete detail had emerged before. At the end of August 1942 Göran von Otter delivered this explosive material to the Foreign Ministry in Stockholm, with the intent that it be forwarded to the British. For security reasons, he delivered the message verbally at a one-to-one meeting with Staffan Söderblom. Von Otter described the conclusion of the meeting to the journalist Gitta Sereny many years later: "Once I had summed up the situation, he asked me to drop the entire matter. He wished me a nice vacation and told me that he would take the necessary action. Later – much later – I learned that he had not done a single thing." Two years later Staffan Söderblom was appointed Sweden's ambassador to Moscow. He went on to play a leading role in the diplomatic dance between Sweden and the Soviet Union that followed Raoul Wallenberg's arrest in January 1945.

*

Raoul Wallenberg spent the first few months of 1942 on a business trip in war-torn Europe. The days shortly before New Year's Eve he travelled through Germany and Switzerland to the city of Vichy in the unoccupied part of France. Vichy was the seat of Marshal Pétain's strongly Nazi-sympathetic and anti-Semitic puppet regime. Many Nazi decrees had been adopted in this southern, so-called "free" part of France, including strict Jewish laws.

Raoul Wallenberg's assignment was fairly clear – he was to try to salvage the promising horse deal. The French now claimed that it was impossible to assemble the necessary rubber tyres that the Swedes were demanding in trade.

Already an experienced negotiator, Raoul had learned to find his way through Swedish regulatory authorities with finesse and he spoke French and German better than most Swedes. Now he quickly learned what was needed in order to hustle the Vichy bureaucracy. According to Lauer, Raoul even managed to present his case to a member of the circle of Admiral Darlan, Pétain's most trusted associate.

Still Wallenberg had to reduce the ambition of their export deal from 2,000 horses to 200.

From France, Raoul travelled for the first time to Budapest on business. He checked in to the Dunapalota-Ritz, one of the renowned hotels on the east bank of the Danube.

In the early spring of 1942, Budapest – just like Stockholm – was something of an oasis of normality in wartime Europe. The Hungarians might be unwillingly fighting alongside the Germans on the Eastern Front (and had just lost an entire army) but the country was not a battlefield and in cosmopolitan Budapest the sparkling restaurant and café life continued as usual. There was an abundance of food, as if the concept of war rations was unknown. In the evenings, the city was filled with the murmur of carefree life, almost always accompanied by the sound of lyrical string music.

The energetic Kálmán Lauer had provided Raoul with a memo of around thirty pages. In it he had written everything Raoul needed to know about Budapest and everything that he was supposed to do. When Raoul returned to Sweden the memo was covered in all kinds of notes in the margins with words underlined in red, white and green – the colours of the Hungarian flag.

There would be at least one more business trip to Budapest for Raoul

Wallenberg. He attended cocktail parties at the Swedish legation on Gellért Hill and he became acquainted with some young wealthy aristocrats and jet-setters who introduced him to Budapest society. In only a short time, Raoul Wallenberg established an interesting Hungarian network, which very likely also included a number of Jacob and Marcus Wallenberg's Hungarian business contacts.

Just as in Budapest, the nightlife in Stockholm continued relatively unaffected by the war, especially when the light returned with spring and summer. Raoul had his parties and dinners on Bragevägen but was also seen out on the town. Raoul, who celebrated his thirtieth birthday at the beginning of August, now counted as one of Stockholm's slightly older and most sought-after bachelors. To judge from Raoul's surviving invitations and thank you notes, there were occasional girlfriends. A Britta, who attended nursing school at Sophiahemmet, wrote a warm greeting to Raoul one night when he had not answered the telephone. The 24-year-old Ulla Collett would frequently be seen by Raoul's side during these years.

Among Raoul's private documents there is also an undated dinner speech in verse that he wrote, dedicated to Woman. All the women present were given their own poetic interpretation along the following lines:

> Maud reminds me
> Of wild strawberry milk
> A tasty taste
> Not sour but sweet
> Not full-bodied
> But fully mature
> Tenacious tamer
> Of three tongues
> Dresses coquettishly
> Cannot cook

Journalists, diplomats and even spies were drawn to Stockholm in growing numbers during these years. The neutral city offered an excellent vantage point for those who wanted to observe the war. The numbers of foreign legations grew by leaps and bounds. The Soviet Union finally had 150 individuals on hand spread across numerous divisions. The American legation grew from ten staff in 1940 to four hundred in 1944. The German representation was almost as large if one counts the families, with sixteen subdivisions and twenty-three official apartments in Stockholm. The British legation doubled its staff several times over and it was in Stockholm that the British had their most important organisation for their wartime surveillance of the European press, the Press Reading Bureau (P.R.B.).

But it was of course not the nerve-racking Swedish war politics that brought the masses to the country. As the Swedish historian Wilhelm Agrell writes in his book *Stockholm: A Magnet for Spies*, "Stockholm was one of the few places in Europe where all the warring parties could be found represented in one place, a Nordic Casablanca where they met on the street, ended up next to each other on trams or realised that they lived in the same building."

For the temporary visitors it was sometimes difficult to interpret public opinion. Diplomats at the British legation in Stockholm were perplexed. On the one hand they had the decided feeling that nine out of ten Swedes sympathised with the British and that the overwhelming German-friendly attitude of the First World War had disappeared. On the other hand it was clear that many of the Swedes they encountered had a chilly, if not outright unfriendly, attitude toward the British representatives. Perhaps they did not know that the Swedish government had encouraged Swedes to be careful about taking a public stance for either side in the war.

From the perspective of the British and Americans, Raoul Wallenberg was an exception to the rule. He was happy to socialise with those employed at the British and American legations. The security police must have been aware of this since they tapped the diplomats' telephones. A couple of the conversations they reported on from the British and American legations during 1942 concerned invitations to Bragevägen 12.

Raoul Wallenberg was also one of the Stockholmers invited in secret to the British legation's private screening of "'Pimpernel' Smith", which was banned in Sweden and which was a modernised version of the classic "The Scarlet Pimpernel". Raoul brought his sister Nina with him to the Grand cinema on Sveavägen. They were enthralled by the film's slight but cunning Professor Smith, who managed to save thousands of Jews from the Nazis. Leslie Howard, who directed the film and played the starring role, was himself the son of a Hungarian Jew. "We thought the film was amazing. When we got up from our seats, Raoul said 'That is the kind of thing that I would like to do,'" Nina Lagergren remembers today.

To judge from their correspondence with various ministries, the most likely trade partners that Mid-European identified were located almost exclusively in German-dominated parts of Europe, above all in countries such as Hungary and Italy, who were allied with Germany and remained unoccupied. This was not a politically motivated position – it was simply how things were, and Raoul Wallenberg was not one to let potential ideological unease stand in the way. When it came to business, he played the cards he was dealt. As paths to the west were blocked, with the exception of a few designated ships a month, there were hardly any alternatives. It was trade in the German zone or no trade at all.

During the first year of the war, the German proportion of Swedish exports increased dramatically. Germany was buying so many war-oriented goods from Sweden – including iron ore and ball bearings – that the Scandinavians were forced to import unexpectedly large quantities of coal and coke.

Grocery imports from Hungary remained the central pillar of the business during Raoul's three years in the company. The Mid-European Trading Company was Sweden's largest importer of Hungarian fowl – from goose, duck and chicken to turkey, broiler hens and guinea fowl. They also purchased foie gras in large quantities and sold this on to the Swedish retail trade. It could add up to around 30,000 tins a year. Dried vegetables and sliced onion were other popular wartime products on their list, on which even fresh Hungarian superior-grade apples sometimes appeared.

The company was doing very well. Their business was growing and they had been making profits since the first year. This would continue for the duration of the war, with the exception of the great slump of 1944. But when Germany occupied Hungary in March 1944 and the deportation of that country's 825,000 Jews was initiated, both Kálmán Lauer and Raoul Wallenberg suddenly had something else to think about.

*

By the winter of 1942–43 it was increasingly clear that the tide of the war had turned against the Germans. In October and November the British prevailed against General Rommel's German–Italian troops at the battle of El Alamein outside Alexandria. Shortly thereafter, Adolf Hitler again experienced torment in the Soviet Union, this time in the battle for Stalingrad. The fighting had been going on since September and had turned from German superiority to bloody defeat. It did not help matters that Hitler forbade the encircled General Paulus to retreat. In Stalingrad, on January 31, 1943, Germany's Sixth Army surrendered.

News of these German setbacks appeared at the same time as the first frank reports of the Holocaust in the Swedish press. In mid-October 1942, the historian Hugo Valentin published an article titled "The War of Extinction Against the Jews" in the Gothenburg daily newspaper, *Göteborgs Handels- och Sjöfartstidning*. In the article he described the German politics of extermination in convincing detail. The article was not the first in the Swedish papers about the ongoing genocide, but it was by far the most comprehensive. It became an important wake-up call for the Swedish public.

It was clear that something significant had taken place. Less than a year earlier, a newspaper with an article similar to the one by Hugo Valentin had been confiscated as "cruelty propaganda" by the government. Now there was no such attempt at censure. After this point, public condemnation of Nazi crimes against the Jews was no longer regarded as a threat to Swedish security.

Towards the end of November 1942, the Swedish press reported that five hundred Norwegian Jews had been forced onto a steamship and deported to Auschwitz. This time, when the atrocities struck a brother nation, emotions ran high. Newspapers that had earlier obediently avoided all criticism of the Nazis now gave full expression to their outrage. Protest meetings were organised and could suddenly even draw support from conservatives.

Once the Allied governments had presented a unified declaration against the genocide of the Jewish people in December 1942, the earlier justification of censorship on the grounds of "cruelty propaganda" lost all validity. Hitler's propaganda minister, Joseph Goebbels, noted in his diary that same month that "The Swedes have [. . .] become exceptionally reserved and insolent as of late."

Even the foreign minister Christian Günther woke up to the situation and began to make some changes. As historian Paul A. Levine has shown, the Swedish Foreign Ministry now turned around completely and initiated a series of bureaucratic rescue missions for affected Jews, and not only in Norway. The foreign minister himself acted discreetly, not even informing the rest of the government. The changes he enacted were primarily to allow these things to take place and from time to time to involve himself in secret.

The Swedish turnaround was historic. Paul Levine observes that "For the first time since Nazi Germany began persecuting its Jewish population in 1933 a sovereign state announced to the Germans, albeit informally and not yet for public knowledge, that it was willing to accept any Jew, from a third country, who could make it to the Swedish border."

This change in Swedish attitude became even more noticeable later in 1943.

On a deeper cultural level, the orientation away from Germany and towards a more Anglo-Saxon direction had been evident in Sweden for a while. A reorientation was also perceptible in the attitude of Swedes to their great neighbour to the east. The Soviet Union's new position in the war, side by side with the Western powers, had not gone unnoticed in Sweden. The arch-enemy was showing itself in a more heroic guise. The Soviet Union had probably never awakened such warm feelings in the Swedish people as in the years just before and just after the end of the war. A certain measure of naïve trust developed, which would present problems for those Swedes who became acquainted with the darker side of Stalinism at the war's end.

There is no evidence that Raoul Wallenberg participated in the public debate during these years. He stayed abreast of the latest war-related news through newspapers and radio broadcasts, but did not adopt any public stance. In private he was far more open. His sister Nina Lagergren remembers how Raoul would storm into her parents' home for dinner and almost immediately launch into an intense discussion of the latest developments. Raoul attentively followed the difficulties of the German troops in the Soviet Union. According to Nina Lagergren, Raoul's position from the beginning was that of an anglophile anti-Nazi, for whom Adolf Hitler was the greatest evil that had afflicted the world. "Raoul was so cosmopolitan, grasping the span of the entire world in a way that was very unusual in Sweden back then," Nina

Lagergren recalls. "He burst in like a whirlwind with all these opinions and scenarios. When he left, we sat there in our calm and ordinary existence. Having discussions was not such a usual occurrence at that time. Life in Stockholm was relatively carefree."

But Raoul Wallenberg restricted his convictions to his private sphere. There were several anti-Nazi-oriented organisations in Stockholm for a young man like Raoul, but none of them appear to have tempted him to join. There was, for example, the anti-Nazi group called the Tuesday Club, a secret society of authors, journalists and intellectuals, who could also be seen at the British legation. But this wasn't quite Raoul Wallenberg's world. He had no interest in committing his opinions to paper in that fashion, nor was he an ideologically motivated public debater.

Raoul Wallenberg appears to have preferred to engage in practical displays of action.

The Swedish armed forces had largely recovered from their years of relative neglect and, by the last few years of the war, the country was reasonably well prepared for an attack that appeared ever less likely. Raoul Wallenberg was regularly called in for a few months of military service. He had no great difficulties in maintaining a decent social life even when he was in the army. But, during the first few months of 1943, Kálmán Lauer had to manage the company on his own, handling the delivery of 15,000 hares from Hungary for example: large plump animals of more than four kilos apiece.

By this point Raoul Wallenberg had established many of his own professional Hungarian contacts. The Mid-European Trading Company had engaged two businessmen as local contacts in Budapest, Josef von Déak and Laszló Kelemen, who received Raoul whenever he came. He had also become acquainted with a young official at the Foreign Ministry and several of Sven Salén's more important business associates, at the Royal Hungarian National and Free Harbour among other places. He had already met Antal Ullein-Reviczky, the future Hungarian minister in Stockholm, along with his wife, at a gathering in Budapest during the autumn of 1943.

Even back in Stockholm, Raoul was beginning to move more and more in Hungarian circles. When the trade commissioner Georg von Pogány at the Hungarian legation was about to leave Stockholm in the spring of 1943 he invited "architect Raoul Wallenberg" to his farewell soirée.

Raoul Wallenberg's social life in Stockholm had also changed character in other ways. His sister Nina Lagergren, who was nine years his junior, noted with some fascination that the female acquaintances of Raoul and his bachelor friends grew younger and younger as their peers got married. Now most of the women were her age or even younger and Nina and Raoul went to more parties together.

The eighteen-year-old singer Caroline Jacobsen was probably the youngest of the women Raoul Wallenberg dated at this time. Caroline Jacobsen toured as a field artist and sang for Swedish soldiers. Sergeant Wallenberg had sought her out after a performance and asked her for a date. Caroline, whose name today is Grinda Christensen, says: "I thought that he was very charming. He was cute when he laughed and looked nice although he didn't have much hair." They continued to meet for a time, between her tours.

One evening Raoul Wallenberg invited Caroline Jacobsen to a restaurant. They ate sole au gratin and talked about life. Once they had finished eating, Raoul began to draw on the paper tablecloth. He sketched a dream house, inspired by the houses in the Diplomatic city quarter. According to Caroline, he fantasised that they could live there once she was done with her singing career, and had perhaps attended a convent in Switzerland, and he had become something like an ambassador. Raoul must have spent about an hour drawing and then he said: "You can tear it off while I take care of the bill." Caroline kept the drawing and today it is securely stored in a safe. The grease stains are still there and it is possible to see that Raoul even pencilled in the points of the compass.

The brothers Marcus and Jacob Wallenberg continued to divide their time between the daily business of the family bank and high-level foreign negotiations. Stockholms Enskilda Bank did well during the war years. It had an international profile and the enterprise as a whole was, according to the professor of economic history Ulf Olsson, "the only private Swedish actor of any significance on the international financial market". Many years later it transpired that certain large Swedish transactions with Nazi Germany had been negotiated in exchange for gold that the Nazis had stolen from Jewish families. Some of these deals had gone through the Stockholms Enskilda Bank.

Another tribulation for the Wallenbergs occurred when the United States entered the war. During 1942 the Americans had seized the newly purchased American Bosch as hostile property since they did not believe that the Wallenberg family was the genuine owner.

Jacob Wallenberg had continued his trips to Berlin and retained his contact with representatives from Bosch and Carl Goerdeler, who opposed the German regime. In mid May 1943, Goerdeler came to Stockholm for the last time. His goal was the same as the year before. The German conspirators wanted to assure themselves that the Western Allies were prepared to come to a peace agreement in the event that they succeeded in their plot to remove Hitler from power. Goerdeler wanted Jacob, via Marcus, to communicate to the British the need for such advance guarantees.

A year earlier, Jacob had judged the plot as hopeless and tried to convince Goerdeler to do everything in the reverse order – first remove Hitler, then negotiate with the West. Now, in May 1943, Goerdeler was agitated and insisted that he be put in contact with Winston Churchill. Jacob wrote a letter to Marcus in London, who did as his brother asked and contacted one of Churchill's advisers. But the British reply was harsh and disappointing – no advance guarantees of any kind could be made. Several months later Jacob learned from Goerdeler that, despite this setback, the plans for the coup against Hitler were under way.

But during the spring and summer of 1943, Jacob and Marcus Wallenberg had other things to think about. Their father Marcus Sr had complained of sciatica and the reason behind the pain was now revealed to be prostate cancer. He died early on the morning of July 22 1943. Crown Prince Gustaf Adolf as well as several statesmen were present at the funeral in Jacobs kyrka. Raoul Wallenberg, his brother's grandson, was also present and had a seat on the left of the chancel.

Raoul had not lost contact with his father's cousins just because the question of his employment had been solved. It was not unusual for him to call on them or to pay a visit to the head office of the Enskilda Bank. He had brought Jacob Wallenberg flowers on his fiftieth birthday in the autumn of 1942, and from time to time he invited the brothers for tea or cocktails at his apartment.

At the same time, Sven Salén was engaging him in new assignments. During the summer of 1943, Raoul Wallenberg was voted onto the board of yet another company that Salén had invested in – the Pacific Trading Company, which, among other things, imported almonds and sardines from Portugal.

In addition to this, Raoul pursued his own projects on the side. He became interested in a small press in southern Sweden and appears to have had an idea about a business printing registers and catalogues; for example, a register of addresses of Swedish schools.

Friends from this period have reported that he was despondent during his last few months in Sweden. There are many indications that he wanted to move on, that trade in horses and turkey at the Mid-European Trading Company was not the professional end point for him. The trip he made to Budapest in the autumn of 1943 can hardly have improved his mood.

It was in fact a time of warm relations between Hungary and Sweden. Swedish singers were enjoying triumphant successes at the Hungarian State Opera in Budapest and the respective national football teams played each other, with the Swedish minister Ivan Danielsson and the Hungarian regent, Miklós Horthy, in attendance.

It is not clear if Raoul Wallenberg met with Minister Ivan Danielsson in Budapest on that occasion. He did however visit the Swedish legation, which was housed in a stylish Art Nouveau villa on Gellért Hill. There he met with the newly appointed deputy, Per Anger, whom he had known for a long time. Anger was a year younger than Raoul and had been an officer in the regiment where Raoul was sergeant. They would often see each other on the Stockholm social scene. Now they had a new professional contact, since Per Anger was responsible for trade issues at the legation. He had participated in the trade negotiations with Hungary from the beginning and had the task of facilitating the relatively substantial volume of trade.

Raoul used the legation as a base during his visit. He turned up at regular intervals and borrowed Per Anger's telephone when he needed to make a call to his Hungarian business partners. Anger noted that Raoul was unusually competent in German, to his ears completely fluent. He was also impressed by the Swedish food importer's finesse during negotiations.

But during this particular visit something appears to have gone wrong. Raoul Wallenberg had scheduled a meeting with the head of the Hungarian foie gras export association, who wanted to sell fifty tons of goose meat to Sweden and the Mid-European Trading Company. The negotiations concerned the price per kilo and unfortunately the communications appear to have broken down. Afterwards a veritable war broke out between the Hungarian trade delegation in Stockholm and the Mid-European Trading Company, since the final price was felt to be "disloyal to Hungarian interests". In Budapest the goose exporter was threatened with closure and cut all ties with Raoul Wallenberg.

These difficulties in Budapest were, for Raoul, also accompanied by alarm at the precarious situation of the Hungarian Jews. On the one hand, the Hungarian regent Horthy had made Hitler furious by stubbornly refusing to agree to deportations, despite repeated and increasingly insistent demands from the German Führer. But on the other, as a German ally, Hungary had in fact been more diligent than most other "free" countries in introducing anti-Jewish laws. Anti-Semitism spread like a heavy blanket across the otherwise so light-hearted daily life in Budapest. An agitated Raoul Wallenberg returned to Stockholm and described several worrying anti-Semitic incidents to his Jewish boss, Kálmán Lauer, who had both in-laws and a sister with small children back in Hungary.

This concern was partly offset by the joyful news of Raoul's younger sister Nina's engagement to Gunnar Lagergren, a clerk at the Swedish National Courts. In December 1943, the couple married in Jacobs kyrka in Stockholm. Raoul was given the task of creating a flower-covered archway that would greet the guests at the dinner afterwards. He finished it at the last minute.

The newlyweds had just made a dramatic decision. The Swedish legation in Berlin needed the reinforcement of an attorney and had turned to Svea Hovrätt, the National Courts, for help. Gunnar Lagergren was asked and he and Nina decided to depart shortly after the wedding: Raoul, who felt the move to Berlin sounded far too adventurous, had advised them to decline.

On New Year's Day 1944, Raoul participated, as he did every year, in the traditional Wallenberg family service, followed by a morning buffet. In the year that lay ahead he himself would turn thirty-two. His cousins of the same age had long since married, but he was far from even contemplating it. Life does not appear to have been particularly happy for Raoul in the first few months of 1944. At Strandvägen 7a, his working days were temporarily brightened by a large shipment of oranges, but otherwise there continued to be every kind of problem with orders of various feathered fowl.

It was a despondent Raoul who, in late February 1944, wrote a birthday letter to his sister Nina in Berlin: "It's terribly boring here without you and the dinner table at home is like a scene from a Strindberg play. Mother is quite depressed as you must understand since, on top of everything else, she has to return to the hospital for perhaps as long as three months and undergo another operation."

He wrote more about his mother's broken leg as well as dinners that he had attended and people that he had met. Among other things he described a discussion that he had had about crime with the wife of a lawyer at a black-tie dinner. "I claimed that every person has their price, so to speak, and that as long as the temptation was great enough, the reason strong enough and the threat of discovery unlikely enough, anyone could be transformed into a criminal," Raoul wrote.

It was February 28, 1944. The only thing that Raoul Wallenberg knew for sure about his immediate future was that he had a few more deliveries of oranges to arrange, and that he was due to go back into the military again at the end of March, for a couple of months' service.

Raoul sent along a present to Nina with his letter. He concluded by saying: "I wish you a very happy birthday and dearly hope that the two of you will make it through the year without any mishaps."

Blasieholmen, May 2010

Raoul Wallenberg was not alone in beginning 1944 with a prayer for the New Year at seven o'clock in the morning. The Wallenberg clan stuck together. Sometimes more than one hundred people turned up at the early morning service at the church and thereafter defied the January cold with a walk to the home of Amalia Wallenberg at Strandvägen 27. Marcus Jr's youngest son, Peter Wallenberg, was one of those who thronged at the breakfast buffet in that sumptuous apartment on January 1, 1944. He was only seventeen then and home for Christmas from his boarding school in Sigtuna. He only had a couple of months left before graduation.

I have asked him for a meeting in order to hear him talk about what he remembers of his second cousin. It is a miserable day at the end of May. Rain is pouring down and in the morning the Stockholm financial markets have taken a shocking tumble. S.E.B., the Wallenberg family bank, sinks furthest of all.

Peter Wallenberg is eighty-four years old and honorary chairman of the Wallenberg family's holding company, Investor. He is the family's current *pater familias* and still has, despite his age, a hand in the game when it comes to important decisions. We have arranged to meet at the head offices of Investor at Blasieholmen, a hop and a skip away from Raoul Wallenbergs torg, the square which holds the monument to Wallenberg by Kirsten Ortwed.

During this spring of European bank crises the head office is wrapped in scaffolding for a complete renovation. In the executive suite on the fourth floor conversations are held as well as they can be, accompanied by thundering drills. I am shown into a conference room with a chandelier and an oriental rug. On the oval mahogany table there are a couple of notebooks and neatly arranged pencils.

The door opens and a tea trolley is brought in. A minute later Peter Wallenberg appears with a canny smile on his lips. He is dressed in a dark suit and tie with a white handkerchief peeping out of his breast pocket.

He is called "Pirre" by all who know him.

"Hi there! he says and lays his cane on the table. "Would you like some tea?"
He refuses to let me help with the trolley.

"This is a job for old guys," he says, pouring out two cups and placing a plate
of biscuits and chocolate in front of me – as well as an ashtray for himself.

Peter Wallenberg sits down, takes out his pipe and carefully packs it with
bourbon tobacco. Then he tries to satisfy my curiosity and recall the New Year's
Day celebration of 1944, since it was probably the only time he exchanged words
with Raoul Wallenberg.

"I remember that he was dressed in uniform, exactly as I would be later, the
same boring grey-blue uniform. That's how it was back then, one only had short
leaves. Everyone walked around in uniform. And ours was about the same as they
had in World War I. He had sergeant's stripes, I think, can that be right? But I can't
remember that I ever met him before."

This is not surprising. When Peter Wallenberg was four years old, Raoul left
for the United States and did not return until 1935, which happened to be a difficult year for Peter and his elder brother. In October his father Marcus Wallenberg moved out of the family home and one year later the divorce was final.
Mother Dorothy moved to England. The eleven-year-old Marc and nine-year-old
Peter were sent to boarding school in Sigtuna.

By New Year's Day 1944, Peter Wallenberg had not seen his mother since 1940.

But this is not a detail he brings up. Instead, Peter begins to describe his
grandmother Amalia Wallenberg with great warmth. He was extremely devoted
to her, just like his cousin Raoul. Her own children may sometimes have found
her strict, but she lavished her care and attention on her grandchildren and more
peripheral relatives. Peter recalls how he was brought for formal visits with her
when he was little, where he was spoiled with sweets and presents. He is convinced that even Raoul went on such "official visits" as a child.

Today's generation of Wallenbergs – Marc and Pirre's children – have done
away with the New Year's Day event. Now Amalia's birthday on May 29 is the
great family reunion, with the same menu every year: lightly smoked salmon,
pheasant with morel sauce and champagne jelly for dessert. Amalia's portrait is
always in the same place, next to a silver vase filled with lilies of the valley. This
year, 2010, she is to be congratulated on her 146th birthday.

"Amalia was a mother. She asked me once if I knew that I had 200 second cousins. She kept track of all of them," Peter Wallenberg tells me.

It is unlikely that this is an exaggeration. Amalia's embrace was at least large enough for Peter's fatherless second cousin Raoul, as evidenced by all the greetings and letters about birthday presents. There was of course a Christmas card from Amalia to Raoul in the batch of mail that never arrived in Budapest in December 1944.

"But for me Raoul Wallenberg was never very close," Peter observes. "We were of the same generation, from a family perspective, but the age difference was great. I can't say that I was particularly aware of him until he went missing. He wasn't someone I heard my father talking about when I was home. But I was at a boarding school, of course, so I never experienced the kind of chit-chat that goes on in everyday family life."

Our meeting is brief. We make plans to see each other again to talk about what happened after the war. Or did not happen. Peter Wallenberg has already warned me. He does not believe that he can be of much use to me, in part because the subject was so hush-hush in the family and in part because he was abroad for much of the fifties and sixties. He worked for Atlas Copco in Central Africa, among others.

"Do you want to know what happened then? It was either 1960 or 1961 and I was going on holiday to Cape Town. I came driving in early one morning without having booked a room in advance. By chance I stopped at a small hotel outside the city that was on a cliff, with the entire Atlantic Ocean below it. In the lobby there was a middle-aged European man. He took a look at my passport and then he said 'Wallenberg? Are you Swedish? Are you a relative of Raoul?'

"'Yes,' I said, 'his second cousin.' Then he beamed at me, this hotel receptionist and said, 'I will make sure that you receive our finest room with a view of the ocean. And whatever you need, Mr Wallenberg, you have only to ask.'"

Peter Wallenberg taps his pipe on the side of the ashtray. The construction workers have paused.

"This came a little unexpectedly and I didn't know very much about Raoul. I must have looked quite puzzled. 'You understand,' the man went on, 'Raoul Wallenberg saved my life.'"

Peter Wallenberg died on January 19, 2015

PART II

WHAT MAKES AN ACT HEROIC?

CHAPTER 9

The Encounter in the Elevator

It has never been completely understood how the whole thing started. There are as many versions as there are tellers. But, to judge from the known facts, the elegantly wrought elevator at Strandvägen 7a in Stockholm played a central role in what was to come. Most likely it was here that all of the separate threads of the situation in Hungary came together in a single solution late in the spring of 1944. It is probably this very elevator that has the honour or blame for the fact that all eyes suddenly fell on Raoul Wallenberg.

None of this, of course, would have come to pass if Adolf Hitler had not lost his patience with his Hungarian ally, the regent Miklós Horthy and – perhaps above all – with his prime minister Miklós Kállay.

There were several points of contention. Despite repeated requests, Horthy had refused to give in to the demands that Hungary's 825,000 Jews be deported as part of the "final solution". Horthy had his reasons. Hungary's large Jewish population was among the most assimilated in the whole of Europe. In the circles of the social elite, in which the regent himself moved, there were plenty of Jewish families. Many had long since stopped reflecting on their Jewish origins, if they were even aware of them. They saw themselves as Hungarians, nothing more. Naturally there was also another way of life represented among the Hungarian Jews: but the Orthodox who resisted assimilation often belonged to the more impoverished social classes and therefore largely existed outside 76-year-old Horthy's social purview.

Admittedly, after the Great War, Hungary became the first country in Europe to introduce anti-Semitic laws. Just as in Germany, it was the substantial Jewish minority that took the blame for the misery that the Hungarians experienced after their defeat. As early as the 1920s, the country restricted the right of Jews to attend university, and other discriminatory laws followed. But the step from this to Hitler's genocide proved too great for Admiral Horthy. There was no possiblity that the country's Jews should be stigmatised by being forced to wear the yellow star. How Hungary treated its Jews was a strictly national question and had nothing to do with Germany. This had been Horthy's message to Hitler.

The existing oppression of Hungarian Jews had strong roots in historic prejudice, though one can also trace elements of a conscious strategy to appease Hitler. If the Hungarians pursued a domestic programme of discrimination against the Jews they could win time, and the country's Jews could be saved from an even more terrible fate.

But by now Hitler's rage was not solely limited to the Jewish question. The Führer was also frustrated by the unsatisfactory Hungarian unwillingness to engage in battle. Hungary had aligned itself with Germany in the hope of being able to regain the territories that had been lost in the Great War. For a leader such as Horthy this strategic decision had been akin to a choice between being infected by cholera or the plague. He despised Hitler and Nazism but he hated the Soviet Bolsheviks even more.

Hungary had enjoyed a number of victories in battle but, after the loss of an army on the Eastern Front in early 1943, the confidence of both the leadership and the common soldier was beginning to falter. Hitler's mood did not improve when the German intelligence service revealed that Miklós Kállay had secretly put out repeated feelers for peace talks with the Allies.

Interestingly enough, one of Kállay's covert avenues for communication had been through Stockholm. In 1943 his press secretary Antal Ullein-Reviczky had been appointed minister of the Hungarian legation in Stockholm. Ullein-Reviczky had played a leading role in these exploratory conversations even earlier and the Germans had demanded his resignation for this reason. Once he was in place in Sweden, Ullein-Reviczky would continue to build contacts with the West.

Some of these Hungarian peace talks were to take place in Raoul Wallenberg's immediate social milieu. Wallenberg had become acquainted with the new Hungarian minister in Sweden during an earlier visit to Budapest in the autumn, and there were also other connections. Raoul's half-siblings had a distant cousin, Nane de Dardel, who was a close friend of Raoul's sister Nina. Nane de Dardel was engaged to the American legation secretary in

Stockholm, Francis Cunningham, and the couple was renting Nina and Gunnar Lagergren's apartment while they were in Berlin. In December 1943, this same Cunningham had brought together Ullein-Reviczky and a Stockholm representative for the American Office of Strategic Services, or O.S.S. (later the C.I.A.). They had met at Strandvägen 7a, where the American legation had its two floors and Raoul Wallenberg his office. The following day Ullein-Reviczky was the guest of honour at a cocktail reception at Raoul Wallenberg's home on Bragevägen 12.

The Hungarian contacts with the West did not enrage just Hitler. The Soviet Union's foreign minister, Vyacheslav Molotov, hit the roof when he got wind of the matter. Molotov made it perfectly clear that under no circumstances were the British and Americans to negotiate an armistice with a nation whose soldiers were still engaged in violence on Soviet territory. If Hungary was seeking peace, this would require unilateral capitulation to all Allied states. The project was therefore hopeless. Hungary could potentially consider surrendering to the British and Americans, but absolutely not to the Soviet Union.

At the beginning of March 1944, the Soviet troops were 160 kilometres from the Hungarian border. Adolf Hitler felt pressured. He no longer trusted his Hungarian partners, and still had trouble getting over the fact that the Italians had overthrown his ally Mussolini the year before. Another betrayal would be too much. He had therefore, some six months earlier, prepared an invasion plan for Hungary, called Operation Margrethe, which he kept in his desk drawer.

When in February 1944 Horthy wrote to Hitler and demanded that the Hungarian troops be recalled from the Eastern Front, the Führer had had enough. He launched into action in mid-March, by luring Horthy out of the country.

On March 15, the Hungarian national day, both the Swedish minister in Hungary, Ivan Danielsson, and his deputy at the Swedish legation, Per Anger, were sitting in the audience at the State Opera in Budapest. Miklós Horthy was also present for the ceremonial premiere of the patriotic opera "Petőfi". During the intermission, a German diplomat delivered an important message to Horthy. Afterwards the Swedish diplomats heard that the regent had been summoned to a meeting with Adolf Hitler. The Führer wanted to meet with him at Schloss Klessheim outside Salzburg within forty-eight hours.

Ostensibly, Hitler wanted to discuss Horthy's request to recall the Hungarian troops. But, when the Hungarian regent arrived in Klessheim, it became apparent that he had been deceived. Adolf Hitler, in Horthy's view much aged and nervous, explained that Hungary's evident betrayal had forced him to enact certain "security measures" against the country. Horthy was quick-witted enough to understand that this meant military occupation. "If only I had brought my revolver, I would have shot that scoundrel; for the rest of my life I have regretted that I was unable to do so," Horthy confessed in an interview many years later.

Instead he felt forced to accept Hitler's disingenuous "compromise": Horthy would be allowed to retain his position and Hungary would formally retain its independence. The current government would, however, be replaced with one aligned with German Nazi principles. As soon as the new government was installed, the German troops would leave the country, the Führer promised.

Hitler accompanied Horthy to the train that same evening, March 18. The trip back to Budapest took more than twelve hours since the Germans made sure the train stopped in several cities and in Vienna almost all night. The delays were enough to present the regent with a fait accompli.

At three o'clock on the night of March 19, 1944, the first German para-troopers floated down onto the Hungarian airfields. A few hours later, Hungarians awoke to the roar of German bombers. On the train, Horthy was introduced to the new German emissary Edmund Veesenmayer. He immediately brought up the question of a Nazi-friendly government, presenting to Horthy the Hungarian minister stationed in Berlin, Döme Sztójay, as his candidate for prime minister. A few days later Sztójay was selected by Horthy to lead Hungary's new puppet government.

In Budapest the airwaves had gone silent. Armed German soldiers marched in the streets, soon followed by German tanks and military vehicles. The Hungarians were given no information but, when Horthy's train pulled into Budapest close to noon, most people already knew that their country was now under occupation. With the exception of a few initial salvos of gunfire, the Germans met with no resistance.

Horthy was escorted by the S.S. to the royal castle, where he withdrew into isolation, uneasy at having to lend legitimacy to a Nazi-friendly government and, for all practical purposes, to transform his country into a subservient German state.

It was almost a given that the new Hungarian regime he approved would swiftly implement Hitler's demands regarding the Jews. Horthy even seems to have given the go-ahead for the transport of 100,000 Jewish labourers for the German war industry. In return, Horthy hoped that Hitler would keep his promise and pull back his troops as soon as the formalities regarding the new government were completed. But things did not turn out exactly as the Hungarian regent had imagined.

In the Austrian concentration camp Mauthausen, Obersturmbannführer Adolf Eichmann was awaiting his marching orders. He was the one who, after the Wannsee Conference, had been appointed administrator of the deportations. On this Sunday, March 19, 1944, he turned thirty-eight years old and faced his greatest challenge yet. His orders from the S.S. leader Heinrich Himmler were clear. Eichmann was to make his way to Hungary and Budapest in order to "comb the country for Jews, from east to west, and, as soon as possible, deport each and every Jew to Auschwitz". He, if anyone, knew what that meant. Eichmann himself had compiled the data and was fully informed that there had been more than eight hundred thousand Jews in Hungary before the war. These would be the most rapid and most comprehensive deportations of the entire Holocaust.

Adolf Eichmann was a delicately built man who had begun his professional career as a travelling salesman for an oil company. He was born in Germany but – just like Adolf Hitler – he had spent his childhood in the Austrian city of Linz. He had even attended the same school as the Führer, although not at the same time.

During his time with the Austrian oil company Eichmann made a name for himself through his diligence and talent for organisation, as well as his passion for paperwork and report writing. These administrative talents had taken him far within the Nazi bureaucracy, which he sought out shortly after Hitler's rise to power in 1933. He had advanced as a practical fixer and as a tireless worker with a large appetite for success and responsibility.

Since the beginning of the war, Eichmann had been charged with the "Jewish questions and evacuations" within the Security Ministry (Reichs-sicherheitshauptamt, R.S.H.A.). He had successfully stepped up to handle the difficult logistics of the deportations from, among other places, Austria, France and the Netherlands. This meant that he had identified which Jews should be apprehended and how, he decided what they were allowed to bring with them, he had synchronised train schedules and reviewed the capacity of the concentration camps. All in all, a macabre résumé.

Despite all this, he was finding it increasingly difficult to conceal his frustration at still being a mid-level S.S. officer. Eichmann had not progressed beyond the rank of Obersturmbannführer, to which he had been promoted in 1941. Now, in Hungary, he had the chance to achieve a notable success at the helm of his unit, the Sondereinsatzkommando, or Special Operations Command. This time Eichmann would also be present in the field, not simply giving orders from behind the desk at Prinz-Albrecht-Strasse in Berlin.

Toward the evening of March 19, 1944, Eichmann's unit began its journey to Budapest. The convoy had close to 200 men, in more than 140 trucks and other vehicles. They met with no resistance and so could take it easy, even stopping along the way. The officers wanted to make a celebratory toast to their leader on his birthday. It was the birthday celebration that Eichmann would remember best from the day. The rest of it was, after all, business as usual.

The deputy at the Swedish legation, Per Anger, was woken up at six o'clock that morning by the ringing of the telephone. The caller was the minister Ivan Danielsson and his message was short and dramatic: "The Germans are in the process of occupying the city. Get down to the office immediately!"

Up to this point the Swedish diplomats had enjoyed a relatively carefree existence in peaceful Budapest. The thirty-year-old Anger and his wife Elena rented a house on Rózsadomb, or Rose Hill, from a baron in the powerful Hungarian-Jewish Weiss family, the dynasty that owned the large Manfréd Weiss factory on Csepel Island in the middle of the Danube. The couple had married the year before and Elena Anger was nine months pregnant. When their daughter Birgitta was born a couple of weeks later, bombs were raining down on the previously idyllic city.

Per Anger was young, energetic and socially talented. He had been sent to the legation in Budapest in November 1942 with the primary assignment of managing any trade issues. Before this he had been stationed for a year in Berlin, so he was not unaccustomed to the war. After four years in the diplomatic corps, Per Anger was convinced that he had chosen the right career path. He found the task of representing Sweden deeply satisfying and his placement in sought-after Budapest was a testament to his successes.

The Swedish minister Ivan Danielsson was separated and approaching the age of retirement. He had a private apartment at the very top of the palatial legation building on Gellért Hill. Even that building was owned by a wealthy Hungarian businessman, Count Dezső Bayer-Krucsay, who had been the Swedish consul general before the war. Minister Danielsson was a diplomat of the old guard, rather more stern and serious than his easygoing young deputy. He was tall and still regarded as a handsome man. He insisted on wearing a monocle and often carried a silver cigarette holder, though he had stopped smoking. Danielsson rarely went far without his beloved poodle, Diana.

Ivan Danielsson had been stationed in Spain during the civil war and in Egypt while the battles raged there. His time in Cairo had come to an unhappy end when the Egyptian government accused Danielsson of making pro-German statements and proclaimed him *persona non grata*.

So far Budapest had lived up to his hopes for more peace and quiet in the final days of his career. The minister was committed to his diplomatic assignment, but had grown weary over the years. He appears to have appreciated Per Anger's youthful energy and often gave his deputy a free hand to act beyond his trading brief. Per Anger was given responsibility for a greater portion of the affairs at the legation than he had expected.

There were also two Swedish secretaries at the legation, Margareta Bauer and Birgit Brulin, as well as a Swedish-speaking Hungarian clerk named Dénes von Mezey. The secretaries had hugely enjoyed their time in Budapest so far, living "a veritable life of luxury in the midst of regular business", as Margareta Bauer wrote later in her unpublished memoirs.

> We often played tennis, tended to our health in the warm baths and
> drank the water that tasted worse than the most terrible mineral

water but which was good for weak stomachs [. . .] We ordered
handmade shoes and let the fashion models strut before us while
we sat back cosily in our fine armchairs.

The social life of the legation was equally busy. Ivan Danielsson had good
contacts among the Hungarian aristocracy. There were dinners and receptions and sometimes Per Anger and Danielsson were invited to weekend
hunting parties at large estates outside Budapest. From time to time one of
the travelling Swedish opera stars came by, not to mention all the Swedish
businessmen who had to be entertained. The telephone call warning of the
Nazis' occupation of Budapest early that Sunday morning in March 1944 put
an end to this carefree diplomatic existence.

Per Anger got dressed and left for the legation. Up to this point he had mostly
spent his work days negotiating quotas for goods, discussing the exchange of
so much Swedish steel for so many Hungarian apples, goose or turkey. From
now the nature of the work altered drastically. The amount and scope of what
he was expected to do would also increase radically.

The day after the occupation, Danielsson paid a visit to Hungary's outgoing foreign minister and, in confidence, was given a summary of events.
After this he wrote his first report to the Foreign Ministry in Stockholm:
"Dramatic and, for Hungary, quite dire events have taken place here these
past few days," Danielsson began. He related the course of events and concluded with a description of the current situation:

Budapest itself is not full of German troops; these have established
camps around the circumference of the capital city. It is, however,
overflowing with S.S. formations and Gestapo agents, and a ruthless
hunt has been instigated against Jews in positions of responsibility.
A number of arrests have even been made of notable Hungarians
within the socialist, liberal and legitimist parties, known for their
entente sympathies, including the minister of domestic affairs [. . .]

There is calm in the city, but one can perceive an acute nervous-
ness among the population, so many of whom must fear for their
lives. Our offices are veritably overrun with people, mostly Jews

and Poles who are either applying for asylum or requesting papers
showing that they are under our protection.

Lines also formed outside the legations of other neutral nations – the Swiss,
Portuguese, Spanish and the Vatican – but the pressure on the Swedish representatives was the greatest. This had in large part to do with the new Swedish
attitude towards the persecuted Jews, which had attracted international attention. But the significant trade relationships between Sweden and Hungary
also played a role. Among those who waited in line, and whom Per Anger
would encounter, were many important Jewish businessmen with whom he
had earlier come into contact regarding business. Now they were desperately
pleading for help.

In March 1944, it was no longer news to the Allies that the Nazi regime
was transporting the Jews of Europe to concentration camps in order to
exterminate them. After the lightning occupation of Hungary it became clear
that Europe's last remaining substantial Jewish population was threatened
by deportation and genocide. The outside world's list of sins of omission
was already embarrassingly long. For far too long, far too many had taken
no action and allowed terrible things to happen. Now the situation could no
longer be tolerated: what was needed was action, or so many international
parties reasoned. They would all converge in Stockholm in different ways.

The American government was one of them. President Roosevelt and his
ministers had at this point known of the ongoing genocide for eighteen
months. And yet it took until January 1944 before any American rescue missions were organised. The Allies had adopted the position that the most
important thing for all parties, including the affected Jews, was that the war
should be won. Thus no resources could be set aside, no concentration
diverted, for humanitarian rescue missions. For fear of fuelling an increased
domestic anti-Semitism, even the American Jewish organisations had
remained relatively passive. According to the historian David S. Wyman, they
had been more concerned about demonstrating their American patriotism
than voicing any demands for rescue operations on behalf of the victims of
the Holocaust.

But, in the final phase of the war, a demand for action among the American public was growing. The increased pressure led President Roosevelt in January 1944 to found the War Refugee Board (W.R.B.), an independent authority with the mandate to coordinate and lead rescue missions for Jews and other persecuted minorities in Europe.

The creation of the War Refugee Board was a relatively unusual measure in the political climate. In the end it was the U.S. secretary of the treasury, the Jew Henry Morgenthau, who managed to convince President Roosevelt of the merits of the project. Both Secretary of State Cordell Hull and Secretary for War Henry Stimson had been sceptical, since they still believed prioritising refugee issues could interfere with American foreign policy and the conduct of the war.

There was, therefore, some friction when the three sparring departments were informed they should now cooperate with the War Refugee Board. Even in March 1944 there wasn't much to show for the new American mission to aid Europe's Jews.

These activities were also at first hampered by a lack of money. The War Refugee Board received federal aid only to support its own administration. The missions themselves required outside support and came to be funded almost entirely by American Jewish organisations. The single largest financier was the American Jewish Joint Distribution Committee, which contributed an impressive fifteen million dollars (almost two hundred million today). These efforts were probably helped by the fact that the secretary of the treasury's father, also named Henry Morgenthau, had thirty years earlier helped to found the American Jewish Joint Distribution Committee, which was now more widely known as Joint.

It had been a slow start, but by the time the Germans marched into Budapest, the War Refugee Board was finally ready. The Hungarian crisis became its first major challenge. That spring, special W.R.B. representatives were appointed and dispatched to neutral countries such as Turkey, Switzerland, Sweden and Portugal.

In Stockholm, the chosen man was the finance attaché at the American legation, Iver Olsen. He was born in northern Norway and, as it happened, had come to Stockholm during Christmas 1943. Like the other American representatives, Olsen had his office at Strandvägen 7a. He could now add the refugee question to his other work duties. Olsen had occasionally shared the elevator with Kálmán Lauer, and perhaps even Raoul Wallenberg, of the Mid-European Trading Company. But it was a while before they discovered what they had in common.

Now the War Refugee Board began to raise its voice abroad. The day after the German occupation of Hungary, the W.R.B. in Washington sent urgent telegrams to several neutral countries with diplomatic representation in Budapest in order to quickly gather situational intelligence. On Friday of that same week, President Roosevelt gave a speech that was cabled out across the world by way of radio stations based in neutral countries. The speech was an important gesture. Roosevelt declared that the United States viewed the Nazi persecution of the Jews as criminal mass murder and that "none who participate in these acts of savagery shall go unpunished". This speech would be used many times by W.R.B. as they sought to influence public opinion. It was broadcast over the airwaves, printed on leaflets and spread by underground resistance groups to countries under German control.

It is unclear if Raoul Wallenberg heard Roosevelt's speech. On the last weekend of March 1944 he was preparing for several months of military service and his days were booked solid with social engagements. Among others, he was meeting with the young singer Caroline Jacobsen. But everything suggests that there was one new female acquaintance in particular who was dominating his thoughts at this time.

During the five last days before being called up, Raoul met the 21-year-old beauty Jeanette von Heidenstam four times. They went to a Chinese restaurant and an art exhibition. As Jeanette remembers, when Raoul went running in Lill-Jans forest in Östermalm she used to follow on a bicycle. Raoul's infatuation lasted all spring and also through the series of coincidences that would lead his life in an unexpected direction.

The events in Hungary came to dominate daily life at the offices of the Mid-European Trading Company. Raoul Wallenberg's partner Kálmán Lauer became increasingly restless, anxious and distraught as time went on. He worried about what would happen to his Jewish in-laws and his sister's family. "In just a week Dr Lauer's dark hair became sprinkled with grey!" one of his secretaries wrote later.

He was, of course, not alone in these concerns among Swedish-Hungarian

Jews in Stockholm. After the German invasion, the Foreign Ministry at Gustav Adolfs torg was overwhelmed with letters from alarmed individuals who wanted to secure the Ministry's protection for their Jewish relatives in Hungary. Lauer probably played an important role in the agitated conversations that were now under way among the Hungarian colony in Stockholm. He had managed to become a fairly established personality in Swedish–Hungarian matters and was not the kind to sit idly by, or lack for ideas, when there ' was a new and difficult situation that required a solution. When the Hungarian minister in Stockholm, Antal Ullein-Reviczky, distanced himself from the new quisling government in Hungary, the Hungarians in Stockholm all sent him letters of support, a gesture that Lauer played a large role in organising. They also saw each other socially.

In April, the outgoing Ullein-Reviczky pleaded with the Swedish government to take measures to improve the situation for the threatened Hungarian Jews. While the Hungarian Jews in Stockholm had, inevitably, nurtured thoughts of collective action, somewhat remarkably the Swedish–Jewish community in Stockholm had so far adopted a hesitant and passive attitude whenever the question of rescue missions for the victims of the Holocaust was raised. The community's leaders had not gained a reputation as eager supporters of a generous Swedish refugee policy vis-à-vis the European Jews. In fact, the Chief Rabbi, Marcus Ehrenpreis, appeared to lean in the opposite direction. Like his American counterparts, he was deeply worried that an invasion of Jewish refugees could trigger anti-Semitism and persecution in Sweden.

When the War Refugee Board began its local work in Stockholm in 1944, the newly appointed Iver Olsen was shocked by the attitude of the leading Swedish Jews. He forwarded his impressions to his boss, John Pehle, in Washington.

The following is for your information only, but it is only too true that the Swedish Jews don't want any more Jews in Sweden. They are very comfortably situated here, have no anti-Semitic problems, and are very much afraid that an influx of Jews will not only be a burden to them, but will create a Jewish problem in Sweden. Consequently, you will find them very interested in Jewish rescue and relief operations, so long as they do not involve bringing them into Sweden.

And indeed it was the German-born fur trader and Zionist Norbert Masur, rather than Ehrenpreis, who first introduced into Jewish circles in Sweden the question of helping the Hungarian Jews. Masur had for many years tried to press for more rescues, but had hitherto always run up against the hesitant Jewish community. In the spring of 1944, Masur realised that Marcus Ehren-preis was finally more receptive to the idea. The Chief Rabbi had, for instance, just been persuaded to form a Swedish chapter of the World Jewish Congress, an activist organisation. This would have been unthinkable only a few years earlier.

The diplomatic Masur began to test the water. He tried various avenues until he arrived at a proposal that he outlined in a letter to the Chief Rabbi on Karlavägen, on April 18, 1944:

> We should find a person, highly skilled, of good reputation, a non-Jew, who is willing to travel to Romania/Hungary in order to lead a rescue mission for the Jews. The person in question must have the confidence of the Utrikesdepartementet, be issued a diplomatic passport, and the Utrikesdepartementet must instruct the legations in Bucharest and Budapest to assist him to the best of their abilities. We must supply this person with a considerable sum, say 500,000 kronor [. . .] I believe that with this plan we will be able to save a few hundred people. The main requirements are: the right man, support from the Utrikesdepartementet, and money. The latter is the least of our concerns as we can most likely secure a large portion of it from the United States. Even support from the Utrikesdepartementet should be possible in light of the helpfulness that is now in evidence. It would, of course, be invaluable if the Utrikesdepartementet were also to authorise the legations in question to prepare a limited number of temporary Swedish passports.

Temporary passports were not a new idea. They were a standard tactic within the diligently applied bureaucratic pressure that Sweden's Utrikesdeparte-mentet, the Foreign Ministry, exercised behind the scenes, most often on behalf of individual Jews. After the deportation of Norwegian Jews began in 1942, the Swedes had changed their attitude and become a source of irritation to the talented killer bureaucrats of the Holocaust. The main weapon employed by the Swedish authorities was to issue persistent, factual, diplomatic enquiries in support of particular Jews with a Swedish connection who, according to the Foreign Ministry, should be exempt and sent to Sweden. This strategy appears to have taken the Germans by surprise. They would have found it easier to manage emotional protests of a general nature than this kind of insistent, legal argumentation.

Already in November and December of 1942, in missions for the Norwegian Jews, Swedish diplomats had sometimes issued temporary passports to Jews with a "Swedish connection". Soon the incidence of pure bluffing increased. With enough creativity and effort, almost all Jews could be connected with some area of Swedish interest. The historian Paul A. Levine observes in his doctoral dissertation about Sweden's diplomatic activities during the Holocaust that, "What developed was a remarkably broad reading of who was eligible for Swedish diplomatic representation." Levine has coined the term "bureaucratic resistance" for these more covert protest activities.

This bureaucratic resistance deliberately occurred out of the spotlight. Success followed from a combination of rational argument and the senior official status of the diplomatic contacts involved. Demands made of the Germans did not include any criticism of Nazi racial ideology. The tone was strictly bureaucratic.

The Germans who, at this difficult stage of the war, were increasingly concerned about maintaining their diplomatic relations with Sweden, had trouble managing these new Swedish tactics. Many hundreds of Jews were saved from the Holocaust in this way. The individual with direct responsibility for the deportations, Adolf Eichmann, was becoming more and more frustrated. He made loud internal protests and accused the Swedes, with their new practice of declaring people Swedish who had never set foot in Sweden, of systematically trying to undermine the German treatment of the Jews.

Eichmann had this Swedish impertinence in mind when he turned his attention to the task of cleansing Hungary of Jews. Only a few months earlier, German bureaucrats had failed in their plan to deport Denmark's 8,000

Jews. Even in that case, actions by the Swedes had hindered the Nazis. For a long time, the Danish Jews had been protected from the German extermination apparatus, in part owing to Hitler's desire to present Denmark as a model protectorate. When the Nazis finally acted at the beginning of October 1943, the Swedish government reacted immediately by declaring themselves willing to take in all the Danish Jews. By that point, most of them had already been warned and had managed to flee across the straits that divided Denmark and Sweden. The Germans only managed to send 474 Danish Jews to concentration camps.

This Swedish gesture had echoed across the world and was widely praised, by the U.S. government among others. An American-Jewish organisation sent the following telegram to the prime minister, Per Albin Hansson:

> During the years of untold suffering of Jews under the Nazis this is the first time that a government officially issued a statement announcing readiness to grant asylum to tortured Jews of a neighbouring country.

Adolf Eichmann learned one thing as he analysed the failures in Denmark. One could not assume that the local population would assist with the German plan for the Jews. The Danes had helped their Jewish brethren flee to Sweden. In Denmark loyalty had deteriorated so far that not even the German officials involved in the occupation had cooperated fully. "It became clear to me that I, as a German, could not require the deportation of Jews from Hungary. To proceed as in Copenhagen would only result in a great fiasco. I left this matter to the Hungarian officials," as Eichmann later expressed himself.

The enthusiasm of the "Hungarian officials" would exceed his wildest expectations. This was a completely different scenario, one that was clearly linked to the fact that any moderate political forces in Hungary had been spirited away. At the beginning of April, busloads of apprehended ministers and parliamentarians, social democrats and liberals, prominent Jews and anti-Nazi aristocrats were sent to newly constructed camps. Ten thousand people were arrested in the first few weeks alone, three thousand of them Jews.

The new Nazi-friendly minister of the interior appointed two well-known Hungarian anti-Semites, László Endre and László Baky, as state secretaries and gave them the responsibility of tackling the Jewish question according to Eichmann's plan. They would take on the task with a determination and drive that amazed even Eichmann, and which meant that the war's largest deportation was undertaken with astonishing ease and in record time. These violent acts by the Nazi puppet regime also gained legitimacy within Hungary from the fact that the regent Horthy remained in his post, to all appearances sympathetic to the events unfolding in his country.

Such was the Hungarian enthusiasm that almost all German soldiers were able to leave Hungary within a month. This was a necessary part of the plan since the situation on the Eastern Front was so perilous that the troops were needed elsewhere. Soon hardly any German uniforms could be seen on the streets. This did not, however, mean that the Germans had disappeared, which had been Horthy's hope. The Defence Corps, or S.S., and Gestapo simply switched to wearing civilian clothing, with a penchant for the leather coats that they confiscated from the Jewish stores.

When the largest part of the army had left Hungary, the German presence in Budapest consisted of the S.S. and the staff at the German legation, under the leadership of Hitler's personal envoy, the minister Edmund Veesenmayer. Veesenmayer used his diplomatic power to push the Hungarians even harder on the Jewish question. Otherwise most of the work fell to Himmler's S.S. or, more precisely, the Reich Security Main Office, R.S.H.A.

The R.S.H.A. was a bureaucratic mishmash of security services and police organisations. It included both the Gestapo and the Security Service, or S.D. After the murder of Himmler's deputy, Reinhard Heydrich, in Prague in 1942, the R.S.H.A. was led by Ernst Kaltenbrunner, who had arrived in Budapest during the first few days of the occupation. There he had invited Adolf Eichmann out to a restaurant and wished him the best of luck in his work.

Eichmann's command was a subunit in the R.S.H.A. He was not even the highest-ranked S.S. representative in Budapest – Eichmann was in fact subordinate to Otto Winkelmann, the R.S.H.A. chief who had been dispatched to Budapest. Eichmann would be given a free hand to deal with the Jews but he still lacked significant power or recognition. His activities were given high priority but, formally, he was still unable to communicate directly with either Hitler or Himmler.

At this time, Eichmann appears to have felt a great need to bolster his own image. As he was waiting to implement the extensive plan in the countryside he went out on a confiscation tour around Budapest with his closest associates. They seized the biggest of the luxury villas that wealthy Jews had been forced to leave. Eichmann moved into a magnificent house on Rózsadomb, with a view of the Danube. He had drivers and servants and would soon indulge in an orgy of luxuries, far from the relatively ascetic existence he had led before.

Eichmann established his main office in the Hotel Majestic, high up on Svábhegy, one of Budapest's many hills. He hung a large map of Hungary on the wall and, together with the eager Hungarian government officials Endre and Baky, he divided the country into six zones. The north-eastern zone, the front closest to the Soviet Union, stood first in line for the deportation plan. Thereafter the annihilation of the Jews continued zone by zone clockwise around Budapest. The plan bore Eichmann's organisational stamp. But it was the Hungarian police and the gendarmes – a half-militarised police force – who would implement the brutal task of rounding up the approximately 400,000 Jews in the countryside and driving them into camps. It would not take them long.

For the plan to succeed, Eichmann had to find a way to keep the leading Jews in Budapest calm and cooperative. Himmler had made it clear that he did not want to see a bloody Jewish uprising like the one that took place in the Warsaw ghetto in 1943. And a repeat of the embarrassing Danish episode was also unacceptable.

Part of the overall strategy was to begin with the deportation of the Orthodox Jews in the countryside. With the exception of some lightning raids during the first few days, the brutal spring arrests occurred out of the sight of Budapest's assimilated Jews. Another strategic move was to use both the carrot and the stick to get the Budapest Jews to form a central Jewish council that would be duped into assisting rather than resisting the campaign of annihilation. On one of the first days, Eichmann sent his co-workers Hermann Krumey and Dieter Wisliceny to the Jewish congregation at Síp utca (Síp Street) in Pest to oversee the formation of a Jewish council with six members. The two Nazis assured the group that nothing bad would befall the Hungarian Jews, as long as the Jewish council cooperated and tolerated certain "temporary restrictions".

On March 31, 1944, Eichmann invited the selected Jewish leaders to an audience with him at his office in the Hotel Majestic. The delegation was led by the newly elected chairman, the – among Budapest's assimilated Jews – highly regarded elder, Samuel Stern. According to David Cesarani's biography, Eichmann gave them a real "bravura performance". The Jewish leaders were spellbound by his false but seductive combination of threats and assurances. They were informed that all Hungarian Jews would henceforth be required to wear a yellow star ten centimetres square in size, "sewn onto the left breast pocket of the outer garment, clearly visible, canary yellow, made of broadcloth, silk or velvet", as the ordinance was worded. Eichmann explained that Jews would be sent to labour centres for the German war industry but that they would be well treated as long as they followed the rules.

It would be the responsibility of the Jewish council to prevent panic from breaking out, Eichmann explained. And did they know, he went on in a honeyed voice, that he had learned Hebrew and had an abiding interest in Jewish art and books?

Historical researchers are perplexed by the tragic credulousness of the Hungarian Jews. News of what happened to deported Jews in other countries had also reached Hungary. But knowledge is not the same as insight. Many dismissed these reports as exaggerated. Among the Hungarian Jews there was a widespread conviction that what had happened to others could never happen in Hungary, where the Jews had been a part of the general population since before anyone could remember. Nothing appeared to alter this conviction, not even the extent of the new restrictions that were promulgated as early as the beginning of April. In the blink of an eye, the Hungarian Jews were robbed of their public employment as well as the right to use cars, taxis and trains, make telephone calls and patronise restaurants. Their radios were confiscated and all Jewish newspapers were censored.

Even so, many Hungarian Jews did not want to accept the truth. The ones who had realised the extent of the danger and tried to warn the others were accused of unnecessarily spreading panic.

*

Late one evening at the beginning of April, somebody knocked on Per Anger's door. It was Hugó Wohl, managing director of Orion, a radio manufacturer within the extensive Hungarian Tungsram conglomerate. Wohl's and Anger's paths had crossed many times before. Ten years earlier, Orion Tungsram had established a sales company in Sweden, Svenska Orion, which had successfully introduced more than a hundred thousand Orion radios into the Swedish market. Even Tungsram's well-known lightbulbs were sold in large quantities in Sweden.

Wohl was known for being a proper and distinguished gentleman. Now he tried to conceal his yellow star with his briefcase. "You have to help me, you absolutely have to help me!" he pleaded.

Per Anger was already deeply involved in the fate of the Hungarian Jews. Recently the exchange of telegrams between the Foreign Ministry in Stockholm and the legation in Budapest had been fast and furious. The head of the legal department at the Ministry, Gösta Engzell, had indicated that officials in Budapest could, in certain exceptional cases, issue temporary passports valid for six months to relatives of Swedish citizens or to a small number of long-serving Hungarian representatives for Swedish companies. But regulations had also been issued regarding severe restrictions for these passports since they were formally connected to citizenship and it was unclear how many the Germans would accept. It was less risky to issue a three-month visa as an alternative, but it offered less protection.

Hugó Wohl did not quite meet the requirements, but Per Anger did not need much time to think before he issued his first temporary passport. He saw no reason to stop there and issued temporary passports to Wohl's entire family. Only afterwards did he seek approval from Ivan Danielsson and the Foreign Ministry in Stockholm. "This is on your conscience," Danielsson told him.

Hugó Wohl's closest associate at the Orion factory, Vilmos Forgács, actually had closer ties to Sweden than his boss. He had travelled to Sweden in the thirties and, among other things, spent eight months in Stockholm launching the radio company's Swedish outpost. It was during this time that he became acquainted with Anger. In Budapest they had socialised at dinners and embarked on mountain hikes together. But Vilmos Forgács was one of the prominent Jewish engineers whom the Germans had arrested in the first days of their occupation. When details of Forgács' situation emerged later in the spring, Anger issued temporary passports to his family, which saved them. Just like the Wohl family they could henceforth remove their yellow stars and move about freely.

Wohl and Forgács belonged to Hungary's business elite. Between the two of them they possessed an unrivalled expertise and eventually became two of Raoul Wallenberg's most important co-workers and confidants.

The Swedish efforts were made easier by the fact that the Germans in Budapest did not reject out of hand these requests for exceptional treatment for Jews from neutral countries. After negotiations with Anger and Danielsson, the Hungarian puppet authorities had also agreed to treat those in possession of temporary passports as Swedish citizens.

But a sudden inflation in the number of these sorts of passports in circulation would eventually reduce their effectiveness. Anger ended up issuing several hundred but also started to construct other kinds of more imaginative protective paperwork. He created a kind of illusory document that was not an actual visa but only an assurance that a certain named Jew had the *right* to a Swedish travel visa and therefore stood under the protection of the Swedish legation.

Per Anger called the new certificates "letters of protection". These letters had absolutely no formal status but they were supplied with impressive stamps and everyone who had spent any time in Hungary knew that, in a critical situation, it could be enough.

In the middle of April, the death machinery started up and hundreds of thousands of Jews in the countryside were driven together into internment camps, the first one located in the city of Kassa in north-eastern Hungary (today Košice in Slovakia). The conditions were indescribable. The Jews were severely beaten, robbed of their valuables and brought to exposed industrial areas where they were forced to live outside. "We lie in the dust, have neither straw mattresses nor covers, and will freeze to death . . . We are so neglected that we do not look human any more," one of the affected Jews wrote in a letter smuggled out from a brick factory in Kassa.

More and more desperate Hungarian Jews turned to representatives from the neutral countries. The pressure on Anger and Danielsson, who had other things besides the long lines outside the legation in Gyopár to think about, increased. Among relatives back in Sweden there was a growing concern in the flood of demands and requests made to the Foreign Ministry.

At the Mid-European Trading Company, a stressed Kálmán Lauer was beginning to feel an urgent need to take action. His director of foreign affairs, Raoul Wallenberg, was still engaged on his military service, but they talked from time to time about the possibility of Raoul travelling to Hungary to try and help Lauer's relatives. On April 25, even Lauer's partner Sven Salén jumped in and wrote a letter to Per Anger in Budapest. He congratulated the legation secretary on the birth of his daughter Birgitta and then asked for protection for Lauer's sister's family and his parents-in-law. Per Anger issued the new letter of protection to each of them and did what he could to follow their fates during the spring. But since Lauer was not a Swedish citizen, there was not much more Anger could do.

In the circles around the fur trader Norbert Masur and the Swedish section of the World Jewish Council, the plans to send a Swedish representative to Hungary had begun to take shape. Now even the Chief Rabbi Marcus Ehrenpreis was in support of the plan. They invited Kálmán Lauer to join their discussions, probably to deepen their knowledge of the situation in Hungary. One day at the beginning of May, Ehrenpreis asked Lauer if he knew of a suitable candidate for the mission in Hungary. Lauer did not have to think hard. He immediately mentioned his colleague Raoul Wallenberg, who was already preparing to travel there on Lauer's behalf.

On May 14, the plans were already so advanced that Raoul wrote a letter to the commander-in-chief of the army seeking permission to travel abroad after the conclusion of his military service. The idea now was that Raoul would travel to Hungary and, once there, form a Swedish aid organisation, perhaps by convincing Save the Children to open an affiliate in Budapest. Raoul would stay for two months, and hopefully have time to recruit a local committee to include a Swede living in Hungary, a handful of "decent-minded Aryans" and a few Jews. "My intention is to travel to Hungary in order to purchase food goods for export to Sweden and also for distribution to the Jews of Hungary by way of the committee that will be formed for this purpose. This is an extremely deserving cause and one that is truly a matter of life and death," Raoul wrote in his application.

A few days later, Marcus Ehrenpreis met with Raoul Wallenberg for the first time. Unfortunately he was far from impressed. When the potential emissary began to talk about how the rescue mission depended on bribes, that it was mostly a question of money, Ehrenpreis became wary. He did not feel that Raoul was mature enough for the assignment.

The Chief Rabbi's daughter, Miriam Nathansson, later described the meeting in an interview with the author Lena Einhorn.

> I was at home that time when Wallenberg came by. Afterwards my father said that he was not really sure that Wallenberg wanted to do this out of a sense of conviction; he did not feel that he had a real sense of connection to Jews. My father thought he was motivated more by a desire for adventure.

Ehrenpreis did not want to give Raoul Wallenberg the green light. He let weeks go by in the hope that a better candidate would appear. And there the process stalled. In late May 1944, Wallenberg's mission was, for the moment, on hold.

The War Refugee Board had held off from pursuing any direct rescue missions in Hungary. The Americans judged this as extremely hard to organise given that the country was surrounded by enemy forces. During the spring, the W.R.B. instead put great effort into conducting psychological warfare, in which different kinds of sharp warnings directed at the Hungarian government were communicated through neutral channels.

In the meantime, the S.S. and the Hungarian gendarmes continued to purge the countryside of Jews. The number of internment camps multiplied and the number of captured Jews was quickly approaching the target of 400,000 that had been set by the Nazis. Hitler's murderers were beginning to feel pressured to begin the transports to Auschwitz. But the considerable logistical challenges involved were not so easily worked out.

Eichmann had tasked his people with arranging the necessary details for four train transports a day from Hungary to Auschwitz. A new railway track was built and the staffing of the gas chambers and crematoria was almost quadrupled.

On May 15 the first deportation trains began to run according to schedule, four overloaded trains a day with approximately three thousand Hungarian Jews in each. The internment camps were slowly emptied and, at the Swedish legation, the personnel were told the most horrifying eyewitness accounts. A week or so later, Per Anger travelled to one of the Hungarian camps, situated at a brick-making factory, to see for himself what was happening.

> While I stood there, a train with empty cattle cars was switched onto a siding that led into the factory area. The doors were opened and as many Jews as possible – men, women and children – were forced into the cars under kicks and blows. Around eighty people were crammed into each car, which looked to only be able to take about half that number. A mother tried to hide her child and prevent it from going along. A soldier saw this, grabbed the child by its legs and threw it into the car.

Adolf Eichmann had reached the brutal peak of his career as emigration expert and the foremost organiser of the Jewish extermination. He impatiently awaited his promotion but even now it was not forthcoming. Instead he became painfully aware that he was no longer the undisputed master in this area of expertise. Alongside Eichmann's deportations, other initiatives in the "Jewish question" had been made that did not involve sending the Jews to extermination camps. The thinking in these cases was to negotiate small-scale business deals in which Hungarian lives were exchanged for money or resources. This task had been assigned to Himmler's deputy, Obersturmbann-führer Kurt Becher, who had been sent to Budapest as representative of the S.S. financial division. When Eichmann realised what had transpired behind his back he became absolutely furious.

Kurt Becher had a background in buying horses for the S.S. Officially he had been sent to Hungary to secure weapons and 40,000 horses to stanch the flow of the German army's catastrophic losses on the Eastern Front. But in May it had been discovered that he was actually involved in secret "negotiations" (the defendant was transferred from a camp to house arrest) with the Jewish director for the Manfréd Weiss conglomerate. Of the Manfréd Weiss factories, 51 per cent were owned by a large Jewish Hungarian family, 49 per cent by the Hungarian state. Since the owners had earlier converted to Christianity, the firm had not hitherto been considered Jewish, but now such leeway was no longer on offer.

The companies owned by Manfréd Weiss manufactured war materials among other things and had more than 30,000 employees. While in close contact with Himmler himself, Kurt Becher now negotiated an agreement which involved turning the Weiss factories over to the S.S. in exchange for allowing some fifty members of the Jewish family to flee to Switzerland and Portugal.

In addition, the families would be given $600,000 in compensation.

The contract was signed on May 17. The Hungarian government was not alone in being enraged by this coup, which deprived the country of one of its most important industries. Eichmann, whose frustration was already threatening to boil over, now suddenly saw his rival Kurt Becher ascend to the position of Heinrich Himmler's favourite.

Adolf Eichmann could not bear to see Becher shine at his expense. If Himmler's intention was to return to regular emigrations surely it was he, Eichmann, who was the expert. Eichmann even had men who had, earlier in the spring, experimented with methods similar to those employed by Becher. In order to mark his territory, he and his staff began business negotiations with selected Jews. He went so far as to offer to release one million Hungarian Jews in exchange for 10,000 trucks that could be sent to the army on the Eastern Front.

Nothing came of these schemes in the end. But the new tactics had gained the approval of Himmler himself. Given that the Manfréd Weiss director Henrik de Wahl was Sven Salén's business partner, it was not impossible that Raoul Wallenberg knew something of this.

In any case, it is clear that the young Swede was absolutely correct to insist on the importance of money to any rescue attempts during his meeting with the Chief Rabbi.

When the deportations from Hungary began in the middle of May, the Americans abruptly changed their strategy. Ten days later, on May 25, the War Refugee Board in Washington sent urgent telegrams to American legations in the neutral cities of Ankara, Bern, Lisbon, Madrid and Stockholm. Secretary of State Cordell Hull was listed as the telegrams' author and he warned that, "according to persistent and seemingly authentic reports, systematic mass-extermination of Jews in Hungary has begun".

The W.R.B. leadership now decided that it was necessary to quickly send as many foreign observers as possible to Hungary in order to try to prevent a process that could threaten the lives of more than 800,000 individuals. All legations were urged to contact the governments in their respective countries in order to convince them to increase immediately, for humanitarian reasons, the number of diplomatic representatives in Hungary and "to the greatest possible extent". There was not much time and Washington wanted to assess the willingness of other governments to cooperate.

This move troubled most of the American diplomatic emissaries. The W.R.B's proposal went against all standard foreign-policy practise. Should countries that had refused to recognise the new quisling regime now be urged to increase their diplomatic presence in Hungary? Turkey and Switzerland responded negatively and the American diplomats in Spain and Portugal thought the idea was so crazy that they did not even bother to relay it. Only Sweden remained.

The American legation in Stockholm was led by Herschel Johnson, who had been stationed in Sweden shortly after the bombing of Pearl Harbor in 1941. He was a broad-shouldered bachelor in his fifties with a "firm handshake and an open smile" and had quickly become popular in the diplomatic community. In contrast to the American diplomats in other neutral countries, he had taken a close personal interest in the work of the War Refugee Board.

At the beginning of May the American minister had actually had a conversation with Marcus Ehrenpreis about Stockholm-based rescue missions for Polish Jews, an initiative that could potentially be extended to Hungary and Romania.

The American minister was also a good friend of Kálmán Lauer's business partner, Sven Salén, who was vice president of the Swedish-American Society. According to the most recent news from Hungary, Lauer's relatives had been seized, which must have affected the temperamental grocery businessman's mood.

Sven Salén had shown concern for Lauer's Hungarian relatives, but he also had his own interests to look out for in occupied Hungary. He had entered into a relationship with a Swedish-Hungarian shipping company. His company had also started to sell Hungarian tinned goods, which was a way of surviving when the trade blockade stopped banana imports. These goods were from the well-known brand Globus, which was part of Manfréd Weiss, the industrial complex that had just fallen into the hands of the S.S.

For the past couple of years, Banan-kompaniet and the Manfréd Weiss conglomerate had jointly run a canning company in Malmö under the name Svenska Globus Inc. This meant that Sven Salén had his own connections to the dramatic events in Hungary.

There are many indications that the Manfréd Weiss family had made use of their connection to the Banakompaniet and Svenska Globus in order to secure portions of their capital in the uncertain war situation. To judge from the Svenska Globus accounts, the Weiss family placed large assets in the Swedish company during the forties, money that in the accounts was listed as debt to "various people". It also appears as if the Weiss family's financial interests in the Swedish company continued after the war.

Banan-kompaniet's Hungarian counterpart in charge of sales was Henrik de Wahl, a nephew of Manfréd Weiss' wife, who had spent long periods of time in Sweden working in the canning business. Henrik was in his fifties, although most people took him for at least sixty. In the autumn of 1943 he had been admitted to a hospital in Stockholm for high blood pressure and had spent several months there before he could return home to Budapest.

Coincidentally, Henrik de Wahl had returned to Stockholm the week before the Hungarian occupation in order to continue his medical treatment and to marry the Swedish woman he had fallen in love with. Now he earned his living at Svenska Globus, was supported by Sven Salén and followed the events unfolding in Hungary with increasing concern. De Wahl not only had the welfare of his relatives on his mind, but also the aftermath of the dramatic sale of the family business, the Manfréd Weiss conglomerate.

In his application for a renewed residency permit on March 16, 1944, Henrik de Wahl had written that during his time in Sweden he not only planned to lead Svenska Globus, but also to negotiate the "postwar programme for trade between Sweden and Hungary". Thus Henrik de Wahl entered the picture just as the rescue mission to Hungary was taking shape. Naturally enough, his future father-in-law had an apartment in Strandvägen 7.

*

It is almost impossible in hindsight to reconstruct exactly what happened after the War Refugee Board sent their alarming telegram on May 25, 1944. One can only state that many were rightly very concerned and that, in different parts of Stockholm, there were thoughts of organising rescue missions in Hungary. One might also observe that Strandvägen 7a began to act as a powerful epicentre for these efforts.

Raoul Wallenberg had already shown goodwill but was, during this time, mostly unconnected with the everyday life of the Mid-European Trading Company. His army unit had begun to wind down, but he was still called in for the entire month of May. This did not prevent him from maintaining contact with Lauer. His placement with the Svea Life Guard meant that he was never far away. One day, for example, he turned up with his platoon at the warehouse on the Frihamnen harbour owned by the Mid-European Trading Company and Banan-kompaniet, in order to practise urban warfare.

Because of this, he was quickly informed when the terrible news came: Lauer's relatives had been taken away. Now their efforts were redoubled. At first Kálmán Lauer had not been a Swedish citizen, which limited his ability to assist his relatives. When the message about the deportations reached Stockholm, Raoul Wallenberg therefore helped his partner to apply for Swedish citizenship. The sooner Lauer could get his citizenship, the greater the chance that his relatives would get temporary Swedish passports and be released from their imprisonment.

Kálmán Lauer had not abandoned the thought of also sending Raoul Wallenberg to Budapest but, after the Chief Rabbi's negative reaction, Lauer now imagined a more focused assignment in which Raoul would help Lauer's in-laws and five-year-old niece to enter Sweden.

In the end it was only a matter of time before all of these disparate dreams were fused into one. Not much was needed before a mission to Hungary appeared necessary to everyone and a soon-to-be 32-year-old architect and businessman, a thin-haired sergeant with the Svea Life Guard, materialised as the only possible candidate – even in the eyes of the Chief Rabbi.

As Kálmán Lauer told it afterwards, it was in the elegantly appointed elevator at Strandvägen 7a that everything fell into place. That was where Lauer had kept bumping into a newly recruited American diplomat for the past six months. There were a couple of hundred Americans at the legation so, according to Lauer, he did not know who Iver Olsen was. But, one day in the elevator, the new refugee attaché asked him if he might possibly be the Mr Lauer he had heard so much about:

> I said yes and he said then that his name was Ivor [sic] Olsen and that he worked at the American legation. He asked me if I wanted to come to his room and have a cigarette. I went with him and it turned out that he knew a great deal about our company and the conglomerate that we belonged to. He also knew that I was born in Hungary. Mr Olsen showed me many reports that they had received from various sources, which described the fate of the Hungarian Jews. He told me that he was a humanitarian attaché at the American Embassy in Stockholm and that his assignment was to help the Hungarians. It was supposed to be done in such a way that the Foreign Ministry in Stockholm would send a humanitarian attaché to the legation in Budapest. He asked me if I could recommend a reliable, energetic and intelligent person who would be suitable for this purpose. I answered immediately that I could and I named Raoul Wallenberg.

CHAPTER 10

The Assignment

The spring had been colder than usual. It was only around Pentecost, which in 1944 fell on one of the last days in May, that the warmth returned to Stockholm, and with it the swarms of sun-seeking travellers to the archipelago. Boats were filled to their last seat and holiday-bound Stockholmers with their gardening tools and fishing equipment crowded on the dock outside the Mid-European Trading Company.

Reports from the war sounded like a muted minor chord in the background, claiming column inches between the bathing-suit and "sun-tanning lotion" advertisements in the newspapers. At the end of May, the Swedes – just like everyone else – eagerly followed the progress of the Allies towards Rome. The advances appear to have given birth to the need for public, if somewhat disingenuous, displays of friendship between the West and the Soviet Union. The British foreign secretary Anthony Eden did what he could to assuage the British fear of the Russians. In a speech in the House of Commons at the end of May he reminded his countrymen that the British and the Russians had fought side by side "in three world conflicts – the Napoleonic war, the last World War, and the present war". The suspicion on both sides was simply a sign that they needed to get to know each other better, Eden said. The Soviet foreign minister, Vyacheslav Molotov, replied with a telegram in the same tone. He explained that the victory of the British–Russian–American coalition over Hitler's Germany "will lay a strong foundation for lasting friendship between all freedom-loving peoples".

This all sounded good, but everyone involved knew that behind the scenes it was evident that Stalin did not completely trust the capitalist countries of the United States and Great Britain, and that the collective war effort had not erased the scepticism of the Western powers toward communism. The situation was not improved when the Soviet Union attempted to use its position in order to circumscribe its allies' plans. In June, for example, the deputy minister of foreign affairs, Andrey Vyshinsky, declared that they would not tolerate any negotiations with the Nazis over the Jews. The Russians could under no circumstances accept Eichmann's proposal to exchange one million rescued Jews for 10,000 trucks. The sharpness of the Soviet position might have been due to Eichmann's promise that the trucks would only be used on the Eastern Front.

The Americans met with the same intransigence when they tried to get the Soviet Union, like the British, to lend support to the newly formed War Refugee Board. Though one should not exaggerate the degree of British enthusiasm for this American initiative, the Russians declared outright that they were unwilling to participate and also made it known that they were sceptical of the W.R.B.'s agenda.

In Hungary, all these contested issues loomed large, which Stalin can hardly have found encouraging. On the one hand there were secret Hungarian peace talks with the West, on the other there were negotiations regarding Hungarian Jews. The Soviet intelligence services had already been able to connect the Swedish family name Wallenberg to these kinds of covert separate peace negotiations, which so provoked Stalin. It was aware of the role played by the "capitalists" Jacob and Marcus Wallenberg in contact between the German resistance and the Western leaders. Soon the name would turn up again, this time in connection with negotiations and rescue efforts on behalf of the Hungarian Jews.

In the spring of 1944, Stalin's patience was already being tried. Since 1942 he had waited for the United States and Great Britain to do as they had promised: open a second front in the west and thereby reduce the pressure on the Soviet troops in the east. But the Western Allies were taking their time and Stalin could not conceal his frustration at the delay.

At ten past midnight on June 6, 1944, the first British soldiers landed just outside the French city of Caën, their faces painted black so that they would not be seen in the dark. D-Day had just begun. Operation Overlord was in motion.

That same afternoon, the first pictures of the invasion forces reached

Stockholm. The B.B.C. was on the alert and booked large advertisements in the Swedish newspapers for the following day. Using the phrase "D-Day" the radio station wanted to publicise its short-wave broadcasts, which were offered in Swedish three times a day.

On Tuesday, 6 June, Stockholmers were as usual celebrating the Day of the Flag (later Sweden's national day). The American Envoy to Stockholm, Herschel Johnson, accompanied his British colleague, Victor Mallet, to the "invasion service" in the English Church. On this historic occasion, the congregation had raised an enormous Union Jack that covered the entire chancel. The church broke all previous attendance records and, after the prayer, some four hundred voices were united for the American and British national anthems.

Raoul Wallenberg also had personal reasons to celebrate that day. He had at last received an answer from the army regarding his request to travel abroad, even though he was still serving in a wartime military position.

The decision was not automatic. Sergeant Raoul Wallenberg was regarded as unusually competent in his position as platoon commander and would be difficult to replace. Raoul's case had to be sent to the commander-in-chief's office for final approval. Permission was granted, though with a caveat: Wallenberg was allowed to spend the remainer of the year in Hungary, but if his unit was mobilised he would have to return immediately.

The following day, Kálmán Lauer wrote a letter to Budapest in order to make arrangements for Raoul's mission, which at this stage still appears to have concerned only Lauer's deported relatives. Lauer wanted to make Raoul's impending trip as easy as possible, so he contacted a man who, over the past few months, had been highly praised in the Swedish-Hungarian colony in Stockholm for his good-hearted work on behalf of the Jews in Budapest. His name was Valdemar Langlet, he was over seventy years old and he had lived in Hungary with his Russian wife Nina for thirteen years. Langlet was a university professor of Swedish in Budapest and was often to be seen at the Swedish legation, where he functioned as a kind of volunteer Swedish cultural attaché. He had round glasses and a greying moustache and was more impulsive in his nature than Swedish bureaucracy ever felt comfortable with.

During the spring, Valdemar Langlet had worked intensively on Per Anger and Ivan Danielsson, trying to press them into doing more for the Hungarian Jews. But Anger was already working around the clock on this matter and the

Swedish legation was beginning to get overrun. In the middle of May, the university professor and his wife instead had the idea of trying to get the Swedish Red Cross involved in this cause. They made enquiries about the possibility of inviting the newly appointed vice chairman of the Swedish Red Cross, Count Folke Bernadotte, to see the hellish situation in Budapest. As they awaited a reply they initiated their own rescue activities together with the Red Cross in Hungary.

Valdemar Langlet had already begun to create his own Swedish letters of protection, with stamps from the Red Cross, which he generously distributed to persecuted Jews. The initiative resembled Per Anger's creative "visa certificates" – seemingly official but in reality completely devoid of any formal status. The Swedes were not alone in thinking along these lines. The first person to issue letters of protection to the Hungarian Jews had been the Swiss diplomat Carl Lutz, whom Anger knew well. Lutz had earlier been the Swiss consul in Palestine. When he was transferred to Budapest in 1942, it had seemed logical for him to become involved in the relatively substantial emigration of the Hungarian Jews to Palestine. Lutz had created a kind of "emigration certificate" that functioned as a letter of protection for those Jews who were in the middle of the application process. They could produce these certificates as they awaited their departure. He had continued to issue the letters of protection even after the arrival of the Germans, although Jews were no longer allowed to leave Hungary.

Valdemar Langlet was probably inspired by both Lutz and Anger when he created his Red Cross passports. But, in contrast to Anger, he saw no reason to restrict the production of his documents. "His kind heart beat for each and all and there was no limit to the number of Red Cross letters of protection that he personally produced and signed," Per Anger wrote of Langlet in his book on his time in Budapest.

Now it was to the idealist Langlet that Kálmán Lauer turned with regard to Raoul Wallenberg's impending trip:

My dear friend Valdemar! The great misfortune that has befallen us all has been particularly hard on my relatives, whom you know to be at liberty no longer. I ask you to assist Mr Wallenberg, so that he may get my parents-in-law, Lajos and Irene Stein, and little Susanna

Mihaly to Sweden. Both Director Salén and I place all of our
resources at your disposal. Raoul Wallenberg, whom I have come to
know these past three years as an honest and kind-hearted person,
will surely do everything in his power to help.

[. . .] You cannot imagine how many people now pray to God
here in Sweden so that He may protect you and enable you to continue your humanitarian work. The friends whom I have spoken
with think of you with the deepest gratitude.

Two weeks had gone by since the American legation in Stockholm had
received the telegram from the War Refugee Board in Washington, with its
demand that they should pressure the Swedish government to extend their
diplomatic representation in Hungary as soon as possible. Herschel Johnson
seems to have delayed broaching this issue and it wasn't until June 9, 1944,
that he scheduled a meeting with the cabinet secretary at the Foreign Ministry, Erik Boheman.

The War Refugee Board received disappointing responses from the American legations in all the other neutral countries that had been contacted. But,
after the meeting with Boheman, Herschel Johnson had encouraging news
to report. Perhaps the American diplomat had read a little too much into the
fact that Boheman had listened with interest and not immediately dismissed
the idea of increasing the number of Swedish diplomats in Budapest. Even if
Johnson's intuition was correct, he could not report any firm promises following the encounter. However his account of Boheman's positive attitude still
seemed to please his superiors in Washington. Boheman had also promised
to forward a report on the situation in Hungary that the Swedish minister on
the ground, Ivan Danielsson, had recently submitted.

When I have received it I will go back again to Mr Boheman and
endeavor to get concrete suggestions from him as to what it may be
practicable to do in Hungary as well as further expression of his
ideas regarding increased Swedish representation.

It would be two weeks before Herschel Johnson received this report, although
Ivan Danielsson had written it on May 26. But things were moving. A couple

of days earlier, the Swedish legation in Budapest had communicated their need for reinforcements, citing an overwhelming workload. There were also voices from several sources asking for a more organised Swedish rescue effort that would be able to cooperate with the Hungarian Red Cross. Ivan Danielsson had sent telegrams to the Foreign Ministry in Stockholm regarding these requests and also suggested that representatives from the Swedish Red Cross and Save the Children be dispatched to Budapest.

In addition, Danielsson's most recent situational report, which most likely had been written by Per Anger, made for unsettling reading. "During the past few weeks, new ordinances have been instituted on a daily basis, intended to exclude the Jewish population from more or less everything that belongs to the natural rights of a member of society," the report began, before explaining that the lives of all members of Hungary's large Jewish population were in danger. Jews were being transported to "Germany" in "sealed freight cars containing seventy people in each and without access to sanitary facilities or food". Danielsson wrote that he had received news that 100,000 Jews had already been transported out of Hungary in this way.

By the time of the meeting between Erik Boheman and Herschel Johnson, ninety-two trains with a total of 289,357 Hungarian Jews had departed Hungary, if one believes the meticulous bookkeeping of the Nazi bureaucrats. The overfilled trains had travelled through eastern Slovakia and passed through Kraków on their way to Auschwitz. Once there, nine out of ten Jews were taken directly to the gas chambers.

In the past week, the tone of the telegrams from Per Anger and Ivan Danielsson had grown sharper with each passing day. The Foreign Ministry, in turn, had asked their diplomats in the country to investigate the practical possibilities for the Red Cross-directed rescue mission that Danielsson had mentioned, after which the Swedish government intended to move quickly to test the proposal.

The Hungary question was increasingly prominent amongst the daily affairs of the Swedish Foreign Ministry at the beginning of June 1944. But it would have been quite understandable if the cabinet secretary Erik Boheman had other things on his mind when the American minister Herschel Johnson visited him that Friday. Relations between the Swedish and American governments had been cold during the spring and Boheman had been in the middle of the conflict. What he had seen of American power plays had horrified him.

The conflict had centred on Swedish exports of ball bearings to Germany. Afterwards, Boheman would use words like "brutal" and "ruthless" to describe the Americans' behaviour. The Allies had pressed Sweden to halve the number of ball bearings that S.K.F., the Swedish ball-bearing factory, were sending to Germany as part of a trade agreement that had been sealed at the end of 1943. But, as D-Day grew closer, Allied demands for Sweden to cease the exports entirely grew more insistent. The Germans used the ball bearings in their warplanes, and the Americans argued that the more German planes they faced, the greater the risk that the invasion would fail. In response the Swedes replied that they had already decreased the exports and that Sweden could not back out of trade agreements just because other warring parties wished them to do so.

Erik Boheman was beyond doubt the shining star of the Foreign Ministry at this time. He was known for his sharp mind, his quick wit and his jovial neighing laugh. During the more uncomfortable Swedish–German flirtations at the start of the war, he had distinguished himself by his Anglo-Saxon orientation.

But in the ball-bearing affair it was Erik Boheman, the Western powers' most trusted partner among the ministry's leadership, who, in his own words, had to shoulder "the burden of the battle". In April he had outlined the Swedish position for Herschel Johnson. Johnson had returned after a week with a stern diplomatic note signed by the American president, that caused the Foreign Ministry to quake. President Roosevelt declared that the issue of the Swedish ball bearings touched the lives of countless Americans. If their demands were not met, the government of the United States would be forced to "take under serious consideration the use of all possible methods to reach the desired results".

"All possible methods." At the Foreign Ministry this could not be interpreted as anything other than an indirect threat of war. The situation was not exactly improved by a parallel, and unusually harsh, American media campaign against Sweden. Günther sent a curtly dismissive reply, and with it the bilateral discussions were halted. Instead an American delegate was sent to Sweden to deal directly with the ball-bearing factory, S.K.F. During the delegate's stay he indicated that "the American government would not hesitate, as a last resort, to bomb the S.K.F. facilities".

It took until June 12 to resolve the conflict. S.K.F. finally agreed to reduce exports to the Germans for four months in return for compensatory orders from the Allies.

This was the atmosphere during those days in which Herschel Johnson tried to get the Foreign Ministry to cooperate in an American rescue mission in Hungary. It is worth noting that majority stakeholders in S.K.F. were the Wallenbergs.

Very few private citizens in Sweden were consulted as frequently on diplomatic matters during the war as Marcus and Jacob Wallenberg. Most recently, during the early spring of 1944, Marcus Wallenberg had proved a valuable link when the Swedish government felt unable to pursue an open peace negotiation between Finland and the Soviet Union. Marcus Wallenberg was good friends with the Soviet ambassador in Stockholm, Alexandra Kollontai, or "Madam Kollontai", as she was generally called after her fourteen years as the most senior Soviet representative in Sweden. Marcus Wallenberg also had a personal relationship with the Finnish president, Risto Ryti, and with the incoming prime minister, Juho Paasikivi.

Jacob Wallenberg had scaled down his involvement in these matters, but he maintained his contacts with the German resistance centred around Carl Goerdeler. They had seen each other on Jacob's visit during the trade negotiations of 1943 in the already fairly hard-hit Berlin. Goerdeler told him then about the two failed assassination attempts against Hitler.

Since then, Goerdeler had sent several indications to Jacob Wallenberg that the sworn members of the group had not given up and still planned to go through with the assassination. It was important to keep Jacob Wallenberg abreast of the news. Goerdeler had asked him to organise a meeting in Stockholm between the new Goerdeler-led German government and the British immediately after the *coup d'état*, assuming it was successful.

Jacob Wallenberg's primary occupation was, however, to lead Stockholm's Enskilda Bank as managing director and to keep a watchful eye on the family conglomerate's affiliated businesses. For the Swedish commercial banks, the war years were a relatively quiet period and Jacob Wallenberg had the freedom to focus on investing the bank's and the family's money.

On one of the first days of June 1944 he received Raoul Wallenberg at the bank headquarters on Kungsträdgårdsgatan. Raoul had concluded his military service only a few days earlier and, to judge from his diary notes, it appears that Jacob again wanted to discuss the idea of purchasing land in the Stockholm suburb of Huvudsta with a view to developing it.

Raoul Wallenberg was otherwise back in his life at Strandvägen 7a and his role as international director at the Mid-European Trading Company. He had resumed his volunteer activities with the Home Guard and was often seen in his field uniform.

The daily business no longer had very much to do with horses, geese or turkeys. Now that Raoul had been given the go-ahead from the army to travel abroad, his mission to Hungary had to be organised. It was an urgent but complex task.

After the meeting between Iver Olsen and Kálmán Lauer, new possibilities emerged that promised to shift Raoul's Hungary trip from a private act of desperation into an indirectly sponsored international initiative, aimed at saving more than just Lauer's relatives. If the Americans successfully managed to press the Swedish government into increasing their representation in Hungary, the trip would be established on a smoother and more secure foundation. If Raoul Wallenberg was selected, he would be issued with an invaluable diplomatic passport. But how could the Foreign Ministry be persuaded to recruit a relatively unknown architect and import/export trader for a diplomatic post?

Iver Olsen had, of course, immediately asked to meet the young director whom Kálmán Lauer had so warmly recommended. According to one of the many stories surrounding Raoul Wallenberg's recruitment, the three of them met for the first time at a dinner hosted by the Manfréd Weiss director Henrik de Wahl, who was temporarily lodged at the Wallenberg-owned Grand Hôtel in Saltsjöbaden, outside Stockholm.

If this story is correct, the meeting appears to have been a success since the dinner is said to have lasted from seven in the evening until five in the morning. But there are strong reasons to hold off from drawing a conclusion. In most accounts that have tried to capture this series of events, fact and fantasy are wildly mixed. The dates vary from one witness to the next, as do the dinner guests and the restaurants – even the sequence of events is sometimes reversed.

Luckily there are a couple of fixed coordinates to cling to. Among these are Raoul Wallenberg's pocket diary for 1944; the telegrams sent by the American legation in Stockholm to the W.R.B. and the State Department in Washington; and the telegrams between the Foreign Ministry in Stockholm and the Swedish Budapest legation. There is also the only document in the Foreign Ministry archives from these weeks of negotiation that bears Raoul Wallenberg's signature – a letter to the cabinet secretary Erik Boheman of June 19.

Alternatively, one can simply observe that, of everyone who has tried to retell this story, only one of them was actually there: Kálmán Lauer.

According to Lauer, the first meeting between Iver Olsen and Raoul Wallenberg was indeed a dinner that lasted from evening until dawn. They discussed rescue strategies all night and Olsen had, according to Lauer, asked Raoul if he would consider being sent to Hungary by the Foreign Ministry. Olsen explained that, if so, the "American legation" would supply "the material foundation of his mission". Raoul indicated that he would be willing to do this.

Kálmán Lauer and Iver Olsen then informed their respective bosses – Sven Salén and Herschel Johnson – who already knew each other well. Salén rang the American minister and it was decided that Johnson would also meet Raoul Wallenberg. On June 12, 1944, Herschel Johnson sent a telegram to Washington on this matter:

[I] have found [a] Swede who is going to Hungary very near future on business trip and who appears willing to lend every possible assistance on Hungarian problem. [I] am having dinner with him on June 11 with Wahl, for the purpose of exploring possibilities and to obtain in some measure his capabilities along those lines. Any instructions which would coordinate approach to Hungarian problem would be helpful.

The first time the impending assignment left any trace in Raoul's diary is recorded in an entry for a dinner with "Mr Olsen" on Monday, June 12 at 6.00

p.m. It must have been the dinner that Herschel Johnson referred to. It happened to take place on the same day that S.K.F. signed the contract and Swedish ball-bearing exports stopped threatening to torpedo Swedish–American relations. Perhaps this was a coincidence, perhaps it wasn't.

Apparently Iver Olsen and the Hungarian businessman Henrik de Wahl were at the table that night. We do not know who the other guests were but, considering the context, it is not improbable that Kálmán Lauer and Sven Salén were also present.

One can only speculate as to why the Hungarian businessman and canning industrialist Henrik de Wahl was always drawn into these discussions. Of course it may have been his knowledge of Hungary and Budapest that lay behind his invitation to the dinner. After all, the American minister had established contact with the Manfréd Weiss director before Raoul entered the picture, in order to receive information about the sale of the business and the flight of the family itself.

But one cannot simply ignore the fact that Henrik de Wahl and Sven Salén also ran a company together. Globus tinned goods would come to play a central role when Raoul Wallenberg eventually had to arrange food for the many thousands of protected Hungarian Jews. According to the first account of the Budapest mission, Rudolph Philipp's book about Raoul Wallenberg of 1946, it was "Henrik de Wahl and his family conglomerate" who arranged for a portion of the War Refugee Board's American dollars to be paid out in Hungarian pengő to Raoul Wallenberg in Budapest.

Perhaps Sven Salén and Henrik de Wahl's involvement stemmed from a desire to contribute to the War Refugee Board's Hungary effort. It is clear from initiatives during the spring and autumn that Salén was personally involved in the fates of several Hungarian families, as Henrik de Wahl must also have been. But one cannot exclude the possibility that they also saw business potential in becoming the supplier for a rescue mission that was backed by a seemingly bottomless fund of American dollars.

The next fixed coordinate in the recruitment process can be found in the diary exactly one week after Raoul Wallenberg's dinner with Herschel Johnson. On Monday, June 19, Raoul Wallenberg sent a letter to Erik Boheman at the Foreign Ministry. "With regard to our conversation, I would like to thank you for the confidence that has been placed in me," Raoul began.

With the help of Kálmán Lauer's recollections, a picture of the events in the interim begin to emerge. At first the American minister appears to have gone home after the dinner in a relatively enthusiastic frame of mind – he had formed a good impression of Raoul Wallenberg. "After this things went fairly quickly," Lauer observes. Herschel Johnson had again sought out Erik Boheman in order to persuade Sweden to increase its diplomatic representation in Hungary. Now he was equipped with the name of a possible candidate, one who was very familiar with Budapest.

Erik Boheman followed Johnson's advice and set up a meeting with Raoul. Some time between June 14 and 16, Raoul Wallenberg was asked by the Foreign Ministry if he was prepared to accept a post as legation secretary in Budapest.

Exactly what Herschel Johnson said to Boheman about the War Refugee Board and the American financial backing for the intended rescue missions is not clear. But the American minister must have had something of substance to communicate on the matter. Erik Boheman was suddenly convinced – about both the project and the candidate. Stockholm was not overflowing with men who were familiar with Budapest and also willing to set off on a risky assignment to the Eastern Front. And in the background there was the insistent pressure from Jews in Stockholm and cries from a hard-pressed legation in Budapest. But the speed of events is nonetheless astonishing. All at once things happened very quickly and the Foreign Ministry was now prepared to recruit a grocery salesman completely inexperienced in foreign affairs for a diplomatic post in a country with which most other nations had severed their ties.

After the approach from the Foreign Ministry, Raoul contacted the boards of both companies in which he was active: the Mid-European Trading Company as well as the small Pacific Trading Company, where he was a member of the board and also the managing director. He was careful to explain that he would "not be able to undertake any business activities during this time". Nobody stood in his way. He also secured clearance for his Budapest trip from Jacob Wallenberg.

After taking the weekend to think it over, he wrote his reply to Erik Boheman. Raoul told him that all the obstacles that accompanied his current responsibilities had been set aside and that, if required, he was also prepared to leave his board assignments for the duration of the Hungary mission. In closing, he wrote, "As soon as the final decision has been made, I would be grateful for a message so that I can make the necessary arrangements with regard to my business activities. Sincerely, Raoul Wallenberg."

Two days later, two telegrams were sent from the Foreign Ministry to the Budapest legation. The first informed them that it had been decided to officially recognise Valdemar Langlet, who was already in the field, as a delegate with responsibility for the Red Cross rescue mission for Jews in Hungary. The second stated the plans to recruit Raoul Wallenberg as a special attaché at the Budapest legation.

The argument for creating the new post was somewhat tangled. The Foreign Ministry mentioned a special mission that would involve "continuous reporting" as well as suggesting "suitable and achievable humanitarian initiatives as well as necessary aid measures for the post-war period". The Foreign Ministry went on to say that the American legation had given the matter a great deal of attention and it was evident that, hard pressed as they were in Budapest, they could not "spare any personnel" for this "special assignment". Ivan Daniels-son and Per Anger, who must have been puzzled by the connection to the American legation, were urged to "telegraph immediately" if they had any objections.

Erik Boheman appears to have assumed a positive reply because, later that same day, he informed Herschel Johnson that Raoul Wallenberg's position at the Budapest legation had been confirmed. At least this was how Johnson understood it, according to the telegram that he sent to Washington shortly after lunch on the same day, June 21. Johnson wrote that Boheman had been at pains to make it clear that the Foreign Ministry was prepared to do everything necessary to make this happen. If any problems arose regarding necessary visas for Raoul Wallenberg, the Swedish government would counter by not accepting Hungary's chargé d'affaires, Boheman had explained. The cabinet secretary had emphasised that the Foreign Ministry and the Swedish government planned to cooperate "in as large a part as possible" in all humanitarian efforts.

Johnson concluded the telegram by saying that:

[t]he appointment of this Attaché is undoubtedly evidence of official Swedish desire to conform to the wishes expressed in Department's telegram 1010, May 25 [. . .] Olsen and I are of opinion that War Refugee Board should be considering ways and means of implementing this action of Swedish Government particularly with respect to financial support it may be possible to arrange for any concrete rescue and relief progress which may be developed.

Erik Boheman did not have to worry about the reaction in Budapest. The Swedish minister Ivan Danielsson asked his deputy Per Anger what he thought about the proposal. "I know Raoul Wallenberg and I think that this is an excellent solution," was his answer.

At the same time, Per Anger commended the impending appointment in a letter to Sven Salén. "It is with the greatest satisfaction that I have received the message that Raoul W. is on his way. He should, however, make all haste."

In Hungary, Eichmann's death machine showed no signs of letting up, even if the numbers from May's record deportations were no longer being matched every day. Over the past two weeks, another 50,000 Hungarian Jews had been forced into the Nazis' freight cars, like cattle on their way to slaughter. Before the end of June, approximately 40,000 more would meet the same fate and, with that, the Hungarian countryside was effectively wiped clean of its Jewish population.

Adolf Eichmann was impressed by the industriousness of the Hungarian gendarmes, the half-militarised police force that mainly handled the practical work involved in the deportations. He was just as impressed by the determination of the two state secretaries at the Ministry of the Interior, László Baky and László Endre, who ran the deportations at a speed that exceeded all Eichmann's earlier work. But the countryside was one thing, the capital city quite another.

As early as April, Eichmann's Sondereinsatzkommando and the leadership of the Hungarian gendarmerie had put forward a plan to create a ghetto in Budapest. But the proposal stalled. With the Western Allies' air raids from the first few days in April fresh in people's minds, it was deemed too risky to separate the Jews from the rest of the population. Isolating them would only make it easier for the enemy to direct their fire at the non-Jewish quarters.

Instead a compromise was reached and two thousand buildings in Budapest's fourteen districts were identified and furnished with black signs bearing large (thirty centimetres in diameter) yellow Stars of David on their doors. On June 16, the Hungarian government issued a new housing decree. Within five days, all Budapest's Jews who did not already live in a starred house would have to leave and crowd together in the newly designated residences. It was not unusual to see ten people to a room. The Jews were also forbidden to come and go as they pleased: excursions were only permitted between two and five in the afternoon. They were not allowed guests and they could not speak to people on the street through the windows.

The starting date for the deportations from Budapest was set for June 30. But now dissenting voices began to make themselves heard. These were not simply a response to the cruelties that were creeping ever closer to the capital's social elite. More detailed information about what awaited the Jews in Auschwitz-Birkenau had leaked out. In April 1944, two Slovakian Jews, Rudolf Vrba and Alfred Wetzler, managed to escape from the camp. Together they wrote a thirty-two-page report with detailed information about the routines and geography of Auschwitz-Birkenau. It was sent to the Jewish council in Budapest and, by the end of the month, would be confirmed by additional witnesses. These eyewitness accounts came to be known under the collective name of the "Auschwitz Protocols".

It took until the second half of June for the contents of the Auschwitz Protocols to spread to Hungary. The reasons for this delay are contested. Rudolf Vrba himself suggested that it was due to the recipient of the report, Rezső Kasztner. Kasztner was one of the Zionists in the rescue committee that was negotiating during the spring with Adolf Eichmann and Kurt Becher about rescuing a group of Hungarian Jews in exchange for money. At the end of June, Kasztner also managed to get Eichmann to "save" a train with around 1,700 Jews, in exchange for money, gold and diamonds. Vrba accused Kasztner of not wanting to make the information in the Auschwitz Protocols public, since it could have threatened the negotiations, something that Kasztner denied.

*

Hungary's head of state, the regent Miklós Horthy, had already declared at the end of March that he "did not want any kind of influence" on the new anti-Jewish politics. Horthy had retreated to the castle. He was not imprisoned there as some rumours had suggested, but he kept himself at a distance in order to avoid being connected with the activities of the puppet regime. The regent had managed to convince the new government to make their decisions as decrees and not as laws, which freed him from the responsibility of signing them.

But Horthy knew what was going on. One of the leaders of the Jewish council, Ernő Pető, socialised privately with Horthy. Pető was a lawyer and also, in a remarkable coincidence, the father of László Pető, the young Hungarian boy whom Raoul Wallenberg met and saved from bullying at his summer course in Thonon-les-Bains in 1929. Ernő Pető provided the regent with detailed information from the Auschwitz Protocols. At the beginning of June, Miklós Horthy was unable to keep silent any longer. He wrote a letter to Prime Minister Sztójay about the atrocities and demanded that they cease the inhumane treatment of the Jews. He also requested that particularly prominent Jews, and Jews that had converted, be excused entirely.

At a parliamentary meeting on June 21, even the deputy foreign minister, Mihály Jungerth-Arnóthy, protested. He explained to his colleagues that it was true that the Hungarian Jews were being sent to Auschwitz and gassed and not, as the Ministry of the Interior insisted, brought to "work in Germany". But the minister of the interior, Andor Jaross, assured everyone that the alleged genocide was no more than a false rumour and repeated the established Nazi lie: the only reason that all Jews, even children and the elderly, were deported was that the Jewish labourers were more productive with their families around them.

On June 20, the *New York Times* began to publish a series of articles based on the Slovakian Jews' report on Auschwitz. At about the same time, portions of the descriptions were printed in Swiss newspapers and an international wave of condemnation rose up. The newly appointed Swedish Red Cross delegate Valdemar Langlet received the entire collection of new eyewitness accounts from the Jewish council in Budapest, translated them and gave them to the Swedish legation to forward to the Foreign Ministry in Stockholm.

On Midsummer's Eve, June 23, Danielsson gave his clearance for the recruitment of Raoul Wallenberg in an encoded telegram. The following day he added the translated Auschwitz Protocols to the report about developments in the Jewish question that he sent back to the Foreign Ministry.

It was a very pessimistic and despondent minister who picked up his pen. Only a week or so earlier, he had felt required to ask permission to be able to increase the distribution of temporary passports in cases of emergency. Now he wrote that all attempts at pressuring the authorities yielded no results and the last thing they had heard was that all foreign Jews who remained in Hungary on July 1 would be interned. Sweden had requested protection for three to four hundred Jews with Swedish papers, but not even the temporary Swedish passports appeared to guarantee any longer that a refugee would be identified as a Swedish citizen. And no-one knew any more if it was the Germans or the Hungarians who were in charge.

The following day, the Swedish minister sent an even more sombre missive. He had worked very hard in order to supply Valdemar Langlet with the necessary documents for his Red Cross efforts, which had also been promised financial support from a "European-American Jewish Aid Organisation". But the message he was waiting for from the Hungarian government had now been postponed for another week. Danielsson waited and agonised. To the ministry he wrote that if they were not ready by the end of the month, "the question should be removed from our list and the poor Jews, who with the gold of their relatives would have been helped to neutral countries and eventually onto America, should be seen as definitively and helplessly lost".

It was becoming ever clearer that Hitler would inevitably lose the war. The Western Allies had enjoyed continued success after the Normandy landings and, on June 22, the Soviet Union began an offensive on the Eastern Front in which Germany lost 130,000 men, one of the largest military defeats in the war. This change in the climate had a positive effect on international willingness to aid the Jews. On June 25, Pope Pius XII sent a letter to Horthy asking him personally to put an end to the brutality. The very next day a threatening President Roosevelt demanded an immediate cessation of the deportations.

According to the American historian Deborah S. Cornelius, it was when

Admiral Horthy's son, Miklós Horthy Jr, gave his father an article from a Swiss newspaper that the regent finally reached his breaking point. In the article, Hungary was lambasted for presenting itself as "a chivalrous nation", whilst allowing itself to become involved in shameful crimes that would "would remain a dark stain on the nation's honour for ever". According to Cornelius, "Horthy, who had always been fiercely proud of Hungary's reputation for honour and chivalry, was appalled."

Horthy called a cabinet meeting of the Hungarian puppet regime on June 26. With distaste he related everything he knew of the terrible treatment of the Jews and mentioned all the international threats that he had received. He did not mince his words: "I shall not tolerate this any further! I shall not permit the deportations to bring further shame on the Hungarians! Let the government take measures for the removal of Baky and Endre! The deportation of the Jews of Budapest must cease! The government must take the necessary steps!"

Admiral Horthy was still generally revered as a strong national symbol, but not as an intellectual giant. He was advanced in age and increasingly slow. His lecture made an impression on the ministers, but for the moment they did not make any moves to stop the deportations. The demands from neutral nations to grant exceptions to certain groups of foreign Jews did, however, begin to be regarded in a different light. Sweden's request for free passage for three to four hundred Jews was suddenly approved by the puppet regime, as was the Swiss legation's request for visas to Palestine for the approximately seven thousand Jews who were already lining up to emigrate. The Hungarians forwarded the decisions to Edmund Veesenmayer at the German headquarters in Budapest, for approval.

The wavering Hungarian government now made the argument to their German allies that they should approve the Swedish demands. But the Swedish case was put aside at the German legation. Veesenmayer needed to communicate with Berlin and reflect further on the matter since the first signals from the foreign minister, von Ribbentrop, had not been in favour of accommodating the requests made by the Swedes or the Swiss.

Ivan Danielsson and Per Anger could meanwhile take some comfort in the fact that the Hungarian government had extended the deadline on imprisoning foreign Jews to August 1. This was a very positive step, especially since the Swedish list was continually growing. It now consisted of 450 individuals with either temporary passports or Swedish visas.

After Midsummer, a torpor had settled over Stockholm. Iver Olsen was shocked by how important people in positions of great responsibility could simply pack up and disappear from the city for several weeks' holiday. Even the foreign minister Christian Günther had taken a break that began on June 8.

At the American legation, the intense activity continued. Iver Olsen was busy with both the impending Budapest mission and an exciting offer from the Germans to save a few thousand Latvian Jews in exchange for two million Swedish kronor. He had also zeroed in on Hermann Göring's 25-year-old Swedish stepson, Thomas Kantzow, who he knew stayed with his stepfather in Germany from time to time. At the end of June 1944, on the eve of one of Kantzow's trips to see Göring, Olsen invited him to his home and warned him that his stepfather would soon be brought to justice and that he should advise him to do everything to minimise the ongoing persecution of the Jews. Olsen was willing to pull any strings that he could in order to get results for the W.R.B.

The month of June had otherwise been characterised by a great number of secret meetings at Strandvägen 7a. Lauer and Wallenberg's co-workers at the Mid-European Trading Company were sent up and down the stairs with letters and messages, from and to "Mr Olsen". Lauer's newly hired twenty-year-old secretary, who came straight from the clandestine activities at the National Defence Radio Establishment (otherwise known as the F.R.A., the contemporary Swedish equivalent of the American N.S.A. or Britain's G.C.H.Q.), felt right at home.

The formalities were concluded at the Foreign Ministry immediately after the Midsummer holiday weekend. Now all that remained were the practical arrangements. Raoul also wanted to take care of various emotional matters before his departure. The day after his notification, according to his diary, he met twice with the object of his spring romance – once at "the parents" and the second time in his home. Much later Jeanette von Heidenstam, who went on to become a well-known Swedish television host and producer, claimed that Raoul Wallenberg proposed to her just before he travelled to Budapest. According to Jeanette, the proposal took place at an outdoor café at

Drottningholm Palace outside Stockholm. Raoul was in her eyes a "very lively person", an intelligent man whom she thought attractive, even if he "was not particularly handsome". She said in a magazine interview more than fifty years later that, "[H]e had very dark hair and nice eyes. We could laugh together and he was enjoyable to talk to."

Jeanette thought the proposal was a piece of fun. She did not think that Raoul was very much in love with her and, for her part, she had no thoughts of marriage yet. She was about to turn twenty-one and he was far older. As she recalled it several decades later, she gave him the following answer: "You know, I'm not at all the age yet where I want to think about such things. It's very nice and flattering that you think it would be fun but I can't even think about getting married to anyone." When they saw each other for the last time she was told of Raoul's plans. "I'm going now and it will be dangerous," he said.

Raoul Wallenberg was not a bad negotiator. He had demonstrated this many times at the Mid-European Trading Company, and now he once again had use for his talents. In connection with the appointment, he was called to a new meeting at the Foreign Ministry, this time with the acting cabinet secretary, Vilhelm Assarsson.

There are no minutes for the meeting in the Foreign Ministry archives but, if one may trust Raoul Wallenberg's own notes, it was not exactly a timid young thing who sat down in the visitor's chair. He had his own agenda. He did not have to be particularly imaginative to realise he had been called to an important, exciting and in no small measure secret task.

Before the meeting, Raoul Wallenberg discussed with Iver Olsen, Marcus Ehrenpreis and Kálmán Lauer how the operational framework might look. He summarised his proposal to Assarsson in nine points:

1) I confirm the concession discussed earlier that I will have the freedom to negotiate and that I cannot be held responsible by the Swedes for bribes that I make.

2) I assume that if I should be required to travel home to provide a report that I may do so without further ado and the costs will be borne by the Foreign Ministry.

3) Given the evident impossibility of securing funds in Sweden, I propose that a propaganda campaign be undertaken in Swedish newspapers and may I ask that, unless anyone has any objections, it be started immediately.

4) I would like to be informed what my rank at the legation will be.

5) Experts at the American and British legations have advised me to contact several people, many of whom are in opposition to the current regime, something that I would like noted.

6) Mr Böhm at the English legation has advised me, regardless of the circumstances, to contact the prime minister Stojaj [sic]. Is this in order?

7) How often may one assume courier service?

Under these typewritten lines, someone, most likely Raoul, has added two brief handwritten notes:

8) The right to asylum.

9) Audience.

Raoul mentioned a meeting with a "Mr Böhm in the English legation." Vilmos Böhm was a Hungarian Social Democrat of Jewish extraction who had lived in exile in Sweden since 1938. He had been minister of defence in the Hungarian Soviet Republic of 1919. Now Böhm belonged to the multitude of refugees from various linguistic areas who worked at the British legation's Press Reading Bureau. Their task was to follow and report on the newspaper coverage in a selection of European countries.

Raoul Wallenberg had been put into contact with Vilmos Böhm by Kálmán Lauer and had asked to meet with him to get his advice before the trip. When they met, Raoul asked for names of anti-Nazi Aryans whom he could look up in Budapest. Böhm wrote out a list of individuals, mainly Hungarian Social Democrats, whom he trusted. Raoul then, according to a British legation report, spoke "fairly openly" about his collaboration with Iver Olsen and the American legation's role in his mission.

This was perhaps somewhat careless. According to the Swedish historian Wilhelm Agrell, Vilmos Böhm was at this point also working for the Stockholm office of the Soviet Security Service (the N.K.V.D.), under the cover name of Orestes. At the same time, Böhm had all the reasons in the world to prevent any suspicion from falling on the young Swede's mission. Once deployed to Budapest, Raoul Wallenberg would be in a position to save not only many of the Social Democrats named by Böhm from the Holocaust, but also his son, Stefan.

At the Swedish Foreign Ministry, interest in what Raoul would actually do in Budapest was surprisingly low. Raoul Wallenberg was appointed legation secretary, a formal position at the Foreign Ministry, and issued with a diplomatic passport that would be valid for six months. His salary was set at 2,000 kronor a month (barely £400 today) and the conditions of employment precluded him from continuing his work for the Mid-European Trading Company or engaging in any business deals. Strangely enough, the Foreign Ministry did not create a dossier on Raoul Wallenberg, which was normal procedure for all new recruits. Nor did he seem to have received any instructions from the Ministry's leadership. It seems as if the Foreign Ministry wanted to avoid creating any documents that had to do with the new special attaché. The entire process in fact left more traces in the official American archives than it did in their Swedish equivalents.

It was to the American legation that Raoul, for understandable reasons, now turned for further instructions. On Wednesday June 28, he had lunch with Herschel Johnson on the beautiful island of Djurgården in Stockholm.

The day before, Johnson had informed Washington that a "local businessman is now going [to Budapest] with full diplomatic status and will devote his entire time to humanitarian efforts". Johnson reported that all formal arrangements with the Hungarian authorities had been taken care of and that Raoul could leave immediately, but that he was eager to be "fully instructed" before he departed. Johnson added that he "[w]ould appreciate very much any further instructions that the W.R.B. can supply for the purpose of implementing this mission".

It appears that Wallenberg and Johnson discussed this question with some intensity during their lunch. That same evening, Johnson wrote another long telegram to the War Refugee Board in Washington that gives an idea of what was said.

We should emphasise that the Swedish Foreign Office in making this assignment feels that it has cooperated fully in lending all possible facilities for the furtherance of an American programme. It is not likely, however, that it will provide the newly appointed attaché with a concrete programme; but instead will probably give him rather general instructions which will not be sufficiently specific to enable him to deal promptly and effectively with situations as they develop in Hungary. The newly designated attaché, Raoul Wallenberg, feels however that he, in effect, is carrying out a humanitarian mission on behalf of the War Refugee Board. Consequently he would like full instructions as to the line of activities he is authorised to carry out and assurances of adequate financial support for these activities so that he will be in a position to develop fully all local possibilities. We are very favourably impressed with Wallenberg's ability to act intelligently and with discretion in carrying out any responsibilities that the W.R.B. may delegate to him and urge strongly that appropriate instructions be forwarded as soon as possible. Arrangements have been made to communicate with him in Budapest through the Swedish Foreign Office and vice versa and it should be possible for us to keep currently informed on developments in Hungary.

With barely a week left before his departure, it remained unclear to Raoul Wallenberg exactly what he was to do in Budapest. If one trusts Johnson, the Foreign Ministry had indicated that the responsibility for settling these questions and delivering more detailed instructions fell primarily to the United States government. Shortly thereafter, Erik Boheman turned to Herschel Johnson and expressly said that if the War Refugee Board could "formulate some form of directive for him [Raoul Wallenberg], which the Foreign Office will be glad to transmit, it would be of great help to Wallenberg."

As Johnson saw it, Raoul's Budapest mission was "an American programme", which the Swedes were facilitating by assisting with the practical framework. The Swedish officials appear to have had more or less the same opinion. It was the Americans who had selected Raoul Wallenberg. The Foreign Ministry paid his salary and gave him Swedish diplomatic status, but it was the Americans who were to instruct him and produce the funds necessary for the humanitarian activities he was expected to undertake.

Raoul Wallenberg was a Swedish diplomat on an American assignment. This was, in truth, a unique recruitment for a neutral state such as Sweden. The official Swedish investigation that sixty years later evaluated the Foreign Ministry's actions observed that "[t]he fact that Boheman (and most likely the prime minister as well as the foreign minister) gave their approval for Wallenberg to receive his instructions from the United States is not only unusual. It can also be viewed as confirmation that instructions were never actually issued from the Swedish side."

When the Foreign Ministry in Stockholm informed the Budapest legation, Raoul's assignment was described as "extremely delicate". But there was no mention of the American involvement.

Of the original Hungarian Jewish population of around 825,000, only the approximately quarter of a million Jews of Budapest remained. The international public outrage after the Auschwitz Protocols awakened some hope that perhaps the Budapest Jews would be spared at the last minute.

In Stockholm's Jewish community, Chief Rabbi Marcus Ehrenpreis was pressured by Jews in other countries who felt that the Swedish king should also act. On Thursday June 29 Ehrenpreis wrote a hurried letter to the Foreign Ministry on the matter. The issue was immediately forwarded to the court at Stockholm Palace.

The following day, King Gustaf V returned from his summer retreat, Solliden, for a cabinet briefing. He was then presented by Prime Minister Per Albin Hansson with a proposal for a personal message directed to Admiral Horthy. The message was composed in French and intended to be conveyed to Budapest on behalf of the king. This letter read in part: *"Je me permets de m'adresser personnellement à Votre Altesse pour La prier au nom de l'humanité de prendre des mesures en faveur de ceux qui restent encore à sauver de cette race malheureuse."* (I turn personally to Your Highness in order to ask of you in the name of humanity to take measures to save those of this unfortunate race that may still be saved.)

Unfortunately, the intended Swedish messenger in Budapest was on holiday. Ivan Danielsson made his way back to the capital as soon as Per Anger contacted him but it still took until July 3 before they were given an opportunity to present King Gustaf V's plea to Admiral Horthy. The regent was, according to their impressions, very tired and deeply saddened. Horthy blamed everything on the Nazis. "It was depressing to hear the old regent assure us that no Hungarian authorities could imagine participating in these crimes," Per Anger wrote much later about this meeting.

But Miklós Horthy was both better informed and more forceful than Anger believed. In reality, listening to the Swedish plea was almost a pleasure in comparison to the kind of pressure that the regent normally felt. The day before, the Americans had carried out a bombing raid over Budapest in order to demonstrate the seriousness of President Roosevelt's protests. Threatening leaflets outlining how those responsible for the deportations would be punished after the war fluttered down over the city. Admiral Horthy was also quickly forced to act to prevent a coup, organised by, among others, the anti-Semitic state secretary László Baky. The plan had been to overthrow the increasingly shaky Hungarian government and pave the way for the right-wing extremists of the national socialist Arrow Cross Party to seize power. In this way they hoped to quash any lingering doubts about the continued deportations.

It is claimed that it was on the evening of July 3 that Miklós Horthy read the Auschwitz Protocols in their entirety for the first time. His daughter-in-law Ilona Horthy gave him the documents, noted the event in her journal and then heard his reaction from her mother-in-law. According to Ilona Horthy's description, her father-in-law emerged from his study deeply agitated. The regent had not been ignorant before, but now he was convinced that not even the most horrifying details in the report were sinister exaggerations. "The deportations must be stopped!" he is said to have exclaimed. Then he busied himself in laying the groundwork so that he could step into action.

Raoul Wallenberg's departure date was set for Friday, July 7, and there was much to do before then. On June 30, his final working day at the Mid-European Trading Company, he received his diplomatic passport. In it, he could read the authoritative language regarding diplomatic immunity in a fine script in several languages. He was identified as being 176 centimetres tall, with chestnut hair, dark brown eyes and an oval, beardless face.

The Foreign Ministry equipped Raoul Wallenberg with the most recent reports from Hungary. He made sure he met with other individuals who possessed situational knowledge, like Vilmos Böhm. He also spoke with the American diplomat Francis Cunningham, who now lived in Raoul's sister Nina's apartment on Brahegatan and who had continued his role as a facilitator between the American intelligence service O.S.S. and Hungarian politicians in exile in Stockholm. Raoul's diary indicates further that he invited to his home the Hungarian journalist and press attaché Andor Gellért, who was part of Cunningham's Stockholm network. Gellért had been a link when the Hungarian peace negotiators sought contact with the West in the autumn of 1943. He functioned as a kind of messenger for briefings from Hungary and cooperated with the Hungarian Vilmos Böhm at the British legation's Press Reading Bureau.

According to Wilhelm Agrell, Böhm had tried to recruit his informant Andor Gellért to the Soviet N.K.V.D. but was prevented from doing so by Moscow.

On the surface, Stockholm was a worry-free Mecca in war-torn Europe. At the same time, this neutral capital was possibly Europe's most intense market for information, a veritable playground for spies and informants with unclear, sometimes multiple, loyalties.

What Raoul Wallenberg saw in all this, no-one can know. Even his closest contact at the American legation, Iver Olsen, wore both visible and invisible costumes. Much later it was revealed that Olsen had a secret parallel assignment for the O.S.S., with the code name "Crispin". The organisation that Raoul was to work with, the War Refugee Board, also had a cover name in the O.S.S. – "Garbo". There is, however, nothing to indicate that Raoul was aware of Olsen's connection to the O.S.S. In the fifties, in a C.I.A. interrogation, Olsen reiterated that his contacts with Raoul Wallenberg only concerned the assignment for the War Refugee Board.

Olsen's colleagues in the O.S.S. had of course considered the fact that the Swede Raoul Wallenberg could perhaps be of use to them. While Raoul was preparing for his departure, the possibility of using this new "Garbo" mission was discussed in at least one encrypted O.S.S. telegram. But the conclusion was that, "from the subject's personal history we suppose he would be of doubtful assistance in our activities".

At this time, unlike during the Cold War, intelligence networks of this kind did not automatically threaten relations between the U.S.A. and the Soviet Union. The O.S.S. was relatively open about sharing its intelligence with the Soviet security services as part of an attempt to create "mutual understanding based on shared war goals". And whatever the Russians did not know they quickly tracked down. As Wilhelm Agrell writes in his book on the circumstances surrounding Raoul Wallenberg's Budapest assignment, "[t]he intelligence gathering of the Western Allies and special operations against Hungary were almost completely infiltrated by the Soviet intelligence agencies".

Raoul Wallenberg now possessed a considerable list of names that extended beyond potential allies in the Hungarian opposition. Once it became known that Raoul would join the legation in Budapest, he was flooded with gifts of money and packages, as well as names and addresses of Swedish-Hungarian relatives in need of assistance.

It was clear that communication with Stockholm could become sensitive and Raoul appears to have felt uncomfortable with the Foreign Ministry's system of cipher telegrams. In the days before his departure, he sat down with Kálmán Lauer and, between the two of them, they created a private code for telegrams and letters.

Their imagination flowed in the process: "Goose liver, special metals, pheasant or partridge" were four different codes for the word "Jew", which they decided had to be varied so that it would not be easily identified. "Invite to a nice lunch" would indicate a bribery attempt. Letters of protection would be referred to as "medicine or bird food", temporary passports would be "pharmaceuticals" and citizenship would be "medicine for rheumatism". The most important Hungarian politicians received their own code names, as did the heads of the Jewish council, and the rest of the main players. Per Anger was called "Helena" and Ivan Danielsson "meine Freundin". The Americans were called "Larsson", the press was "Anderson" and Vilmos Böhm was given the name "Gustafsson". The Foreign Ministry was dubbed "the administration" and when the Germans were added to the list it was under the name of "Plauen & Co", after Maj, Raoul Wallenberg's favourite cousin in Berlin.

They numbered the internment camps and gave names to all the Hungarian ghettos. Finally, they decided to use the sentence "my sciatica is flaring up" as a secret signal for when a message was encoded and needed attention.

They also gave some thought to the greater risks of the project. If Raoul was in danger and needed to hide or travel, the alarm would be: "I am in need of a bath."

Three days before his departure, they went together to a weapon store in Nybrogatan and bought a 9mm Browning pistol and 200 rounds. Raoul added them to his luggage.

To judge from his telegrams to Washington, Herschel Johnson was becoming ever more convinced that Raoul Wallenberg was the right person for the job. A couple of days after their lunch, when he again reminded the W.R.B. about the need for instructions from the American side to Raoul, Johnson wrote, "There is no doubt in my mind as to the sincerity of Wallenberg's purpose because I have talked to him myself. I was told by Wallenberg that he wanted to be able to help effectively and to save lives and that he was not interested in going to Budapest merely to write reports to be sent to the Foreign Office. He himself is half Jewish, incidentally."

The information about Raoul's Jewish heritage was of course a modification of the truth. He had only a very small proportion of Jewish blood in his veins. Indeed, very few knew about even this weakest of connections. To Marcus Ehrenpreis, for example, Raoul Wallenberg had initially appeared more as a naïve adventurer than someone who cared about the Jewish cause. But by this point, when the project finally appeared to be taking shape, Ehrenpreis had adjusted this evaluation. Raoul Wallenberg met the Chief Rabbi again during one of his final days in Sweden. He did so together with Kálmán Lauer and the Zionist Norbert Masur among others. Ehrenpreis recited the Lord's Blessing over Raoul and his mission. According to the Hungarian writer Lévai Jenő's 1948 book about Raoul Wallenberg, Ehrenpreis also recited some words from the Talmud: "those men who prepare to travel in the service of mankind do so under the special protection of the Lord."

Raoul packed his things into two backpacks of the same model that he had used in the army. He arranged a reception at Bragevägen 12. Stockholm was paralysed by a heat wave and, many decades later, his cousin Lennart Hagströmer still recalls how crowded it was out on the terrace. The day before he left, his parents, Maj and Fredrik von Dardel, gave a farewell dinner attended by guests including Kálmán Lauer and Antal Ullein-Reviczky.

*

It is clear that the lack of written documentation for the assignment bothered Raoul Wallenberg. On July 6, as an extra piece of security, he wrote a letter to Boheman:

> So that no misunderstandings may occur, I will allow myself to con-
> firm a few of those matters that have been discussed at our meet-
> ings. It has thus been agreed that I have a certain freedom to negoti-
> ate in accordance with the programme that was earlier outlined by
> Professor Ehrenpreis, Mr Olsen, Dr Lauer and myself. In addition, I
> have the right to employ those means that I bring with me for the
> purpose of assisting these individuals, in the way that appears to me
> to best lead to the desired result and that, according to Mr Olsen
> and Professor Ehrenpreis, have shown themselves to be necessary
> under similar circumstances. The payments will largely be made by
> intermediaries so that my position as an official with the Foreign
> Ministry will not be compromised. Travel costs will be borne by the
> Foreign Ministry. Furthermore, it has also been agreed that I may
> quit my post after two months, that is, on September 6, if I should
> so desire.
>
> Sincerely, Raoul Wallenberg.

On Friday morning, July 7, no instructions had yet arrived from the War Refugee Board. Stockholm awoke to yet another day of over thirty-degree heat. Raoul spent the hours before he set off for Bromma Airport trying to settle upon an agreement regarding the printing company in Vadstena that he had become involved in. This was only one of the many colourful ideas that over the years had characterised the businessman Raoul Wallenberg.

His partner Kálmán Lauer accompanied him to the airport. Raoul was said to have been dressed in a grey-green raincoat and a brown "Anthony Eden" Homburg. He was wearing boots and with his two backpacks – one on his back and one in his hand – he looked more like a scoutmaster than a professional diplomat.

In Budapest, Friday 7 July, 1944, was the day when the news of regent Miklós Horthy's decision to stop the deportations was publicly released. This time the regent did not simply make a plea. The order that overrode the government had been issued the day before. On the morning of July 7, Prime Minister Sztójay informed the German representative Edmund Veesenmayer of the new situation.

At 2 p.m., ten minutes after the scheduled time, the Lufthansa Junkers Ju 52 took off from Bromma Airport, just outside Stockholm. It made a left turn over the tops of the houses and then continued in a south-westerly direction towards Berlin. Among the ten passengers was a thin-haired 31-year-old architect and businessman who, in all haste, had been transformed into a newly fledged Swedish diplomat on a secret American mission.

Djursholm, October 2010

Nina Lagergren is standing on the balcony and waving when I arrive. She has moved from her house now, to an apartment in central Djursholm. The harsh winter settled the issue. I remember the snow banks in February, the ones she insisted on shovelling herself, despite the fact that they far exceeded what might be called "moderate healthy exercise" for an 89-year-old.

To prepare for the move, Nina and her children sorted papers. She found some letters from 1944 that I am going to be allowed to look at. I am most curious about what she wrote in July 1944 about Raoul's visit to Berlin.

When Raoul Wallenberg was appointed legation secretary in Budapest, his sister Nina and her husband Gunnar Lagergren had spent six months in the German capital. Gunnar Lagergren had been recruited at short notice to the Swedish legation from his position at the Swedish Courts in Stockholm. The situation in Berlin had deteriorated and a few vacancies had opened up when Swedish diplomats with families had been advised to return home. But Gunnar and Nina Lagergren were not exactly faint of heart. They had accepted the challenge and travelled in the opposite direction.

"At the time, Berlin was already being destroyed by bombs and the staff had been evacuated to the suburb of Altdöbern. But, during the spring, we moved to a gardener's house by a small castle outside Potsdam. It was beautifully situated by a lake. The area was called Caputh so we used to say that we lived in 'Klein Caputh, bei Gross Caputh, Berlin,'" Nina Lagergren tells me and I can't help laughing at these words.

On the kitchen table there is a scrapbook with copies of some of her letters from that time. She says that it was only a few days before her brother came that she heard from the minister in Berlin, Arvid Richert, that Raoul was going to stop over on his way to Hungary.

Nina shows me a letter from the same month.

"We had been told that Raoul would come down on Friday. I hardly dared believe it was true," she reads from the letter, "On Friday, we cleaned in the heat and lifted furniture around and I picked countless wild flowers so that everything would look nice when Raoul arrived. He was given the small flowery bedroom next to our bedroom. It was possibly even warmer that day when we drove in the evening to pick him up."

Towards the end of the war, Lufthansa's reputation in Sweden had diminished. The company's daily Berlin flights were called "flying coffins" and, later during the autumn, a passenger plane crashed on its way to Sweden. Things were not quite so bad on this particular day. Raoul Wallenberg was thoroughly shaken but landed in one piece at Tempelhof airport. There Nina and Gunnar were waiting with their Opel. Nina was seven months pregnant and would be sent back to Sweden for reasons of safety only a week or so later.

"It was so wonderful to see him again and he had so many interesting things to tell in the car on the way home! He had had a terrible flight and was enjoying the leafy greenery and the coolness and a refreshing swim at our idyllic little bathing spot, with the weeping willows and the charmingly dilapidated West Indian boathouse," Nina wrote in her letter a few weeks later.

"When we sat in the car he could talk without anyone listening and it was the first time I heard about his assignment in Budapest and everything he had before him, that he was going to save as many people as possible. And it wasn't just something that he said. It was with the greatest seriousness. As a person, he was fully engaged", Nina tells me.

There were great hopes riding on Raoul's mission and he placed high expectations on himself. Nina recalls that he seemed very stressed when he arrived. He had informed the legation in Berlin that he wanted to continue travelling on Saturday and had asked them to book him a seat on the train to Vienna.

But Richert thought it would be nice for Nina if Raoul stayed two nights, so he had changed the reservation to Sunday without saying anything. Raoul became furious when he discovered this. "I have to leave as soon as possible," he said.

"So it was only one night. But it was a wonderful evening, with a beautiful sunset and everything," Nina tells me.

I keep reading the letter that Nina wrote to Gunnar in Berlin from the summer house in the Stockholm archipelago a few weeks later. They had agreed that she would write down what they had experienced, which could then be committed to the shared diary they kept of their time abroad:

"Then we were all very hungry and the dinner, to which Dr Ehlers was also invited, was delicious. Afterwards we drank coffee on the large patio outside Raoul's room, in the mild summer evening with the mirror-like lake and its beautiful green shores providing a delightful view. Eventually we turned in for the night but even in our pyjamas we had so much to tell each other, the three of us, Raoul in his funny newly purchased fire-red silk pyjamas that made him look like a flame! When everything was finally dark, it did not take long for the sirens to start up."

Caputh lay six kilometres south of Potsdam and it was known as a peaceful idyll. Nina leafs through to some beautiful photographs from her wartime summer there – swimming down at the bathhouse and croquet on the lawn. When the air-raid sirens went off late in the evening on 7 July, 1944 it was the first time that it had happened during the entire time that Gunnar and Nina had lived there. Nina will never forget that moment.

"Then we had to get up and make our way to the castle again, to a cellar there. We saw how they dropped flares, which were called Christmas trees, one flare in each corner of a square. Then the planes came through and dropped their bombs within the square. They were British planes. The Americans came in the daytime, the British at night," Nina tells me.

This air raid is of course mentioned in Nina's summer letter to her husband Gunnar from 1944. "Do you remember that we thought it was a smashing success to invite Raoul to this sensation? The park was completely illuminated by the moon and everything was so calm and magical and heavenly until the anti-aircraft guns started to thunder and you took my hand and we quickly set off for the cellar.

"After a while the noise stopped and we could go back and go to bed again. It was probably the first time that Raoul had come into close contact with the real war. I remember that he did not think it was pleasant," Nina says.

The following day Raoul Wallenberg had lunch with Arvid Richert. The train to Vienna that Raoul insisted he take left at 5.21 p.m. Gunnar drove him to the station.

"But then he had no tickets and it was completely filled with German soldiers who were going to the front, so he sat in the corridor with his backpacks. It would be a very difficult journey for him," Nina continues.

"Yes, that was the short while he was with us. That was the last time I saw him."

CHAPTER 11

Save As Many As Possible

On Sunday, July 9, 1944, Raoul Wallenberg arrived in Budapest having taken the train from Vienna. The improvised departure from Berlin had not been cheap and he summed up the additional costs in his diary: the ticket at Vienna, the baggage, porters and taxi. Now there was also the tip for the porter who received him when he arrived at the Swedish legation on Gellért Hill in Buda.

The building had the address Gyopár utca 8 (today Minerva utca 3a) and was an impressive creation, a four-storey palace with finely wrought iron gates and arched doorways. When the villa was constructed in 1907 it was written up in architectural publications on account of the groundbreaking combination of Art Nouveau and modern conveniences such as a lift and central heating. No expense had been spared, either on the stained-glass windows or the hardwood details. The marble staircase up to the large reception room was edged with exquisite green ceramic tiles. The legation's cars were parked on a paved yard in front of the main entrance and squirrels ran around in the lush garden. From the terrace one could enjoy, at that time, an enchanting view of the Danube and all of Pest.

Per Anger had his office next to the cupboard with the cipher machine, half a storey up from the office on the main floor. During Danielsson's holiday, Anger was the legation's chargé d'affaires and it was therefore he who received the new legation secretary. He had some heartening news for Raoul: it seemed that the deportations had been called off. But he was quick to add that everything depended on what the Germans had in mind. It was hardly credible that they would spare the capital's Jews in the end.

The legation had been sent certain parameters from Stockholm regarding Raoul Wallenberg's role in the diplomatic corps. He would be installed "as

usual" as secretary at the legation. He would be subordinate to Ivan Danielsson and would keep the minister informed about his activities. His assignment was to stay for "a couple of months . . . follow the developments in the
Jewish question and report back to Stockholm". But that this was not the
whole truth was evident from the end of the letter. "Since an activity of the
special nature with which Mr. Wallenberg has been entrusted is naturally very
delicate, the legation's support from the chargé d'affaires Anger, Budapest, is
of the greatest significance. Every intermezzo with the authorities is to be
avoided and I am counting on you to supply Wallenberg with the necessary
directives in this area," the interim director for the political department wrote.

The standard activity of writing reports could hardly be described as
either delicate or combined with risks of "intermezzo with the authorities".
Per Anger must have known that there were humanitarian ambitions invested
in this new recruit, but according to his own account he remained unaware of
the extent of the American involvement for the remainder of the war.

The following day Raoul met Ivan Danielsson for lunch. Afterwards Anger
reflected upon the impressive flexibility that the relatively conservative senior
diplomat was displaying. Of course it was possible that internationally prominent businessmen might be assigned diplomatic positions in countries in
which they were already well connected. But for the Foreign Ministry to bring
in someone who could at best be regarded as an unknown upstart in the
business world – this was something that neither of them had experienced
before. In an interview many decades later Per Anger praised Ivan Danielsson's ability to adapt:

> Here a businessman suddenly appeared as a secretary, the same
> rank as myself, and negotiates with the Hungarian Foreign Ministry
> and acts independently. He had to inform minister Danielsson of
> course . . . But he went his own way . . . In the beginning it was, of
> course, a shock for Danielsson . . . that here he had a man with
> extraordinary powers, that this was something the Foreign Ministry
> had agreed upon, to appoint him and all that. But, step by step, he
> became convinced that this was the only way of doing this, to save
> people.

*

Raoul Wallenberg checked in to the Hotel Gellért, which was only a few hundred metres from the legation. In the evening he sent a telegram to Kálmán Lauer: *"gut angekommen vorlaeufig Gellert Wallenberg"* (arrived safely provisionally Gellért Wallenberg).

The Hungarian minister of the interior Andor Jaross and his two state secretaries Baky and Endre had fought until the end. In opposition to Admiral Horthy's express order they had allowed the death machinery to continue for two more days. Only on Saturday, July 8, did the final trains depart, sending another 25,000 Jews from the suburbs of Budapest to the gas chambers in Auschwitz.

The final count was beyond all reasonable comprehension: 437,000 Hungarian Jews deported in barely seven weeks.

The prickly Adolf Eichmann did not take kindly to the Hungarian decision to stop the deportations. For him it was a signal that the S.S. should act with greater firmness. Several days after the order to stop the deportations, he decided to test Miklós Horthy's resolve and gave the order to deport 1,500 Jews, many from the camp at Kistarcsa on the outskirts of Budapest. The train left but Horthy was informed and acted. Hungarian gendarmes stopped the train after forty kilometres and made sure that it returned. Unfortunately, on his second attempt, Eichmann had better luck.

The Jews of Budapest had little confidence that the halt in deportations would hold indefinitely. Rumours circulated that the date for the resumption of the deportations had already been set for August 5. And with the unpredictable Eichmann in the city one could never be sure. Eichmann's stay in Budapest had degenerated into a quintessential study in moral decay. He drank without moderation, spent time at brothels and held night-long sex orgies.

Eichmann was unstable. The halt to the deportations enraged him. But he was also irritated that the Swedish and Swiss legations had the nerve to demand protection – even emigration visas – for "foreign" Jews. And as if that were not enough, the Hungarian government was supporting these requests and had asked the Germans to sanction them. Eichmann was sceptical. He had heard this Swedish song before. He was certain that if one scraped the surface one would find that many of these proclaimed "Swedish" Jews would turn out never to have set foot in Sweden. The German envoy Edmund Veesenmayer had reported this same suspicion to Berlin at the beginning of July.

Somewhere the thought occurred to the Germans that, if the Hungarian government was so eager to grant free passage to a couple of hundred "Swedish" Jews, they would have to offer something in return. The same would also be true if the Hungarians insisted on allowing free passage to the 7,000 emigrants on their way to Palestine, who had been granted emigration visas by the Swiss legation, but denied the right to leave the country.

Certainly we can consider these things, the Germans said. But we will hold off making practical arrangements until the deportation of the rest of the Jews has been resumed. The Nazis' evil equation could be written out in this way: they would consider allowing a few thousand "Swedish" and "Swiss" Jews to escape if they were given free rein to exterminate the remaining 200,000–250,000 Jews in exchange.

By this point the Swedish diplomats had basically given up hope that the Germans would give the 450 Jews on the Swedish list the green light to travel to Sweden. Forecasts from the Hungarians continued to be gloomy. But, four days after Raoul Wallenberg's arrival, Per Anger was called to an evening meeting at the Hungarian Foreign Ministry where he was abruptly informed that the answer from the Germans was a yes. The Swedish legation now had only a couple of days to submit a final list so that German visas could be prepared. These protected Jews would have to leave Hungary no later than August 1.

"Basically this news . . . struck the office like a bomb going off," Per Anger wrote to Stockholm.

No-one could yet discern the cynical thinking behind these decisions.

Raoul Wallenberg immediately set to work. From Tuesday, July 11, 1944, his relatively sparsely filled diary changes markedly, and in his tight, microscopic writing one can follow the intense network-building he engaged in during this early phase. Over the first few days he had one or two long sessions with Valdemar Langlet, the newly appointed Red Cross representative. Langlet's spirits had soured substantially, as the Foreign Ministry had just restricted the legation's quantity of temporary passports. In Stockholm they were worried that passport inflation would undermine the value of genuine Swedish passports and thereby reduce security for all Swedish citizens. But Valdemar Langlet found these calls for restraint "disobliging" and bureaucratic. In this university lecturer's humanitarian mission there was a great self-sacrificing courage but also a maverick instinct that was not always so easy for the Swedish diplomats to support.

On Tuesday evening, Per Anger invited Raoul Wallenberg to his home in Rose Hill above Margaret Island. There, according to the diary, Raoul met Géza Soós, one of the representatives of the anti-Nazi underground movement M.F.M., the Movement for Hungary's Independence. Soós was a lawyer and had earlier been an adviser at the Hungarian Foreign Ministry, but had chosen to go underground when the Germans arrived. The resistance fighter Soós told Raoul that many Jews in Budapest, probably around 50,000, were being hidden by Christian friends. Raoul remembered this and later used these numbers in a report that he submitted to the Foreign Ministry. He conducted a handful of such interviews in his first week. He questioned several individuals, including the Mid-European Trading Company's representatives, László Kelemen and Josef von Deák, as well as Vilmos Böhms' Social Democrat contact, Miklós Kertész, about the persecutions and the nature of the deportations. And, naturally, he paid a visit to the Jewish Council in their headquarters at Síp utca 12, down in Pest.

According to eyewitnesses, the day Raoul Wallenberg arrived, the place was crowded with people. He had brought a greeting from Marcus Ehrenpreis to the chairman of the Jewish Council, Samuel Stern. In the letter, Ehrenpreis asked the council to receive Raoul Wallenberg and give him all the information that he might need.

One of Samuel Stern's closest associates, the lawyer Ernő Pető, recognised Raoul Wallenberg's name and summoned his son. The young László Pető had not forgotten the somewhat older Swede from the French summer course in Thonon-les-Bains in 1929. He had not heard from him since then, but now the Swede had suddenly turned up again, in the darkest of circumstances.

The leaders of the Jewish Council told Raoul Wallenberg what they knew about the deportations. Raoul learned that people only received one loaf of bread and one bucket of water per freight car for a trip that took five days and that therefore many of them died during the transportation. They told

him about a new "deal" with the Gestapo that they had heard about. Approximately one thousand Hungarian Jews had paid 80,000 Hungarian pengő
each to the Germans in order to be able to travel to Spain. But now they had
been informed that the train was still standing on a track in Hanover. Their
experiences with bribes were relatively murky. They knew of several cases
where Jews had paid sums of money for their salvation but had still been
killed.

As Raoul Wallenberg left the Jewish Council he was given a secret letter
to take back to King Gustaf V. It was a cry for help in which the Jewish Council pleaded for greater intervention. They wrote that in the current situation,
emigration appeared the only possible solution for the Jews of Budapest. They
hoped for a coordinated rescue effort by several of the neutral European
countries and perhaps King Gustaf V could again add his voice.

Raoul Wallenberg himself soon changed his mind. Emigration, he would
come to believe, was not the best way to save the Jewish population of
Budapest.

Some of the Jews that had been issued with temporary passports now willingly offered their labour to the Swedish legation. They had been freed of
their yellow stars and could come and go as they pleased, in contrast to the
majority of Budapest's Jews who could not stay out for more than three hours
a day. Included in this group of Swedish passport holders was the managing
director of the Orion radio factory, Hugó Wohl. He was the man who had
knocked on Per Anger's door that night in April, beside himself with fear.
Recently, Wohl's colleague at Orion, the engineer Vilmos Forgács, had joined
them.

Forgács had been arrested by the Nazis back in March, interned in north
Buda for several months, and was on the verge of being deported in one of
the last transports from the outskirts of Budapest. But then he had had the
presence of mind to run back to the hiding place where he kept his temporary
Swedish passport. He had presented this and successfully protested to the
gendarmes when they tried to seize this "foreign citizen".

From now on, Hugó Wohl, Vilmos Forgács and several other protected
Jews came to the Swedish legation every day in order to work. They assisted
with the urgent repatriation list which had continued to grow and now

included 649 Jews for whom "the nature of the connection to Sweden varied", as the Foreign Ministry's legal head, Gösta Engzell, diplomatically put it.

When Raoul Wallenberg arrived, he was put in charge of a new section at the legation, the "humanitarian department". On the street outside, the crowds of Jews seeking aid remained considerable. The thought was that Raoul would handle this work, thereby taking the pressure off Per Anger, who had other important questions to tackle, not least the plans for a potential evacuation of the legation.

The radio directors Hugó Wohl and Vilmos Forgács had been among the first to receive temporary passports from Per Anger. It felt natural to include them at the heart of the team that Raoul now started to build. The Hungarian-Slovakian lawyer Dr Pál Hegedűs also came to be one of Raoul's closest associates in the humanitarian department. Hegedűs was Hungarian but, until recently, he had resided in Czechoslovakia. There, in light of his Hungarian nationality, he had been exempted from the anti-Jewish laws, a privilege that he managed to maintain even when he returned to Budapest. He now put his services at Raoul's disposal.

These were no innocent doves that Raoul gathered around him. They were all influential, talented and accomplished men a generation older than he was. They were all Jews and were there of their own free will. One might say that they offered the Swedes their labour as a token of gratitude. A very special feeling of camaraderie would grow between them and the new Swedish legation secretary.

Hugó Wohl, the diminutive radio director, with his sharp wit and his dominant position in the Hungarian business world, was the clear leader of the group. He was a brilliant but also very strict and quiet man who was not overly generous with his smiles. The large and loud lawyer Pál Hegedűs was his complete opposite. Hegedűs was always close to laughter and possessed a diplomatic and analytical talent that made him an important sounding board and adviser to Raoul Wallenberg. And in Vilmos Forgács, the team had a highly industrious associate who never left anything undone.

Raoul Wallenberg recruited individuals from other quarters as well. In the Hungarian network around the Swedish legation, there had been for many years some more or less blue-blooded aristocrats. In the middle of Úri utca (or "gentleman's walk") behind the palace, for example, was the residence of

1924. Raoul Wallenberg is twelve years old and a student at Nya Elementarskolan in Stockholm. His life has been strongly marked by a family tragedy. Three months before Raoul was born, his father, Raoul Oscar Wallenberg, died of cancer. As a young schoolboy, Raoul was regarded as slightly anxious by his classmates. He often described himself as a coward, even when he was older.

Raoul Oscar Wallenberg and Maj Wising married in September 1911. In May 1912, Raoul Oscar died, about three months before the birth of his son Raoul Gustaf Wallenberg.

Newly widowed Maj Wallenberg spent the first few months of her son's life in mourning. During his first years Maj raised Raoul alone. In October 1918, she married Fredrik von Dardel.

Raoul Wallenberg was born on August 4, 1912, on the second floor of Per and Sophie Wising's summer house in Kappsta on Lidingö island. Kappsta was a thirteen-acre beachfront property purchased at the end of the nineteenth century. Sophie Wising can be seen in front of the house.

When Raoul was four years old he met his grandfather Gustaf Wallenberg for the first time. Gustaf was the demanding father figure in Raoul's life, until his death in 1937.

Raoul's cousins, Gösta, Anders and Lennart Hagströmer, were significant for him as he was growing up. Above left they are pictured in their caps next to Raoul. His half-brother Guy was born when he was seven years old. His mother Maj congratulates him on his graduation in May 1930. Seventeen-year-old Raoul is also pictured in a suit.

In autumn 1931, Raoul Wallenberg travelled to the United States for three and a half years of studies at the University of Michigan's College of Architecture in Ann Arbor. During his vacations he hitchhiked around the States, for security reasons often dressed in the uniformed shirt of the Reserve Officers' Training Corps.

During his student years in Ann Arbor, Bernice Ringman (top left) and Raoul were close friends, in fact they were thought of as a couple. After graduation, he travelled abroad for professional experience. Raoul took the boat to and from South Africa and then spent half a year in the Palestinian port of Haifa (top right). On the photo from the ship (bottom), Raoul has indicated himself with an X.

Christmas Eve at grandmother Matilda von Dardel's at Humlegårdsgatan, 1938. From the left: Matilda, Maj, Fredrik's sister Elsa, Raoul, Fredrik and Guy. Behind Guy von Dardel there is a glimpse of Fredrik's uncle Nils. The walking club took skiing trips in the winter. Raoul is at the very front to the right with his friend Lars Pilz. To the left in a white hood is Nina von Dardel, today Lagergren.

Raoul Wallenberg frequently entertained in his apartment at Bragevägen 12. Here are guest lists from a cocktail reception in 1943 and for a tea party, most likely from the same year. The documents have been preserved in Guy von Dardel's private archives.

Towards the end of the 1930s, Raoul Wallenberg often spent time with his cousin Lennart Hagströmer. They sailed in the Stockholm archipelago on Lennart's boat "Nunne", here with cousin Ander's girlfriend Madeleine and Lennart's girlfriend Gunnel as companions. These photographs, which have never before been published, were made available to the author from the late Lennart Hagströmer's archive.

In spring 1935, the newly graduated architect Raoul Wallenberg presented a proposal for an outdoor swimming centre at Riddarholmen. He continued to draw as often as he could. Below is his "dream house", sketched during a dinner with Caroline Jacobsen.

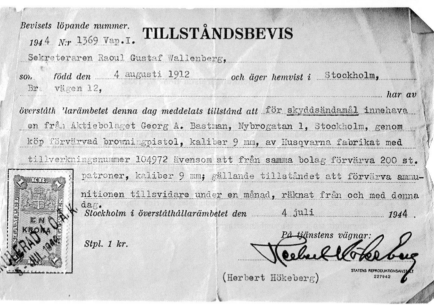

During the 1940s, sergeant Raoul Wallenberg served as a Home Guard instructor in his spare time. Three days before his departure to Budapest, he purchased a pistol in a firearms shop on Nybrogatan in Stockholm.

Tillverkare:

Erste Ungarische Conservenfabrik
und Metallwarenfabrik des

MANFRED WEISS A.G.
BUDAPEST – UNGARN

Generalagent för Sverige
A.-B. BANAN-KOMPANIET

At long last, Raoul Wallenberg was hired as a director of foreign operations at the Mid-European Trading Company, which imported Hungarian foodstuffs. The company offices were located on Strandvägen in Stockholm and were owned by Sven Salén (right), who also sold Hungarian Globus tinned foods. The Hungarian Kálmán Lauer was Raoul's boss and colleague.

Half-siblings Raoul Wallenberg and Nina von Dardel were nine years apart. They grew close during the 1940s. One of the last pictures of Wallenberg is from a visa application to Hungary in 1943. The Swedish coalition government during the war was led by Per Albin Hansson (with briefcase). The Swedish Minister of Foreign Affairs was Christian Günther (to the left of Per Albin.)

Artistically inclined Raoul Wallenberg created a new Swedish protective passport when the Hungarian authorities protested against the many strange provisional documents that circulated in Budapest in the summer of 1944. Raoul's "skyddspass" was regarded as the most credible of all the newly created documents in Budapest that autumn. But the crowns from the Swedish coat of arms were accidentally transposed. Note Raoul Wallenberg's hasty signature bottom left.

The Hungarian regent Miklós Horthy with Adolf Hitler at a parade in Berlin 1938. Hungary was Germany's ally during the war. The country adopted many anti-Semitic measures but opposed Hitler's demands that Hungarian Jews should be deported. Finally Hitler was pushed too far. On Sunday March 19, 1944, German troops invaded Hungary.

Adolf Eichmann soon arrived in Budapest and began to plan for the largest deportation project of World War II. In seven weeks, more than 400,000 Hungarian Jews were transported in cattle cars to Auschwitz. Below: the arrival of one of these trains. Above: the yellow Star of David that Jews were forced to wear prominently displayed on the left side of the chest on their outer layer of clothing.

Tibor von Berg, who felt a great degree of closeness to Sweden. His grand-father's sister had married a man employed by the Swedish court in Stock-holm. The relationship was so strong that Prince Gustaf Adolf (the present king's father) had come out to visit the von Berg family in Budapest in the early 1930s. Even Per Anger had a distant family relationship with the baron, as the result of this Swedish–Hungarian marriage.

Baron von Berg had a young relative, the Countess Erzsébet Nákó, who lived with him in his beautiful medieval house at Úri utca 15. Raoul was invited to a dinner there on one of his first evenings, and afterwards Countess Nákó became a member of Raoul's closest circle. The 22-year-old was a stocky and energetic woman, a fixer of prodigious ingenuity. She spoke quickly, moved rapidly and would come to function as a kind of "social secretary" for Raoul Wallenberg, working alongside German-born Frau Falk, his older, sterner and more typewriter-oriented administrative aide.

Existing staff members at the Swedish legation were also affected when the intense Raoul Wallenberg flew in. During the new secretary's first week, the office assistant Margareta Bauer noted her overtime in her diary: July 13 "worked until 2.30 a.m.", July 16 "worked until 4.30 a.m." and July 20 "my name day, worked all night."

Towards the end of July the heat was as oppressive in Budapest as it had been in Stockholm before Raoul Wallenberg left. The tasks the "humanitarian department" set themselves only grew. Raoul worked night and day and it was not long before he was sending desperate messages back to Kálmán Lauer about needing more funds. His real task did not end with the paperwork for those queuing up outside Gyopár utca 8. Although the current discussion at the legation centred on the 649 Jews on their list, Raoul Wallenberg was already making calculations regarding thousands more. In one of his very first letters home, he wrote to Lauer that they had to avoid speaking to each other on the telephone, "because I am fairly certain that the large administration down here will have become vigilant".

The War Refugee Board had managed to get neither instructions nor money to Raoul Wallenberg before he departed from Stockholm. "Wallen-berg left in a hell of a hurry," Iver Olsen observed later. He put 10,000 kronor (£15,000 today) at Raoul Wallenberg's disposal so that he would not be completely without funds as he was starting out, money that he had received from President Roosevelt's "special fund".

The American instructions arrived at the legation in Stockholm on the very same day that Raoul Wallenberg left, in the form of a telegram from the U.S. State Department and the War Refugee Board, signed by Secretary of State Cordell Hull. Had they arrived in time, Raoul would have been saved some financial worries. Hull explained that the War Refugee Board intended to send an additional 50,000 kronor (£75,000 today) to Iver Olsen, which he should use with "discretion" for "less substantial transactions" in connection with the Hungary mission. Hull went on to write on behalf of the War Refugee Board that, when larger projects began to take shape along with calculations for budget requests, additional funds would be made available.

The problem was how to get the American money to Raoul Wallenberg in Budapest. The Swedish currency laws did not permit large international money transfers without prior notice. The transfers required a smart solution. As Raoul saw it, it was best not to involve people in the Foreign Ministry since "they have to be much more formal than what would be needed if the matter were handled privately". Slow bureaucratic processes were out of the question. The transfer had to happen quickly, Raoul emphasised. "There are many to help here, and great suffering."

Raoul suggested himself, in a letter to Kálmán Lauer, that the money should be deposited into his account at Stockholms Enskilda Bank and then shuffled on to him in stages. He would earmark the sums in question in his account in Stockholm for a certain named individual who, in turn, would receive a corresponding sum in Swiss francs in Switzerland. Iver Olsen, however, tried to solve the problem by using middlemen who were "in a position in which they could satisfactorily receive a good exchange value in [Hungarian] pengő". According to Rudolph Philipp, these middlemen were the Hungarian businessman Henrik de Wahl and his family conglomerate. In view of the escalating inflation of the Hungarian pengő, such alternatives were not a bad idea.

Unfortunately it would take a while for the transfers to work, to Raoul Wallenberg's great frustration. The original agreement was that the Swedish legation was only going to cover the administrative overheads. For everything else, Raoul was dependent on the Americans. Raoul, who was standing face to face with the unabated misery of the Hungarian Jews, thought it unbearable to have to wait and so he didn't. He simply counted on the fact that the money would soon be coming in.

The telegram also included instructions to Raoul Wallenberg regarding the rescue work itself. It mentioned potential escape routes from Budapest and suggested suitable individuals to seek contact with in the new Hungarian administration. It was thought, among other things, that Raoul should investigate the possibility of making use of the ships and barges that were now mostly empty on the Danube. A Hungarian informant had indicated that one could approach the ship owners "on a financial basis" and in this way convince them to take on a limited number of Jews, perhaps dressed as the crew.

The W.R.B. had been tipped off in a similar way about the possibility of approaching train operators on the railway line between Budapest and the city of Mohács on the southern border of Hungary. The telegram urged Raoul Wallenberg to bring copies of President Roosevelt's strong statement from March 24 as well as a similar message issued on July 1 by the U.S. Senate's Committee on Foreign Relations. The thought was that Raoul could use these documents as a source of pressure. It could not hurt to remind contacts that the President of the U.S.A. regarded the Holocaust as mass murder, for which those guilty would be punished after the war.

It is clear from the telegram that Raoul was expected to respond to the War Refugee Board with concrete suggestions for the rescue missions. The W.R.B. wanted to approve any operations that required more "substantial financial agreements" or promises to Hungarian officials about "favourable treatment after the war". According to the instructions, Raoul was to explain to those he met that the Americans meant business regarding their threats of repercussions after the war, but at the same time try to tempt them with the message that "helpful conduct now may result in more favourable consideration than actions hitherto might warrant".

In addition, the War Refugee Board mentioned a number of Hungarians in senior positions who were known to assist Jews and who, officially or unofficially, could be of use to Raoul Wallenberg. A police chief who had been shifted to the Ministry for Internal Affairs was mentioned, as was a state prosecutor and a businessman who was close to the Hungarian minister of trade.

The instructions also emphasised that Raoul was not allowed to appear openly as a representative of the War Refugee Board or act in the name of the organisation. If needed, he could imply that, as a Swede, it was possible for him to communicate with the representative of the War Refugee Board in Stockholm and to convey proposals to him.

These instructions were included as a measure of protection, not as a disclaimer. As the Foreign Ministry in Stockholm had already implied, the assignment and thereby Raoul Wallenberg's situation was diplomatically "delicate". The American instructions were yet another indication of this. The much later official investigation regarding Sweden's actions in the case of Raoul Wallenberg observed that, "Wallenberg was therefore to explain his presence in Budapest in terms of a construction that to all extents was purely American. There are no indications that Wallenberg in his work would refer to statements by the Swedish prime minister or the foreign minister." Quite the opposite, one might add. The Swedes had explained to the Americans that their newly appointed special attaché in Budapest "was available for any work the War Refugee Board might wish to assign to him".

It is easy to believe that one or other of his Swedish colleagues may have raised their eyebrows as Raoul Wallenberg's mission gathered momentum.

It is hard to know if Raoul Wallenberg followed all the details in the American instructions to the letter. His address book for 1944 features none of the names that the W.R.B. listed, nor do they appear in his diary. But in the very first week Raoul, or possibly his secretary, noted the address and telephone number of a contact at the trade ministry, which may indicate that the American message came through. And he did meet the head of the harbour in Budapest, Félix Bornemissza, twice before the end of the month.

Raoul Wallenberg had been in contact with Bornemissza before. A few years earlier his top boss, Sven Salén, had begun to collaborate with the harbour chief, who had set up a shipping company. The contact with Bornemissza was worth its weight in gold for Raoul Wallenberg in his new situation. Salén's partner was a close friend of Horthy's son, Miklós Horthy Jr, or

"Junior" as he was mostly called. Bornemissza had also been a vocal force among the leading Hungarian Jews who called for Hungary to leave the alliance with Germany.

Salén had, for his part, written to Raoul and added names of Hungarian Jews he wanted him to help. He was not alone in this. Wallenberg already had a long list with him when he arrived. The highest priority was, of course, Lauer's family.

On July 14, Kálmán Lauer had finally become a Swedish citizen, which made it easier to arrange Swedish protective documents for his family. Raoul had run himself ragged the first week, going to the Foreign Ministry, the Ministry for Internal Affairs and the Traffic Ministry, as well as meeting with the German legation official Theodor Grell. He now had both good and bad news to share. Lauer's sister and brother-in-law were safe, as was their daughter. All three received temporary Swedish passports. But unfortunately things looked darker for Lauer's parents-in-law. Raoul had tried to track down the trains that had left their hometown but could only conclude that they had been deported and had already left Hungary. Shaken, he wrote home and asked his mother to invite Lauer and his wife to dinner, as a gesture to recognise the great sorrow that had befallen them.

Lauer refused to give up. He wrote to the Foreign Ministry and pleaded on behalf of his in-laws and at the same time sent new names to Raoul of individuals who also needed rescuing. In Stockholm, rumours had circulated that 200 Jewish children were going to be released to Sweden. Lauer wrote down the names of several small children that he felt Raoul should try to arrange passage for. He also named other Jews who he knew were in danger and needed temporary passports. And so it continued. For Lauer, to judge from his letters, Raoul's rescue work was always about responding to tragic individual circumstances. It cannot always have been easy for Raoul Wallenberg to balance the intense pressure his boss exerted on behalf of specific cases with the more general mission that he was expected to pursue and at which he was passionate to succeed.

Raoul had also begun to question whether investing so much time, money and effort into these emotionally charged, but small-scale escape attempts, was the best way to accomplish the task he had been given.

Exactly where these doubts came from is unclear. Perhaps it was the Jewish

Council's stories about hopeful emigrants who had paid for their salvation and still met with death. Perhaps there was something about the promises that the Germans had made that made him feel queasy? Did Raoul sense that the German emissary Edmund Veesenmayer was disingenuous? Or was it simply that, if one had the goal of saving as many as possible of Budapest's 200,000–250,000 Jews, it was blindingly clear that trying to rescue the country's Jews one by one was both prohibitively expensive and guaranteed to benefit only a very small minority of those at risk.

In Raoul's second week in Hungary, his work took a new turn. He wanted to use his money to acquire safe housing for the Jews in Budapest rather than spend everything on bribes and international tickets, he explained. He envisaged both a Red Cross camp and organising private residences in existing houses. As he wrote home to Lauer, "I am convinced that in this way we can save many. The costs for each person will naturally be significantly lower than if we try to get them out of the country."

In fact, Valdemar Langlet had already started aid work in a similar vein. It was not hard to come by residences, apartments or even houses in Budapest at the end of the summer of 1944. Jewish families who needed to go underground often turned their homes over to the administrative agencies of neutral states or unimpeachable international aid organisations. The Swedish Red Cross was held in high regard and received many offers, according to Valdemar Langlet and his book *Verk och dagar i Budapest* (Work and days in Budapest):

> Soon we had taken possession of a dozen villas and apartments in different areas of the city for our office needs; in addition, there were also a large number of established or planned safe houses. Jokingly, one started to call us the largest homeowner in the city and our envoy, who worried about what he called "inflation in localities" made increasingly vehement objections when I asked for his signature on our protective certificates.

At lunchtime on Thursday, July 20, 1944, Colonel Claus Schenk Graf von Stauffenberg placed a briefcase with a bomb under the map table in Adolf Hitler's Eastern Front headquarters. Twenty minutes later it exploded. Four people died but Adolf Hitler survived, albeit with an injured left arm and burst eardrums. The news reached the Germans in Budapest the same day and at first triggered a heightened state of alert. David Cesarini writes in his biography of Eichmann that "for several hours Eichmann had to prepare the defence of his offices and his men but it soon became apparent that the German army units stationed in the country were loyal to the Führer and the Hungarians remained friendly".

The failed assassination attempt was earth-shattering news, even for the bank director Jacob Wallenberg in Stockholm. He had been in contact with the conspirators by way of his friend Carl Goerdeler during the spring. He had promised Goerdeler he would arrange a meeting in Stockholm in order to bring the new German government together with the British as soon as possible after the hopefully successful coup. Nothing went as they had planned. Goerdeler was arrested, tried that same autumn and executed in February 1945. And a shaken Jacob Wallenberg did not dare to travel to Germany for the remainder of the war.

It is highly unlikely that Raoul Wallenberg knew any of this, but his relative's possible involvement in the planned aftermath of the assassination did not, of course, make Raoul's work in Budapest any less risky.

The day before the assassination attempt, Wallenberg set off for Pest, for a meeting with a lieutenant colonel in the Hungarian gendarmerie, the 46-year-old turncoat László Ferenczy. It was Ferenczy who had personally assumed responsibility for the mass deportations from the Hungarian countryside. It was his gendarmes who had undertaken the work and it was he who had submitted the grotesque daily reports from the field, which were added to the extermination statistics compiled by the Ministry of the Interior and the German legation.

On the door to Ferenczy's office, which was not far from the Great Synagogue in Budapest, there was, for some unfathomable reason, a sign with the text "*Nemzetközi Beraktározási és Szállítmányozási Kft*" (International Warehouse and Transport Company). For the sake of efficiency, he had another office right next to Eichmann's at Svábhegy in Buda.

Eichmann had praised Ferenczy for his impressive arrests and raids, but after Miklós Horthy had stepped in and put an end to the deportations, the Hungarian gendarme in charge had got cold feet. Perhaps the American message about punishments had reached him, via leaflets or the communiqués. For whatever reason, Ferenczy had decided to approach the Jewish Council in order to convince them of his genuine desire to save the Jews of Budapest.

As the historian Randolph Braham describes the events, it was when Raoul Wallenberg turned up with his list of 649 "Swedish" Jews that Ferenczy was given a perfect opportunity to cooperate with the Jewish Council and show that he was now a sympathiser. He asked the Jewish Council to arrange some houses to hold the foreign Jews as they awaited departure. During the late summer and autumn, Raoul Wallenberg would cooperate closely with some of Ferenczy's gendarme officers, above all Captain Batizfalvy.

It was a time of violent swings from hope to despair for the Budapest Jews. All kinds of rumours circulated. One of the more persistent ones concerned peace negotiations between the Nazis, the Americans and the Russians. Raoul Wallenberg relayed this rumour back to Stockholm in the special cipher language that he had created with Kálmán Lauer.

At first glance, it looked as if Raoul wanted Lauer to ask a certain Larsson to intercede with his subsidiary "East Josephson Company" in the event that "an agreement regarding market distribution may have been entered into with Plauen & Co". If that were the case, a non-negotiable requirement, according to the subsidiary, was that "calm be established on the Hungarian goose liver market". But between Lauer and Raoul Wallenberg, "Larsson" meant the Americans, "Plauen & Co" stood for the Nazis, "East Josephson Company" was the Russians and "goose liver" was the Jews. What Raoul was really asking Lauer was to contact the American Embassy, inform them of the peace rumour in Budapest and assure himself that the Americans were including the cessation of the deportations in any armistice negotiations they might be involved in.

This seemingly innocent information spread like wildfire on the intelligence market in Stockholm. Kálmán Lauer contacted the Hungarian Vilmos Böhm at the British legation's Press Reading Bureau, who in turn transmitted the contents to a British legation official, and he wrote a report about the matter to his superior. There was no discretion with the Wallenberg source and, like a game of Chinese whispers, facts were distorted in the process:

Mr Boehm informs me he has just seen cipher telegram from M. Wallenberg to Dr Lauer in which it is stated that, since Saturday, 22 July, rumours are circulating in Budapest to the effect that Germany wishes to sign an armistice with Russia. M. Wallenberg asks that the attention of Mr Olsen of the U.S. Legation should be drawn to this fact and that everything should be done to ensure the safety of the Jews in Hungary at the conclusion of peace ... As the telegram was shown to Mr Boehm in strict confidence he asks that the information should be treated likewise in any discussions that may take place with the Americans so as not to compromise the source.

It was of course information that, in the wrong hands, could give a strange impression of the new humanitarian attaché at the Swedish legation in Budapest.

Toward the end of July, exchanges in German telegraph traffic regarding the Swedish and Swiss emigration lists increased in intensity. Edmund Veesenmayer was not happy with the Hungarian government's decision to allow all these "foreign" Jews to leave Hungary, but he had felt compelled to comply. For now there was only a verbal agreement. The formalities still remained. The emigrants needed German transit visas before they could set off for Sweden. And the days went by. Since Veesenmayer had declared that all foreign Jews who had not left Hungary by August 1 would be interned, there was some urgency.

Veesenmayer had a colleague working on the Jewish question at the legation by the name of Theodor Grell. Raoul Wallenberg had met him in his very first week in Budapest. Grell now sent a lengthy account of the situation back to Germany. In it he observed with dismay that the number of foreign Jews with connections to these neutral countries continued to grow. "Among the foreign Jews, the Swedes at this point are in a unique position," he wrote from Budapest on July 24, "because the local Swedish legation has issued a number of purported Swedish passports to Jews after March 19, 1944. They claim that there are certain provisions in Swedish law that extend citizenship to individuals with family or financial connections to Sweden. The extent to which these naturalisations should be recognised from our side is still a question of discussion between the Auswärtiges Amt [foreign ministry] and R.S.H.A."

The actions of the Swiss at this time were, if that were possible, even more irritating to the Germans. The highly active consul Carl Lutz was, unlike the Swedes, quite circumspect about granting Swiss citizenship, so from a legal perspective his actions were less provocative than those of the Scandinavians. But they concerned exponentially more Jews. Before the war Lutz had been closely involved with the emigration of European Jews to Palestine, in coop-eration with the Zionist Jewish Agency. He had continued with this "second-ary task" in Budapest. When the Germans occupied Hungary in March 1944, Carl Lutz had as many as 7,000 Jews with emigration certificates to Palestine on his books, and their chances of securing an exit visa looked to have receded rapidly.

Confronted with this new situation, Lutz became more ambitious. Switz-erland was a protective power for the United States as well as others and had moved its legation to the former American legation's imposing building, which stood among the financial palaces at Szabadság tér (Liberty Square) in central Pest. When the deportations began he had allowed the Jewish Agency's Budapest representatives to have space in the legation quarters. Carl Lutz simply renamed the Jewish Agency "The Swiss Legation's Emigration Department", which meant that the Zionists continued their work under diplomatic protection. He also ensured that its leaders – Ottó Komoly, Rezső Kasztner and Miklós Krausz – received Swiss protective passports so that they could move freely in Budapest. The 7,000, soon to be 8,000, travellers await-ing passage to Palestine received special protective letters, or *Schutzbriefe*. Lutz had successfully negotiated with the Hungarian authorities and had been promised that the letters would save the Jews from deportation pending departure.

The formalities dragged on but the Germans had, despite everything, reluctantly granted approval for the emigration. Technical preparations for the journey were underway at both the Swedish and Swiss legations. To Adolf Eichmann, all this was insanity. He could not understand why Veesenmayer did not put his foot down.

From his barbed-wire-ringed office in the Hotel Majestic, Eichmann wrote a furious letter to the R.S.H.A. in Berlin, not so subtly directed at his own legation based at Úri utca behind the Royal Palace. Eichmann criticised his compatriot's yielding on this position. He explained, not without some sharpness, that he felt it was high time to clarify that the emigrations that Sweden and Switzerland demanded would not take place until the rest of the Jewish deportations had resumed. Eichmann pointed out that the Germans had the ability to meet force with force. No emigrations could happen unless Veesenmayer and his colleagues issued German transit visas to the travellers.

While for Eichmann the German legation's relatively weak reactions were a disappointment, at the neutral legations they had fostered a feeling of possibility. In a manoeuvre as smart as it was bold, Carl Lutz now tried to increase the number of Jews with Palestine certificates from 8,000 to 40,000. The idea came from his new colleagues at the Jewish Agency. Lutz simply claimed that an embarrassing typographical error had occurred. The documents stated that the Swiss had applied for exit visas for 8,000 individuals, Lutz explained, but this actually referred to 8,000 families.

This was a significantly more audacious move than the incremental increases of the Swedish repatriation list. The ploy was not successful, but it demonstrated that Carl Lutz was a creative man, very much to Raoul Wallenberg's taste. He was almost twenty years older than Raoul but, according to Per Anger, the two of them got to know each other relatively quickly and thereafter had contact almost daily.

Creativity was sorely needed. There was no opportunity to rest and, in the aftermath of Eichmann's outburst, the Germans adopted a more aggressive tone. On Thursday, July 27, Per Anger sent a telegram to Stockholm warning that he had heard the Germans were planning to drive a hard bargain over the emigrations to Sweden and Palestine. The Germans' price for letting the Swedish- and Swiss-protected Jews go was that the Hungarians resume the deportations so that the remainder of Budapest's 200,000 Jews could be transported to Auschwitz. As a despondent Raoul Wallenberg wrote in his report a few days later, "[w]ith this, the question of transports home will have to be tabled for now".

The Swedish diplomats in Berlin had been engaged to help their colleagues in Budapest drive through the transit visas. They were also to taste the hardened German attitude. The deputy at the Swedish legation in Berlin visited Eberhard von Thadden, the specialist on Jewish Affairs at the Auswärtiges

Amt, or Foreign Ministry. Von Thadden had been on location in Budapest at the end of May and admired the mass deportations. Now he did not conceal his aversion for the Swedish requests for exemption. He was particularly critical of the strange Swedish documents that he heard were in circulation among Jews in Budapest: "some peculiar certificates from the Swedish legation in Budapest" which signified "that they 'very likely' were Swedish citizens" von Thadden scoffed, according to the Swedish Berlin legation's telegram on the matter.

It was evident that the credibility of the Swedish legation in Budapest was suffering as a result of the profusion of protective documents that they were issuing in ever greater numbers. Recently a kind of collective passport designed to expedite the bureaucracy involved in the journey home had been added to the existing panoply of paperwork. Instead of individual passports, the emigrants were given a certificate stating that they were named on a collective passport, and were therefore under Swedish protection. Perhaps this initiative was a step too far, because before long the Hungarian Authority for Foreigners refused to accept these odd Swedish quasi-documents. Raoul Wallenberg was informed that only an individual Swedish "protective passport", with a photograph and signatures, would be enough to exempt a Jew from having to wear the yellow star.

The Hungarian authorities were actually asking for official Swedish passports, but the Swedes in Budapest did not have the diplomatic authority to issue these to anyone other than Swedish citizens. What was needed was a new kind of Swedish passport that was not in fact a passport. Luckily, the new legation secretary Raoul Wallenberg was richly endowed with both imagination and artistic flair.

The challenge was to find a way of operating with more daring and wit, but without unnecessarily challenging existing regulations and thereby undermining Swedish diplomatic credibility. Raoul Wallenberg already understood that these were the rules of the game. But any lingering doubts he may have had were dispelled once he had managed to uncover the Germans' bluff over the postcards.

It was a brilliant move. Raoul had heard that the German legation's Jewish affairs specialist, Grell, had made public assurances that the deported Jews were well treated during their labour in Germany. As proof of this, Grell had mentioned that the deportees enjoyed free postage and could write to their relatives. A few postcards from the deportees had in fact arrived. But Raoul Wallenberg decided to examine this claim and so conducted his own investigation. Around 400,000 Jews had been deported during the period May 15–July 12, but Raoul's calculations showed that the Hungarian mail service had only delivered around 14,000 postcards. It therefore seemed that only some 3 per cent of the victims had cared enough to write to their concerned family members and friends. Raoul's conclusion was self-evident. He sent it to the Foreign Ministry in Stockholm: "There must, therefore, be no free postage if one is to believe the official German claim that the majority of the Jews are still alive."

The new addition to the Swedish legation was a clever, clear-sighted and analytic player, not a hesitant diplomat of the docile and gullible variety. This made a difference.

Raoul and his colleagues now worked on producing a new document that would satisfy both the Hungarian and Swedish authorities. They put a great deal of effort into the visual representation of formality. The new passport was a bone-white A4-sized document with blue lettering, in which the official text was placed in four yellow boxes lined with blue – an inverted Swedish flag of sorts. The passports were numbered and labelled "SCHUTZ-PASS". In one of the yellow boxes there was space for a photograph that would then be stamped by the Swedish legation. Next to it there was an official space for the personal details usually recorded in passports, written in German and Hungarian: name, address, birthdate, birthplace, height, hair colour, eye colour. In the two lower areas there was the following text, in German and Hungarian: "The Royal Swedish Legation in Budapest hereby confirms that the person listed above intends to depart for Sweden in accordance with the repatriation process authorised by the Royal Swedish Foreign Ministry. A Collective Passport has been issued to this person. Until his/her departure, this person and his/her residence is under the formal protection of the Royal Swedish Legation." And then some subtle and sly additions: "Expires 14 days after arrival in Sweden," as well as, "Valid only for travel in combination with the Collective Passport. Arrival visa only to be entered into the Collective Passport."

The "cross" of the flag was decorated in its centre with three yellow Swedish crowns, encircled by the country's name, SCHWEDEN (in German) and SVÉDORSZÁG (in Hungarian). In the chaos of Budapest almost no-one had time to puzzle over the fact that not even the name Sweden was written in Swedish in what was claimed to be an official Swedish document. Still fewer noticed that Raoul and his co-workers managed to arrange the crowns of the Swedish national symbol incorrectly. "We were in such a hurry," Per Anger laughingly explained in an interview in 2002. "The three crowns should be . . . two up and one down. And then we put one up and two underneath, like that. Nobody noticed and nobody thought of it."

The passport form was sent over to the Budapest printing company Antiqua Nyomda. According to Per Anger, Raoul Wallenberg printed several thousand such forms straight away. These new protective passports had the same undetermined formal status as the earlier Swedish documents that had no photographs. But they were so convincing in their professional appearance, especially since they now included photographs, stamps and signatures, that they were far superior to any of the rescue documents that had been seen in Budapest up to that point.

Raoul's collaborator at the Swiss legation, Carl Lutz, was inspired. He had encountered the same problems with his protective letters, which were linked to Palestine certificates. Now he improved them, connected them to collective passports, numbered them and declared them comparable to a real Swiss passport.

The Swedish legation's new humanitarian department had ingeniously managed to create a Swedish passport that was not a passport.

Rumour had it that Eichmann and his special command unit were preparing to defy Horthy's order and resume the deportations on August 5, which did not exactly reduce the flood of aid-seeking Jews outside the Swedish legation building. Despite the curfew, large numbers of people were gathered outside the gates by dawn. "It was constantly crowded down on the street and people stood in a long line all the way down to the corner, then we couldn't see any more," the office assistant Margareta Bauer later wrote in her unpublished memoirs.

Raoul Wallenberg's department was growing and even the regular staff at the legation were under pressure. The piles of papers only grew and all the new local staff members and the hopeful applicants made the office crowded. The long working days became especially trying in the summer heat that had hit Budapest. Raoul had to turn on the charm, promising the office assistants Margareta Bauer and Birgit Brulin wage increases from his own budget in return for their extraordinary efforts. The young office workers appreciated this thoughtful gesture. They thought that the new legation secretary was friendly, although very proper, and they were impressed at how effective and insightful he was, how quickly he grasped the overall situation. But didn't he go a little bit too far?

Margareta Bauer and Birgit Brulin rented an apartment at the very top of the brick building that was next to the Swedish legation. It was owned by a sister of János and Béla Zwack, the Jewish brothers who ran Hungary's largest liquor factory, Zwack. When the deportations began, the sister and her family hid in the attic of the building. According to Margareta Bauer, the family lived "in complete isolation, sneaking quietly as mice out into the garden at night for air, otherwise they huddled in a corner of the loft". The brother János had also moved in during the summer, but he had adopted the cellar as the hiding place for himself and his family. This meant that Henrik de Wahl's sister, who happened to be married to János, was down there. On the first floor, however, the grand apartment stood empty, with several rooms and a beautiful oriel window facing the enchanting city view.

It was decided that Raoul's expanding operation would move from the legation building and rent part of the half-empty Zwack villa. Ivan Danielsson even managed to get the Hungarian Foreign Ministry to reclassify the villa as Swedish diplomatic territory, which was a boon both for the legation and the hidden Jewish families. The move was essential: the staff was being doubled every week and by the beginning of August the new humanitarian department had over forty employees. These were all Hungarian Jews who, thanks to Swedish papers, had been freed of their stars, and willingly volunteered their help. Raoul borrowed a dozen or so typewriters, desks and chairs, but could not avoid some costs – such as installing telephones and buying office materials. He knew that he was testing the limits of the Foreign Ministry, which had agreed to cover the basic administration costs, but which perhaps had a different sense of his mission's scope. No American money had yet arrived. "It is unfortunate that those who have been the most interested in my travelling here do not appear to understand the necessity of money. Here there is boundless suffering to try to assuage," Raoul wrote in a report around this time.

Since the Germans had at first delayed and then made unreasonable demands in return for exit visas, the humanitarian department had already begun to redirect its work toward protecting Jews in situ, The main task was to find lodgings for the 649 people on the list. Raoul Wallenberg's thoughts were racing far beyond this number and, even before the Germans adopted a more intransigent stance, he had, via Kálmán Lauer, tried to sound out the Americans about establishing a rescue camp for one thousand people under the protection of the Swedish legation. He had even directed enquiries to the Foreign Ministry.

Raoul was worried about the apathy that he thought he detected in the Budapest Jews, an inability to act that, in his eyes, could only stem from a sense of hopelessness in the face of their fate. "In the Jews, we must combat their feeling of being forgotten," he wrote.

> The simple fact that the Swiss and Swedish legations have received Jews, questioned them and registered them has encouraged them and those who are willing to help. A successful small repatriation mission or the creation of a Red Cross camp or financial assistance would, in my estimation, have the greatest significance, in that one could by these means instil hope in the hearts of one hundred thousand Jews and awaken their temporarily paralysed sense of self-preservation.

As Raoul saw it, the recurring threat of reprisals in the Western Allies' propaganda was also a problem. It created a deadlock, since it was so one-sidedly judgemental and unforgiving. "The Russian propaganda that emphasises magnanimity and a love of peace is considered better. If at least some promises of future aid could be offered to those who now help the Jews, the propaganda would surely do more good," he observed.

*

In reality the current situation was not as bleak as many of Budapest's Jews imagined it to be. The setbacks in the war had weakened the position of the Germans in Hungary. After Horthy's order to end the deportations, the Hungarian gendarmes were no longer as willing to back up Adolf Eichmann and his *Sondereinsatzkommando*. The head of the gendarmerie himself had begun to cooperate with the Jewish Council, and the feared state secretaries at the Ministry of the Interior, László Baky and László Endre, were out of the game after their attempted coup. Soon, even the minister of the interior would be replaced.

The country was gripped by a power struggle. Fairly soon after his intervention against the deportations, Miklós Horthy had sent signals to the German authorities demanding that the Hungarian puppet regime, with Prime Minister Sztójay at the helm, be removed. Hitler's response was immediate and furious. The regent was told that, if he was serious about his betrayal, Hitler would ensure that Hungary ceased to exist as an independent nation. This caused a shaken Horthy to withdraw for the moment, but without completely giving up on his plans.

The atmosphere became tense, expectant. The assigned date for the new deportations, August 5, came and went without any trains leaving. But at this point Prime Minister Sztójay mustered his courage. He promised the Germans that the deportations could resume "within eight to fourteen days", at the latest. After some quibbling, it was decided that August 25 would now be the new day of terror for the Jews of Budapest.

According to the historian Randolph Braham, the date was selected in part with the transit visas for the Swedish- and Swiss-protected Jews in mind. They were due to be ready on August 25 and, by discharging this obligation, the Germans felt they had met the Hungarian demands. It only remained for the Hungarians to live up to their part of the "bargain" and "deliver" the remainder of the Jewish population of Budapest.

After the Nazis' chilling conditions became known, enthusiasm for the travel plan cooled considerably in the Swedish camp – in Stockholm as well as in the Budapest legation. The Foreign Ministry did not want to give up just yet. It was still possible that the transit visas would be issued without special conditions attached. But they also sanctioned the idea of building a camp locally to protect the Jews that were on the list. "The Swedish Red Cross stand ready to assist with staff for organisation," the Foreign Ministry wrote in a cipher telegram to Budapest at the beginning of August.

Budapest happened to be a city filled with abandoned apartments and property, a tragic consequence of June's forced relocation of Jews to yellow-starred houses. When the Swedish legation took up the discussion about safe houses for Jews on the Swedish list, they were well received. According to the report that followed, the Hungarian authorities promised to "find particular, fine houses for our Jews".

Valdemar Langlet, of the Swedish Red Cross, had already taken advantage of such spare residences for various kinds of protected housing. He had placed signs bearing Ivan Danielsson's signature, and stating that the locale was under the protection of the Swedish Red Cross, at hospitals, institutions and ordinary buildings. He handed out these signs in the same frenetic manner that he passed out protective passports emblazoned with the emblem of the Swedish Red Cross. Langlet's enthusiasm was both an inspiration for Raoul Wallenberg and, after a while, a source of anxiety. Per Anger remembers clearly how concerns about Valdemar Langlet's lack of restraint increased, both at the legation and at the Red Cross in Stockholm.

> . . . in the beginning it worked, but when it spread and he started to put signs on far too many houses and so on, he naturally encountered problems. So we told him that he . . . should try to be more restrictive and limit it to specific categories of people, not to go too far . . . But it was very hard for him, I must say. And he did save people's lives, there is no doubt about that. But at the same time he risked the entire operation by allowing it to spill out in the way that he did.

Raoul Wallenberg had a few years of close combat with the Swedish grocery business' bureaucracy behind him. He had led many more or less undisciplined military recruits. The man who had successfully planned a schedule down to the minute for a Home Guard exercise for one thousand men in the centre of Stockholm, did not stand helpless in the face of this new organisational task. There was order in the new offices at Minerva utca and no question of an uncontrolled inflation in the dissemination of the new home-made protective passports.

Raoul wrote strict rules for the processes governing the distribution of the protective passports. Particular application forms had been developed for this purpose, which each person in the queue had to fill out and submit. The purpose of these forms was to prove the applicant's connection to Sweden, whether through family or business association. If it was business, there were several conditions that had to be met: the money they made from their Swedish operations had to represent a demonstrably significant proportion of the Hungarian company's business transactions; the relationship had to have lasted over several years; and the applicant had to have had an important role in the firm. Raoul also introduced a third category for protection, aimed at artists, "theatre agents" and other people working in the arts. This dossier was marked with the letters K.L., which stood for *Kulturleute* (cultural people).

Each case was examined by a panel consisting of four of Raoul Wallenberg's closest colleagues, among them Hugó Wohl, Vilmos Forgács and Pál Hegedűs. Three out of the four had to be in agreement for an application to be approved. In time, when Raoul had extended and refined his bureaucratic construction, the panel's decision would also be scrutinised by additional reviewers and auditors, but he was not at this point yet. Finally, Raoul Wallenberg himself determined the fate of the applicant with his own signature. Only then could the protective passport be handed over to Danielsson for a final stamp and signature.

Raoul Wallenberg had no intention of starting an ill-considered lightning action. His idea of saving lives was based on effective and accurate bureaucracy, at least at this stage. The stringent conditions he was forced to adopt were necessary for credibility, but they also came with certain consequences. To those who read the conditions, it was clear that only the well-to-do in Budapest could be considered for the Swedish protective passports. Therefore Raoul Wallenberg and his colleagues had to contend with the rumour that the Swedish rescue mission was not interested in helping poor Jews.

From the outset, the plan had been for Raoul to return to Sweden after a few weeks to make an initial report to the Americans. This was not to be. At the beginning of August, however, Per Anger travelled home to Stockholm in order to bring his family to safety. During the summer, Budapest had experienced more than one bombing and Per Anger was the only member of staff who had a family. His wife Elena had spent a great deal of time with their three-month-old daughter Birgitta at the Swedish legation's evacuation house on Lake Balaton. But this was not a sustainable solution.

By now, Raoul had told Per Anger so much about his mission that he could ask him to meet with Iver Olsen in Stockholm and update him on the situation. He also gave Anger some points to make at his meeting with the Foreign Ministry. Among other things Raoul wanted to rid the home diplomats of any illusions: the Germans were, and would remain, opposed to the transports to Sweden. This meant that the Swedes would only ever be able to assist a very small number of individuals by these means. If they were to help a much larger number, they would have to focus on arranging local protection, within the limits imposed by available resources. He observed that, "[i]t is also not in Swedish interests to take in too large a number of Jews".

Per Anger was asked to arrange things so that the Foreign Ministry would forward Raoul's Budapest reports to Kálmán Lauer, "as he needs this information to collect additional funds and he is the only one who can manage the money". In the greeting that he sent to Lauer via Anger, Raoul told him emphatically that he urgently needed the money from the Americans in one way or another.

Raoul wrote that he would use the sum made available for the office costs. In addition he wanted to purchase tinned goods, in order to be able to distribute these according to need. It also was not cheap to secure housing for the Jewish families that now were to be placed under Swedish protection: Raoul calculated the cost of housing 2,000 individuals and estimated that he needed about 75,000 Swedish kronor for the whole operation (approximately £115,000 today). "The 'rich' Jews have no money since this has been confiscated," Raoul pointed out.

He asked Lauer to send him one thousand cigarettes, two kilograms of coffee, a couple of soaps and a thousand pages of standard typewriter paper.

Despite the tragic circumstances and the many financial obstacles, it was, by all indications, a healthy and stimulated Raoul who finally added a letter to his mother to Per Anger's collection of documents for the trip home. "I have here experienced perhaps the three or four most interesting weeks of my life. Although there is a tragedy of unimaginable proportions all around us, my days and nights are so filled with work that one can only reflect on this now and then," he began.

Anyone reading the letter could not help but see that Raoul enjoyed the camaraderie at the humanitarian department. His days were so intense and meaningful that he almost forgot about his birthday on August 4.

> My birthday has been very enjoyable because, by a coincidence, I only realised the date that very afternoon and mentioned it to my very capable secretary, Countess Nákó. Two hours later there was a very fine collection on my desk, consisting of a briefcase, diary, ink-well etc.; as well as a bottle of champagne and flowers.

He told his mother that he had now rented a "very beautiful eighteenth-century house on Várhegy (Castle Hill) with the most exquisite furniture, a wonderful little garden and a breathtaking view, and here I sometimes hold official dinner parties".

The stone villa that Raoul wrote to her about had the address Ostrom utca 9–11 and it lay on the north slope of Várhegy. It was undeniably an impressive residence, with chandeliers and stoves in almost all the rooms and marble statues in the garden. Raoul rented the villa from a justice of the court, Aurél Balázs Sr, who was a wealthy man with an important role in Budapest business life. He was the director and Hungarian representative for many foreign corporations in the technical industry, none of them Swedish, however.

Raoul knew this Jewish family through their 25-year-old son, Aurél Balázs Jr, who was known as Relli and belonged to the cosmopolitan circle of young jetsetters that Raoul Wallenberg had acquainted himself with during his business trips to Budapest in 1942 and 1943. Balázs Jr was regarded as a playboy. He was handsome but that's all, his friends would say. Even his father thought him too much of a party boy. Raoul gave him a job as a chauffeur and he was therefore eligible for a protective passport.

The Swedish protection meant that the family could remain in the other building on the property when Raoul moved in.

The Foreign Ministry in Stockholm had called Raoul Wallenberg's assignment "delicate". Even after a few weeks it was clear to everyone in Raoul's immediate surroundings that his work in Budapest would not stop at writing dry evaluations of the situation in the country.

Back in Stockholm, Iver Olsen was notified that not everyone at the Foreign Ministry liked what they saw. He forwarded these impressions to the War Refugee Board's head office, in a letter dated August 10, 1944:

I get the impression indirectly that the Swedish foreign office is somewhat uneasy about Wallenberg's activities in Budapest, and perhaps feels that he has jumped in with too big a splash. They would prefer, of course, to approach the Jewish problem in the finest traditions of European diplomacy, which wouldn't help too much. On the other hand, there is much to be said for moving around quietly in this type of work. In any case, I feel that Wallenberg is working like hell and doing some good, which is the measure.

CHAPTER 12

"Your Relation to Sweden is the Kanthal Company"

The nineteen-year-old Jew Alice Korányi had never heard of a company called Kanthal in the Swedish industrial village of Hallstahammar. She knew neither her father's nor her new father-in-law's foreign affairs well enough. She hardly even knew where Sweden was and she did not, of course, know Wallenberg, the new diplomat at the Swedish Budapest legation. How could she? At the beginning of August 1944 she had already been held captive for several weeks in the Kistarcsa camp on the outskirts of Budapest. Like thousands of her unfortunate co-believers she had been placed there awaiting transport to Auschwitz – as soon as the trains started to roll again.

Alice had black shoulder-length hair and steel-grey eyes and she was living on borrowed time. She had been in Budapest when the Germans invaded in March, staying in a girl's boarding house. She came from the little Hungarian town of Körmend, which lay near the Austrian border. But Alice was from a bourgeois family and her parents had sent their daughter to school in Budapest.

For a while Alice had lived an idyllic student existence in the capital city, with courses in anthropology and archaeology and lively evening conversations about books and classical music. On Sunday, March 19, 1944, all this had changed. The same day that the Germans crossed the Hungarian border, the son of the boarding-house owner went to Alice's room. Neither Alice nor her roommate Adrienne Mátyás was welcome any longer, he said. This was only natural, he said. They were, after all, Jews.

In March, Alice was still unmarried and her last name was Breuer. She was thrown out onto the street and she could only think of trying to return to the little town of Körmend, to her mother, father and younger sister Ibi. This was no simple task in the spring of 1944, not for a young Jewish woman who now had to wear a large yellow star on her coat pocket and who had lost the right to use public transport. But in the end she managed, only to discover that her family was now interned in one of the many ghettos in the Hungarian countryside, in preparation for the mass deportations. Alice moved in there, with her mother, father and little sister. And awaited their shared fate.

Alice Breuer's sudden trip home made her boyfriend Erwin Korányi desperate. He saw the danger and did not lack for initiative. He thought for a while and then stole some letterheaded paper and stamps. With the help of these he created a fake official letter from the university in Budapest to the ghetto commandant in Körmend. The letter exhorted the "medical student" Alice Breuer to report to the university chancellor as soon as possible "in the interests of the nation".

Stamps and authoritative letterheads made an impression on the often quite uneducated gendarmes. Alice was given ten days of furlough and returned to the capital. "If we get married, you can stay in Budapest," said Erwin Korányi, and there it was. Ten days later they were man and wife and from the ghetto in Körmend there came a letter and a cake, which her mother Cecil in some extraordinary way had managed to bake and smuggle out. "Take care of my Lici," Cecil wrote to Erwin. "From now on you are responsible for her."

A few days later yet another overfull train left Körmend for Auschwitz. Alice's mother, father and sister Ibi were crowded into one of the cars. They never returned.

The newly married Alice Korányi moved in with Erwin and his parents. They had recently had to leave their beautiful home in Budapest in order to, in Erwin's words, live "in a crowded, run-down hole in a pathetic building" in Pest. This miserable building was marked with a large yellow star on a black background.

One day in July, Alice was waiting at the front entrance of the building at 11 a.m., as she was careful not to disobey the curfew for Jews. Once the clock had struck the appointed time she went out – only to be arrested a minute later. "Too early," the gendarmes said, and it was in this way that Alice ended up in the Kistarca camp, awaiting transport to Auschwitz. Again the situation seemed dark. She suffered abuse as the days went by.

After three weeks a guard came and called out her name. She thought it was because it was her turn to be deported, but outside there were two police officers who said that Alice was a pending Swedish citizen and that she would therefore be taken to the Swedish legation in Budapest. Alice, who had been severely assaulted after the arrest, believed in all seriousness that she had suffered brain damage.

"They said that I was Swedish. I knew nothing of Sweden and I had no idea where my father-in-law, who was an ironmonger, purchased his steel. I was completely bewildered," she later said of the situation.

It was of course Erwin's doing. Erwin's father bought special steel from the Kanthal company in the Swedish village of Hallstahammar. Luckily he had done so for many years, and he had the documents to prove it. Erwin Korányi had made his way to Raoul Wallenberg's office. He had this Swedish connection approved and thereafter received a promise from the legation to help his young wife. He had spoken with Raoul Wallenberg himself and regarded the Swede as "an energetic man, clearly driven by a deep inner force".

The police now brought nineteen-year-old Alice Korányi to the humanitarian department's new offices. There she saw a thin-haired man behind a desk, soft-spoken and cultivated. He offered her some chocolate from a box and said that her husband had been to see him three times already. He explained that from this point forward no-one could do anything to her, since she was under the protection of a neutral country. And then he handed her a certificate on an A4-sized piece of paper. She felt nauseous and dizzy. Sweden, was that in Scandinavia? When she was about to leave, Raoul Wallenberg told her: "Remember, your relation to Sweden is the Kanthal company in Hallstahammar."

Raoul Wallenberg was familiar with Kanthal. He knew the owner, Hans von Kantzow, and had met his son and daughters socially. Von Kantzow had played an important role in the autumn of 1938, when Raoul helped the German-Jewish engineer Erik Philippi to escape to Sweden from a German concentration camp.

With the document in her hand, a dazed Alice staggered out into the street where her young husband Erwin caught up with her. After a much-needed delousing, she again moved in with her in-laws in the shabby hole over in Pest. From that day forward, the whole Korányi family practised the phrase, "the Kanthal company in Hallstahammar". It became their mantra. Each and every one of them gained protection from their connection with this firm.

Soon Alice – just like her husband – was in possession of the new Swedish protective passport. It was the first, but not the last, time that Raoul Wallenberg came to their aid.

In August, work in the humanitarian department at Minerva utca began to settle into a routine. Raoul Wallenberg was the hub of the activities. He talked continuously on the telephone, made notes or gave instructions in his fluent but, to his co-workers' ears, almost American-accented German, "a kind of business jargon from the other side of the sea", as Gábor Forgács' brother Pál would describe it. ". . . a language that nonetheless suited him in a funny kind of way, just like the windcheater and the soft felt hat, or later, the grey steel helmet and the sleeping bag."

When Raoul was not writing, he drew. Just as back at the Mid-European Trading Company, his desk became littered with his quick sketches and doodles. "As soon as he spoke on the telephone or listened to a report, when he talked, yes, even when he was thinking, he always drew," his secretary Frau Falk said later.

Many of Raoul's co-workers were also interested in art. If he ever had a moment's peace he liked to chat with them about masterpieces from architectural history. And he often drew small sketches to show what he was thinking. But for the most part he maintained a high tempo. He walked quickly, thought quickly and made quick decisions, without losing his organisational grip. Some found him tense, others interpreted his somewhat serious attitude as an expression of his focus and determination. From the beginning, his colleagues were impressed by his tireless energy and capacity for work.

Raoul Wallenberg had his office further back in the villa, with a large desk and his own telephone. In the room outside, there were female typists lined up in a row. These had the task of accepting the applications for protective passports and sorting any telegrams that came through from supposed relatives or business partners in Sweden. A porter ran back and forth between the humanitarian department and the real legation next door, since that was where the telegraph office was.

Some of the typists had been recruited by Raoul from among Valdemar

Langlet's Swedish students. They played an important role when the protective passport processing began in the middle of August because they could read Swedish and thus sort the telegram replies into those where the Swedish association had been confirmed and others where it had not. The applicants who were accepted had to submit two photographs.

Gabriella Kassius, at that time Gabriella Margalit, was one of the Swedish students who, in August 1944, started to work for Raoul Wallenberg. She recalls how they pasted the snapshots into the passports, typed out the name and next attached the replies from Sweden with a paperclip. Raoul then reviewed the documents and signed them. According to Gabriella Kassius, he was very firm and always stressed how important it was that there be no fudging, that it was a matter of life and death. Raoul was anxious lest the staff begin their own rescue activities. He did not want the protective passports to suffer the same loss of credibility as the Red Cross letters. That would ruin things for everyone, he said.

Every evening, Raoul Wallenberg went to Ivan Danielsson in the legation villa with that day's harvest of protective passports in big bundles. He had them stamped and signed, one after the other, without the minister asking so much as a single tricky question.

Sometimes, as in the case of Alice Korányi, there was a need for direct contact with the internment camps so that prisoners with Swedish connections could be pulled out. Raoul Wallenberg soon worked up a set routine for these cases. He wrote a letter of verification confirming that the passport had been issued, made sure that authoritative stamps were placed where they should be, sent the original to the passport ministry and a copy via courier to the commanding officer of the actual camp.

By the beginning of August, Raoul had forty employees and the department was growing continuously. Raoul the skilled administrator had, from the start, divided them up. There were the "reception section, registration section, accounts, archive, correspondence section, as well as the transportation and housing section". This kind of disciplined approach was essential. Raoul had 4,000 applications on his desk and, on average, there were 600 new applications per day. The pressure was so severe that the office ran out of application forms and the applicants had to copy the documents from each other with an old-fashioned hectograph.

The transportation and housing section was also not sitting idle. The Swedish legation had just received a concrete promise about a building down in Pest that was to be emptied in order to house the protected Swedish Jews. "In time, the nearby buildings on the same street will be transformed into Swedish transit camps," Raoul Wallenberg wrote in a report home on August 6, 1944.

The Americans remained considerably more interested in influencing the direction of Raoul Wallenberg's work than the Swedish Foreign Ministry. The War Refugee Board in Washington soon sent additional instructions to Iver Olsen to forward to the newly recruited emissary in Budapest. One of the points raised was that Raoul Wallenberg should seek out cooperation from the Portuguese legation since the U.S. State Department had noted that the Portuguese were covertly acting on behalf of the Jews. In a special telegram signed by Vice Secretary of State Edward Stettinius Jr, Olsen was asked to "express the W.R.B.'s great appreciation for Wallenberg's efforts".

The hope of the War Refugee Board had always been that Raoul Wallenberg would manage to facilitate the departure of large groups of Jews from Hungary. But now Washington gave the green light to Raoul's desire to build a camp in Budapest to protect the Jews. The W.R.B. wrote that they were happy to receive an "estimate of cost of operating suggested experimental camp as well as your views as to the extent to which it might be financed without supplying free foreign exchange to the enemy. Need of protection would appear to be proper basis of selection."

The War Refugee Board still insisted that the main direction of Raoul's work should be to assist the Hungarian Jews in fleeing the country. It was a given that this could require pure "business" negotiations. In the telegram signed by Stettinius, the Americans therefore suggested that Raoul Wallenberg should look up Vilmos Billitz, of the Manfréd Weiss conglomerate.

Billitz was the man who had facilitated the contacts between the Jewish family that owned the Manfréd Weiss conglomerate and Himmler's main business negotiator, the S.S. officer Kurt Becher. That negotiation ended in May with the S.S. taking over Hungary's largest industrial venture, the Manfréd Weiss factories, in exchange for ensuring free passage for some fifty members of the owners' families. Billitz had then helped to organise the flight of the families to Switzerland and Portugal. He still held a position in the Manfréd Weiss operation and was the appointed link to Kurt Becher who, after his success in May, had continued with more of these "business negotiations".

This advice was something that Raoul Wallenberg would soon follow.

An impatient Iver Olsen sat in Stockholm, trying to piece together what he knew of Raoul's work and match it with how he had imagined the rescue mission unfolding. He had difficulty concealing a rising sense of concern over Raoul Wallenberg's clearly bureaucratic bent. Up to this point, he had supplied the young Swede with 10,000 kronor from President Roosevelt's secret funds so that he could save Jews in Budapest. He had informed the Foreign Ministry that more money, another 50,000 kronor, was en route. But Olsen had definitely not imagined that this cash would be spent on a bunch of forms, typists and telephones at the Swedish legation. Finally he called the head of the legal department at the Foreign Ministry, told him what he had heard about the volume of Wallenberg's administration and underscored that the Americans were not prepared to accept the costs for this kind of low-level paperwork.

A few days later, Iver Olsen had lunch with Per Anger, who had come home to Sweden in order to bring his family to safety. A clearer picture began to emerge. Per Anger had promised Raoul he would inform Olsen about the situation. Now he explained to Olsen that it was basically impossible to try to transport the Jews under Swedish protection to Sweden. There were already so many of them. To date, the middle of August, almost 2,000 Hungarian Jews had received Swedish protective documents. There was also the Germans' unpleasant ultimatum to consider. Exit visas for these 2,000 could cost the lives of the remaining 200,000 Hungarian Jews.

Per Anger tried to convince Olsen that the only constructive move in this situation was to try to place as many Jews as possible under Swedish protection in view of the coming deportations, the start date of which was still August 25.

During his time in Stockholm, Per Anger also met the former Hungarian minister to Sweden, Antal Ullein-Reviczky. Ullein-Reviczky had resigned from his diplomatic position in Sweden earlier that spring in protest against the German invasion and the new puppet regime in Hungary. In his meeting with Per Anger, Ullein-Reviczky said that he, personally, only saw one way to salvation for Hungary. And it was a route they needed to follow urgently. As Ullein-Reviczky saw it, the time had come for Horthy to depose the puppet government and form his own military government, which could enter into peace negotiations.

Ullein-Reviczky had written a letter to his friend, the regent's son, Miklós Horthy Jr, and had asked him to convince his father to follow this advice. Now Ullein-Reviczky wondered if Per Anger was willing to bring the letter back to Budapest and deliver it personally. "I did so, with the blessing of the Foreign Ministry," Per Anger remembered later.

On August 21, Per Anger was to return to Budapest after his holiday. He had managed to drum up reinforcements from the Foreign Ministry and therefore was accompanied by two newly appointed colleagues, the clerk Göte Carlsson and the attaché Lars Berg. Berg was only twenty-six years old, but had several years of foreign ministry experience behind him and had already "smelled the gunpowder" at the legation in Berlin.

The new recruits would help out at the so-called protective division in Budapest. Sweden was now a designated protective authority for seven countries in Hungary – warring parties that had appointed neutral Sweden to protect their interests. As early as the summer of 1941, the Swedish legation in Budapest had, for example, assumed the protection of Soviet interests in Hungary. This meant, in practical terms, that the Swedes retained all property that had belonged to the Soviet diplomatic representatives, including the silver cutlery, and that Sweden would look out for the Soviet Union's local interests. Providing protective services for seven countries was not a negligible task, so Berg and Carlsson were welcome additions.

Even the Swedish Red Cross took the opportunity to send some reinforcements with Per Anger. Valdemar Langlet would henceforth receive help from the Swedish Red Cross's great poster figure, Asta Nilsson. She was already well known among the Hungarians, since she had been praised for her rescue work with Hungarian children during the Great War.

The new American funds took their time to arrive, which created problems for Raoul Wallenberg. He was still managing on the initial 10,000 kronor that he had received when he departed for Budapest, but it would not last much longer. For a while, Kálmán Lauer believed the delay to be due to logistical problems in transferring the money to Raoul in Budapest, that the Americans wanted to see a solution first. Since the thought had been that the Foreign Ministry should be kept out of the financial transactions, the task of organising the transfer had fallen to Lauer. He had a number of creative suggestions. One idea was to turn to Marcus Ehrenpreis, who could potentially funnel the American sums to Raoul through Swedish Red Cross channels. In such a case, Lauer suggested, secret transfers could be sent in coded texts via the Mid-European Trading Company's representative in Budapest, Josef von Deák.

But the problem remained theoretical since the money was still not forthcoming. It was highly unusual for such a range of slippery and circuitous financial transactions to occur at this senior diplomatic level. At first Lauer heard that everything was completed, and that the Americans were going to be paying out 50,000 kronor to him personally on August 22, which he could forward to Raoul in Budapest. But the following day, Olsen refused to perform the transfer, in protest against the fact that he had not received any reports about the work in Budapest from Raoul Wallenberg himself.

Kálmán Lauer, who was not exactly phlegmatic by nature, grew furious and wrote a seething letter to Olsen. He explained that Raoul Wallenberg was toiling away to help people, often sixteen to seventeen hours a day, and that he did not have time to spend writing separate reports to Olsen. If the Foreign Ministry did not forward the reports that Wallenberg was writing, it was hardly Raoul's fault. "If you lack confidence in Mr Wallenberg, it would definitely be better for you to let me know so that he may conclude his work in Budapest and return," Lauer wrote. "You must understand that Mr Wallenberg is not only spending time and effort on helping the suffering, he is also, in certain circumstances, risking his life. Personally I feel a moral responsibility for this mission and I therefore feel very strongly that Mr Wallenberg should not continue his work in Budapest if he does not enjoy your trust and your assistance."

The letter received a good response. Only a day or so later, Iver Olsen transferred the 50,000 kronor to Lauer, who in turn deposited them into Raoul Wallenberg's personal account in Stockholms Enskilda Bank. But Iver Olson, who was fairly agitated, then contacted the Foreign Ministry and asked that, in future, Lauer should not be involved in the handling of the

Hungary money. He pressed for another solution, one that kept the Foreign Ministry out of the actual transfers but formalised the processes around them.

It ended with Raoul being asked to open a separate account for the American Hungary money, "Raoul Wallenberg's Special Account". Olsen would deposit the money there himself, after which S.E.B. would send a confirmation to the Foreign Ministry.

A month later this account held close to 250,000 kronor (almost £375,000 today). Just as with the rest of the W.R.B.'s programmes, the majority of the money came from the American Jewish Joint Distribution Committee, or Joint. According to Iver Olsen, Joint eventually went so far as to open their own account at S.E.B., from which Olsen could withdraw funds whenever Raoul needed it.

It is clear from Kálmán Lauer's letters to Raoul at this time that he was worried about the safety of his colleague. He reminded Raoul that there were plenty of untrustworthy people in Hungary and that he had to be careful when handling money. There was the risk that he could encounter provocations by spies, Lauer warned. And on no account was Raoul to use the American money in a way that benefited the Nazis. The Americans had made this very clear. "You must therefore be very careful before you throw yourself into anything, as a diplomat's word cannot be compared to that of a businessman," Lauer wrote.

Kálmán Lauer told Raoul that his telephone was ringing non-stop and that he had made enemies out of a great many people in Stockholm since he did not want to hand out Raoul's address to those wishing to speak to him about personal affairs. That did not prevent him from filling his own letters with favours he asked of Raoul on behalf of certain Jews in Budapest. Some were Lauer's personal friends and relatives, others he forwarded for someone else. He strongly endorsed a list of fifty names, for example, the closest friends of the Hungarian exiled politician Vilmos Böhm, who were all to be regarded as "people of the future".

Long before Raoul Wallenberg arrived in Budapest, the possibility of receiving American financial aid for rescue missions had been mentioned in the telegram exchanges between Stockholm and Budapest. Nobody talked more about the subject than was strictly necessary, but most people soon realised that a great deal of money was streaming in from the U.S.A. to the coffers that Raoul Wallenberg controlled. But the fact that the new legation secretary was also acting on behalf of the American government was something that even the legation deputy Per Anger claimed not to have realised. It is possible that Ivan Danielsson was better informed. He had orders from Stockholm to give Raoul Wallenberg a free hand, and he must have had enough insight to realise why the Foreign Ministry called Raoul's mission "special" and "extremely delicate".

In the information vacuum created around Raoul Wallenberg's mission, there was fertile ground for misunderstandings and irritation. Raoul took the steps that the Americans expected, but to those who did not have a clear picture, his aggressive actions began to feel provocative. After only a month he could write back to Stockholm and talk about his private audience with Miklós Horthy (probably the son), as well as his private meeting with Jaross, the minister of the interior. Horthy had demanded an anonymous written proposal for security measures, and the minister of the interior had confirmed the promise of certain houses for Jews under Swedish protection, Raoul Wallenberg reported. Simply having these kinds of contacts broke with the traditional diplomatic hierarchy at the legation.

It was also Raoul Wallenberg who was the driving force behind the collective statement of protest against the planned deportations of Jews that the diplomatic authorities of the neutral states and the papal nuncio managed to muster in August 1944. It was signed by Sweden, Switzerland, Spain, Portugal and the papal office, and in it the nations demanded that the Hungarian government definitively end "these actions which in the name of decency and for humanitarian reasons should never have been undertaken". Ivan Danielsson and the papal nuncio delivered the protest, but one does not have to read very far to sense Raoul Wallenberg's pen behind the lively formulations.

> The undersigned accredited representatives for the neutral powers in Budapest have to their embarrassed astonishment learned that there is an intention to resume the deportation of the Hungarian Jews. We have also learned – and this from a more secure source – what the consequences of the deportations are in the most cases, even if they are camouflaged under the name of "international labour".

*

Raoul Wallenberg was starting to settle in. But the time of political surprises was not yet over.

As promised, Per Anger brought the letter from Ullein-Reviczky to Miklós Horthy Jr. It fell on fertile ground. Ever since the beginning of July, his father had been planning to implement just such changes and secretly had an alternative prime minister in the wings. He had let the politically inexperienced but loyal General Géza Lakatos believe that he wanted to see him installed as prime minister. Now both Lakatos and Horthy were biding their time.

On August 23, a possibility presented itself. The neighbouring country of Romania's Nazi-friendly dictator was overthrown and the new government declared war on Germany. This in turn opened up space for political action in Hungary. "It gave me a much longed-for possibility to act," Horthy wrote in his memoirs.

The following day, Horthy demanded that the puppet government step down and called in Lakatos. It happened to be the same day as the Allied troops rolled into Paris and this time the weakened Germans in Budapest chose not to fight. On August 29, a new "unpolitical" Hungarian government was sworn in, a government that was half military, half officials. As soon as Lakatos had been appointed prime minister, the new government put a stop to all plans to resume the deportations. The German legation forwarded the demand to the head of the S.S., Heinrich Himmler, for an official German response.

Now a kind of political theatre began. The new government of supposedly obedient Hungary spoke with a double tongue. On the one hand, it tried to assuage German ears with propagandistic declarations about the Hungarian willingness to wage war; on the other, it was putting out feelers about the possibilities of an armistice, beginning with the Western Allies.

In Germany, Heinrich Himmler was becoming increasingly influential. The Hungarian demand for a continued postponement of the deportations landed on the S.S. leader's desk in a drastically altered strategic situation. It was clear to Himmler that the Germans could not afford to lose yet another ally after Romania. It was also the case that Himmler himself was playing double at this point of the war. In secret, he was trying to achieve an armistice with the Western powers. His attitude toward the "Jewish question" had also changed. Only a week or so earlier, he had sent his favourite emissary, Kurt Becher, to a bridge at the Swiss border for "business" negotiations with a representative for Joint. Becher had dusted off the old idea of an exchange in return for 10,000 trucks, in this case for all the Hungarian Jews. The negotiations had been fruitless thus far, Himmler had just been informed, but Becher made a gesture of goodwill and put a couple of hundred Hungarian Jews from Bergen-Belsen concentration camp on a train to Switzerland.

For Himmler, back in Berlin, these kinds of negotiation strategies were becoming more and more appealing. He had realised that in certain circumstances, the Nazis could have more use for living Jews than for dead ones. Once more faced with the Hungarians' demands, he decided in this case to accede to their wishes and personally informed the German representation in Budapest that the deportations would now be postponed. The German minister Edmund Veesenmayer was so shocked by this message that he asked Himmler to repeat it.

"Himmler's order appears to indicate that in some high S.S. circles, the fanatic effort to exterminate all Jews in Europe fell into second place behind the prospect of financial profit. The hypocrisy of 'mercy' and 'rescuing', the elements of which had been present earlier, now became more prominent. Human trade had undeniably come to form an essential part of what the S.S. expected to achieve through implementation of the *Endlösung*," writes the Hungarian historian Szabólcs Szita in his analysis of these events.

As far as Adolf Eichmann was concerned, Himmler's decision was the last straw. He had had to watch as Kurt Becher and his negotiations on the side were afforded the recognition his own efforts had been denied. Now Eichmann's central mission had been as good as negated – by Himmler himself. Eichmann felt humiliated. He informed Veesenmayer that, in the current situation, he felt superfluous and demanded to be reassigned. Almost immediately, Eichmann and several of his closest men from Budapest were shifted to the Hungarian–Romanian border, with orders to evacuate the German population in the area.

With Eichmann gone, the threat of the deportations lifted. All at once the future looked brighter for the Hungarian Jews who, at this point, were limited to the roughly 200,000 still residing in Budapest. Towards the end of August, these Budapest Jews were either crowded together in "star houses", interned in camps, placed under international protection by, above all, the Swedish and Swiss legations, or drafted into Jewish labour units. If they were not in hiding.

There was still a curfew in place for Jews for the majority of the day, as well as the requirement to wear the yellow star. The Jews were still barred from all public life and had lost their civic rights. But at this time, even the smallest symbolic act, the first sign of relief, felt like manna from heaven. When the new minister of the interior decided to release a couple of hundred Jews from the camp in Kistarcsa there was jubilation.

Who had the energy to think too much about the fact that the new ministers were talking about forcing all the Jews in Budapest into ghettos outside the city? Or that they wanted to exploit even more Jews in forced labour?

The relief affected the mood of the Hungarian Jews to the extent that the new foreign minister, Árpád Henney, began to grow uncomfortable. In a conversation with Ivan Danielsson in early September, Henney said that he noted that the Hungarian Jews had become more confident and bolder in their appearance since the situation had improved. According to Henney this was unfortunate since, as he put it, the trustworthiness of the Jews was still "doubtful". This meant that the government would be forced to "retain a very strict control over them".

The Lakatos government may have dropped the murder plans, but Hungarian politics still rested on a horrifyingly solid anti-Semitic foundation. For Ivan Danielsson, the meeting with Henney was nonetheless positive. He had recently received word that the new government was planning to respect the Swedish government's protective actions. The protective passports were sufficient for a Hungarian Jew to be regarded as a Swedish citizen and be released from internment camps and the requirement to wear the yellow star. The provision of housing was taking a long time, but now the foreign minister promised that secure accommodation would be found for the Swedish Jews as they awaited their journey to Sweden. Although he added that he presumed the Swedish Jews could also contribute to the forced-labour plans.

The need for the houses was urgent. Raoul Wallenberg's humanitarian department was now handling almost 9,000 applications for protective passports.

Vilmos Forgács was one of the protected Hungarian Jews who was working at Minerva utca and helping Raoul Wallenberg's swelling bureaucracy. He was a part of the small group of four or five people who kept the wheels turning under the direction of Hugó Wohl. Wallenberg himself was often out and about, visiting ministries and other legations or meeting resistance fighters. He also spent a great deal of time and money on networking. "A substantial portion of the expenses so far have consisted of dinners and lunches for various influential officials, especially officials responsible for the Jewish question. No money has been used for bribes, but a certain number of gifts of sardines have been distributed," Raoul wrote in an account to Iver Olsen on September 12.

Vilmos Forgács had a strong connection to Sweden and in June had received a temporary Swedish passport from Per Anger, both for himself and his family. He had only one problem. His eldest son, eighteen-year-old Gábor Forgács, had been forced into a Jewish labour unit in a coal mine in western Hungary. Since May he had been compelled to engage in the kind of work that, for several years, had been the anti-Semitic alternative to military service for Jewish men. Vilmos did not know exact details about his son's experience, but he knew that Per Anger had sent a lawyer to provide Gábor with a temporary Swedish passport. And yet his son was still there.

Gábor Forgács did not have an easy existence. Every day he and the other two thousand forced labourers were roused at 4 a.m., forced to walk seven kilometres to the mine, work for ten hours and then make the same trip back to the barracks again. He had lost fifteen kilogrammes, even though he was given two cooked meals a day. But Gábor had many good friends in the same predicament and he did not feel that his life was in danger. He had sewn the temporary passport into his jacket, not sure if it was a good idea to show it to his superiors or not. Gábor had learned that Per Anger would soon come to get him, so he let the matter rest until then.

Early on the morning of September 6, half the men in the labour unit were awakened and asked to pack their things. After a ten-kilometre walk from the barracks they found a train waiting for them. They were told that they were going to be relocated to the front in Serbia.

The young Gábor Forgács was put in an open car near the back. When the train passed through Budapest he managed to jump off, luckily without anyone noticing and without hurting himself. In the letter with the passport there was the address for the apartment where his parents were and soon he had found his way there. The next day he was woken up by his father: "There are your clothes, Gábor. Shave and come with me."

They made their way to Raoul Wallenberg's humanitarian department at Minerva utca 1a, where Gábor was brought on board as a messenger boy. His father did not have time to provide him with a more general introduction. Gábor had to sit in a corner of the room, looking at the typists as he waited to be called for his next errand. There the middle-aged Frau Falk walked to and fro in her elegant suits, like a professional executive assistant in a large company. And there was Countess Nákó, Raoul's young and cheerful fixer, in one colourful and flowery outfit after another, which matched her extroverted and exuberant personality. Gábor Forgács noted that Raoul's inner circle – which included his father Vilmos, Hugó Wohl and the lawyer Pál Hegedűs – always turned up freshly shaven and impeccably dressed in pressed shirts, handsome suits and ties.

The overall impression was more business elite than aid organisation, a style that even Raoul Wallenberg was at pains to maintain. Gábor admired the Swedish legation secretary's sporty "button-down" shirts, an American style that he had never seen before. He noted that Raoul often looked serious, that he never arrived smiling at the legation. But from time to time loud laughter from Raoul's office could be heard over the sound of the typewriters. Gábor had the impression that, more than anyone else, Pál Hegedűs and Raoul Wallenberg had connected in a deep and meaningful way.

On rare occasions, the "Miracle" stopped by. Her name was Berber Smit and she was the daughter of Lolle Smit, the head of the Dutch radio manufacturer Philips' subsidiary in Budapest. Since Sweden was the protective power for Holland, Ivan Danielsson had formally placed the Smit family's private residence under Swedish protection in the week after the German invasion in March. At the beginning of June, Lolle Smit left Budapest to look after Philips' interests in Bucharest. But the family remained behind and it was a common occurrence for the Dutch in Budapest to be seen at the Swedish legation. By the beginning of September, Raoul Wallenberg had already asked the young beauty Berber Smit out twice. They would continue to see each other during a large part of the autumn.

"When Berber came to the office the atmosphere changed completely," Gábor Forgács recalls. "She was the kind of woman one never forgets, tall with shining green eyes and a mysterious smile. Her legs, well, they were aesthetically perfect, like a sculpture. I was eighteen years old and had spent several months in a labour camp. I thought she was a miracle."

The father of this miracle was at least as interesting, if in a less apparent way. At this point, Lolle Smit had been an agent for the British Secret Intelligence Service (S.I.S.) for a while, a connection he shared with others among the expat Dutch in Budapest. The recruitment of Lolle Smit was a success for the British: a businessman who travelled a great deal in Europe and had many German friends. A few years later, he was decorated by the British for his efforts on behalf of S.I.S. during the war. But the undercover assignment was not publicly known until 2010, when the intelligence researcher Craig G. McKay brought the entire story to light.

Lolle Smit had left the city when Raoul Wallenberg arrived, and there is no indication that Raoul knew anything about it. But it was impossible for anyone to be involved in the Jewish rescue efforts in Budapest at this time without in one way or another coming into contact with the many tangled webs of the various intelligence services of the warring nations.

American money, contact with the family of a Dutch spy and relatives who exported ball-bearings to the Germans as well as conveying peace feelers to the West – to a well-informed Soviet agent with a conspiratorial mindset and a good ear, the Swedish rescue operation's leader would have looked suspicious. Soon Raoul Wallenberg would also enter into discussions with Himmler's "business negotiator", Kurt Becher. This kind of wheeling and dealing with Nazis about the Jews' fate had already provoked Stalin's wrath.

With the stop in deportations and relief for certain groups of Jews, the situation became somewhat calmer at the Swedish legation. At the same time, everyone was painfully aware that, in Budapest in 1944, almost everything could change in an instant. One day every foreign Jew left in the country was to be interned, the next they were to be transported out of the country. But nothing came of this, other than the new government making good on its threats of forced labour with a general call for all Jews capable of working – in the countryside, at the front or in Budapest's war industry.

Raoul's employees with families now numbered some 250 people, and the department was working round the clock. Part of the administration was forced to move to a building at Tigris utca on the hill behind the castle. But the protective passport application operation remained at Minerva utca 1a, next to the Swedish legation. The stream of applicants never seemed to cease. When it was at its worst, Ivan Danielsson's office assistants Margareta Bauer and Birgit Brulin could hardly make their way up the stairs to their apartment.

In the calmer political situation, there was more room to manoeuvre and this increased the courage and, to a certain extent, the boldness at the humanitarian department. The more careful and diplomatically trained Per Anger was astonished when he came back from his holiday and realised what proportions Raoul's venture had acquired in such a short amount of time. He tried to restrain Raoul, who he felt "pushed on like they do in business when everything is about getting as much as possible". Lars Berg, newly arrived, appreciated Anger's attempts to temper Raoul Wallenberg's eagerness. Berg said later that he had been worried about what it meant for the protection of Swedish interests if "every other person in Budapest had Swedish papers". He also noted that, "with his forcefulness, his intelligence and his persuasiveness, Raoul managed at every opportunity to convince the minister to give his approval for his plans. And then Anger couldn't do anything but relent."

A new rumour was spreading in Budapest that Raoul, despite his title, did not in fact belong to the diplomatic corps. Anger told him that he had to be more careful, but he might as well have been talking to a brick wall. As was so often the case, these admonishing conversations ended with Raoul starting to joke, and then they would laugh together and Raoul would call him "the old diplomat". They decided to adopt these roles. Anger would be the strict, correct official who followed diplomatic regulations, to all outward appearances keeping some distance from the "freelancer" Raoul Wallenberg's more improvisational and audacious rescue work. If things heated up, Raoul could be dismissed as not belonging to the "regular embassy".

But Anger was also impressed by Raoul's level of ambition and how well he had organised his operation – how meticulous his control was over both the budget and the passport bureaucracy. He saw real leadership talent in Raoul and admired his ability to get things done.

The aid operation had grown to an entire industry. Raoul sat in his office like the head of a company, receiving his colleagues, giving instructions and listening to presentations. And it was exactly in this direction that Raoul wanted to take his mission. The ambition was to save as many people as possible. Therefore it was important to have a well-developed organisational capacity and a sure grip on the overall situation. "Time does not allow me to devote myself to single cases when it is a question of life or death for all of Budapest's Jewish population," Raoul Wallenberg said to Per Anger. His closest colleagues were firmly informed that, even among the management, there could be no private rescue missions for relatives or acquaintances, that all those seeking help should be treated in the same manner and follow the same application process.

Raoul was not the kind to stop in the overcrowded stairwell and spend a half hour of his empathy on a sad, abandoned teenage girl. He steeled himself and elbowed his way to his office without a word, where he instead worked on another hundred passports in order to save not only her but everyone who was lined up outside. This single-mindedness could sometimes be perceived as cool, but it also impressed many of his colleagues.

With an ever-growing organisation it was inevitable – despite all the controls – that some less trustworthy individuals managed to find their way in. Rumours started about a black market in Raoul's Swedish protective passports, about falsifications. The Swedish legation prepared them free of charge, but false passports were selling in town for 1,000 pengő and above.

Birgit Brulin did not like what she saw. On September 6 she wrote home and complained to the businessman Lennart Larsson, who had been Raoul Wallenberg's rival in Budapest for many years and had even been seen a great deal at the legation.

> There are many times when Margareta and I feel terribly sad that you are not here condemning what is happening here right now. When you went home it was all child's play compared to what it is

right now. The queues outside the gates are no shorter and the buying and selling continues at much higher rates than before. There are today 120 Jews employed here to manage the work, and there are no words to describe the corruption and protection and bootlegging that goes on . . . And your good friend Berg, who appears to be a good man, has already reacted strongly to the whole thing and can't understand how these things can take place at a Swedish legation. If there is even any use in protesting. At any rate, our nice little colony has now been increased to around 3,000 people.

Hugó Wohl managed to identify some of the individuals who were guilty of the passport falsification. They were sharply dealt with by Raoul Wallenberg and forbidden to come into contact with the legation documents again. Raoul decided to increase security. He appointed a higher command under the direction of Vilmos Forgács, who was tasked with double-checking his colleagues' decisions in the passport applications, according to a meticulous bureaucratic process designed by Raoul. He also tightened the rules. Only people with Swedish business connections with over 2,000 pengő per employee per annum could be considered. Claims of family relationship had to be verified with signed documents. An applicant who did not have a closer association than, for example, an uncle or cousin in Sweden could only claim protection for himself, his spouse and his children.

But the problem with the black-market trades did not go away and Raoul Wallenberg therefore recruited a special security officer, who had the responsibility of informing him of all that he saw and heard regarding passport sales. After a while the black-market activities led to police involvement. Three people were arrested, among them a well-known murderer who was caught with some of the falsified protective passports during a search.

The handling of the protective passports was a difficult balancing act. While zealous control was essential, at the same time there was no point in being counter-productively holier-than-thou when faced with the death-bringing and dishonest ways of the Nazis. Occasionally applicants were handed Stockholm telephone books and asked to close their eyes and point in order to locate the names of their "relatives". According to the author Jenő Lévai, Raoul Wallenberg himself sometimes issued protective passports without applications, including for 105 anti-Nazi Social Democrats who were under political persecution. He stored these protective passports in a safe in case of future need. But these were exceptions; generally Raoul made sure to stay within the rules.

When things heated up around the issue of the falsified protective passports, he immediately received support from Ivan Danielsson. And more than that. One day the minister was confronted by some Hungarian immigration officials, who showed him a fake Swedish document and asked him if the falsified signature at the bottom of the page was his. Ivan Danielsson, realising that he probably held a person's fate in his hands, lied without blinking: "Yes, of course I have signed this."

At the German legation the minister Edmund Veesenmayer became very irritated. On September 15 he complained about the Swedish documentation in a telegram, informing Berlin that the numbers of passports had increased from the known figure of 650 to around 6,000. Ivan Danielsson was severely reprimanded because he "in a conspicuous way allows his protected Jews – those individuals who because of their protected status have removed the Jewish star from their clothing – to be seen in public". Veesenmayer also pointed out that there were stubborn rumours about falsified Swedish documents – that one appeared to be able to obtain citizenship in return for payment at the Swedish legation.

Raoul Wallenberg was well aware that there was a limit to how many protective passports he could get away with distributing. More than once Hungarian officials had forced their way into his office. He had always managed to drive them out again, but who knew what would be next?

They decided to close the passport application office on September 17. The Swedish legation had received about 11,000 applications and had managed to issue 3,500 passports. Now the intake would be stopped, the piles of outstanding applications worked through and the activities at the humanitarian division steered towards providing care and assistance to all Jews under Swedish protection. This included overseeing moving those that had been promised housing into the Swedish safe houses in Pest. In response to a rumour circulating about an impending lack of food, Raoul started organising food supplies and set aside an amount worth 65,000 pengő (at most £13,000 today) of the American money to buy tinned goods among other things.

Two months had gone by since Raoul arrived in Budapest and he now had, according to the agreement with the Foreign Ministry, the possibility of concluding his mission and returning home. Raoul appears to have been tempted to do so. Recently, Kálmán Lauer had both called and sent telegrams regarding exciting new possibilities that looked likely to open up for Raoul in Stockholm. Salén was travelling abroad for several months and Lauer was going to assume leadership of both Banan-kompaniet and the tinned goods factory Svenska Globus. This could also mean a new role for Raoul.

Raoul reflected on the assignment that Jacob Wallenberg wanted to give him as part of the Huvudsta project. If he stayed away too long, there was the risk that this opportunity would disappear. He made some rapid calculations and sent a telegram to his business partner informing him that he should be able to depart relatively soon. "Likely coming home 2 weeks at the earliest stop."

At Raoul's urging, Kálmán Lauer contacted Jacob Wallenberg about the Huvudsta project. In fact, Lauer did more than that. He asked Jacob to intervene with the Foreign Ministry in order to expedite Raoul's return, whether it was necessary for the construction plans at Huvudsta or not. Lauer wrote that the Russians were approaching and he considered the return to be necessary for "Raoul's preservation". He explained to Jacob Wallenberg that he felt a moral responsibility for Raoul's trip as, "I convinced him to take on this mission."

Jacob Wallenberg had himself long harboured concerns about Raoul's assignment in Hungary. So much so that he had actually made contact with an S.S. officer close to Himmler that he knew, Walter Schellenberg, and asked him to protect Raoul against the Nazis. Now he complied with Lauer's wishes and spoke with Gösta Engzell, head of the legal division at the Foreign Ministry. Afterwards, Jacob Wallenberg wrote a doubly reassuring response to Lauer. First, there was no rush with the Huvudsta project. Second, Engzell had informed Jacob that Raoul was employed as a legation secretary in Budapest and that, as such, he enjoyed diplomatic immunity.

The war situation worsened week by week for Germany. Hot on Romania's heels, even Bulgaria had stepped into the Soviet camp and declared war on Germany. In addition, only a few weeks later, at the beginning of September, Finland left the alliance with Germany and could, after many months of drawn-out negotiations, sign an armistice with the Soviet Union.

Hungary's strategic importance to Germany was only growing. At the same time Budapest received news that Russian troops were making their way through Hungarian lines of defence and were now marching through northern Transylvania. For Miklós Horthy there was only one solution. Hungary had to take itself out of the war and actively seek negotiations for a ceasefire, primarily with the Western Allies. Russia was, according to Horthy, "a cancer to be excised, a poison to be removed from the system, a vile Mafia run by the scum of society", an opinion shared by the majority of the government and large portions of the Hungarian population.

This was not how the Swedish diplomats saw the matter. They nurtured strictly positive feelings for – even looked forward to – the arrival of the Soviets. They saw them as the longed-for allies of the U.S.A. and Great Britain, as the liberators who would finally come and crush the Nazis.

Still, Miklós Horthy's policy of seeking peace with the United States and Great Britain alone met internal opposition. The new Hungarian government voted against his proposal for negotiations and threatened to resign en masse if he drove it through. When he then sent his own covert emissary to the Western Allies he was rebuffed by them too. No peace agreements without the Russians, was the reply.

Reluctantly, Miklós Horthy decided to send his undercover negotiators to Moscow. This had to take place with the greatest discretion, so that neither the Germans nor the Hungarian government would discover what he was doing. Horthy gathered at the palace in secret a small peace unit of his closest associates. His son, Miklós Horthy Jr, played an important role as the inner circle's link to the various Hungarian opposition groups. These were factions that even Raoul Wallenberg had contact with. In fact, Raoul visited Miklós Horthy Jr at the palace during the days on which the regent embarked on these sensitive dealings.

Hungary had tried to put out feelers for armistice agreements with the West earlier in the war: Albert Szent-Györgyi, the 1937 Nobel Prize recipient for Medicine, had been one of the most important messengers. But, after the German occupation in March, Szent-Györgyi had realised that his life was in danger. He went underground and, invoking his Nobel Prize, had sought protection from the Swedish legation. Disguised by a beard and horn-rimmed glasses, Szent-Györgyi had then been allowed to walk around as "archivist" at the legation's house at Lake Balaton.

Now he was needed again. In the middle of September Horthy sent word to Szent-Györgyi and asked him to travel to Moscow for peace negotiations. But before he could leave, the Germans sensed that something was up, and Szent-Györgyi had to be hidden. This time he was placed in the cipher room at the Swedish legation. Szent-Györgyi was called "Svensson" and was said to be a Swedish businessman from southern Hungary whose house had been bombed. He stayed for two months and was supplied in secret with tea and food by Margareta Bauer and Birgit Brulin.

Raoul Wallenberg was not the only one playing a high-stakes game in the Swedish camp.

The Hungarian military-dominated government wanted, just like Horthy, to arrive at a quick armistice agreement, but had chosen another – to their mind smarter – strategy. They formulated what they believed was an unreasonable demand. They told the Germans that they had only twenty-four hours to send a considerable military reinforcement to Hungary, otherwise Hungary would be forced to seek a ceasefire since the country could no longer be defended. But they did not receive the reaction they had anticipated: the Germans unexpectedly promised to meet the demand immediately.

The German emissary Veesenmayer had long made it known that, for his part, he envisaged the young Hungarian Nazi leader and chairman of the feared Arrow Cross, Ferenc Szálasi, as the new prime minister. Now the Germans saw the Hungarian demand for reinforcements as an excellent opportunity to both strengthen the position of the Arrow Cross party and further their own interests.

On September 20, a German force arrived with express orders to arm the Arrow Cross and have them infiltrate the Hungarian army as a prelude to seizing power. They arrived at almost the same time as the Russian army crossed the Hungarian border.

Only a few weeks earlier, Raoul Wallenberg had determined that his assignment in Budapest was nearing its end. All that remained was to launch the efforts to provide food and housing for the protected Jews, as well as dismantling large parts of the bureaucracy he had created. Then he could head home and transfer the ongoing administration to his trusted colleagues. He wanted to try to leave before the arrival of the Russians so that he could take the faster route back through Germany. But Raoul's American sponsors had other ideas.

On 20 September, the W.R.B. sent additional instructions to Raoul Wallenberg via Olsen in Stockholm. Raoul had received such American messages on several occasions since his arrival in Budapest. These had concerned new possible escape routes into Romania, new names to contact and had also included some nice words of praise, praise that the American government also had the good taste to formulate in a separate letter to the minister of foreign affairs, Christian Günther.

Up to this point the instructions from the W.R.B. had not been particularly disruptive. Raoul Wallenberg had been asked several questions regarding the situation in Hungary and he had been urged to try to agitate for more relief in the political tactics against the Jews. But the new batch was characterised by a different and alarmist sensibility.

The W.R.B. had received reports that the Germans had changed their position again and that new deportations from Hungary were imminent. Both Iver Olsen and Raoul Wallenberg were asked to "convey to appropriate individual German officials through all channels that may be available to you the strongest possible representation against these deportations. You should make clear this government's unflinching determination to see to it that all persons participating in any form whatsoever in these deportations or in any other form of persecution are apprehended and punished." From the American perspective, Raoul's assignment was far from over.

Furthermore, things were not completely peaceful in the capital. September had seen repeated air-raid warnings and bombings. Time and again Raoul and his colleagues were forced to leave their offices and rush down the small hill to the shelter in the cellar of the legation's house. They could end up sitting there some three or four hours. Often the attacks came late at night. Soon they had learned to distinguish the "heavy engine noise of the bombers from the angry buzz of the fighter planes", as Lars Berg later put it.

The air raids interrupted the otherwise relatively mundane pace in Budapest. Once the all-clear was given, life returned to normal. Even in September

1944, Budapest's restaurants opened as usual and, as quickly as the planes disappeared, the murmur of the crowds rose again, accompanied by the ever-present strings.

In the middle of September, Raoul invited his Swedish colleagues at the legation home for dinner. Margareta Bauer and Birgit Brulin were both there that Friday evening. Their scepticism about the extent of his aid operation did not prevent them from enjoying his company. But the apparent life and soul of the party at the legation's numerous private dinners appears to have been Per Anger who, with his humour and his warmth, "made all of us forget our fatigue and our worries".

Berber Smit's name continued to appear in Raoul's diary throughout September and October. Now and then Raoul and the others at the legation also played a game of bridge with the Jewish liquor manufacturer Zwack, on the nights he dared to emerge from his hiding place in the cellar at Minerva utca. But otherwise, evenings simply meant more work and business-related entertaining for Raoul Wallenberg.

"I have arranged some very nice dinners at home for various officials who are important for my operation. A few days ago I had invited a very interesting creature from the higher ranks, namely Himmler's representative. Unfortunately he was delayed by work at the last minute and was unable to come. He is a very entertaining man who, by his own acount, is planning to shoot himself in the near future," Raoul Wallenberg wrote to his mother in a letter dated September 29.

Himmler's representative was Kurt Becher. According to Raoul's diary, they most likely met for the first time a week or so earlier. At least that was when Raoul had noted that he was to meet Becher's associate, the Hungarian Vilmos Billitz, "with Gestapo" one evening.

It was unusual for Raoul Wallenberg to meet with Germans. He spent more of his time trying to influence Hungarian officials. But Obersturmführer Kurt Becher and Raoul Wallenberg appeared to have achieved some kind of a rapport, at least socially. There was only three years between them and they had a great deal in common. Both had a past in the export business and had been involved in selling horses on the continent during the war.

The day after the cancelled dinner, Raoul Wallenberg visited Kurt Becher's office. There he encountered Vilmos Billitz and, most likely, Becher. In an interview with the Swedish historian Bernt Schiller many years later, Kurt Becher related that, in his first meeting with Raoul Wallenberg, he had talked about whether or not a hundred employees from the Manfréd Weiss conglomerate could be brought to Sweden with Swedish protective passports. One can sense Kálmán Lauer and Sven Salén in the background.

Later that autumn they saw each other again. But this time the negotiations took a more businesslike form – they concerned free passage for a few hundred Swedish-protected Jews in exchange for 1,000 Swiss francs per head. There were many of these kinds of "business" deals in the works at this time. During the autumn, a proposal from Veesenmayer reached the Foreign Ministry in Stockholm. It suggested the release of a passenger car containing certain Hungarian Jews in exchange for a shipment of Swedish goods to needy Hungary,

By the beginning of October Raoul had not yet had time to begin preparations for his trip back home, and it began to appear more and more unlikely that he would leave Budapest at all. Joint had just donated even more money to the W.R.B.'s Hungarian mission. When Raoul received an offer to purchase a large shipment of groceries for a good price, all he had to do was send a message via the Foreign Ministry and Iver Olsson deposited 200,000 kronor (almost £3.2 million today) in the special account in Stockholm.

The large infusion of funds was an extra encouragement for Raoul to continue. The problem with the practical issues regarding the transfer of money into a Budapest marked by war and inflation, however, remained. In the end, this was solved by adopting Raoul's own suggestion whereby the Foreign Ministry used Stockholms Enskilda Bank as a conduit to move money to a bank in Switzerland. Raoul Wallenberg could then purchase goods or borrow Hungarian pengő in Budapest, but pay for the whole thing with transfers to Swiss bank accounts that were opened in the seller's or lender's names. It was a scheme that relied on a generous measure of confidence in Raoul Wallenberg and his assurances.

In terms of practical matters, things were coming together for Raoul Wallenberg in his humanitarian work. At the same time, the clamour of suffering was only increasing. The Jewish Council needed assistance in order to buy food and clothing for all Jews in need, and not just those under Swedish protection. A Jewish orphanage had just been bombed and could not afford to rebuild. Many of Raoul's employees, despite their protective documents, had been forced into manual work on the outskirts of the city. Raoul had to drive around in a borrowed maroon Studebaker in order to try to free them.

Winter was approaching, and with it came new difficulties that would demand well-organised responses. The Swedish legation learnt that 18,000 Hungarian Jews were in a labour camp in Austria, with only ragged summer clothing and clogs. They were housed in unheated barracks and would not be able to survive the cold nights that were coming.

Raoul Wallenberg did what he could to try to send warm clothes to those in most need. First he earmarked 35,000 kronor (around £55,000 today) and asked the Foreign Ministry to buy in used clothing and so-called paper vests (warming utility garments constructed from several layers of newsprint). Then he alerted Kálmán Lauer and asked him to solve the administrative issues surrounding the transport to Vienna. "I am very aware of the fact that the matter is impossible, but still we have to try. In my opinion, the lack of clothing in south-eastern Europe will be so great this winter that in this case we have to take on the responsibility for the dispatch of the goods," he wrote to Lauer.

On Tuesday, October 11, 1944, Budapest was still buzzing with rumours that the deportations would soon be resumed. On the streets, one could tell that something was afoot. The presence of German soldiers was suddenly very noticeable. Something important had also occurred. Few knew about it but, in Moscow, Horthy's secret delegates had – after a week of negotiations – just agreed an armistice with Vyacheslav Molotov.

The following day, some couriered mail left the Swedish Budapest legation bound for Stockholm. A dejected Raoul Wallenberg sent a few lines to his mother. He warned her that he believed he would have trouble getting back as soon as he had hoped, but wrote that he still anticipated he would be able to leave before the arrival of the Russians. "If not, I will try to make my way to Sweden through Russia as soon as possible after they march in. I assume that such a journey would take considerable time."

Buda, June 2010

Gábor Forgács has an unusually infectious laugh. It cascades from the car's front seat, where he is playing with his walking stick. We have stopped at a red light not far from Budapest's Hotel Gellért and will soon turn up towards the castle. It is Gábor's wife Kati who is driving. The Budapest traffic is difficult, especially this year as the Danube has risen several metres and men in yellow vests have to pile up sand bags in order to protect the city's quays.

In north-eastern Hungary some 20,000 people are already homeless, Kati tells me. She is worried about her relatives.

Gábor Forgács switches back and forth between 2010 and 1944 in his stories and now his shoulders are jumping again. We all laugh and I am thinking that certain people have a rare ability to make others feel good, regardless of how life has tested them.

Gábor is eighty-two years old and has many years as director of a Hungarian car firm behind him. It is sixty-six years since the morning he jumped from the train heading toward the Southern Front and became one of the employees of Raoul Wallenberg's humanitarian department. It has been sixty-six years since he sat in a corner of the room at Minerva utca and waited for the next trip to get the mail.

I have just been up to take a look at the red-brick house where they worked that autumn. The house is almost impossible to spot behind overgrown vegetation. The Zwack family no longer lives there. After the war, the communist regime confiscated both the liquor factories and the house at Minerva utca, and most of the Zwack siblings left Hungary. János Zwack's son, Péter Zwack, was able to buy the factories back in 1991, but the villa on Gellért Hill is now owned by an American banker. He has retained the small apartments that the Russians created and now several families with children rent them. I glimpsed a few toys on the lawn, but no-one was at home.

Kati takes us on narrow side streets behind Gellért Hill, up towards Várhegy, Castle Hill. We turn onto Tárnok utca, past the house where the papal nuncio, then the 72-year-old Angelo Rotta, had his seat during the last autumn of the war. From what I have understood of post-war scrutiny, Pope Pius XII's attitude toward the Holocaust left a great deal to be desired. But his envoy in Budapest had substantial inner strength. It is probably very much thanks to Angelo Rotta that the Pope, at the eleventh hour, realised that the Christian world could not remain silent before the Nazi genocide. The passionate note Angelo Rotta sent to the Hungarian government in May 1944 was the first protest from the papacy against the deportations of the Jews during the entire war. Pope Pius XII had met even the Nazis' cleansing of Jews from Rome with silence.

Raoul Wallenberg probably came here several times. At least I know that he came more than once during the final siege to a cellar in one of the houses on Tárnok utca. It was here, to Prince Esterházy's palace, that the Swiss moved their offices when the capital city became a battlefield and their minister went home. The palace had a spacious bomb shelter where Ivan Danielsson, Margareta Bauer and several others from the Swedish legation hid during the worst days of the Siege of Budapest.

I try to pick out the correct barred window but there are too many. Many thousands of people hid up here, then in all the underground chambers and tunnels. The whole place is "like a Swiss cheese with the palace on top", I am told.

By the end of the war, these picturesque streets were dominated by bomb craters and horse cadavers. I admire the pastel-coloured houses of today and try to imagine the transformation when Kati turns the corner around Maria Magdalena kyrka and back onto Úri utca, the "Gentlemen's Street". Úri utca is, if possible, even more charming. Almost directly to the right, in the pale pink building numbered 66, is where Edmund Veesenmayer had his headquarters. The German eagle can be seen from far away, because the embassy is actually still there. I realise that the German diplomats worked only a few hundred metres from the medieval building at 15 Úri utca in which Raoul Wallenberg's "social" secretary Erzsébet Nákó lived, the 26-year-old with the colourful dresses.

A relative of Erzsébet's, Gloria von Berg, is waiting outside number 15. She was born after the war but is the spitting image of Raoul's secretary, according to Gábor Forgács.

The summer heat strikes us as we step out of the car. We are to visit the apartment on the left. Today it belongs to Gloria von Berg but in the second half of

1944 Per Anger rented it from Tibor von Berg, Gloria's father. Gloria has heard that Raoul Wallenberg stayed there for a couple of days at the beginning, before the arrangements with the house at Ostrom utca were completed. Otherwise it was Per Anger's intention that the small one-bedroom apartment should be reserved for refugees in need, such as the Nobel Prize-winner Albert Szent-Györgyi when the cipher scrub at the legation was no longer deemed secure.

Erzsébet Nákó lived with her relatives one floor up. She was close to Tibor von Berg. He had previously been married to her sister, before he met Gloria's mother. On his third evening in Budapest Raoul Wallenberg was invited to dinner here, according to his diary.

In the hall there is the rectangular sign that was attached to the outside of the building during the latter part of 1944. It is badly rusted but wonderful in its charming absurdity. On the left there is a Swedish flag and then the text [in bad Swedish]: "DETTA UTRYMMAR STOR ONDER SVENSK SKYDD" ("This plaijs stend undar Sweden protection." [sic])

Gloria von Berg offers us sparkling wine and strawberries. She shows us around and talks about her relatives and antiques with an enthusiasm that surpasses even that of Gábor Forgács. On the table by the Chippendale sofa there is the official housing registry from 1944 with its worn black covers. In it we find Per Anger's name in a sprawling script, and, of course, Erzsébet Nákó. But no Wallenberg. Gloria takes out yet another treasure from her chiffonier, a well-thumbed telephone directory from 1944. We turn the pages eagerly and find most of them: Hugó Wohl, Pál Hegedűs and also Vilmos Forgács at Eszter utca 29, with the telephone number 157 244.

They were all very much there.

On a bureau in the apartment there is a framed and signed photograph of the Crown Prince Gustaf Adolf, father of the current Swedish king. Gustaf Adolf gave it to Gloria's father during a visit to Budapest in the 1930s. Her father's contact with the Swedish court endured, Gloria von Berg tells me.

"When I was little after the war I received packages of used clothing from the royal family in Sweden," she says and her laughter rings out across the table. "I actually fled Hungary in 1956 dressed in a pair of light-brown boots that had belonged to the Swedish royal family!"

*

Gábor Forgács has a thin, greying beard and a striped summer shirt, and now he recalls a strong memory that he has of Gloria's relation, Erzsébet Nákó. It is a scene that took place at the humanitarian department on Minerva utca. As he remembers it, Raoul Wallenberg's inner circle was to have dinner together at the Hotel Gellért. It was at the beginning of October 1944, in the relative calm before the storm: around the time when the Dutch "Miracle" – the graceful Berber Smit – had entered Raoul Wallenberg's life.

Raoul suddenly says that he can't come along to the dinner, that he is busy that evening. When Nákó finds out, she goes ballistic, Gábor Forgács says.

He forms his hands into claws and shows how the jealous and impetuous Nákó grabs hold of Raoul. He raises his voice as he imitates her outburst.

"*Das kannst du mich nicht antun!*" she yelled. You can't do that to me!

Gábor readjusts his facial expression.

"That was when I started to suspect that Raoul Wallenberg had a very special relationship with Berber Smit."

Gloria smiles at the story.

"And Nákó was apparently crazy about Raoul Wallenberg that autumn," she says.

"That is something I have heard before, that she was hopelessly in love with him. She moved to Munich later, after the war, and opened a Hungarian restaurant."

Finally I make contact with one of the families in Zwack's villa. I am told I am welcome to come and look inside. One day I stand there on the parquet floor in what was once the humanitarian department.

The main room has now been converted into rental apartments, but the mouldings on the ceilings are still there, as are the beautiful glass doors with dark wooden frames. Behind them Raoul and his closest associates most likely had their offices, I think, stepping over a toy monkey. Through the arched window frames I see a swing set in the garden.

I walk around the room and try to imagine where Gábor sat waiting and where Nákó had her outburst, then the family says they have to leave.

The past and present swirl in my head. It was here it all took place, before the events of October 15, 1944 turned life in Budapest upside down.

Gábor Forgács died on February 27, 2013.

CHAPTER 13

Savagery

Admiral Miklós Horthy had achieved his goal. A preliminary armistice between Hungary and the Soviet Union had been signed in secrecy in Moscow. Now the only question that remained was when it would take effect, when the sensational news that even Hungary had changed sides in the war would be made public.

The regent knew that the Germans would do anything in their power to stop such an agreement and had therefore asked for a couple of days of respite. The Russians wanted to speed the process up, but Horthy preferred to wait with the proclamation until October 20 in order to be better prepared. In the meantime, he asked the Red Army to call a halt to its attacks. In this way, Hungarian military units would have time to retreat and provide reinforcements in Budapest in case anything should happen.

Horthy had his suspicions and prepared for a tough reaction from Hitler. Yet, as he saw it, this side deal was inevitable. He deemed it impossible for Germany to win the war against the Soviet Union. "If I wished to spare Hungary from the horrors of war on home soil and ensure that the victor should acknowledge Hungary's existence as a state, then this was my absolutely final opportunity," Horthy wrote in his memoirs.

Afterwards, the naïve Horthy would be astonished at how well informed the Germans had been. Perhaps he even played into their hands when he suddenly brought the date forward, most likely in response to hearing about German troop reinforcements assembling around Budapest. On the morning of October 14, Admiral Horthy decided that his announcement could wait no longer. At lunchtime on the following day, a proclamation to the nation was scheduled for broadcast on the radio. But Horthy was always very careful to make sure that everything be done correctly, including informing his alliance partner in advance. He contacted Veesenmayer and summoned him to the palace at 12 a.m. the next day, shortly before the radio broadcast.

The Germans were well prepared. They had been working for weeks to strengthen the Hungarian Nazis' Arrow Cross, in preparation for a counter-action that they had dubbed Operation Panzerfaust. By the time Horthy's invitation arrived, Edmund Veesenmayer had already received his final instructions.

On Sunday, October 15, which, according to those who remember, was a beautiful day, Operation Panzerfaust was set in action. It started in the morning. Admiral Horthy's son, Miklós Horthy Jr, had planned a meeting with some of the Yugoslavian partisans led by the resistance leader, Josip Tito. Tito would shortly march into Belgrade with the Red Army and become a national hero.

The meeting took place at the office of Félix Bornemissza, the Budapest harbour master. He belonged to those among the Hungarian establishment who had fought early on to get Hungary to abandon its collaboration with Germany.

On this particular morning, Bornemissza's office was encircled by S.S. soldiers. They took Miklós Horthy Jr by surprise, assaulted him, rolled him into a rug and drove him to the airport for transportation to Mauthausen concentration camp in Austria.

Back at the palace, his father had called a cabinet meeting at 11 a.m., before the radio broadcast and Veesenmayer's visit. News of his son's capture reached Horthy just before the cabinet meeting, which had to be postponed for half an hour. When Veesenmayer arrived shortly thereafter he was met by the regent's outrage at the kidnapping. Veesenmayer replied with bewilderment, stating that he knew nothing about what Admiral Horthy was telling him. But, he added, if it were true it would, in his estimation, be a justified arrest, as it was known that Horthy Jr had conspired with the enemy.

Admiral Horthy then told him about the Hungarian armistice with the Soviet Union. He had the impression that it was a surprise to Veesenmayer, who grew pale and asked him to wait. But Horthy was adamant. At 1 p.m. he read the proclamation about the coming armistice on the radio, surprising most Hungarian families in the middle of their family Sunday lunch. Scenes of celebration ensued. Cakes were baked and bottles of Tokay opened. Many Jews tore off their yellow stars.

Shortly after lunch, the Swedish legation's Per Anger, Göte Carlsson and Lars Berg found themselves in the midst of chaos at the railway station. With the Russians on their way, the risk of fighting breaking out in Budapest was deemed too great and the legation had decided to call home all women and children from the Swedish families. Their departure would be guarded and the train compartments sealed off from the German soldiers, who were filling the trains to bursting point. Elbows would be needed, as Per Anger and his colleagues knew.

Then a rumour spread along the platform, in increasingly loud voices. "Hungary has capitulated, the war is over. THE WAR IS OVER." The Swedes began to hesitate. Did they dare to send away their families with a German troop transport train under the new circumstances? Per Anger made the difficult decision. He let the women and children go. He would not regret it.

News of the ceasefire was received with joy, even among the employees at the legation, not least because it meant that Raoul Wallenberg and Valdemar Langlet had succeeded in their work. They had saved a substantial number of Budapest's Jews from the Holocaust. Neither of them was, however, present at the station. No-one could later account for Raoul's whereabouts on that dramatic Sunday. The only note in his diary is an untimed meeting with Berber Smit.

The celebration came to a halt only a few hours later. Operation Panzerfaust was in full swing, the Hungarian military was successfully infiltrated and the Arrow Cross armed. They met with no resistance to speak of. Soon German troops had assumed all strategic positions, among them the radio station. During the late afternoon, all the Hungarian broadcasts were interrupted for the second time that day. Now there was a new announcement, an order to resume the war issued by the Arrow Cross leader, Ferenc Szálasi.

Towards evening, the German troops had surrounded the castle and the palace and finally Admiral Horthy was forced to surrender. Early in the morning of October 16, 1944, the 76-year-old regent was apprehended by Veesenmayer. The German said that he wanted to spare Horthy "the pain of witnessing the occupation of the palace". Against the promise that his son's life would be spared if he did so, Horthy signed his abdication and proclaimed Ferenc Szálasi as the new government leader. *"Heil Hitler! Éljen Szálasi!"* the announcer exclaimed on Hungarian radio that evening.

On October 17, Admiral Miklós Horthy left Hungary to spend the remainder of the war under house arrest in Germany. He would never return to his homeland and nor did he see his son again until the Nuremberg trials after the war.

What awaited the Jews of Budapest were for them the worst months of the entire war.

Raoul Wallenberg had come so far in his plans for a return home that he had obtained a visa for travel through Germany, valid October 13–29, 1944. It is not impossible that he sensed something was afoot. A few days before the dramatic Sunday events, he had had a meeting with Horthy's cabinet secretary. At the same time it was clear to all that the Russians would soon be standing on the outskirts of Budapest. Anyone who, like Raoul Wallenberg, was eager to leave the city before this did not have much time.

The days leading up to the Arrow Cross coup had been hectic for Raoul Wallenberg. Many Jews under Swedish protection had been rounded up into new forced labour units and Raoul had had to halt the shutting down of his department and employ new staff in order to free them. In the long run, however, there was no way to avoid the labour camps altogether. Realising this, Raoul negotiated a compromise. Jews under Swedish protection were to be placed in a particular Swedish labour unit with special benefits.

But on the Friday prior to the coup, things heated up for this Swedish labour unit, which was housed in a synagogue at Aréna út in the eastern part of Pest. The unit consisted of around one hundred people and, up to this point, they had been allowed to move about freely and had been treated relatively well. Now they were interned together with more than one thousand Jewish soldiers who had returned from the failed Southern Front. They received no food, had to share a single toilet and were being overseen by guards with bayonets.

Some of those imprisoned there managed to get out and call the Swedish legation. After a while, Raoul Wallenberg turned up. His arrival happened to coincide with an order regarding the temporary rearrangement of the guards. To the thousand-odd Jews who were locked in the synagogue, it appeared as if the guards became frightened and fled at the sight of Raoul when he opened the doors to assess the situation. They felt it was magical.

Of the funds in the well-stocked bank account in Stockholm 150,000 kronor (around £225,000 today) had now been transferred to Raoul's special account in Switzerland. The money was largely used to purchase food. Raoul had established a dedicated section for the purchase of food and medicine, and had managed to recruit the former Swedish consul in Zagreb, Yngve Ekmark, to manage it. In the days before the Arrow Cross coup, Ekmark purchased food for 300,000 Hungarian pengő.

Ekmark was a representative of the Swedish Match firm and had been delayed in Budapest on his way home from Zagreb. He was not the only Swedish businessman who had been called home from war-torn Europe. The Swedish export trade had been very negatively affected by the latest developments; the exports to Germany that had evoked so much criticism from the Allies ceased completely. The diplomats in Budapest who were eagerly awaiting the arrival of the Russians probably drew a sigh of relief when the Svenska Kullagerfabriken halted all exports of ball-bearings to Germany in the middle of October.

Since the course of the war had turned, maintaining good relations with the Soviet Union became a high priority in Swedish political life. The foreign minister Günther now came under severe criticism for the German-friendly tone of the first few years of the war. Swedish newspapers reported the Russian advances in Hungary in a positive manner. Only the "pusztan" (The Pannonian steppe) remained before the Soviet troops reached Budapest, was the optimistic assessment of the Swedish media.

This sudden warmth towards the Soviet Union also left its mark in the Swedish chancellery. Only a few days earlier, 900 Soviet war refugees had secretly been handed over to the Soviet Union from the harbour in Gävle. It was a departure from the earlier Swedish line that "those who wanted to stay here should be allowed to do so".

Raoul Wallenberg had hoped to return soon to the calm of Sweden, but reality was always tripping him up. And if he had been suffering from homesickness before, it must surely have grown stronger on the evening of October 14. His brother-in-law Gunnar Lagergren suddenly contacted him from Berlin in a personal telephone call under official pretences. Raoul's sister Nina Lagergren had given birth to a healthy baby girl, who would be called Nane, after Nina's favourite cousin, Nane de Dardel.

Raoul Wallenberg was far from that idyll. In Budapest the killing had started on the first day after the coup. The Arrow Cross' recruitment wave had attracted a mob of young anti-Semitic hooligans, who were more interested in weapons and blood than political discussion. In truth, Ferenc Szálasi was no devotee of Hitler's "Final Solution". Instead, his anti-Semitic political plan consisted of expelling all Jews from Hungary at the end of the war: until then they could provide forced labour. But the mob had little time for this kind of thinking and no-one can honestly assert that the bloodbath that followed occurred against the will of the new prime minister.

Several thousand Jews were apprehended in the first couple of days. The Arrow Cross dragged many of them down to the banks of the Danube, where they were shot and allowed to fall into the water. Entire labour units were slaughtered and all the star houses were locked. Nobody was allowed to leave the buildings, and the rest of Budapest's Jews were now told they were to be moved there, without exception.

Panic broke out in Raoul Wallenberg's humanitarian department. When Szálasi assumed power, the Swedish labour unit was still interned in the synagogue at Aréna út. This group included Gábor Forgács. By sheer chance, Gábor had been able to escape during the day and find safety, but his father did not know this.

According to witnesses, Raoul Wallenberg wrote out self-produced "leave authorisation" notes for the threatened Swedish unit. He then sent Lars Berg and Hugó Wohl, among others, to the synagogue to save everyone inside with the fake documents. When Berg opened the door and called out for the "Swedes", he also urged the other prisoners to leave.

It was in the nick of time. Those who were there could see ever greater numbers of Arrow Cross and S.S. assembling outside. It was not difficult to imagine what they had in mind.

The Arrow Cross coup had dramatic consequences for Raoul's department. Large numbers of the staff had disappeared and no-one dared to move freely in the city any longer. For his closest associates, including the Wohl and Forgács families, Raoul Wallenberg arranged a temporary refuge in a house belonging to one of Budapest's most prominent dermatologists, Professor Nékám. He led them there early in the morning of October 16 but, after he had seen Arrow Cross men surrounding the house, did not dare leave in his car. Professor Nékám's daughter lent him her bicycle. "The whole first day yours truly had to ride around on a woman's bicycle on the bandit-infested streets in order to finish tying up loose ends. The second day I spent transporting any staff who were in danger to safer hiding places and dragged around food supplies for them in a bag," Raoul Wallenberg wrote in his report to the Foreign Ministry on October 22.

Hugó Wohl and Vilmos Forgács spent their time in hiding planning the next step in the rescue mission. The great interest that the Arrow Cross showed in the "Jewish legation" at Minerva utca meant that it was impossible to continue the operation from there.

It was not long before Adolf Eichmann was back in Budapest. An intoxicated Eichmann is reported to have proclaimed smugly to the Jewish Council that, "as you can see I have returned . . . The Jews in Budapest shall be deported." He then added: "This time on foot. We need our vehicles for other purposes!" That autumn Adolf Eichmann appears to have regarded the world through a veil of cognac, which did not make him any less choleric. But he acted swiftly. The day after his arrival, he had already reached an agreement with the new minister of the interior, Gábor Vajna, about an initial transport of 50,000 Jews who would replace worn-out Russian prisoners of war serving in German industry. The Germans' cynical plan was to have Eichmann continuously demand batches of 50,000 forced labourers until all the Jews were eliminated.

In a public statement later that same day, Gábor Vajna made it clear that the Arrow Cross intended to solve the Jewish question with "the ruthlessness that the Jews deserve", and that he would not differentiate between Jews. There would be no question of exceptions for Jews with foreign protection.

It was a desperate situation that needed to be approached systematically. Raoul Wallenberg first took on the task of saving his staff and their families. He had grown close to them and could not manage his work without them.

Only after this did he turn to help the thousands of Jews under Swedish protection. Some fortuitous coincidences played into his hands. Among the "Swedish" Hungarian Jews there was a book publisher who tipped him off that the 34-year-old minister of external affairs in the Arrow Cross regime, Gábor Kemény, was married to a former employee of his. She was a baroness, two years younger than Raoul Wallenberg, by the name of Elisabeth Kemény-Fuchs.

It is possible that Raoul Wallenberg had encountered the beautiful Baroness Kemény-Fuchs before. But, in any case, he was quick to take advantage of this informal line of contact with the newly appointed minister. In a conversation a week after the coup, Raoul mentioned to Gábor Kemény that his staff was to be excused from the demands both to wear the yellow star and to reside in the star houses, according to earlier agreements. He emphasised that the Swedish legation presumed that this agreement still stood since there had been no formal notification to the contrary.

Apparently Raoul managed to converse with Kemény twice over the first few days, without Ivan Danielsson reacting significantly to the fact that Raoul had gone over his head. Wallenberg was also successful in having his demands met, at least according to the report that was dispatched to Stockholm. The hundreds of employees of the humanitarian department and their families could breathe more easily for the moment.

The next task was to reinstate the exceptions for all of the thousands of Jews who had either already received, or applied for, Swedish protective passports. A new race against the clock ensued. Almost every day there were new draft orders issued by the Arrow Cross authorities and, by October 26, nearly 35,000 Jews had been mobilised for various labour assignments. Almost every day, Raoul Wallenberg issued new diplomatic protest letters to the Hungarian Foreign Ministry, which he signed personally on behalf of the Swedish legation. Sometimes he sent in long lists naming "Swedish" Jews who had been forcibly removed, sometimes he reminded the Ministry more generally about the demand that the Swedish protective passports be respected in the same way as before. Officials at the Ministry had their hands full keeping up with the flood of correspondence.

Under these alarming circumstances, energy and focus mattered more than diplomatic rank. Raoul did not give up, even when the electricity failed and he had to sit at his desk in candlelight. His efforts appeared to yield results. When Ivan Danielsson had his first official meeting with the new foreign minister on October 26, he was told that the Arrow Cross had decided to accept the protective passports and emigration demands of the neutral countries.

But there was still brutal anarchy in the streets and it did not seem as if the government's message to the Swedes had reached the reckless Arrow Cross militia, who preferred to kill first and ask questions later. Something had to be done quickly: both to stop the excessive violence, and to find a way to bind the government more firmly to its promise.

Raoul Wallenberg had earlier asked the Hungarian Foreign Ministry to make an announcement on the radio about respecting the protective passports of the neutral countries. Now he repeated this idea to Baroness Kemény at a meeting towards the end of October. She promised to convince her husband, the foreign minister, in exchange for a kilogramme of meat and seven protective passports for some relatives. The message was sent over the radio twice a day for the next few days.

The new prime minister, Ferenc Szálasi, had not wanted to meet Eichmann's demands of deportations immediately, since he needed to make use of the Jewish forced labourers on the home front first. The majority of the 35,000 Hungarian Jews drafted into forced labour were now put to work digging trenches and building fortifications around Budapest, under the ruthless oversight of the Arrow Cross. They worked under miserable conditions. Many died early on from torture, hunger or exhaustion, and they had to sleep out in the open air.

The fortifications they were to erect were directed at the Soviet troops, whose progress now appeared to have slowed somewhat. In the days after the coup, the Red Army had taken the city of Debrecen in eastern Hungary, but had also suffered considerably greater losses than the Germans. During the period that Soviet troops had spent waiting for the armistice that never was, Hitler had had time to send reinforcements to Hungary.

For now, though, there was peace in the vicinity of Budapest. Too peaceful, according to Joseph Stalin, who was eager to acquire large parts of central Europe before the U.S.A. and Great Britain got there. Stalin felt that the commander of the 2nd Ukrainian Front, General Rodion Malinovsky, was advancing too slowly. On the morning of October 28, therefore, Stalin called his general and ordered an immediate attack on Budapest.

Malinovsky tried to object. His soldiers were exhausted and there was a great risk that they would get stuck in protracted battles along the way if the attack was too hurried. But he did as he was told and, by November 2, 1944, Soviet troops were only fifteen kilometres from the capital. On the streets of Budapest one could hear the faint roar of the artillery. The Jewish labour units were moved closer to the city by Arrow Cross guards, who amused themselves with target practice on the Jewish labourers as they walked across Budapest's bridges.

Many of the 35,000 labourers, those who had not fallen dead into the Danube, were eventually brought to various holding camps, in the first instance Óbuda, the large brick factory in north Budapest. According to Szálasi's agreement with Eichmann, they were to be "loaned out" for six months of labour in the Third Reich. The next large-scale deportation from Hungary was imminent. This time the description of labour in Germany was at least not a euphemism for the gas chambers of Auschwitz. It was not widely known in the field in Hungary but, on November 2, 1944, the gas chambers were used for the last time before they were destroyed on the orders of Himmler.

The Germans could no longer spare any trains for the deportation of the Jewish labourers. So, starting on November 8, the Arrow Cross instead sent 2,000 Jews a day on foot to Hegyeshalom, a town on the border between Hungary and Austria. Eichmann planned to use the men to build fortifications along the border, and the women were to be placed in the German war manufacturing industry. But many never made it that far. Two hundred kilometres on foot in icy November rain, without food or warm clothing and, in many cases, no shoes, amounts to a description of hell. One saw women staggering along in high heels, men without overcoats and, despite the claims of the Arrow Cross, many starving children in torn clothing. The groups were followed by gendarmes and S.S. guards who struck any Jews who started to fall behind with the butts of their rifles. Before long, the road to Hegyeshalom was lined with corpses.

*

The advances made by Soviet troops prompted the Swedes to try to ensure that the victorious Russians were in no doubt about Swedish neutrality.

In the days after the Arrow Cross coup, the Soviet legation in Stockholm received specific information about Sweden's activities in Hungary from the head of the Foreign Ministry's political division. Officials there thought it necessary to make it completely clear to the Soviets that Sweden distanced itself from the Arrow Cross government, and that the Swedish legation in Budapest was dedicated to humanitarian aid work. This position became even more emphatic when Sweden banished all Hungarian diplomats who were loyal to the Arrow Cross regime. Those humiliated in this way included László Vöczköndy who, two months later, became the Arrow Cross' foreign minister. This would not make the situation any easier for those Swedish diplomats who were on the ground in Budapest.

After Germany declared war on the Soviet Union in 1941, and Soviet diplomats left German-allied countries, the task of defending Russian interests had been given over to Sweden. Matters regarding protective power were managed by attaché Lars Berg at the B-division of the legation. He now had eight countries to look after, since even the Finns had left the city on signing their armistice with the Soviet Union. The closer the Russian troops came, the more tasks on behalf of the Soviets were laid on young Berg's shoulders. Among other things, the number of Russian prisoners of war in Hungary increased exponentially.

Lars Berg had moved to the abandoned Finnish legation house. There his B-division shared space with Yngve Ekmark, who managed Raoul Wallenberg's operations regarding purchases of food supplies. Lars Berg now created a special Russian section at his B-division, recruiting a number of Russian-speaking colleagues to translate certificates and signs into Russian and to act as interpreters when the Red Army arrived.

They were a colourful and varied group. One went under the name of Henry Thomsen and claimed to have been born in Norway, but actually came from the Soviet Union. The Russian-born Count Mikhail Tolstoy-Kutuzov was another recruit, a Belgian citizen living in Budapest. He was given responsibility for the prisoner-of-war hospital managed in Pest by the Swedes as part of their responsibilities as protecting power.

Neither Lars Berg nor Ivan Danielsson appear to have thought about the wisdom of allowing Soviet staff into the Swedish legation. It was only after the war that the Swedes would come to suspect that at least one of these men had been an agent for Soviet intelligence.

Raoul Wallenberg had not yet begun to plan for the arrival of the Russians. He had his hands full trying to bring order to the chaos that had erupted among the Jews under Swedish protection after the Arrow Cross coup. The dramatic development had compelled him to drop all the normal rules of diplomatic contact. As second legation secretary, he now began a kind of improvised diplomatic solo performance far above his rank. His persistence eventually opened doors to Arrow Cross connections at the highest level.

He was not alone in continuing these efforts. The Swiss consul Carl Lutz worked hard for his 8,000 protected Jews with Palestine certificates. The two of them collaborated closely and were in almost daily contact: it was imperative that the actions of the neutral countries were coordinated. Despite the radio announcements, it was still relatively unclear what was to become of the Jews protected by neutral powers. And the Arrow Cross mob that drove around on the streets of Budapest meant that no-one could feel safe. According to Per Anger, Wallenberg was often the driving force behind the neutral powers' collective actions.

On Saturday, 30 October, Raoul Wallenberg and Carl Lutz were called to the Hungarian Foreign Ministry. They were then told that the Szálasi government was willing to consider allowing 4,500 Jews with Swedish protective passports and 7,000 Jews with Palestine certificates to leave Hungary. Until their departure, these protected Jews would receive the same special treatment as before. But the conditions for this were twofold: first, that the 11,500 Jews would leave Hungary by 15 November at the latest, and second, that, before this date, the Arrow Cross government hoped that Sweden as well as Switzerland would recognise the new government in Hungary.

The proposal may have appeared promising but it presented far too many problems. Recognition of the Arrow Cross government was a particular issue. Ivan Danielsson sent telegrams and enquiries, but at the Foreign Ministry in Stockholm the reply was unambiguous: Swedish recognition of the Arrow Cross government was out of the question.

Another problem was the allotted number of 4,500 Swedish protective passports, which now appeared as if written in stone in all official German and Hungarian documents. In reality the number of Jews under Swedish protection was far higher than that. By way of a clever doubling of the number series in the Swedish passport register, Raoul's humanitarian division was able to keep to the allowed number while the quantity of those under protection was doubled. In reality there were always two Swedish protective passports with the same number. Carl Lutz and his colleagues at the Swiss "emigration department" had used the same method of employing parallel number series in their protective documents. According to the author Jenő Lévai, by the end of October there were 8,000 Jews under Swedish protection.

Ivan Danielsson was growing increasingly worried about the situation. The indiscriminate attacks on the Jews by the Arrow Cross showed no signs of abating, and frequently even those with Swedish protective passports were targeted. The humanitarian department had so far managed to get more than one thousand Jews back under Swedish protection. In a telegram sent to Stockholm, Danielsson used the word terror and again asked for some kind of superficial acknowledgment of the regime from the Swedish side so that the protected Jews could be brought to Sweden.

After the coup, the humanitarian department had to leave the Zwack family's villa on Minerva utca. The staff had been scattered to the winds and Raoul Wallenberg temporarily used an affiliate in the house on Tigris utca that had been put at his disposal back in September. Now they were regrouping.

Sweden was the protective power for the Netherlands too, and was now invited to take over several floors of a building in Pest, Üllői út 2–4, that had belonged to a Hungarian-Dutch insurance company, but which now stood empty. There Raoul and his staff could spread out over several hundred square metres. Many of them moved their families into the small apartments in the same building. Marianne Vaney, at that time the secretarial assistant Marianne Bach, remembers that two or three families crowded into one apartment. They were arranged around an open courtyard with raised walkways, a gallery-like construction resembling the one that Raoul Wallenberg would meet in the Moscow prison Lefortovo the following year.

The insurance company's elegant executive office was on the second floor, in the corner closest to Kálvin tér (Kalvin Square). It was furnished with a

Persian rug, a large Flemish desk in Renaissance style, a small toilet and shower. Behind a concealed door there was also a large safe. This magnificent room became Raoul Wallenberg's impressive office, giving him a more private workplace than before.

In order to get to Raoul's office, his colleagues had to walk through a larger room that housed Hugó Wohl, Vilmos Forgács and Pál Hegedűs. The Jewish psychoanalyst Ottó Fleischmann, who had found a place as adviser and discussion partner in Raoul's inner circle, also worked there.

The other staff spread over the rest of the available space. Two empty apartments with separate telephone lines were dedicated to Raoul's newly established security service, the "Security Protocol" (*Schützlingsprotokoll*). The organisation had been created by a reserve officer and had the task of following up on reports of Jews under Swedish protection who had disappeared, tracking them down and rescuing them. The name came from the fact that the unit was to write daily "protocols" to Raoul Wallenberg about the incidents, a kind of bookkeeping of crimes. The workers in the Security Protocol could count on support from recently defected anti-Nazi gendarmes on their more risky raids, but armed operations required special permission from Raoul Wallenberg.

Raoul included in the Security Protocol some friends he knew from his time with the Mid-European Trading Company. The brothers András and László Geiger came from a rich Hungarian family in the grocery business and Iván Székely was the son of the owner of a large pharmacy chain. In total, there were almost twenty people in this "attack commando". They worked in shifts and manned the phones round the clock. When there was a report they contacted Raoul Wallenberg, who decided if they were going to set out and, if so, how. They went many times to the Óbuda brick factory in cars with diplomatic signs and Swedish flags. When the death marches began they drove further and further down the road to Hegyeshalom.

Raoul Wallenberg's instructions for the Security Protocol stated that "[t]he members of this division must be in service round the clock. There is no time off. If someone fails he cannot count on much assistance; if he does good work he cannot count on much gratitude."

It was more common that Raoul dispatched his security patrols than that he himself set off on rescue missions, but this did happen. He even took his

Hungarian driving test at the beginning of November, most likely in order to become more mobile. He had two large cars at his disposal, which the owners had lent to him so that they would not be seized: a maroon American Studebaker and a Czech Tatra. A small D.K.W. was also available for errands. At this time the job of chauffeur was shared by the engineer, Vilmos Langfelder, and Tibor Jobbágy, who was called Teddy.

On November 4, 1944, Raoul Wallenberg is said to have undertaken a rescue mission himself. Ignoring the proclamations of the government, the Arrow Cross mob had arrested around one hundred Jews, who were under Swedish protection, and interned them in the Great Synagogue in central Pest. According to Jenő Lévai, Raoul Wallenberg travelled there, walked up to the altar, cited the agreement with the Hungarian government, called out all the Swedish-protected Jews and spirited them away under police escort.

If this is true, it was a busy day. That same morning the wife of one of Raoul's Jewish colleagues had given birth to a baby girl in his bed. When her labour pains started, the stress level at Tigris utca, where the couple was staying, had risen considerably. It was felt to be far too risky for a Jewish woman to try to get to a hospital. Instead, they called for a physician and Raoul Wallenberg opened his home. "She looks like my grandmother," Raoul is said to have exclaimed when the girl was born. When the parents asked him for ideas, Raoul Wallenberg suggested they name the child either Nina or Maria.

The barbarism on the streets of Budapest spoke a plain language. Only the naïve believed that the Arrow Cross government's talk of repatriation and special protection for the Jews from neutral countries was truly the end of the story.

At dinner time on November 7, the lieutenant colonel of the gendarmerie, László Ferenczy, called a meeting with the Jewish Council. Ferenczy had been responsible for the practicalities of the record deportations from Hungary that spring, but had had a change of heart after the political turmoil in July and then approached the Jewish Council as a reformed saviour. Now, after the Arrow Cross coup, the turncoat was back among the Nazis again.

Ferenczy's message to the Jewish Council was insidious. Jews under neutral protection would receive the promised special treatment, but first had to be placed in a particular international ghetto. Before November 15 they would all be moved into starred houses in the vicinity of Szent István park in northern Pest: neighbourhoods where the Swedes and Swiss had already been assigned specific houses.

The Arrow Cross government had counted up all the exceptions and the relocation would, according to their lists, include some 15,000 Jews: 4,500 of them were under Swedish protection; 7,800 under Swiss; 800 under Spanish and Portuguese; and 2,500 were either under the protection of the Vatican or counted as war heroes and had, for that reason, been blessed by Horthy. The Jews who currently lived in the houses in question would be driven from their homes and brought to the collection camp for deportation to Hegyeshalom.

The houses around the Szent István Park were, of course, heaven in comparison to the brick factory in Óbuda. Finding houses for the protected Jews had been high on the humanitarian department's list of priorities since the end of the summer and the amount of lodging received so far had been far from satisfactory. But this shattering piece of news still evoked horror. Other Jews would have to pay a high price for the special treatment of the protected Jews. Who knew when the houses would be emptied next time? The relocation order happened to coincide with the Arrow Cross leader Szálasi's first "delivery" of 50,000 Jews to Eichmann, that is to say, the first death marches to Hegyeshalom. In Budapest in November 1944 no forced relocations of Jews were good news.

But since those who had not moved before November 15 would surely be deported, it was imperative to relocate the protected Jews quickly. Raoul called in one of his colleagues, Rezső Müller, and asked him to create a separate social division in a location closer to the residences, and take charge of the question of distributing the promised housing.

Müller was sworn to secrecy and told that Raoul's rescue operation was financed with American money from the War Refugee Board, and that these funds were also intended for "necessary assistance in the post-war period". Raoul asked his colleague to begin planning a larger aid operation, which would be implemented after the liberation by the Russians. This would start to take shape in the coming weeks and was known by staff as "The Wallenberg Institution for Aid and Reconstruction".

*

The actions of the Arrow Cross were full of contradictions. If what they were suggesting was taken at face value, then 4,500 Swedish-protected Jews, who were currently being relocated to the international ghetto, would leave Hungary for Sweden by November 15 at the latest. Not even the Arrow Cross themselves believed this. The promise of departure appeared to be empty Hungarian rhetoric, since everyone knew that it was ultimately the Germans who determined the issue. Thus far Berlin had granted only 400 transit visas to Jews under Swedish protection.

But it was important to play the game, if only to win time. Raoul Wallenberg in particular was well prepared for this task. He had received superb training in skilful bureaucratic correspondence during his years at the Mid-European Trading Company. He now wrote a diplomatic letter to the Hungarian foreign minister and informed him that the Swedish-protected Jews would begin their homeward journey by train on November 15, exactly as agreed. He was counting on being able to send off around 300 people by train every other day, until all 4,500 had left the country. One could almost see Raoul's sly smile as he added the question: "Is an export licence required for the food rations that will be accompanying them on the journey? The legation is intending to provide the first train with a three-week supply."

In truth there were no available trains to be found. A repeat of the long trudge towards the Austrian border seemed on the cards.

The Spanish and Portuguese diplomatic envoys had decided to leave Hungary. Only Switzerland, Sweden and Turkey remained. The front was now creeping closer to Budapest. German and Hungarian troops were fleeing the Soviet forces and even the Arrow Cross government began to consider plans to move their seat to a more secure area in Western Hungary.

Ivan Danielsson was asked if the Swedish legation would relocate in the event that the Hungarian government was evacuated to another location. He forwarded the query to the Foreign Ministry in Stockholm, who simply urged him to remain in place. It was apparent that the leadership was unable to appreciate fully the conditions in Hungary. "The roar of artillery can be heard. The city is in the process of being surrounded and is likely to fall shortly," the Budapest legation wrote in an alarming message to Stockholm on November 9, 1944.

*

The courier service between Stockholm and Budapest was still working, and occasionally deliveries contained private letters to the employees of the legation. In this way Raoul Wallenberg received a long letter of complaint from his boss in Stockholm, Kálmán Lauer. Lauer was bemoaning his demanding existence.

Lauer grumbled that the promise he had made to manage Banan-kompaniet for Sven Salén meant he did not have time to manage the Mid-European Trading Company's affairs. "You can well imagine that I lie sleepless sometimes thinking about what surprises the morning will bring and from which direction they will come," Lauer wrote in his litany.

This was probably how Raoul Wallenberg felt at the time. But for completely different reasons.

Lauer asked nothing of how things were going for Raoul. He just underlined that he hoped Raoul would soon be able to join him so that they could run the Banankompaniet together. The future looked bright – if only the war would end. Lauer wrote about the impending deliveries of millions of bananas, of Californian fruit and the possibility of a licence to sell Kellogg's cornflakes.

But for this the Banan-kompaniet would need competent people, especially for the canning factory. Could Raoul keep an eye out for "a capable fruit preserve man"? He instructed Raoul that Soor of the Manfréd Weiss conglomerate would very likely be able to recommend "particularly well-suited people" who could be assisted with immigration papers.

It is difficult in hindsight to decipher what Kálmán Lauer meant, especially since the two partners had established a private code. But earlier in the autumn Raoul Wallenberg had negotiated with Kurt Becher for protective passports and emigration visas for one hundred employees with Swedish connections at the Manfréd Weiss conglomerate. Very likely this was yet another attempt by Lauer to recruit workers of the kind that he had referred to as "people of the future". He was not alone in this kind of thinking. Earlier in the autumn, the Foreign Ministry had heard from another source about a proposal to exchange Swedish goods for a trainload of freed Jews. A list of suggested names was attached to the proposal and in the document a Foreign Ministry official had commented that the people in question were "upstanding individuals".

It is likely that Kálmán Lauer was among those who wanted to exploit the desperate situation in Hungary in a macabre process of cherry-picking, in which priority was given to saving those Hungarian Jews who would be assets for Swedish trade, industry and finance. This was in stark contrast to the ethos underpinning Raoul Wallenberg's rescue mission. As Per Anger observed in his book about his time in Budapest, Raoul repeated as a mantra that the humanitarian department did not have time to devote itself to individual cases when life hung in the balance for the Jews of Budapest. A month later Raoul would, with some sharpness, explain this to his partner in a letter.

Otherwise, Lauer's thoughts – like those of everyone at this time – were directed to the east. He told Raoul that he had negotiated with the Russian trade representation in Stockholm and had ordered 1,000 kilos of caviar for Christmas. Apparently, bigger deals were in the works, in which Lauer was hoping for Raoul's involvement. "If you can't get away in time, you must travel through Russia, Moscow, and it would be good if you could undertake some investigations for us there," Lauer wrote, not ruling out the idea that he could join Raoul if the latter was there. He never told Raoul this but, during his discussions with the Russians at the trade representation, Lauer actually mentioned Raoul Wallenberg's rescue mission to save the Hungarian Jews. According to Lauer, the Russians had stated that Raoul Wallenberg "personally as well as his mission enjoyed their greatest sympathies". This was only a partial truth, as events would soon make clear.

Praise from the Americans now rained down on Raoul Wallenberg. The American legation wrote a special letter to the cabinet secretary at the Foreign Ministry and expressed their great appreciation for the Swedish government's humanitarian activities, "and for the ingenuity and courage which Mr Wallenberg has shown in rendering assistance to persecuted Jews".

This praise could not have arrived at a better time. At the Foreign Ministry, there had recently been some grumbling over the unusual financial transactions connected with Raoul's operation. Raoul's first financial statements were not considered to be satisfactory.

Even Iver Olsen had questioned the bookkeeping. In addition, he was irritated that Kálmán Lauer had contacted him yet again to demand another 15,000 kronor on Raoul's behalf. It was a complex matter to manage the transfers of funds from the Americans, via two different countries, to individuals who were more often than not residents of Budapest. Sometimes the recipients' involvement in Raoul Wallenberg's operation could not be revealed. In these cases, an anonymous numbered account was all the Swiss bank had to go on when it was asked to deposit the Swiss francs sent as repayment for the goods or Hungarian pengő that Raoul had borrowed in Budapest.

It was not that the Foreign Ministry doubted the integrity of Raoul's affairs, Engzell emphasised in a letter. But one can surmise from his comments that the arrangement was considered somewhat unorthodox. The entire operation was an anomaly among the Swedish state agencies, but one that the country's leadership had not hesitated to support. The situation was extreme, the solution temporary: so there was not much else to say. Now it was simply a matter of all the parties involved holding out until the Russians arrived and "liberated" Budapest.

On November 13, a total of 27,000 men and women had left Budapest to walk on foot to the border town of Hegyeshalom. They were said to be Hungarian labourers destined for the German war effort, but the description was far from convincing in view of the large numbers of children, old and sick among them. From time to time, patrols from Raoul Wallenberg's Security Protocol arrived and either invoked the protective passports of some of the Jews or distributed new ones. In this way they managed to save some of those who were being deported. Similar raids were conducted by the staff of the Swiss legation's "emigration division".

The sights they encountered horrified even the most hardened members of the Security Protocol. One of the daily reports detailed "[t]he starving, sick, miserable people from twelve-year-old children to 74-year-old women marching without any equipment, ragged and dirty". Others testified to the kilometre-long rows of walking skeletons with swollen legs, and feet that had been rubbed raw in shoes that were falling apart. Many Jews collapsed in the chilly rain and were left dying of starvation and exhaustion in the ditches, or were shot by the gendarmes and S.S. guards when they could not manage to walk any further.

The Swedish and Swiss rescue efforts did not go unnoticed in Berlin. After only a couple of days, rumours of a "great leak" from the marching Jews had reached Joachim von Ribbentrop. He urged Veesenmayer to immediately broach this matter with Szálasi and pointed out the undesirable consequences that the acknowledgement of the protective passports had had. He told Veesenmayer to recommend to Szálasi that he adopt a threatening posture toward the Swiss in particular. Von Ribbentrop added that Szálasi should clearly express the Hungarians' great surprise at this sabotage of the Hungarian and German war efforts, one that did not sit well with their supposed neutrality. Shortly thereafter his colleague Horst Wagner returned with a clear order that the Hungarians were not allowed to accept any protective passports: they only created problems and the neutral nations had neither cooperated with the Hungarians nor acknowledged the new government.

Veesenmayer dutifully sought out Ferenc Szálasi, who complained loudly and said that he was tired of the Swedish, Swiss and papal interventions. Szálasi promised to call a meeting with all involved and make it very clear that he had had enough.

Ivan Danielsson at the Swedish legation had wished for a more peaceful and comfortable life in his old age. Now he could glimpse the flashes from artillery fire on the front line, while at the same time Sweden had slipped into a diplomatic impasse with Hungary that was starting to put the legation at risk. There was a rumour that the Arrow Cross would attack the neutral legations after November 15, as part of their hunt for Jews that had not been relocated to the international ghetto. The Szálasi regime continued to demand political recognition and now the tone was so insistent that, if it had been up to Danielsson, he would have the Swedish government give in. Otherwise the days of the protected Jews were numbered. Sweden could at least offer a little more flowery language about a desire for cooperation, something akin to what the Spaniards had done to alleviate their situation, Danielsson thought.

But the Foreign Ministry in Stockholm was unwavering in its position. Recognition was out of the question, and instead Danielsson was given the order to delay the issue. On November 16, the minister could report home that, officially, 4,500 protected Jews had been relocated to the international ghetto. But he counted up to 15,000 Jews that Sweden had helped to liberate from forced labour or deportations, either through surreptitious interventions or the actions of the Security Protocol.

The following day, the neutral legations were called to a meeting with the

Arrow Cross. The Swedes were now informed that the departure of the 4,500 was entirely due to the development of diplomatic relations. There would be no more protective passports. The Szálasi regime had had enough and the remaining 70,000–100,000 Jews left in Budapest would now be gathered in one big ghetto in the area surrounding the Great Synagogue in central Pest.

During the weekend that followed, the windows of the Swedish legation house on Gyopár utca were shattered when a bomb fell close by. Soon it was clear that the Arrow Cross were not leaving Jews in the protected houses in peace. They had dragged a number of them down into the cellars, beaten them bloody and stolen their belongings. The legation also received additional indications from the Arrow Cross that their patience was definitely at an end. The foreign minister, Gábor Kemény, had an outburst in a private meeting. He said that he was intending very shortly to call Danielsson and explain to him that, if the Swedish government did not recognise the Arrow Cross within a certain time frame, then "all Sweden's protected Jews would . . . be drowned in the Danube".

Ivan Danielsson found this piece of information so alarming that he immediately informed Stockholm. He also asked that the Foreign Ministry should inform Iver Olsen at the American legation. Danielsson pleaded to at least be allowed to tell the Hungarians that the continuing Swedish presence could be viewed as a form of recognition. But the Foreign Ministry was not prepared to let the word "recognition" cross his lips.

The hellish scenes on the road to Hegyeshalom had shaken even the officers in the circles closest to Ferenczy. The gendarme commander Captain Nándor Batizfalvy had fulfilled his duty as one of Ferenczy's officers during the spring deportations. He had adjusted accordingly to his commander's approach to the Jewish Council during the summer and thereafter collaborated somewhat with Raoul Wallenberg. But when, after the October coup, Ferenczy took on the role of Nazi executioner for a second time, Batizfalvy could stand by no longer. Batizfalvy contacted Raoul Wallenberg, told him what he knew about the death marches and offered to assist in the rescue missions of the neutral countries.

On November 22, at 6 p.m., Raoul invited representatives from the Swiss, Spanish and Portuguese legations to Üllői út in order to meet with Batizfalvy.

Since the minutes have been preserved we know that Batizfalvy told them that almost 10,000 Jews had reached the border and been handed over to the Germans. An equal number had perished along the way, according to his estimate, and about 13,000 were still walking. They received at most about three to four bowls of soup on the entire journey. Batizfalvy had been forbidden by his commander Ferenczy to release the Jews with protective passports, but he explained that he was now prepared to disobey this order and at least attempt it. In answer to a direct question from Raoul Wallenberg, Batizfalvy replied that he would also consider distributing food.

The agreement was that two delegates from each legation would arm themselves with typewriters and blank protective passports and leave with Captain Batizfalvy. A shipment of rations would quickly be prepared in collaboration with the International Red Cross and five trucks would leave Budapest that same night with food and medicine for the deported Jews walking along the road.

Raoul Wallenberg took Per Anger in his car, which was driven by one of the tougher members of the Security Protocol, the pharmacist's son, Iván Székely. They followed the trucks, stopping first at the so-called "death ships" along the way. These were two barges on the Danube where the deported Jews spent the night in the rainy and windy November cold. It was known that many voluntarily threw themselves overboard into the icy water to escape more suffering. Others were helped along by their brutal guards.

Trucks halted in the fog, and blankets as well as boxes of food and medicine were unloaded. It was forbidden to help the Jews while they were being deported, but Batizfalvy's authoritative presence did its work. Raoul Wallenberg and Per Anger did their part by bribing the guards with rum and cigarettes. They then dragged tinned goods and medicine over to the Jews and even gave them a few sips of rum. They worked in the company of staff from the International Red Cross and colleagues from the legations of the other neutral countries, above all those from the active Swiss legation. But none of the others sent any of their diplomats.

The convoy of trucks then continued toward Hegyeshalom. Anger and Wallenberg noted that many of the guards that accompanied the death march appeared unmotivated, in particular those who had been recruited from the regular Hungarian army. "I saw, for example, how an elderly woman was supported by a soldier who gave her his arm to lean on. He steadied her and they marched on together, the two of them, he with a rifle on one side and the woman on the other," Per Anger related later.

Raoul Wallenberg was horrified. Eight days on the road. There was no shelter along the way and seldom anything to eat. One by one the Jews on the march died of starvation and related diseases. "On a barge . . . there are around one hundred severely ill individuals without enough to eat, without medicine, without doctors and living under terrible conditions . . . People are so far gone that they are almost forced to an animalistic state," he reported afterwards in an uncensored letter of protest to the Hungarian Ministry of the Interior.

He described how fights had broken out among the crowd as he and Anger tried to distribute small sandwich packets.

In Hegyeshalom, the deported Jews were handed over to Adolf Eichmann's Sondereinsatzkommando. Somewhat unexpectedly, a train was waiting for them. According to the Swiss who were present, it was Dieter Wisliceny, Eichmann's close colleague, who counted the exhausted Jews on the platform.

Per Anger remembers Raoul Wallenberg bringing a register of issued protective passports with him onto the platform. It was fairly large, with black covers. Raoul asked for Jews with Swedish protective passports, consulted his list and sometimes bluffed or sometimes referred to real passports. In this way they managed to extract around one hundred deported Jews whom, with the help of Captain Batizfalvy, they could transport back to Budapest.

Afterwards, Per Anger would reflect on how Raoul Wallenberg was so clearly the right man at the right time in Budapest that autumn of 1944, even though few who had known him before would have thought so.

He was courageous, he had imagination and he always found solutions. In peacetime you often don't notice this kind of person . . . But when it came to a war-time situation, as here in Budapest . . . then these hidden qualities are developed . . . He was a very warm person, but could at the same time be very formal, a cold organiser and negotiator. And then he was an actor. Absolutely. He could transform himself into a very brutal [person]. When he spoke with the Germans he used their language . . . and screamed at them.

*

Captain Batizfalvy would remain a very important contact for Raoul Wallenberg. He was not the only gendarme or military officer who faltered in his loyalty towards the Arrow Cross regime, as a personal protest against the atrocities. And cooperation was not without its risks, either for Batizfalvy or for the Swedish diplomats. There was a thin line between their humanitarian efforts and actions that could be labelled as political resistance.

At this time the previously fragmented and weak Hungarian resistance movement gathered strength under an umbrella organisation called the "Liberation Committee of the National Hungarian Uprising" (Magyar nemzeti felkelés felszabadító bizottsága, or M.N.F.F.B.). The Wallenberg researcher Gellért Kovács has studied the Hungarian resistance movement's contacts with the Swedish legation and established that it is possible to identify many who, in one way or another, had a connection with Raoul Wallenberg.

There was Géza Soós, active in the Hungarian Reformed Church and with a past career in the Foreign Ministry. He had a leading position in the bourgeois branch of the resistance – indeed Raoul Wallenberg met him at a dinner at Per Anger's on one of his very first days in Budapest. Soós was active in a variety of ways. During the spring, he had supplied exiled Hungarians in Stockholm with intelligence, among them the journalist and press attaché Andor Gellért, whom Wallenberg had met before he left.

Both Soós and Gellért had, later that autumn, been involved in the American O.S.S.'s various attempts to smuggle radio transmitters into Hungary. It was an operation coordinated by the O.S.S. staff in Stockholm, including Iver Olsen. In a telegram dated November 1944, the O.S.S. wrote this about Géza Soós:

> He may be contacted only through per [sic] Anger Swedish Legation Budapest. Raoul Wallenberg of the same legation will know if he is not in Budapest. Soos had Swedish signal plan, whole affair was administered by Sweds [sic]. Concerning the signal plan, Nagy, former secretary of the Hungarian legation should contact Captain Thernberg in Stockholm.

This was not innocuous information if it fell into the wrong hands.

Another member of the resistance movement's bourgeois branch was Professor Albert Szent-Györgyi, the Nobel Prize-winner who had been hidden in the cipher room at the Swedish legation. There was also an aristocrat and journalist by the name of Gyula Dessewffy, whom the Germans were hunting and whom Raoul Wallenberg hid in a tower room on the other side of the garden at Ostrom utca for a couple of weeks.

Per Anger and Raoul Wallenberg did not differentiate between the various resistance groups, unaware of the fact that only the uprising's communist branch would be considered acceptable by the approaching Russians.

The resistance fighters also created a military wing with a number of Arrow Cross officers as its core. The idea was to organise an armed uprising to coincide with the arrival of the Russians. But the group was not careful enough and, at a meeting on November 22, the same evening as the neutral legations' convoy of rations and medicine departed for Hegyeshalom, the leading officers were arrested by the Arrow Cross. They were executed a week later.

Responsibility for the military branch now devolved to a captain in the defence unit by the name of Zoltán Mikó, who is said to have been both anti-Nazi and a Hungarian nationalist. Therefore he played a double game. At the same time as Mikó earned the confidence of the Arrow Cross by organising the Hungarian National Guard, he was building up resistance cells within the armed section of the liberation committee. This was not difficult since many in the military had a sceptical attitude towards the new leadership. Among other things, Mikó had been assigned the task of organising a kind of home guard, called the K.I.S.K.A., in all Budapest's districts. Some of these units consisted almost entirely of resistance fighters. It is estimated that Zoltán Mikó had 800 armed resistance fighters ready by the end of November.

A colleague of Zoltán Mikó has described Mikó's close contact with Raoul Wallenberg and his humanitarian division. Mikó arranged for the Swedish houses in Pest to receive deliveries of food items from military supplies. He claimed that it was through Mikó's intervention that the humanitarian department's new offices at Üllői út were supplied with armed guards by the gendarmes. The same colleague also asserted that Mikó transported sensitive documents to and from Raoul Wallenberg's safe. Mikó would therefore have known that, among all the documents about the abuses of the Arrow Cross, Raoul kept Polish emigrants' witness accounts about the Soviet mass murder of Polish officers in Katyn in the spring of 1940. These are claimed to have been found by Soviet soldiers during the siege of Budapest, but this cannot be confirmed. Zoltán Mikó was executed by the Russians in Odessa in 1945.

Staying in Budapest at the end of 1944 was highly dangerous. But now it was only a matter of weeks before the Russians arrived and Raoul's task would be completed. Diplomats at the Swedish legation could not imagine that the Russians would do anything other than applaud the rescue mission and understand the tactics that had been used.

At the same time, a world war continued to rage and more and more names appeared in Raoul Wallenberg's diary and address book that would have made not only the Arrow Cross and the Nazis suspicious, but also the Russians. Raoul did not hesitate to negotiate with the enemy. Quite the opposite, it was an integral part of his audacious strategy. Among his contacts, he now counted both the foreign minister in the Arrow Cross government, the gendarme officer Batizfalvy, Himmler's emissary Kurt Becher and even Adolf Eichmann himself. In his address book, Raoul Wallenberg had no fewer than three telephone numbers noted under the name of Eichmann.

Per Anger has recounted that Raoul both spoke on the telephone with Eichmann and met him in person, something that Anger himself avoided. They agreed in their internal division of labour that Raoul would be the more daring "non-diplomat", who would act off the record.

Relations between Raoul Wallenberg and Adolf Eichmann do not appear to have been particularly cordial. Rezső Kasztner, one of the Zionists at Carl Lutz's "emigration division", witnessed one of Eichmann's many furious outbursts towards the end of November. This time it was over "the abuse of protective passports". The moody Eichmann had screamed that he would hold Carl Lutz and Raoul Wallenberg – "the representative of the Swedish Red Cross" – responsible for their outrageous actions.

Two of Raoul Wallenberg's diplomatic colleagues at the Swedish legation in Budapest, Göte Carlsson and Lars Berg from the B-division, have in interviews and memoirs described how, on Raoul's orders, they arranged a dinner for him and Adolf Eichmann. This is said to have taken place during the latter

PART II: WHAT MAKES AN ACT HEROIC?

half of November 1944. Göte Carlsson remembered this dinner some twenty years later, when he was interviewed for a documentary:

> There were hard-hitting discussions that evening, especially between Wallenberg and Eichmann and I remember very well how Wallenberg – and for that matter all of us – walked up to a window that faced east and where the sky and horizon were completely red from the gunfire of the Russians . . . There in the dark and with a gesture towards the proximity of the Russians, Wallenberg argued with Eichmann for Eichmann to put a stop to these meaningless deportations.

According to Lars Berg, Eichmann ended the discussion after this by saying that he would do everything in his power to thwart Raoul Wallenberg and that Wallenberg's Swedish diplomatic passport would not be any protection if Eichmann felt it necessary to get Wallenberg out of the way. "Accidents can always happen, even to a neutral diplomat," Berg quoted him as saying, and went on: "With these words, Eichmann stood up to leave but not at all in a state of anger. With the unwavering courtesy of a well-mannered German, he bid Raoul goodbye and thanked all of us for the most delightful evening."

Wallenberg experts debate whether it really was Adolf Eichmann that Lars Berg and Göte Carlsson met that evening. By this time Eichmann was severely alcoholic and was almost always intoxicated. His frequent rages were well known and inspired terror. This does not fit well with the description of "the unwavering courtesy of a well-mannered German". Many find it likely that the person in question was instead the more polished Kurt Becher. There is something to be said for this. Raoul Wallenberg had invited him to dinner once before, but Becher had cancelled at the last minute. It is also relevant that Raoul Wallenberg had had some dealings with Becher in November over negotiations to "buy" transit visas to Sweden for 400 Jews with Swedish temporary passports.

Regardless of who confronted Raoul Wallenberg at this particular dinner, the account of what was said fits well with what Eichmann had expressed about the Swedish legation secretary at this time. And things would get worse.

CHAPTER 14

Thirty-one Houses and Ten Thousand Bellies to Fill

The humanitarian department's new offices were located in the hustle and bustle of southern Pest, a lively city environment that was in stark contrast to the lush gardens of the upper-class villas in Buda. It took about fifteen minutes to walk there from the legation at Gyopár utca. To do so one walked down the hill, past the Swedes' B-division at the Finnish legation building, past the outdoor swimming pools of Hotel Gellért and across Szabadság híd (Liberty Bridge), where there were no longer so many romantic couples as before. On the other side of the Danube, one continued past the large market hall until one arrived at Kálvin tér. There, in the corner building on the right-hand side of the square, Raoul Wallenberg and his department were now based.

The offices at Üllői út 2–4 were enormous compared to the brick house on Minerva utca. According to Marianne Vaney, there was also a more sober atmosphere than they had been accustomed to in the offices in Buda. This was not only a result of the increasingly hellish circumstances: the rooms were darker, the interactions less intimate and both of the entrances to the office area were guarded, often by armed gendarmes. In addition, the central heating and hot water failed after a time.

Raoul's aid operation had continued to expand and, with more than 300 employees, was now regarded as an entire industry. The distances within the organisation naturally grew, as did a degree of suspicion and a need for secrecy. The colleagues who could walk into Raoul Wallenberg's office unannounced these days could be counted on the fingers of one hand. What was important now was hard work and a focus on the task at hand, if the employees were to have a chance of keeping up with Raoul Wallenberg's increasingly hectic tempo.

Thirty-one houses in the international ghetto by Szent István park had been made available to the 8,000–9,000 Jews under Swedish protection. They all bore Swedish extra-territorial plaques and were to be regarded as Swedish diplomatic territory. Valdemar and Nina Langlet had received an additional eight houses for the 2,000 protected Jews of the Swedish Red Cross, but these were still far too few for so many people. The Swiss had twice as many houses.

Raoul's associate responsible for social issues, Rezső Müller, had prepared two housing offices for issuing apartments. But then there was everything else that needed to be authorised, in large part also for the Red Cross houses: the security issues, providing food rations, storing food supplies, the common kitchen areas, the house checks, courier service, bookkeeping, the archive, staffing questions, supervision of children, legal issues and then all the technical challenges, such as heating the houses and repairing broken windows.

The humanitarian department opened a new office inside the international ghetto (Tátra utca 6) as well as two branch offices in the already established Swedish house in Pest (Jókai utca 1 and Arany János utca 16). The undertaking was enormous. A whole society, with the population of a small Swedish city, was being built. This feat would also have to be performed under the most difficult circumstances imaginable. The staff grew to more than 350 individuals.

Every house had an appointed house manager and a deputy. They were responsible for implementing all directives from Raoul's head office. They were also to keep detailed records of the residents, so that the Swedes could not be accused of filling their houses with anyone other than the approved protected Jews.

Special inspectors were appointed. They were given four houses each and the task of gathering all the records and writing up daily housing reports for Raoul's central office. Each morning a courier was dispatched with mail and messages from Üllői út to the three branch offices. Each evening the couriers made the same trip, this time transporting the daily reports to the head office from the field offices and the ghetto. In view of all of the unpredictable Arrow Cross mobs roaming the city, these were life-threatening journeys.

Each day there were morning meetings at Üllői út at which the daily reports and questions from the field were discussed and decisions made.

Erzsébet Nákó kept the increasingly significant archive of documents and accounts at her Buda residence, in a large roller-shutter cupboard in the medieval building's bomb-proof cellar. She also took care of the petty cash. The humanitarian department's accountant was in Pest and authorised payment orders that the couriers could then cash with Countess Nákó in Buda.

The distribution of food was perhaps the most vexing challenge. The Jews in the international ghetto could not survive without food deliveries from the outside. They were only permitted to move freely in the city for an hour or so a day and within the ghetto their ration cards did not go very far. The humanitarian department was prepared for this. At the beginning of October, Raoul Wallenberg had asked the consul Yngve Ekmark to purchase and store basic necessities. This work had exceeded their expectations, thanks to Iver Olsen's generous financial backing. Now there was already enough food on hand to keep seven hundred people going for three months. Several tons of tinned goods, puréed tomatoes, beans, biscuits, powdered milk and soup had been driven to the three warehouses that Raoul's humanitarian department had managed to secure. Even Danielsson's cellar in the Swedish legation had been stocked to the brim with potatoes, rice, tinned food and other staples.

It cannot be ruled out that Sven Salén and the tinned goods factory Svenska Globus A.B. in some way profited from Raoul's large orders for the Swedish protected houses. One of Raoul's colleagues noted that the tinned items brought into the ghetto were often of the Globus brand. These Globus tinned goods were usually manufactured and sold in Hungary by the Manfréd Weiss canning factory, but were also marketed in Sweden. They were manufactured there by way of a licence agreement with Svenska Globus A.B., a company that the Hungarians had started with Sven Salén's Banan-kompaniet. There are several indications that the Manfréd Weiss group had transferred a large part of their stock value to the Swedish company before the occupation.

It is most likely that Sven Salén and the very business-oriented Lauer, who was managing Svenska Globus that autumn, surely saw financial opportunities in the American support for food to Jews under Swedish protection. But one could also argue that it is most likely that it was only thanks to Raoul Wallenberg's professional past that the humanitarian department had the opportunity to purchase as much food as they needed in food-scarce Hungary.

The Hungarian canning factory was still the cornerstone of the Manfréd Weiss empire, which was now run by the S.S. officer Kurt Becher. Kurt Becher had gone so far as to move into the company's head offices and could be regarded as its top executive. At the same time he was Himmler's envoy with the task of negotiating an agreement where Jews were saved in return for money or goods.

At the end of November, Raoul Wallenberg had again entered into such negotiations with Kurt Becher, this time about "buying" a trip home for the 400 protected Swedish Jews who had real, temporary passports. The price tag had been set at 1,000 Swiss francs per person. Raoul Wallenberg had even gone so far as to contact the International Red Cross and ask for help to find companions who could protect the group at train changes in Vienna. He had also gathered all the temporary passports and dropped them off at the German legation for visas.

The largest food warehouse was in the complex of the chocolate and sugar factory Stühmers at Szentkirályi utca, a few blocks from the office at Üllői út. The couriers were sent there several times a week with authorised orders. Gábor Forgács, who was one of them, remember how they had their carts filled according to the items on the list and then had to walk the carts back through the entire city, to the collection depot in the international ghetto.

The food shortages quickly grew acute, especially in the main ghetto, where Budapest's other 100,000 Jews had been relocated. At the end of November, the member of the Jewish Council who was responsible for food distribution called Raoul Wallenberg and asked for help. They were going to need food worth about 500,000 pengő per day in order to keep starvation at bay. The Jewish Council received aid from the International Red Cross but it was not enough. At Raoul's request, Ivan Danielsson immediately sent a telegram to Stockholm asking for a new, larger infusion of cash from the American War Refugee Board's account. Raoul had calculated that he would need another 450,000 Swiss francs (almost £700,000 today) for the main ghetto.

The Foreign Ministry contacted Stockholm's Enskilda Bank, but it is unclear if the sum was ever transferred to Raoul Wallenberg's special account. Like other groups, the humanitarian department would nonetheless, with whatever means were available, contribute provisions to the starving people in the main ghetto. It was a difficult task, since the Arrow Cross guards stationed outside the ghetto stopped all food deliveries. The food rations for the more than 100,000 Jews in the main ghetto bordered on starvation levels: only 690 calories per day. People died from the lack of food. The main ghetto developed into an overpopulated death trap.

At the humanitarian department, great care was taken with the bookkeeping of the food operation. According to Gábor Forgács, it was impossible to make off with even a single egg. In the archives of the Foreign Ministry there are detailed stock listings from December 1, 1944 that are a sight to behold. All the quantities of tinned meat stew, bags of potatoes, lentil soup, goulashes and hundreds of other items are listed almost down to the gram.

"Only when there is order around me can I work properly," Raoul Wallenberg is said to have told his secretary once. There was indeed order and he worked thoroughly. Colleagues have later testified to Raoul Wallenberg's extremely high capacity for work, and how they had an increasingly difficult time keeping up with him. But his level of ambition also inspired and motivated them. They were pulled along and could, on his orders, perform "assignments that had previously been deemed impossible". They knew that for Wallenberg the word impossible did not exist. "Under his influence the staff overcame their fear and hesitations – which were completely understandable – and instead tried to reach results with Wallenberg's methods."

Responsibility for the distribution of the food fell to the house managers, who were required to keep their accounts just as thoroughly. But it was not possible for all the protected Jews to cook in the crowded conditions in which they lived. Therefore a large-scale kitchen with commercial cookware was organised, where breakfast, lunch and dinner was made for 1,500 people every day. Bread was a problem for a long time – until it was decided to begin daily baking sessions in a factory.

Raoul and his closest associates appear to have thought of everything. The managers were asked to appoint people in every house with the task of fixing any broken pipes, locks and windows. They organised the distribution of fuel, special housing for the elderly, and arranged childcare. Raoul also established a clothing depot, where those in need could receive used clothing and shoes, which a shoemaker among the protected Jews supplied him with. The organisation of the entire operation was a first-rate administrative undertaking. And yet it was only later, when healthcare was added, that Raoul Wallenberg displayed the full extent of his abilities.

It was actually just in one area that Raoul became more lax, not to say consciously sloppy, as time went on. The senselessly violent raids by the Arrow Cross mobs had made him rethink the matter of the protective passports. The Swedish protective houses were definitely not exempt. Before any time at all had elapsed, the Arrow Cross had seized several hundred people with Swedish protective passports, dragged them back to their headquarters and beaten them to a pulp. Raoul Wallenberg peppered the Hungarian Foreign Ministry with letters of protest over the matter but it was clear that the regulations were no longer being respected.

Publically, in front of the Arrow Cross inspectors, they kept the formal aspects of the protective passport process as rigorous as ever. But back at the humanitarian department it became clear that the bar had been lowered substantially. Now it was not only the applicants who looked for relatives in the Stockholm telephone directories. Raoul himself would send telegrams to Kálmán Lauer for the names of Swedes who could pretend to be relatives of Jews in need. Lauer would then call known anti-Nazis in Stockholm and say that he needed "Swedish relatives for twenty-five people" delivered by telegram the following morning. A simple printing press was set up at Üllői út and a kind of "field passport" was developed, which the patrols of the Security Protocol could employ in tense situations.

As late as the beginning of November, Ivan Danielsson wrote to Stockholm and complained about the obstinate Red Cross delegate Valdemar Langlet, who never stopped producing protective documents. Now the restraints of Raoul's disciplined operation also loosened. This development was not confined to the Swedes. Raoul was in daily contact with the Swiss legation, either with Carl Lutz himself or with the Zionists Miklós Krausz and Rezső Kasztner at the fictitious "emigration department". Their rescue operation had also moved out of their former legation building, and was now located in the so-called Glass House, a former glass factory some streets away. At the Swiss legation, they were now said to have issued up to 65,000 protective documents of various kinds. Raoul was told that the Swiss had 26,000 Jews living in their protective houses by Szent István park.

To those who were close to Raoul Wallenberg it is clear that a significant change occurred after his mission on the road to Hegyeshalom. The man who returned was not quite the same. There was a new darkness that deepened with the Arrow Cross attacks on the Jews in the protected Swedish houses.

Up to the end of November, Vilmos Forgács and Hugó Wohl had consistently followed Raoul's established requirements and inspection routines in the protective passport process. Gábor Forgács has described how his father and Wohl were sitting in a meeting around that time, as usual with a pile of applications that they were supposed sort into those that would be accepted or declined. Then Raoul Wallenberg entered the room and asked them to stop. He said: "If anyone is capable of making their way to our door and submitting an application for a protective passport, the answer from now on will always be yes."

The deported Jews saved from the death marches by the Security Protocol's patrols were often so emaciated and exhausted that they would not survive without hospital care. On one of the last days of November, there came an emergency call to Raoul Wallenberg's office at Üllői út. The hospital that had been used until this point was now filled beyond capacity and those turned away risked having to spend the night in the courtyard.

Raoul decided to empty six apartments at Tátra utca 14–16, one of the houses under Swedish–Swiss protection. "Practically within the course of a couple of hours, he transformed the apartments at Tátra utca into a hospital, with furniture from private residences and borrowed equipment from other public hospitals in Budapest," one of his colleagues later said. A hospital with fifty beds was prepared, an arrangement that would soon have to be tripled in capacity.

By coincidence, Raoul had only a few days earlier sent a patrol from the Security Protocol to save some Jewish physicians. Since the summer, they had been engaged in forced labour at a military hospital, but now the Arrow Cross had arrested them. It was the chief of the hospital himself who had notified Raoul Wallenberg that the doctors had been taken to the brick factory at Óbuda. Now he was worried that they were on their way to Hegyeshalom.

Raoul activated one of the Security Protocol's patrol units and reinforced them with a former, and probably bribed, armed gendarme. Since one of the doctors was Vilmos Forgács' brother-in-law, Wallenberg asked his son, Gábor Forgács, to accompany them in order to help make the identifications. The patrol unit drove several tens of kilometres along the death march, in the humanitarian department's small D.K.W., which was disguised for the day by the red-and-white pennants of the Arrow Cross. When Gábor caught sight of his uncle by the side of the road, they stopped. The uniformed gendarme put on a performance for the Arrow Cross guards, approaching the doctor and starting to kick him. "You there, get up!" The uncle, a professor and expert in diseases of the lung, spotted Gábor and understood. But his colleague, a professor of surgery, fell into a tearful state of shock at the same treatment. He was hysterical as, under feigned blows, he was brought to the "Arrow Cross" car. But the "arrest" was standard procedure for Raoul Wallenberg's Security Protocol and their lives were saved.

The surgery professor's name was Lipót Schischa and he was now the man who was given the responsibility of leading the humanitarian department's "Swedish hospital" at Tátra utca. To assist him there were some forty physicians with protective passports, and at least as many nurses. They wrote lists of the equipment and medicine that were needed. Incredibly, almost all of it arrived. A witness has stated that "Wallenberg charmed his associates with his personality. He had the ability to motivate them so that they could, in the shortest possible time, and as if by magic, supply equipment, medicines and food in spite of the completely impossible circumstances." Raoul himself managed to procure the surgical instruments. An achievement that must have been facilitated by the fact that one of the co-workers in the Security Protocol, Iván Székely, was a pharmacist and also the son of the owner of a large chain of pharmacies. It was not long before the hospital staff could hang up a sign that read: "The Swedish Hospital has opened. It enjoys full extra-territorial status."

The Arrow Cross were suspicious of the Security Protocol's so-called recall orders from the death marches. The humanitarian department knew there was a risk that those who had been recalled could be deported again. Then Raoul Wallenberg had an idea. If they were to spread the rumour that there was typhoid fever among the recalled, then the Arrow Cross would be likely to leave them alone. He even turned up at the Swedish hospital with a fake typhoid patient. The doctors became alarmed about what the Arrow Cross would do to the protected Swedish Jews if they were told that they carried typhoid fever. They managed to convince Raoul to change the illness to dysentery instead.

Incidents of violence were now starting to become so frequent and so serious that Raoul Wallenberg felt the need to begin documenting them. It was dangerous to take photographs, but the more active resistance groups had already been secretly recording the crimes of the Arrow Cross and had hidden the pictures pending post-war scrutiny. Raoul also felt that the images could convince the American parties about the value of his work.

Per Anger had earlier issued a temporary Swedish passport to Horthy's Jewish court photographer, Pál Veres, who knew many Swedes and had taken photographs for the Swedish legation. The court photographer himself was not available, but Raoul Wallenberg had taken care of his seventeen-year-old son, Tamás Veres, after the Arrow Cross coup in October and had assigned him the task of taking photographs for the protective passports.

As December approached, Raoul Wallenberg received bad news that would yield an opportunity for such documentation. In Budapest there were still groups of Jews who were being drafted into forced labour units involved in defence work for the city. Raoul Wallenberg had, at an earlier stage, given in and let a few protected Swedish Jews go to such a unit, the Swedish Labour Unit. It was made up of several hundred and, until now, with some exceptions, the majority had been safe. But on November 28 and 29, Adolf Eichmann's Sondereinsatzkommando called all of the Jews protected by Sweden in the unit to Józsefváros train station. They were to be deported to Hegyeshalom, together with seventeen thousand others drafted into labour.

Raoul Wallenberg dived into the bureaucratic work. He dug out an old diplomatic note from his intensive correspondence with the foreign minister. Using this as foundation, he claimed that these "Swedish" labour draftees certainly could not be "loaned out to the Germans", and that they had to remain at the disposal of the Swedish legation. Therefore he made an arrangement with the gendarme commander Ferenczy that the Swedish legation would dispatch a "legitimation committee" to Józsefváros station "consisting of myself and two legation officials. This commission will determine which of those awaiting deportation hold, or have held, protective or temporary passports. Once they have been identified, these individuals will step down and under suitable escort be transported to one of the protective houses."

On the morning of November 28, Tamás Veres received a note from Raoul Wallenberg's secretary. In it Raoul had written: "Meet me at József-város station. Bring your camera." Tamás put his Leica in his bag and took the tram to the station, which recently had become a new assembly point for the deportations.

Rumours about the horrifying death marches had reached Berlin and, by now, these descriptions raised objections even there. Himmler had lately become more concerned with Germany's image than with the extermination of the Jews. He had just ordered the gas chambers of Auschwitz to be dismantled. Jews who walked 200 kilometres on foot without food in the bitter cold would not be capable of labour. Without the solution offered by Auschwitz, they would only become a burden for the Germans, or so Himmler's office argued. In order to soften this criticism, Eichmann had managed to free some trains from Vienna and the intenttion was that the 17,000 labourers would be transported to Germany in sealed boxcars.

Józsefváros train station was surrounded by gendarmes and the Arrow Cross. Tamás Veres hid his camera in his scarf and approached the guards. In order to make his way past them, he spoke German with a Swedish accent and claimed that he was a Swedish diplomat who needed to see Raoul Wallenberg. They let him in.

There, in the November fog, the loading of the boxcars had already begun. Tamás caught sight of Raoul who was arranging a table and some chairs in preparation for the "legitimisation". The legation's protective passport registers, bound into a large black folder, lay on the table. "All those who belong to me line up in a queue here. All you have to do is show me your Swedish protective passports!" Raoul shouted, according to Tamás. Another of Raoul's colleagues walked along the cars and explained that all those with Swedish protective passports should present themselves for identification and wait in line. To Tamás Veres, Raoul whispered, "Take as many pictures as you can!"

Tamás walked over to Raoul Wallenberg's maroon Studebaker, where the driver Vilmos Langfelder was waiting. He dug out a penknife and made an opening in his scarf for the lens, before he again hid the camera. Then he walked around as calmly as possible and took photographs of what he was seeing through his scarf. He was especially careful when he recognised one of Eichmann's S.S. inspectors, Hauptsturmführer Theodor Dannecker. Tamás had met him once before, when the German came to his father to be photographed in his uniform.

Raoul Wallenberg was not content just to sit at the table with the protective passport register. As Tamás Veres recalls, he elbowed his way through the crowds outside the cars: "You there, I have your name, where is your document?" Bewildered men reached into their pockets and held out letters of any kind to Raoul. "Excellent. Next!"

According to Tamás Veres, they managed to save almost 500 people before the day was over. Those who were freed could then walk through Budapest to the protected houses, escorted by the police.

The following day, Raoul and his associates were back at the station. Tamás Veres was considerably more brave this time. Among the Jews in the crowd he discovered many well-known Hungarians and some friends, whom he spontaneously grabbed and dragged up into the line in front of Raoul Wallenberg. According to Tamás Veres, he himself finally became so daring that he climbed up onto one of the box cars and then jumped down on the lock so that the door opened and the people streamed out.

A gendarme discovered what he was doing. He roared and aimed his weapon at the young man: "Stop that!" Then Raoul Wallenberg tucked his black register under his arm and the Swedish "legitimisation committee" quickly left, not as successful on the second day as on the first.

Of the seventeen thousand who had been called to Józsefváros station on those days it is claimed that only the 500 protected Swedish Jews managed to escape.

Hauptsturmführer Theodor Dannecker was a full-blooded Nazi who had served as a "Jewish expert" in Eichmann's murder unit in both France and Italy. Raoul Wallenberg's monumental audacity at the Józsefváros station infuriated him and he made no attempt to hide this from his superior. Adolf Eichmann soured at the news. Already frustrated by the actions of Wallenberg and the other neutral legations, Eichmann ordered Dannecker to hit back by staging raids in the international ghetto.

The month of December began with a new series of terror-like attacks on the Swedish and Swiss blocks. They went under the rubric of "inspections" and were conducted by the local police. In one house at Tátra utca, for example, fifty-four of the residents were arrested and forced, with their arms above their heads, to Teleki tér, a square that was one of the many "collection and plundering places" of the Arrow Cross. In another of the Swedish houses, all of the women under fifty and all of the men under sixty were ordered "to make themselves ready for a long journey" and gather in the courtyard. In a third house, thirty-eight people were taken to a village outside Budapest, where they were beaten for five days.

And on it went. Not a day went by without fresh assaults. Sometimes the Security Protocol's patrols managed to rescue those who had been arrested, sometimes not.

For a while they were at a loss as to how to deal with this violent turn of events. Though Raoul Wallenberg had managed to become very good friends with the foreign minister's wife, Baroness Elizabeth Kemény-Fuchs, he had now unfortunately lost this special access to the Arrow Cross government. The Baroness was pregnant and so her husband sent her to South Tyrol at the end of November. But Raoul Wallenberg's network of contacts did not stand and fall with the baroness. Despite his junior diplomatic rank, Raoul Wallenberg had visited a surprising number of Hungarian ministers after the transferral of power.

Yet, in view of the daily terrors his charges were forced to endure, it was no longer enough to pressure the government. It became increasingly necessary to make contacts in the field, among police, paramilitary gendarmes and the local Arrow Cross militia. Raoul Wallenberg appears to have pursued a multi-pronged approach. He bombarded the Ministry of the Interior with protest letters about the violence, while at the same time sending security patrols into the field. He also began to do daily inspections himself. In this way, Wallenberg and his associates became well-known names and faces among the field officers in the Arrow Cross, just as they had among the afflicted Jews.

According to the author Jenő Lévai, Raoul left every morning for a round of the brick factory in Óbuda and the collection place at Teleki tér. He visited the Swedish houses as well as the main ghetto, where the relocation was now complete and work was under way to erect a wall around the area. Conditions in this large ghetto defied all description.

The international ghetto was located in Budapest's thirteenth district. There the name of the local police inspector was Zoltán Tarpataky. He had earlier shown himself to be approachable and had tried to give Raoul's associates advance notice of any threatening developments. On December 3 he received an ominous order. Tarpataky was now on a daily basis to order 300 Jews from the Swedish houses to report for forced labour: 100 women and 200 men. They were to be placed at the "German labour unit's" disposal.

Faced with this clear threat of deportation, Raoul Wallenberg reached for his best weapon – bureaucratic guile. He negotiated on the spot with Police Inspector Tarpataky and suggested a compromise. Raoul promised to provide him with 300 labourers every day, as long as he received a receipt for each and every one of them and a promise that they would be promptly returned to the Swedish houses each evening. Tarpataky not only accepted the proposal but also honoured it. The police inspector developed such respect for Wallenberg that he thereafter began helping him whenever he could.

Great risks were associated with any kind of forced labour and Raoul Wallenberg knew this. He therefore developed a new document that would serve as an additional insurance for the Jews under Swedish protection:

The Royal Swedish Legation in Budapest hereby certifies that . . . who is born . . . year . . . in . . . (mother's name . . .) and proves his/her identity with protective passport number . . . by way of the Royal Hungarian Defence Minister's regulation number 152 730/eln 42/1944 and this complementary and properly authorised agreement, has been recalled from service.

Budapest, 4 December, 1944. Raoul Wallenberg. Legation secretary.

It sounded convincing but was nothing more than a bluff. The regulations in question actually pertained to something completely different, but he was gambling on the Arrow Cross not having time to verify this. The members of the Security Protocol had also begun to engage in this kind of bold dissembling and often turned up during their rescue raids in clerical dress or Arrow Cross uniforms with red-and-white armbands.

Unfortunately, there were setbacks. One evening in December, the humanitarian department received a report about a freight train with Jews in sealed boxcars that had been parked for several days at a station outside Budapest. The informant spoke about indescribable conditions. The people imprisoned there had not received anything to eat for several days. Raoul Wallenberg quickly arranged a food delivery and drove out with an associate. They were allowed to distribute the food but could not bring any of the protected Swedish Jews back with them. Raoul reported that there were fifty cars with several thousand deportees, among them many with Swedish protective passports. The humanitarian department fought for several days and enlisted the help of the gendarme captain Batizfalvy, just as they did in the mission to Hegyeshalom. But it was in vain. At last they sadly heard the news that the freight train had departed for an unknown fate.

These kinds of panic missions became more numerous. Each setback was followed by despair. Everything now centred around gaining time and holding out for liberation. Unfortunately that was taking longer than expected. The Russian troops had been delayed, as they had unexpectedly encountered stiff resistance in the last approach to Budapest. But no-one doubted that they would make it and Raoul's mission would soon be at an end.

The Americans appeared to see things the same way. The head of the American War Refugee Board in Washington, John Pehle, wrote to Raoul Wallenberg personally and thanked him for his "difficult and important work" and for performing the assignment with such "personal devotion".

> I think that no-one who has participated in this great task can escape some feeling of frustration in that, because of circumstances beyond our control, our efforts have not met with complete success. On the other hand, there have been measurable achievements in the face of the obstacles which had to be encountered, and it is our conviction that you have made a very great personal contribution to the success which has been realised in these endeavors. On behalf of the War Refugee Board I wish to express to you our very deep appreciation for your splendid cooperation and for the vigor and ingenuity which you brought to our common humanitarian undertaking.

The letter was sent to the American legation in Stockholm on December 6. It is not known why – it could have been the war or simply Christmas preparations – but Herschel Johnson did not manage to get Pehle's letter over to the Foreign Ministry before December 30. Therefore it is quite certain that Raoul Wallenberg never had the opportunity to read it.

The Swedish diplomats could not know it but the final courier post from the Budapest legation to Stockholm went out on Friday, December 8. There was a considerable quantity of mail to the Foreign Ministry from Raoul Wallenberg. Apart from his usual report on the situation of the Hungarian Jews he also sent a financial statement for the humanitarian department, correct as of November 15. It included the most recent inventory of food purchases, the staff list of his now 335 employees (excluding the forty or so physicians and house managers) as well as a detailed description of the arrangement for the financial transfers through Switzerland.

In view of the circumstances, the orderliness of this paperwork is almost unnatural.

Up to this point, the humanitarian department had purchased food for almost two million pengő, Raoul Wallenberg wrote, a sum that corresponds to 250,000 Swedish kronor (about £375,000 today). Raoul pointed out that the majority of Jews were completely penniless after their relocation to the ghettos and the scenario was, as far as he could tell, on the verge of becoming catastrophic.

Including families, he had a total of 700 individuals living in the building at Üllői út 2–4. This time he did not massage the number but simply admitted that at least 7,000 people were living in the Swedish protected houses and that there were another 2,000 in the house of the Swedish Red Cross. Under the heading "achieved results", Raoul Wallenberg wrote that 2,000 people had been saved through patrol rescue missions of various kinds, "of which around 500 from Hegyeshalom". The humanitarian department had also managed to get the defence minister to release an order that all Jews with foreign papers who were in forced labour units should be recalled to Budapest. "After a military person, dispatched in one of the department's cars, distributed the order, around 15,000 Jews returned," he noted.

In the package of mail sent to the Foreign Ministry, he included a few of the shots that the photographer Tamás Veres had snapped during their recent rescue mission.

Raoul managed to write his last two personal letters home to Sweden before the courier left from Budapest. They were both composed in German, since he was pressed for time, and typed by Frau Falk. One was addressed to Kálmán Lauer. Raoul told Lauer that a few of his relatives had been employed by the legation and also wrote about a couple of families that he had protected in this way. He asked not to be sent any more such requests as he did not have the time to dedicate to individual cases. The situation in the city was "extremely dangerous", Raoul wrote. He told his business partner that his plan was now to spend another couple of months in Budapest after the arrival of the Russians and start "an organisation for the return of Jewish property". In conclusion he asked Lauer to once again enquire with Jacob Wallenberg about the Huvudsta position "since I will be gone for so long". Raoul wanted to have a telegram reply on the matter.

The letter to his mother Maj von Dardel was also dictated in German. This is what Raoul Wallenberg wrote:

KÖNIGLICH
SCHWEDISCHE GESANDTSCHAFT

Budapest, 8 Dec. 1944

Dearest Mother!

I really don't know when I will make up for my sins. Today yet another courier departs and again all you will get from me is a few hasty lines.

The situation is exciting and dangerous, my workload almost inhuman. Bandits roam the city, whipping, abusing and shooting people. Just among my staff, I have had 40 cases of kidnapping and assault. All in all, however, our morale is good and we are happy for the fight.

I have sent a telegram in which I agree to the proposal of taking on the Lagergren's apartment. The conditions must be as follows. My own apartment should be rented out by a rental agency, for which Mr Eriksson must give his approval. Furthermore, I ask you to engage Frey's Express to handle the entire move. I don't want anyone to be burdened with it, so the whole matter should be left to Frey's Express.

Day and night we hear the gunfire of the approaching Russians.

The diplomatic operation has become very lively since Szálasi's arrival. I represent the legation with the ministers almost by myself. Up to this point, I have been some 10x to the foreign minister, 2x to the acting ministerial president, 2x at the minister of the interior, 1x at the minister of supply and services, 1x at the finance minister, etc.

I am fairly good friends with the foreign minister's wife. Unfortunately she has left for Merano.

The food shortage in Budapest is acute. But we have accumulated a respectable stockpile of goods in the nick of time. After the invasion I have the feeling that it will be hard to get home so I think that it will take me until Easter to get back to Stockholm. But this is all speculation. No-one yet knows how the occupation will develop. I will certainly try to start thinking about the trip home as soon as possible.

Today it is still impossible to make any plans. I was convinced that I would be back with you by Christmas. That is why I must send you my Christmas greetings like this and also my best wishes for the New Year. Hopefully the much longed-for peace is now no longer so distant.

My dearest Mother, I enclose another 2 photographs for you which are fairly recent. You see me there at my desk surrounded by my colleagues and staff.

With all of this work, time goes by very quickly, and it also happens fairly frequently that I am invited for supper where I am served suckling pig and other Hungarian specialities.

Darling Mother, I will bid you goodbye for today, the courier sack must now be made ready. I send you my greetings and my heartiest and warmest kisses to you and the entire family.

Your

2 photographs   R. Wallenberg

Many kisses to Nina and the little girl

P.S. It is very likely that I will stay here for quite a while longer.*

---

* Handwritten notes added by Raoul Wallenberg in Swedish, at the end of the letter and in the left-hand margin.

Joseph Stalin was disappointed in General Rodion Malinovsky. Malinovsky led one of the Red Army's most formidable units, the 2nd Ukrainian Front, but had advanced astonishingly slowly toward the Hungarian capital. The Soviet headquarters had therefore also summoned the general for the 3rd Ukrainian Front, Fyodor Tolbuchin.

General Tolbuchin's forces were approaching Budapest from the southwest, Malinovsky's from the east. It took time, but slowly they surrounded the Hungarian capital in an offensive that would be characterised as much by competition as by cooperation between them. Malinovsky, who had just turned forty-six, was far from happy at the prospect of sharing the glory of conquering Budapest. Tolbuchin was a challenging opponent. He was a few years older and a highly respected general, known for his calm, his thoroughness and his ability to get along well with others.

Afterwards, many would observe that those foreign diplomats in the areas of the city where Tolbuchin arrived first were better off than those in Pest, who instead met with Malinovsky's forces.

German and Hungarian soldiers fled headlong in the face of the Soviet tanks. At the beginning of December, it was starting to look more and more likely that the final battles would take place on the streets of Budapest. In the field the opinion was that such a development should be avoided and the city spared. German officers had, just as in the battle at Stalingrad, pleaded to their commanders to be allowed to retreat in the event that the lines of defence around Budapest were broken. But Hitler was merciless. His harsh message was that not a house in Budapest should be lost without a fight, regardless of the cost in material destruction and civilian casualties. In Hitler's eyes, Budapest was a fortress.

By the middle of December 1944, the Soviet Union had taken two-thirds of Hungary. In the city of Debrecen in eastern Hungary, Hungarian communists and Social Democrats had started to prepare a temporary Hungarian government, with representatives from the occupied regions, which would take over after the invasion.

The Soviet foreign minister Vyacheslav Molotov had supplied a vanguard of Hungarian communists who had been living in the Soviet Union. They would be needed – the Hungarian communist party was still a weak movement numbering only 4,000 members in 1944. This temporary Hungarian government would compete with General Malinovsky's army leadership for rooms at Debrecen's best hotel, Arany Bika, the "Golden Bull".

Raoul Wallenberg was also looking ahead to the time after the Soviet invasion. The plan for post-war aid assistance that he had written about in the letter to Kálmán Lauer was beginning to take shape. As Wallenberg saw it, such aid would encompass not only the protected Swedish Jews and their deported relatives, but also all the other Jews and the 200,000 Hungarians who had fled to the West during the war. One would get them home, give them work and help those who were destitute to get back on their feet. Jewish valuables confiscated by the Germans would be returned. Raoul Wallenberg saw this as a task resembling the heroic contribution of the Norwegian explorer Fridtjof Nansen after the First World War. Nansen organised the journey home for hundreds of thousands of refugees and prisoners of war.

This time Raoul Wallenberg wanted to build up a private aid organisation unconnected to the Swedish legation and the restrictions imposed by diplomatic protocol. As early as the end of November, his colleague Rezső Müller had been assigned the task of drawing up plans for it. Now, in December, the idea was intensely discussed in Raoul Wallenberg's inner circle. But the bustle at the overfilled Üllői út office did not lend itself to discretion. Müller had therefore been asked to find another location where those in the know could work on the details in peace.

The choice fell on the Hazai Bank ("the national bank") in central Pest. It stood on Vörösmarty tér, a square a few streets north of Üllői út, next to the exclusive Budapest confectioners, Café Gerbeaud.

With the Soviet troops approaching, the Hazai Bank – like other banks – had been ordered to hand over gold, cash and foreign currency to the Hungarian central bank. Since all normal activity had been suspended, the bank's director was prepared to rent out the entire office level on the third floor to Raoul and his associates. They also had access to a bomb shelter in the bank's vaults. They put up a Swedish flag outside and the bank became yet another of the humanitarian department's many branch offices.

After the Spanish and Portuguese diplomats had left Hungary, only Sweden, Switzerland, Turkey and the papal nuncio had retained their representation. Even the Swiss minister, Jäger, now left Budapest, although his subordinates remained, among them Raoul Wallenberg's collaborator, the consul Carl Lutz, and the increasingly active legation secretary Harald Feller.

To anyone who counted the number of houses flying Swedish flags in Budapest it must have looked as if Sweden had extended its diplomatic representation in Hungary. Questions were raised in the Soviet Union. The Soviet legation in Stockholm sent a diplomatic note to the Foreign Ministry and asked for an explanation as to why the Swedes had remained in Budapest when all the other diplomats had left. Was not Sweden said to have broken off diplomatic relations with the Arrow Cross? The Foreign Ministry responded by saying that Sweden remained for two reasons: to protect the Hungarian Jews they were responsible for, and in order to continue its work as protective power for several countries, among them the Soviet Union.

Ivan Danielsson and his deputy Per Anger found themselves in hot water in the course of their diplomatic games with the Arrow Cross regime. Raoul Wallenberg often participated in the tense negotiations and played a central role, according to Anger. Their lives were made more difficult by a lack of understanding from the leadership in Stockholm. It does not seem as if the foreign minister Christian Günther and his closest associates fully understood what kind of bandits they were dealing with, nor that the Swedish legation had actually been the target of repeated threats.

For instance, at the beginning of December the Arrow Cross had, for security reasons, moved the seat of government to the city of Szombathely on the Austrian border. When Sweden ignored their order to accompany them, the Arrow Cross let it be known that they regarded this as an unfriendly act. The Swedes were therefore quite astonished when, not long after, they received an invitation to a wild-boar hunt with Ferenc Szálasi. They were to report to the Hungarian Foreign Ministry "dressed warmly with clothes suitable for the hunt". The Swedes sensed that something was afoot and avoided sending a reply. They were later told that the Arrow Cross plan had been to kidnap the Swedish diplomats and take them by force to Szombathely.

The Arrow Cross became more and more aggressive about the Swedes' continuing refusal to extend diplomatic recognition to their regime. Signal after signal arrived threatening that the Swedish legation and the Swedish Red Cross could count on a violent response if Sweden did not give in. Ivan Danielsson had already sent a telegram back to Sweden warning that this could mean a storming of the Swedish houses and violence against the protected Swedish Jews. But so far the Foreign Ministry had replied only that they would consider the question – as if this were just a run-of-the-mill diplomatic issue.

On December 11, Ivan Danielsson was called to see the Foreign Minister Gábor Kemény. Kemény expressed with considerable displeasure his astonishment at the fact that Sweden had not yet recognised the new Hungarian government. He informed Danielsson that the Arrow Cross regime now intended to evacuate all Jews from Budapest, including those under Swedish protection. He also demanded that Hungary should be compensated for the brutal manner in which Sweden had deported the Arrow Cross diplomats from Stockholm in October.

Ivan Danielsson understood this as an ultimatum. He sent an anxious telegram back home and explained that he really had to give an answer on the recognition question within a couple of days. If the Swedish answer was no, he was afraid that the relations would be completely broken, with unforeseeable consequences. Ivan Danielsson and his colleagues all felt that acknowledging the regime was a cheap price to pay for saving lives. But the answer from the Foreign Ministry was laconic and rather unhelpful: "You should seek to prevent the question from coming to a head."

The first attack came on the night of December 14. Shortly after midnight, police and militia broke into one of the Swedish Red Cross premises outside the international ghetto. They arrested all the Hungarian staff and the protected Jews. At the same time the Arrow Cross government sent a formal diplomatic note to the Swedish legation. The Swedish diplomats were told that the activities of the Swedish Red Cross were now prohibited. The reason given was that the Swedish aid organisation had indiscriminately distributed protective passports and also hoarded food supplies that were needed for Hungary's citizens. This could no longer be tolerated.

According to the writer Jenő Lévai, it was Raoul Wallenberg who went to the besieged Red Cross house in the middle of the night. He managed to convince the police that they should, at the very least, drive those Jews who possessed Langlet's protective letters to the international ghetto. But the staff were dragged off and jailed. The following day, the police returned and took food supplies, medicine and the entire archives of the Swedish Red Cross. They claimed later that they had found documents that were highly incriminating for the Swedes.

Nina and Valdemar Langlet were elsewhere and managed to avoid the attack but would thereafter be "defenceless against any kind of future attacks", as Valdemar Langlet wrote in his memoirs. They continued their work as well as they could but, from then on, they mainly hid in a basement at Üllői út.

A very shaken Ivan Danielsson called the Swedish legation in Berlin, who forwarded his emergency call to the Foreign Ministry. But, even now, neither support nor understanding was forthcoming. The telephone message that was sent back to Budapest via Berlin that same day instructed that:

> No changes will be made in the acknowledgement question. You must decide yourself if the circumstances are such that the legation or its members should depart. Protest against the raid of the Red Cross premises. The Red Cross operations may be concluded if you, after consultation with its representatives, no longer find it possible to continue.

The Swedish diplomats in Budapest felt abandoned. Until then, their own judgement had been that Sweden's representatives could not leave Hungary. It risked becoming the trigger that would send thousands of Jews under Swedish protection to their deaths. But now it was clear that even the lives of the diplomats could be in danger.

After Raoul Wallenberg's intervention at Józsefváros train station, someone had tried to run him over several times. People around him thought they recognised Hauptsturmführer Theodor Dannecker's large car and warned Wallenberg. The warning was justified. The day after the raid at the Swedish Red Cross, Adolf Eichmann lost his temper in front of one of the Red Cross employees. Discernably angry, he made it clear that he intended to "have that Jew-dog Wallenberg shot".

It is very likely that the drunken and erratic Eichmann was more volatile than usual during this period. His conflict with Himmler's representative Kurt Becher had reached its peak. Becher had reacted to the Hegyeshalom death marches and told his colleague that he had to put a stop to "this miserable exodus of Jews from the city". Eichmann refused and the situation between them became untenable. Both had then been ordered to come to a meeting with Himmler. There are conflicting accounts of what exactly was said during this meeting, but Eichmann was certainly upbraided in some way by the S.S. chief. When he returned to Budapest the city was almost completely surrounded by the Red Army. However much Eichmann wanted to continue the deportations, it was now a practical impossibility.

It was during this period that the outburst directed at Raoul Wallenberg occurred. That the Swedish legation secretary's rescue operation irritated the frustrated S.S. officer was hardly news. But one could not dismiss the clearly articulated formulation, "have that Jew-dog Wallenberg shot", as a passing comment made in anger. Colleagues at the legation could testify that they had heard Eichmann's representative say something along the same lines. In addition, one of Raoul Wallenberg's Hungarian employees had recently been shot at the Chain Bridge, together with three family members who had all then been thrown into the Danube.

This time the Foreign Ministry in Stockholm took Danielsson's concerns seriously. Arvid Richert in Berlin was asked to immediately contact the Auswärtiges Amt, relay his protest and require that Eichmann's S.S. unit be ordered to respect legation personnel. It was a Sunday, so Richert visited an official from the German ministry at his home. At first the German had tried to make light of the entire affair, reminding Richert of the saying that "dogs who bark don't bite" and suggesting that the words were surely not seriously intended. But he did as the Swede requested and sent a telegram to Budapest censuring Eichmann's actions.

The German envoy in Budapest, Edmund Veesenmayer, took Eichmann's side. He informed Berlin that Eichmann and his colleagues had lately "often had reason to direct justified criticism" at the Swedish legation's "Jewish office", and in particular towards Raoul Wallenberg. According to Veesemayer, Raoul Wallenberg had "interested himself to an unusual degree in the Hungarian Jews who were ordered to serve in labour units at the border". Veesenmayer claimed that Raoul Wallenberg, "with absolutely illegal methods, had tried to snatch them [the Jews] out of the legal labour force by handing out protective passports".

The whole affair still seems to have ended with Adolf Eichmann receiving a reprimand from the Auswärtiges Amt.

Only a week remained until Christmas. In Stockholm most families had lit the third candle of Advent and were starting to think about their decorations. The Swedish diplomats in Budapest were far removed from that atmosphere. They received daily reminders that their service for Sweden in Hungary posed a danger to their lives.

The legation was now told by an official at the Hungarian Foreign Ministry that the recent raid against the Swedish Red Cross had only been the beginning. The Arrow Cross wanted to "liquidate the Swedish operation": punishment for the fact that so many Jews were illegally residing in Swedish houses, and because Sweden had humiliated the Hungarian diplomats in Stockholm.

The following day, the Arrow Cross forced their way into a Swedish house with an extra-territorial sign, where officials from the humanitarian department lived with their families. They were robbed of all their valuables. As the thugs left the building, the families were told that the Arrow Cross did not "foresee a glowing future" for the Swedes.

Until now, Ivan Danielsson had felt that the Swedish diplomats could not leave Budapest without it being seen as a provocation against the Arrow Cross government. The Swedes had stretched formalities as far as they could and had encouraged the impression that their remaining was in itself a way of recognising the new regime. "If we had left, they would immediately have realised that everything was one big bluff," Per Anger explained in a television interview many years later. "Then they would have sent thousands of Jews under Swedish protection to a certain death."

But could Danielsson really expose the entire Swedish representation to danger? After the threat that the Swedish operation was going to be "liquidated", the legation tentatively began to discuss a departure. At the same time, it was clear that it would be only a matter of days before the Red Army took Budapest, after which Eichmann's death threats and the Arrow Cross raids would be history. How would the Russians perceive the matter if the Swedish fled with the enemy at the moment of liberation?

It was not an easy decision for the 64-year-old senior diplomat, who would rather have spent his last days in the service at carefree cocktail receptions than in the midst of a raging world war. He may have appeared rather worn-down, but he did not lack courage. According to Per Anger, there was really never any doubt that they would stay. Early in December, the minister had urged the female Swedish secretaries to go home, but that was all. Birgit Brulin had obeyed this order but Margareta Bauer had stayed, arguing that she wanted to "experience something exciting".

The Swedish diplomats armed themselves instead. For some time now, Raoul Wallenberg had alternated between several different residences in order to make things harder for those who were pursuing him. Aside from the villa at Ostrom utca he had access to another house on a hill behind the palace. But sometimes he spent the night at the Hazai Bank or elsewhere. Raoul had packed up some necessities, including a few tins of food, in a backpack that he always carried with him. And he asked his associates always to wear boots, as he did himself. He had seen enough tattered shoes on the death marches to Hegyeshalom to realise how such a detail could seal a person's fate. "We never know when these marches will be repeated, so everyone has to be prepared," was his message. He is said to have always carried the pistol he bought at Nybrogatan in Stockholm before he left.

Raoul Wallenberg was not alone in arming himself. Per Anger had bought some Russian machine guns on the black market for the Swedish legation. One of his contacts in the resistance movement had taught him how to shoot them at his father's hunting estate a few weeks earlier. Now, in December, Anger had set his colleagues to weapons training. Brave Margareta Bauer spent part of her birthday in the legation's garden with a machine gun. The Swedish-speaking office worker Dénes von Mezey had been given the assignment of teaching her to shoot.

Margareta struggled valiantly with her task. She found the machine gun extremely heavy and difficult to hold still. It was almost impossible to aim. However hard she tried, she could not master all the small knobs and levers. She did not understand how she was supposed to manage, how she would have time to get it right if "a hoard of Arrow Cross or Russians or whatever it was going to be, were to attack me!"

Raoul Wallenberg Square, January 2010

The snow is falling thickly and settling like balls of cotton over Raoul Wallenbergs torg, a square in central Stockholm. Those assembled there are huddled under hoods and thick shawls. It is −12°C and very few are speaking to each other. Someone tries to stamp the snow off or stamp warmth into their frozen feet.

It is Holocaust Remembrance Day, January 27, 2010, and the snow is falling so heavily over Stockholm that the photographers have to wrap plastic bags around their lenses. The January-dark water of Nybroviken bay disappears from sight even though we are so close. The stubborn flakes find their way in every-where.

The square is flanked by tall white banners. These are one-metre-high por-traits of the ten Swedes who have received Yad Vashem's honorary designation "Righteous Among the Nations" because they risked their own lives to save Jews during the Holocaust.

I count them. Six worked in Budapest: Per Anger, Lars Berg, Ivan Danielsson, Nina Langlet, Valdemar Langlet and Raoul Wallenberg.

"What drove them individually is hard to say. But I think there was a common denominator: when it came down to it, they did not feel that they had a choice. The strength of their empathy made it a necessity," says Eskil Franck, superinten-dent at the Forum for Living History, in his introductory speech.

Kate Wacz is listening, standing almost at the front. She has a fur hat and a dark warm coat and her handbag is tightly clenched in her hands. In it she keeps copies of some Swedish protective passports from that dark autumn of war in Budapest. She is seventy-eight years old and one of those who was saved. After coming to Sweden in 1951 she worked mainly in the cosmetics industry.

Afterwards, those assembled carry lanterns in different colours and set them on the Raoul Wallenberg monument. Kate Wacz goes up to the introductory speaker, Eskil Franck.

"I have some protective passports in my bag. Can we show them?" she asks.

Eskil Franck tries to blink away the snow in his face.

"I think it will be hard in this weather," he says and gestures toward the sky.

"But these are copies," Kate says, dejectedly.

They part. Kate's brother, Gustav Kadelburger, comes over and takes her arm. He was a messenger boy for Raoul Wallenberg and that was how they came to live in one of the Swedish houses. Kate and Gustav take a couple of steps to the side. Her husband, Niklas, joins them and absentmindedly starts to brush the snow from Kate's shoulders.

"This is how it was," she says suddenly.

Niklas keep brushing.

"It was snowing just like this!"

"What do you mean?" Niklas asks.

"This is exactly how it was in Budapest in January 1945."

CHAPTER 15

"I am a Swede, Son of a Neutral Nation."

They had managed to keep the Christmas present a secret, probably because they made it in the cellar under the main office at Üllői út. There, Raoul Wallenberg's humanitarian department had created a small graphic-design office, thoroughly equipped with the paper, pens and ink bottles that the Dutch insurance company had left behind. Vilmos Forgács' two sons, Pál and Gábor, spent time in the cellar, printing forms and anything else that was required. Most recently they had been working on a Christmas present for Raoul Wallenberg alongside their regular duties.

Péter Sugár, one of the employees in the Security Protocol, had come up with the idea. He was the same age as Raoul and had been a professor of German Literature before the anti-Jewish laws had deprived him of his post. Péter wanted to write a Christmas elegy about protective passports for Raoul as a Christmas present, a heroic poem in the spirit of Goethe. It would praise Raoul Wallenberg's mission and depict the fictitious history of the protective passports. One of the secretaries would write the poem neatly in German in old-fashioned *Fraktur* script.

The Forgács brothers and two of Raoul's co-workers who were artistically inclined made up their minds to do it. They would contribute illustrative drawings to accompany Sugár's poem – on the theme of "The Protective Passport in Art History". No-one who worked closely with Raoul Wallenberg could ignore his artistic inclinations. He liked to chat about art and architecture and was quick to laugh and make jokes when the circumstances allowed. They knew exactly how they were going to approach this. They would make an offbeat and funny "history of art", with paintings and droll catalogue descriptions: the kind of intellectual humour that Raoul enjoyed. Everyone contributed paintings or quasi-learned art analyses. They created nineteen pieces of art from different epochs, beginning with an invented cave-painting of a bull described as "world history's first protective passport (10,000 BC)" that, "with its contrasting light and dark colours", was said to be "typical of all prehistoric artistic works".

In the finished collection of imaginary reproductions there was everything from antique vases to wood blocks, through to medieval church windows and lyrical seventeenth-century landscapes – all with different protective passport motifs. In the midst of all the misery, Raoul's colleagues excelled in their witticisms. They knew that Raoul Wallenberg would chuckle at the book being printed by the "Schutzpass Verlag 1944", with Raoul's own signature as the logo. He would love the fact that, at the end of the fake scientific references in the footnotes, there was a book by the author "R. Wallenberg" that bore the title "A Humanitarian Mission in the Land of the Savages" and was published in Stockholm in 1946.

The compliment that the artists wanted to convey above all was to be found in this attention to detail. "It was our intention to give something to our guardian protector, Raoul Wallenberg, who embodied St George for us, that he could keep as a memento of this time long into his old age," Gábor Forgács explained later.

The Christmas present was finally ready on Thursday, December 21. The artists went together to Raoul Wallenberg's office but encountered him in the hallway outside in the process of leaving. He had already put on his coat. "We have a gift for you," Péter Sugár said. "Thank you," Raoul Wallenberg replied unsentimentally, taking the book and leaving without a single comment. But subsequently the disappointed artists heard from others that he liked it.

Later on that December day, Péter Sugár participated in a rescue mission with the Security Protocol to assist two Jews with protective passports who were being held prisoner at an Arrow Cross location. He never returned. The Arrow Cross shot him dead during the operation. It would take several days before this information reached the Swedish legation and Raoul Wallenberg.

Having left Budapest, the members of the Arrow Cross government were now staying in various small towns along the Austrian border, including Szombathely. Remaining in the capital city there were instead various acting government representatives from this Hungarian Nazi party. The evacuations did not, unfortunately, bring any sense of relief to the Swedish diplomats, who had recently heard that the Arrow Cross intended to "liquidate the entire Swedish operation". Ominously, the acting foreign minister was the former military attaché, Vöczköndy, who had been deported from Sweden under humiliating circumstances after the Arrow Cross coup on October 15.

Edmund Veesenmayer and his diplomats were also in a hurry to leave now that the Soviet troops were approaching. They burned their confidential documents and followed the Hungarian government west in the last few days before Christmas. Ironically, Veesenmayer asked the Swedish legation to become Germany's protective power and defend its interests in Hungary. They did not have much choice, since most of the other neutral states had fled the field. Per Anger went to pick up keys to the German legation building from an unexpectedly gracious and conciliatory Edmund Veesenmayer.

Otherwise there were few noticeable preparations for the impending Soviet invasion. In Buda, people were out doing their Christmas shopping. Fathers were carrying their Christmas trees home and on the radio there was Christmas music. The day before Christmas Eve, the State Opera of Budapest gave a performance of Verdi's "Aida" and even at the cinema films were screened as usual. For Budapest's non-Jewish population, life was by no means shattered.

The tens of thousands of Jews in the large central ghetto, however, were fighting for their lives under the vilest of conditions. Raoul Wallenberg drew attention to this ongoing humanitarian catastrophe with disgust in his final missive to the Hungarian Foreign Ministry, dated December 22:

> There [in the main ghetto] lie not hundreds but thousands of sick people in unheated rooms without mattresses, without blankets, with minimal health care and food rations, provided by official distribution, that consist of a quarter of what is considered a normal nutritional requirement. At the Danube quay, Jewish people are often shot without due process, even without so much as a drumhead court-martial. One such individual who was shot and subsequently pulled out of the Danube – moreover the mother of an employee at the legation – is still lying in hospital with a bullet in her back.

*

Life was considerably more tolerable for the approximately 35,000 Jews living in the Swedish and Swiss houses in the international ghetto.

It seems from the letter Raoul sent to the Hungarian Foreign Ministry that he wished to provide something of an overview of the critical situation, and an explanation for the Swedish activities, not simply to protest against individual incidents. Reading between the lines, one can sense that he is addressing both the current and the future ruling authorities from the super-power to the east.

Raoul Wallenberg observed that neutral Sweden had always seen it as its duty in wartime to help those who were suffering in other countries. The Swedish humanitarian action in Budapest should therefore be regarded as a continuation of Sweden's many rescue missions in the First World War. With a diplomatic nod to communists as well as Nazis he mentioned the Swedish nurse Elsa Brändström's heroic work in Russia and Siberia – "even during the revolution" – and the Swedish Red Cross' efforts for vulnerable "Aryan" Hungarian children in the years following the First World War. He did not miss the chance to mention that Asta Nilsson from the Swedish Red Cross, who had led the work then, was now back in Hungary as the leader of the Red Cross' orphanage operation. In his overview of Swedish aid operations he also mentioned the collection of funds for Finland in 1939.

It was in this historical context that the Swedish decision to organise a humanitarian operation in Hungary should be viewed, Raoul went on. After the inhumane deportations of the spring it was natural to direct aid to Hun-gary's Jews. He told them about the important function of the protective passports. Sweden wanted to send home all these protected individuals, he asserted, but had encountered difficulties in finding trains for their transpor-tation to Sweden.

In fact, the Swedish legation had actually wanted to extend its aid oper-ation. The thinking had been to supply food and clothing to other groups of Hungarians as well as the Jews but, unfortunately, the Hungarian government had always declined. It was, however, not too late, he stated, not even if the Russians occupied Budapest. Sweden had been appointed the protective power for the Soviet Union in Hungary. This meant that "in the event of a temporary occupation of Budapest" – read the arrival of the Red Army – then

Sweden would be in a good position to be able to continue its humanitarian operation.

Raoul Wallenberg was not alone in his optimistic attitude towards the Soviet Union. At the Swedish legation, everyone was convinced that, when the Russians arrived, they would endorse the Swedish rescue operation for the Hungarian Jews. And Raoul had thought further than this. He had been working with colleagues on ideas for rebuilding Hungary after the war, which he wanted to convey to the Russians as soon as possible. Nothing indicates that he expected anything other than applause.

The thought was that the cooperative "Wallenberg Institute for Aid and Reconstruction" would offer the needy temporary loans. The same day Raoul Wallenberg wrote his last lines to the Hungarian Foreign Ministry, he also sent a telegram to the Swiss bank and asked them to transfer his portion of the initial capital for the cooperative, around 100,000 kronor (over £1.5 million today). This would be taken from the American money and deposited in a new, separate account in his name.

Unfortunately, this was easier said than done. The transfer of American money via the Swiss banks did not work flawlessly. An irritated Raoul had begun to receive claims for damages from Hungarian merchants who had provided the Swedish legation with several tons of bacon, tinned meat or pork fat in exchange for promised deposits in Swiss bank accounts. But, for an unknown reason, the payment had not materialised. Money was a difficult subject for Raoul Wallenberg. Even by the beginning of December, the Foreign Ministry had not paid out a single one of the monthly salaries that he had been promised when he left Sweden.

Raoul Wallenberg concluded his final letter to the Hungarian Foreign Ministry with a protest against the growing brutality towards Jewish children in Budapest. The humanitarian department's Security Protocol had, a few days earlier, received a cry for help from a Catholic orphanage that was under the Swedish legation's protection. When the unit arrived, they were told that eighty Jewish children and forty ordained Catholic brothers had been taken away. They were told that the Arrow Cross was planning to bring all the Jewish orphans to the main ghetto.

In his note, Raoul pleaded with the Foreign Ministry that all the orphanages under Swedish protection be left in peace. As usual, he skipped any emotional appeals to the Arrow Cross' limited powers of empathy, discussing instead how complicated the manoeuvre was from a purely technical standpoint. Many children were so young that they could not yet walk and there were no prams, Raoul observed. He also played on their anti-Semitism, warning them about the unfortunate consequences that the relocation would have for Aryan children in the Swedish orphanages, since the staff were also being relocated to the main ghetto.

He ended with an attempt at something approaching a diplomatic carrot: "If these differences of opinion that have emerged can be cleared out of the way, Sweden will continue its humanitarian operations in Hungary in recognition of the great mutual sympathies that exist between both countries."

But shortly thereafter the orphanage of the Swedish Red Cross was also stormed. All the children who lived there were removed together with six men and six women from the staff, though luckily not the Swedish chief, Asta Nilsson. Raoul Wallenberg sped "like lightning from one Arrow Cross and police authority to the next" in order to save those who had been taken away. In the coming days more Jewish orphanages would be targeted in similar operations.

By December 23, Generals Tolbuchin and Malinovsky had largely succeeded in surrounding Budapest. Only one clear way out of the city remained, west towards Vienna. This was under constant Russian artillery fire and it was clear that there were not many hours left before this final avenue for evacuation was also closed.

In the afternoon, both Per Anger and Raoul Wallenberg were called to the Foreign Ministry by Vöczköndy. They were driven there by the Jewish engineer, Vilmos Langfelder, a protected Swedish Jew who had recently stepped into the role of Raoul Wallenberg's driver. Langfelder had strawberry-blond, slicked-back hair and prominent cheekbones. He was the same age as Raoul and came from a well-to-do Jewish family that had made its fortune with steam-driven industrial saws at the beginning of the twentieth century. The young engineer had been given his chauffeuring duties at the humanitarian department because he spoke both English and German and therefore could also function as an interpreter. He had become a confidant of Raoul Wallenberg and it was clear that they enjoyed each other's company.

When they arrived at the Foreign Ministry on Várhegy they were greeted with the message that the meeting had been postponed for a few hours. During this time, Wallenberg and Anger went their separate ways to try to do something for the increasingly threatened Jewish orphanages. Per Anger went to the papal nuncio, Angelo Rotta. Ivan Danielsson, among others, was already there, writing a letter of protest from the neutral legations, in response to the merciless treatment of Jewish children. Wallenberg, Langfelder and a member of the Security Protocol went up to the Hotel Majestic. It was there that not only Adolf Eichmann but also the Hungarian secret police had their offices. They met with a police chief and Raoul conveyed his demand that the Jewish children should be freed. But they received only dismissive responses. When Vöczköndy finally received them at 5.30 p.m. they were convinced that the orphanages would be the topic of discussion.

Vöczköndy was obviously stressed, though the reason for this was not the orphanages, but the Swedish diplomats. In agitated tones he demanded that the Swedish legation leave Budapest that same night. Anything else would be seen as deeply provocative. The Arrow Cross government had ordered a complete evacuation of all official bodies from the capital, the minister reminded them. Per Anger replied gently that the Swedish diplomats did not have any such instructions from the Swedish government and their intentions were to stay. And even if they were not, he added, an evacuation that same evening would be technically impossible to arrange.

Then Vöczköndy became contemptuous. He had only been given an hour to pack his things when the Swedish government deported him in October. Now it was only right that the Swedish legation was treated in the same way. Vöczköndy made it clear that, if they refused, he could not be responsible for the consequences. When Anger wondered if he meant that they would be subjected to violence, Vöczköndy answered evasively.

Anger and Wallenberg interpreted this as indirect confirmation. Per Anger immediately returned to the legation, summoned all of his Swedish colleagues and told them about the threat. During the next twenty-four hours, he said, no-one was allowed to stay in the legation building and the best thing would be if they spent the night somewhere other than their regular residences. At around 10 p.m. they all left.

During this time Vilmos Langfelder had driven Raoul Wallenberg to the

Swiss consul Carl Lutz to discuss the new threat. Lutz confirmed that he had also heard that the Arrow Cross were going to undertake an operation against the diplomats. "It looks as if everything could be over," Raoul Wallenberg is supposed to have said when he emerged from the meeting with Lutz a few hours later.

That evening, Raoul Wallenberg drove to the main office at Üllői út in order to warn his staff, just as Per Anger had done. According to Jenő Lévai, Raoul told them that the legation was in danger and that it looked as if the rescue operations would have to cease. He told his colleagues to take care of themselves and try to find a secure place to stay. Everyone started to pack. The leadership group, including Hugó Wohl and Vilmos Forgács, were already in the new branch office at the Hazai Bank most of the time. Raoul Wallenberg himself decided to move over to Pest and spend the Christmas holiday with Pál Hegedűs and his family, in his apartment a few streets north of the Üllői út office. Per Anger moved into the one-bedroom apartment he had rented, in part to put up refugees, in the building at Úri utca where Erzsébet Nákó lived.

Later that evening, Ivan Danielsson sent a telegram to the Foreign Ministry in Stockholm about the Hungarian ultimatum and the hints of violent reprisals against the Swedish legation. But, unfortunately, the telegram would not reach the Ministry until the following day.

The only communication that arrived in Stockholm on the evening of December 23 was a telephone message that had been called in from Budapest via the Berlin legation. The Foreign Ministry's official on duty in Stockholm wrote it down by hand at 7.40 p.m. It concluded in the following way: "The attachés Anger and Wallenberg would like to send their regards to Mrs Anger and Wallenberg's parents (Dardel) respectively and wish them a merry Christmas."

It was decided that the Swedish staff at the legation would celebrate Christmas together. At 10.30 a.m. on December 24, they planned to begin their Christmas Eve celebrations at Margareta Bauer's place. She still lived in the apartment in the Zwack family's villa, which was next to the legation house at Gyopár utca. Margareta had baked Christmas biscuits and set the table with candles, Christmas decorations and spruce branches. She had hosted Asta

Nilsson from the Swedish Red Cross the night before. Clearly the apartment at Minerva utca was regarded as safe.

In the afternoon, the Christmas festivities would be moved to Lars Berg's and Göte Carlsson's house, beginning at around 4 p.m. Lars Berg and Göte Carlsson had been at the urgent meeting at the legation the night before but had decided not to heed Anger's advice to seek out a different place to spend the night – they had weapons with which to defend themselves and also needed to prepare for the Christmas party. Both were up until 4 a.m. wrapping packages, composing Christmas rhymes and decorating a large Christmas tree that a secretary had managed to procure. Snow falling gently over Budapest added to the Christmas spirit.

On Christmas Eve, at 6 a.m., Lars Berg was awakened by the telephone. The porter at the B-division screamed that Berg had to come down immediately. The Arrow Cross had broken into the building and were now dragging out all the occupants.

Berg and Carlsson were soon there. Outside the old Finnish legation house, where the Swedish legation's protective power department was housed, there were armed Arrow Cross men in uniform with their red-and-white armbands. The two Swedes decided that Göte Carlsson would wait in the car and Lars Berg would make his way inside.

There he found a dozen plainclothes and uniformed gendarmes. Lars Berg managed to get to a telephone and called the legation house at Gyopár utca, a hundred metres up the street. He reached the chef de mission. Yes, the Arrow Cross had broken in there too a few hours earlier. They had searched the entire house for Danielsson, who was not there. The Arrow Cross had helped themselves to the drinks cabinet and then continued on to the protective power department. "Wait, Mr Berg," the chef de mission said, as he saw the Arrow Cross returning, "Now they are taking Mr Carlsson as well."

A stone's throw from the drama, Margareta Bauer was lying in her bed, asleep. Suddenly she felt someone tugging on her arm. "Are you Margareta Bauer?" A man was addressing her in broken German. She opened her eyes. In the bedroom there were five armed Arrow Cross men. "Get up, you're coming with us."

Asta Nilsson, who was lying in Bauer's guest room, received the same brusque awakening. Groggily, they joined each other in their nightgowns.

Then the telephone rang. It was Lars Berg. "Have they made it there yet?" he asked. He advised Margareta to try to delay the Arrow Cross for as long as she could, so that someone would have time to get there and help them.

Lars Berg managed to get in a call to Per Anger at Úri utca before a gendarme laid his rifle barrel over the telephone and stopped him. "Do not come to the legation," Berg had time to say, "I've just been arrested."

Berg was disarmed and the intruders explained that several groups of gendarmes and Arrow Cross had been sent out to seize the Swedish diplomats and take them to Szombathely. The bus was already waiting outside the legation house. They asked where Anger and Danielsson were and Lars Berg realised that he had to give them an answer. In order to confuse them he gave them the address of his shoemaker.

The Finnish diplomats' cars were still in the garage as well as Lars Berg's private car. When the Arrow Cross found them they decided to transport Lars Berg to Szombathely alone by car. The bus could be used for the others. They reluctantly agreed to Berg's plea to be able to get his clothes from his apartment. Escorted by armed guards, he drove his Opel Capitan through snow-covered Buda. He had a machine gun aimed at his midriff during the entire trip.

Margareta Bauer and Asta Nilsson followed Lars Berg's advice. They got dressed as slowly as they could. For a while things looked promising because the drunken Arrow Cross men had fallen asleep on the sofa next to the table set for Christmas breakfast. But they woke up and ordered them to leave. Sixty-four-year-old Asta Nilsson had nothing more than high-heeled shoes to wear as she made her way through the snow.

The first stop was the protective power department in the Finnish legation house. It looked as if a bomb had gone off. Hoards of intoxicated Arrow Cross men were feasting on the food and drink from the pantry. Objects lay spread out over the entire floor – writing materials, tablecloths and silver candelabras all in a jumble. The women waited in the midst of this mess for several hours. The Arrow Cross had plans for them, but were first going to collect some ten or twenty other, in their view suspicious, people that they had scraped together during the night.

In the end there were eighteen of them. They were ordered to march two by two, with armed Arrow Cross guards on either side, through the city. Only when they reached one of the Arrow Cross houses in Pest did they come to a stop. There the Swedes had to leave their passports and were taken to a barracks courtyard. Margareta and Asta looked around and caught sight of a pile of dead bodies in a corner. Their horror grew as their group of eighteen was asked to turn to face the wall of the barracks and stand perfectly still, lined up in a row. A multitude of thoughts were swirling in Margareta Bauer's head.

> Dear Father and Mother, what will you think of this? You will never find out where we will be buried. It is soon our turn. Thank you my beloved parents . . . I pray to God. Help us, dear God, both Asta and me.

They stood like this for a long time. But nothing happened. Instead there were new orders: to set off on a march to the main ghetto. Again they had to walk two by two, surrounded by armed militia. "What now, aren't we going to be shot?" Margareta Bauer wondered.

Lars Berg did not drive home in his car but instead went to the headquarters of the German army leaders, where he jumped out, identified himself and reported the attack on the Swedish diplomatic representation. When he informed them that Sweden had been entrusted with the keys to the newly abandoned German legation, his story gained traction. The keys were in fact in a safe in Lars Berg's office, which had now been plundered.

The German military immediately freed him from the Arrow Cross men and made sure that he was given back his weapon. Lars Berg was even promised a military escort back to his office in order to locate the German legation's keys. Alarming news of the progress of the Russian armies, however, meant that he eventually had to make his way back on his own. But a German officer supplied him with documents written in German and Hungarian that declared that their bearer was under the protection of the German military.

Per Anger had, of course, not sat idle after the telephone call in the morning. He too went to the German military headquarters and demanded to speak to the general. His aim was to get the Germans to intervene in the unconstitutional attack by the Arrow Cross on Swedish territory. Unfortunately he was not successful. The general simply had his aide inform Anger that the attack was an internal Hungarian matter and that the Swedish diplomat should apply to the Hungarian authorities. But the Hungarian military leadership did not even want to listen to Per Anger's protests, much less take action. Anger then went to the home of the Swiss chargé d'affaires, Harald Feller, and interrupted him in the midst of his Christmas preparations.

By this point, Lars Berg had returned to the now abandoned and plundered office. His desk had been forced open, and the empty drawers were hanging out. Everything of value in the building was gone, the Arrow Cross had not even left the painstakingly wrapped Christmas presents. In the midst of all the mess he found one of the staff and the cook who, terrified, helped him to pack his car for departure. When they had finished, Lars Berg placed a case of champagne on top of the load of bags and filled his tanks with petrol. His thought was to drive to the Swedish general consulate in Vienna. But before he left, he wanted to find the others.

Raoul Wallenberg had spent the morning of Christmas Eve with the Hegedűs family in an apartment in Pest. He was not present when word about the attacks on the Swedish diplomats reached the offices at the Hazai Bank. And there was still no sign of him when, shortly after that, Hugó Wohl and his colleagues were notified that Margareta Bauer and Asta Nilsson had been taken to the main ghetto. He may have been involved in a hunt for kidnapped children – early on Christmas Eve, the Arrow Cross had attacked more orphanages – but, wherever he was, the situation was now too serious for Wohl to wait for him any longer.

The large central ghetto was under close surveillance and was almost impossible to enter. At the Hazai Bank, they therefore decided to alert the International Red Cross – one of the few organisations that had access to the sealed areas. The I.R.C. was led by the Swiss Friedrich Born, who worked close to the Swiss legation. Wohl and his colleagues went to Friedrich Born's home in Buda in order to persuade him to save the two Swedes.

Raoul Wallenberg turned up at the Hazai Bank after they had left. He had heard about the operation and, according to witnesses, looked very serious. His colleagues recognised this look. Wallenberg had had such moments before, when everything fell apart and his will to fight disappeared, and he became darkly pessimistic. But they knew that these attacks of gloom did not tend to last very long. At the first positive sign, his spirit returned.

Up in Buda, Hugó Wohl was having difficulty convincing Friedrich Born to intervene on behalf of Margareta Bauer and Asta Nilsson. At the very least, Born objected, such a request should not come from a locally employed Hungarian but from the Swedish government. A Swedish request was far from straightforward for Wohl to obtain, especially now that the legation house was under the control of the Arrow Cross. At the Swiss legation, Per Anger and Harald Feller had arrived at the same solution, possibly in consultation with Ivan Danielsson, who also found his way there over the course of the day: it had to be Friedrich Born who intervened.

The all-important telephone call appears to have come in the middle of Hugó Wohl's attempts to convince Born. With this, the discussion was over. Friedrich Born left for the main ghetto.

At the ghetto, Margareta Bauer and Asta Nilsson had been received warmly and had even each been given a serving of spaghetti with tomato sauce. But now the afternoon was turning into evening. It was dark outside and they were worried. Then they heard someone calling for them. It was Friedrich Born, who had managed to obtain permission to take them both out of the ghetto. Relieved, they climbed into Born's car for transportation to his combined villa and work place in Buda. When Margareta Bauer and Asta Nilsson stepped into the safety of his dining room, they both broke down. Tears ran down their cheeks as they stood in front of a table spread with food and lit by candles. Once they had eaten, they were each shown to a bed with embroidered silk sheets.

As Christmas Eve came to an end, the first Russian tanks had reached the outskirts of Buda. The sky was illuminated by rockets launched by *Katyushas*, the Soviet artillery system that the Germans had dubbed "Stalin's organ". At Raoul Wallenberg's newly founded Swedish hospital in Pest, the staff had just gathered for a Christmas dinner with soy sausage and puréed peas when all the windows were suddenly blown out by a Russian bombing raid. They were veterans now, but the attack still came as a shock. They had to rush out into the snow and take care of all the dead and injured from the bombed building next door.

The last escape route to Vienna had been cut off a couple of hours earlier and was completely under Russian control. The drunken Obersturmbann-führer Adolf Eichmann had managed to flee in his Jeep only a few hours before the roads closed. Eichmann's driver had to take a slalom course through the terrain in order to avoid the volleys of Russian rockets. Not until Christmas Day did the director of the mass deportations arrive at the German Security Service's temporary offices by the Austrian border. By then, his colleagues had already given him up for dead.

There are several versions of what happened to the other Swedes and where they later met up. According to Per Anger and Margareta Bauer, it was in Anger's secret apartment at Úri utca, in Countess Nákó's house, that they eventually all gathered between late Christmas Eve and early Christmas Day. So, too, Raoul Wallenberg. Margareta Bauer and Asta Nilsson arrived last of all. They were brought there in the early morning hours by Per Anger's driver since their colleagues at the legation had become seriously worried about the Russian bombing raids.

Everyone had come through the ordeal unscathed. It turned out that Göte Carlsson had been joined in the morning by Raoul's food buyer, the consul Yngve Ekmark, in the occupied legation house at Gyopár utca. But Ekmark had managed to flee during the day by pretending to be severely ill. Göte Carlsson had had recourse to another strategy. In the evening he had tempted his Arrow Cross guards with a secret stash of legation alcohol. The guards had eventually fallen asleep and Carlsson could leave.

It was not an easy prospect that awaited the Swedish diplomats once Christmas morning arrived and everyone had told their stories. They knew that they somehow had to retake the Swedish diplomatic territory. At the same time they had to continue to keep themselves out of sight. Budapest was not only a city in the grip of war with all the government authorities evacuated, it was also a city in the hands of the criminal and violent Arrow Cross hooligans – they had already shown what they were capable of. Simply reciting diplomatic laws was no longer viable: the Arrow Cross most likely did not even know what crimes against international law were.

The staff members could not all crowd into Per Anger's apartment at Úri utca. But the new quarters of the Swiss, located behind Count Eszterházy's palace, were deemed to be safe. It had large bomb shelters and, from the cellar, the Swiss had contact with the labyrinthine tunnels under the palace district where several thousands of people were hidden. Ivan Danielsson, Margareta Bauer, Asta Nilsson and Yngve Ekmark had moved there already on Christmas Day. But Raoul Wallenberg was stubborn. He did not want to go underground. He wanted to go to his colleagues in Pest.

At the humanitarian department's Üllői út office the telephone operator Edith Wohl, daughter of Hugó Wohl, had held the fort alone during the dramatic events of Christmas Eve. The rest of the Hungarian staff began to return as evening fell, despite the order to go underground. They had nowhere else to go.

It had often been the case in the circle around Raoul Wallenberg that unexpectedly useful contacts had materialised in times of crisis. During the last month, Raoul and his "security service", the well-staffed Security Protocol, had had several successful collaborations with police and even gendarmes who had been alienated by the actions of the Arrow Cross and become double agents.

Loyalty within the regular Hungarian police was so fragile by this point that the Arrow Cross had been forced to put them under the supervision of a 29-year-old party official called Pál Szalai. But, confronted by the unbridled atrocities that the Arrow Cross mob were perpetrating, even he was starting to get cold feet.

A typewriter technician who had occasionally been hired by the Swedish legation now turned up and offered to help. His name was Károly Szabó, he was twenty-eight years old and had happened to spend his teenage years in the same scout troop as Pál Szalai. Károly Szabó was not himself of Jewish extraction but he had assisted in some earlier rescue missions. The police coordinator, Szalai, had equipped him with a kind of police identification that he made great use of. Szalai had also warned Szabó in advance of the party's planned violent operations.

Károly Szabó had an athletic build and blond hair. He had just invested in a long black leather coat and the final result was that many assumed he was a Gestapo officer. On Christmas day he drove up to the Swedish legation together with the psychoanalyst Fleischmann, one of Wallenberg's closest associates. Dressed in the leather coat and a Tyrolean hat, Károly Szabó walked right into Ivan Danielsson's office and ordered the intoxicated Arrow Cross men to leave the legation. The trick worked and, via his friend Szalai, Szabó then called the police. The telephone call from Ottó Fleischmann made Raoul Wallenberg and his colleagues cheer: "We have won back the legation!"

The following day, the Swedish diplomats gathered for a council of war. They decided that Lars Berg, who had received a German protective order, would return to the legation and guard it, together with the Hungarian official von Mezey. Per Anger would remain at Úri utca and handle any resulting contact with Hungarian and German military leaders. The rest would stay in the palace that the Swiss had rented.

They did not lack for much, at least not in the beginning. Count Eszterházy was still living in the residence and, in the first days, before the kitchen was bombed, the diplomats were served four-course dinners. The Swiss gave them secret codes to crack, as a way of lightening the mood. Margareta Bauer did however note that Danielsson paced anxiously and "rapidly around the garden like a prisoner".

Raoul Wallenberg now became extremely interested in Pál Szalai and asked Károly Szabó to arrange a meeting with him. Close to midnight on Boxing Day, Szabó and Ottó Fleischmann went to the police chief's office in the town hall and fetched Szalai. Raoul Wallenberg was waiting in the repossessed Swedish legation house, where the power was out. Much later, Pál Szalai would remember the rows of trembling Jews who illuminated the stairwell with candles in the darkened building. It was apparent that they became terrified when they realised who had come.

On the night when Raoul Wallenberg and Pál Szalai met for the first time, only about three weeks of Raoul Wallenberg's thirty-two years of freedom remained. These would be three of the most difficult. During that time, the Szabó and Szalai duo would play a central role in the Swedish rescue operations. Wallenberg's handshake agreement with Szalai could perhaps be regarded as controversial after all that had happened, but it would save the lives of many Hungarian Jews.

While still in the hallway, Szalai emphasised that he had not come to see Wallenberg in his official capacity, but as a friend. By the fire in Ivan Danielsson's office, Szalai expressed horror at all the unruly thugs who had joined the Arrow Cross and now drifted about like murderous barbarians on the streets of Budapest. He said that everyone's life was in danger and that henceforth he wanted to work with the Swedish legation and Raoul Wallenberg. He said that he knew that at least one of the senior police chiefs in the city felt the same way. They agreed that Raoul would send word to Szalai as soon as he needed anything.

Szalai did not leave the legation at Gyopár utca until 2 a.m. As he departed he asked the two police officers who had accompanied him to stay behind as bodyguards for Raoul Wallenberg. It is not clear if it was Szalai's initiative or someone else's, but for the next while both the legation building in Buda and Raoul's office in Pest were under twenty-four-hour surveillance by dozens of police and gendarmes.

The staff at Üllői út could temporarily breathe easy and remain in the building with their families. From this point on, Raoul Wallenberg slept in different locations and rarely moved around without bodyguards. He had assembled his necessities in a backpack that he always carried with him.

During the coming weeks, Pál Szalai and Raoul Wallenberg met several times a day. Raoul was also eager to share his new contact. He saw to it that Szalai got in touch with the Swiss legation as well as some of the leaders from the Jewish Council.

"What was so typical of him [Raoul Wallenberg] was that he, unlike the Swiss and the others, wanted to help everyone. He wanted to help the ghetto in a way that meant he helped the Swiss as well as the Swedes, and everyone else who was persecuted," Pál Szalai said in an interview many years later.

At the Foreign Ministry in Stockholm, concern was growing with each passing day at the lack of contact from the legation in Budapest. The telephones had been cut off and telegrams did not seem to be getting through. Ministry officials anxiously recalled the information about the threat of violent retribution. When four days of silence had gone by, the evacuated Swedish minister in Berlin, Arvid Richter, was asked to look into the fate of the Budapest Swedes with the Auswärtiges Amt. The consulate in Vienna was also asked to investigate whether the Swedish diplomats had possibly made their way to the Austrian border.

The Auswärtiges Amt quickly received word from the evacuated German representation in Szombathely. The German envoys had spoken to the Hungarians and could relate that, "the Swedish minister is in hiding in an undisclosed location in Budapest and the legation secretary Wallenberg from the Swedish Embassy has placed himself under German protection (Waffen S.S.)." The German foreign official was trying out an explanation: "This should be seen in connection with certain actions from the Hungarian police regarding the Arrow Cross."

The Siege of Budapest had now begun in earnest. On the outskirts of the surrounded city, both German and Hungarian troops fought hard as they tried to follow Hitler's express order that not a single street corner of Budapest was to be given up. But the Red Army was a formidable opponent. General Rodion Malinovsky had broken through important lines of defence in the eastern suburbs and his troops had engaged in brutal street battles. And to the west General Tolbukhin had continued his advance.

Nonetheless, the Soviet war leaders wanted to try another way of capturing the city. On December 29, leaflets fluttered down over Budapest, urging the Germans and Hungarians to capitulate. Generals Malinovsky and Tolbukhin followed up by each sending an officer to the German-Hungarian military leaders. They travelled under a white flag and brought the Germans an ultimatum: immediate surrender in exchange for favourable treatment. But the Germans flatly refused. Neither of the two Soviet messengers returned alive.

With this, the fate of Budapest was sealed. The streets of the city would become a battlefield. That day, snow fell heavily over Budapest. It was -4°C out- side and almost impossible to orient oneself in the midst of all the white. Moving around in the poor visibility was associated with almost immediate danger.

A Soviet bomb had obliterated both the kitchen and guest room in Count Eszterházy's palace and forced everyone down into the cold and damp cellar. There the Swedes played bridge and sang songs to distract themselves. Raoul Wallenberg and the Swiss chargé d'affaires, Harald Feller, held a war council in the original Swiss legation house in Pest. They discussed various plans of action together with the two leading Hungarian Jews – Miklós Krausz from the Swiss "emigration department" and Károly Wilhelm from the Jewish Council. By the light of the fluttering candles, they talked through the ways in which Feller and Wallenberg would be able to make their way to the Russians in order to inform them of the situation. A few hours later, Harald Feller and his fiancée were apprehended and taken to an Arrow Cross location where he was beaten unconscious. He was only released after he threatened that the Arrow Cross consul in Switzerland would be hanged if they continued.

There was complete chaos in the Hungarian capital. People who had been injured in the various bombing raids streamed to the Swedish hospital in the international ghetto. On some days, close to five hundred patients shared the fifty beds. The doctors had to hang rugs and blankets to keep the cold from entering through the bomb-shattered windows. On one of the last days of 1944, the doctors performed four amputations, one operation to remove shrapnel from someone's back, four chest operations (bullets) and ten to twelve operations to remove grenade fragments. They also had to deal with the birth of a premature baby.

The day the first injured Arrow Cross man knocked on the door and received help, a barrier came down. Soon Raoul Wallenberg's staff were also taking care of sixty injured soldiers at a military hospital next door, which had been abandoned when the original staff had fled.

During the last weekend of the year, the acts of violence against the Swedish-protected Jews intensified. The day before New Year's Eve, eight Arrow Cross men armed with machine guns stormed into one of the Swedish houses in the international ghetto. All 170 people who lived there – sick as well as healthy, the elderly as well as infants – were forced out into the courtyard, deprived of all of their goods and ordered to line up. After a few hours in one of the Arrow Cross headquarters, at midnight they were taken down to an area close to the Danube quay. There they were bundled out onto the quay in groups, bound together with leather belts, shot and allowed to fall like sheaves of wheat into the cold water.

Neighbours alerted Raoul Wallenberg to the arrests. He made some inquiries at the Hungarian Foreign Ministry. But, according to eyewitnesses, it was more likely his contacts with "military formations in the underground movement" that put a stop to the killings before all the Swedish Jews had been exterminated. Similar operations were directed at other Swedish houses. That weekend, several hundred Jews with Swedish protective passports were shot on the Danube quay. And many others fell victim to the same fate.

Raoul Wallenberg contacted his new ally, the police coordinator Szalai, who was in the town hall in Pest. Szalai was sceptical. There were not sufficient numbers of sympathetic police officers and gendarmes to protect all the houses in the international ghetto. He advised Raoul to move all of the Jews under international protection, including the Swiss, to the main ghetto. Raoul was painfully aware of the living conditions in the main ghetto and Szalai's suggestion filled him with horror.

On New Year's Eve, Margareta Bauer, Ivan Danielsson and the others played yet another game of bridge in their dank cellar. As a gesture of gratitude, Margareta deliberately allowed Count Esterházy to win. Back in the legation building, Lars Berg went to bed after an attempt to normalise his existence with an elegant dinner. As usual, he went to sleep with his boots on and a machine gun close to hand. Raoul Wallenberg had again switched residences and was going to celebrate the New Year in a palace in northern Pest with Hugó Wohl. But, during the night, the house was bombed and they had to leave.

A few hours before midnight, the Swiss ambassador to Sweden called the Foreign Ministry in Stockholm. He had received a telegram about Budapest with a single barely legible sentence: "No members of the Swedish legation are injured." This message was forwarded that same evening to the next of kin.

While the Swedish diplomats in Budapest were filled with an almost naïvely positive sense of anticipation concerning the Soviet "liberators", their colleagues in the Soviet Union, who were now brought into the situation, had more mixed feelings.

Staffan Söderblom, Sweden's minister in Moscow, was forty-four years old and had been the head of the political department at the Swedish Foreign Ministry for a large part of the war. For the first few war years, Söderblom had argued vociferously that a strategic policy of appeasement vis-à-vis Germany was the best way to keep Sweden out of the war. This position had made him a favourite of Christian Günther. He maintained this stance until 1942, when Swedish foreign policy was slowly reoriented as it became increasingly clear that Germany was heading for defeat.

There were those who labelled Söderblom a Nazi for what was construed as his German-friendly position, but nothing could have been further from the truth. If perhaps he occasionally went too far in accommodating the Germans, it was always for pragmatic, not ideological, reasons. Söderblom had no problems changing his political strategy when the war turned and had been active in the Swedish rescue operation for the Danish Jews in October 1943.

Söderblom had also been an enthusiastic anglophile since he was a child. At sixteen he translated his idol William Shakespeare's sonnets and gave them to his mother as a present. The young Staffan Söderblom often said that one should throw a lasso around the British Isles, tow them to the Swedish west coast and anchor them there. A decidedly gentlemanly aura radiated from his person. He dressed smartly and walked with a straight back, like the cavalry officer he was.

On New Year's Eve 1944, Söderblom had been in his new post for barely six months. He had left Sweden around the same time as Raoul Wallenberg, the man whose fate would soon land on his desk.

When Staffan Söderblom had arrived in Moscow in the summer of 1944, the diplomatic relations between Sweden and the Soviet Union were uncomfortably strained. At the end of 1943, his predecessor, Vilhelm Assarsson, had been declared *persona non grata* after the Russians claimed to have discovered that the Swedes were leaking Soviet military secrets to Germany.

Staffan Söderblom entered into his new assignment in Moscow with vigour. He was determined to be the man to deliver what Christian Günther and Prime Minister Per Albin Hansson most desired: radically improved and trusting relations with the Soviet Union.

Within the Foreign Ministry, Söderblom was known as a great talent, a driven and diligent worker. He spoke French, English, German and Russian and was quick-witted in both his thinking and speech. Perhaps too quick: his humorous British understatements and ironic utterances were often misunderstood and occasionally gave offence.

Söderblom generally came across as confident, even superior. But he had other dimensions, marked as he was by being one of ten children of the great Archbishop Nathan Söderblom. Growing up with a successful father, who was adored by the public and whom he himself boundlessly admired (though, as an agnostic, he did not share his father's strong Christian faith), had left an impression. He had a need for affirmation and high, self-imposed expectations of performance, recognition and success. There were moments of searing self-criticism, darkness and pessimism. And there was a vulnerability that he did everything he could to conceal. "Staffan was a friendly and obliging person, courteous, I would say. But he did not approach life lightly. He was anything but thick-skinned, very controlled. One could tell that he had very strong emotions on the inside," a relative recalls.

Staffan Söderblom's realpolitik-inspired stance towards Germany was, in many ways, consistent with his outwardly somewhat servile persona. He felt that one should "avoid unnecessary difficulties and antagonisms", and this had been his motto during his concession-driven relationship with Germany. That strategy would be employed again in Moscow, he had explained to his colleagues at the legation when he arrived in July 1944. They would no longer waste time getting bogged down in recriminations. Instead they would seize on everything that was positive and not utter a single word that the Russians could use against them. "Rather brush away the difficulties than be felled by them," is how the then deputy, Ingemar Hägglöf, remembers the Söderblomian programme.

In the beginning, things had gone well. The new minister had praised the modernised Soviet Union in his reports back home with a fervour that caused his colleagues to draw the conclusion that he was under surveillance. Which he most likely was. "In Söderblom's mirror everything was good: people, public statements, events, landscapes, the weather. All those involved were friendly and funny, intelligent and honest. Even Stalin appeared human and forthright," as one of them wrote later.

Staffan Söderblom also benefited from the fact that discreet Swedish diplomatic mediation had strongly contributed to the Finnish–Soviet armistice of September 1944. And, in November 1944, Sweden had presented a generous proposal for a Swedish–Soviet trade agreement that could not be seen as anything other than a gesture of friendship.

Söderblom's enthusiasm had continued unabated during the December visit to Stockholm that he had just concluded. He was so exuberant that his successor at the Foreign Ministry, Sven Grafström, commented on it in his journal:

Söderblom is gracing Stockholm with his presence. He is completely gripped by a messianic conviction when it comes to the Soviets. To anyone who will listen he sings Russia's praises and holds forth on how extraordinary our relations with Moscow are. I think he is going to be outright dangerous when our relations with the Russians require a firm grip – and that day is coming.

So far, Söderblom's enthusiasm had correlated fairly closely with the glorified view of the Soviet Union held by his colleagues in Budapest. But now it was New Year's Eve and, over the past few weeks, he had experienced one setback after another.

It had started on December 12. That was when Söderblom visited the deputy foreign minister,* Vladimir Dekanozov, who was responsible for northern Europe. Suddenly the cordial atmosphere from earlier meetings had vanished. Instead Söderblom encountered irritation and pointed comments. Dekanozov wanted to talk about the 30,000 Baltic people who, faced by Soviet advances in the autumn, had fled to Sweden in boats across the sea. Their proper home was back in the Soviet Union, Dekanozov observed sharply. Sweden should never have received them and it was imperative that they should be sent back. Visibly agitated, Dekanozov claimed that the Swedes had, "by hook or by crook", prevented the refugees from returning.

Söderblom had replied that Sweden was not planning to force the refugees out of the country. Dekanozov could not understand this. "Did the Swedish government really intend to give way to sentimental feelings rather than tend the good relations with the Soviets?"

The frosty mood remained during the next meeting the following week. When Söderblom returned from the Foreign Ministry that day, Hägglöf noted that he was "despondent and pessimistic". In his report to Stockholm, Söderblom described the unfriendly reception as inexplicable. "I will not be in a hurry to return to see the gentlemen in question."

But, only a week later, he was forced to get in touch with them again. The

* Until 1946 the formal title for this role in the Soviet Union was Deputy People's Commissar of Foreign Affairs (with the Ministry known as the People's Commissariat of Foreign Affairs), but to avoid confusion I have used foreign minister and Foreign Ministry throughout.

day before New Year's Eve, the Swedish foreign minister sent a telegram to Moscow saying that the Budapest legation had gone underground after violent threats. Söderblom was given the task of asking the Russians to help the Swedish diplomats once they had liberated Budapest. To be safe, a complete list of names was sent over. The Foreign Ministry also supplied Söderblom with a couple of helpful arguments. He was to say that the only reason that the Swedish legation was still in Budapest was that Sweden wanted to see through its assignment to act as protective power for the Soviet Union, as well as aid the fifteen thousand or more Jews that had been placed under Swedish protection.

Staffan Söderblom presented this request in a written note to Dekanozov. On January 2, 1945, the Generals Tolbukhin and Malinovsky at the fronts in Budapest each received a telegram in a cipher from the Red Army's headquarters in Moscow. The telegram informed them that the Swedish diplomatic mission had remained in the beleaguered city. They were given the names of all staff members, urged to report when they were encountered and then wait for further instructions regarding precautions to safeguard them.

Not even Raoul Wallenberg could continue to ignore the fact that the situation had become more hopeless. The Arrow Cross who had taken over in Budapest appeared to want to use the short time they had left in power to exterminate as many Jews as possible.

In addition, he had a series of death threats issued against him. A number of Arrow Cross leaders were convinced that Wallenberg was spying for the Allies and had radio transmitters in the cellar at the legation. The Swedes and the groups under their protection were now fair game. From the Arrow Cross perspective their extra-territorial rights had expired once the Swedish legation had refused to follow the government to the west.

For safety's sake, Raoul was careful to stay on the move, but he did not go underground. He was followed by his bodyguard police officers or by armed gendarmes, and he had the engineer and chauffeur Vilmos Langfelder constantly by his side. They drove around in the maroon Studebaker with the number plate AY 152. It was plastered with diplomatic and courier signage and other protective information. Raoul was intent on keeping himself abreast of the siege's progress and he often turned up at Pál Szalai's Arrow Cross headquarters, where he could follow the Russian advances marked by flags on a map mounted on one of the walls. But he was also daring enough to drive up Gellért Hill so he could see for himself how far the Red Army had advanced into Pest.

On January 2, the Hazai Bank was bombed. In the attack, another legation driver was killed and Raoul Wallenberg's colleagues now had to move down into the bank vaults for safety. There, behind a half-metre-thick armoured door with multiple locks, there were some twenty to forty people crowded on straw mattresses. Sometimes Pál Szalai came to the bank vault for negotiations. The first time Wallenberg opened the heavy iron door, he delightedly pointed out to Szalai that the vault contained far greater riches than money: people.

The year 1945 had certainly not begun hopefully for Raoul Wallenberg. Within hours the Arrow Cross ordered that all Jews in the international ghetto were to be relocated to the main ghetto. This was a serious setback. Raoul foresaw a dramatic starvation catastrophe. The food transports of the International Red Cross to the closed-off ghetto had just been halted because no suppliers dared to take on the job. Raoul made an approximate calculation and arrived at the conclusion that the main ghetto's 70,000 imprisoned Jews would find themselves on the brink of starvation in only a few days. To relocate the 35,000 Jews under international protection under these circumstances could not be viewed as anything other than a deliberate act of mass murder.

On January 3 Raoul Wallenberg contacted the military authorities in order to try to avert the situation. The German military commander was informed that "this plan must from a humanitarian perspective be regarded as inhuman and senseless. It is not known to the Royal Legation [Sweden's diplomatic representation] that such a plan has ever been carried out by the government of a civilised nation." Raoul threatened to hold the Hungarian army leadership responsible for the 100,000 lives that would probably be lost.

But the decision appeared irrevocable. From police in the area there came word that something was about to happen. Raoul Wallenberg saw no other option than to give way, at least temporarily. If he resisted, there was the risk that matters would end even more badly.

The following day, a message went out to the Swedish neighbourhoods that everyone should prepare to move to the main ghetto. The protected Jews were urged to pack their essential belongings in parcels or backpacks and not to bring more than they could carry for long stretches. They were to write their names on the rest of their belongings and leave them where they were. A few hours later, the first four houses were evacuated. The head of the management office for the Swedish houses in the international ghetto became so distraught at this fatal turn of events that he took his own life.

But Raoul Wallenberg had not given up completely. He continued his negotiations even after the decision to let the protected Jews be relocated. Now he turned directly to the most senior members of the Arrow Cross left in Budapest, the city commander, Ernő Vajna, and the head of the militia, Imre Nidosi. They were holed up in the bomb shelter under the town hall in Pest, at the feared address Városház utca 14.

Raoul Wallenberg played the best card he had: food. Even the Arrow Cross were hungry. When Raoul promised them a portion of the humanitarian department's supplies, he finally managed to arrange at least a forty-eight-hour postponement of the planned evacuation. This reprieve also held for the Swiss houses. A couple of signed protective passports were probably included in these negotiations.

In the town hall, Wallenberg met an Italian, Giorgio Perlasca, who had taken over as de facto chargé d'affaires when the Spanish diplomats had left. He was now responsible for two hundred or so Jews under Spanish protection. Raoul Wallenberg had helped him by, among other things, putting him in touch with the high-ranking police chief Szalai.

Raoul now told Giorgio Perlasca about the threats he had received. He asked if the Spanish legation could offer him a haven for a couple of days. Perlasca promised to take him in. The days went by and Perlasca waited, but Raoul Wallenberg never turned up.

The evacuation of the international ghetto had been postponed but the situation was highly uncertain. They were dealing with unbridled barbarians who had completely lost touch with whatever sense of humanity they had once possessed. The militia leader Imre Nidosi was one of the very worst. He had previously run the renowned Gellért baths in Buda. When the Arrow Cross government left Budapest shortly before Christmas, he had appointed himself the commander of all the Arrow Cross units. The rumour was that it was he who had incited the Arrow Cross militia to indiscriminate killings by printing leaflets with the words "execute all traitors where they stand". Refusal to obey this order supposedly carried a death sentence.

A handshake carried no weight in this hell and the most extensive attack on the Swedish houses came on the night of January 8. Armed Arrow Cross units stormed into the Swedish humanitarian department's administrative offices at Jókai utca 1. Just like the head office at Üllői út, Jókai utca was outside the area in Pest that constituted the international ghetto. But the house was protected nonetheless. A large Swedish flag hung outside, as did a sign outlining Swedish extra-territorial rights.

Some 260–290 people lived at Jókai utca, all Jews under Swedish protection and, in many cases, employed by Raoul Wallenberg's department. A sense of anxiety had spread in the house the day before the attack when the gendarme guards had suddenly been called away. In addition, a week earlier, the house manager had been arrested and shot. The building's occupants knew that something was afoot.

The Arrow Cross unit now searched the entire house and ordered all the residents to report to the courtyard "within three minutes". Most of them had been sheltering in the cellar from the bombing, when they were forced out into the winter night, shaking in equal measure from cold and terror.

From the courtyard they were forced to march out into the snow-covered streets and on towards an unknown destination. They were all certain that the journey would end at the Danube quay. But first they had to spend the night standing crowded together at the Arrow Cross headquarters at Városház utca 14. There they were assaulted and robbed of their valuables, before they were sent in small groups to meet their fate.

Among those in this crowd was twelve-year-old Kati Kadelburger (today Kate Wacz). Sixty-five years after the attack she could still remember the drama and snowfall over Budapest in January 1945. "We were packed like sardines. Then they started screaming for the children. I went up to an Arrow Cross woman who looked terrifying and I had to take off my necklace. In the pocket of my brown pullover I had a few hazelnuts. There was also a small potassium cyanide ampule that my mother had given me when the Arrow

Cross came into power. All these I had to hand over. Then the horrible woman ordered me to remove my boots. 'But how will I be able to walk?' I asked her. 'If you don't take them off I will shoot you,' she screamed."

Kati's mother and brother were sent in the same group and ordered to walk. Kati had to march in her socks through the snowdrifts, towards the Danube quay and, she believed, her death. Instead the Arrow Cross guards stopped in front of a high wall. A door opened and the group was let inside. Kati saw streets lined with corpses and understood where they had come. In a sudden gesture of "empathy" the Arrow Cross had taken the women and children to the main ghetto. But at least 180 of the Swedish Jews seized during those days were executed at the Danube quay.

According to the typewriter technician Károly Szabó, Raoul Wallenberg visited the militia leader Imre Nidosi in the shelter at Városház utca that night, without knowing that the protected Jews from Jókai utca were being kept prisoner there. They went there together, as Raoul wanted to protest against the attack. Szabó would never forget the visit to the dark, vaulted cellar. "In the half-dark room we first spotted Nidosi's girlfriend, who was lying on a divan eating biscuits. At the table, around which Nidosi and other Arrow Cross leaders, including Kurt Rettmann and Second Lieutenant Darabont, were sitting, there were burning candles arranged around a skull. Nidosi's group asserted that they 'had no knowledge of the case of Jókai utca 1'.

A few of the residents of Jókai utca 1 had managed to remain hidden during the entire raid. Nineteen-year-old newly-wed Alice Korányi and her husband Erwin, for example. Alice had been saved from a forced labour camp in August after Raoul Wallenberg had issued her with a protective passport. After the Arrow Cross coup, the young couple had been moving between various hiding places and had finally ended up in a room on the fourth floor of the Swedish house at Jókai utca 1. This was where they were on the night the Arrow Cross unit came.

Erwin acted quickly. He looked around and discovered a bathroom window, one and a half square metres in size. Then he tied a sheet around Alice, fastened it to the window and they both crawled out. For two hours she hung outside, in a narrow four-storey-high gap with a slender and over-loaded iron bar as her only support. It helped that Erwin Korányi was an elite gymnast. He propped himself up by pushing his back against one wall and his feet against the other. Sweat poured down their bodies and their hands froze to ice in the January cold. They heard pistol shots and loud screams. Alice felt sheer panic.

Then everything fell silent. They thought they could hear each other's heartbeats. They waited a little while longer before they dared to crawl back inside. In the house they found the rest of Erwin's family, who had all managed to hide.

The following day, January 8, they made their way to Raoul Wallenberg's head office at Üllői út. Most of the protected Jews were staying there in a shelter in the cellar. Erwin and Alice were now completely exhausted but they felt that they could relax in this new and, at the same time, familiarly Swedish-tinged milieu.

Unfortunately things did not stay calm for long. Just as had happened at the house at Jókai utca the night before, the armed gendarmes guarding the house were called away before the Arrow Cross made their assault. All the 156 Swedish Jews in the house were seized and taken away. They were beaten in a barracks cellar before they were directed to a darkened "dressing room" in an Arrow Cross house. This time Alice and Erwin had not managed to escape. Along with Gábor Forgács they were among those who now stood there in their shirtsleeves and heard the Arrow Cross talking about the Danube.

But news of the storming of Üllői út had reached one of Raoul Wallenberg's colleagues. Of his own accord he informed Pál Szalai, who reacted swiftly and ordered the local police chief to free the Swedish Jews with the help of an armed unit. To Alice Korányi it seemed as if it was once again Raoul Wallenberg who saved her life.

The police escorted them all back to Üllői út but explained that they could no longer protect them. If they wanted to stay, they would be doing so at their own risk.

Raoul Wallenberg was thinking intensely about how to get to the Russians early. On Wednesday, January 10, 1945 he asked Károly Szabó to come to the shelter in the vault at the Hazai Bank. Raoul wanted his help to reach the Red Army.

Raoul had several pressing issues that he wanted to present to the Soviet leadership in Debrecen as soon as possible. He wanted the attacks on the house that belonged to the Swedish legation to stop and he wanted to discuss how to save the people in the ghetto. Last but not least, he wanted to present his plan for an aid programme in Hungary after the war. In his briefcase he had a detailed memo about the proposed "Wallenberg Institute". He had also written a personal appeal to the Hungarian people that he hoped to be able to publish once he had been given clearance from the Russians and the provisional Hungarian government in Debrecen.

In the countless documents he had authored during the autumn, Raoul Wallenberg had always kept a low profile. Not once had he beaten his chest or highlighted his personal efforts. Now, in the appeal, it was time to take that step.

I beg your indulgence for the fact that I here, for the first and last time, in this ostentatious way, address the public in the first person. But I feel it is necessary for the sake of those who are suffering, since my name is known from the Royal Swedish Embassy's humanitarian operation, the leader of which I have been until now. Many thousands have shown great faith in my rescue mission and I appeal to this faith for the following undertaking. I am a Swede, the son of a neutral nation. My country and I have never viewed neutrality as a comfortable, passive state. On the contrary . . . For several months now I have seen the suffering of the Hungarian people and – if I may say so – have been as emotionally engaged as if they were my own. I now see clearly the areas in which urgent assistance is needed.

Raoul listed a long series of tasks that his new, private aid organisation would help with. It included assistance in locating lost family members, especially reuniting children with their parents. It mentioned such things as pensions for war invalids, help to reconstruct business connections, assistance to create employment opportunities, large-scale food programmes, assistance with the housing shortage, the collection and distribution of furniture, repatriation and emigration, the care of orphans, medical assistance for individuals and municipalities, control of epidemics, assistance with pharmaceuticals, planning and construction assistance, emergency camps and temporary hospitals.

He clarified that this was not a question of charity. The initial capital that he and his colleagues provided was only to be viewed as a loan. "If you would like to apply to our organisation for self-help, then please contact our information division," Raoul Wallenberg concluded his appeal.

The typewriter technician Károly Szabó turned up at the Hazai Bank a little later that same day. Raoul Wallenberg asked him to try to arrange transportation to the Russians and Szabó left in order to do some reconnaisance.

Raoul Wallenberg had another task to take care of: with Per Anger he was to pay a visit to the German military headquarters in a final attempt to extract a promise about not killing any more of the Jews under Swedish protection. Their trip took them through the horrifying streets up by the castle. Time and again they had to brake for "dead people, horses, uprooted trees and bombed-out houses". Per Anger tried to persuade Raoul Wallenberg to stay with the other Swedes on the Buda side, but Raoul refused. He was heading back to Pest. He said that he did not want to hear afterwards that he had not done everything that he could.

On that same day, Raoul Wallenberg's name came up in Berlin. Adolf Eichmann had now returned to his office at Prinz-Albrecht-Strasse. There he lifted the receiver and called von Thadden at the Auswärtiges Amt. Eichmann wanted to know what had become of the Swedish Jew-saviour Raoul Wallenberg. Von Thadden made enquiries and several days later could give Eichmann the same message as the Swedish Foreign Ministry had received earlier: "Wallenberg had placed himself under German protection, Waffen S.S."

Per Anger and Raoul Wallenberg's meeting with the German general was brief and fairly unsuccessful. The general was upset by the fact that he had heard that Raoul Wallenberg had hidden one of the Hungarian resistance fighters, Gyula Dessewffy, in his house at Ostrom utca. The rumour was true, the resistance fighter had stayed in the tower room, but Raoul Wallenberg denied this convincingly.

After the meeting, Per Anger and Raoul Wallenberg parted. They never saw each other again.

*

Károly Szabó had been somewhat more successful. On the evening of January 10 he came back to the Hazai Bank and said that the front was now no more than ten kilometres from Városliget (City Park) in Pest. He had located a friend who was planning to make his way over to the Russian side and who had offered to take Raoul Wallenberg and his driver Vilmos Langfelder. A heated discussion broke out among the staff, who all tried to dissuade Wallenberg from such a reckless undertaking. Eventually Raoul decided to decline this offer, but did not drop the idea altogether.

That same evening, Langfelder and Wallenberg drove to a garage and prepared the car "for a longer journey". They packed food and are said to have hidden some gold and jewels in the reserve petrol tank. They told the garage owner that Wallenberg was heading "to Debrecen and then on to Sweden to file reports".

Raoul now moved east in Pest, to what would become his last address, Benczúr utca 16. The house was only a few hundred metres from Városliget in the eastern part of Pest. It was owned by a Hungarian captain, László Ocskay, with whom Raoul Wallenberg had earlier had some contact. Captain Ocskay belonged to those Hungarian military men who were critical of the Arrow Cross. He had led a Jewish forced labour unit with responsibility for repairing German and Hungarian uniforms. Ocskay's unit had become more of a protective refuge than a torture chamber for the Jews in question. According to the Hungarian author Mária Ember, Ocskay was said to have rescued 2,000 Jews with his "forced labour".

Some time earlier Captain Ocskay had put parts of his house at Benczúr utca 16 at the disposal of the International Red Cross' transportation organisation. On the evening of January 11, Raoul Wallenberg turned up in order, as he said, to stay there for a couple of days. It was not just for security reasons that he had moved again. Ocskay's house suited him, he said, since those parts of Budapest would soon be liberated. From there he would quickly be able to get in touch with the Russians.

The following day, Raoul Wallenberg undertook something resembling a first round of farewells. He made his way through a city that was under constant gunfire, in itself a feat for a person who often called himself a coward at heart. He was driven, most likely by Vilmos Langfelder, to the shelter at Üllői út 2–4, among other places. The main office was now partly in ruins after the section of the building that faced Kálvin tér had been badly damaged by a bombing raid. There was not much left of Raoul Wallenberg's old office. About a hundred resident Jews were still taking shelter in the cellar of Üllői út 4. The stores of food were low but they had found a well with potable water under the cinema next door.

During Raoul's visit to the cellar his co-workers asked him to issue a few more protective passports and to extend those temporary passports that expired on January 15. According to Jenő Lévai, Raoul felt that this was "unnecessary" but arranged it all the same. "A historic moment – I sign protective passports in the ruins of Stalingrad," Raoul Wallenberg is claimed to have said afterwards.

Raoul's own diplomatic passport expired on New Year's Eve but at the last minute Per Anger had made sure that it was extended for another six months. Raoul now had diplomatic immunity until June 30, 1945.

In the afternoon he stopped by the Swiss legation's "emigration department" in the so-called Glass House in Pest. There he met Miklós Krausz, who was in possession of 200,000 pengő and some documents which Raoul had previously given him for safe keeping. Raoul now needed them back. Krausz learned that the Swede was planning to make his way to General Malinovsky in Debrecen.

Finally Raoul met with Pál Szalai and Károly Szabó for a bite to eat. Most sources say this was a late dinner at the Swedish legation house in Buda. Dinner is probably an exaggeration. All Raoul Wallenberg could find to offer was some Swedish bread, a bit of Hungarian cheese and a bottle of Hungarian wine. He presented the meal as a kind of testament to Hungarian–Swedish friendship.

Raoul Wallenberg told Szalai and Szabó that he was planning to meet General Malinovsky in Debrecen. Raoul outlined his plans for a larger aid operation. In an interview much later, Pál Szalai said that Raoul had told them that some of the "assistance for self help" would involve food deliveries from Sweden. "He said that his original profession was grocery import/exports. When he returned to Pest he would get in touch with the Russians and offer them deliveries of food supplies in great quantities from Sweden to Hungary. First as free assistance and later for purchase.

At some point Raoul Wallenberg must have realised that it was not completely unproblematic from a diplomatic perspective that he, as low-ranking legation secretary, would be the first Swede to meet with the Soviet general. Such an initiative needed to be sanctioned from above. He sent a message to Ivan Danielsson and informed the minister that he viewed the situation as untenable and that he now wanted to cross the front line to the Russians. From his cellar, Ivan Danielsson sent word that, if this was how he judged the situation, he should do it.

Russian bombs were now raining down on Budapest without cease and several of the bridges over the Danube were impassable. German and Hungarian troops retreated further and further west in Pest ahead of the Russian troops' slow but steady advance towards the centre.

In Városliget, only one street from Raoul Wallenberg's new dwellings at Benczúr utca, hard close-quarters fighting had been going on for several days. Almost all the animals in the zoo had perished. By the morning of January 13, the entire park was in Soviet hands. Before long, the first Soviet soldiers emerged between the acacia trees at Benczúr utca. The time for Raoul Wallenberg's planned contact attempt was at hand.

The facts about what happened next are somewhat hazy, the pieces of the puzzle many and the lapses in memory evident. In Russian documents one can easily get lost amid the Red Army's rank and unit registers. But, with a little patience, one can more or less piece together what happened.

According to staff at the International Red Cross it was close to lunchtime when the first Soviet soldiers forced their way into the building at Benczúr utca 16 where Raoul Wallenberg was. Raoul then turned to the soldier who appeared to hold the highest rank and explained, with the help of an intepreter, that the building was occupied by "the Swiss Red Cross" and the Swedish legation. Raoul showed them his diplomatic identification, which had previously been translated into Russian. Then he asked to speak to a superior.

Later that day, Major Dmitry Demchenko of the 581st Infantry Regiment arrived at Benczúr utca 16. Raoul Wallenberg repeated that he was a Swedish diplomat and that he wanted to get in touch with General Malinovsky. Major Demchenko appears to have received this appeal without making any protest. At Raoul Wallenberg's request, he posted two Soviet guards outside the building before he left.

In the evening, the Soviet major returned. The Red Cross staff and Wallenberg gave him something to eat and everything appears to have been congenial. Witnesses have reported that both Major Demchenko and Wallenberg stood and delivered short, interpreted speeches.

The following day, Raoul Wallenberg and Vilmos Langfelder left with Major Demchenko. Raoul had his usual backpack, as well as a briefcase where, among other things, he kept his written plan for the assistance programme. Before leaving he left a few hundred thousand pengő with the senior I.R.C. staff member in the building.

So far, everything appeared to have gone well. When Demchenko's superior gave a report later in the day it stated that they "took him on 13.1.45 at Benczúr utca (he crossed the front line himself)". It is possible that their exchanges had been so relaxed that Demchenko had let Wallenberg and Landfelder make their own way to the next stop up the military hierarchy. There are some accounts that indicate that Wallenberg and Langfelder drove off in their diplomat-marked car only to be stopped a little while later by other Soviet soldiers, who ordered them to get out. Raoul Wallenberg and Vilmos Langfelder refused. Only when machine guns were aimed at them did they leave the car. It is said that the soldiers then slashed their tyres.

The car was seized, but Raoul Wallenberg and Vilmos Langfelder nonetheless arrived at the infantry regiment Demchenko had directed them to. The unit was located in the suburb of Rákosszentmihály, about eight kilo-metres east of Városliget. The unit's commander greeted them with friendliness and consideration. When he heard that Raoul Wallenberg was demanding to see General Malinovsky, he contacted his superiors in the division for further instructions. According to the regiment's political commissar, the officers were instructed to treat the Swede and his driver humanely for the time being. They should show respect for his diplomatic immunity and not interrogate him.

Towards evening, two officers and four soldiers took Wallenberg and Langfelder to their next stop in the Red Army, the headquarters of the 151st Infantry Division. They were received by Kislitsa, the unit's head of counter-intelligence (SMERSH) before they were allowed to meet Podshivalov, the division commander. According to Russian witness accounts it was a warm reception and it is said that all Soviet officers who met Raoul Wallenberg this first day observed "the greatest correctness and kindliness possible given the circumstances of the war". Some of the counter-intelligence officers had carefully expressed some doubts, but the SMERSH chief had, according to those present, shown "the greatest tact toward the diplomat". One can understand why the cordiality was noted. The word SMERSH. was an acronym for "Death to Spies".

In a matter of hours, Raoul Wallenberg and Vilmos Langfelder had managed to make swift progress in their mission to make contact with the Soviets.

A Hungarian interpreter from the 30th Army Corps intelligence division was brought to the house where Wallenberg and Langfelder were waiting. His name was Michail Danilash and, if one can believe him, their meeting took place in a room in one of the Red Army's office buildings in Rákosszentmihály. This is how Danilash remembered the conversation when he gave his testimony for a joint Swedish–Russian investigation some forty years later:

> I walked into the room. There, sitting (leaning forward somewhat) by the middle of a table, was a man in a black suit, dark-haired, in his thirties, thin, not particularly pale (slightly dark-toned skin) while to the left . . . there was a substantial man in a black leather jacket. The man politely informed me that he was secretary Wallenberg of the Swedish Embassy and introduced the other as his driver . . . Wallenberg spoke to his driver in German and the driver spoke to me in Hungarian, after which he translated back to Wallenberg in German. Most of all, Wallenberg wanted to know where I was from and how I ended up in this Red Army unit . . . Then he asked me the following question: "How can you explain the fact that the Red Army has advanced so quickly – is it because you are so strong or is it because the Germans are so weak?" I answered what I had heard from our officers, that after the Germans lost Stalingrad the German army lost its fighting spirit and it was now too late to regain it. Then came the next question: "How does the Red Army view the population and the prisoners of war in the occupied areas, is there any persecution of religious groups, Jews, etc?" I answered that, during the short time that our field office had been stationed in different places, I had not

noticed anything negative in regard to these issues. After this Wallenberg told me the following: "When the Red Army's troops entered Budapest, my official car was taken from me. I have done everything imaginable to try to get it back, but instead of my own car I have been given a car that was seized as war booty. This is something I do not find acceptable . . . I demand that my car be returned to me and will not accept any kind of substitute. Secondly, I demand to meet with General Malinovsky immediately. I ask that you forward my wishes to your superiors, and that they in turn give them to their superiors." . . . When he spoke, Wallenberg appeared both persuasive and forceful. He was a person who presented himself with all the power of authority afforded by his position. He then thanked me for the conversation and suggested that I drink a glass of wine with him.

If it was true that Raoul Wallenberg had stuffed the petrol tank full of gold and diamonds then one can understand his stubborn insistence that the car be returned.

It seems as if it was when Wallenberg and Langfelder finally were able to meet with the division's commander, Podshivalov, that Raoul presented his case in a more collected manner. According to witnesses, he had a bulging briefcase with him. He showed that it contained many important documents and said that he was prepared to hand them over to the Soviet military commanders. Raoul repeated his demand to be put in contact with General Malinovsky and had elaborated on his operation in Budapest. To judge from the report that was sent that same day to the leadership of the 7th Guards Army, Raoul Wallenberg said that the Swedish legation "represented those Jews who were in the main ghetto" and had nine offices in Budapest. Raoul had explained that he wanted to meet with the senior officer in order to discuss among other things how best to rescue the ghetto.

The head of the 151st Infantry Division was also told that the Swedish minister Ivan Danielsson had taken shelter in a cellar in Buda and that the Swedish legation house was guarded by the attaché Lars Berg. Wallenberg then produced a telegram in German that he asked the Soviets to forward to Stockholm. Raoul wanted them to let Stockholm know that everything was fine and that he was in liberated territory. To the Soviet military he said that he could not leave the front because "seven thousand Swedish citizens were under his responsibility and protection in the eastern part of the city".

A witness later testified that Raoul Wallenberg inspired confidence in the division's leadership. This "despite the fact that the front-line troops were very suspicious, trained to see spies everywhere". When it was later reported that the Swede Raoul Wallenberg and his driver had been placed under protection, it was most likely exactly what happened and not a euphemism for imprisonment.

As the division's staff waited for word from further up the Soviet hierarchy, Wallenberg and Langfelder stayed overnight in a house at Erzsébet Királyné útja, in the area east of Városliget.

On January 15, at about the same time that the Red Army reached Üllői út and the Swedish-protected Jews, a new edge became discernible in the tone of the Soviet military's attitude toward Raoul Wallenberg. The man who had voluntarily sought out the Red Army in order to help all Budapest's Jews would not himself experience the hour of liberation, either for the protected Jews at Üllői út that Monday or in the international ghetto the next day.

At Üllői út, the past few days had been a bombed-out hell. For at least twenty-four hours, the main office had been right in the middle of the battle; grenades had hailed down and one of the legation doctors had to perform serious operations on German and Russian soldiers, one after the other, on a worn kitchen table in the dilapidated bomb shelter.

Early that afternoon, the first Soviet soldiers stormed into the ruins of the old head office. On the first and second floors, violent bouts of close combat broke out between Soviet and German soldiers, while the Swedish staff and their families tried to take shelter in the cellar as well as they could. For them "liberation" was within reach now. For their Swedish boss and leader it was the exact opposite.

Around the same time, the message about Raoul Wallenberg's request for contact had been up the Soviet command chain and come back down again. But it had not been received with the unequivocally positive reaction that Raoul had expected. A certain duplicity can now be detected in the internal Soviet communications as well as a more adamantine attitude in the orders dispatched down the ranks.

Kupriyanov at the field office of the 7th Guards Army ordered that Raoul Wallenberg and his driver should immediately, although under comfortable circumstances, be relocated to another corps. He made it clear that Wallenberg was henceforth forbidden to have any contact with the outside world. The telegram to Stockholm should "for now" not be sent anywhere. Two named "comrades" were given the assignment of finding out what kind of secretary he really was.

It is possible that this move towards isolation was a kind of safety measure imposed while waiting for definitive word from above. But in this case one cannot rule out the instruction having come from Moscow. Whatever the truth, that day the field office chief for the 2nd Ukrainian Front reported back to headquarters in Moscow that they had encountered Raoul Wallenberg, and also that measures had been taken to protect him and his property. That is to say, acting exactly according to the orders regarding the protection of Swedes that had been issued from Moscow after Staffan Söderblom had applied pressure.

The information that Raoul Wallenberg had been taken into protective custody reached the political leadership in Moscow. Dekanozov, the deputy foreign minister, was known for acting quickly. Perhaps he acted just a little bit too fast in this case. On January 16, Dekanozov wrote a note to Staffan Söderblom. He forwarded the information that the Red Army had encountered Raoul Wallenberg and that measures had been taken to protect him and his property. He also conveyed the news that the rest of the legation was in the western part of Budapest. But he wrote nothing about the fact that they had isolated Wallenberg. It is not clear if he even knew this.

At the Swedish legation in Moscow, Staffan Söderblom had not yet recovered from the humiliating treatment that he had suffered at the Soviet Foreign Ministry before Christmas. On January 15, his deputy Ingemar Hägglöf had anxiously noted in his journal that it seemed as if Söderblom no longer dared to go to the Foreign Ministry, that a whole month had gone by without his visiting it.

The fighting down in Pest was nearing its final phase, but the three hills in Buda – Gellért Hill, Castle Hill and Rose Hill, were still in German hands. The

Swedish diplomats did not often dare to go out, but when they did so they could see Red Army soldiers on the streets of Pest. Several thousand people had sought protection in the tunnels under the castle. The food shortage was severe.

Per Anger had now retreated to the cellar under the building at Úri utca 15. There they had fortunately been able to dig a wood-burning stove out of the bombed-out ruins. Countess Nákó prepared food on it in the courtyard when the situation allowed. They subsisted on tinned foods, watery soups and meat from a dead horse on the street outside. In the cellar under Prince Eszter-házy's palace, Margareta Bauer, Ivan Danielsson and the others from the legation were surviving on water and bread that was sometimes mouldy. Occasionally the nobleman's family brought cheer to their existence with some fine cognac.

From time to time the Swedes would sneak across the vaulted cellar to the Swiss, where they played brain-teasing games and told amusing stories. Raoul Wallenberg's food buyer Yngve Ekmark taught Margareta Bauer to sing descant. Such pastimes were sorely needed. It would be almost another month before they could leave their hiding place.

With Pest's fall imminent, a rumour that had been circulating for a while gained in strength. It was claimed that the Germans and the Arrow Cross were planning a large-scale mass killing in the main ghetto as a final act of revenge before they retreated. The rumour turned out to be true. On January 16, Pál Szalai received a visit from an agitated police officer in his office in the headquarters under the town hall. The policeman told him that he had heard that there were five hundred German soldiers with machine guns at the Hotel Royal who were only standing by for orders to begin the mass killings. Two hundred Arrow Cross men and police were also to be dispatched. Clearly there was little time left.

Pál Szalai had earlier made an arrangement with Raoul Wallenberg that he could refer to the Swede if he found himself in a difficult situation. Now he went to the German General Gerhard Schmidhuber, who had his office in the same shelter under the town hall. Szalai explained to Schmidhuber that he came as a proxy for Raoul Wallenberg. He asked if the General knew that his troops were planning a mass murder in the main ghetto.

The name "Wallenberg" was by this time well known in Budapest, even to

General Schmidhuber. He had met the Swede before on one of his visits to see Szalai. The latter noticed that Schmidhuber's face grew red as he posed his question. "I told him that when the war ended he would not be judged as a soldier but as a war criminal. And I said that this was a message from Wallenberg," Szalai said later in an interview. "Did this message really come from Wallenberg or did you make it up?" the interviewer asked. "I made it up but Wallenberg had given me permission to do so and he would probably have said the same thing. But by this time I could no longer get in touch with him," Pál Szalai answered.

After this, General Schmidhuber called together the German and Hungarian commanders and put a stop to the planned mass murder. The following morning, Russian troops reached the outskirts of the ghetto. It took less than a day for the sealed ghetto with its 70,000 emaciated inhabitants to be liberated. Since approximately 35,000 protected Jews had just been liberated in the other ghetto it meant that more than 100,000 of Budapest's Jews had survived the Holocaust.

Raoul Wallenberg had been successful in his protests against the seizure of his vehicle. On the morning of Wednesday, January 17, he and Vilmos Langfelder drove back to the building on Benczúr utca 16, where Raoul had been living most recently. But they did not come alone. The car was followed by three armed Soviet officers on a motorcycle, one of whom was in a sidecar. Raoul went up to his room in order to collect his things and to explain to his colleagues at the International Red Cross that he was heading on towards the Soviet headquarters.

The Red Cross staff recognised one of the Soviet officers in the escort as the "gracious" Major Demeshenko who had had dinner with them only a few days earlier. Raoul Wallenberg collected the money that he had left behind and then came through the vaulted entrance at Benczúr utca with his backpack, briefcase and another three bags. He was, it is claimed, in a wonderful mood and, as he often did, sprinkled witticisms around him. Everything indicated that he was undertaking this trip willingly. The Soviet officers had remained in the street and so, if Raoul Wallenberg had been suspicious that something was going on, he could easily have alerted the Red Cross staff or even fled.

Out on the street, beside the motorcycle, Raoul encountered László Pető, the Hungarian friend he had met on a language course in Switzerland in his teens. During the autumn, Raoul had had dinner from time to time with László and his family. A certain worry must have been gnawing at Raoul because, as he proudly displayed his impressive escort to Pető, he said in German: "These have been ordered here on my account. I do not know if it is to protect me or to guard me. I do not know if I am a guest or a prisoner." Raoul had also told the Red Cross staff that Langfelder and he had been placed in separate rooms at Erzsébet Királyné útja and that they had not been allowed to speak to each other.

László Pető and Raoul Wallenberg spoke about the liberation of the international ghetto the previous day. When Pető was told that Raoul planned to pass through there before he travelled on to Debrecen he asked if he could come along. Raoul Wallenberg suggested that he should come all the way to General Malinovsky. He said that the central ghetto would soon be liberated and that Pető would be able to assist in the organisation of the necessary food and medical provisions.

They left and László Pető noted that Vilmos Langfelder had switched to another car. The Studebaker was not suitable for the trip that they were going to make, Raoul explained. The motorcycle escort followed them to the Swedish legation's office in the international ghetto. This time too the Soviet officers remained outside on the street. They gave Raoul Wallenberg and László Pető half an hour before they had to leave again.

At the office, Raoul Wallenberg met with some of his co-workers. He told them how happy he was that the international ghetto had been liberated and that the majority of the protected Jews were therefore safe from the Arrow Cross. He wanted to hear more about how it had happened, but was unfortunately in a hurry, he said, as the car was waiting outside. Raoul told them that he was going to Debrecen in order to make contact with Soviets at the highest level. He said that he hoped to be back very soon, but most likely in a week at the earliest. He asked them to carry on the work themselves and enquired if they needed any money.

The visit ended with Raoul Wallenberg giving 100,000 pengő to the cashier and receiving an invoice in return. His colleagues thought they saw quite a bit of money left in the briefcase. Before Raoul left the office at Tátra utca he ensured that the office staff knew that there were also "diamonds and valuables" in the Hazai vault.

The Soviet officers were growing impatient. But Raoul Wallenberg could not stop himself from looking in at the Swedish hospital only a few doors away. He asked about the situation and was given a report. Perhaps it was stress that caused him to slip and fall on the icy pavement on the way back.

In the car, which according to witnesses was light blue, Vilmos Langfelder said that he had discussed the war situation with the officers in the escort. Apparently it would not be long before the Soviet troops would also conquer Buda. László Pető, whose parents were hiding in Buda, began to hesitate. Finally he said to Raoul Wallenberg that if Buda's liberation was so close he could not come with him to Debrecen. He had to find out what had happened to his parents.

They drove back east through Pest and passed the magnificent monument at Heroes' Square before Langfelder pulled over at the corner of Aréna út (today called Dózsa György út) and Benczúr utca. There they let László Pető get out. László Pető described the moment to author Jenő Lévai only a year or so later: "We bid each other an exceedingly fond farewell and I wished him all the best for what, under the circumstances, was a very adventurous journey. After that the car disappeared from view."

During this time, the Soviet government machinery in Moscow had continued to work on the issue of Wallenberg and Langfelder. On Wednesday, 17 January, 1945, a telegram was sent by the Soviet Defence Ministry to the commander of the 2nd Ukrainian Front. The sender was the deputy defence minister Nikolai Bulganin and the telegram contained an arrest order, with a copy sent to the head of SMERSH, Viktor Abakumov:

> Raoul Wallenberg, who has been encountered at Benczúr utca in the eastern part of Budapest, shall, in accordance with information from the counter-espionage agency "SMERSH", be arrested and sent to Moscow. Secure the necessary means for the completion of this assignment. Report the time for departure to Moscow as well as the name of the responsible officer. Bulganin.

It is interesting that one sentence from the original draft of the telegram was eliminated before it was sent. In the draft, Raoul Wallenberg was referred to as "secretary at the Swedish legation". Shortly thereafter another telegram arrived from Bulganin, in which he ordered that the two Swiss diplomats Harald Feller and Max Meier should be arrested and sent "in the same way as Wallenberg to Moscow". Nor were these men given any diplomatic titles in the message. It eventually emerged, in a subsequent letter from Abakumov, that these arrest orders had been issued by Joseph Stalin.

In a single day, Dekanozov's assurance that Raoul Wallenberg was safe and under the protection of Soviet troops had ceased to be true. But information about this radical change did not of course enter the Swedish diplomatic communication channels.

Staffan Söderblom, the humiliated Moscow minister, had received Dekanozov's positive message by now. But for some reason it was almost midnight on Wednesday, January 17, before he managed to get his own cipher telegram off to Stockholm. It did not arrive at the Foreign Ministry until 7 a.m. the following day. By then, Raoul Wallenberg and Vilmos Langfelder had long since left freedom in Budapest behind.

In the morning of January 18, 1945, an official at the Swedish Foreign Ministry called Raoul's mother, Maj von Dardel. He probably told her, exactly as explained in the telegram, that they had heard from Moscow that Raoul Wallenberg had been encountered at Benczúr utca in Budapest. Soviet military authorities had now taken precautions to protect Wallenberg and his belongings. Minister Söderblom in Moscow had recommended that they should not announce this news in the media before all of Budapest was liberated.

Maj von Dardel cannot have found the telephone call anything other than joyous.

Ostrom utca, autumn 2010

The building is difficult to spot. The stone villa that Raoul Wallenberg rented for most of his time in Budapest lies concealed behind a high wall. I try to stand on tiptoes on the steep incline but can only catch sight of the brick tiled roof. A cupola-shaped tower peeps out of the greenery. It must have been there that the journalist and resistance fighter Gyula Dessewffy was in hiding.

It is of course a mere coincidence that the street on which Raoul Wallenberg lived was called Ostrom utca, "Siege Street". And that it ends at Moszkva tér (today Széll Kálmán tér). After Christmas 1944 Raoul never came back here. But I cannot rid myself of the thought that he may have left some trace behind.

The detective within me fires up. Soon I have an e-mail address for someone who should be able to open the door in the wall for me. His name is Richard, he is in his twenties and represents the younger generation of the family that has owned the house since the fifties. During the day he sells soft drinks, when he is not working as a swimming instructor. But certainly he can assist me, if I insist.

A chilly morning in September, the wooden door is opened. Richard smiles in welcome and we walk through the garden between lightly greying Roman marble statues. The spruce is so high that it must have been here sixty-five years ago, I think. The statues were also there and definitely the magnificent stone terrace in front of the entrance, the one that, with its sculpted columns, gives everything the air of a grand mansion.

The door to what is today a white house is wide open. A black-and-white cat scampers in ahead of us. My host apologises and says that not much has been done inside. As far as he knows, most of it has been left untouched since the end of the war. That was when his family took over. Then communism came and it was not so easy to renovate houses any more.

It is not without a feeling of awe that I cross the threshold and pass into the salon to the left. The style has something of a rococo revival. Sideboards and bookcases in dark wood stand against the walls. There is beige medallion wallpaper, and patterned carpets over dark parquet floors. There are armchairs and chandeliers, sconces and landscape paintings, easy chairs and tapestries. And isn't that a bust of Napoleon in the corner?

I look around for traces of Raoul. The large green ceramic stove must have been here when he held his dinners, I think. Perhaps Raoul did some writing at the delicate secretaire? Or browsed through some of the old books with French bindings?

In the kitchen I catch my breath when I see the mahogany dresser. It is decorated with carved garlands and is at least two and a half metres tall. Suddenly I know what Raoul meant when he referred to "the beautiful furniture" in the letter he sent his mother in August. For surely they did not have the energy to move this hundred-kilo piece?

The furthest room is round and brick-coloured. It is dominated by a rust-red stuffed divan large enough for two. Richard believes but cannot swear that it was already there in 1944.

"So can this have been Raoul Wallenberg's bed?" I ask.

At that point my guide has already disappeared up the narrow stairs to the rooftop terrace. I follow. Up there one certainly has, as Raoul wrote to his mother, "a wonderful view of the entire city". But I am beginning to feel disappointed. As yet there is no concrete reminder of Raoul Wallenberg and really nothing of the war.

On the way back through the salon, Richard stops at a sombre watercolour painting in a gilded frame. It is of a Hungarian mountain landscape. At first I don't understand what Richard is pointing at. I can see a few geese and a lake. Then I walk closer and I see the damage. Three substantial holes.

"There," Richard says. "Those are bullet holes from the Russian siege of 1945."

PART III

WHAT DETERMINES A PERSON'S FATE?

CHAPTER 16

From Protected to Missing

When the Soviet soldiers reached central Pest in January 1945, they were surprised to see Swedish or Swiss flags on practically every other house. Special signs, sometimes looking suspiciously home-made, declared extra-territoriality. On the streets, people walked around with blue and yellow ribbons on their clothes and called themselves Swedes. Had Budapest already been occupied?

It did not take long before the Russians began to think that there was something strange about the Swedish – and, for that matter, the Swiss – diplomatic representation. Raoul Wallenberg had realised that the considerable rescue operation would need to be explained to the newly arrived Russians. But he knew very little about how either his country or his rescue mission was regarded in the Kremlin, something that would have a profound bearing on his chances of success.

Around the beginning of 1945, the Soviet attitude to Sweden had undergone a radical change. As the Swedes had gratefully noted, the Soviet Union had not yet taken Sweden to task for its policy of compromise with the Germans. According to the Russian historian Maxim Korobochkin, the relatively conciliatory Soviet attitude had been steered by a political desire not to frighten Sweden into the arms of Germany. But, with the war nearing its end, things were different. Now it was high time that Sweden should pay for its disingenuous "neutrality", or so the Kremlin argued. The Soviet Union was a conquering nation and, if Sweden wanted to have any kind of relationship, it would necessarily have to be on Soviet terms.

The iciness that Staffan Söderblom had encountered in the Foreign Ministry in December can be viewed as an expression of this shift. But this was not the only negative Soviet reaction. It may have been a coincidence, but on the same day that the arrest order for Raoul Wallenberg was issued, the Soviet government took up two more sharply drawn political positions towards Sweden.

That Wednesday the Soviet Union shocked Sweden by rejecting its proposal for a new trade and credit agreement. It was a painful message that the Soviet ambassador in Stockholm, Alexandra Kollontai, was forced to deliver to Ernst Wigforss, the finance minister. For Kollontai, it was a stinging personal failure. She had wagered all her prestige on the Soviet acceptance of the proposal.

But the tensions did not end with the failed trade agreement. On January 17, the Soviets began making enquiries regarding a delicate exchange issue. The person in question was a young refugee from the Baltic region, the fifteen-year-old Lydia Makarova, who was originally from the Soviet Union. For the next few years, the Russians would repeatedly – with increasing irritation – demand the "return" of young Lydia Makarova to her father in the Soviet Union. Not infrequently, these demands would be made in connection with discussions between the two countries about Raoul Wallenberg.

When, that same day, Raoul Wallenberg voluntarily crossed the Soviets' front line for the second time, he was unaware of the fact that Moscow had put out an order for his arrest. Nor did he know anything of the grim new tone of Swedish–Hungarian relations. He was simply returning with the aim of repeating his important proposal to General Rodion Malinovsky in Debrecen.

Wallenberg planned to draw on all the legitimacy that he had earned during the rescue operation in the autumn in order to convince the Russians to give him the go-ahead for his plan for the reconstruction of Hungary after the war. He most likely saw a trump card in the fact that this venture, just like the earlier one, would be financed by American funds from the War Refugee Board. After all, the United States was an ally of the Soviet Union.

Unfortunately, these kinds of proposals were no longer looked on favourably by the Soviets.

It was no secret to the Russians that the Americans had founded the War Refugee Board a year earlier, as a kind of last-minute action to save the European Jews. The American government had conscientiously informed their eastern ally and invited the Soviets to participate. But to the Kremlin all Western dealings with the Nazis smelled suspiciously like betrayal.

During the autumn of 1944 Soviet suspicions about W.R.B. had grown stronger. This process was linked to the case of the 30,000 Baltic citizens who fled to Sweden when the Red Army arrived in September. In October the Swedish communist newspaper *Ny Dag* revealed that there were many "fascistic elements" among those fleeing, and that the American legation in Stockholm was involved. *Ny Dag* was able to prove that the War Refugee Board's Stockholm representative Iver Olsen had contributed 900,000 Swedish kronor (around 1.5 million pounds today) to help facilitate the sudden flight of people from the Baltic region. In the Soviet newspapers it was said that the American legation had invested money in "an anti-Russian Baltic organisation in Sweden".

The same Iver Olsen supplied Raoul Wallenberg with large sums of money. He paid for almost the entire operation in Budapest, one that had basically come into being as an American assignment for the War Refugee Board. The revelation in *Ny Dag* was naturally not helpful for Raoul Wallenberg, who was now planning to sell a new rescue operation to the Soviet army leaders.

In the middle of January 1945, the Soviet legation in Stockholm issued a protest to the Swedish Foreign Ministry over the supposed anti-Soviet propaganda circulated by the Baltic refugees in Sweden.

It was two days before SMERSH acted on the order from the Kremlin and arrested Raoul Wallenberg and his driver, Vilmos Langfelder. On January 19 they were apparently forced to leave their hitherto relatively comfortable Red Army quarters, where they had even been assigned kitchen staff, and instead were locked up in a temporary N.K.V.D. prison. Even if the officers assured them they would not be considered prisoners, that they were only being moved to a "protective holding facility", the worsening conditions must have alarmed them.

Either this isolation was not absolute in the beginning, or else Raoul Wallenberg had early doubts, because, at some point around January 20, he was apparently able to send word to his trusted collaborator, Pál Szalai. In an interview with the Hungarian journalist Mária Ember many years later, Szalai said that around that time he received a message informing him that Raoul

Wallenberg had run into problems. "But who of us could do anything then, in that chaos?" Szalai said apologetically.

Officials at the Foreign Ministry in Stockholm were reassured by the message from Deputy Foreign Minister Dekanozov. At least Raoul Wallenberg was in safe hands. "Measures to protect Mr Wallenberg and his belongings have been taken by the Soviet military authorities," was what Dekanozov had written. The Foreign Ministry did not even reply to Söderblom's telegram on the matter. They simply appear to have noted that Wallenberg was in apparent safety.

The Foreign Ministry officials seemed more focused on forwarding the news about Raoul Wallenberg to the Americans, as if the matter was of greater concern to them than even to the Swedes. On January 20, Herschel Johnson, the United States envoy in Stockholm, sent a telegram with the good news to his new foreign minister, Edward R. Stettinius. He wrote: "Wallenberg is safe and sound in that part of Budapest occupied by Russians." The Swedes had therefore recommended that, in future, the Americans should communicate their instructions to Wallenberg's aid operation by way of the American legation in Moscow.

If one bears in mind that the strained relations between the Soviet Union and the Western Allies were becoming increasingly difficult to hide, these responses by the Swedes and Americans seem very naïve, especially in view of what we know of the reach of the Soviet Intelligence Service.

At the Swedish legation in Moscow, the mood had not improved after the setback of the failed trade agreement. Staffan Söderblom had avoided getting in touch with the Soviet Foreign Ministry for as long as possible, out of fear of provoking any further hard-edged demands about the Baltic refugees. But, finally, he had no choice but to request a meeting with Dekanozov. The matter that forced his hand was a planned visit by the head of the Red Cross, Count Folke Bernadotte, to Moscow in May.

On January 26, a nervous Söderblom left his sheltered existence in the "Mindovsky Mansion", a beautiful turn-of-the-century villa in central Moscow where the Swedish legation had been located since the 1920s. He set off on shaky legs for the Soviet Foreign Ministry, which at this time was housed in a government building a stone's throw from the large Lubyanka prison.

Vladimir Dekanozov was a short man of around forty-five with thinning red-blond hair. He belonged to the inner circle of Stalin's security chief Beria and had a past in the N.K.V.D. Dekanozov was a Georgian, like Stalin and Beria. After a few war years as envoy to Berlin he was now the acting authority on behalf of Foreign Minister Molotov.

To Söderblom's enormous relief, Dekanozov made no mention of the Baltic refugees at their meeting. Söderblom himself set the tone for the encounter by thanking the Russians for listening to Sweden's request for protection for Raoul Wallenberg. He said that he hoped that they would show the same care to the other Swedes from the Budapest legation.

After the initial niceties the meeting appears to have continued in a relatively relaxed atmosphere, focusing on topics unlikely to raise adrenalin levels, such as visa issues and the impending visit of Folke Bernadotte. But towards the end of the audience, Dekanozov raised yet another matter that was causing Soviet displeasure. This time it was in relation to five Soviet sailors who had defected, but whom the Swedes refused to hand back to Russia.

Söderblom countered by saying that he did not know anything about the matter and promised to contact Stockholm about it. After this he appears to have done what he could in order to restore the positive atmosphere. According to the Soviets' minutes, Staffan Söderblom ended the meeting by maintaining that "the Soviet military successes make a deep impression on the entire world and that news of these victories for the Red Army take up a large amount of space in the Swedish press".

Some of the officials at Gustaf Adolfs torg were growing increasingly irritated by Söderblom's grovelling. Above all, his servility appears to have exasperated the acting head of the political department, Sven Grafström. As Grafström saw it, it was clear that the Russians were now attempting to intimidate the Swedes into obedience just as the Germans had done at the beginning of the war. The only way to handle these Soviet tactics was to answer hardness with hardness, Grafström said. But he was fairly isolated in this opinion at the Foreign Ministry in Stockholm, where there were still hopes of being able to achieve a trade agreement. Grafström appears to have used his private journal in order to express the distaste he felt at Söderblom's obsequiousness, however much this behaviour was supported by their superiors:

One may be fairly sure that the Kremlin views Söderblom as one looks at a louse under a magnifying glass to see how it writhes. They cannot be blind to the fact that he, although he himself may have forgotten it, personified the administration's policy of compromise toward Germany. And what do they see? A wriggling little insect but not a louse, absolutely not a creature that can bite. A devoted ladybird ... Any unsteadiness from our side will give them [the Russians] the impression that they can manipulate us with threats. Söderblom is therefore, according to my humble opinion, an extremely dangerous representative for us in Moscow. He is overcome with Messianic feelings, he sees everything through rose-tinted glasses and wants to do anything he can to please. He is intelligent but not smart.

A week had passed since Raoul Wallenberg and Vilmos Langfelder had driven away through the snow in eastern Budapest. The arrest order from the defence minister Bulganin stated that Raoul Wallenberg was to be sent to Moscow and that the leadership of the 2nd Ukrainian Front should report the time of departure from Budapest. At midnight on January 26, 1945, the message was sent. General Malinovsky's chief of staff wrote to Moscow that Raoul Wallenberg had been sent off that same day and that a Captain Zenkov was responsible for the convoy. In addition to Captain Zenkov, four Soviet soldiers were assigned to escort Wallenberg and Langfelder.

The party travelled east by train, aiming to stop first in the Romanian town of Iaşi. During the trip Raoul Wallenberg and his driver would again be told that they should not regard themselves as prisoners.

On Saturday January 27, 1945, the Red Army opened the gates to the Polish concentration camp Auschwitz and liberated the 7,500 emaciated prisoners. After an aggressive offensive on the Eastern Front, the German troops had been forced to retreat all the way to the river Oder and the Red Army was now only seventy kilometres from Berlin. The end of the Second World War seemed close.

In the grand political arena, the anticipated winners began to redraw the world order according to the new power relations. The Soviet Union's dictator Joseph Stalin entered these negotiations with his head held particularly high.

Staffan Söderblom was not alone in tiptoeing around the victor of the Eastern Front. Even the president of the United States, Franklin D. Roosevelt, belonged to the ranks of his admirers.

Roosevelt had decided that Stalin had to be a good man. If one could only handle the Soviet leader in the right way, he would work for democracy and peace in the world together with the United States. Roosevelt used to call Joseph Stalin "Uncle Joe", and it says something about the tone of that era that *Time* magazine selected Joseph Stalin as their "Man of the Year" for 1942. Roosevelt preferred to interpret Winston Churchill's more sceptical attitude toward the communist dictator as a lack of personal chemistry. "I think I can personally handle Stalin better than your Foreign Office or my State Department. Stalin hates the guts of all your top people. He thinks he likes me better, and I hope he will continue to do so," Roosevelt wrote to Churchill in 1942.

At the beginning of February 1945 the three gathered for a conference at the Soviet seaside resort of Yalta to divide post-war Europe into discrete spheres of interest. Stalin had no trouble getting the others to dance to his tune. Just as at the earlier conference in Teheran in 1943, he arranged the location of the negotiations and made the others travel further, although Roosevelt was confined to a wheelchair. He also managed to have the susceptible American president stay in a palace riddled with Soviet microphones, another similarity to the Teheran conference. Every morning Stalin received thorough transcripts of everything that had been said in Roosevelt's suite. This was normal practice for a dictator who saw spies everywhere, who himself had spies everywhere, and who only had to lift the telephone under his desk in the Kremlin to listen to the private conversations of members of the Politburo.

Roosevelt was in poor physical condition, weakened by heart problems and high blood pressure. He had only ten weeks to live and was in no condition to be forceful. The American president's foremost ambition for the meeting in Yalta was to build friendship between the leaders of the world powers, to be manifested in the new United Nations. He did this by showing goodwill and humility and confidence in Stalin, when it came to other matters on the agenda. The future of Eastern Europe for example. When the Soviet dictator promised to allow free elections in Poland "as soon as possible", Roosevelt was convinced that he meant it. In response to a direct question the Soviet dictator had even answered that the elections would be held within a month.

When Stalin signed a declaration stating that free democratic elections were the goal for all liberated countries, the American president did not worry about potential differences of interpretation. Even Churchill, who was more suspicious, allowed himself to be persuaded. "Poor Neville Chamberlain believed he could trust Hitler. He was wrong. But I don't think I'm wrong about Stalin," was Churchill's comment regarding the Poland promise.

The major powers were still intriguing in Yalta when the train with Raoul Wallenberg and Vilmos Langfelder pulled into Moscow's Kiev Station on one of the first days in February 1945. There is no indication that the journey was anything other than relatively pleasant. They had been allowed to disembark at the Romanian town of Iaşi and spend a few hours at a restaurant called Luther. The men were allowed to travel in first class and had been served the best food from the restaurant car. Later, Raoul told a fellow prisoner that he had spent his free time on the train writing a spy novel. He had also tried to write down his memories of the time in Budapest.

The soldiers in the escort continued to be friendly. When they left the train, they showed Wallenberg and Langfelder the Metro, the pride of Moscow. But, from what we know, the convoy preferred to walk at least part of the distance to the headquarters of the N.K.V.D.

The dark yellow turn-of-the-century palace at Lubyanka Square had once been the head office of a large insurance company. But, after the Revolution of 1917, the feared security service – at that time called the Cheka (Extraordinary Commission) – had moved in. It was still there but was now called N.K.V.D. (later the K.G.B.). The counter-espionage agency SMERSH also had its headquarters in the N.K.V.D. building, which was now connected to other, newer structures, so that the tentacles of the security service stretched around the whole block. The notorious prison of the N.K.V.D. was located in the inner courtyard. It was the starting point for the journey out into the hell of the Gulag system for countless victims during Stalin's Terror.

On Tuesday, February 6, 1945, Raoul Wallenberg and Vilmos Langfelder walked across Lubyanka Square with their luggage. The head of the security service, the ruthless Lavrentiy Beria, had his office on the third floor of the main building. But, on the day when Raoul Wallenberg arrived, Beria was at the conference in Yalta, where Stalin introduced him to President Roosevelt as "my Himmler".

It is most likely that Beria was nonetheless informed of the Swede's arrival. It was no ordinary prisoner who was recorded in his register that day. The instruction to arrest him had come from Stalin himself and the head of SMERSH, Abakumov, had been informed. Surely Beria was aware of the decision to defy diplomatic immunity and imprison a diplomat from a neutral country? It was a sensitive situation, one that in all likelihood even the foreign minister Molotov must have been told about. But what about Deputy Foreign Minister Dekanozov, who had assured the Swedes that Raoul Wallenberg was in safe hands? Did he know that the case had taken a new turn?

What we know is that the Wallenberg case was veiled in great secrecy. But we also know that the buildings of the security service and Foreign Ministry stood so close to each other that they were referred to as "the neighbours". Beria was barely a minute's walk away from Dekanozov, who was his trusted associate and also a former N.K.V.D. colleague.

Maybe Wallenberg and Langfelder believed they would only be spending the night at the Lubyanka. But, when the doors closed behind them, it was for ever. Fairly soon they were separated. In the future, they would, with a few exceptions, be able to find out about each other only by asking other prisoners.

The Russian author Alexander Solzhenitsyn, who also arrived at the Lubyanka in February 1945, would later describe the prison in his book *The First Circle*, in which he cited Dante's injunction: "Abandon all hope, ye who enter here." According to Solzhenitsyn, the Lubyanka's holding area consisted of adjacent cells of minimal dimensions. These were concealed behind grey-green doors with oval number plates. Inside "was a night stand and a stool and they took up almost all the floor space. If one sat down on the stool, one could not stretch out one's legs." It resembled nothing so much as a morgue.

Now, as the end of the war approached, the N.K.V.D. was working round the clock. In Poland alone some 27,000 supposed "security risks" were arrested and taken away that spring. Most of the undesirable elements, whether domestic or foreign, would pass through the Lubyanka before they were either executed or sent to the Gulag. The routines on entry were therefore necessarily practised and quick. The prisoners had to remove all of their clothing and were then subjected like animals to a "medical" examination of every part of their body. Fillings were prised out of teeth, shoe heels were cut in two and jacket linings were ripped open in the hunt for secrets that could be used later. The arrival procedure ended with the prisoners being placed under a pipe with running water and being asked to wash themselves.

Raoul Wallenberg was registered as the "war prisoner" Raoul Gustaf Wallenberg. It is clear that SMERSH had begun to doubt his status as legation secretary because, on the registration card, he is titled "diplomatic observer" and not the more usual "diplomatic official".

Both Raoul Wallenberg and Vilmos Langfelder had to give up their possessions. The money that Raoul had brought with him from Budapest was seized, as was his backpack containing "the necessities": his diplomatic passport, Hungarian driver's licence, pocket diary and address book. They also seized a cigarette case that the non-smoker Raoul used as a way to grease the wheels. The spy novel, as well as his notes from Budapest, were lost.

As was his practice, Raoul Wallenberg had some tins of food in his backpack. They belonged to the category of "forbidden goods", but Raoul managed to negotiate to keep them before being led to Lubyanka prison cell number 121. Another contemporary prisoner, Alexander Dolgun, who was an employee at the American Embassy, has described the process of being taken to his cell in this way:

> During this trip, from the shower to my first cell, I became aware that I was, in fact, in a huge prison. I would catch glimpses of long, gloomy corridors, lined with doors, each door with its peephole and food slot with a sliding metal panel. All the hallways were carpeted and almost the only sound as we moved along was the guard's clucking of his tongue – the signal used at Lubyanka to let it be known that a prisoner was under escort ... All those metal doors were grey, battleship grey, and the effect of the gloom and the silence and the grey doors repeating themselves down the corridors until they merged with the shadows was oppressive and discouraging.

*

Prisoners were kept in the Lubyanka during the investigative process and were moved to other prisons or camps once they had been sentenced. The prison took up six floors in the inner courtyard. There were exercise areas for the inmates, both in the courtyard and up on the roof. Those who were there at the same time as Raoul Wallenberg have estimated that it could hold some five hundred prisoners, spread out over twenty or so cells per floor. But the walls were thick and the guards attentive, so they had great difficulty in communicating with each other.

In his book *The Gulag Archipelago* Alexander Solzhenitsyn describes his experience of the Lubyanka in the spring of 1945. He mentions the chimney of the prison that spewed out ash flakes from all the documents and novels that were burned in the prison ovens:

> We walked in the shadow of that chimney – in a concrete box on top of Big Lubyanka's roof, six floors up. Here the walls were also as tall as three grown men. Our ears heard Moscow – the cars signalling to each other. All we saw was this chimney, the sentry up in his tower on the seventh floor and the confounded little piece of God's sky allowed to be visible above the Lubyanka.

Raoul shared his cell with a German diplomat and S.S. captain who had been stationed as a police attaché in Romania. His name was Gustav Richter and he was a devoted Nazi who had assisted Adolf Eichmann in the planning of deportations of Jews from Romania, fortunately without great success. He was also, according to what his colleagues stated in Soviet interrogations, a senior official in the S.D. (the German security service), with a network of agents under him. A spy, in other words.

When the Swedish Foreign Ministry managed to track down Gustav Richter ten years later he said that he and Raoul had become very good friends during that short time in cell 121. He recalled that the Swede had barely entered the cell before he had started to compose a letter to the prison director. In it Raoul Wallenberg protested against his arrest and demanded to be able to get in touch with the Swedish legation in Moscow immediately. He referred to the fact that he was a Swedish diplomat and added that he, as a Swedish citizen, should be given better food.

Gustav Richter read what Raoul had written and thought his cell-mate had stated his points too harshly. He advised him to use more "objective" formulations. Richter felt that this would have a much greater impact. Raoul accepted the criticism and softened the language before he gave the document to the officer on duty on the first floor of the Lubyanka prison.

Two days after his arrival, Raoul Wallenberg was taken to a night interrogation by an officer and lead interrogator who spoke excellent German. Plucking a prisoner from his sleep was a typical Soviet torture tactic.

The interrogation with Raoul Wallenberg lasted from 1 a.m. to 4.30 a.m. on the morning of February 8. When Raoul returned to his cell he was pale. He told his cellmates that the blond interrogation leader, who was named Sverchuk, was "a terrible man". Sverchuk had accused Raoul Wallenberg of spying. "You are known to us. You belong to a big capitalist family in Sweden," the officer had said.

The Wallenberg family was by no means unknown in Moscow. For several years, one of the main assignments of N.K.V.D. agents in Sweden had been to try to infiltrate the family behind Sweden's mightiest financial empire. The Soviet Foreign Ministry had reported on the brothers Jacob and Marcus Wallenberg in special memos. On the one hand they had awakened suspicion after their attempts to contribute to an armistice between Germany and the Western Allies, on the other they gained respect for the liaison role that Marcus Wallenberg had played in the peace negotiations between the Soviet Union and Finland. And behind this all there was of course the ideological distaste of the communist leaders for capitalism.

After Raoul Wallenberg it was Vilmos Langfelder's turn to suffer the same treatment. He was fetched from his cell the following day and also accused of spying. In this case, as his cellmates recall, it was supposed to be on behalf of the Americans, or possibly the British.

Raoul Wallenberg did not allow himself to be broken down. During the first period of time he spent in cell 121 he was cheerful. He exercised every day in order to stay in shape and he exchanged addresses with his cellmates so that they would be able to see each other after they were released. "Raoul Wallenberg, The Swedish Foreign Ministry", was what he wrote on the note that he gave to Gustav Richter. They spent their time playing chess and telling their life stories to each other.

When they talked about their families, Raoul Wallenberg spoke particularly about his mother, Maj von Dardel. Gustav Richter noticed that he was worried. "What will my family say when they are told that I am in prison?" Raoul asked on several occasions. "I comforted him with . . . the fact that, under the current circumstances, there was certainly no shame in it," Gustav Richter told the Foreign Ministry's investigator many years later.

There was only a kilometre or so between cell 121 in the Lubyanka and the Mindovsky Mansion, where – with its grandiose conservatory and staircase lined with bronze lion masks – the ambassador Staffan Söderblom lived a comfortable life in the most exquisite of interiors.

Söderblom believed that his diplomatic colleague Raoul Wallenberg remained in safety among the Soviet troops in Budapest. Still, after several weeks of silence from Stockholm, it was the anxious Söderblom who, against all odds, took the first initiative. And he happened to do so on the same day that Raoul was undergoing his first interrogation in Moscow, just a few streets away.

Söderblom thought it was high time that Raoul Wallenberg was sent a sign of life from the Foreign Ministry, or some sort of instruction. As a Swedish representative, perhaps he could be asked to establish connections with the new Hungarian government? That was what he wrote to Stockholm.

It took five days for the Foreign Ministry to reply to Söderblom's telegram. And when it did, it was only a curt request that Söderblom clarify his "hazy" suggestion. However, Söderblom received explicit orders to find out as soon as possible what had happened to Ivan Danielsson, Per Anger and the rest of the Budapest staff members. It was clear where their concerns lay.

When Staffan Söderblom clarified his thinking about Raoul Wallenberg, there was finally a reaction from Stockholm. The question had provoked a certain amount of handwringing in the ministry. There, the understanding was that Wallenberg was still with the Red Army in Budapest and there was a fair amount of uncertainty regarding how Sweden should relate to the new Hungarian government. But on February 17, exactly one month after Raoul Wallenberg had disappeared, the Foreign Ministry wrote to Söderblom in

Moscow: "If you are able to establish contact with Wallenberg . . . please forward our gratitude, greetings from his family and the message that further instructions will be forthcoming once Danielsson has been located."

Söderblom did as he was told. He sent a diplomatic note to the Soviet Foreign Ministry asking his contacts to let "Legation Secretary Wallenberg" know about "the ministry's thanks, greetings from the family", as well as the information that he would have to wait for further instructions until Danielsson was reinstalled.

There was good reason for the concern about the fate of the diplomats in Budapest. Minister Ivan Danielsson had in fact been "located", but not in the way that the Foreign Ministry would have wished. After a month of fighting, the Red Army had finally conquered Buda. During the final battles, German soldiers were entrenched in the house next to the Swedish legation on Gyopár: the Zwack family's villa that, earlier in the autumn, had housed Raoul Wallenberg's humanitarian department. Soviet soldiers had responded by taking up a position inside the Swedish legation building. They ran up to the bombed-out remains of Danielsson's bedroom, where they opened fire on the Germans.

When the German's resistance had been overcome, the Swedish legation building was filled with Soviet soldiers in white battledress. It did not take them very long to find Ivan Danielsson's substantial wine and spirits store, which contained 150 bottles of cognac. The Soviet military command had given their soldiers a few days of "free licence to plunder" after the conquest of Buda, and that was what they now expected to do. It did not help that the legation guard on duty, Lars Berg, had hung signs in Russian that said that this was Swedish diplomatic territory and that Sweden was a protective power for the Soviet Union in Hungary. Drunken soldiers ran around the building with bottles in their hands, ripping open suitcases and throwing clothes, silver and silk on the floor.

A Hungarian maid was raped twice. The safes were opened "like tins of sardines" and everything of any value was wrapped in torn sheets and driven away in trucks. Ironically, the soldiers even took the silverware that actually belonged to the Soviet legation in Budapest.

Intoxicated Soviet soldiers had also stumbled into the underground shelter in Prince Esterházy's palace. There the Swedes who were hiding out had put up a sign in Russian that said: "The Swedish Legation. Acting protective authority with regard to Soviet interests." The exhausted Ivan Danielsson, who had been preparing himself to receive a Russian command unit, lost a shoe in the darkness of the cellar and now stood barefoot on a heap of gravel as the soldiers ran amok, searching for clocks and guns.

Lars Berg had left the occupied legation building to look for a higher-ranking Soviet unit and request protection for the Swedish legation. He was sent to see a commander down in Pest. There he met his Russian colleague, Count Tolstoy-Kutuzov, whom he had employed at the Swedish legation in October for interpretation and translation work. Tolstoy-Kutuzov told him that he had appealed to the Soviets but had been jailed and interrogated for several days. He said that the Russians had accused the Swedish legation of spying for the Germans and that it was above all Raoul Wallenberg and Lars Berg who were the targets of suspicion. Now Tolstoy-Kutuzov was free again and had been recruited by the Red Army to run a foreign affairs bureau. Berg began to feel uncomfortable.

> Strangely enough Tolstoy did not seem completely happy to see me again. He had changed in some strange way. He was no longer the friendly and always extremely helpful colleague. Nervously he asked me if the Russians knew that I was with him.

Per Anger, Göte Carlsson and Yngve Ekmark had been driven out to the countryside by a Soviet major and housed in a barracks under military protection. A few days later, Ivan Danielsson and a clerk, Mezey, were brought in. They were then all moved over to new quarters in the town of Dunavecse, seventy kilometres south of the capital. There the group stayed put, guarded by soldiers.

Margareta Bauer had made her way back to the legation building at Gyopár utca alone, kitted out with a sheepskin coat, a bucket and a spade. She was the only one of the Swedes to remain in Buda and she spent her days burning documents from S.K.F., the Swedish ball-bearing factory, which the legation had stored.

*

Several weeks had gone by since the Foreign Ministry had called Maj von Dardel with the news that her son had been received into the custody of Soviet troops. But still there was no word or even a greeting from Raoul himself. In February she decided to look up the Soviet ambassador in Stockholm, the legendary Alexandra Kollontai.

Madame Kollontai had her office and residence in the Soviet legation's stone villa, located in Stockholm's fashionable Östermalm district. Kollontai had been a minister in the Bolshevik government after the revolution of 1917, the first female government member in Europe. After a wave of executions and unexplained deaths, she was now one of the few remaining original revolutionary leaders.

For two years, Kollontai had been able to call herself "Ambassador". She was the centre of diplomatic life in Stockholm. Colleagues recall that she held well-attended receptions on every conceivable Soviet holiday. Madame Kollontai would receive her guests like an empress in her raised chair, surrounded by subordinates in dark-blue uniforms.

In March 1945 she would turn seventy-three. She still attracted attention but was marked by illness. Two and a half years earlier she had survived a stroke, which left her partly paralysed on her left side, but two months later she still managed to celebrate from her wheelchair the anniversary of the October Revolution with a magnificent party for four hundred people at the Grand Hôtel. Russian caviar was served in silver bowls and the wine flowed.

At the time that Maj von Dardel came to see her, the Soviet leadership's growing displeasure at Alexandra Kollontai's autonomous actions was becoming clear. The most recent incident in this regard was when the Soviet Union declined the trade agreement with Sweden. Kollontai had softened the message and told the Swedes that it should not be viewed as a political statement, that it was simply the terms of the loan that the Soviet Union opposed. This action was seen as a violation of her instructions and unleashed rage at the Foreign Ministry in Moscow. "She weakened the strength of our reply. She reduced the question to a mere commercial level without trying to use our answer to further our political interests," the head of the Scandinavian division, Mikhail Vetrov, wrote in a stern memorandum. He named both the Baltic and Soviet prisoners of war as potential Swedish concessions that Kollontai had gambled away.

Maj von Dardel and Alexandra Kollontai had certain personal connections. These were primarily through Nanna Svartz, the physician who had successfully cared for Kollontai after her stroke in 1942, and thereafter become her friend. Nanna Svartz was a well-known figure in Swedish medical circles. She was a professor and head of the medical clinic at the Karolinska Hospital. This meant that she worked closely with Fredrik von Dardel, Maj's husband, who had been appointed director general of Karolinska when it opened in 1940.

Nanna Svartz was the first female university professor in Sweden, no easy position to hold in such a stiff and thoroughly male faculty. But Fredrik von Dardel had supported her. A friendship was born between the two and their families. Nanna Svartz also became Maj and Fredrik von Dardel's primary physician.

A further personal connection came from the fact that Alexandra Kollontai counted Marcus Wallenberg among her personal friends – a result of all their contacts during the peace negotiations between the Soviet Union and Finland in the autumn of 1944.

At the meeting on Villagatan 17, Kollontai was persuasive. She told Maj von Dardel that she should not be worried. Raoul Wallenberg was safe and sound in Russia. At around this time, Alexandra Kollontai also invited Ingrid, Christian Günther's wife, to tea. This is how Ingrid Günther later described the meeting:

When I was there she asked me to tell my husband the following: that Raoul Wallenberg was in Russia and that it would be better for him if the Swedish government did not argue about this matter. Naturally I forwarded this message, which Christian tried to follow as far as he could. Madame Kollontai added: I assure you that he is alive and is treated well.

History does not record what happened to this information after the tea. But Kollontai's most crucial message – that Raoul Wallenberg was in the Soviet Union and not with the Red Army in Hungary – was never noted in the Foreign Ministry records. It would be several years before this became known.

*

The Soviet SMERSH agents in Budapest interrogated several of the staff from the Swedish legation and the Swedish Red Cross, not just the mysterious Count Tolstoy-Kutuzov. But it seems that Berg's intuition was correct. According to an officer at the N.K.V.D., Pavel Sudoplatov, for many years one of the most senior in the intelligence service, Tolstoy-Kutuzov had been a Soviet agent since the twenties. During the latter half of the autumn of 1944, Tolstoy-Kutuzov had described Raoul Wallenberg's work in Budapest as "suspect" in his reports. Tolstoy-Kutuzov had informed them that the Swede had frequent contact with the German intelligence services and that he was most probably engaged in duplicitous activities.

By February 19, the SMERSH operation for the 2nd Ukrainian Front could deliver a fairly damning intelligence report on the Swedish legation to its superior in Debrecen. This was forwarded to the Lubyanka in Moscow. It was based in large part on a witness account from a source, who was very likely Tolstoy-Kutuzov, but also on information from Henry Thomsen, another of the Russians that Lars Berg had employed at the protective powers department. Thomsen had been arrested by the Russians at the end of January and even he was subject to fierce interrogation.

Both Thomsen and Tolstoy-Kutuzov appear to have filtered what they had seen through murky Soviet glasses. Possibly the SMERSH agents' interpretation of the intelligence at hand was influenced by the fact that the agency saw its purpose as being to catch as many spies as possible. This tended to increase the number of suspects.

In a report titled "Special Messages", a Colonel Mukhortov now wrote to Moscow that SMERSH had received "intelligence that compromises activities at the Swedish embassy and the Swedish Red Cross in Hungary". He went on:

The Swedish Embassy has extended protection to a significant number of civilians in Budapest, persons who have absolutely no relation to Sweden, and issued various kinds of documents to them such as passports, papers of identifications and "letters of protection". In this category there are known members from fascist organisations in Hungary, certain staff and agents for the intelligence services and counter-espionage sections of enemy nations as well as other counter-revolutionary elements.

*

The SMERSH colonel referred to an agent who, only a week or so earlier, reported that the Swedish embassy had sold at least 20,000 passports for between 2,000 to 20,000 Hungarian pengő apiece. The agent claimed that wealthy Jews, such as those belonging to the Manfréd Weiss family, had been granted Swedish citizenship for 200,000 pengő. The clearly misinformed but imaginative agent then named the officials who had been involved in the passport sales and grouped "Countess NAKO, Doctor FLEISCHMANN under the leadership of the director FORGACS as well as the office manager MEZEY and even, according to certain accounts, minister DANIELSSON himself."

In his report, Colonel Mukhortov wrote that most of the people who had been granted Swedish citizenship had departed with a German transit visa just before the Red Army encircled Budapest. Several pages are devoted to "evidence" that the Swedes were fascist collaborators. Staff at the legation itself who, "until very recently were fascists", were named, as were Red Cross employees with supposed fascists in their families who "always have been open enemies to Soviet Russia".

The Swedes were quick to point to their role as protective power for the Soviet Union, but the counter-espionage investigators did not give this much weight. Help for Russian prisoners of war was limited to ten shirts and twenty boxes of sardines, they stated sourly. "From the above demonstrated but still incomplete facts it is evident that instead of protecting the Soviet Union and Hungary's interests, the Swedish embassy and the Swedish Red Cross take enemies of the Soviet Union and the Hungarian people under their wings and offer them refuge and safety. On these grounds we are taking steps to arrest persons of interest who possess protective papers issued by the Swedish embassy," Colonel Mukhortov concluded his report. He was given orders to gather more information.

Valdemar Langlet, the elderly and somewhat loquacious delegate for the Swedish Red Cross, had, against all odds, managed to make his way to Debrecen on bomb-damaged roads. There he had established contact with the new Hungarian government and asked for permission to continue his humanitarian work. The Soviet-supported Hungarian ministers had expressed their genuine gratitude for the Swedish rescue operation and their "great admiration for Danielsson's heroic actions".

Now the warm-hearted Langlet was back in Pest again and was soon one of those interrogated by the Russians. The Soviet military leaders had got hold of a letter about Raoul Wallenberg apparently written by Langlet. The letter claimed that Wallenberg had travelled under Soviet escort to General Malinovsky's headquarters.

Langlet had to wait for hours before he saw the Soviet major who was conducting the interrogations. "Where was that Wallenberg, where was he living and why was he staying away?" Langlet later remembered the major asking. When Langlet replied that he did not know but had heard that Wallenberg had gone to see General Malinovsky, the major sharpened his tone. "Then you should not have written as you did, since you did not know if it was true!"

Every morning, the Lubyanka's prisoners were awakened by a guard who shouted "*Podyom!*" (Get up!) and opened the food slot. A canister of tasteless "tea", as well as a small loaf of bread for each prisoner was pushed onto the shelf inside. For dinner there were different varieties of thin soup. In between there was nothing.

The carpets in the corridor outside dampened all sounds. In the Lubyanka, silence and desolation reigned. The guards held firmly to the principle that the prisoners should not encounter anyone other than their cell mates as they were led to interrogations, to exercise or to the so-called bath that occurred on every tenth day. When the bolts on the cell doors were slid aside no-one knew what was coming. They never knew if the prisoner would return or not.

On Tuesday, March 6, the daily routine was interrupted for the Swedish prisoner Raoul Wallenberg in cell 121. Up to this point, not much had happened in his month-long prison stay. If his case was being investigated, it was happening in slow motion. Raoul Wallenberg had not been interrogated once after the night-time ordeals of the first few days. Now he was to be moved to one of the neighbouring cells, number 123.

He had not been completely forgotten. Staffan Söderblom had made an attempt to get a message to Raoul through the Soviet Foreign Ministry. But it appears that the message containing the Foreign Ministry's thanks and the greetings from his family did not reach him in the Lubyanka. And Söderblom had not asked to be allowed to see his fellow diplomat. He had no instructions to do so and perhaps this did not even occur to him. He was still under the impression that Raoul was in Hungary.

On the same day that Raoul Wallenberg switched cells in the Lubyanka, Swedes who read the newspapers received the first detailed account of his actions. Under the headline "Heroic Swedish Feat in Hungary", the newspaper *Dagens Nyheter* printed an interview with a Hungarian who had managed to escape from Budapest. He praised the Swedish efforts to save the Hungarian Jews, particularly the work of Raoul Wallenberg and Valdemar Langlet. The majority of the article was about Raoul. "Nothing was impossible for Wallenberg. During those troubled days, he received anonymous death threats, stones were thrown at his car, they did everything they could to make it impossible for him to go and see the people he was protecting: armed gangsters were sent to follow him, but nothing could compel him to give in," said the Hungarian, who claimed to have worked at a printing shop in Budapest and to have had contact with Wallenberg.

The first accounts of what happened to the rest of the legation had now reached Stockholm by way of the Swedish minister in Romania, Patrik Reuterswärd. He had received second-hand reports from some of Raoul's charges who had made their way across the border, as well as a letter from Valdemar Langlet. It was now stated, incorrectly, that all the Swedish diplomats, with the exception of Raoul Wallenberg, were in safety at the papal nuncio's residence in Budapest, news that was immediately announced by Swedish Radio. To the Foreign Ministry, Reuterswärd also reported rumours that Raoul Wallenberg had departed by car to an unknown destination.

Staffan Söderblom received instructions from Stockholm to communicate the news to the Soviet Foreign Ministry. On one of the first days in March he went to see the head of the Scandinavian division on Kuznetsky Most. Söderblom informed him that all Swedish diplomats in Hungary had now been located, with the exception of Raoul Wallenberg, "about whom we have received information long ago through the Foreign Ministry's dedicated efforts". The Swedish minister made it sound as if Raoul Wallenberg was a completed case.

Only a day or so later, Söderblom returned to the Soviet Foreign Ministry. Söderblom was instructed to ask the Russians to tell Raoul that he was "eagerly expected" at home and that Sven Salén was asking when he might arrive. Söderblom, however, chose to pass the question along to the minister in Romania. Why bother Moscow again when Raoul Wallenberg was somewhere in Hungary? His pre-eminent task in Moscow was to achieve noticeably improved relations between Sweden and the Soviet Union. It made no sense to inconvenience them unnecessarily.

Protected or disappeared? It was becoming increasingly clear that the Russians wanted to distance themselves from the quick, calming message that Deputy Foreign Minister Dekanozov had sent and that Ambassador Kollontai had repeated during her tea parties in February. It was a troubling fact for the Russians that the Swedes had received written confirmation that Raoul Wallenberg had been taken under the protection of the Red Army. But could one glide away from this clear position and into a vague fog?

Disinformation was a speciality of the Soviet intelligence service. At 10.30 p.m. on March 8, news about the Swedish Budapest colony suddenly turned up in a broadcast from the now Soviet-controlled Hungarian Kossuth Radio. Under the title of "Conversations: Man-hunting terrorism. Swedish diplomat on the Hungarian Deportations", the programme related information about the situation in Budapest that Valdemar Langlet had given during his visit to the new Hungarian government in Debrecen. Langlet was said to have estimated that half a million Hungarian Jews had been deported by "Hitler and the Arrow Cross bandits". Then the radio station reported that one of the leaders of the "Red Cross initiative" in Budapest, Raoul Wallenberg, had disappeared "without a trace" on January 17. The studio reporter's conclusion was bewildering. "All signs indicate that Gestapo agents murdered him," the journalist said without hesitation.

From protected to missing – a new Soviet position on Raoul Wallenberg was starting to take shape. Now they only had to get the strategic disinformation to spread to the right person. Shortly after the broadcast, the Stockholm-based Hungarian exile Vilmos Böhm called the Foreign Ministry and tipped them off about the Hungarian radio programme. Böhm, the former Hungarian minister who now worked at the British embassy's Press Reading Bureau in Stockholm was later revealed to be working as an agent of the Soviet intelligence service in Stockholm.

The rumour that Raoul Wallenberg could have been murdered by the Gestapo had reached its mark, but at this stage it does not appear to have been deemed particularly credible by the Foreign Ministry. More attention was paid to the indication that Raoul Wallenberg was perhaps missing and not, after all, under the protection of Soviet troops. Confusion did not exactly lessen when contradictory information about minister Danielsson and the other Swedish diplomats started to trickle in. It was claimed that they were no longer in safety at the papal nuncio's residence in Budapest. The sense of concern in Stockholm was growing. A new telegram was dispatched from the Foreign Ministry in Stockholm to Söderblom in Moscow: "As contradictory rumours regarding the staff of the Budapest legation swirl here, you are requested to energetically pursue information to establish the whereabouts of Danielsson, Anger, Wallenberg."

Raoul Wallenberg had now been moved and replaced Vilmos Langfelder in the Lubyanka prison's cell 123. He shared the tiny room with Willy Rödel, one of his former cell mate Gustav Richter's German co-workers. Rödel was a large man in his fifties who, like Richter, had been stationed as a diplomat in the Romanian capital Bucharest. There he had been a political adviser to the German minster and distinguished himself as an expert on the "Jewish question". He was later identified as a spy by his diplomatic colleagues when they were interrogated by the N.K.V.D.

The third prisoner in cell 123 was a Czech interpreter from a German signal surveillance company. Jan Loyda, as he was called, was Raoul's age and dubbed "The Czech", even though he had been a German citizen since his twenties.

The fact that a diplomat from neutral Sweden was in the Lubyanka attracted a certain amount of attention among the prisoners. The new cell mates understood from Raoul Wallenberg that he regarded his arrest as an inexplicable mistake. Raoul told Rödel and Loyda that he was convinced that the mistake would be rectified and that he would soon be able to begin the negotiations he had planned.

Raoul Wallenberg was still keeping his spirits up. Even in the new cell, he exercised every day. His cell mate Jan Loyda has said that Raoul began to sketch a victory monument in honour of the Red Army during his time in cell 123. He often sang – mostly Swedish folk songs – and took the opportunity to dust off his schoolboy Russian. The two cell mates agreed that Loyda would teach Raoul Russian and Raoul teach Loyda English.

It was now mid-March 1945. Spring was approaching and, outside the high walls of the Lubyanka, the snow had started to melt. In Budapest, the change in the weather had created such intense spring flooding that the Danube almost burst its banks. There, in the Hungarian capital, Raoul's colleagues Lars Berg and Margareta Bauer had kept things going while the higher-ranked diplomats of the legation played cards and made corncob pipes during their "protective custody" in the Hungarian countryside. Lars Berg had stayed in Pest, in the building of the Swedish Red Cross on Üllői út, only a few streets from Raoul Wallenberg's now bombed-out headquarters. Margareta Bauer, who had managed on her own in the legation house for a long time, joined him there.

It was with some concern that Berg noted that the Swedish Red Cross' operation had again started to "swell up in an uncontrolled fashion". Even worse, when he walked out on the street he saw a Swedish flag only a few buildings away. On the door there was a sign which stated in Hungarian, Russian and German that this was "The Royal Swedish Legation". He walked in and found Raoul's Hungarian co-worker Otto Fleischmann at a desk, in the midst of completing a document that bore the legation's stamp and even a copy of Raoul Wallenberg's signature. He then met a few of the others in the circle closest to Raoul – Hugó Wohl and Pál Hegedűs – who told him that they wanted to resume their work: to operate a hospital, community kitchen and orphanage in the way that Raoul Wallenberg had planned.

Lars Berg had never concealed his scepticism over what he regarded as excesses in Raoul Wallenberg's explosively growing humanitarian operation. He had not changed his opinion. Berg knew that the Russians suspected them of spying and that his and Raoul Wallenberg's names were considered particularly dubious. He asked Fleischmann to shut down operations immediately. After this he wrote a diplomatic notice and put an announcement in the paper declaring that all Swedish protective passports were henceforth invalid.

Before they parted, Pál Hegedűs took Lars Berg to the ruins of the Hazai Bank. Hegedűs wanted to give him a package that Raoul Wallenberg had stored at the bank and that the Russians had missed during their plundering. Lars Berg opened it on the spot. "It turned out to contain 870,000 pengő in bills, a ring set with an unusually large diamond, a copper plate, as well as a bound piece of writing depicting Raoul's deeds in Hungary in verse and unusually artistic illustrations. Apparently it was a Christmas present from some of his staff and admirers," Lars Berg noted in his book *What Happened in Budapest*.

On Thursday, March 15, Per Anger was suddenly standing at the door of Lars Berg's new office in Pest. After a month of waiting in Soviet "protective custody" they had finally been told that all the Swedish diplomats would return to Sweden via Romania and the Soviet Union. "A truck is waiting on the street," Per Anger told Margareta Bauer and Lars Berg. Since neither of them owned more than the clothes on their backs, they could leave almost immediately. Margareta Bauer looked around the flatbed of the truck, where Ivan Danielsson and the others were waiting. Where was Raoul Wallenberg? She posed the question to the Soviet officer who was going to be escorting them. He saluted and answered that Wallenberg had already been taken care of. He was in southern Hungary and would arrive in Sweden before them.

Valdemar Langlet had long thought that Raoul Wallenberg would turn up again. But now he changed his opinion and put forth a new theory. "It may be possible that in reality he has fallen into the hands of disguised Arrow Cross, in which case one must fear the worst for his fate."

The Red Cross delegate was ill and would therefore remain for another two months in Budapest. They said goodbye and the truck with the somewhat tousled Swedish diplomats set off on a farewell tour of Budapest – to Prince Esterházy's damaged palace and the bombed and plundered legation buildings on Gellért Hill.

They had a week-long trip to Bucharest on the back of a rickety truck before them. The first night they slept on bags of straw.

*

The Kremlin's irritation over Ambassador Kollontai's independent actions in Stockholm had now grown into outright mistrust. Her apparent betrayal in connection with the trade negotiations was a factor, her openness about Raoul Wallenberg's whereabouts was another. According to the author Arkady Vaksberg, Kollontai had told Foreign Minister Molotov what she had said about Raoul Wallenberg to his mother and to Ingrid Günther. Molotov had become irritated and ordered her not to speak with anyone about such things.

Kollontai's outspokenness was now a problem and it was felt she was too friendly with too many important Swedes. Stalin wanted her to leave her post immediately and return to Moscow. The problem was that Kollontai had come down with pneumonia. Her physician, Nanna Svartz, now had to drop everything else and escort her famous patient back to the Soviet Union. The Soviet military plane left Stockholm on March 18.

Staffan Söderblom still felt his situation in Moscow was "anything but easy". The Soviets had not responded to any of his enquiries about Raoul Wallenberg and the rest of the Budapest staff. He was becoming more unwilling to send them any further questions.

Instead, Söderblom paid a visit to the newly returned Kollontai. He presented all his topics to the convalescing 73-year-old diplomat – the imminent United Nations conference, the Baltic refugees and Folke Bernadotte's visa. Finally he mentioned that he had submitted enquiries to the Soviet Foreign Ministry regarding the whereabouts of Danielsson, Anger and Wallenberg, but that he had not received an answer. Afterwards Söderblom wrote to Stockholm that Kollontai had promised "to expedite the investigation into the Budapest Swedes".

At the same time, the Russian rewriting of Wallenberg's fate was in full swing. The Russian strategy appears to have been to give the new version of reality legitimacy by way of unofficial channels and rumours, with the goal of convincing the Foreign Ministry that Dekanozov's account was fiction. At a cocktail party in Bucharest in mid-March, for example, Soviet diplomats told their Swedish colleagues that no-one knew anything about Wallenberg in Moscow, that he had "gone missing somewhere".

It did not take long for the new Soviet version of reality to take on a life of its own in the Foreign Ministry. When the truck from Budapest arrived in Romania, Staffan Söderblom picked up his pen and wrote a kind of final report to the head of the Scandinavian division at the Soviet Foreign Ministry. He listed the names of everyone who was reported to have arrived safely in Romania and mentioned that Valdemar Langlet had remained in Budapest. Then he came to Raoul Wallenberg and suddenly it was as if Dekanozov's clear message from January had never existed. It did not matter that the deputy foreign minister had actually provided a written receipt to the effect that Wallenberg was under Soviet protection. It did not seem to matter that this receipt indicated that, if Raoul Wallenberg was now missing, it was the Russians who should know what had happened and were obliged to inform the Swedes. Söderblom did not demand any information. Instead he wrote that Raoul Wallenberg "according to the Swedish legation in Budapest" had been "missing since January 17 when he said he intended to leave and travel by car". By the end of March, the word in the corridors of the Foreign Ministry was that there was a lack of "sufficient intelligence" on Raoul Wallenberg.

The process was now complete. Raoul Wallenberg was no longer under Soviet protection. He was missing.

On Thursday, April 12, Franklin D. Roosevelt died from a massive stroke while on holiday in Georgia. During the last few weeks of his life, he had seen superior allied forces completely wipe out the formerly so feared German army. But the successes on the battlefield were accompanied by increasingly abrasive verbal exchanges between the United States and the Soviet Union. Stalin, it seemed, had changed his tune. He refused to allow American officers into Poland in order to assist American prisoners of war. He refused to let any ministers join the Polish government other than those hand-picked by the Soviet Union. The high-minded democratic phrases that Stalin had used were starting to look like over-inflated, perhaps already punctured, balloons. The mood gave a taste of the cold war to come.

In a letter sent in early April, Stalin had not hesitated to accuse President Roosevelt of making secret attempts to negotiate a separate agreement with the Germans. An offended Roosevelt sent a reply only a few days before he died.

Finally I would say this: it would be one of the great tragedies of history if at the very moment of victory now within our grasp, such distrust, such lack of faith should prejudice the entire undertaking after the colossal losses of life, material and treasure involved. Frankly I cannot avoid a feeling of bitter resentment toward your informers, whoever they are, for such vile misrepresentations of my actions or those of my trusted subordinates.

Stalin's allegations did not completely lack substance. The Germans had sent out a number of feelers to see if a separate treaty could be agreed. Some of these went through Stockholm. As the historian Bernt Schiller has shown, in February 1945 Raoul Wallenberg's relative Jacob Wallenberg received a visit from an envoy sent by Foreign Minister Joachim von Ribbentrop. The German wanted to get a message to Winston Churchill that Hitler was willing to consider a separate agreement with the British and Americans, one founded on their shared interests in stopping the Russian advances. Earlier in the war, the Wallenberg brothers had proved themselves to be effective communication channels for such matters. When Jacob Wallenberg dismissed the idea as unworkable, von Ribbentrop's envoy made his way to Iver Olsen at the American legation instead.

The contacts continued in April. With Folke Bernadotte as his channel, Heinrich Himmler and his associate Walter Schellenberg attempted to negotiate an armistice with the Western Allies. Walter Schellenberg had been one of Jacob Wallenberg's channels into the German S.S. When Raoul Wallenberg departed for Budapest in the autumn of 1944, Jacob Wallenberg had just asked Schellenberg to protect his cousin.

No-one can say how much of this was known to the Soviet intelligence service. But, for a well-informed counter-espionage operation, guided by the conspiratorial mindset that permeated Stalin's Russia, it would not have been hard to uncover associations that could hardly have helped the case of the young Swede in the Lubyanka prison. That the connection was coincidental and without importance would not have mattered. In Stalin's Soviet Union, an interpretation of the truth could be as significant as the truth itself.

At the American legation in Stockholm, the news that Raoul Wallenberg was missing had caused some concern. Herschel Johnson felt responsible and took action. He wrote to the State Department in Washington, where the secretary of state was now Edward Stettinius. Johnson stressed that he felt the American embassy in Moscow should offer Staffan Söderblom assistance "since we have a particular interest in Wallenberg's Budapest mission". The message hit its mark. The secretary of the treasury, Henry Morgenthau, who originally oversaw the creation of the War Refugee Board, attached a special note to Johnson's telegram: "Let Stettinius know that I am personally interested in this man."

The U.S.A.'s ambassador to Moscow, Averell Harriman, did as he was told, but Staffan Söderblom declined the offer of American assistance. "The Swedes say that they have no reason to suspect that the Russians are not doing what they can and they do not feel that an approach to the Soviet Foreign Ministry from our side would be desirable," Harriman reported back to Washington.

Shortly before lunch on Friday, April 13, a group disembarked at the Kiev Station in Moscow: Per Anger, Ivan Danielsson, Margareta Bauer, Asta Nilsson, Yngve Ekmark, Dénes von Mezey and Göte Carlsson. The only one missing was Raoul Wallenberg. The journey had gone well. They had been given their own blue carriage, an "old tsarist Russian model", and had stayed in Odessa for three days on the way, where they had seen a performance of "Madame Butterfly".

Staffan Söderblom and Ingeman Hägglöf were waiting on the platform. They were slightly tense, mainly because Söderblom had become worried that the Russians would steer the Swedish diplomatic carriage on towards Siberia. Söderblom invited everyone to lunch at the Mindovsky Mansion and spent the afternoon in various meetings with Ivan Danielsson. Söderblom and Danielsson met with Vetrov, among others, who was head of the Scandinavian division at the Foreign Ministry, which was in the same area as Lubyanka prison. The meeting lasted five minutes. No-one mentioned Raoul Wallenberg's case.

Still, in their private talks, the Swedish diplomats must have addressed the issue. Danielsson communicated a new angle on the mysterious disappearance of Raoul Wallenberg to Söderblom – the rumour that Valdemar Langlet had heard, about him being led away by disguised Arrow Cross men. If this was the case, almost anything could have happened and Raoul would very likely not have survived. Staffan Söderblom listened and felt more and more convinced. The only conclusion, as he saw it, was that Raoul Wallenberg was dead.

On the platform that evening, Staffan Söderblom turned to Per Anger. "Remember this when you arrive back in Sweden – not one bad word about the Russians!" The following day, Söderblom sent this latest piece of information back to Stockholm:

> Wallenberg, who had been the target of death threats from the Germans and the Arrow Cross, went over to the Russians on his own initiative. As soon as he was encountered, I received official notification. After this, Wallenberg appears to have departed by car for Debrecen and is feared to have perished during the trip. There are various theories: car crash (very likely), robbery-murder, ambush by the Arrow Cross etc. I am afraid that we may never know the truth.

The Budapest Swedes were expected home the following week. Up until the very end, Maj von Dardel nurtured hopes that her son was also on his way back. But, on the Tuesday, she was notified that the Budapest legation would be arriving by boat from Finland the next day and that Raoul Wallenberg was unfortunately not among them.

Maj and Fredrik von Dardel nonetheless went down to Skeppsbron quay in order to greet the S.S. *Arcturus* on Wednesday morning, April 18. The quay was overflowing with relatives carrying flowers and presents. They waved vigorously and cheered as the ship approached. In front of the customs booth there was a small greeting committee from the Foreign Ministry and in the crowd there were also many exiled Hungarians who were hoping for news about family members.

In the middle of the quay stood Per Anger's wife Elena, with their one-year-old daughter Birgitta, who had a dewy red rose tucked into the brim of her little hat. Lars Berg's mother cried as she hugged her son. Out of the corner of his eye, Berg noticed Maj and Fredrik von Dardel, who were silently watching the others. "The tears that ran down the cheeks of Raoul's mother were those of the heaviest grief," he wrote many years later.

When an appropriate number of days had gone by, Maj von Dardel made an attempt to invite Ivan Danielsson to her home in order to hear more about Raoul. He politely declined, using the contrived excuse that he did not have "any suitable clothes".

The Foreign Ministry's official press release about Raoul Wallenberg only came out on that Friday evening. It "struck Stockholm like a bomb" according to the newspaper *Expressen*. The information that Raoul Wallenberg had been taken into protective custody by the Red Army had been comforting. His relatives had been told that there were no "direct reasons to worry". Now they heard instead that "there is no further information and the possibility that Mr Wallenberg is still alive must be considered limited".

A press conference with Per Anger and Ivan Danielsson took place on Friday. "Not a bad word about the Russians," Staffan Söderblom had urged and those words rang in their ears. The encounter was dominated by revelations of the dramatic events in Budapest. Anger and Danielsson touched on Raoul Wallenberg's enormous contribution but refrained from elaborating on the fact that he had not been on the ship.

The following day, Raoul Wallenberg was praised for his actions by both Swedish and foreign papers. A headline in the *New York Times* read: "Raoul Wallenberg. Architect. Led the rescue of 20,000 from the Nazis". "An imperishable honour is connected to his name and memory," *Svenska Dagbladet* wrote in an editorial.

At the same time, the Foreign Ministry took a sharper tone towards Söderblom in Moscow. With the rest of the Budapest legation safely home, the need to establish why one of the diplomats had *not* returned grew stronger. The Russians had, after all, made assurances that Raoul Wallenberg was in their custody. So, what had happened? By all accounts it was Foreign Minister Christian Günther himself who was driving this. Söderblom now received strict orders, or "definitive instructions", as the Foreign Ministry put it, to follow up with Dekanozov, refer to his message of January 17 and demand "a thorough investigation" into Raoul Wallenberg's "later fate".

Staffan Söderblom must have groaned. He had tried to indicate to Stockholm that he thought this question should be handled through other means and not be allowed to disturb the difficult and sensitive contacts at the top level in Moscow. Especially not now when so much pointed to the fact that Raoul Wallenberg had been killed, either in an accident or by the Arrow Cross. Wasn't the new Hungarian government in Debrecen a better source of information?

Reluctantly he agreed to do as he was instructed, though not without his customary conciliatory gestures. Söderblom was given a meeting with Dekanozov on April 25. He began the meeting by handing over a letter that contained an official Swedish demand that the Soviet side would take measures to search for Raoul Wallenberg. Dekanozov promised to do this. But Söderblom did not stop there. He had only recently informed the Soviet Foreign Ministry that Wallenberg was very likely missing. So he must have felt compelled to give an explanation for the new demand.

Afterwards Dekanozov made the following notes about the thoughts regarding Raoul Wallenberg that Staffan Söderblom had shared with him:

> Possibly he had suffered an accident. The Swedes had received information regarding such an incident from Jews who had come from Budapest to Bucharest. I asked what kind of incident Söderblom meant. Söderblom clarified that, according to witnesses that he had, Wallenberg – after he had been encountered – had died in a car crash.

Maj von Dardel loved her son, but she was not an oversensitive mother, the kind of bundle of nerves who would air her concerns whether or not there was any basis for them. Quite the opposite. Raoul's mother had been through more in life than most and was, by nature, a fairly tough and straightforward person. Over the years she had demonstrated that she could withstand farewells and long separations if she knew it was in her child's best interest. She had after all sent Raoul off into the world when he was twelve years old.

But the experience of the *Arcturus* was too much, as were her suspicions that something terrible had happened. It did not fit with what she had heard from Madame Kollontai.

Those who were close to Maj von Dardel unanimously describe her as an unusually energetic and vigorous person, a quick and instinctive problem-solver. Naturally she must have felt it necessary to take the matter into her own hands.

Maj von Dardel now sent a message to the Soviet legation at Villagatan and asked for information about Raoul Wallenberg. When the diplomats sent the question on to Moscow, the reply was:

> He was last seen in an automobile belonging to the Swedish legation, in which he is said to have left the German zone for the zone encircled by the Soviet troops. In Sweden, Wallenberg is rumoured to have been seen in connection with a troop movement on its way to the U.S.S.R. Since this time, he has not been heard from.

Perhaps it was simply a coincidence but, the following day, the Soviet legation in Stockholm wrote to the Foreign Ministry and demanded for the second time the return of one of the Baltic refugees, Lydia Makarova. The Soviets' interest in this teenage girl, who had fled the Soviet Union when her mother died, is curious. Perhaps she was regarded as a good moral example since she was a minor? In any event, it was not the last time that the Russians would respond to an enquiry about Wallenberg with a question regarding Makarova. It was as if the Soviets wanted to send a message: if we get her, you will get him.

Maj von Dardel had not been able to meet with Ivan Danielsson, but she did see some of Raoul's other diplomatic colleagues from Budapest. It seems that Per Anger visited the von Dardel family on one of the first days after he came home. Even Lars Berg is assumed to have come to Raoul's family home. After all, he had managed to bring back the ring, the plate and the beautiful Christmas book from the Hazai Bank.

Fredrik and Maj von Dardel heard the speculations of the Budapest Swedes. But they also heard Per Anger's new theory. The Foreign Ministry in Stockholm had received intelligence to the effect that the Swiss diplomats Harald Feller and Max Meier had also disappeared from Budapest. Apparently this was after they "had been offered the chance to inspect a certain office location in Pest, under Russian escort". Anger was starting to sense a logical connection, that all three were imprisoned. But when he tried to establish the theory at the Foreign Ministry, no-one wanted to listen. Per Anger was correct in his speculations. Harald Feller and Max Meier had been sitting in a cell at the Lubyanka prison since March 4.

Now Raoul's famous relatives leapt into action. Staffan Söderblom had suggested that Marcus Wallenberg write a letter to his friend, Madame Kollontai – probably as a way to try to clarify the situation without Söderblom having to confront the senior ranks of the Soviet Foreign Ministry. Marcus Wallenberg did not hesitate. He consulted Raoul's boss, Kálmán Lauer, about the details of the Budapest mission before he wrote his letter. Lauer described the entire story from the beginning, as he remembered it. Then he speculated as to what might have happened. Lauer told Marcus Wallenberg that Raoul had "some notes and photographs of the atrocities that the German and Hungarian Nazis had committed and it is possible that he suffered an accident on the way to Debrecen".

Marcus Wallenberg's letter, which he had written in French, arrived by courier in Moscow on Friday, April 27. Staffan Söderblom visited Alexandra Kollontai on Saturday in order to deliver it. Wallenberg explained that he was writing to her on "a strictly personal" matter and asked Kollontai to exercise her considerable influence to investigate Raoul Wallenberg's case, since the family was becoming exceedingly worried.

The messenger Söderblom felt he had already sized up the situation. When he reported back to the Foreign Ministry about the visit to Kollontai he concluded: "As I have maintained earlier, it is unfortunately possible that the matter will remain an unsolved mystery."

When prisoners in the Lubyanka were brought to interrogations, they would usually be escorted to some of the rooms higher up in "Big Lubyanka" by guards from the "Inner Prison". The procedure was carefully recorded. The length of the interrogation was noted in the ledger and the prisoner had to sign his name. Often the exercise ended with the prisoner being given a piece of paper and asked to write down his life history. It was a deliberate move to ensure that the story did not change. The interrogators leaders liked to remind new inmates that the acronym SMERSH stood for "Death to spies".

On the last Saturday in April 1945, shortly after 3 p.m., the guards came for Raoul Wallenberg for the second time during his months in prison. He was brought face to face with the chief interrogator, Kuzmishin, who was the head of a section at SMERSH's 3rd Division. Perhaps the recent tumult in Stockholm had precipitated the session. Or perhaps there was a connection between

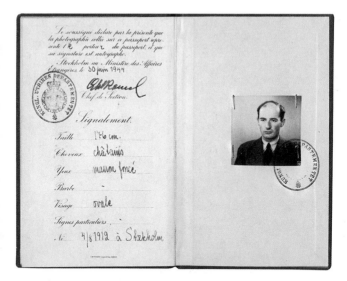

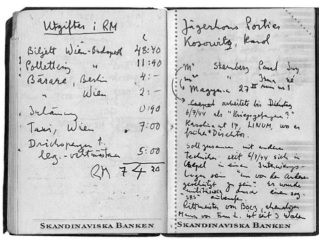

Raoul Wallenberg's diplomatic passport was issued only a week before he left for Budapest. Both the chief rabbi in Stockholm's Jewish community, Marcus Ehrenpreis (1), and the American ambassador to Stockholm, Herschel Johnson (2), were involved in the negotiations that led to Raoul's appointment. Marcus Wallenberg Jr. (3) and Jacob Wallenberg (4) were Raoul Wallenberg's father's cousins. They tested Raoul in various small projects but never fulfilled their promises of a permanent position. Raoul meticulously tracked all his expenses, even during the final phase of his journey to Budapest, as his notebook shows.

Until October 15, 1944, Raoul Wallenberg maintained his head office at Minerva utca 1a (today Minerva utca 5). Long lines of aid-seeking Jews formed on the street outside. The young boy just in front of the gate with his face turned towards the camera is Gustav Kadelburger.

The Swedish legation in Budapest was located in Baron Bayer Krucsay's villa at Gyopar utca 8 (today Minerva utca 3a). Thirty-year-old Per Anger was first secretary at the legation and the minister was Ivan Danielsson, here in a snapshot taken by Per Anger at the soccer match Hungary–Sweden in 1943, with the Hungarian regent Miklós Horthy at his side. Sweden won 7–2.

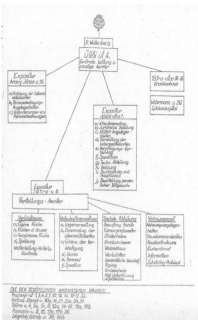

Swiss diplomat Carl Lutz (top left) ran another considerable rescue operation and cooperated closely with Raoul Wallenberg. The ranks of the humanitarian division swelled after the Arrow Cross coup and the establishment of the International Ghetto. At the end of November Raoul was photographed at his desk at Üllöi út, surrounded by colleagues. Front row: Hugó Wohl, Vilmos Forgács, Pál Hegedüs and Otto Fleischmann. Back row: Dezsö Donnenberg, unknown, and Tibor Vandor.

Raoul Wallenberg had three numbers for Adolf Eichmann written down in his telephone book. The German minister Edmund Veesenmayer and Heinrich Himmler's special envoy, Kurt Becher, were two other central Nazi figures in Budapest, 1944. The photo was taken in October 1945. Some of the staff of the Swedish legation that autumn are assembled on the balcony of the legation building, from left: Birgit Brulin, Per Anger, Margareta Bauer, Göte Carlsson and Asta Nilsson from the Swedish Red Cross.

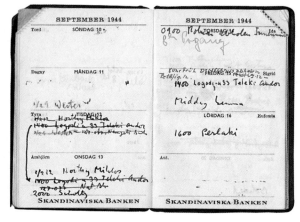

Raoul Wallenberg rented a house at Ostrom utca 9–11, photographed here at around that time. Later he gained access to additional places of residence. The Dutchwoman Berber Smit figures frequently in his diary in fall 1944. A meeting with Miklós Horthy, most likely the regent's son, is also mentioned.

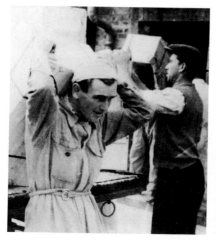

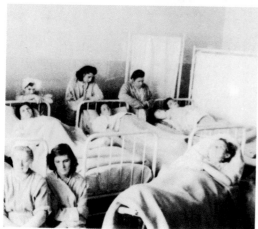
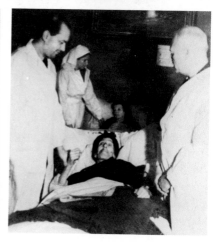

Raoul's humanitarian division had a hand in organising almost everything. Food was delivered from a variety of warehouses around Budapest, and a central kitchen prepared breakfast, lunch and dinner for 1,500 people every day. Some forty physicians tended to the seriously ill at the special Swedish hospital where beds were crowded together in order to maximise the number of patients. These pictures were taken on location and sent back to the Swedish Foreign Ministry by courier in December 1944.

Raoul Wallenberg moved his headquarters to Pest after the Arrow Cross coup, to the abandoned offices of a Dutch insurance company at Üllöi út 2–4, at the corner of Kálvin tér. The balcony one floor up was probably outside Raoul Wallenberg's office. At the beginning of January, the neighbourhood was bombed and the offices were completely destroyed. Alice Breuer (photographed in 2006) and the delivery boy Gábor Forgács (photographed in 2010) hid in the cellar at Üllöi út during the worst of the January events. They both survived thanks to Swedish protective papers.

The leader of the Arrow Cross, Ferenc Szálasi, is sworn in as the new prime minister of Hungary after the coup on 15 October, 1944. A new period of brutal oppression, deportations and executions awaited the Hungarian Jews. Sometimes Raoul Wallenberg himself went out into the field; here he can be seen in a hat and with his hands clasped behind his back, most likely at Józsefváros railway station on November 28, 1944. The typist Károly Szabó provided valuable assistance to Raoul Wallenberg during his last few months in Budapest.

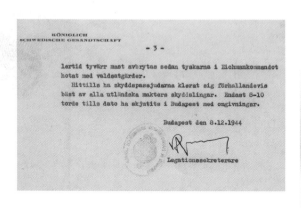

A group of Jews turn back relieved after a threat of deportation has been averted, here most likely from Józsefváros station on November 28, 1944. The photographer was the young Tamás Veres, whom Raoul Wallenberg had instructed to covertly document the rescue operation. The final situation reports signed by Raoul Wallenberg were dispatched by courier on December 8, 1944. As a Christmas present, Raoul was given a tongue-in-cheek book about the "history of the schutzpass", hand-written and illustrated by his colleagues. This picture depicts St. George with a dragon and a protective passport.

The prison card that registered Raoul Wallenberg in the Lubyanka prison on February 6, 1945. The original was shown to the author at a visit to the F.S.B. archive in Moscow. Raoul's driver, Vilmos Langfelder, met the same fate as his employer. The remaining Swedes at the legation in Budapest were greeted with bouquets of flowers at Skeppsbron quay in Stockholm in April 1945.

Sweden's envoy to Moscow 1944–1946, Minister Staffan Söderblom, with his letter of credence in July 1944. To his right is the Russian Deputy Foreign Minister Vladimir Dekanozov. Söderblom's residence and offices were located in the so-called Mindovsky mansion at Ulitsa Vorovskogo, today Povarskaya, in central Moscow. At a historic opportunity, Söderblom was given an audience with Joseph Stalin and raised the Raoul Wallenberg case. Ambassador Rolf Sohlman with his wife Zina, his son Mischa (Michael) and the dog Tarras in their home in Moscow in 1953.

Raoul Wallenberg's cell mate for two years, the German diplomat Willy Rödel, was a legation official in Romania during the war. He is said to have died of "heart paralysis" in October 1947.

The Smoltsov report (top left) was long claimed to be the only document that had been found in Russian archives. The temperamental author Rudolph Philipp (in the dark jacket) became, for better or worse, Maj and Fredrik von Dardel's private investigator. The trio are here seen (bottom) conferring in the von Dardels' garden in 1956.

Professor Nanna Svartz greets the Soviet leader Nikita Krushchev during his visit to Sweden in 1964, where the conversation was dominated by new information in the Raoul Wallenberg case that she had obtained three years earlier. During this visit, the newspaper Expressen *ran the headline "Where is Raoul Wallenberg?" Östen Undén was Sweden's foreign minister in 1924–1926 and again in 1945–1962. Tage Erlander was Sweden's prime minister 1946–1969.*

Guy von Dardel is pictured outside the Lubyanka on his visit to Moscow in October 1989, when he and his sister Nina Lagergren were invited by the K.G.B. They were presented with a box of Raoul's belongings, among these his diplomatic passport. In 2012, the anniversary of Raoul Wallenberg's birth was commemorated with a stamp, among other items.

The author with Raoul Wallenberg's half-sister Nina Lagergren, taken in 2009. They are sitting on the foundations of the house in which Raoul was born in Kappsta, Lidingö. It burned down in the 1930s.

Nina Lagergren, half-sister of Raoul Wallenberg, shows President Barack Obama her brother's diplomatic passport, diary and address book at the Great Synagogue of Stockholm, September 4, 2013. Participants include: Swedish Prime Minister Fredrik Reinfeld; Gustav Kadelburger, errand boy for Wallenberg in Budapest; Kate Wacz, sister of Gustav Kadelburger, lived in sheltered houses in Budapest; Alice Breuer, saved by Raoul Wallenberg in 1944 and 1945, and Gabriella Kassius, who worked with Wallenberg in Budapest issuing protective passports.
Photograph: Thomas Karlsson.

President Barack Obama greets Nina Lagergren after he delivers remarks at the Holocaust Memorial at the Great Synagogue of Stockholm, Sweden, September 4, 2013.
Official White House Photograph by Pete Souza.

the need to interrogate the Swede and the persistent Soviet attempts to get Sweden to surrender its Baltic refugees. These 30,000 refugees were regularly mentioned in diplomatic exchanges. Soviet diplomacy often centred on this sort of deal. They did not give anything without expecting to receive something else in return.

Major Kuzmishin was not particularly fluent in German and often had an interpreter by his side. Even so, his questioning of the 32-year-old Raoul Wallenberg went relatively quickly by SMERSH standards: the interrogation only lasted an hour and twenty-five minutes. Raoul appears to have taken the opportunity to protest against his arrest. To his fellow inmates, Raoul later said that he declared that the Russians "did not have any reason to keep him imprisoned. He had worked for the Russians in Budapest." But Kuzmishin was not receptive to this line of argument.

Shortly thereafter, Raoul's cell mate Jan Loyda was also interrogated. The interrogator asked him whom he shared a cell with. "Two diplomats, Wallenberg and Rödel," Loyda answered. To Loyda's astonishment, the interrogator countered, "Wallenberg is no diplomat. He is a Swede who helped rich Jews in Hungary."

At this point, Jan Loyda had got to know his Swedish cell mate and appreciated him a great deal. Afterwards he would describe him as a "very friendly, comradely and helpful" person. For example, Raoul Wallenberg routinely asked the guards to give his cigarette rations to Vilmos Langfelder. When Loyda returned to his cell, he told Raoul what the interrogator had said, "so that he would better understand his position with regard to the Soviet authorities".

Outside the Lubyanka's walls, there was a celebratory feeling in the air that weekend. Moscow residents streamed out into the streets in the unusually beautiful spring weather and began their victory celebrations, even though the official German surrender had yet to be declared, and there was still a day or so left before Soviet troops finally seized Berlin. "There was a mood of spring, victory and joy everywhere. It was as if the entire Russian people was revelling after years of tribulation, darkness and endless labour," Ingeman Hägglöf, the deputy at the Swedish legation, wrote in his memoirs.

A week later, peace was confirmed. On the afternoon of May 7, Stockholm exploded in a joyous frenzy. Kungsgatan was filled with so many people that it had to be closed to traffic. Waste paper baskets were emptied out of the windows so "the air between the buildings glittered with a snowfall of paper". People were waving flags from every window. Paper boys strapped headlines to their chests and ran around. Champagne corks popped on the balconies and on Strandvägen, below the offices of the Mid-European Training Company, "there were flags on every pram". One family refrained from joining in the festivities that day. In Maj and Fredrik von Dardel's home, the news of the armistice had not brought the same sense of joy.

Maj von Dardel had begun to receive letters of praise for her son's work. Iver Olsen had already written to her in April and thanked her for Raoul's contribution that, "from the American side", was recognised as one of the greatest of its kind during the entire war. The World Jewish Congress executive committee wrote to the Swedish government with a special word of thanks to the Swedish legation in Budapest and especially Raoul Wallenberg, Valdemar Langlet and Asta Nilsson for their "holy" rescue operations: "The Jewish people will never forget the men and women who did their best to help us survive the inferno of the last few years, despite the difficulties and even personal risk which beset their paths all too often."

The practical Maj von Dardel stubbornly refused to believe those who claimed that her son was already dead. She now contacted the Foreign Ministry on a more prosaic matter. She felt that it would be appropriate for the government to pay the bills for her son's life insurance – from the remaining salary that he was owed.

Staffan Söderblom celebrated the peace with a large luncheon at the Swedish legation's villa for his diplomatic colleagues. In general, however, he felt that his situation was both stressful and difficult.

Shortly before the weekend, he concluded yet another trying meeting with Dekanozov. Söderblom had verbally asked Dekanozov for information on several matters, among them Raoul Wallenberg. But Dekanozov was irritated and seemed on the verge of an outburst several times. His anger stemmed from the ongoing dispute over the 30,000 Baltic refugees in Sweden.

The Soviet Foreign Ministry indicated that other bilateral matters, requests for transit visas for example, would be made considerably easier if Sweden was cooperative and, at the very least, allowed the Russians to contact people in the refugee camps. It was a clear offer of an exchange of concessions. But, when the question came up again, Staffan Söderblom answered that he felt that it was unfortunate "in the international context to connect one issue with another".

Dekanozov had another view of the matter. He now toughened his tone towards Söderblom and angrily pointed out that the Russians could not accept the Swedish refusal to allow the Soviet diplomats to get in touch with the Baltic refugees. He asked Söderblom to "look past the specifics of the refugee issue" and instead elevate the question to a theoretical plane. Söderblom reported the exchange back to Stockholm in the following way:

> "What would you say if there were Swedes here with whom you were denied personal contact?" Mr Dekanozov asked. I explained that, to the extent that there were Swedes who wished to live in the Soviet Union, I would surely not wish to compel them to return home. Mr Dekanozov replied that there could definitely be cases where I would wish to have personal contact.

Certainly there was one increasingly famous case where Staffan Söderblom might have wished to be able to make personal contact. The case in question was even on the agenda. But, unfortunately, the true significance of Dekanozov's question appears to have eluded Söderblom.

On Tuesday, May 29, the three inmates in cell 123 – Willy Rödel, Jan Loyda and Raoul Wallenberg – were asked to report for departure. It is likely they each carried a bundle containing their clothes and other belongings. Outside in the Lubyanka's inner courtyard, a prison van was waiting, its back doors open. None of their cases were completed yet and no sentences had been given. But now they were to be moved from the Lubyanka to the large remand prison in Moscow, Lefortovo.

Two weeks later, the Swedish staff of the Budapest legation gathered for a reunion at a restaurant in Stockholm. In this circle there were at this time ambivalent feelings regarding Raoul Wallenberg's operation in Budapest. About a week or so before the dinner, Margareta Bauer had given expression to her thoughts in a letter to a diplomatic colleague. "Documents were falsified right and left and sold for several thousand pengő . . . To be honest I don't think that either of the gentlemen at the Foreign Ministry have yet heard the entire situation and the pre-history." One year later the recipient of her letter would become responsible for the Wallenberg matter at the Foreign Ministry.

The evening was a jovial affair. Lars Berg entertained his colleagues with a long poem about their fates and adventures that he dedicated to Ivan Danielsson. "Once in Budapest so gay, life was a party every day," Berg rhymed. He described all of his colleagues in verse, even Raoul Wallenberg: "But I must say it was Wallenberg/who had the worst of the worry/he was rarely seen to rest/no, only hurry."

One can hear the peals of laughter as this was read. Despite everything that happened, the end of the adventure was basically a happy one, the poet Lars Berg appears to have implied:

> Yes, Budapest it was destroyed
> And one of us went missing
> But by and large our gang, it seems,
> Escaped the cataclysm.

Lefortovo Prison, April 2011

There are several roads to the district of Lefortovo in east Moscow. From Lub-yanka Square, one can drive out to the circular road Garden Ring and then con-tinue east, where the narrow tributary Yauza joins the Moskva River. It is a stretch of about nine kilometres. When Raoul Wallenberg arrived here at the end of May 1945, the journey took roughly fifteen minutes.

We drive along the Yauza early one morning in April 2011, my interpreter Maria and I, rolling towards the remand prison under a whitish-grey impenetra-ble spring sky. The water snakes beneath small arched bridges, which Raoul may have been able to glimpse between the cracks of the prison van if he was lucky. Nowadays there are mainly industrial areas and military facilities in the area of Lefortovo, as well as grim collections of the Soviet era's depressing concrete apartment blocks.

Lefortovo has roots stretching back to the early eighteenth century, which is hard to believe when one enters the area. The park of the same name, which is situated next to the Yauza, was created to honour Peter the Great – only a year or so before the battle of Poltava, 1709, I can't help but note. Poltava – a defining moment in the struggle for power between Sweden and Russia. And one that Sweden lost.

If one is heading to Lefortovo prison, one does not see much of the park, even through freshly cleaned car windows. To be honest, one does not see much of the prison either. It takes a while to find the way, but then suddenly it looms up behind a playground, the perfectly-strung barbed wire above the wall. Today it holds 180 prisoners.

When Raoul Wallenberg came here, he was greeted by a gate with heavy iron fittings and the words "LE FORT" in raised, old-fashioned letters.

Maria parks in front of the three-metre-high wall. The bricks are crumbling and at chest level someone has scribbled the words "LEFORTOVO. WHITE POWER", in Russian. I stand on tiptoe. Through the barbed wire I can see the metal roof and a piece of the dirty yellow stone façade of Lefortovo prison's four-storey main building. I have seen in sketches that the prison is shaped like the letter K. Two three-storey wings radiate out from the middle of the building. There, in the centre of the "star", a guard was posted in Raoul's time. He could see all two hundred cells, it is claimed, since the Lefortovo prison was built as an open gallery with raised walkways outside the rows of cells.

According to contemporary inmates, the Lubyanka was a like a hotel in comparison to the hell of Lefortovo. Here one sat while awaiting sentencing. The treatment was such that most began to long for both the trial and the banishment to the Gulag they expected would follow.

We can see the uppermost storey where Raoul was held but, unfortunately, not all the way to his cell, number 203. I zoom in on a cell window with my camera. The bars have rusted and what, from far away, looked like glass panes, now appears as a mute and opaque surface in my lens. Back then, in 1945, there were three prisoners in each cell, sharing a space of three by three and a half metres. One sixty-centimetre gap between the cots was the only space to move. "Six steps forward – six steps back – in a goose step hour after hour, that was our only relaxation," wrote the inhabitant of a cell one floor below Raoul's, the Italian diplomat Claudio de Mohr, who was later released.

In the winter, the prisoners froze. The heating pipes were a joke and the prisoners had to be grateful for every degree above freezing the temperature crept to in the cells. Light was as rare as fresh air, according to de Mohr.

There was always half-darkness in our cell. On the outside, the window was covered with a metal plate, which was to prevent us gazing out into the world beyond our cell . . . Nine out of twelve months of the year we thus spent both day and night in the uncertain and reddish light of a weak little electric lamp . . . It was only during the short Russian summer that the strong light from the sun and the blue sky penetrated into our cell, but weakened, anaemic, only a hint of the light world outside.

We notice that the spring in Moscow can be bitingly cold, not to say outright inhospitable. Our fingers quickly grow stiff. We need to move and continue along the wall, walking through the playground, with its colourful climbing structures, and around the corner onto ulitsa Val Lefortovsky (Lefortov Rampart Street). Perhaps I can catch a glimpse of Raoul's cell window from the other side?

A police car drives by through an entrance in the wall. Some dry year-old leaves are still hanging on the birch trees along the pavement. The cold eats in through our shoes, and around the next corner some street cleaners are shovelling old snow out of the gutters. We stop by one of them. His name is Fyodor and he is from Uzbekistan. He frowns when we ask if he has heard of Raoul Wallenberg. The name is familiar he says, but he can't place it.

"Wallenberg, was he the one who made clocks?"

Fyodor lives nearby but almost never sees any of Lefortovo's prisoners. Everything to do with the prison is a bit secret, he explains and continues shovelling.

We meet several young mothers with pushchairs on their way to or from Lefortovo park. None of them has ever heard the name Raoul Wallenberg before. But outside the Sputnik, the local cinema, we spot a 94-year-old war veteran, Dmitry, who is walking slowly with a brown stick and a grey cap. He is a retired major in the Russian Army and took part in the battle for Berlin in the spring of 1945. Since then he has lived in this area.

"Of course I know the name Raoul Wallenberg!" he exclaims and becomes animated.

"It was very wrong that they arrested him for no reason. Why did they do that to a person who helped Jews like me? Did they ever let him go?"

"No," I reply. "It is claimed that he died of a heart attack in prison in 1947—"

"Nonsense!" Dmitry says with irritation and waves his hand. "I don't believe that for a second. You should know that there were many people who were executed here after the war, despite their heroism. It makes me angry. And see how things have gone here in Russia. Potatoes cost forty rubles now. I never thought that things would get so bad."

He says goodbye and heads towards a park bench a little further away. We make a final attempt to catch a glimpse of the prison from the side where Raoul's cell was. But we never manage to get close enough.

Raoul Wallenberg arrived here on 29 May, 1945. It was not until March 1947 that he left. "This existence in an eternal dusk, or in the weak illumination of a lamp that sends out a kind of vague red beam of dusty light, while outside the sun may be shining and nature blooming in all her majesty – this existence is what is most depressing and brings despair to a person who has not yet managed to reach the degree of resignation where one is only and simply an animal, but still has within oneself a soul, an ability to feel and suffer. This existence was our fate," wrote his fellow inmate Claudio de Mohr.

CHAPTER 17

To Behold the Face of God

Maj von Dardel refused to believe that Raoul was dead. The messages from Dekanozov and Madame Kollontai had been extremely clear and she had definitely not been presented with any certain evidence that Raoul had died or been killed.

Madame Kollontai had suggested the Swedes should lie low and the Foreign Ministry had advised the family not to go to the press. But to keep quiet and avoid making one's own contacts was not the same as sitting idle. Maj von Dardel decided to request a meeting with Staffan Söderblom, who was coming to Stockholm for a short visit at Midsummer.

She took out the last letter that she had received from Raoul in Budapest. In it, Raoul had included two newly taken photographs that Maj now had enlarged and brought to her meeting with Staffan Söderblom. She asked him to give the pictures to the Soviet Foreign Ministry in order to hasten the investigation.

Staffan Söderblom felt ambivalent about Maj von Dardel's request, not only because his intuition told him that Raoul Wallenberg had died. There were so many rumours about Raoul Wallenberg and the Swedish legation in Budapest that complicated the situation. The fact was that, of late, the Budapest Swedes in general had been an uncomfortable topic of conversation in Moscow.

The legation staff from Budapest had been asked to keep silent about the plundering of the Swedish legation by Soviet troops in February 1945. But, despite all the secrecy surrounding this episode, news about the Russian thefts and rapes in Swedish diplomatic territory had leaked out in the middle of May. The headlines in the press were as could be expected.

Pressured by the attention, the Foreign Ministry officials in Sweden had ordered Söderblom to toughen the diplomatic tone and, in a so-called démarche, demand an investigation of the incident by the Russians. Söderblom did not appreciate these instructions. Naturally the Russians would have been offended by the Swedish press accusations levelled against them. Söderblom had read a Soviet army paper that taunted the "anti-Soviet" Swedish press campaign about the plunder.

Söderblom did as he was asked. But he followed up with a toned-down letter home to Stockholm where he explained that all of the accounts of the Red Army's violent actions had to be taken with a pinch of salt. They were most often exaggerations.

The Soviet circles drew a different conclusion. Dekanozov had demanded an investigation as soon as he heard the accusations of theft and rape – so that he would be able to construct a counter-attack. It had turned out that the Swedish papers were correct. The events had been quite as brutal as described. But Dekanozov chose to refrain from sharing this.

The unpleasantness associated with the accusations in Swedish newspapers was not the only reason that Söderblom hesitated in taking a hard line on the Raoul Wallenberg case. Since the Budapest Swedes had returned home in April 1945, the operations of the rescue mission itself had started to come under scrutiny. It was not exactly news that many of Raoul's colleagues at the Swedish legation had been sceptical of his wide-ranging and at times rather risky venture. Now they unburdened themselves here and there. Rumours started to circulate that the Arrow Cross attack on Christmas Eve was revenge for a suspected black-market trade in Swedish protective passports at Raoul Wallenberg's humanitarian department. It was remembered that Wallenberg was a foreign element in the diplomatic corps anyway, a grocery trader at the periphery of the business world who had been stationed in Budapest without any experience. What had he really been doing there?

Such rumours had already reached Staffan Söderblom in Moscow. He now wrote to the deputy cabinet secretary that he felt the protective passport operation should be properly investigated and that he wanted a "sign" from the government about the appropriateness of the venture that had been undertaken in Budapest.

Six months later, Sweden's new ambassador to Hungary, Rolf Arfwedson, would investigate these rumours. He established that the accusations of uncontrolled abuse of Swedish protective documents had exclusively been directed at Valdemar Langlet of the Swedish Red Cross. "By contrast, Wallenberg's department appears to have been very competently managed and the checks there were good. I would like to establish this . . . so that no shadow may fall on a person who cannot speak in his own defence," Arfwedson wrote in a letter in January 1946. But what good did that do now, in the summer of 1945?

At the beginning of July, Staffan Söderblom returned from his visit to Sweden back to the legation in Moscow. He retained strongly ambivalent feelings about the Raoul Wallenberg case, but he had his orders. He had just begun to put Maj von Dardel's photographs in order when he was given a telegram from the ministry in Stockholm. It was with regard to a new piece of information that had come in via Swedish diplomats in Switzerland. An "absolutely trustworthy witness" had met a person who had encountered Wallenberg in the spring. Wallenberg was claimed to be "healthy and free" and "hiding under a secure disguise in Pest". If this were true, Söderblom could end up in a very bad light if he troubled his contacts within the Soviet Foreign Ministry. "It goes without saying that I will for now refrain from passing along the photographs or otherwise engage myself further in the matter," he stated.

And so the final word had been spoken, at least for the moment.

The three inmates of cell 123 in the Lubyanka prison had been placed in separate prison vehicles that had caravanned their way in a bumpy ride through Moscow. When they pulled up in front of the Lefortovo prison, Jan Loyda saw through a gap in his van that Raoul Wallenberg and Willy Rödel were being unloaded. He himself continued on to another prison.

Lefortovo was regarded as the central remand prison for the Soviet intelligence service. Many "political enemies" and "suspected spies" were held here, awaiting what the Soviet system could provide in terms of reasonable trials and sentencing. Thereafter, those who were not simply imprisoned or executed could expect a trip to the camps of the Gulag. The intake process in Lefortovo was similar to the one at the Lubyanka. Otherwise the two gaols had little in common. If the "Inner Prison" in the Lubyanka was silent and light, Lefortovo was echoing noise and darkness. In the Lubyanka there was central heating, in Lefortovo the cold in the cells could be oppressive even during the summer, especially on the lower levels.

Newly arrived prisoners were given a wooden spoon, a wooden bowl and a rolled-up, worn mattress. Raoul Wallenberg and Willy Rödel were lucky in the midst of their misfortune and were brought by the guards to cell 203 on the fourth floor, away from the worst of the cold. The way there was, according to other inmates, similar to a walk in the bowels of a large ship. The guards clattered their keys against their belts and the prisoners walked with their hands behind their backs along narrow metal bridges outside the cells. Beyond, a deep chasm opened up onto a seemingly endless space. The dizzying impulse to throw oneself off was thwarted by steel mesh.

Cell 203 was located in the main area, which was in the straight part of the building's K formation. When Wallenberg and Rödel arrived at the metal door to the cell, the guard would have pulled back two heavy sliding locks, a deafening noise that echoed on into all the cells nearby. Inside, there were three narrow cots along the walls. Not much else could fit into the roughly seven square metre space. On the far side, there was a tiny window with bars that, unfortunately, was almost completely covered with a metal plate. Only a thin strip of light from outside found its way in. In the Lubyanka it had been difficult to sleep in the strong light. Here it would be hard even to see.

The days came and went. The morning tea that was pushed through the food slot at 7 a.m. was similar to that at the Lubyanka – warm water "faintly coloured by some revolting surrogate made from the roasted shells of nuts". But Lefortovo's sticky prison bread had many longing for the "Inner Prison". The rest of the rations consisted of sour soup that smelled of fish and cabbage, or a kind of millet porridge that often arrived covered in mould. "For eighteen months straight, from spring 1945 to November 1946, we were given this mouldy inedible porridge every day," Claudio de Mohr told a Swedish newspaper in 1953.

A twenty-minute walk was part of the routine, even at Lefortovo. The prisoners were led out to the inner courtyard, where there were eight small exercise pens, hardly larger than the prison cells, lined with wooden planks and surrounded by a three-metre-high wall.

Lefortovo's prison regime in general was stricter than in the Lubyanka.

The prisoners were forbidden to speak to the guards. The interrogations were the only opportunity for a prisoner like Raoul to express himself to the authority that carried his fate in its hands. But it would take over a year before he was called to his first interrogation at Lefortovo prison.

For Raoul Wallenberg, this desolate atmosphere must soon have become intolerable.

In one way the Lefortovo prison was more humane than the Lubyanka. For some strange reason, the prison authorities had overlooked the fact that the walls between the cells were so thin that one could communicate through them. The prisoners could "speak" with their nearest neighbours – above, below or to either side – simply by knocking on the walls. The cell ceilings were arched and the walls were brick, which made communication easier. Up on the fourth floor, where Raoul Wallenberg and Willy Rödel were, the Lefortovo prisoners could sometimes also take advantage of the poor water pressure in the pipes. In the cells there was a tap and a primitive, stinking toilet. In the summers it was sometimes possible to open the tap and speak to the next cell through the water pipes.

But one had to be careful. All communication between the cells was forbidden and the guards kept a suffocatingly close watch on the prisoners through the peephole in the door. A winning strategy had been established to combat this. The prisoners sat on their cot with their back to the wall and arranged the sleeve of their shirt that was furthest from the door so that the guard could not see that the arm had been slipped out. In this fashion they could then knock on the wall behind their back, for example with the shaft of a toothbrush, in simple code. In Lefortovo the most frequent code employed was the "idiot system". One knock meant "A", two knocks were "B", and so on through the entire alphabet. Raoul Wallenberg would eventually become a very active knocker.

In this way, some unusually chilly summer months went by. It was only in August that Moscow warmed up. In his book *Beria's Gardens*, the Finnish prisoner Uno Parvilahti writes about everyday life in Lefortovo that summer. Day and night the inmates were bothered by the engine roar from the aeroplane construction site next door. Parvilahti says that there were stories about the noise being a deliberate tactic to conceal the anguished screams from the interrogation block. But sometimes the cries broke through.

One night in particular has fixed itself in my memory. It was a summer night that happened to be very quiet, for some reason the engines were not going. In one of the interrogation blocks a window must have been open, because one could clearly hear a coarse, drunken man's voice that yelled, "*Gavarij, gavarij!*" (Speak, speak!); the sounds of blows; and a woman's cries that went on hour after hour and finally gave way to a kind of mindless howl. That evening not a single one of us was able to sleep. The sun was already high overhead when the unbearable noise finally ceased.

After the war, normality was restored to Swedish party politics. The circumstances were no longer extraordinary and, one overcast Tuesday morning at the end of July 1945, the coalition government of the war years came to an end. A purely Social Democratic government stepped in, led by the same prime minister – Per Albin Hansson. His new foreign minister was the 61-year-old international law expert Östen Undén.

Undén was one of those who had been most critical of the outgoing minister Christian Günther and his concilatory stance towards Germany during the war. But soon Undén would have similar criticisms levelled against himself – for his obsequious position vis-à-vis the Soviet Union. Östen Undén knew Staffan Söderblom relatively well and had sent him a personal letter congratulating him on his appointment the year before. The two appear to have been fairly united in their conviction that the Soviet leaders should be appeased as much as possible. The Kremlin would need to be convinced that Sweden did not one-sidedly favour the Western allies.

Though a new recruit, Undén was something of a heavyweight. He had been foreign minister as well as minister of justice for a couple of years in the '20s. As both a professor of civil law and a university chancellor he had been generally respected and often admired for his considerable expertise. Bound by principles and somewhat humourless, he could easily become inflexible, but the von Dardel family had no particular grounds to fear his appointment. Undén had supported Nina's husband Gunnar Lagergren very generously in his career as an internationally renowned laywer.

Undén's ethical stance, however, had the potential to prove problematic for the family. He found it unthinkable to compromise one's higher values and moral principles in matters of foreign policy. He disliked the idea of agreeing to temporary concessions in order to gain advantages for Sweden. This meant, for example, that Undén was against all proposals to exchange prisoners since he believed it immoral to "exchange a life for a life".

Maj von Dardel continued to nurture hope. She was given the news about the claim of a disguised Raoul in Budapest when she visited the Foreign Ministry one day. This sounded far-fetched but could be interpreted as positive.

With her husband Fredrik, Maj tried to get the Foreign Ministry to dig further into this but was given the answer that Staffan Söderblom in Moscow could, for the moment, do no more.

The family had obediently followed the advice they had been given and refrained from making a public fuss over the situation. Maj von Dardel had forwarded the Foreign Ministry's injunctions to Marcus and Jacob Wallenberg. But, even had they wished to, Raoul's relatives in the Enskilda Bank's leadership were no longer in a position to pursue this issue. The Wallenberg purchase of the American subsidiary of the German electronics giant Bosch at the beginning of the war had been a ticking time bomb for several years. The Americans had suspected early on that the whole deal was a front to conceal German ownership. Now the Bosch archives had been seized by American troops and the scandal was upon them. On August 31, the first article on the matter came out in the American press. It was revealed that, as part of the deal, the Enskilda Bank had concealed a repurchase agreement that secured American Bosch in German hands.

Jacob and Marcus Wallenberg would spend the greater part of the autumn 1945 in the United States in order to sort out their affairs. The scandal had several dimensions. In the eyes of the Americans, the respected Swedish banking family had suddenly acquired a pro-Nazi patina that could not be easily washed away. The Bosch affair would plague the Wallenberg family for many years.

The events in the United States meant that these influential relatives could not be counted on for much during the Raoul Wallenberg's first crucial years of imprisonment. Jacob and Marcus Wallenberg were simply too preoccupied with their own catastrophe to have the energy to involve themselves in the fate of their cousin's son.

Towards the end of the summer, Kálmán Lauer returned from a trip to

Switzerland with some promising news. He had met the head of the Hungarian central bank, who claimed that Raoul Wallenberg was very much alive and that he had been taken "by the Russians, with all his notes and documents". According to the Hungarian bank director, the Russians were planning to use Raoul Wallenberg's materials in the trials against the Arrow Cross. His recommendation was that Sweden refrain from public enquiries and instead tried to intervene "through private channels".

An unpleasant catch-22 now presented itself. In Stockholm, there were Maj and Fredrik von Dardel, who wanted nothing more than to devote all their energies to trying to get Raoul home. But they had been strongly advised not to pursue any personal initiatives, for Raoul's sake. The matter was said to be being handled by the Foreign Ministry, but now they heard from Staffan Söderblom that he could not for the moment make any more official enquiries into the case.

What were they to do? The family and Kálmán Lauer became involved in the work of sending the first aid convoys to Hungary organised by the International Red Cross. But at the same time they refused to believe that the official channels were closed. Staffan Söderblom had a boss, hadn't he? In September, Maj and Fredrik von Dardel demanded to see the new foreign minister, Östen Undén. They asked Undén to take serious steps to free Raoul Wallenberg. But, according to the writer Rudolph Philipp, who would eventually become the von Dardel family's private investigator, Undén simply replied that he did not know if Sweden had any chance of forcing an answer from the Russians.

A conflict with the Soviet Union was not the note on which Östen Undén had been dreaming of beginning his time as foreign minister. He had inherited a number of sore spots relating to Swedish–Soviet relations from his predecessor, among them the issue of the 30,000 civilian Baltic refugees that the Soviet Union was demanding be returned. During the summer, this list had acquired yet another, even more pressing, demand: the Soviet Union had asked that Sweden send them almost three thousand German soldiers who had fled there to escape the Russians.

Among these soldiers were 167 individuals of Baltic origin that the Germans had forced into service. In the months before Undén was appointed, the Swedish government agreed to hand over all the soldiers – who were seen as part of Germany's capitulation agreement – but reaffirmed that the 30,000 Baltic refugees would remain under their protection..

As far as Undén was concerned, there were already far too many complications. His ambition was to steer a course between the Soviet Union and the Western Allies that demonstrated to Stalin that Sweden should not be counted among the partisans of the United States and Great Britain.

This was one of the reasons behind Undén's decision to make a big speech in October 1945 in which he effectively fluttered his eyelashes at the superpower to the east. Undén assured his audience that Sweden, first and foremost, strove to improve relations with the Soviet Union. He said that he hoped for increased trade and increased cultural exchange and added, temptingly, that Sweden was in a position to offer significant credits to the Soviet Union. To ensure that the message reached its target, a copy of the speech in its entirety was delivered to the Foreign Ministry in Moscow.

But this attempt at charm did not impress Madame Kollontai's successor in Stockholm, Ilya Chernyshev. Since the end of the war, he had peppered Moscow with warnings that these kinds of pronouncements from Sweden were only shallow gestures. As he saw it, Sweden had an anti-Soviet attitude and its orientation over time had only become more British-American. The new government had not made any difference in this regard, Chernyshev maintained. After Undén's speech, he sent a list back to Moscow of requirements he felt the Swedes should fulfil before relations could be improved. Chernyshev demanded that Sweden should purge its army, police and state apparatus of fascist elements, immediately put an end to all anti-Soviet propaganda in the media and, as soon as possible, return the 30,000 Baltic refugees.

Sweden was acting from a position of considerable disadvantage. It was not the best context for a concerned mother to make a plea for greater efforts to bring home her son.

In October, the Politburo approved some holiday for Joseph Stalin. After a lengthy war, and after the almost euphoric state of the past six months, the dictator was worn out. Towards the end of June 1945, only a few days after the Red Army's triumphant victory parade on the Red Square, the modestly reluctant Joseph Stalin had been promoted to "Generalissimus". With this, the Stalin cult reached its absolute zenith.

This boundless worship had left traces on the Generalissimus. His successor, Nikita Khrushchev, remembered how, in 1945, Stalin appeared to believe that "he was in the same position as Alexander I after his victory over Napoleon and that he could dictate the rules of the game for the whole of Europe". His hubris made him even more tyrannical, manipulative and unpredictable. At the same time, his health started to falter. It has been claimed that Stalin had his first heart attack shortly before the military parade in June. Now, during the holiday in October, he had his second.

Relations with their U.S. allies had quickly grown frosty. Stalin missed Franklin D. Roosevelt, who had died so swiftly. His successor, Harry S. Truman, had, from the start, shown a tougher attitude towards the Soviet Union's claims on Eastern Europe. There were rumours in Washington about a radically altered view of the Soviet Union. When the Allied leaders met in Potsdam to discuss the terms of surrender for Germany, Stalin was far from impressed with the new incumbent of the White House. "Truman is neither educated nor clever," was Stalin's dismayed comment.

The atom bombs in Hiroshima and Nagasaki in August 1945 had not improved relations between the two countries. "We felt humiliated that the Americans, although they were our allies in the war against Germany, kept their advances in the atomic bomb area secret from us," Pavel Sudoplatov, the former head of SMERSH, wrote in his memoirs. During the autumn, Stalin repeatedly tested the patience of the Allies with his attempts to enlarge the Soviet security zone. The irritation of the West was palpable.

Stalin used his autumn holiday at his dacha by the Black Sea to recover from the heart attack. He did not return to Moscow until December. During his recuperation, he observed with growing displeasure how Molotov appeared to bask in the international spotlight, how he struck an almost obsequious attitude towards the Western Allies. Stalin himself now mostly wanted to break the bonds of friendship.

He decided to shake up Molotov. He explained that he no longer had any confidence in him. He let the foreign minister squirm for several days before he took him back into his good graces. Stalin enjoyed playing those closest to him off against each other and, after Molotov, he would continue with Lavrenty Beria, head of the N.K.V.D. After the new year, Beria had to leave his office in Lubyanka in order to oversee the new Soviet atomic bomb programme. He lost parts of his domain and had to watch his rival, Viktor Abakumov, be promoted to new security minister and head of counterespionage. "The coming atrocities were Abakumov's doing, not Beria's, even though most histories blame the latter," Simon Sebag Montefiore points out in his biography of Stalin.

Staffan Söderblom had allowed almost the entire autumn to go by without altering his passive attitude towards the Raoul Wallenberg case. In his estimation, Raoul was probably dead, or possibly in hiding in Budapest. If contact was to be made, it should be with the new Hungarian government. And that was not his department.

After his strong statement during the summer, Söderblom had only grown more convinced of his opinion. In September, Valdemar Langlet had earned a great deal of attention in Sweden with some articles about the mission in Budapest. When even Langlet asserted that Raoul Wallenberg had probably fallen victim to the Nazis or the Arrow Cross, this explanation seemed even more convincing. It was now a common view in the corridors of the Foreign Ministry, even if it was not the only one in circulation.

During the autumn, news had emerged regarding other Swedes who were imprisoned in the Soviet Union. Among them was the journalist Edward af Sandeberg, who had been in Berlin when the Russians seized the city, and was now claimed to be sitting in a camp in Krasnogorsk. For af Sandeberg, Staffan Söderblom does not seem to have felt any of the reticence he had displayed over Wallenberg's disappearance. During the autumn of 1945, he appears to have churned out a torrent of diplomatic démarches, notes and reminders that af Sandeberg should be sent back to Sweden. In fact, his persistence was not dissimilar to the way that the Soviet legation in Stockholm had handled the case of the young Miss Makarova.

But, towards the end of October 1945, something happened in the Wallenberg case that apparently jolted the few doubters at the Foreign Ministry. Ironically, it is possible that the catalyst was the fact that the Russians had sent another pointed request about the sixteen-year-old Lydia Makarova. Or perhaps it was a fresh tip that indicated Raoul had been in the company of his driver Langfelder when he disappeared. Either way, suddenly feverish activity broke out at the Foreign Ministry. What was known of the sequence of events surrounding Raoul's disappearance was plotted, day by day, and a swift order was sent to the legation in Moscow: dig up Dekanozov's soothing message from January 16, demand an exhaustive account of the entire investigation into Raoul Wallenberg's case.

This belated escalation happened to coincide with Söderblom being called back to Stockholm for a few weeks of debriefing. The task of raising the level of urgency fell instead to his deputy, the chargé d'affaires Ulf Barck-Holst. Barck-Holst did as he was told, reminded Dekanozov about his note and demanded – on behalf of the Swedish government – information regarding results from investigations about Raoul Wallenberg. Now a strange exchange was set in motion. A few days later, the Russians replied with yet another demand about the young Makarova. And, later in November, the Stockholm envoy Chernyshev took the case of the young woman to ministerial level when he met with Östen Undén.

It was clear that the new Swedish impetus over the Wallenberg case had been taken seriously in Moscow. The Russians had not received any official enquiries about Raoul Wallenberg since May and, even then, Söderblom had appended to his demands his belief that the missing man had died in a car crash. The new Swedish enquiry unleashed a flurry of activity in the Soviet Foreign Ministry. Dekanozov wrote a letter to the chief of espionage Abakumov. He asked him to supply facts and information regarding this Raoul Wallenberg that the Swedes were asking about. How Abakumov replied is, unfortunately, unknown.

Perhaps the Russians saw this intensified concern as an invitation to negotiate with the Swedish government. The Soviet Union was in the concluding phase of a similar diplomatic discussion with Switzerland with regard to Raoul Wallenberg's colleagues at the Swiss legation in Budapest, Harald Feller and Max Meier, who had also been held at the Lefortovo prison since the spring of 1945.

The Swiss held better cards than the Swedes, since they had received information from trusted sources that their diplomats had been taken to Moscow and put in prison. This meant that the Swiss were not quite as credulous when the Russians denied any knowledge of them. Just as for the Swedes, the Swiss were involved in more extensive exchange negotiations with the Soviet Union at the same time. But it was something that they, in contrast to the Swedes, chose to take advantage of.

The Swiss had declared from the outset that they did not intend to review any Soviet demands positively if Feller and Meier were not set free. The Russians had countered by listing six Soviet citizens in prison in Switzerland that they wanted to see released. Switzerland then added additional names and the Soviet Union answered with similar demands. The game went on in this way and now, in November 1945, they were close to an agreement.

In the ongoing discussions between the Soviet Union and Sweden, several cards were already on the table. Raoul Wallenberg and the young Miss Makarova were two. But there was also af Sandberg, the journalist; the 30,000 Baltic refugees; and the transport of the 3,000 German soldiers, including the 167 forced Baltic recruits.

Unfortunately the Swedish diplomatic leaders did not appear to have asked themselves whether the Soviet Union might be waiting for the Swedes to make the opening move. Such ideas directly contradicted the foreign minister's morals. In any case, Östen Undén soon had other things to think about.

In mid-November the press revealed that Sweden had decided to turn over the 3,000 German soldiers to the Soviet Union. A public outcry ensued, above all out of sympathy for the 167 Baltic men who had been conscripted against their will. The newspapers filled countless column inches while the Baltic legionnaires themselves went on a hunger strike and threatened to commit suicide.

The government was shaken, the king lay sleepless and, for a while, even Undén wanted to retract the decision. This despite the fact that he had worked so hard to strengthen the friendship with the Soviet Union. Ultimately, however, Undén's ambitions for greater amity between the two nations prevailed. A U-turn would have serious political consequences for Sweden, the foreign minister explained. The decision was upheld, and the 167 Baltic soldiers were extradited to the Soviet Union on January 25, 1946 without Sweden having demanded a single repatriation in return.

*

The Lefortovo prison cells were dangerously cold in the winter. The prisoners would walk back and forth in the narrow passage between the cots in order to stay warm. Walks in the so-called exercise yards were often cancelled, especially at the weekends. During the winter, this was a relief. The prisoners had to walk without socks, and in leaky shoes. In sub-zero temperatures and snow, the exercise sessions could become hellish.

As Christmas 1945 approached, Raoul Wallenberg had been imprisoned for over ten months, approximately six of them in Lefortovo. But not once since his relocation to the new prison had he been called to an interrogation. Not once had he been able to articulate his protest against his imprisonment, or his wishes to be put in touch with the Swedish legation.

He tapped messages expressing his frustration to the men next door and in the cell below. It turned out that Raoul Wallenberg had been placed in the same part of the prison as the German and Italian diplomats who had been apprehended during their service in Romania or Bulgaria. Many of them, like Willy Rödel, were suspected of spying. In the cell below and across from Willy Rödel and Raoul Wallenberg's, for example, there was Ernst Wallenstein, who had worked with Willy Rödel at the German legation in Bucharest. As soon as the new arrivals had learned how to tap in the "idiot language", they began daily contact. Raoul Wallenberg and Ernst Wallenstein realised that they had met before, during a flight to Budapest or Vienna in conjunction with one of Raoul's business trips for the Mid-European Trading Company.

Raoul tapped in German and impressed those around him with his vocabulary. Every prisoner had their own greeting, so that others would know who they were speaking with: Raoul always began with five rapid taps. Other prisoners were surprised to hear that there was a diplomat from a neutral country in their midst. They were told that Raoul Wallenberg had protested against his imprisonment and that, to this point, he had refused to speak any further in the interrogations.

As in the Lubyanka, the prisoners exchanged addresses. Raoul said that what was best in his case would be to use: "The Wallenberg Banking Firm", or just "Mr Wallenberg, Stockholm". In Lefortovo, the prisoners had realised that they could write down their neighbours' addresses with the burnt ends of a match on a patch of fabric, which they then sewed into the sleeves of their jackets. They made the sewing needles out of fish bones from the thin soup that they were given. Matches accompanied the weekly ration of fifty Russian *papirosa* cigarettes that each prisoner was given. They promised each other that whichever one was set free first would contact the relatives of the others.

In Lefortovo, there were no chess sets to while away the hours. Sometimes the prisoners could borrow books from the prison library, but these were all in Russian and, in the dim light, it was difficult to see well enough to read. Every tenth day, they were taken to the prison baths in the cellar, where they would take the opportunity to call out their names to each other. The prison also had a barber, who kept the hair and beards of the prisoners cropped.

Normally pen and paper in the cells were forbidden. Once every fourteenth day the prisoners were given writing materials, but only in order to communicate with the prison management. At the end of 1945, Raoul Wallenberg took this chance. He had perhaps done so before, but now he involved all of his cellmates in his work. Raoul Wallenberg explained that he wanted to cite his diplomatic status and demand to be interrogated. But he did not quite know to whom he should turn. A discussion broke out between the cells and, finally, they agreed that Raoul should direct his protest missive directly to Stalin. It was decided that Raoul would write in French.

One of his neighbours spoke French. He suggested that the letter begin with the phrase "*Monsieur le Président*": Raoul wrote accordingly. "A polite phrase?" he tapped. "*Agréez, Monsieur le Président, l'expression de ma très haute considération,*" his neighbour suggested. "Mr Chairman, please receive these assurances of my exceedingly high estimation."

Staffan Söderblom returned to Moscow in mid-December, around the same time as Joseph Stalin. Officially, the re-energised Swedish enquiry about Raoul Wallenberg still lay on his desk. His deputy Ulf Barck-Holst had even sent a reminder at the end of November. There was also the memo that had been drawn up in Stockholm, with its meticulous day-by-day account of what had hitherto been undertaken in regard to Raoul Wallenberg. The games could begin. The next move would be crucial.

But Söderblom did not appear completely satisfied with this turn of events. He had probably hoped to be able to resume his Moscow contacts on a more positive note and, instead, he was now preparing arguments as to why he should not have to continue the Barck-Holst offensive. In his first letter home to Stockholm, Staffan Söderblom indicated that a series of new documents had been added to the Raoul Wallenberg case. Above all he named an article in the *Stockholms-Tidningen* paper by Valdemar Langlet's son Emil, which he had read shortly before his departure. In it Emil Langlet had developed a theory that Wallenberg had died on the way to Debrecen. Staffan Söderblom pointed out to the Foreign Ministry that Langlet dismissed the idea that Raoul Wallenberg could have been imprisoned for ten months without contact with the outside world. In addition, Langlet had heard that the Russians had asked the Budapest Swedes where Wallenberg was holed up. Surely there would have been no need for this if they already knew?

Söderblom reminded them that the Hungarians wanted to name streets after Raoul Wallenberg, and that Swedish newspapers had recently published pictures of a statue that was going to be erected in Budapest in his memory. He did not come right out and say it, but between the lines his question emerged clearly: wasn't it obvious that the man was dead?

Among his papers, Söderblom still had the photographs that Maj von Dardel had given him in June. "I would be grateful for your reply as to whether or not, under the current circumstances, these should be forwarded to the Soviet Foreign Ministry," he wrote to the head of the ministry's political division, Sven Grafström. Since the mail was infrequent it was after the New Year before he received the obvious answer: "Yes".

On December 26, Staffan Söderblom had set up a meeting with the new head of the Soviet Foreign Ministry's Scandinavian division, Alexander Abramov. Söderblom had a number of issues to discuss. He did not bring Maj von Dardel's photographs of Raoul Wallenberg, but nor did he arrive empty-handed. During his recent stay in Stockholm, Söderblom had gone to the labour movement's archives and rifled through any Russian documents that could be of interest to the Soviet leadership. Among other things, he had found a letter to a Swedish prime minister with Vladimir Lenin's signature, of which he had had a copy made.

Söderblom began the meeting by presenting his gift and also praising the new telephone line between Stockholm and Moscow. Then he urged Abramov to try to hurry along any word of the journalist Edward af Sandeberg and also another Swede who was said to be held in a camp. Finally he took up the case of Raoul Wallenberg.

When one reads the Soviet transcript of the conversation it feels as though Söderblom took a deep breath before he started. What he now said about Raoul Wallenberg was not something that he would relay back to Stockholm. Abramov's colleague, however, waited intently.

"During my time in Sweden I tried to investigate this case, and gather and review all the facts as a prosecutor or head of an investigative team would have done," Söderblom began.

He said that he had heard eyewitnesses who had seen Raoul Wallenberg in a group of three hundred people, who the Soviet military leaders were sending to Debrecen in cars. "I would like to be open about my opinion of this case," Söderblom continued, and just this part of the conversation would be recorded word for word in the summary prepared by Abramov's colleague. "I know of course that my opinion cannot be of a private nature but, in this case, I would like to see it as private. I presume that Wallenberg is no longer alive. It is possible that he died as a result of a German bombing raid, or after an attack by a Hungarian or German military company that may have turned up behind Soviet lines," he said.

Just to be sure, the Swedish minister reminded his listener that the Red Army had begun a broad offensive at the same time. This could explain why it was not possible to find out what had happened after January 16, 1945. Since all staff and archives were being moved, it was simply difficult to ascertain any information about Raoul Wallenberg. Abramov must have been somewhat astonished.

Then Söderblom came to his personal request:

> It would be excellent if the mission could receive word to this effect, namely that Wallenberg has died. This is necessary, primarily to assuage Wallenberg's mother, who is still hoping that her son lives, and who expends her health and energy on this fruitless search. A couple of days ago I consulted with Madame Kollontai on this matter. She agreed with me and recommended that I share this with you, which I have now done. I emphasise again that my request for an answer from the Soviet government and the content of

this answer is a personal request and my personal opinion.

Söderblom concluded the conversation by talking about his rough flight from Stockholm. He did not report anything about his actions regarding Raoul Wallenberg's case to the Foreign Ministry in Stockholm.

Two days later, the Soviet Union and Switzerland reached an agreement in their hard-nosed exchange negotiations that concerned, among others, Raoul Wallenberg's diplomatic colleagues Harald Feller and Max Meier. Feller and Meier were now being held in a cell on the first floor of Lefortovo prison. At the end of January 1946, they were given their personal belongings and moved from the prison to a location in Moscow. Shortly afterwards they were flown to Berlin, where their escorts handed them over as free men to the Swiss legation.

It was only then, at the end of January 1946, that Staffan Söderblom gave Maj von Dardel's photographs to the Soviet Foreign Ministry. One showed Raoul Wallenberg sitting at a desk surrounded by standing colleagues. There were also two portraits of him, one small and one enlarged.

The chill intensified between the developing superpowers. In early 1946, President Truman had had enough of Stalin's provocative expansion attempts in countries such as Turkey and Iran. The United States now veered towards a more confrontational approach with the express ambition of defending Europe from the threat of communism. The altered atmosphere between East and West became apparent to everyone in March 1946 when the former British prime minister Winston Churchill delivered a fiery speech denouncing Soviet politics. President Truman's presence in the room reinforced Churchill's message:

> From Stettin in the Baltic to Trieste in the Adriatic, an iron curtain has descended across the Continent. Behind that line lie all the capitals of the ancient states of Central and Eastern Europe. Warsaw, Berlin, Prague, Vienna, Budapest, Belgrade, Bucharest and Sofia, all these famous cities and the populations around them lie in what I must call the Soviet sphere, and all are subject, in one form or another, not only to Soviet influence but to a very high, and in some

cases increasing measure of control from Moscow . . . Whatever conclusions may be drawn from these facts – and facts they are – this is certainly not the Liberated Europe we fought to build up. Nor is it one which contains the essentials of permanent peace.

At the Soviet Foreign Ministry, the head of the Scandinavian division, Abramov, quickly spotted the risk that the new British–American position would influence Sweden and the rest of the countries in his area of responsibility. The Nordic countries were starting to cooperate more closely, in a way that he felt was clearly indicative of a more Anglo-Saxon orientation.

The Soviet Union needed to act. Abramov analysed the policies that the Soviet Union had pursued with regard to Sweden during the past year. It was clear that the aggressive position that they had taken – the strategy of making tough demands and ignoring Swedish gestures of friendship – had not worked. While the Russians had secured the return of the 167 Baltic soldiers in the face of public uproar, this had been the sole success. For instance, the Soviet Union's rejection of the trade agreement had only really profited the Swedish economy, since the country had instead more than doubled its trade with the West.

Abramov wrote a letter to his superiors and suggested a radical reorientation of political tactics vis-à-vis Sweden. In the current situation the Soviet Union should hold out a hand, not coldly turn its back on Sweden. He was supported in this by the legation in Stockholm. In his own memo to the foreign minister, Molotov, the Stockholm envoy Chernyshev wrote lists of possible gestures of goodwill.

Foreign Minister Molotov pruned the list but approved the new, friendly political approach. By the time the Politburo had approved the resolution "Regarding our relations to Sweden", in April 1946, the more gentle approach was already in place. The repatriation of the 30,000 Baltic refugees quietly disappeared from the Soviet lists of demands. And soon an official telegram to Stockholm from Moscow confirmed the recent subtle signs: the Soviet Union wanted to re-enter the trade negotiations. They also let it be known at the same time that they wanted the Swedish minister in Moscow, Staffan Söderblom, to be replaced.

A week or so later, the Swedish government had decided to replace Staffan

Söderblom with Gunnar Hägglöf. According to the journals of the minister of education, Tage Erlander, many of the ministers felt that Söderblom had been disturbingly weak during his spell in Russia. Undén's hope was that Hägglöf would take a more "objective and clear" view of the situation in Moscow.

The transition was scheduled to take place in the summer.

Raoul Wallenberg's name was of course still on the list when the Soviet Union altered their policies towards Sweden in April 1946. A great deal of interesting new information had also flowed in during the first few months of the year. To begin with, Sweden now had a new minister in Budapest, Rolf Arfwedson. He had swiftly been able to scotch the rumour that Raoul Wallenberg was hiding out in Hungary. He had also managed to get the names of the three Soviet officers who had escorted Raoul Wallenberg when he disappeared. Raoul Wallenberg's brother-in-law was able to contribute a few more details about Raoul's final days in Budapest once he came back from his trip with the Red Cross convoy to Budapest.

But none of this had altered Staffan Söderblom's basic position. He continued to take great pains to ask about Edward af Sandeberg. In January he approached the Soviet Foreign Ministry twice over the af Sandeberg case. But when it came to Raoul Wallenberg's case he kept pretty quiet. He had turned over the list of names of the Soviet soldiers in Wallenberg's escort during a brief meeting with Abramov at the beginning of March, but did so with an apologetic flourish: "I have yet again been convinced that Wallenberg most likely is dead. But since his relatives, in particular his mother, still hopes to find him, I have decided to forward to you a few more details about him that have been recovered from eyewitnesses. Perhaps these details will help to establish the circumstances under which he died."

The new Soviet stance toward Sweden did have an impact on other repatriation cases though. During the spring, Edward af Sandeberg was suddenly freed. He arrived in Sweden in June and could describe his travails in a Soviet prison camp. Many were amazed at his story. While the Russians had, at an early stage, indirectly confirmed that af Sandeberg had been in the Soviet Union, until he was released they had consistently maintained that they had no new information.

*

At last even Staffan Söderblom appears to have seen things more clearly. Slowly he had begun to understand how the Russians wanted to play the game – a name for a name, exchange for exchange. This was clearly confirmed for him when, at the end of March, he thanked Abramov at the Foreign Ministry for the fact that af Sandeberg had been released. Abramov immediately responded by asking about Makarova, whom Sweden had not yet sent home. Even if the Swedes were reluctant to engage in this kind of trade in people, it was clear that the Russians preferred to follow this method.

Before long, there were more indications that Soviet officials were not always telling the truth when they claimed to have no knowledge about a particular case. The newly released Swiss diplomat Harald Feller visited the Swedish legation in Bern and explained that the Russians had always told Switzerland that they did not know anything about his case, even though he had demonstrably been imprisoned in Lefortovo the whole time. It would be no great leap to draw the same conclusion for Raoul Wallenberg. Perhaps he wasn't dead after all?

At the end of April, the Foreign Ministry in Stockholm undertook a new analysis of the Raoul Wallenberg case and came to the conclusion that the list of names of the Soviet officers in the escort was the best clue they had. It should not be impossible for the Russians to contact these three and find out what had happened. The Moscow minister was asked to remind Abramov of their identities.

Staffan Söderblom had now been informed that he would be transferred from Moscow to Bern in Switzerland. He must have felt disappointed at this move, but he kept up appearances. To his mother, he even expressed some fear that the transfer would not go through. "What needed to be done here in the transition from war to peace has been done. I am tired and should be allowed to withdraw to a more peaceful life."

At the beginning of May, he was to go back to Sweden one last time before wrapping things up in Moscow. On the day of Walpurgis Night, 30 April, just before he left, he met Abramov at the Foreign Ministry, among other things in order to remind him of the new clue in the Wallenberg case. But Abramov dismissed the question and said that, as far as Raoul Wallenberg was concerned, there was nothing new to report.

This time Söderblom stood his ground, however, and explained how important the matter was, and how much attention it had attracted in Sweden. Abramov countered by observing that the Swedish journalist af Sandeberg "has probably already arrived in Sweden". This caused Söderblom to react. He was suddenly struck by the feeling that Abramov was trying to tell him something, an impression that did not diminish when Abramov repeated the demand to repatriate Lydia Makarova. "This is something that could be interpreted as a sign that Wallenberg is alive after all and has been identified in a camp or some such," a dazed Söderblom later wrote in his account of the meeting.

It was with this completely new impression that Staffan Söderblom returned to Sweden in early May 1946. At the Foreign Ministry in Stockholm, morale was high. They were pleased that the Russians were now far friendlier and that negotiations about a trade credit for the Soviet Union would be resumed.

Neither Staffan Söderblom nor Östen Undén could have known what had gone on behind the scenes at the Kremlin during the spring – that the Soviet Union had made a deliberate political choice and decided to start listening to Sweden's demands. If they had, the Swedes might have straightened their backs a little. As it was, Sweden's attitude toward its large neighbour to the east was still anxiously careful, as if the sunshine was temporary and the slightest irritation could extinguish the new-found warmth between the two countries.

On one of his first days back, Sunday, May 5, Söderblom visited Undén, apparently at his home. Both of them had fresh impressions of meetings with representatives of the Soviet foreign relations leadership to convey. The Soviet minister in Stockholm, Chernyshev, had been to see Undén at the beginning of the week and reminded him of the Lydia Makarova case, as well as another urgent repatriation case of five Soviet sailors who were imprisoned in Sweden. But, above all, Undén and Chernyshev had talked about the coming trade negotiations and agreed how important it was that the two countries reach a positive result. In his journal, Undén wrote that he "fervently" wished for this. Undén even exerted himself socially: Chernyshev and Undén managed to squeeze in three private dinners in May 1946 alone.

Söderblom, for his part, was burdened with new doubts about the credibility of the Kremlin officials, at least in the Raoul Wallenberg case. He had brought his report from the meeting with Abramov and he gave this to Undén. He probably said what he had written before, that he believed that Abramov had tried to imply that Raoul Wallenberg was alive.

It is not known how the rest of the conversation proceeded between the two men that Sunday. But the circumstances did not lend themselves to Söder-blom being able to persuade Undén. It was not just that Undén had previously shown his displeasure and removed Söderblom from his assigned post. Amidst the new bilateral warmth he was hardly likely to be receptive to critical comments about the Soviet Union.

In Yngve Möller's biography of Östen Undén, Sven Dahlman, who was head of the Foreign Ministry's Press Bureau between 1946 and 1948, talks about Undén's relationship to the Raoul Wallenberg case around this time. He was able to note Undén's scepticism on several occasions. "Undén displayed every indication of unease and displeasure when he had to deal with the Wallenberg case ... Undén dis-liked being drawn into opposition with the Soviets through this case and he became abrupt and dismissive in his dealings with it," Dahlman told Yngve Möller.

It would not be a wild guess that Undén simply waved away Söderblom's new doubts concerning Raoul Wallenberg when they met that Sunday. Undén was a man of principle, not known for changing tack in the face of a light breeze. Had Staffan Söderblom not always claimed that he believed that Raoul Wallenberg was dead? Was it really reasonable of Sweden to suspect the Soviet Union of something as outrageous as having imprisoned a Swedish diplomat?

At the end of May, Staffan Söderblom returned one final time to Moscow. Since he was single and had no children, his move to Bern did not present a great logistical challenge. But it must have chipped away at his self-confidence, regardless of what he expressed outwardly.

Those who were close to him describe him as a psychologically complicated person. His shell of confidence was hard to crack, a kind of protection that he had armoured himself with in order to conceal his sensitivity and vulnerability. He had a great need to be affirmed.

It was perhaps in order to compensate for the humiliation he felt that he indulged in so many excesses in his last few weeks. He started to fill his letters back to Stockholm with the polite farewell comments made by the Russians as evidence for his personal successes in Moscow. And he was now on the hunt for a final triumph with the right amount of lustre.

On June 6, Sweden's National Holiday, Molotov received Söderblom at the standard farewell meeting in the Kremlin, probably in his large office with the wall clock. Molotov had a short, somewhat square physique. He wore a small pince-nez. Staffan Söderblom found him a "highly cultivated but not particularly accessible person". They had a long conversation of a general nature. Towards the end, Molotov asked Söderblom if he had any particular wishes. Söderblom replied that in fact he did: a meeting with Stalin was at the top of his wish list.

It was a daring request, even arrogant. Generalissimus Stalin almost never granted audiences to foreign diplomats. No Swedish diplomat had ever managed to secure a hearing with the dictator. But, for unclear reasons, Molotov reacted positively, assured Söderblom that it should be possible and passed along his request.

One week later, on June 13, the leading members of the Politburo met with Joseph Stalin, among them Molotov, Beria, Dekanozov and the minister for foreign trade, Mikoyan. According to the Russian members of a Swedish–Russian Working Group that investigated Wallenberg's fate in the 1990s, there are indirect indications that the audience Söderblom had requested with Stalin was mentioned at the meeting, as, perhaps, was the Wallenberg case itself.

The next day, the protocol department at the Soviet Foreign Ministry called the Swedish legation. Stalin had said yes. Söderblom was welcome at the Kremlin the following evening, at 9 p.m.

This was nothing less than a sensation, but it came on quickly and Söderblom hardly had time to prepare. He did not even confer with Foreign Minister Undén before he left for the Kremlin with his deputy Barck-Holst the following evening. He had met with Undén relatively recently and knew where he stood, and he felt there was no need to establish an agenda. As Söderblom saw it, the sudden appointment with Stalin was an unusually strong symbolic expression of the improved relations between Sweden and the Soviet Union. He really had no other agenda other than capitalising on the meeting itself.

Söderblom decided not to appear aggressive and risk disrupting the mood. But one question was still unresolved and could perhaps finally be clarified – Raoul Wallenberg. Söderblom thought that, if he presented this issue to the most powerful person in the Soviet Union, then nobody could accuse him of not having done all that he could.

The Swedish diplomats were met at the south-west entrance to the Kremlin by two officers, who led them up to one of the palaces behind the Kremlin walls. They took the elevator up two floors and walked at a slow marching pace down a long corridor to a reception room where there were English, American and French newspapers on the table. At exactly 9 p.m., the door to the meeting room opened to show Joseph Stalin sitting at the far end of a long conference table, with another deputy foreign minister, Solomon Lozovsky, at his side. According to Simon Sebag Montefiore's biography of Stalin, Lozovsky was "a grizzled old Bolshevik with a biblical beard" and "the token Jew in the highest echelons of Molotov's Foreign Commissariat". He was responsible for Stalin's Jewish Anti-Fascist Committee. The two had reserved a whole hour for the meeting with Staffan Söderblom.

Stalin stood up and walked over to meet Söderblom, holding out his hand and introducing himself in "his low but distinct voice 'Stalin.' I almost started to laugh. There was almost something comical in the otherwise so serious situation that such a famous man would have to introduce himself," Söderblom recalled in an interview in 1980. "He was wearing a marshal's uniform with the star of the Order of Victory on his chest. Not a big man but a very well-proportioned body. He was actually quite handsome."

Staffan Söderblom chose to speak to Stalin in Russian from the start.

"I would like to thank Your Excellency for being willing to receive me before my departure. I do not want to take your valuable time for granted since I have no reason to make any particular proposals or present any particularly difficult problems," Söderblom began, according to the contemporary Swedish translation.

Then he presented the Swedish government's desire for neighbourly relations, a friendliness that Joseph Stalin immediately returned. "I can only say that we share the same desire on our side. We would like to maintain peaceful, friendly relations with Sweden. Our two countries may be of mutual benefit to each other through exchange."

Generalissimus Stalin then asked Staffan Söderblom if there was anything he wanted. The Swedish minister said not really, but now that Stalin asked, he did want to "mention one thing". Söderblom told him about the Swedish rescue mission for Jews in Budapest and mentioned that one of those who had participated in the operation was the Swedish diplomat Wallenberg.

"Was his name Wallenberg, did you say?" Stalin interrupted and asked him to spell it. Stalin wrote the name down in his notebook.

Söderblom went on and told him how Dekanozov had informed them that Wallenberg had been encountered and how, in January 1945, Wallenberg had been seen in a car with the Russian military, but that he had remained missing since then.

"I am sure that you know that we gave the order that Swedes should be protected," Stalin said, as if to show that he was briefed on the case.

"Yes, and I am personally convinced that Wallenberg has fallen victim to an accident or an assailant." Söderblom replied, as if he felt that the positive mood was in jeopardy.

"Have you not had any further messages on the matter from us?" Stalin asked.

"No, I feel that it is likely that the Soviet military authorities do not have any further information about Wallenberg's fate to share," Söderblom said. He mentioned as an example that the Soviet military had asked Swedes left in Budapest if they knew what had happened to Wallenberg – with the implication that if the Russians had known, they would not have had to ask.

"I would, however, like to see," he went on, "an official communication listing all of the measures that have been taken in the investigation of his case, even if they have unfortunately not yielded any results."

He added that he also wanted to assure himself that the Russians would inform Sweden as soon as they knew something more on Wallenberg.

"This lies in your own interest since there are people who, in the absence of such information, would be able to draw incorrect conclusions," Söderblom said.

"I assure you that the matter shall be looked into and cleared up," Stalin answered.

Söderblom noted that Sweden did not have any other issues of that kind to take up with the Soviets, not when the rest of the Swedish diplomats – in Budapest as well as Berlin – had made it home.

"I promise that I shall look into the Wallenberg matter," Stalin said yet again.

Only five minutes of the allotted hour had gone by. But Söderblom had nothing else to discuss. He ended by expressing his thanks for the kindness with which he had been met in Moscow and confessed that he would leave the city with regret.

"It is not according to your wishes?" Stalin asked.

"No," Staffan Söderblom said.

"Duty calls you to new tasks?"

"Yes."

Then Söderblom and Barck-Holst bade farewell and left the room. Joseph Stalin and Solomon Lozovsky remained for the rest of the fifty-five minutes that were left of the reserved meeting time. "It seems that they couldn't help but evaluate the conversation," the Russian members of the Wallenberg Working Group commented sixty-five years later. "Most likely the conversation inspired . . . astonishment and perhaps even irritation on Stalin's side. Not a single important question had been raised," the Russians observed and went on:

> One cannot avoid noting the ambivalent attitude towards the R. Wallenberg question: on the one hand the stated desire to clear up the case, on the other a note in the form of a "personal opinion" that the diplomat probably died in Budapest . . . On the Soviet side it was not at this time possible on a political level to have any "personal opinions". According to the Soviet diplomatic rule book, Soviet representatives could only express a "personal opinion" if it was supported by the leadership. The "leader" could therefore not imagine anything else, not even for a diplomat from another country. It is therefore logical to assume that he [Stalin] took this . . . to mean that the Swedish leadership was in this way letting him know that questions about his [Wallenberg's] fate were being posed to "keep their conscience clear" before his relatives and the general public.

*

For his part, Staffan Söderblom was pleased with the meeting, even when it was reviewed critically several decades later. After all, Stalin had promised to clear up the Raoul Wallenberg case.

In the meeting with Stalin I do not think I could have expressed myself very differently. When one is fortunate enough to be admitted to the highest levels it is exceedingly unwise to meet such a favour with accusations that the Russian authorities had killed Raoul Wallenberg or some such. I took pains to keep the door open to continued negotiations and did not want to say anything that could have worsened the situation . . . Anyway, I believe that I expressed the *possibility* that Wallenberg was dead. I did not say to Stalin that we *knew* that he was dead.

Three days after the appointment with Stalin, the transcript of the conversation was ready and Staffan Söderblom sent his report to Stockholm. He added his own impression of the Soviet Union's leader:

Stalin appeared healthy and spry, in full vigour. His short but proportionate figure and symmetrical features make a particularly pleasant effect. His voice and gaze gave the impression of a friendly attitude towards his visitors . . . The announcement on the radio and the press that I have been received by Stalin has drawn great attention here. It is viewed as visible evidence that Swedish–Russian connections are excellent.

A few weeks later, when he travelled through Stockholm on his way to his post in Bern, Staffan Söderblom was still overcome by his visit. Even Foreign Minister Östen Undén responded to this. "Went by the department for a while – met Söderblom who had just come from Moscow. He described his visit to Stalin as if he had gazed upon the face of God."

Undén does not, however, appear to have been surprised by what Söderblom said to Stalin about Raoul Wallenberg. On the contrary, Undén must have thought that Söderblom by and large communicated the government's opinion in the case. Perhaps it even reminded him of how he had expressed himself when he met with Söderblom in May. If Undén felt that the words about Wallenberg possibly succumbing to an accident had been a departure from the government's line, he should immediately have ordered the Moscow legation to correct the misunderstanding. He never did.

CHAPTER 18

"No-one is Interested in You"

"RAOUL WALLENBERG LIVES – IN THE SOVIET UNION." This head-line, written in capitals, covered the front page of the *Stockholms-Tidningen* paper on June 28, 1946. The earth-shattering news was based on information from the Swedish journalist Edward af Sandeberg, who had been released from Krasnogorsk prison camp outside Moscow.

Edward af Sandeberg had come to Sweden ten days earlier after a long and laborious journey through Poland. In his first interview, he said that he had met prisoners in the Soviet Union who spoke of a Swede whom they had met by the name of Raoul Wallenberg. Sandeberg had not recognised the name at the time, but realised when he came home who the prisoners had been talking about. He had met two inmates who had mentioned Raoul Wallen-berg and, independently of each other, also spoken about Raoul's "chauffeur". Later it would turn out that one of them had even shared a cell with Langfelder.

Sandeberg's information attracted a great deal of attention, not least because Hungary's new minister in Stockholm, Vilmos Böhm, had just announced information to the contrary. Böhm had claimed that one could now once and for all establish that Wallenberg had died, since the belongings of the missing Soviet soldiers in his escort on the way to Debrecen had been recovered.

The revelations in the *Stockholms-Tidningen* were news for everyone except Maj and Fredrik von Dardel. Af Sandeberg had visited Maj and Fredrik von Dardel before the article was published and told them what he knew. "Obviously it made her very happy," af Sandeberg said in the newspaper inter-view. "Mrs Von Dardel explained to me that she had never doubted that her son was still alive."

Raoul Wallenberg's name was suddenly everywhere. The evening before,

Swedish Radio had broadcast a gala concert that had been arranged in Buda-pest a few weeks earlier in honour of Raoul Wallenberg. Vilmos Forgács' son, Pál, had written an emotional speech about the man in the windbreaker and the soft felt hat whose appearance suggested an American sportsman but whose mask concealed a hero. A Hungarian actor read his text.

That same Friday, Maj von Dardel received an invitation from King Gustaf V, who wanted to see her and Edward af Sandeberg in an audience at the Royal Palace the following day. On the other side of the Norrbro bridge, in the Arvfurstens Palace (the seat of the Foreign Ministry), the phones were ringing non-stop. Questions from journalists were flying and the Foreign Ministry were doing what they could to convince everyone that Stockholm was in constant contact with the legations in Moscow and Budapest about Raoul Wallenberg.

It seemed as if change was in the air.

Friday, June 28, also became a wake-up call for the publisher Arvid Fred-borg. He had recently received a proposal for a book about the "problem of Raoul Wallenberg" from a Social Democratic journalist. Fredborg called the reporter, whose name was Rudolph Philipp, that afternoon and gave him the go-ahead. The same evening, Philipp was sitting on a sofa in the home of Maj and Fredrik von Dardel.

The fifty-year-old Rudolph Philipp was a multi-faceted person. His varied past is perhaps best captured in a few facts from the personal file that the Swedish Security Police, or Säpo, had started several years earlier: a former Austrian citizen, Jewish on his father's side, a stateless writer, artillery officer, Social Democratic journalist, an alleged Trotskyite, active in the Shoes and Leather International, "supports himself . . . mainly as a teacher of Italian fencing". Säpo noted that Philipp had come to Sweden as a "political refugee" in 1937 and communist sources claimed that he behaved "very aggressively and ruthlessly toward 'Moscow's lackeys and the bloody dictator Stalin'".

To Maj and Fredrik von Dardel, Rudolph Philipp appeared like a gift from heaven. This journalist without a country was convinced that Raoul Wallen-berg was alive in the Soviet Union and he wanted to write about it. He now plunged in with boundless energy and would, for better or worse, not let go of the Raoul Wallenberg case for several decades.

Philipp stayed for several hours at the von Dardels', and did not leave until shortly before midnight. He wanted to know everything about Raoul's life, his work in Budapest, what Maj and Fredrik knew about the Foreign Ministry's investigations and what they had learned from the Ministry's documents. Philipp was planning a book but first, on July 5, 1946, he published a lengthy article on the subject in his publisher Arvid Fredborg's conservative cultural journal *OBS!* Using the title "Raoul's Fate" he described Wallenberg's life and work in Budapest up until that day in January when he disappeared without a trace. "Although seventeen months have gone by since then, there has been no confirmation whether he is dead or still alive," Philipp wrote. He demanded positive verification of what had happened.

> Somewhere there must be someone who is pouring sand into the investigative machinery. There is no other way to explain the many contradictory versions from official, half-official and private instances, and witnesses who are now changing their initial explanations since Raoul's disappearance . . . and that so many traces have not been pursued systematically.

Raoul Wallenberg had now been in the Lefortovo prison for over a year. But, in early 1946, he had at least managed to dispatch his written protest to Stalin. He knew that it had been received because, one day, the guards turned up at his cell with a confirmation of delivery. There was, however, no response. Now it was July and Raoul Wallenberg had still not been questioned although he had expressly requested it. This was unusual. In Lefortovo there were inmates who suffered through several hours of interrogation sessions every day.

The prisoners in Lefortovo had various ways to keep track of time. It was easy to scratch a line in the blackened wall of the cell to mark each day that went by. Monthly routines also offered a way to gain a perspective on time. More or less every tenth day, the prisoners were brought down into the cellar for showers, always with a lump of the same foul-smelling soap.

The prisoners exchanged tips on how best to manage an interrogation. Everyone knew that the heavy locks on the cell doors could be released at any moment and the obligatory questions would ensue – "Family name? Birth year? Nationality?" – followed by the notification that the prisoner was to be brought in for questioning. It was not unusual for the guards to throw open the door in the middle of the night.

One piece of advice was to not tell the questioner anything that he did not already know. "If they pick up the end of a thread, they will know to start winding and then you will have no peace, either night or day." The best answers in Russian were spread by way of tapping between the cells. *Ne znayu* (I don't know), *ne pomnyu* (I don't remember) and *ne ponimayu* (I don't understand). "You will be prompted repeatedly to write down your life story. Do this in as few words as possible and identically each time."

On the morning of July 17, 1946, it suddenly happened. Prisoner Raoul Gustaf Wallenberg was summoned for questioning in Lefortovo prison. He would have had to walk along the metal walkway outside his cell with his hands behind his back, and then through a corridor towards the interrogation section, which was located in a newer part of the prison. First they stopped by the caretaker in the reception area. The caretaker had a large book, an interrogation ledger, on the table where he wrote down the prisoner's name and the exact time of the start of the session. The same procedure was repeated when the session ended. On both occasions the prisoner had to sign his name.

The interrogation ledger was almost completely concealed beneath a metal plate. There was a rectangular hole where only the row pertaining to the current prisoner could be seen. In this way, the names of the other prisoners who were brought in remained secret. On the wall in the reception room there was a clock: sometimes the prisoners actually longed to be brought in for questioning so that they could see it and regain a sense of time. Others looked forward to the self-affirming act of writing their names.

When Raoul Wallenberg was led into one of the many chambers in the interrogation wing, it was 10.30 a.m. The interrogation chambers in Lefortovo were furnished with a desk, a few chairs and a chaise longue. The window was covered with thick curtains. The doors had a mattress attached to their backs and were covered with a waxed cloth, presumably as a precaution.

On this day, the German-speaking interrogator Daniel Kopelyansky was sitting behind the desk. He was of Jewish extraction and would lose his job under Stalin's anti-Semitic purges a few years later. He was employed in the security ministry that was by now referred to as the M.G.B. (later K.G.B.). For a while, SMERSH was a subdivision of the M.G.B. Kopelyansky worked on the interrogations of prisoners of war.

Unfortunately, no records of the interrogations with Raoul Wallenberg have been located in Russian archives. The only thing that can be confirmed is that the session lasted two and a half hours, and that Raoul Wallenberg had company for the last forty minutes. It must have been a fond reunion as it was his driver, Vilmos Langfelder, who was led into the room. What is also known is that Raoul Wallenberg's cell mate Willy Rödel was brought to Kopelyansky's interrogation room the following day.

Inmates in neighbouring cells nonetheless managed to ascertain a portion of what had transpired. By tapping, they learned that Raoul Wallenberg had demanded to be put in touch with the Swedish legation in Moscow, at least by way of writing. According to these neighbours, Kopelyansky had replied: "If the Swedish government or its legation had any interest in you, they would have established contact with you long ago. No-one is interested in you and there is no-one who is trying to reach you." Raoul was told that his case was straightforward. He had been arrested for spying in Budapest and, if he felt that he was innocent, it was up to him to prove it. The view of the M.G.B. was that the Swedish government's unwillingness to do anything for him was the best evidence of his guilt.

This same Kopelyansky interrogated Raoul once more that summer, for one hour and forty minutes on August 30. In connection with this session, Raoul Wallenberg apparently asked an interrogation officer if he would be sentenced or not. "You will never be sentenced. You are a political case," was his reply.

Raoul Wallenberg's family had hoped for a positive change in the case's fortunes but, after the commotion during the summer, the Foreign Ministry's work on the matter collapsed like a soufflé. Time and again Maj and Fredrik von Dardel hit a brick wall, despite there being so many new signs that Raoul could be alive. An employee of the International Red Cross had, for example, visited Stockholm over the summer and told them that he had met a Hungarian border official who claimed to have been held in a Russian jail in Budapest with Raoul Wallenberg in January 1945. But when Maj von Dardel took the Red Cross employee to a meeting at the Foreign Ministry, the reaction was muted. According to Rudolph Philipp, she was told that the Foreign Ministry had done everything possible and that there was no hope that Raoul was still alive. Maj and Fredrik von Dardel then tried to contact the new Moscow envoy, Gunnar Hägglöf. But Hägglöf did not reply to their letters and let it be known that he did not want to meet them.

Towards the end of July, when Rudolph Philipp tried to interview the clerk Margareta Bauer about her experiences in Budapest and about Raoul Wallenberg's work she answered: "I'm not allowed to. Too much has already been written and the Foreign Ministry has done everything." It almost seemed as if an order to keep things quiet had been issued. Even Kálmán Lauer was starting to falter and told the family that he believed that Raoul was dead.

The dramatic change that they had been hoping for simply petered out. In certain official settings, one did not dare take the journalist Edward af Sandeberg's new information seriously. The Russians had, through unofficial channels, accused af Sandeberg of willingly participating in the war on the side of the Germans. At the Foreign Ministry, many were convinced that the right thing to do was to hold off. If Stalin had promised to clear up the matter, this would surely be the case. And anyway, the priority was to bring the trade negotiations to a successful conclusion.

Maj von Dardel tried everything. During the summer, she sent copies of a letter that she had received from Lars Berg, who was now stationed in Lima. Lars Berg wrote that he was sure that her son was alive and he was convinced that the Russians were fully capable of lying about holding him. Lars Berg remembered how much they had been asked about Raoul Wallenberg in their interrogations after the siege of Budapest.

"The Russians' great interest in Raoul in February–March 1945 must have been a sign that he was still alive at that time. They had no other reason to interest themselves in a person who was missing without a trace," Maj von Dardel wrote in August 1946 to the Swedish consul general and business magnate Axel Ax:son Johnson. Ax:son Johnson was on his way to Moscow and had promised to try to help. "Dear Axel," she went on, "I hope so much for what you, with your great power, can do to clear up the uncertainties surrounding my beloved boy. You may even have him with you on your way back from Moscow!"

The family's confidence in the Foreign Ministry was crumbling.

*

During the autumn of 1946, Raoul's younger half-brother, the civil engineer Guy von Dardel, moved back to Stockholm from Linköping. He had been recruited to the Defence Ministry's research institute in order to study how one could use the advances associated with the atom bomb to produce energy. In conjunction with this he had the possibility of continuing the work of his doctoral dissertation on the interactions of neutrons. Guy von Dardel had just turned twenty-seven years old and was a dark-haired, thin man. He was now drawn into Rudolph Philipp's dogged research for the book. Guy was a considerably milder, more academically inclined person than the intense Austrian. But he was equally stubborn.

Shortly after that, the family was notified of some startling news. Rudolph Philipp had received information from a Hungarian policeman who claimed to know where Raoul Wallenberg was. They were put in touch through intermediaries. The policeman promised that he would be able to free Raoul if only he could get the 60,000 kronor required to bribe the prison guards.

The offer made the family alter their strategy. Rudolph Philipp's book was ready for publication, but now the family and the writer felt that they had the happy ending of their story within reach. First Raoul would be liberated. Then those in power could be handed the criticism they richly deserved. Philipp even wrote the concluding words "Raoul is free!" in his manuscript.

In early October, Guy von Dardel applied for a cabinet passport to travel to Budapest – officially in order to investigate the fate of his brother, but secretly in order to meet with the Hungarian and to hand over the money. Outwardly, Guy said that he was going to meet with Raoul's colleagues in Budapest.

The Foreign Ministry had no objections to issuing Guy with a cabinet passport, but advised him not to travel to Budapest since it could be counterproductive for Raoul's case. Guy chose to fly to Prague instead.

The Hungarian border official had said that he wanted 60,000 Swedish kronor from the family (around £90,000 today). The money would be placed in the bottom of a basket filled with apples at an agreed location by the Hungarian border. Guy von Dardel prepared everything according to the instructions and drove from Prague to the meeting place where he found the Hungarian. Guy gave him a basket of apples with the 60,000 kronor. The border official promised that Raoul would soon be returning to Sweden by plane from the Soviet Union.

On Sunday October 27, 1946, Maj and Fredrik von Dardel went out to Bromma Airport in order to meet their son. It was said that he would be on the same plane from Moscow as the Swedish trade delegation. But Raoul never appeared. The Hungarian police officer had swindled them. Their action had been as desperate as it was naïve.

Then the family decided to publish Philipp's book.

The publication caused an uproar in November. It was an inopportune moment for the Swedish government. Sweden and the Soviet Union had, only a few weeks earlier, managed to settle a trade agreement that involved a trade credit to the Soviet Union worth one billion kronor. Unfortunately it had not become the domestic triumph that was hoped for. The press campaign against the "Russian agreement" had not been kind. The furore had only just started to dissipate when Rudolph Philipp's book about Raoul Wallenberg landed in the bookshops.

In the Swedish chancellery, the Raoul Wallenberg case that autumn had mostly revolved around money. Hungarians who had provided cash or goods for Raoul's aid operation felt duped. They had contacted lawyers to demand the promised repayment in Swiss francs from the Swedish state. But they were turned down. Gösta Engzell, the head of the legal department at the ministry, had earlier written to Arfwedson in Budapest and asked him to disclaim responsibility. "In particular, you should maintain . . . that Wallenberg's operation was not undertaken by the Swedish state, which is why we cannot be held responsible for settling any agreements entered into by him in Hungary."

This telegram spoke volumes about the attitude to Raoul Wallenberg in the Foreign Ministry. Luckily the American Jewish aid organisation, Joint, came to the rescue. Joint, which had come up with the majority of the funds for Raoul's operation, promised to repay the creditors. In November, Joint also donated 2,500 dollars to the von Dardel family to fund investigations for Raoul Wallenberg.

Rudolph Philipp's book, *Raoul Wallenberg: Diplomat, Champion, Samaritan* was as much a celebration of Raoul's deeds as it was an attack on the Swedish government – especially the Foreign Ministry. Philipp maintained that all the signs indicated that Raoul Wallenberg was still alive. Philipp had had access to the Foreign Ministry documents through the von Dardel family, and in the book he gave a devastating depiction of the actions of the Swedish authorities during the almost two years that had gone by since Raoul Wallenberg's disappearance. "Those forces that allowed Raoul to disappear have managed to draw a thick curtain of fog over the riddle that surrounds him. The Swedish Foreign Ministry has not only not dispersed this mist but has contributed to allowing it to grow more impenetrable," Philipp wrote in his summary. He observed that Söderblom had devoted "a large portion of his energy, not to solving the problem but to creating new arguments for why one should allow the problem to rest, that is to say, do nothing."

In this way, the Raoul Wallenberg case came to be the first headache for Tage Erlander, the new prime minister, who had succeeded Per Albin Hansson after Hansson's sudden death in October.

Rudolph Philipp's book had transformed the Raoul Wallenberg case into an "affair" in the papers. For the first time, the Wallenberg story now also became a parliamentary question. A right-wing M.P., Elis Håstad, stated that it was time for the government to be transparent about what it had done to save Raoul Wallenberg's life or "establish his fate".

Prime Minister Tage Erlander had to handle this parliamentary debate himself since his foreign minister was at a United Nations meeting in New York. A few days before the debate, Philipp was invited to meet with the members of the cabinet in order to present his materials. Among the documents that the prime minister and the minister of justice sent back and forth across the table were Maj von Dardel's description of her meeting with Madame Kollontai in February – the tea when the Soviet envoy had assured Maj that Raoul Wallenberg was in the Soviet Union. This, together with Dekanozov's note, were evidence enough, Philipp said. He asked the government to take action and explicitly demand that the Soviet Union send home Raoul Wallenberg. Tage Erlander commented on Philipp's vivid presentation in his journal a few days later: "I was not particularly convinced of its value."

Prime Minister Erlander used his allotted time in the Raoul Wallenberg debate to give a detailed day-by-day account of the Swedish activity thus far. Not all the voices of the press were convinced. It was said afterwards that the Foreign Ministry had acted as if it were "beating around the bush". In view of the good relations between Sweden and the Soviet Union, it surely was not impossible to find out what had happened? *Stockholms-Tidningen* suggested that the government should free Raoul Wallenberg from all accusations of German spying "which appears to be the source of the issue".

But the facts remained what they were. Almost two years had gone by without the Swedish government even once formally requesting that Raoul Wallenberg be returned from the Soviet Union. Instead they had confined themselves to asking the Russians politely how the investigations were going. Over the past six months, they had not even done that. Gunnar Hägglöf justified this passivity by saying that the question resided with Joseph Stalin, that no Soviet officials therefore dared touch it and that one could only "await word from on high – if it is even forthcoming".

In the autumn of 1946, Stalin took another three months of holiday.

The Soviet diplomats in Stockholm were not as restrained as the Swedes. Ever since the end of the war they had lined up one demand for repatriation after another during their interactions with the Foreign Ministry. Yet another was added just as the worst of the uproar around Rudolph Philipp's book raged on. The man in question was a Soviet sailor, Anatoly Granovsky, who had defected in Stockholm during the autumn when his ship was in the Värtahamnen port. The Russians had demanded his extradition on repeated occasions and claimed that he was guilty of larceny and rape in his homeland.

If Undén had his way, the sailor would immediately have been sent back to the Soviet Union without asking for anything in exchange. But the rest of the government regarded Granovsky as a political refugee and the decision made in early November was to refuse the Soviet demands. The Russians did not back down. In the days around the Wallenberg parliamentary debate, Chernyshev took the Granovsky case to the highest level, both with Prime Minister Tage Erlander and the cabinet secretary in the Foreign Ministry, Karl Ivan Westman.

Cabinet secretary Westman did the unexpected, something that no-one on the Swedish side had dared to do to this point. He connected the two cases and pointed out to Chernyshev that "answers regarding Wallenberg's whereabouts . . . have not yet been received from Moscow". But this defiance did not go beyond a daring comment. According to the Russian investigators in the Swedish–Russian Working Group on the Wallenberg case from the 1990s, it would have been "particularly timely to raise the question officially, but this did not occur".

The tumult surrounding Philipp's book had definitely mobilised new forces in the Foreign Ministry. For a while one could even discern something approaching a diplomatic offensive. But willingness to take action only went so far. The head of the political division, Sven Grafström, for example, sent a telegram to Undén at the United Nations meeting in New York recommending that he raise the Wallenberg case with his colleague Molotov before they both went home. Undén had two personal meetings with Molotov in New York, one before and one after Grafström's telegram. But he did not mention Raoul Wallenberg at either of them. Undén did, however, praise the result of the trade negotiations.

In December, when Undén had returned to Sweden, even the Moscow envoy Gunnar Hägglöf appears to have woken up. According to his later claims, he suggested pressuring the Russians into providing information, for example by suggesting the kind of exchange that the Swiss had participated in. But, according to Hägglöf, Undén did not want to entertain such an idea. Sweden does not engage in "human trade", was his response.

Undén did not want to entertain an exchange but, after the parliamentary debate about Wallenberg at the end of November, the Moscow legation received orders from Stockholm to at least make a new enquiry. This was something that Ulf Barck-Holst had to take care of as Hägglöf had gone back to Sweden for a while. Barck-Holst had earlier shown initiative in the Raoul Wallenberg case, a sense of drive that he still possessed.

His instructions were to exploit the Swedish media storm around Raoul Wallenberg, something it was assumed that the Russians had not missed. Barck-Holst was to pressure them for information and remind them of Dekanozov's note from January 1945, in which the Russians assured the Swedes that Wallenberg had been taken into protective custody by the Red Army. Barck-Holst was to try to engineer a meeting "as high up as possible", and bring along Tage Erlander's closing words about Dekanozov's note in the debate, translated into Russian.

But Dekanozov was suddenly not available. The first time that Barck-Holst tried, Dekanozov was said to be suffering from flu. The next time Barck-Holst asked for a meeting, he was asked whether it was in regard to Wallenberg. When he answered in the affirmative, the response was that Dekanozov was unfortunately otherwise occupied. Instead, Barck-Holst was sent to a subordinate at the Foreign Ministry's Scandinavian division. Barck-Holst launched into the issue. When he once again received demands for the young Makarova and the sailor Granovsky, in return he grew angry. Was he supposed to understand from this that Raoul Wallenberg was alive and that the Soviet Union was proposing an exchange? When he asked this, the Soviet official backed down and said that there was absolutely no connection. Barck-Holst had the impression that the Russian was taken by surprise.

The Swedish diplomat did not give up. On December 13, Barck-Holst managed to get a meeting with Lozovsky, the bearded leader of Stalin's Jewish Anti-Fascist Committee, who had been present at Staffan Söderblom's audience with Stalin. He was now head of Stalin's powerful intelligence bureau. Like Barck-Holst, he had heard Stalin give his promise to look into the matter back in June.

This time, Barck-Holst brought up that promise immediately. He asked about the results of the promised investigations. Barck-Holst described the enormous media pressure back in Sweden and observed that it would be a pity if the improved relations between Sweden and the Soviet Union were now muddied by the Wallenberg affair. Barck-Holst added that, after the storm surrounding the trade agreement, they did not want Raoul Wallenberg to become a prominent topic in the press and parliament.

The seventy-year-old Lozovsky replied that he could very well remember the meeting with Staffan Söderblom, as well as the promise that Stalin had made regarding the Wallenberg case. Lozovsky made some notes and promised to inform both Stalin and Dekanozov, since Molotov had not yet returned from New York.

Almost two years had gone by since the day when Raoul Wallenberg was last seen in Budapest. Ulf Barck-Holst had the definite impression that the Soviet machinery was starting to move. Perhaps the Russians were preparing some kind of statement? A hopeful Barck-Holst wrote to the Foreign Ministry in Stockholm and asked his colleagues to silence all newspaper articles on the matter since, at this interesting juncture, they risked causing "harm rather than help" to the Wallenberg case.

He was right. Something was afoot. Molotov had returned from New York and was, among other things, informed of the new Swedish demands. In early January 1947 he had asked his subordinates for "a review and suggestion" of the Wallenberg case. If one is to believe the analysis of the Russian side of the Working Group on the Wallenberg case in the 1990s it was only now that the rest of the Foreign Ministry learned that Raoul Wallenberg actually was in the Soviet Union, in one of the M.G.B.'s many prisons. It is claimed in some quarters that not even Molotov knew this, but most other sources dismiss this as unlikely.

Molotov's deputy minister Dekanozov now turned to Viktor Abakumov and asked him "to relay what is known of this matter in a presentation to Comrade Molotov". This was not the first time that the Soviet Foreign Ministry had asked the M.G.B. or SMERSH with questions about Raoul Wallenberg. In the past year they had sent over both Maj von Dardel's photographs and the list of names of the Soviet military officers who were thought to have escorted Raoul. Thus far, the security services had either not answered or simply let it be known that information about the requested person was lacking. But, after Barck-Holst's enquiries in December 1946, an official at SMERSH had gone so far as to say that it was perhaps advisable for the deputy foreign minister to call Abakumov about the Raoul Wallenberg case. It was clear that the matter was sensitive. When the head of the Foreign Ministry's Scandinavian section, Mikhail Vetrov, was asked to enquire about Wallenberg "with our other agencies", he was asked to avoid using the telephone.

At the end of January 1947, the Swedish envoy Gunnar Hägglöf returned to Moscow for a short period. He had decided to leave his post for personal reasons after only half a year in the Soviet capital. In the inflamed Swedish debate about the Raoul Wallenberg case, Gunnar Hägglöf had been harshly criticised for his passivity. Now he pulled himself together one last time and visited the Soviet Foreign Ministry almost immediately. He was able to meet with an official and continue along the path that his deputy Barck-Holst had started to go down. Hägglöf informed his hosts that Sweden found it very odd that the Russians had not managed to get any information about Raoul

Wallenberg. Hägglöf even said that the Wallenberg case was now threatening to affect relations between Sweden and the Soviet Union.

Since he was going to leave Moscow, Hägglöf also asked for a final meeting with Molotov. He implied that he preferred not to have to bring up the Raoul Wallenberg case at that time. "What is this about? It is necessary to find plausible explanations," one of Molotov's deputies noted on the internal report on the meeting with Hägglöf.

Officials at the Soviet Foreign Minstry were now ordered to prepare Molotov for the meeting with the Swedish minister. On Friday, February 8, 1947, Vetrov finished his preparatory memorandum. It only needed to be reviewed by his superiors before it was given to Molotov.

Vetrov addressed four current issues that one could expect Gunnar Hägglöf to bring up. The Raoul Wallenberg case was at the top of the list. He made a brief summary of what had been said about Wallenberg from the Soviet side, which is to say nothing. He also mentioned that one of the Foreign Ministry officials had speculated in front of the Swedes that Wallenberg had probably died in a bombing raid.

But the memo was returned to Vetrov. A large portion of his account of the Wallenberg case was now redacted. Instead his superior had written in an alternative text by hand between the lines, a completely new message to Molotov:

> According the information from Comrade Fedotov [at the M.G.B.], Wallenberg is in M.G.B. custody. Fedotov has promised to convey the reasons for Wallenberg's detention as well as to suggest further actions in this case.

As far as is known, this was the first time that the truth about Raoul Wallenberg was set down in writing in a document at the Soviet Foreign Ministry. The information was considered extremely sensitive and Vetrov was given special instructions as to how to handle it:

> Send a fresh copy with my edits. Seal the letter personally and send it to Podtserob. Do not involve your secretary in this matter, have it prepared at Vyshinsky's [another of the many deputy foreign ministers] office.

It was as if Molotov's ministers and officials were sending around a bomb. But in spite of all this, the document did not come to play a decisive role at this time. The promised explanations and suggestions from Abakumov's M.G.B. would be a very long time coming. And the meeting between Hägglöf and Molotov never took place.

Yet another bitter Moscow winter began to draw slowly to a close. But even far into March the temperature was still below freezing and there was snow on the streets of the Soviet capital.

Unfortunately there are no reports about the mood of the inmates of cell 203 from this time. But more than two years had gone by, two years of mouldy porridge and thin soups, occasionally replaced by sauerkraut or possibly raw fish. It appears likely that these days were now dominated by despair, even for a firebrand like Raoul Wallenberg.

After the two closely scheduled sessions during the summer, the interrogation division at Lefortovo had left Wallenberg alone. The last he had heard was that he was a political case and that he would never be brought forward for sentencing. According to employees at the M.G.B. at this time, a prolonged pause in interrogations could indicate that an order had been issued from Stalin not to proceed without special instructions. Occasionally foreign prisoners ended up waiting for long periods without questioning, only to be used in political exchanges later.

According to a neighbouring inmate, Raoul had made repeated attempts to try to find out what was to happen to him. The prison commissioner had comforted him by saying that he could expect an answer after the big foreign affairs summit in Moscow in March 1947. The four victorious nations from the war would convene in the Soviet capital and try to reach an agreement about several as yet unresolved questions regarding Germany's future. It was said that the prisoners' fate would be determined at this time too.

While the highly sensitive briefing for Molotov was being prepared, there was only one month remaining until the summit was to take place. It is not clear if this was a contributing factor, but shortly afterwards, on February 24, a relocation order for prisoners Wallenberg and Rödel was issued by one of the highest-ranked officials at the division for military counter-espionage within the M.G.B. His name was Kartashov, he was fair-haired and heavy-set and worked directly under Abakumov in the Lubyanka's main building. It was staff from his unit who had interrogated Raoul when he was being held in the Lubyanka in the spring of 1945.

"Request that the war prisoners RÖDEL Willy and WALLENBERG Raoul in cell 203 of Lefortovo Prison be moved to the inner prison of the Soviet Union's Ministry for State Security, placed together there in cell number 7 and registered for officer food rations for prisoners of war," Kartashov wrote to the prison chiefs at Lefortovo and the Lubyanka. Two days later, Lefortovo staff noted in their ledgers that the two prisoners would be moved with their belongings and "their documents". But, at the last minute, Raoul Wallenberg was retained. He was not moved to Lubyanka's "Inner Prison" until March 1, 1947.

Cell number 7 was on the ground floor of the Lubyanka prison. In his memoirs, the former Soviet spy chief Pavel Sudoplatov has said that the cell block that Rödel and Wallenberg now came to was akin to a hotel. "The rooms were not cells in the normal sense of that word; the ceilings were high and they were equipped with furniture and amenities." The "officer food rations" meant, according to Sudoplatov, that the security service cafeteria and restaurant supplied the food, which was "incomparably better than normal prison fare". Sudoplatov claims that it was into these cells that particularly highly ranked prisoners were placed, "before recruitment or liquidation". Others say that these were cells where the administration placed prisoners that they knew would be subject to intense interrogations.

Raoul Wallenberg was registered as "special prisoner number 206" and Willy Rödel as number 205. The day after Raoul's relocation, even his belongings were noted in the register. But what these consisted of at this point, and what happened to them subsequently, does not appear in the registration ledger that, in later years, was painstakingly restored. When the investigators in the Swedish–Russian Working Group started to delve into the Soviet prison archives in the 1990s, they discovered that almost all the references to Raoul Wallenberg had been rendered illegible by thick marker. This was a highly unusual sight in the Soviet archives.

A week after Raoul Wallenberg was moved to the Lubyanka, the British foreign minister, Ernest Bevin, arrived in wintry Moscow as the first prominent guest at the foreign affairs summit. He was greeted by the Soviet Union's deputy foreign minister, Andrey Vyshinsky, who stood out in his shiny uniform cap among all the fur hats on the platform.

Andrey Vyshinsky spoke both English and French and would be at Molotov's side during the conference. He was sixty-four years old and had a past as a state prosecutor in Stalin's purge trials during the Great Terror at the end of the 1930s. It was hardly a coincidence that the Foreign Ministry's Scandinavian division head had been asked to write out the delicate Raoul Wallenberg note at Vyshinsky's offices. From this point on, it was from here that this sensitive case would be handled, to the extent that it came up at all.

The Moscow conference had been under way for one day when Raoul Wallenberg was brought to the fifth interrogation of his imprisonment. At 2 p.m. on Tuesday, March 11, he was led by guards to interrogation room 671 on the sixth floor of the Lubyanka's large main building. There he met with the same interrogator from Kartashov's department as last time in Lubyanka, but with a new interpreter.

These interrogation records have also not been found, but the interpreter later recalled that the session was a kind of standard review. Raoul Wallenberg had been dressed in a suit and had looked relatively healthy. The interrogator systematically touched on facts that the Swedish diplomat had disclosed earlier. In particular, the questions focused on "documents of lists that had been recovered at the time of the arrest". According to the interpreter, the interrogator had been particularly interested in Raoul Wallenberg's contacts with Germans and Americans. Everything proceeded calmly and the conversation went on for one hour and forty-five minutes. After that, Raoul Wallenberg returned to an existence that was as uneventful as before, now in the Lubyanka's "Inner Prison".

The Moscow summit that the prison staff had suggested might push Raoul Wallenberg's case forwards ended in yet another setback, after a few weeks of tiresome round-table negotiations. Relations between East and West were poor and were not improved by suspicions about Soviet involvement in the ongoing Greek Civil War. The atmosphere probably deteriorated further when Truman stiffened the tone of his foreign policy in a speech to Congress during the first days of the summit.

This was dubbed the Truman Doctrine and is regarded by many as the formal start of the cold war. The American president delivered a promise: if necessary, the United States would support countries such as Greece with money and military assistance in order to avoid them being forced into the Soviet sphere of influence. Truman drew a much sharper line between east and west than before: "At the present moment in world history, nearly every nation must choose between alternative ways of life. The choice is too often not a free one." He used a black-and-white brush as he painted the alternatives. In one vision, people could live in free democracies with representative governments, free elections and human rights and freedoms. In the other, darker world, however, a minority ruled by terror and repression, controlled media and rigged elections. There, human rights were not even an option. "I believe that it must be the policy of the United States to support free peoples who are resisting attempted subjugation by armed minorities or by outside pressures," said the president. There was, of course, no mistaking to whom these comments were directed.

The Truman doctrine immediately impacted upon the Soviet evaluation of the small, neutral country Sweden. In the days after the speech, Chernyshev, the Soviet envoy in Stockholm, sent a relatively pessimistic analysis of the situation in Sweden to Moscow. In a heightened conflict between East and West, Sweden could not be counted on, he said. The American and British influence was far too strong: "If there is war between the Anglo-Saxons and the Soviet Union, Sweden will be in the Anglo-Saxon camp."

In April, the new American secretary of state George Marshall flew home after the unsuccessful conference in Moscow. There had been no progress to speak of. But, as usual, there was a press contingent waiting at the foot of the plane's steps. At first George Marshall was unwilling to say anything. Finally he walked hesitantly to the microphone without altering his dour expression. He kept his hat on and cleared his throat. "I am glad to be returning home," was his first comment.

In the spring of 1947, Raoul Wallenberg's stepfather Fredrik von Dardel, now sixty-two years old, became very sick. The diagnosis was stomach cancer: Maj von Dardel knew all too well what that meant. In the months before Raoul was born, she had sat by her first husband's deathbed. Like Raoul Oscar Wallenberg, Fredrik von Dardel quickly grew worse. The doctors did not give him a high chance of survival and, towards the end of April, his condition had grown critical. A swiftly arranged operation saved his life at the last minute. Afterwards Fredrik von Dardel said that he had decided from the beginning never to give up. He knew how much Maj needed him.

The relationship between Raoul's family and the Foreign Ministry had turned icy after the publication of Rudolph Philipp's book. The family did not feel that the Foreign Ministry had dealt correctly with Raoul's case. Therefore it was not so strange that the family had begun to feel a desperate need to act on their own, even in the wider political arena. If the Foreign Ministry stumbled, then others had to step forward, Guy von Dardel appears to have reasoned. At the beginning of 1947 he had travelled to the United States on a fellowship to conduct research in atomic physics at Cornell University. There he tried to rouse an American response. Among other things, he wrote a personal letter to Truman and asked him to demand information about Raoul Wallenberg from the Russians. He even contacted the Jewish Nobel laureate Albert Einstein at Princeton University who, after a while, wrote a letter about Raoul Wallenberg to Joseph Stalin.

Guy von Dardel's actions received some attention in both American and Swedish newspapers – and were naturally also registered in the Soviet Union. In the United States the initiative was received with expressions of gratitude from the State Department, regarding Raoul Wallenberg's honourable work in collaboration with the American War Refugee Board. The W.R.B.'s Stockholm representative, Iver Olsen, was interviewed and said that it was as much the duty of the United States as it was of Sweden to come to Raoul Wallenberg's aid.

At the Soviet Foreign Ministry, Guy's letter to Truman was duly noted, especially certain key sentences. "Wallenberg was sent to Hungary in July 1944 as the representative of Roosevelt's organisation, the War Refugee Board," was one of them.

But Guy was not the only family member taking action. Maj von Dardel had managed to elicit a half-promise from the Soviet consulate in New York that the Russian Red Cross would make enquiries regarding her son. She subsequently wrote a letter to the Red Cross in Moscow and told them the whole story of her son Raoul and his disappearance. This was translated and sent on to Vyshinsky. In the internal Soviet commentary on her letter, her words were slanted according to Soviet perceptions. Maj von Dardel was claimed to have written that the W.R.B. representative Iver Olsen had "suggested that Wallenberg assume leadership for that which was called saving Jews in Hungary," as well as that it was "in order to protect him in this risky assignment that the Swedish government appointed him secretary at the Swedish legation in Budapest". The Russians had apparently made up their minds on this matter.

When official Sweden failed to deliver, the private initiatives assumed even more importance. But an important group was missing on this front. Raoul Wallenberg's supporters at the humanitarian department in Budapest had fallen significantly silent.

Both Hugó Wohl and Vilmos Forgács had been to Sweden for a visit. They had formed a Wallenberg committee in Budapest, arranged a memorial concert and ordered a statue of a Saint George figure – all to honour Raoul Wallenberg's fight against the Nazis and the Arrow Cross. A book about his deeds was also in progress. But, the more time went by, the more anti-democratic the increasingly Soviet-influenced Hungary became. Gradually Raoul Wallenberg became a risky and sensitive topic. One by one the former co-workers withdrew in order to try to save their own skins.

Stalin's security minister Viktor Abakumov used to say that there were only two ways to thank a spy – cover him in medals or cut his head off. According to Simon Sebag Montefiore, he even trumped his predecessor Beria's aggressiveness and thirst for blood. Abakumov possessed "all Beria's sadism but less of his intelligence", Montefiore wrote in his biography of Stalin. In Stalin's eyes, one of Abakumov's advantages was that even Beria, who was still on the powerful ministerial council and had overall responsibility for state security, was afraid of him.

Abakumov's security ministry, the M.G.B., had only just started to prepare their promised presentation to Molotov about the Raoul Wallenberg case. By mid-May, deputy foreign minister Vyshinsky grew tired of waiting and wrote to Molotov. He reminded him how insistent the Swedes were and told him that a new parliamentary debate on the Raoul Wallenberg case was to take place in Sweden in the summer. The press campaign threatened to reach the same high level as when "a book by a certain Rudolf Philipp" came out.

For these reasons, Vyshinsky said, it was high time for Molotov to schedule the presentation that Abakumov's ministry had promised as early as February. The M.G.B. was to explain the motivations behind Wallenberg's arrest, but also provide suggestions for what further measures could be taken. Vyshinsky stressed the latter. Now he wrote bluntly that Molotov should demand Abakumov's "proposal to resolve" the Wallenberg case. The deputy foreign minister actually used the Russian word *likvidatsiya*, which could be taken to mean either "liquidation" of the bureaucratic matter or liquidation of a person. Vyshinsky probably meant a liquidation of the case, but there is every possibility that Abakumov understood it differently.

The following day Molotov forwarded Vyshinsky's letter to Abakumov and asked him to present his report.

Vyshinsky's predictions about a Swedish campaign in the press were correct. Swedish newspapers had again begun to make enquiries about Wallenberg. A few of all of the false leads that streamed into the Foreign Ministry had turned up as juicy titbits in the newspaper columns – one day Raoul sat imprisoned in a Slovakian palace, the next he was in a camp outside Moscow. And, in April, the new Swedish minister Rolf Sohlman arrived in Moscow with fresh energies and high ambitions. His arrival was followed by the Swedish–Soviet decision to raise the status of their respective ministers to ambassador level. The scene was set for a new Swedish offensive that could perhaps at last force an honest answer from the Soviets.

Rolf Sohlman was no flash in the pan like his predecessors. The new Swedish ambassador would stay for seventeen years and became well known in Moscow's diplomatic circles. The Moscow posting suited Sohlman exceptionally well. Since his university years he had been very interested in Russia and Russian culture. He was married to a Russian, Zina, and at the Foreign Ministry there were rumours that Sohlman was such a Russophile that he did not think Sweden should mount a defence if the Soviet Union attacked. But, for Sohlman, admiring Russian culture was not the same as celebrating the Soviet Union and communism. He knew something about the difference. His wife Zina came from a liberal family where not everyone had managed to escape persecution by the Russian Bolsheviks. At the same time, Rolf Sohlman was a close associate and favourite of Östen Undén. He shared Undén's view of the world and saw improving relations between Sweden and the Soviet Union as his foremost diplomatic task.

Before Rolf Sohlman travelled to Moscow in April, he had met Maj von Dardel. Sohlman thought it was a good meeting. He had made it clear that he would pursue the question with the assumption that Raoul was still alive. But, he had added, it was important that the Foreign Ministry and the family were reading from the same script. Maj agreed. Sohlman felt they reached an understanding and Maj said that she was "grateful for the conversation and that she now for the first time felt she had a sympathetic response on the part of the Foreign Ministry".

Sohlman's intention had been to raise the Raoul Wallenberg question as soon as the necessary rituals of politeness had been performed.

Unfortunately this plan stalled. Once he was in Moscow, Rolf Sohlman read about the American attention paid to Guy von Dardel's letter to President Truman. His immediate reaction was that this was incredibly unfortunate in the current tense situation. He recalled that, at the meeting immediately before he left, he had advised Maj not to involve the Americans, at least as long as the political tension was high. And here was this.

Sohlman capitulated. He wrote back home that he felt he could not very well go to the Russians with the case after this. "To pursue a tandem enquiry with the Americans here can hardly benefit Wallenberg or Sweden," Sohlman observed and suggested that he lie low until von Dardel's letter had "fallen into oblivion".

Two weeks later the Swedish ambassador lost more momentum. His nine-teen-year-old daughter had met a couple of Hungarians on a bus trip and had started to discuss the Raoul Wallenberg case. One of the Hungarians had told him that a friend of his had "seen Raoul Wallenberg's corpse" in a prison camp in Hungary. According to what the Hungarian had heard, Wallenberg had been one of the many prisoners who had died of illness and malnutrition in the camp.

Rolf Sohlman immediately informed Stockholm of this news and then spent considerable, though fruitless, efforts tracking down the Hungarian source.

This was why it took until June 14, 1947 for the otherwise so energetic Rolf Sohlman to approach the Soviet Foreign Ministry with a request regarding Raoul Wallenberg. Perhaps, by this time, the Russians had repressed their memories of the media attention around Guy von Dardel's letter to President Truman.

*

George Marshall, the U.S. secretary of state, was despondent over the lack of success in the Moscow negotiations. He was also anxious about the economic situation in war-torn Europe. Cities lay in ruins. People were suffering. And the misery only appeared to fuel the Soviet Union's influence in Europe. "The patient is sinking while the doctors deliberate," George Marshall observed.

Now he saw a potential solution, at once strategic and humanitarian. The United States should offer to support a large-scale reconstruction programme in the European countries, in order to stop the spread of communism and prevent a depression. President Truman gave the green light for this idea. In early June 1947, the foreign minister launched the "Marshall Plan" in a speech at Harvard University. The programme was presented as assistance for "self-help". In order to pre-empt political overreactions from the Kremlin, the Soviet Union was invited to participate.

At first Joseph Stalin was positive towards the initiative. Perhaps even the Soviet Union could take advantage of the American venture. Foreign Minister Molotov was therefore dispatched to Paris at the end of June in order to sound out the situation before the summit on economic issues, that was to begin on July 13. But it did not take long for Stalin to perform an about-face. The reports from Molotov about the Marshall Plan were, in his eyes, as alarming as those he had received from his intelligence service. The Marshall Plan was not an aid programme, it was a threat against the Soviet Union. According to Molotov's report, President Truman and his ministers were "eager to use this situation to make their way into the economies of the European nations, particularly to control the flow of European trade according to their own interests". The intelligence service had intercepted secret conversations and supplemented these with descriptions of the Marshall Plan as a far-reaching proposal for economic and political integration in Europe, a strategy that, in the largest sense, was intended to increase the influence of the United States at the expense of the Soviet Union.

Joseph Stalin reared up. Molotov was called home from Paris and, on July 7, 1947, sent directives to all countries in the Soviet sphere of interest informing them that they should skip the Paris summit. He warned that the Marshall Plan was only a cover. The underlying intention of the United States was to build a Western European political bloc that was hostile towards the Soviet Union.

The cold war was now an indisputable reality.

Perhaps it was a coincidence, but the Soviet boycott of the Marshall Plan coincided, almost to the day, with the final act of what, to this point, has been documented of Raoul Wallenberg's fate.

On Monday, July 7, 1947, Deputy Foreign Minister Andrey Vyshinsky looked up the Raoul Wallenberg case in his piles of paper. There may have been many reasons for this. The Swedish ambassador had been making enquiries. One week earlier, the case had been debated in the Swedish parliament for the second time and, just as Vyshinsky had anticipated, this had been accompanied by new Swedish newspaper headlines. In addition, in June the former American commerce secretary Henry Wallace had contacted the Soviet embassy in Washington, D.C. and asked what had happened to Raoul Wallenberg.

The question was again on the table and the Soviet Union would soon have to come up with an answer. Once more, Vyshinsky wrote to Abakumov and asked for the report on Wallenberg. Now there was also an international political dimension to the Raoul Wallenberg case.

Of the documentary traces that have emerged from the Soviet archives, it appears that Abakumov now chose to bring the resolution of the Raoul Wallenberg case directly to Molotov. He did so in a "personal letter" ten days later after he had received the first note. It is a good guess that it was Joseph Stalin himself who in the end sealed Raoul Wallenberg's fate, perhaps in a discussion with Molotov.

Who was the Swede Raoul Wallenberg and what had he been doing in Budapest? The decision regarding his fate did not so much depend on the truth behind the answers to those questions as it did the *appearance* of the truth to Stalin and his henchmen. Fish or fowl? Altruistic aid worker or American spy?

Those who were so inclined and who had heard Raoul Wallenberg's arguments could of course see the resemblance between the new Marshall Plan and the reconstruction programme for Hungary that the imprisoned Swede had been so eager to present to the Russians. That George Marshall surely had never heard of Raoul Wallenberg's plan was of no consequence. The ideas were similar. For any one with a conspiratorial mind (and there was an abundance of these in Stalin's Soviet Union) it would not have been such a stretch of the imagination to think the following: had Raoul Wallenberg's project been in the works from the start? Why was Raoul Wallenberg's fate as much of a priority for the United States as it was for Sweden? And why had the American finance minister suddenly started to ask questions about the fate of the Swede, only days before Marshall's speech at Harvard University?

Not much more than suspicion was required for strange things to happen to people in Stalin's Soviet Union. Not least when Viktor Abakumov was involved.

How would the Raoul Wallenberg case be resolved? It was not so long since Stalin's blood-besmirched security minister Abakumov had been confronted with a similar issue. Then the matter had concerned the American prisoner of war Esau Oggins, who had been sentenced to eight years in a Soviet prison camp in 1939. The Americans had pressed for his release but the Russians had hesitated because Oggins had cooperated with the Soviet security service.

In May 1947, Abakumov had presented his proposal to Molotov and Stalin. His recommendation was that the American be liquidated by lethal injection, but that the Americans should be told that Oggins had died in 1946 from tuberculosis. Abakumov could create a falsified medical report and death certificate that would support the Soviet explanation. These kinds of manipulations were routine for him; heart attack was another commonly fabricated cause of death.

In Stalin's Soviet Union the truth was a relative concept and, therefore, so were lies. Very little was allowed to stand in the way of the overarching collective goal for an ideal communist state. "Truth", in the Stalinist sense, was simply everything that furthered this ambition. If a lie was required to get there, it was excused, or even considered "true" because it was "expedient".

Prisoner Oggins' liberation had not been deemed "expedient", nor was the truth about his fate. In such situations it was not unusual for yet another famous Stalinist saying to be put into action: *nyet cheloveka, nyet problemy,* or, "if there is no person, there is no problem." This usually meant that the prisoner was executed. But not always. Another alternative was to hide the prisoner in the Soviet camp system and erase all traces of their existence.

Oggins met the former fate. "Stalin and Molotov decided to eliminate Oggins and, during a routine medical check-up in the prison in 1947, Mairanovsky poisoned him by injection," Pavel Sudoplatov said in his memoirs. These things sometimes happened in Lubyanka's "Inner Prison". Esau Oggins was not the first to fall victim to Colonel Mairanovsky's poisonous injections. Grigory Mairanovsky was the head of "Laboratory X", which was located practically around the corner from the Lubyanka. He went under the nickname "Doctor Death", and it is not uninteresting to note that, for the majority of his victims, "heart attack" was given as the cause of death.

By mid-July 1947 Raoul Wallenberg had spent four months in cell 7 of the "Inner Prison". Viktor Abakumov would shortly present his proposal regarding the Swedish prisoner.

Maj von Dardel spent the summer caring for her ailing husband, who was struggling to recover from his cancer operation. They were planning a recreational visit to a monastery at Lake Garda. But she did not drop the fight to free her imprisoned son Raoul, who would turn thirty-five in only a couple of weeks.

In June, Maj had written letters to all the Swedish women's associations and had asked them to raise their voices in support of her son's liberation. The chairwoman of the International Association of Women for Peace and Freedom, Birgitta Bellander, took the helm. By mid-July she had coordinated sixteen organisations to sign an appeal for Raoul Wallenberg to Generalissimus Stalin. This meant the signatures of over one million "democratic and anti-Fascist" Swedes, which were turned over to the Soviet embassy in Stockholm.

It was a time of summer holidays and, in Moscow, Ambassador Rolf Sohlman had packed his bags for a trip home. Before his departure he paid a visit to the Soviet Foreign Ministry's Scandinavian division head, Vetrov. Sohlman's preliminary phrases of politeness almost reached Söderblomian proportions. He explained that he did not have "any particularly new" issue to raise. He had not had any mail from home for fourteen days.

Thereafter Sohlman asked if anything new had turned up in the Wallenberg affair. "Absolutely nothing," Vetrov replied, and repeated that the battles around Budapest had been fierce in the latter half of January 1945 and Raoul Wallenberg had probably died in the bombardment. Sohlman had nothing more to add. It was Wednesday, July 16, 1947 and Sweden had still not submitted a single formal demand for the repatriation of Raoul Wallenberg.

Maj von Dardel placed a great deal of hope in the Swedish women's organisations' appeal to Stalin. The author of a forthcoming Hungarian book about Raoul Wallenberg, Jenő Lévais, had recently visited Stockholm and said that it was only when the Hungarian women's associations made demands that Stalin had sent home the Hungarian prisoners of war. She decided to add a personal letter to Stalin that she sent through the Swedish embassy in Moscow. "To Generalissimus Joseph Stalin," Maj began. She explained in brief terms what had happened and when Raoul was last seen alive.

My confidence in the powerful Soviet Union has been so great that, despite my considerable concern, I have been convinced that I will see him again. Since I presume that delays in his return stem from misunderstandings by subordinate authorities, I now turn to the ruler of the Soviet Union with a prayer that my son may be sent back to Sweden and his pining mother. Respectfully. Maj von Dardel.

Unfortunately the holidays complicated matters. When Rolf Sohlman returned in August, Maj's letter to Stalin was still sitting in the piles of paper at the legation in Moscow.

On Thursday, July 17, 1947, something dramatic happened to special prisoner 206, Raoul Wallenberg. But exactly what it was that occurred in the Lubyanka prison that day has not been proven, at least not beyond all reasonable doubt.

Certain details are well known. Viktor Abakumov was working, but Joseph Stalin had left the city the day before for a three-month-long holiday. He was planning to drive around the Soviet Union and meet his people. At the same time, he was wrestling with a new paranoid suspicion. Stalin had started to see a connection between the Marshall Plan, the American ambitions in Europe and the Jewish intelligentsia in the Soviet Union. Didn't the Soviet Jews have unusually strong networks of relatives in the United States? Wasn't it all an American-Zionist conspiracy against the Soviet Union?

Abakumov had, therefore, been assigned the task of gathering evidence against Soviet Jews, in the first place against those in the Stalin-sponsored

Jewish Anti-Fascist Committee. During Stalin's road trip, Abakumov would, among other things, devote himself to torturing Soviet Jews in order to extract the "truth" of the plot. When the Soviet leader returned, the first execution order would be issued. But now, in mid-July, Abakumov also had a report to finish for the Soviet Foreign Ministry.

It is known that an answer regarding Raoul Wallenberg was sent from Abakumov's office to Molotov on July 17, 1947. The letter itself is said to have been lost, but the correspondence is referenced in short handwritten notes on two documents in Soviet archives. It cannot have been a routine report because, in one of the notes, Abakumov's answer is called a "personal letter". It had the title "Regarding the case of the Swedish citizen Wallenberg" and is stamped with the registration number 3044.

One additional document about what happened on July 17, 1947 was presented ten years later in Moscow. This document is called the "Smoltsov Report" and is said to have been created on this exact day. The Smoltsov Report has been put through forensic tests in two different countries without being able to reach 100 per cent certainty as to whether it is a forgery or not. It has not even been established if the report could have been created several years later or not. The letter, with the title "Report", is a handwritten message from the prison physician at the Lubyanka at the time, Colonel A. Smoltsov, to Abakumov.

Smoltsov was only working on a limited basis at the Lubyanka that summer, since he suffered from heart problems. In an interview in the summer of 1992, Smoltsov's son recalled that, despite this, his father had been unexpectedly called to the prison one evening in July 1947. He remembers the event because his father only came back the following day and then told him that a Swede had died in the "Inner Prison".

If the son's memory is right, there is reason to believe that the dating on the prison physician's letter is in fact correct. But that is not to say that everything else that Colonel Smoltsov set down in his beautifully even handwriting on that Thursday can be trusted. Abakumov was not unfamiliar with the practice of eliciting fabricated documents from his medical staff, certificates that matched that day's measure of an "expedient" truth.

So what did Smoltsov write to Abakumov? His report in its entirety read as follows:

I report that tonight the prisoner Walenberg [sic], with whom you are familiar, last night suddenly expired in his cell, most likely as a result of a myocardial infarction [heart attack]. With regard to your instructions personally to supervise Walenberg [sic] I request indication as to whom to entrust the autopsy to establish cause of death.

As a death certificate, Smoltsov's report represented a break with routine, and not only because it took the form of a handwritten letter. It was not standard practice for a subordinate physician to write directly to the minister. Nor was any record of this important prisoner's death made in the prison's registration ledger. The letter also appears not to have been sent. Instead, Smoltsov wrote a new comment at the very bottom, across the document. "Have personally informed the minister. Have been ordered to cremate the corpse without an autopsy. Smoltsov."

It is not possible to say in what form the Soviet "truth" appears in this document. One might possibly, like the Swedish–Russian Working Group on Raoul Wallenberg's disappearance, observe that the odds that a healthy 35-year-old man without a family history of heart disease would suddenly die of a heart attack are something approaching a million to one. One may also observe that the odds of survival in the Moscow blocks where Mairanovsky had his poison laboratory were pretty much the opposite. It is hard to ignore that a fabricated medical report listing "heart attack" as the cause of death was a daily routine in the Lubyanka. They could mask an execution. But they could also be used to erase the traces of a complicated prisoner, one who needed to be hidden from the world but kept alive.

For whatever reason, Stalin and his henchmen had not judged the liberation of Raoul Wallenberg to be useful. They now needed to create a truth about the Swedish prisoner that was both useful and that could be presented to the Swedes.

Deputy Foreign Minister Vyshinsky does not appear to have been informed of any fateful events in the Lubyanka prison on July 17, 1947. After the weekend, he wrote yet another reminder to his colleague, Abakumov, asking him to hurry his answer since the Raoul Wallenberg case had again flared up in Sweden.

On Friday, July 18, the newspaper *Svenska Dagbladet* had published an interesting document, which was said to have been written by Raoul Wallenberg. It was the draft of a presentation on an aid programme for Hungary called "The Wallenberg Institute for Rescue and Reconstruction" and signed "R.W." The Hungarian writer Jenő Lévai had presented these documents during his July visit to Sweden and almost all the newspapers covered it.

The aid operation was presented in the draft as offering assistance to support self-help. It emphasised that no humanitarian effort could be effective without a basis in a financial aid organisation. "R.W." wrote that he hoped for financial backing from Swedish and also international authorities. It was said that this was the plan that Raoul Wallenberg had wanted General Malinovsky to review.

On Tuesday, July 22, Andrey Vyshinsky's reminder was dispatched to the security ministry. That same evening, intense activity broke out at the Lubyanka prison and Lefortovo. It began around 7.00 p.m., according to a planned schedule. In the Lubyanka, the prisoners Ernst Huber and Willy Rödel were brought to an interrogation and, in Lefortovo, there were a number of brief evening interrogations with, among others, Gustav Richter and Raoul's driver in Budapest, Vilmos Langfelder. Everyone who was interrogated on this evening had either shared a cell with Raoul Wallenberg or Vilmos Langfelder.

An interpreter later recalled how a colleague of the interrogator Kartashov had drawn a large diagram detailing which prisoners had shared cells with Raoul Wallenberg. The interpreter who was questioned in the 1990s also said that he was asked to bring a packet of papers and personal documents about Raoul Wallenberg to the head of the M.G.B.'s archives. On the package there had been the note: "Package of materials regarding the arrest of no. 7; may only be opened with the permission of the M.G.B. authorities."

The first to be called in on Tuesday evening was a prisoner who was only referred to by the code "prisoner no. 7" and who was interrogated for twenty minutes before he was joined by Willy Rödel. It appears that this prisoner no. 7 and Willy Rödel were questioned together for five minutes by Kartashov.

Unfortunately Rödel died that same autumn during a transport to a prison camp and has therefore not been able to testify about these interrogations. But some of the prisoners who were questioned that July evening were released many years later and could describe their experiences. The interrogator asked whom they had shared a cell with during their prison stay. "I listed the names and these included Wallenberg. One asked me then to say to whom I had told something about Wallenberg, and what Wallenberg had told me," the German prisoner of war Gustav Richter has recalled.

When the interrogation was ended, after twenty minutes, Richter was placed in an isolation cell for eight months. Other prisoners testified to almost identical treatment – questions about cell mates, follow-up questions about Wallenberg and then an isolation cell for several months.

The next round of interrogations began at 2 a.m. But, that time, only three of the prisoners who had been questioned earlier in the evening were pulled out again. Vilmos Langfelder was one of them. He had been taken to the Lubyanka from Lefortovo prison some time after 10 p.m., when his interrogation there had finished. On the way over, he was accompanied by a cell mate, Sandor Katona, who had also been interrogated that Tuesday evening. A third prisoner was also woken up to be questioned in the middle of the night. He was already in the Lubyanka and had been interrogated there the night before. He was not allowed to write his real name in the interrogation ledger this time either. He was simply called "prisoner number 7."

All three were interrogated by Colonel Kartashov. This indicates that the sessions were considered to be of importance: usually Kartashov's subordinate handled the work. Kartashov could not speak German, so there was also an interpreter in the room. First, prisoner number 7 was led into the interrogation room. Twenty-five minutes later Langfelder joined him and, after another twenty minutes, so did Katona. The three prisoners were interrogated for sixteen hours before they were allowed to leave the room together at 7.30 p.m. on 23 July, 1947. Neither Vilmos Langfelder nor Sandor Katona ever regained his freedom.

Who was "prisoner number 7"? Today, some sixty years later, those responsible for the archives of the Russian security service (F.S.B.) assume that this prisoner number 7 was, "in all likelihood", Raoul Wallenberg, thereby indicating that Wallenberg may not have died on July 17. But they are careful to wrap their statements in a cloud of ambiguity. They are not certain, and no facts have ever been established. "It is at least more true than not true," was the message from the F.S.B. archive in autumn 2011.

*

Protected, missing or dead? Raoul Wallenberg's family felt that there had long been enough evidence to indicate that Raoul Wallenberg was imprisoned in the Soviet Union. This was also what Guy von Dardel wrote in an open letter to American newspapers during the summer: "We have ascertained that Raoul Wallenberg is in prison and has been put to work by the Russians," was his contention. But, when he returned to Sweden again at the beginning of August, he was sharply admonished on a visit to the Foreign Ministry. There was no basis for such a firm conclusion, not in the material that the Foreign Ministry had seen, he was told.

However the adviser at the Foreign Ministry also assured him that the department was energetically pursuing all leads. He asked for more photographs of Raoul and perhaps a description. Guy answered with a letter:

> The following description is from when we saw him last in the summer of 1944: Height 177 cm, brown eyes, dark hair, incipient baldness, a sharply defined chin and lower lip, fairly large nose. My brother had a tendency towards strong facial hair growth, which means it is possible that he has a beard. No particular distinguishing features such as scars etc. Healthy teeth.

Finally Andrey Vyshinsky was given the go-ahead to prepare an answer to Sweden. On August 9 he presented a suggestion to Molotov. They awaited Ambassador Sohlman's return from holiday before Vyshinsky sent over a personal message to the Swedish embassy in the Mindovsky Mansion. The most significant sentence appeared towards the end of the first paragraph: "As the result of a thorough investigation it has been established that Wallenberg is not in the Soviet Union and he is unknown to us."

Vyshinsky blamed the violent battles in Budapest. He could confirm the message from January 1945 stating that Raoul Wallenberg had been encountered, but thereafter there were no traces of him. The officer who had reported on the matter had not been able to be located. There was no Wallenberg in the camps for prisoners of war and internees. "One may only conclude that Wallenberg, in the midst of the battles in the city of Budapest, has either died or been imprisoned by Szálasi's followers," Vyshinsky wrote.

Thus far, there was no trace of Smoltsov's death certificate. It cannot be ruled out that it was fabricated later in the Kremlin's infamously professional falsification workshop. There, decades later, there would have been no problem in taking out paper and ink that could be dated to 1947. But it is also possible that, while the death certificate was genuine, it was viewed as "not expedient" for the moment, and was instead set aside in case it was needed in the future.

After two and a half years, Sweden had finally received an official answer from the Soviet government: Raoul Wallenberg was not in the Soviet Union. As soon as Vyshinsky's note reached Stockholm, a Foreign Ministry official telephoned the family and read the entire text aloud. The von Dardel household was plunged into despondency. This could not be true, not if one put together all of the facts that they had. The answer was so bald. With the writer Rudolph Philipp, the family immediately wrote a public statement in which they listed all the known facts that spoke against the Soviet declaration.

But they were relatively alone in speaking out critically about Vyshinsky's note. On the editorial pages of the Swedish newspapers, the attitude was that the official end of the tragic Raoul Wallenberg case had now been reached. "The note that the Soviet Union's Foreign Ministry dispatched in response to the enquiries about Raoul Wallenberg completely meets the Swedish desire for a clear statement from the Soviet government and is therefore met with appreciation from the Swedish side," as the *Stockholms-Tidningen* paper put it. The dominant feeling was that one had to be grateful, although everyone had wished for a different response.

Almost at once, the spotlight dimmed. When the analyses of the Soviet message were completed, the Raoul Wallenberg case quickly fell off the front pages of the Swedish papers. But the von Dardel family refused to give up hope. They were not just driven by visceral emotions. The family could not comprehend how Vyshinsky's note could be thought to prove that Raoul was dead. Maj and Fredrik von Dardel did not feel that they could drop the matter after such a weak pronouncement. They were supported in this by the women's associations that had organised the petition to Stalin over the summer. At the start of the autumn, they held a meeting and decided to continue the fight for Raoul under the name of the Wallenberg Action. An investigative committee was given the assignment of critically reviewing all known documents in respect of the case, and all evidence that Raoul Wallenberg was in the Soviet Union.

This review was completed by the end of October. The Wallenberg Action drew the conclusion that there was compelling evidence that Raoul Wallenberg had been in the Soviet Union and that he had been alive "at least as recently as a couple of months ago". The results flared in the press for a moment before even they sank into oblivion. The investigation did, however, cause Östen Undén to invite the members of the Wallenberg Action to a meeting.

It turned out to be a stormy encounter. One of the group's members said that he had been struck by a vision as he worked on the investigation. "A man is lying in water, drowning, and by the side of the shore there are a couple of gentlemen in striped, well-pressed trousers, and they do not want to stretch out a hand to help the drowning fellow because they are afraid of getting their clothes wet."

At this, Undén's face became blood red, if the Wallenberg Action's meeting notes are to be believed. He half-stood, yelling loudly, his eyes boring into the dreamer's, who became equally agitated.

"This so-called Wallenberg Action – what is it good for? Only to whip the public into a frenzy of emotion," Undén spat, after he had collected himself somewhat.

"We are not whipping anyone up into a frenzy. We base our cause on facts and evidence. But it certainly wouldn't hurt to see a bit more emotion in this case from your side," the chairwoman of the Wallenberg Action, Birgitta Bellander, said and went on: "We place greater weight on the statements of four trustworthy and well-regarded Swedish citizens, that is to say this committee, than the words of a representative for a dictator state who has every reason in the world to lie his way out of any responsibility."

"Does Mrs Bellander mean to imply that Vyshinsky is lying?" Undén asked.

"Yes, that is exactly what I mean."

"But that's outrageous! Outrageous!"

Donskoy Cemetery, April 2011

It is almost Easter and across the gates to the Donskoy Monastery's domed cathedral someone has hung a yellow banner with a blue text: Christ is risen!

Times have changed. During long periods of the atheistic Stalin epoch the medieval cathedral was used as a factory. In the summer of 1947, the Donskoy Monastery in southern Moscow was also the location of the city's only crematorium. Thousands of victims of Stalin's terror were transported here. The corpses arrived in the night, in trucks driven by M.G.B. officials.

I do not expect any results. The facts that have been presented thus far do not reveal what Abakumov wrote about Raoul Wallenberg in his personal letter to Molotov in July 1947. We do not know if the Swede at that point was dead or "missing". But what if Dr Smoltsov's report was not a lie fabricated at a later date, what if he actually received an order from Abakumov to "cremate the body without an autopsy"?

In that case, it was here, to the Donskoy Monastery's crematorium, that Raoul Wallenberg's body would have been brought that night.

If Smoltsov's notes are correct, the ashes of the Swedish diplomat would probably have come to rest in an anonymous mass grave. The Donskoy cemetery has three such mass graves, all with the inscription, "here lie the ashes of those whose relatives have not been heard from". One could take that view. The reigning Soviet truth was that Raoul Wallenberg had not been seen in the country at all.

The birds are chirping, there is a hint of spring. I walk around for a good while between the rows of high gravestones. Many have portraits engraved on the face. Then I spot an area bordered with high spruce trees. Large, impressive boulders arranged around the statue of a kneeling woman. I have found the right place. Mass grave number three: "To the memory of the victims of the political repressions 1945–1953."

Fresh white and red roses lie strewn in the melting snow. German and

Austrian citizens, Japanese soldiers and members of Stalin's Jewish Anti-Fascist Committee are honoured on the gravestones.

By the entrance I see laminated lists of names. I realise that they represent only a small proportion of the deceased, but I can't help but turn to the Russian letter "В" for Валленберг, Рауль (Wallenberg, Raoul). The pages are damp. My heart beats insistently as I let my finger travel down the line, although I already know the answer. Of course there is no Raoul Wallenberg.

CHAPTER 19

A Swede and a Soviet Wall to Break Down

Per Anger had followed the drama surrounding Raoul Wallenberg at a distance for the first couple of years. Shortly after the end of the war he had been offered the ministerial post in Cairo and had departed with his growing family, and with his belongings packed into a shipping container. It had felt good to leave Sweden again. Per Anger had found it hard to acclimatise to the sheltered environment at the Foreign Ministry in Stockholm after his experiences in wartime Budapest. He harboured many difficult memories, but at home in peaceful Stockholm very few knew what he was talking about.

By the summer of 1945, Per Anger had already become convinced that Raoul Wallenberg was imprisoned in the Soviet Union. But no-one had wanted to listen to him when he launched into his arguments. He had not changed his opinion after returning from Cairo in 1948, so it was with some trepidation that he accepted his new assignment at the Foreign Ministry. "Now you will take over the Raoul Wallenberg case," Sven Grafström declared.

This did not turn out to be an easy task. He was taking over the assignment six months after the Soviet Union's reply of August 1947, which was called "Vyshinsky's note". After this, silence had fallen on the Raoul Wallenberg case. The Foreign Ministry continued following up the leads and traces that streamed in, turning into one blind alley after another. But it was a limited operation. It would be untrue to say that it incited any degree of involvement on the part of the ministry's leadership and in Moscow nothing was done. "One almost had the feeling that Undén wanted to believe Vyshinsky's answer that Wallenberg was not on Russian soil," Per Anger wrote later in his book about Raoul Wallenberg.

Anger's frustration only grew. The picture of what had happened only became murkier. There appeared to be a never ceasing stream of mytho-maniacs who had Raoul Wallenberg on the brain. Strange people reached out and claimed with great conviction to have seen Raoul in Czechoslovakia, Kiev, or dying in southern Poland. And then a Hungarian district court, without the least amount of evidence, confirmed in the late autumn of 1948 that the Swedish diplomat had been murdered by the Nazis in January 1945. It was a big mess.

Per Anger himself was convinced that Vyshinsky was lying. It was in the Soviet Union one should look. With the stubbornness of a mule he tried to persuade the leadership of his doubts, but, after two dismal years as the administrator of the Raoul Wallenberg case, he was now, in the autumn of 1950, close to giving up. From the beginning he had felt a greater solidarity with the doubters in the Wallenberg Action and with Raoul's family, whom he knew privately. Until this point he had advised Maj and Fredrik von Dardel to avoid publicity and to allow the Foreign Ministry to work quietly. But to what end?

Then an opportunity arrived. Late that autumn he was to be allowed to accompany Östen Undén to a meeting of foreign ministers in Norway. Foreign Minister Undén, who had heard from his associates that Anger had strong opinions on the case, invited him into his train compartment and asked him to give his opinion on what had happened to Raoul Wallenberg. Per Anger told everything from the beginning, about Raoul Wallenberg's operation in Budapest and his view of what happened after. Then he made it clear that he believed "fully and completely" that Raoul was still imprisoned in the Soviet Union. He said that Sweden should take a harder line since this was the only language that the Russians understood. Anger reminded him that Switzerland as well as Italy and Denmark had managed to extract imprisoned citizens by exchanges. Perhaps Sweden could also pursue this tactic? "The Swedish government does not engage in such actions," Undén answered.

It was an attitude that Per Anger could not support. In January 1951 the now 37-year-old diplomat went to the head of the political division and resigned from his post.

There were several reasons behind Per Anger's drastic decision. Towards the end of 1950, both Raoul's family and the Wallenberg Action had had enough.

For three years, in order to increase the Foreign Ministry's chances of success, they had refrained from any activity in the media – but to no avail. Now they had no intention of waiting any longer. Now the world deserved to know how poorly the Ministry had handled the case of the missing diplomat, Maj von Dardel's son. They prepared several long articles for the press.

Per Anger decided not to advise them to hold off any longer. He realised that he could not imagine answering on behalf of the Foreign Ministry when the family levied their criticisms. He chose to follow his own convictions.

Maj and Fredrik von Dardel had gone through a few terrible years. After Vyshinsky's note in August 1947 a disquieting silence had fallen, even in their private social sphere. People went out of their way in order not to have contact. When the family continued to maintain that Raoul Wallenberg had been imprisoned in the Soviet Union it was received as an attack on the Swedish establishment. In society circles, the family's protests felt both uncomfortable and dissonant, not the note one wanted at polite gatherings.

There were fewer invitations. Maj and Fredrik von Dardel isolated themselves more and more and dedicated themselves completely to the fight for their son. "Everyone disappeared. We didn't have friends any more," their daughter Nina Lagergren recalls. "People seemed to think that what Raoul had done was unnecessary, that he had only himself to blame since he had put himself in that situation. So Mother and Father had an enormous burden to bear. There is probably no comparison to their pain."

Ever since 1948 the family had tried to do as they were told and keep quiet. At the same time, behind the scenes they had continued to do what they could in order to advance, or at least not fall behind. They felt that it was extremely important to comment on, or to try to erase, any claims that Raoul was dead, so that the claim did not take hold and grow into a truth. They fought against statues and memorials. Sometimes they found unexpected assistance. In April 1949 the first statue to honour Raoul Wallenberg's memory was ready to be unveiled in the Szent István Park in Budapest. But, during the night before the ceremony, the Hungarian Communist Party arranged to have the statue taken away, most likely on orders from Moscow. It was not returned to its original place until 1999.

From time to time the struggle against the declarations of his death took drastic form. For instance, a morally indignant Birgitta Bellander managed, with threats and admonitions, to convince a book publisher to cut a chapter in the translation of the first Hungarian book about Raoul Wallenberg. In it, the author Jenő Lévai had written as if it were an established truth that Raoul Wallenberg had died in Budapest in 1945.

The poor relations between the Foreign Ministry and the Wallenberg Action had, in part, to do with the family and the organisation's claims. Rudolph Philipp, the author who had become a central figure in the fight for Raoul Wallenberg, refused to hand over their evidence. The Foreign Ministry had earlier leaked some sensitive information he had given them regarding names, his sources got into trouble, and he was now unmovable on this point. Witnesses on the other side of the Iron Curtain had to be protected, he maintained.

The Wallenberg Action also felt that the previously existing evidence was more than sufficient to question both the Ministry's and the Soviet Union's actions. To this they added Dekanozov's original "receipt" from January 1945, when the Russians officially declared that they had taken Raoul Wallenberg into custody. They also included Madame Kollontai's message from February 1945 that Raoul was in the Soviet Union. And the latter's information had only grown more convincing. For a long time the family believed that Madame Kollontai had given her message to Maj von Dardel alone, perhaps in a moment of compassion. But, in October 1948, Nina Lagergren had been to a cocktail party in Rome at the residence of the former foreign minister Christian Günther, who was now Sweden's ambassador to Italy. Ingrid Günther had then told her that she had been invited to tea with Madame Kollontai at around the same time that Maj von Dardel had seen her, that is to say February 1945. Mrs Günther revealed to Nina Lagergren that she had been called there because Kollontai had something in particular that she wanted to convey.

The message had been identical to the one that Maj had heard. Kollontai had asked Ingrid Günther to forward to her husband the message that Raoul Wallenberg was currently in the Soviet Union. Madame Kollontai added that the only thing that could harm Wallenberg in this situation was action from the Swedish government. "If you stay calm, perhaps Wallenberg will come back one day," Kollontai told the foreign minister's wife. This news from Rome hit the von Dardel family like a bomb. Suddenly Kollontai's message took on a pronounced official tone. She had, after all, been the Soviet Union's ambassador to Sweden and had conveyed her message to Sweden's foreign minister, even if it was through an intermediary.

Nina Lagergren asked Ingrid Günther to write down this recollection in a letter, which she did, although with some reluctance given the promise of secrecy that she had given Kollontai. But not even this significant piece of evidence convinced the Foreign Ministry officials. They had not found any follow-up to Kollontai's directive in the ministry's archives. "Of course Mrs von Dardel clutches at any straw in order to throw some light on her son's fate," the head of the political department wrote almost apologetically in his letter on the matter to Günther.

Christian Günther replied after a month that he had not given any thought to Kollontai's message since his wife's conversation had not indicated any "new way to gain clarity in the matter". This new piece of evidence was simply added to the case files, and, just as they had agreed, Maj and Fredrik von Dardel kept quiet.

Now, the situation was different. At the start of 1951, the family and the Wallenberg Action broke their silence. Madame Kollontai's message to the foreign minister's wife in February 1945 became front-page news when the Wallenberg Action started their considerable media push in January and February 1951. The magazine *Vecko-Journalen* published a facsimile of Ingrid Günther's letter and at once the debate about Raoul Wallenberg took on new life. It was no longer considered a certainty that Vyshinsky had spoken the truth when he claimed that the Russians had not found any traces of Raoul Wallenberg in the Soviet Union. And what had the Swedish government been doing? Hadn't the foreign minister himself allowed one of the most important pieces of evidence that Raoul was alive to languish?

Rudolph Philipp followed the scoop by an article in the press observing that the Swedish government had not once in these six years formally asked the Soviet Union to return Raoul Wallenberg to Sweden. Some newspapers wrote that they could not believe that this was true. Of course the government must have demanded his return, it would be absurd to think otherwise. Many voiced their support when the Wallenberg committee demanded, in a public statement, that this step should finally be taken.

But, like all media storms, even this one eventually died down and not much changed. No new demands were made to the Soviet Union. In the parliamentary debate that followed, the foreign minister surprisingly made the assurance that, in the preceding years, the Ministry had not in any way been influenced by any of the rumours that Wallenberg was dead. He even went so far as to say that the Ministry worked on the assumption that Raoul Wallenberg could still be alive.

At this point, the foreign minister was interrupted by an angry shout from the gallery: "That is not true!"

One evening in the autumn of 1951, the telephone rang in the von Dardel household. The call was from the wife of a Polish general who lived outside Stockholm. She had sensational news. The general's wife said that she had received a letter from a Polish friend who had been to a cocktail party in Rome (this story's second key cocktail party in Rome). The friend had met an Italian cultural attaché there who had been released in an exchange after six years in a Soviet prison. The name of the cultural attaché was Claudio de Mohr. In the letter, the friend wrote that de Mohr had told her that he had been in the neighbouring cell to Raoul Wallenberg in Lefortovo prison, and that he had been in contact with him by tapping almost every day.

This information stirred up strong feelings in the von Dardel family. Was this really true? Guy von Dardel was given the task of flying to Rome and confronting this unexpected witness. In early December 1952, Raoul Wallenberg's half brother met the dignified 51-year-old diplomat, whose lined face still bore traces of his long prison stay, although over a year had gone by since his release. Guy von Dardel felt an immediate affinity with him. Claudio de Mohr could recount so many details about his brother that what he said had to be true. The Italian promised to come to Stockholm and tell his story if need be, in order to free Raoul. "You do not have to thank me. For me, his return would be the greatest of satisfactions, and it would be the greatest of joys to help bring a smile to a mother's lips," the poetically inclined de Mohr added in his follow-up letter.

But he emphasised the need for discretion. Not a word to anyone and definitely not to the press, he advised. Moscow was not to suspect anything. "I know these people and they are capable of anything," he warned.

A pleased and hopeful Guy returned home. He brought with him two signed witness accounts. De Mohr was the best witness to date, clear proof that Raoul had been held in a Soviet prison. Now, if ever, the Foreign Ministry would surely act.

At the Foreign Ministry, the new year had brought with it a significant staffing change with regard to the Wallenberg case. The newly appointed cabinet secretary Arne S. Lundberg came in with a much more engaged attitude towards the matter and at once the manpower behind the scenes was doubled.

One of the first things that Arne Lundberg did was to appoint a special workforce to approach the Wallenberg case more systematically. Inspector Otto Danielsson of Säpo was brought on board.

Arne Lundberg took the new information from Italy very seriously, even though the von Dardel family allowed it to be conveyed by the volatile and impetuous Rudolph Philipp. Lundberg even agreed to sign a confidentiality agreement. Inspector Otto Danielsson was asked to prepare himself for a trip to Rome in a few days and Lundberg could do nothing but let Philipp accompany him. Claudio de Mohr's instructions regarding the greatest discretion were respected. The trip was undertaken under the radar and not even the Swedish embassy in Rome was fully informed.

But the caution was meaningless, the secrecy already lost. On the same day that they departed, the magazine *Vecko-Journalen* was able to publish a facsimile of "the Italian diplomat's" witness account, although it did not give his name. This attracted a great deal of attention, of course, and Swedish journalists in Rome did not have any trouble tracking down the diplomat, photographing him and revealing his name. Claudio de Mohr was completely taken by surprise. He became distraught at the unexpected revelation that had perhaps ruined the chances of saving Raoul Wallenberg. One wonders what the Italian diplomat would have thought if he had been told that it was one of the inner circle, Rudolph Philipp, who had sold the information to *Vecko-Journalen* before he flew to Rome. "Truly, if he is still alive, Wallenberg has reason to beg God for protection from his friends," a newspaper wrote in the ensuing coverage.

For Raoul Wallenberg's family, Rudolph Philipp's uncontrollable actions were becoming a problem. But what should they do? The Austrian writer was one of the few who had engaged himself in the case of their missing son and brother. And he had been right about so much.

Since October 1951 Sweden had been ruled by a coalition government between the Social Democrats and *Bondeförbundet* (the Farmer's League). Foreign affairs were still directed with a steady hand by Östen Undén, the principled Social Democrat.

Undén had a firm perspective on the world situation. As he saw it, it was primarily the West that bore the responsibility for the worsening relations between the superpowers. It was the expansion-oriented politics of the United States that had forced the Soviet Union to build up its arms and strengthen its grip on Eastern Europe.

Sweden's response was to keep itself outside the conflict. The country was to practise "non-alignment in times of peace, aiming for neutrality in war". This attitude had already been displayed when N.A.T.O. was formed in 1949: the neighbouring countries Denmark and Norway both joined but not Sweden. And, in the ongoing Korean War, Sweden had abstained in the United Nations when the Western Bloc pushed for sanctions against China.

In the past year, Sweden had also actually acted assertively in relation to the Soviet Union. In the autumn of 1951, a non-commissioned officer in the Swedish Navy had been found to be a Soviet spy and had been sentenced to lifetime imprisonment. Would Sweden dare to do more now in the Raoul Wallenberg case?

Otto Danielsson, the police inspector, and the others in Lundberg's special Raoul Wallenberg group had made a clear assessment. More Italian former prisoners had now been questioned. Once all the existing material had been compiled there were now too many witnesses who independently corroborated the information for it to be dismissed. All the facts pointed in one clear direction – Moscow.

Arne Lundberg looked up the von Dardel family. After the group's analysis, he had started to work on a new, tougher démarche to the Soviet Union and he wanted to check with Raoul's next of kin to make sure they were prepared to take the risks that were associated with this tactic. No-one knew how the Russians would react if Sweden took up a case that the Soviet Union had dismissed with such vehemence in 1947. If Wallenberg were alive, perhaps they would hurt him.

The family was prepared to take the risk. They praised Lundberg for bringing such a positive and energetic attitude to the case. This time Lundberg had also unexpectedly managed to get the minister himself to agree with the plan.

Three days later, on February 11, 1952, Foreign Minister Östen Undén quietly summoned the Soviet ambassador Rodionov to the Ministry. The press was not informed about the new Swedish tactics, since part of the strategy was to offer the Russians the possibility of returning Raoul Wallenberg without losing face. Undén approached the matter directly. Armed with the convincing Italian evidence he now had an entirely new power behind his words. Then he handed over his document, in which he explained that there were now several sources that confirmed that, from 1945 onwards, Raoul Wallenberg had "been held in custody in Moscow".

For the first time in seven years the right formulations were in place. There was no more pleading or anxious skirting around the subject. For the first time, Sweden's government put its foot down and presented the Soviet Union with a formal demand to return the imprisoned diplomat Raoul Wallenberg. "I added that I personally had inspected the most important materials and could not doubt their authenticity," Undén wrote in an internal memo afterwards.

Rodionov replied that he would obviously send the message on to the foreign minister in Moscow, but that the Soviet answer from 1947 had been so categorical that he did not think the new Swedish material would alter anything. He found it very hard to imagine that Wallenberg was in a prison or prisoner-of-war camp without their having found him. "He has perhaps been sentenced for some action and placed among regular criminals," the Swedish prime minister suggested.

In Moscow, Joseph Stalin had continued to shuffle the deck. Vyacheslav Molotov had fallen out of favour a few years earlier and been replaced by the man who signed the Soviet note about Raoul Wallenberg in August 1947 – Andrey Vyshinsky. Indirectly Undén's new tactic therefore meant that the Swedish government was questioning the integrity of Soviet Union's serving foreign minister.

Molotov had not completely disappeared from the corridors of power, but he had lost his ministerial post and was no longer invited to Stalin's late dinners at his dacha, where so many important political decisions were made. Stalin had said that he suspected that Molotov was "an American Imperialist agent". A couple of years earlier, Molotov's wife Polina had been arrested during Stalin's wave of terror against Soviet Jewish intellectuals.

It is not known how Andrey Vyshinsky initially reacted to the Swedish demand for repatriation. But, on February 26, 1952, one of his deputy foreign ministers, the young Andrey Gromyko, sent a letter about Raoul Wallenberg to the M.G.B. Gromyko asked if there was reason now to change their answer to the Swedish side about Wallenberg.

Even there, in the Lubyanka, Stalin had made some changes. Viktor Abakumov had been arrested the previous summer, suspected of cooperating with one of the many American-Jewish plots that the paranoid and increasingly sickly dictator saw around him. It was Abakumov's replacement, the new security minister Semion Ignatiev, who had to answer the Foreign Ministry and he did so within a few days. No, the M.G.B. did not feel that "it was useful in any way to alter the character of the answer that the Swedes had been given regarding Wallenberg".

Thereafter Vyshinsky himself took on the question. What should they do? What should they tell the Swedes? Vyshinsky turned directly to Joseph Stalin. In March 1952 he wrote a secret memo to the Generalissimus and gave an account of the new situation. The foreign minister was clearly irritated. Even though he had himself officially explained that Raoul Wallenberg was not on Soviet soil and although a Hungarian court had established that Raoul Wallenberg had been killed by the Nazis, the Swedes now returned and demanded that the Swedish diplomat be sent home. "This is done in view of the material that the Swedish government shall retain control over, which indicates that Wallenberg is in the U.S.S.R." he observed. Vyshinsky mentioned that the Swedes had emphasised that the question was important to them and that a happy outcome would strengthen relations between Sweden and the Soviet Union.

But Vyshinsky did not allow himself to be impressed. In his memo he dismissed the Swedish démarche as a reactionary campaign and wrote that the Foreign Ministry shared the M.G.B.'s view that it was not "useful" to change the Soviet position.

*

In the ever more frosty cold war climate of the early fifties, the Soviet Union saw neutral Sweden as a not inconsequential but relatively unreliable international player. Stalin had recently been heard to say that he saw Sweden "as an enemy if anything were to happen" and, at the Soviet embassy in Stockholm, reports referred to Sweden as a "secret member" of N.A.T.O. Nor had the Russians concealed that they viewed the increasing cooperation between the Scandinavian countries, exemplified by the newly formed Nordic Council, with suspicion. Both Norway and Denmark were of course members of N.A.T.O.

At the same time, the Soviet leaders could not ignore the fact that the existence of a neutral state in such close proximity had become all the more important after the outbreak of the Korean War. At the Foreign Ministry in Moscow there were memos about how they could increase the Soviet social and cultural presence in Sweden. It was regarded as important, both in order to get a better sense of what Swedish cooperation with the West actually looked like, and to get the Swedish general public to realise that it was equally important to manage its relations with the giant to its east.

But, during the spring of 1952 it was another, more negative, Soviet presence that came to characterise Swedish–Soviet relations. A new spy scandal, the so-called Enbom affair, had been exposed at the beginning of the year. Seven Swedes with communist sympathies had, for a period of ten years, handed over information about Swedish defence fortifications to the Soviet embassy in Stockholm. During the summer, six of them were sentenced to prison terms of varying lengths.

Relations between the two countries were therefore already somewhat strained when the new Soviet answer about Raoul Wallenberg finally arrived in the middle of April. It was brief, only a few lines, and it was delivered to Rolf Sohlman in Moscow. The Russians had not allowed themselves to be frightened by the new information from Italian diplomats. In the answer, it was only observed that Vyshinsky's earlier message still held and that the Soviet authorities "do not possess any additional information about Raoul Wallenberg's fate".

But this time Sweden did not intend to back down. The evidence was so compelling that it was impossible to set the case aside. At the Foreign

Ministry, ideas about a tougher approach were already being discussed.

In contrast to the spy affair that dominated the newspapers during the spring, the Wallenberg enquiry was managed at a secure distance from curious journalists.

On Friday, May 23, 1952, Foreign Minister Östen Undén again summoned Rodionov the Soviet ambassador to the Ministry and handed him the new Swedish demand. This time Undén's tone was more insistent than in February. Rodionov was reminded of the obstacle that the attention-grabbing spy stories already presented to Swedish–Soviet relations, and Undén observed that they would only deteriorate "in an unfortunate way" if the Raoul Wallenberg case did not reach "a satisfactory conclusion".

The Swedish government expressed great astonishment at the Russian answer from April. As far as the circumstances around Wallenberg's disappearance in January 1945 were concerned, there could "be absolutely no doubt that he was taken into custody by Soviet authorities". How could the Soviet Union maintain that they did not know anything about him? No, Sweden emphatically repeated its demand that the Soviet Union return the Swedish diplomat that they had patently imprisoned. The least that could be asked was that the Russians take the Swedish enquiries seriously and begin a thorough investigation.

The enquiry had been planned as a tandem attack in both Stockholm and Moscow, in order to underscore its seriousness. On Monday, Sohlman repeated the new Swedish démarche in a meeting in Moscow with Zorin, one of the deputy foreign ministers. The Moscow enquiry triggered, in the Swede's diplomatic formulation, "a three-quarters-of-an-hour-long, in part very animated, conversation." In translation this meant that Zorin flew into a rage and launched a counter-attack. He charged Sweden with destroying Swedish–Soviet relations. There was no end to the accusations. Zorin claimed to know that the Foreign Ministry lay behind the anti-Soviet media campaigns in Sweden. How could it be otherwise when it was clear that facts in relation to the Wallenberg case, which only the Foreign Ministry knew about, had been leaked to the media? And, speaking of the spy affair, Zorin went on, the "Soviet authorities had in their hands complete information regarding a Swedish spy campaign directed against the Soviet Union".

They parted acrimoniously.

*

This counter-attack aside, the new Swedish demands in the Wallenberg case were taken seriously by the Soviet Foreign Ministry. The question was handled at the highest level, again by Andrey Vyshinsky. An official at the Scandinavian division was ordered to go through all of the material and prepare a multi-page edited memo about the Wallenberg case. Then Vyshinsky turned once more to Stalin to delineate the Soviet position in the Raoul Wallenberg question. This was the second time in only a couple of months that the foreign minister bothered the dictator with a discussion about the Swedish diplomat. How would the Soviet Union reply this time?

One can discern from Vyshinsky's actions at this time that he was troubled. Sweden's recurring enquiries about the missing diplomat were, as he saw it, an example of anti-Soviet aggression, nothing else. He made this point in the analysis of the situation that he presented to Stalin on June 10, 1952. The foreign minister repeated that "reactionary Swedish forces in the question of Wallenberg's fate had instigated an extensive campaign of a hostile nature towards the U.S.S.R." He mentioned that even prominent Americans such as the US secretary of commerce Henry Wallace and the Nobel Prize-winner Albert Einstein had become involved in the campaign.

The enraged Vyshinsky had made up his mind. The Soviet Union should ignore the new Swedish document. In his report to Stalin he wrote that the Foreign Ministry did not think it was "useful" to respond to Sweden's new note in any way. Sweden had received the answer that mattered, both in August 1947 and now in April 1952.

Another consequence of the prevailing mood between the two countries occurred only three days later. On the morning of June 13, 1952 an unarmed Swedish military plane, a DC-3, disappeared during a surveillance mission over the Baltic Sea. During the resulting searches another Swedish military plane, a Catalina, was shot down by a Soviet fighter. The crew of the Catalina managed to make an emergency landing and all five onboard survived. None of the eight on the DC-3 were found alive.

A Swedish accident investigation commission established during the summer that a Soviet plane had shot down both of the planes. But the Soviet Union denied all involvement in the disappearance of the DC-3 and would continue to do so until 1991. They defended the incident with the Catalina, however, by arguing that the plane had violated Soviet airspace.

The missing DC-3 was one of the planes that, according to a secret agreement between Sweden and the United States, flew with American surveillance equipment on board. Sweden did not of course mention the secret assignment in the official commentary. It was said that the plane was out for navigation training. The wreckage was not found until 2004.

Foreign Minister Andrey Vyshinsky must have been thoroughly tired of being reminded of the Raoul Wallenberg case. There are several indications that he now decided to proceed in order to silence the Swedes once and for all.

Just like the other Bolsheviks elevated by Stalin, Vyshinsky had the experience of a bloody past. He had been state prosecutor during Stalin's "sham trials" of the thirties, where "the enemies of the revolution" were accused of and sentenced for crimes that everyone present knew they had not committed. "Confession is the queen of evidence," was Vyshinsky's legal motto, and he had become a master of extorting suitable confessions.

Perhaps he could find something in the old toolkit now that diplomatic language no longer seemed sufficient? According to the Hungarian author Mária Ember, it was most likely Vyshinsky who, at this stage, concocted the idea of a trial in Hungary against Wallenberg's "murderer". Mária Ember suggests that Vyshinsky's rationale may have run like this: "A turning point is needed so that the hostile imperialistic environment can no longer knock on our door and ask for a Swedish diplomat. We must prove to the world that the Soviet Union has always spoken the truth about this case."

Towards the end of the summer of 1952, a show trial about the "murder" of the Swedish diplomat Raoul Wallenberg began in Hungary. Raoul Wallenberg's old associate among the Arrow Cross, the police coordinator Pál Szalai, was arrested by the Hungarian security police, the A.V.H., which had ties to Moscow. He was taken to the A.V.H.'s feared "terror house" on the elegant street Andrássy út in Budapest, the same house that the Arrow Cross had used to torture people during the war. According to Ember, who has based her narrative on an interview with Szalai, he was subjected to beatings and death threats in order to "freshen his memory". The Hungarian security police assaulted him and asked him about his contact with the C.I.A. and what he knew about the murder of Raoul Wallenberg.

Exactly what he was to be tortured into remembering was not immediately clear. For a while, the Soviet-led A.V.H. had been planning to accuse the Arrow Cross of Raoul Wallenberg's murder. But, in the end, it was decided to place the blame on several Budapest Jews. This was aligned with the trials against Jews that at this time were being conducted both in the Soviet Union and in Hungary.

Pál Szalai was therefore to be whipped into remembering that one January day in 1945 he had come to the former American embassy in Budapest (then the Swiss legation) and found Raoul Wallenberg's dead body in the cellar. He was tortured into recalling that he had seen two prominent members of the Jewish council in Budapest, Lajos Stöckler and Miksa Domonkos next to Wallenberg's corpse and that they had each been holding a "smoking gun" in their hands.

Preparations for the show trials were completed with the arrests of both Stöckler and Domonkos several months later. They were accused of Raoul Wallenberg's murder and of being American spies. Wallenberg's former colleague, the typewriter specialist Károly Szabó, was also seized by the security service and tortured in order to be used as a witness.

The preparation for the grand trial of Raoul Wallenberg's murderers had been completed when Joseph Stalin died at the beginning of March 1953. After that the trial was postponed and eventually quietly forgotten about.

At home in Stockholm, Maj and Fredrik von Dardel had many other creative accounts of their son's death to combat. But they were unwavering. As long as no concrete evidence for their son's death emerged, the assumption had to be that he was still alive.

The setback after the government's insistent spring efforts in 1952 was difficult for them to cope with. They were pleased that the Foreign Ministry finally, after seven years of doubts, had come to share their belief that Raoul had been imprisoned by the Russians. They could also perhaps find some satisfaction in the fact that Sweden had finally formally asked for their son to be returned. But what did it really matter? To date these efforts had not yielded any results.

There were no alternatives for Maj and Fredrik von Dardel. They had to keep fighting. Fredrik von Dardel was now sixty-seven and, having retired from his position as executive director of the Karolinska hospital, could devote more time to Raoul's case – when he wasn't deep into history books or painting his watercolours.

Maj, who was six years younger, had a hard time letting a day go by without anything being said or done for Raoul. She tried to distract herself by thinking of a steady stream of practical tasks – she sewed things for the entire extended family, made marmalade, reupholstered furniture, made new furniture, climbed ladders and put up shelving. Maj cried often but she did not lose her sense of humour. She could shift abruptly between laughter and tears when the family came together.

In the autumn of 1952, Fredrik von Dardel started a journal. On Friday, October 24 he sat down at his desk in the apartment on Sveavägen and summed up what had happened in his even handwriting.

"Today it is thirty-four years since my and Maj's wedding day. I have every reason to feel grateful for that day and for the companion through life that I then received and whom I hope always to keep," he began. He also wrote about the grief over his stepson's fate as the persistent dark cloud over the family's existence. "The many bitter disappointments that we have experienced during this time have darkened our lives, especially Maj's, and have exacerbated the melancholy to which she is predisposed."

The setback had been painful, but an important aspect of the situation had nonetheless improved for the family. Their struggle was no longer questioned. Several reminders were dispatched from the Foreign Ministry to their Soviet equivalents during the autumn of 1952, although none received a response.

At the same time, rumours could trickle out from Foreign Ministry sources that deeply injured the family. One of the women involved in the Wallenberg Action met several Foreign Ministry officials who claimed that Raoul Wallenberg was deliberately staying away as he did not dare go home out of fear of reprisal for his professional misconduct. After all, Raoul Wallenberg had issued protective passports to Nazis, they claimed.

For the family it was starting to feel as if every step forward was always followed by an equally big step back. One moment it was all so clear, there was evidence and it might sound as if Raoul could be expected home within a couple of weeks. Then time would go by without anything of significance happening. Even the process of speaking with diplomats was tricky to navigate. One had to wait for the right moment, the right people and the right mode of communication. Reminders and enquiries were always being postponed, for one reason or another.

Arne Lundberg was in touch now and again. He would happily announce promising new leads but then remember that something else was needed before he could make anything of it. Sharply worded démarches were always in the pipeline but never seemed to amount to anything of substance. And silence fell again. Not even Joseph Stalin's death in March 1953 appeared to unleash any serious new attempts to get Raoul home.

On repeated occasions the family tried to engage the help of Raoul's influential relatives in the Wallenberg family but without success. Birgitta Bellander in the Wallenberg Action had written several times to Jacob and Marcus Wallenberg and requested a meeting to discuss the campaign for the son of their cousin, Raoul Wallenberg. The lack of involvement of these relatives pained Maj and Fredrik. They could not understand the silence and would carry their disappointment for decades.

Why was the Wallenberg family so glaringly absent from the Raoul Wallenberg campaigns for so many years? According to Marcus Wallenberg's son Peter, the explanation is simple. "We often heard that the family had never done anything. But Maj von Dardel had explicitly asked Jacob and Marcus *not* to do anything since they could risk Raoul's life. That was what my father gave as a reason," Peter Wallenberg later recalled. "It was also the case that Jacob and Marcus had a great deal to do with the government. It's hard to imagine that they would not have been fully briefed. But, as it was an affair of the state, the brothers must have been asked not to talk about it, that it was very sensitive."

Rudolph Philipp was one of the few that the von Dardel family could turn to. Fredrik viewed the situation with some concern. The unpredictable Philipp was making enemies all over the place and they were beginning to understand why. He could call the von Dardels and scream that he had lost his ability to support himself because of them, even though they paid him as well as they could for his efforts. In addition, he had developed the bad habit of calling Foreign Ministry officials in the middle of the night if he felt it was warranted. "Philipp is starting to become a most difficult problem," Fredrik von Dardel noted in his journal.

At the same time he remained their great hope. When the rest of the world turned away from Philipp's excesses, Fredrik and Maj stayed by his side. They chose to see the criticism of the temperamental writer as yet another expression of the Swedish unwillingness to do something for Raoul.

In autumn 1954 the deadlocked situation again looked as if it were about to be resolved. During the summer, Foreign Minister Undén had provoked the von Dardel family by travelling to the Soviet Union "on holiday". But the controversial trip had actually also involved official meetings, including one with the Soviet deputy foreign minister. At that meeting Undén repeated the demand that Raoul Wallenberg be returned, and now he thought he could discern a new response. This time there was no reference to the note from 1947. Instead he was told that the Soviet Union would examine the new material that Sweden claimed to possess.

It seems that even Jacob Wallenberg had secretly started to act on Raoul's behalf. He "believed that he could reach the Russians about this matter by way of businessmen", as the initiative was articulated in an internal report by the security police in 1954. These secret contacts would be managed partly by a Swedish businessman who travelled in Eastern Europe, and partly by a retired major at the Defence Ministry's headquarters. In reports from the security police, it was said that the "Wallenberg family was prepared to make great sacrifices to secure Raoul's retrieval". Maj and Fredrik von Dardel do not appear to have known about any of this. Jacob Wallenberg's initiative remained unsuccessful but it does prove there was a certain degree of willingness to act, even in this part of the family.

During the summer, the Swedish body of evidence had been radically improved. Rudolph Philipp had managed to track down a newly released German prisoner of war, Erhard Hille, who was said by several people to have news of Raoul Wallenberg from Lefortovo prison. Philipp had travelled to Berlin in July and met Hille, who had shared a cell with Raoul's driver, Langfelder, and who therefore knew quite a bit about Raoul. What Hille related fitted well with Claudio de Mohr's witness account. More pieces of the puzzle were falling into place.

Now the Swedish Foreign Ministry reviewed all possible and impossible witness accounts. Six believable witnesses emerged who independently corroborated the theory that Raoul Wallenberg had been locked up in a Soviet prison. It was decided that they should get to work once more and gather all the facts in a new missive to the Russians. It was a grim memo that Rolf Sohlman handed to the Foreign Ministry in Moscow during the autumn of 1954 and it appeared to have an effect. A new letter was dispatched from the Soviet Foreign Ministry to the security ministry, which by now had changed its name to the K.G.B. In the internal correspondence there was no mincing of words. The Foreign Ministry asked the K.G.B. outright to state "where and under what circumstances Raoul Wallenberg had died".

There was some movement behind the scenes in Moscow, but not enough. The communist machinery produced the same old message to the Swedes: no traces of Wallenberg. One can almost hear the deep sigh both in the Foreign Ministry and in the von Dardel home. It does not appear to have mattered how many times Sweden applied pressure, how many facts were laid on the table. Finally it was almost ridiculous.

"What should I believe? I *know* that Wallenberg has been in the Soviet Union for several years," Arne Lundberg said to the Soviet ambassador in Stockholm, Konstantin Rodionov, in March 1955.

"I can only tell you that there are no traces of him," the ambassador replied.

Just like before, the confident official pronouncements were paired with another, more indirect, "answer." Hardly a week after Lundberg's meeting with Rodionov in March, the former Swedish envoy to Budapest, Ivan Danielsson, had received a letter from Count Mikhail Tolstoy-Kutuzov, one of the two Russian interpreters who had worked at the Swedish legation during the autumn of 1944. Tolstoy-Kutuzov had already attracted the suspicion of the Budapest Swedes for his strange behaviour. Now he was living in Dublin and, for some reason, wished to inform the retired Ivan Danielsson of his search for Raoul Wallenberg.

Tolstoy-Kutuzov wrote to Danielsson that he had been searching for Wallenberg for four years only to arrive at the conclusion that he was murdered in January 1945, most likely by the Arrow Cross. It did not take Arne Lundberg many months to gather evidence that Tolstoy-Kutuzov was a Soviet agent, dispatched to silence the Swedes. To Wallenberg's family Lundberg said that he was sure that it was Tolstoy-Kutuzov who had betrayed Raoul.

More than ten years had gone by since Raoul Wallenberg disappeared and the Swedes had never been surer of themselves. The Soviet wall still seemed impossible to move, but the day would come when there were so many witnesses, and the Swedish evidence became so overwhelming, that not even the powerful Soviet Union could hold out any longer.

CHAPTER 20

What Will Do as a Half-Truth?

In the second week of October 1955, huge crowds of expectant relatives thronged the streets of the German city of Friedland. Church bells were ringing and the crowds were cheering as the first buses of German prisoners of war drove up. In total there were 9,000 prisoners who had spent ten years in Soviet prisons. Now they were coming home again. The West German chancellor Konrad Adenauer had managed to persuade the Soviet leadership to set them free in return for normalised relations between the countries.

The relatives were carrying home-made signs with photographs of men in German uniforms and asking questions: "Who knows Lieutenant Heinz Kruger?", "Has anyone seen my son?"

News of the repatriation did not go unnoticed by the Swedish Foreign Ministry. The new man in charge of the Wallenberg case, Gunnar Lorentzon, was sent to Germany as soon as the Foreign Ministry had heard about the expected arrival of the prisoners. He was accompanied by two assistants, one of whom was a policeman. They were going to try to round up all the prisoners who had been in contact with Swedes and question them about Raoul Wallenberg.

It had to be handled quietly. Lorentzon had been issued with a false I.D. as a representative of the Swedish Red Cross, since only Red Cross officials were being allowed into the German prisoners' arrival camp. The Red Cross and the world's media, one might add. In Friedland the Foreign Ministry's team had to contend with much bolder and more enterprising reporters. The Associated Press had fifteen men at the scene and they besieged the buses when they arrived: "Has anyone seen a Swede by the name of Wallenberg?" the reporters yelled. When Ernst Wallenstein got off his bus he answered yes and was immediately taken away by the journalists. Wallenstein had sat in the cell below and to the side of Wallenberg's in Lefortovo prison. He was not let back into the Friedland camp until the news bureau had managed to interview him and cable out the details of his witness account across the world. A Swedish evening paper was also moving about in the crowd and carried several articles in the first few days.

Lorentzon and his two assistants were nonetheless successful in their assignment. After years of stumbling in the footsteps of fantasists, they felt the mists were clearing. As early as the first week, several of Raoul Wallenberg's closest fellow inmates were identified and had time to give important information to the Swedes before their relatives dragged them off. Gustav Richter could relate in haste that he had been Raoul Wallenberg's cell mate in the Lubyanka for a month at the beginning of 1945. Raoul had been in good spirits, Richter told Lorentzon and called his Swedish cell mate a "very funny" person. The German was able to relay that Raoul had been accused of spying.

Lorentzon and his associates also met Bernhard Rensinghoff, who had been on the floor beneath Raoul in Lefortovo prison and had tapped out messages to him and Willy Rödel. Rensinghoff could not at first comprehend the Swedes' questions about Wallenberg. It took a while for him to understand that Wallenberg had not yet returned. He had been convinced that the Swede had already been released.

Two more inmates were interviewed. The Swedish questioners could report back home that Raoul Wallenberg had been accused of spying and that he had heard from the interrogators that the Soviet Union regarded Sweden's passivity in his case as a clear proof that he was guilty.

Maj and Fredrik von Dardel were awakened at home by reporters from the evening papers who vied to trump each other's fantastic stories. The papers were filled with witness accounts that were far from true. At first it was hard for them. "People who had formerly only been glimpsed as shadows in the dismal world of prison now appear in the flesh," Fredrik wrote in his journal. Then hope returned. Now, if ever, there was enough evidence to demand Raoul's return. At the same time it pained them to hear that the lassitude of the Foreign Ministry had apparently complicated his situation.

At a meeting with Östen Undén at the end of October 1955 Maj von Dardel could not hold back her emotions. She explained how poorly she felt she had been treated by the Foreign Ministry over the years and that she now had the right to demand that they did their utmost to free Raoul. "In Germany there were a few who worked and managed to get many to come home. Here in Sweden it appears as if many are now working but they have not managed to get home one person who is in prison," Maj von Dardel said.

Prime Minister Tage Erlander had long been scheduled to make an official visit to Moscow in Easter 1956. It was to be a historic trip, the first ever prime ministerial visit to the Soviet Union. His coalition partner, the leader of the Bondeförbundet, Gunnar Hedlund, was to accompany him. The expectations were that the great breakthrough in the Wallenberg case was imminent.

Erlander and Hedlund were to travel to a Soviet Union that, since the death of Stalin, was in many ways a changed nation. After a power struggle lasting several months in 1953, Nikita Khrushchev had secured the position of First Secretary of the Central Committee of the Communist Party: the Soviet Union's leader. Vyacheslav Molotov had crawled back up on the podium in the days after Stalin's death in March 1953 and was again the foreign minister. He had asked for his birthday that his wife be freed, a request that was granted.

The new leaders had not let the executioners rest. During the three years that had gone by since Stalin's death, several figures central to the Wallenberg case had lost their lives. Abakumov had been executed in December 1954, ironically enough after spending several years as "special prisoner 15" in the Lubyanka prison. His predecessor and rival Beria had been toppled the year before. Beria's subsequent execution was a fate shared by all his closest associates, including former deputy foreign minister Dekanozov.

Even the master of intrigue himself, Andrey Vyshinsky, had died, by all accounts quite unexpectedly. He had been sidelined after Stalin's death and transferred to the United Nations in New York. There he had suddenly died one November morning in 1954, at seventy-one years of age, from "acute disturbances in heart circulation". His wife thought differently. "He has been murdered!" she exclaimed by his dead body. Perhaps she was wrong. In contrast to the others, Vyshinsky was honoured with a state funeral in Moscow with both Molotov and Khrushchev in attendance, though in the Soviet Union this was no guarantee he had died a natural death.

At the time of the Swedish visit in 1956, the new Soviet leader Khrushchev was sixty-two years old. He came from a poor peasant family in the Ukraine, was poorly educated, and had mainly been known as an agricultural expert. Khrushchev made a sympathetic and slightly provincial impression but in this case appearances were deceiving. He compensated for his simple origins and lack of education with an almost manic capacity for work and socialising. At the same time, the warm social signals he sent out could not hide the fact that he had had more than a finger in Stalin's bloody terror. He was a man of many sides. "Quick but not intelligent", was the assessment of the then British ambassador.

The invitation to the Swedish prime minister coincided with both a Soviet and an international thaw. At the end of February 1956 Khrushchev had emphatically distanced himself from the brutal Stalinist period in his historic "secret" speech at the twentieth party congress. For four hours he had shocked the participants by listing and denouncing Stalin's crimes against the people – the torture, terror, mass murders, absolute power and cult of personality. Secret or not, the speech was passed to higher party officials during the spring and read aloud at party meetings across the country.

This turn of events created an extensive mental shift in the Soviet Union. Thousands of political prisoners who had been in camps since the terror years of the thirties started to appear on the streets of Moscow and in other cities. Soon almost all would be released and those who had been executed would be "rehabilitated".

None of this was, of course, known to Tage Erlander as he prepared for his trip to Moscow. But circumstances could not have been better for the most serious effort to date in the Raoul Wallenberg case.

The strong Swedish collection of evidence had been compiled into a report that was going to be presented during the course of the trip. In it there were facts that the Russians would not be able to dismiss. The Swedes now had the numbers for the cells in the Lubyanka and Lefortovo prison where Raoul had been held. They had the names of the interrogators. And they had all the convincing and detailed witness accounts of released German and Austrian prisoners of war. They had even asked two independent justices of the Supreme Court to evaluate the file and had included their state-ments. The justices had both concluded that there "was no doubt that Raoul Wallenberg . . . has been a prisoner in the Soviet Union and that the cited material according to Swedish law is conclusive proof thereof".

Östen Undén had tried to prepare for success by suggesting a suitable line of defence to the Soviet ambassador. The Soviet Union could, for example, blame Wallenberg's arrest on the mass murderer Beria, the foreign minister suggested. "You have yourself condemned Beria's regime. Beria . . . persecuted innocent Soviet citizens. You could confess that he was capable of doing the same to foreigners."

On the Saturday of the week before Erlander's departure, Maj and Fredrik von Dardel met with him. They both felt that Erlander appeared alarmingly ignorant of their son's case but did not mention this.

Maj and Fredrik had prepared a letter to Raoul that they asked Erlander to give to their now 43-year-old son if he were to be set free. The prime minister promised to do so.

Fredrik had written it. It was dated March 24, 1956 and began:

> Our dear, beloved Raoul. After many years of misery and ceaseless longing for you we have now come so far that government leader Prime Minister Erlander and Minister Hedlund are travelling to Moscow to finally see to it that you are allowed to return home. May they succeed and may your suffering now be at an end. We have never given up the hope that we would see you again, although to our great sorrow all our efforts to get in contact with you thus far have failed.

Maj and Fredrik told their missing son of all the efforts that had been made to recover him and about his fellow inmates who had borne witness. They warned him about the reporters who were accompanying the ministers. "We ask that you do not allow them to interview you. You should say that you must first provide a report to the Foreign Ministry and also need to rest and recuperate."

Then they updated him on his siblings Guy and Nina who now both had several children. Guy had recently moved to Switzerland with his family for a position as nuclear physicist at the recently formed nuclear research facility, C.E.R.N.

"There is a room here waiting for you when you return with the prime minister," Maj and Fredrik wrote to Raoul. "You must understand how we have all longed for this day when your suffering and our suffering comes to an end and we may again live together as in former, happy days. Your ever-loving mother and your warmly devoted father."

The Scandinavian Airlines plane chartered by the Swedish government for the trip took off on Holy Thursday. Foreign Minister Molotov and Prime Minister Nikolai Bulganin made up the reception committee at the airport outside Moscow. From the plane it was said that they looked like mushrooms as they stood there side by side in the snow slush, short and stout with their round hats. Incidentally, Bulganin was the man who had prepared the arrest order for Raoul Wallenberg on January 17, 1945.

Negotiations began on Friday shortly before lunch and a young Olof Palme served as secretary in the conference room at the Kremlin. The prime minister took up the Wallenberg case after the initial polite exchanges and explained that the Swedes now had convincing material to present. Bulganin, who can hardly have forgotten his arrest order, immediately adopted a dismissive tone. "We cannot understand why you think it necessary to bring up this question again . . . We have nothing to add."

When Erlander insisted that the Russians needed to inspect the new evidence, Khrushchev took over and gave his view of the state of affairs between the two countries. "Our relations appear very good as long as you do not plan to repeat the attack on Poltava" the Soviet leader declared, cunningly. Khrushchev explained that he too could not understand why the Wallenberg case was always raised. "We have told you everything in complete honesty. Should I, as I once offered in a conversation with Sohlman, in God's name declare that I am speaking the truth? I do not want to hurt your feelings but we have an idea that there may be motives stemming from internal politics behind all this. Internal politics are your business but that is not a reason to place us in this embarrassing position," he said.

Tage Erlander assured him that Sweden did not wish for a new Poltava. But the Wallenberg affair was an irritant in the relations between the two countries that should be possible to clear up. Erlander underscored that Sweden took up the Wallenberg case in order to strengthen, not weaken, relations. And the point they were discussing was, after all, simply a matter of respecting and reviewing the new evidence that the Swedes had brought along.

Finally Khrushchev acquiesced. It was decided that Molotov would take a first look at the new evidence together with Hedlund. "If it could help our relations, I would not hesitate even to commit a theft in order to produce Wallenberg," said the somewhat lively Khrushchev.

At one of the last meetings, there came a final assurance from the Soviet hosts. Bulganin explained to the Swedish prime minister that, if Wallenberg had been in Russian custody, they would have joyfully "presented him on a plate". They knew how eager the Swedes were to recover him.

Tage Erlander did not bring Raoul Wallenberg back home to Maj and Fredrik von Dardel. The only thing Sweden managed to extract was a promise from the Soviet leaders to thoroughly review the Swedish evidence. The Soviet Union had also promised that, if it turned out that Wallenberg was in the country, he could "obviously be allowed to return home".

Even before the Swedish prime minister had left the country, Molotov reported on the new Swedish evidence to the central committee. The party's highest body now gave the K.G.B. two weeks to inspect the new material and propose a response. When the review was completed, the head of the K.G.B., Ivan Serov, asked for a meeting with Molotov. Together, the men wrote a memo to the party's central committee about what they had concluded and how they felt that the Soviet strategy should take shape.

The Swedes were right, Molotov and Serov concluded without any equivocation. They informed the central committee that the witness accounts by the German prisoners of war "coincides more or less with the real circumstances around the arrest and detention of Wallenberg in prison in the U.S.S.R.".

So, after eleven years of deliberate lies, the truth was admitted, once and for all, at least internally.

Molotov and Serov recommended that they should delay in revealing this fact to the Swedes. During the autumn there would be parliamentary elections in Sweden and, in order not to play into the hands of reactionary forces on the right, it was wise to wait. There were several ways of delaying the process. Molotov and Serov had already formed a plan: at the beginning of May, the Soviet embassy in Stockholm would ask the Foreign Ministry to send additional materials in the form of photographs and a description of

Raoul Wallenberg. In this way they could give the impression of an ambitious and exhaustive investigation. During the summer, the embassy in Stockholm could keep the Swedes busy with references to intense interrogations and investigations. Some two, three months after the elections would be a suitable moment to drop the bomb, they felt.

They even wrote a proposal about how the final answer could be expressed. At that time, in April 1956, Molotov and Serov felt that the Soviet Union should blame the executed Abakumov, who had arrested Wallenberg "in conflict with the law". They could write that the Soviet investigation had shown that Raoul died at the prison infirmary in Lefortovo (!) in July 1947 and that his body had been cremated. They could also blame Abakumov for having destroyed all documents about Wallenberg.

The strategy was adopted by the Central Committee and would be followed in large part. It was only the location and explanation of what had happened to Raoul Wallenberg that would be altered. A K.G.B. official who was pulled into the process told the Swedish–Russian working group in the 1990s that in 1956 he was given the task of going through the records from the infirmary of Lefortovo prison, among others. He was to try to find out if Raoul Wallenberg had been suffering from any disease. But the only things he found were incidental, that Raoul had occasionally complained of tooth-ache or a cold. When the officials were asked to come up with a suggested cause of death, they picked "pneumonia." According to another K.G.B. official, the work was now dedicated to fabricating a version for the Swedes that "would do as a half-truth".

The Soviet strategy worked much better than expected. The Swedes swallowed the bait. The family was delighted with the unexpected requests for photographs and a description of Raoul from the Soviet embassy in Stockholm in early May. It appeared serious, a different tone from before. "It was at least the first time that there was a reaction from their side," as Guy von Dardel wrote to his parents in a letter from Switzerland.

The Swedish parliamentary elections in 1956 were a huge success for the Swedish Conservative Party. The Social Democrats suffered their first defeat since 1946, but managed to hold on to power thanks to the coalition with Bondeförbundet (the Farmer's League, later the Centre Party). This meant, from a Soviet perspective, that the threat of a "reactionary" shift in power was neutralised. And that meant in turn that it was time for Moscow to deliver the final answer about Raoul Wallenberg.

In October a fresh proposal was presented to the Central Committee. Now the idea was to blame the difficulties in finding Raoul Wallenberg on his having been imprisoned under another name. According to the new version, Abakumov had also deliberately withheld the truth from the Foreign Ministry. The idea was to write to the Swedes that it was only now, after the investigation, that the Russians knew that Raoul Wallenberg had been held in Lefortovo prison and that he had died. Suddenly there was also a date of death, July 17, 1947. The proposal was rejected. "This is not a sufficient answer," the foreign minister noted by hand on the memo.

New drafts of an answer were prepared. According to a K.G.B. source who was later interviewed, the Soviet leaders had trouble deciding how the message should be articulated. The Russians did not know how much the Swedes knew. They even tried to use informal contacts to find out how the Swedish side wanted to have the answer prepared.

But, in January 1957, a framework for the "half-truth" they were looking for was put in place. For the first time in official Russian circles, the death certificate for Raoul Wallenberg, signed by the Lubyanka's chief physician Smoltsov, was mentioned.

The Soviet Union built their entire answer on this single handwritten piece of paper.

The telegram from the embassy in Moscow arrived at the Foreign Ministry on Wednesday morning, February 6, 1957. Rolf Sohlman was hastily being summoned to see Andrey Gromyko, the new foreign minister, at 3 p.m. No reason was given.

At the appointed time, Rolf Sohlman went to the Soviet Foreign Ministry, which had been moved from its location by the Lubyanka to one of Moscow's seven new "Stalin-scrapers". It was as he thought. Gromyko wanted to hand him the Soviet answer with regard to Raoul Wallenberg.

The investigations had been extremely exhaustive, Gromyko assured the Swedish ambassador. "We have combed through a very large number of archival documents."

The Soviet message was brief and only took two typewritten pages. It stated that the Soviet authorities had now reviewed all the prison registers as well as interrogated a large number of individuals without any facts emerging to indicate Raoul Wallenberg's presence in the Soviet Union. None of those who had been questioned had heard of him.

There was a single exception, the Russians claimed in their answer. At certain institutions they had widened the search to include all existing archives, not only the prison registers. In the Lubyanka prison's infirmary quarters they had then found a handwritten letter about Raoul Wallenberg. It was addressed to the former security minister Abakumov and signed by the Lubyanka prison head physician, Smoltsov. The letter was the only existing trace of the Swede, the Soviets claimed.

Sohlman was never shown Smoltsov's handwritten death certificate in the original. The Russians cited it in its entirety and the Swedish ambassador was satisfied. He returned to the embassy and only an hour later he sent a translation of what would be called "Gromyko's memorandum" to Stockholm.

It was shattering reading, even for seasoned Foreign Ministry veterans. The Soviet leaders had drawn the conclusion that Raoul Wallenberg had died of a heart attack in July 1947. They held the notoriously brutal Viktor Abakumov responsible for the fact that Wallenberg had been imprisoned and for the fact that incorrect information had been transmitted all these years. And they added that Abakumov had been executed by firing squad for all his crimes a couple of years earlier. Sohlman also included the concluding excuse in his translation: "The Soviet government extends its sincere condolences over what has transpired and expresses its deepest sympathy to the Swedish government as well as to Raoul Wallenberg's relatives."

Fredrik and Maj von Dardel were not informed until the next day. They were summoned to the Foreign Ministry, where Östen Undén gave them each a copy of the Soviet response. They read these and shook their heads. Surely no-one believed any of this?

As they saw it, the Russians had made things easy for themselves. They had only produced a single document. And it was suspiciously well matched to the Swedish collection of evidence, which currently did not extend beyond

1947. Fredrik and Maj asked if Undén himself believed this answer and came to understand that he did.

"The death certificate corroborates our own evidence," he stated contentedly, if one is to believe Fredrik von Dardel's journal entry. "And the Russians have no reason not to send Raoul home if he is still alive."

It was with the deepest misgivings that Raoul Wallenberg's parents received the Foreign Ministry's assurance that Sweden, despite this, was not planning to close the Raoul Wallenberg case, that they would continue to demand further information. Maj muttered something about Sweden not yet being "a satellite state" and Östen Undén appeared offended. "He said that he had another meeting, after which I left without shaking the bastard's hand", Fredrik noted in his journal.

When the foreign minister thereafter informed Gustaf VI Adolf, Undén noticed that the king appeared "almost relieved by the answer. He had never believed that W. was alive." Prime Minister Tage Erlander's immediate reaction was similar: "Disappointing but nonetheless acceptable," he wrote in his journal about the news. "Strange that our senses can be so deeply affected by his fate. We have experienced so many tragedies and so many other examples of how brute force has felt itself able to take down an individual." Most Swedish newspapers also accepted the confirmation of his death. Pages were filled with lengthy descriptions in honour of Raoul Wallenberg's actions and comments such as "the long period of waiting dissolves into a moment of pain".

The outgoing cabinet secretary Arne S. Lundberg, the man who six years earlier had energised the Swedish investigations, was not as convinced that the final word had been said. In an analysis titled "Peculiarities in the Russian Answer", he aired his suspicions that the so-called Smoltsov report was fabricated. The handwritten paper that had apparently been found by accident contained exactly what the Soviet side needed in order to placate the Swedes. "It is a remarkable coincidence, that a single piece of evidence should be so conclusive," Lundberg observed critically. And was it really credible that the Soviet investigators had not managed to uncover any other documents and not a single witness who had known Wallenberg, although he had clearly been imprisoned in that country for two and a half years?

Maybe the most likely answer is that Raoul is dead, Lundberg said. But one should also not dismiss the idea that the Russians may have produced the answer because they had lost him or because he was in very poor condition.

Some of Arne Lundberg's doubts found their way into the official Swedish reaction to the Soviet Union a week or so later: "The Swedish government find it difficult to believe that all other documentation regarding Wallenberg's time in Soviet prisons . . . would be completely obliterated."

Shortly thereafter, the Foreign Ministry published a white paper consisting of the most important documents and witness accounts from the now twelve-year history of the Raoul Wallenberg case. A child could list all of the central questions that had been left unanswered in the Soviet note. Concern in the Kremlin for a new wave of Swedish anti-Sovietism was not unwarranted. Regardless of the perception of the death confirmation, almost all the significant voices in Swedish life displayed a growing contempt for the Soviet Union and the country's horrifying treatment of a Swedish diplomat and war hero.

On the other side of the Atlantic, the C.I.A. was following the Swedish developments in the Wallenberg case with interest. Since 1951, the C.I.A.'s Stockholm office had had a relatively good insight into the Foreign Ministry's investigation of Raoul Wallenberg. They had their network of well-placed, attentive agents who, under code names, reported back on what was happening in the search for the Swedish diplomat. In C.I.A. language they were called T.I.E.B.A.R.S. and were made up of "staff at the Swedish defence agency", according to reports that were later made public.

Most commonly these agents were found in close proximity to the so-called T-office, which was the name of the Swedish defence agency's secret intelligence service at this time. But the definition of a T.I.E.B.A.R. was wider than this. One of the C.I.A.'s regular Swedish informants in the Wallenberg questions, "T.I.E.B.A.R./20", was said in telegrams to work for the Foreign Ministry on the Wallenberg case. He had been one of those who had spent several months in Germany during the autumn of 1955 in order to interview prisoners of war, and was plainly part of the Ministry's inner circles.

In December 1956, this agent had met with the C.I.A. in a safe house in Stockholm. There the Swede had said that he believed he had evidence indicating Wallenberg was alive as late as 1949. The agent had been well informed on the current internal Foreign Ministry discussions and was, on this occasion, fairly chatty. T.I.E.B.A.R./20 condemned the Swedish ambassador Sohlman and called him pro-Soviet – he went on to mention Foreign Ministry rumours that Sohlman was going to be kicked upstairs to the United Nations in New York. He also revealed that the Swedish government was soon planning to publish its white paper on the case.

It was not surprising that the Raoul Wallenberg case interested the C.I.A. At this time the C.I.A.'s Stockholm representatives had noted the Soviet approaches to Sweden with anxiety. Increasing numbers of Swedish–Soviet cultural exchanges had been arranged, more official visits and several important meetings. These approaches seemed to be part of Khrushchev's plan to create a Soviet-friendly neutral zone between the Eastern and Western Blocs. The C.I.A.'s Stockholm representatives were given the assignment of countering this, to strengthen the anti-Soviet sentiments that existed and to "awaken the Swedish public to the true nature of the Soviet threat and create public opposition to the Soviet Union exploiting Sweden for its own cause".

Gromyko had played into the hands of the American intelligence agents with his murky memorandum.

The day after the news of the Swedish answer, the C.I.A.'s headquarters in Washington received a telegram about the Raoul Wallenberg case from their western European station in Germany. The Wallenberg story should now be "maximally exploited" in the service of fanning the flames of anti-Sovietism, it said. The Soviet Union should not be allowed to get away with the ridiculous explanation that everything was Abakumov's fault.

The head of the C.I.A.'s western European operations suggested a plan of action in order to maximise anti-Soviet reactions, above all in Sweden. In the first phase, plan A, the C.I.A. contacts within "SHUBA–100" (code name for anti-communist exiled Russians) would pressure the "Swedes" and remind them of the insulting attitude the Soviets had taken towards Sweden in the Raoul Wallenberg case since 1945. "The Swedes" must be persuaded that the illegal and inhumane treatment of Wallenberg should change the Swedish position towards the Soviet Union. If "the Swedes" did not buy this line, they would move on to plan B. In that case, the C.I.A.'s partner SHUBA–100 would find other ways to ridicule Sweden for its incomprehensible action "in light of the Wallenberg case". As a third option, media in other Western countries should be persuaded to draw attention to the story.

The press was an important tool in the C.I.A.'s work of fuelling anti-Soviet feelings in countries such as Sweden. This kind of influence was undertaken within the framework of the C.I.A.'s "psychological and paramilitary operations". Shortly before Christmas 1956 the C.I.A.'s representatives in Stockholm reported on a promising new source that could be useful in this area. An anonymous Swedish journalist had been recruited to "plant news" of an anti-Soviet nature in the Swedish media. According to the report, Raoul Wallenberg was one of the topics that the enthusiastic journalist was going to cover.

The identity of the journalist is still secret. All we know is that it was most likely not Rudolph Philipp. He needed no pressure from the C.I.A. to explode in the media over Gromyko's memorandum. And not only there. The day after the Soviet message, he called Prime Minister Erlander and informed him that he was in possession of compromising documents that concerned the Foreign Ministry's man in charge of the Wallenberg case. They would be made public unless an investigating committee for the Wallenberg case was appointed. "Blackmail, in other words", a troubled Erlander noted in his journal.

A few weeks later Philipp solidified this threat during a visit to the man in question, Arne Lundberg. He said that he had for many years been recording their telephone conversations onto gramophone records that were stored abroad. "Everyone makes mistakes," Philipp observed maliciously.

In this way the choleric Austrian managed to lose the trust of one of the few in the circle around Undén who was applying pressure to continue the fight in the Raoul Wallenberg case.

One cannot rule out the possibility that Philipp's collision with Arne Lundberg that day came to affect the continuation of the case. The day after his threats against Lundberg, on February 26, 1957, Östen Undén presented his final assessment on the Wallenberg case to the Foreign Relations Council. The head of the C.I.A.'s European operations was disappointed by what he heard. Sweden was not planning to change its attitude towards the Soviet Union, despite its humiliating treatment. The Americans' Plan A was already dead in the water by the end of February.

To begin with, Undén stated that the Soviet message meant that Raoul Wallenberg was dead. If anything new were to emerge that indicated something else, one would have to take it up at that time, he said. "But in my opinion we have no reason to keep up a continuing quarrel with the Soviet Union once we have said our piece about where the responsibility lies. We ourselves bear a responsibility to develop our relationship with the Soviets. It is one of our most important foreign relations tasks to retain or build up a friendly relationship with the Soviets to the extent that this is possible without sacrificing our essential values. We should not create the impression that the Swedish nation is prepared to regard the Soviet Union as a hostile power," said Undén, according to the written accounts of the meeting.

In other words, the foreign minister was back where he started.

Beside the Lubyanka, April 2011

We are to meet at 11 a.m in the reading room of the F.S.B. archives. Vasily Khristoforov is the head of the archives for the Russian intelligence service and he knows that I am interested in original documents about Raoul Wallenberg. It has been known for a long time that the Soviet government lied in their answer in February 1957. Even then, the Smoltsov report was not the only written record regarding Raoul Wallenberg in the Soviet archives.

It is with a feeling of expectation that I cross Lubyanka Square and take a left immediately after the old K.G.B. prison, the F.S.B.'s main office. The reading room is on Kuznetsky Most, a few metres from the building where the Soviet Foreign Ministry was located in the 1940s. The words, "The Russian Federal Security Service. Citizens received around the clock," are on a door that I walk past.

The door to the reading room has a spy hole and is padded on the inside. At the wooden tables there are a handful of curious individuals, leafing through files they have requested. Vasily Khristoforov greets me and shows me into a bare office where someone has set out teacups and a dish with chocolates. But no documents. Khristoforov says that if I submit a special request I will be shown some of the originals the next time I come back.

"You will not be allowed to handle them yourself but we will show them to you," he says, and his gaze is velvety soft.

We sit across from each other. Khristoforov explains that the problem with the Wallenberg case is that his personal file is missing. There should have been a collected dossier for him in the F.S.B. archive, replete with his prisoner identification card, the arrest order, interrogation reports, prosecution, sentence and, potentially, a death certificate. This was obligatory protocol for each prisoner in the well-documented Gulag.

"It is not the case that we haven't located it or that it has been destroyed. It never existed. Because if it had existed and had been destroyed we would have found an account to this effect in the registration ledger," Khristoforov says.

"As a result, he is a very rare case, I would say an exception. Raoul Wallenberg was never indicted and there was never a trial. His case did not exist. For other prisoners there is almost always an indictment. It can be more or less well grounded, but it exists."

Khristoforov tells me that the documents regarding Raoul Wallenberg that have been discovered have been spread around several files and different archives. They have not only found the Smoltsov report, but also his prisoner card as well as interrogation and prison ledgers with a notation of Raoul Wallenberg's name. In several cases the name has been crossed out, which is also a very unusual measure.

"It is still a mystery to me why the Soviet Union concealed information about him for so long," he says.

"Where was the Smoltsov report found?" I ask and Khristoforov remains silent for a moment.

"Among the archival documents," he replies in a monotone.

Rolf Sohlman never asked to see the original of the prison doctor's handwritten report from February 1957. There was no forensic examination of the historical document until the early 1990s. Today we know that Smoltsov used the Stalin era's almost square "Writing Paper No. 1". He neatly wrote out the main text with a fountain pen and used an ink based on the colour methyl violet. The additional note about Abakumov ordering a cremation was written with a somewhat thicker dark-blue pen. The paper, ink and pen were common in the 1940s, but could have been used much later in the Communist Party's well-equipped forgery studio.

Two independent handwriting analyses – one Russian and one Swedish – have, however, led to the conclusion that both of the texts on the Smoltsov report were probably written by the same person. A comparison with Dr Smoltsov's handwritten C.V. also speaks for the fact that he was the author in question, in which case the report cannot have been fabricated as late as 1957. Smoltsov died in 1953.

But was he writing the truth? In the past few years, the F.S.B. archive has publicly indicated doubts on the matter. The doubts concern "prisoner no. 7" who, according to the Lubyanka's prison registers, was interrogated on July 22 and 23, 1947, several days after Raoul Wallenberg's supposed death. In a much-publicised letter to the Wallenberg researchers Susanne Berger and Vadim

Birstein in 2009, the F.S.B. archive wrote that prisoner no. 7 "in great likelihood can only refer to Raoul Wallenberg".

"But we have not been able to prove this," Khristoforov says emphatically and I have the impression that he would like to retract this piece of information.

"So when and how do you believe that Raoul Wallenberg died?" I ask.

"We have the official version, the one that is expressed in the Smoltsov report," Khristoforov replies.

"You mean that he died of a heart attack on 17 July, 1947?"

"Yes, at least for now."

CHAPTER 21

The Duel of the Professors

On Monday, January 30, 1961, Nanna Svartz, professor of medicine, asked for an urgent meeting with Prime Minister Tage Erlander. It was not unusual for them to see each other. Nanna Svartz had, for several decades, been one of Sweden's most respected physicians and researchers. Celebrities flocked to her. It was widely known that she had been called to the sickbed of King Gustaf V and that she had been handpicked when the legendary Soviet ambassador Madame Kollontai needed medical attention. Now she had been the Swedish prime minister's personal physician during his entire fifteen-year span of service.

Erlander, who was prone to hypochondria, had seen her twice during the past month. Professor Svartz had tried to address the stomach upset that he had struggled with since his holiday in Tunisia over the New Year. But when they last saw each other, she had proclaimed him healthy. This time it was about Raoul Wallenberg.

Nanna Svartz was seventy years old, but still lived for her work just as she had done for her entire career. Over the years she had held six leadership positions at the Karolinska Hospital and worked fourteen hours a day, six days a week. She was described as a determined and "spiritually broad-shouldered" woman. She referred to herself as a workaholic, not without some pride and satisfaction.

Professor Svartz had just returned from a rheumatism conference in Moscow. This was nothing unusual. Her research on rheumatism was world-renowned. If Nanna Svartz was invited to an international medical congress it was not as a regular participant but as a member of the executive committee or in order to give a paper. This year in Moscow was no different.

But it was not a conference-related development that brought Nanna

Svartz to request a meeting with the prime minister. It was a conversation with her colleague Alexander Myasnikov. Professor Myasnikov also belonged to an international research elite, in part through Nanna Svartz's generous introductions. He had been one of the doctors at Stalin's deathbed and, as far as Nanna Svartz knew, also had the current Soviet leader Nikita Khruschev as a patient.

Alexander Myasnikov and Nanna Svartz knew each other well. In his memoirs, Myasnikov describes his Swedish colleague as a "cultivated individual" and a "substantial woman". He said that she loved art and architecture and that at a visit to his home she had admired the mahogany furniture he had that was made in the time of Peter the Great. The two professors would speak German with each other when they met and often the conversation flowed without any problem. During the medical congress, Myasnikov had given a speech in honour of his Swedish colleague.

On Friday, January 27, Nanna Svartz had visited Professor Myasnikov's research institute in Moscow. They had then ended up sitting for a while in Myasnikov's office. After they had finished their usual conversation, about conferences and research, Nanna Svartz decided to take a chance and ask about Raoul Wallenberg. It was not a sudden impulse. Early on she had resolved to employ her Moscow visit for this purpose and she had obtained the Swedish government's white paper from 1957 before she left. Nanna Svartz apologised for bringing up a non-medical question, but explained that what she now wanted to talk about was very important to her and other Swedes. Then she told him about the Raoul Wallenberg case and asked her Soviet colleague if he knew about it.

Professor Myasnikov nodded.

"I asked him then if he could give me any advice about how I could go about gaining some clarity regarding Wallenberg's whereabouts," Nanna Svartz later wrote in her report to the Swedish government. She told him that Sweden had information indicating that Wallenberg had still been alive at least a couple of years before. Then she asked if Myasnikov could make enquiries.

He then said that he knew the case and that the person I asked about was "in a very poor condition". "Would you like to meet him?" I answered that this was perhaps not so important, that the main thing would be to find a way to bring him back home regardless of his condition. Professor M. then said in a very low voice: "He is in a mental institution."

At this point in the conversation, Professor Myasnikov had stood up and gone to fetch a colleague, a Professor Danishevsky, and left him with Nanna Svartz. Danishevsky sat down across from her, asked her where Raoul Wallenberg had served and asked her to write down his name. Professor Svartz wrote "Attaché Raoul Wallenberg" in "large, clear letters" on a piece of paper. She said that the diplomat's mother was one of her patients and that she needed "peace and to have full knowledge". "Even if her son is sick it would be a blessing for her and the rest of Sweden if he could be nursed in his home country", she went on, according to her own account.

They continued to talk. Nanna Svartz mentioned that she was acquainted with Semyonov, the Soviet Union's acting foreign minister, who had been stationed in Sweden. Danishevsky recommended that she try to get in touch with him. Before they concluded, she asked Danishevsky if he thought that she, as the Wallenberg family's doctor, could be allowed to bring Raoul to Sweden. "If he is still alive, this should not be impossible," he had replied.

From the hotel room, Nanna Svartz called Semyonov's secretary. Unfortunately he was abroad, she was told. During the congress banquet that same evening, Danishevsky looked her up and asked how it had gone. Reluctantly he agreed to her instead writing a letter to Semyonov in which she mentioned that she had spoken with Danishevsky and Myasnikov. Danishevsky said that the two of them had discussed the matter and arrived at the conclusion that, if Raoul Wallenberg was alive, any resulting move to Sweden would have to be arranged by diplomats.

Nanna Svartz was shaken by what she had heard. It appeared that Raoul Wallenberg was still alive, confined to a mental institution. She felt she should stay behind and sort everything out, but her plane ticket was already booked for Saturday and impossible to change. She also realised that the new information she had was of such an extraordinary nature that Tage Erlander should be informed. She told her Soviet colleagues that she would be back again in only a few days.

*

Immediately after lunch on Monday, Erlander summoned Östen Undén. Nanna Svartz had demanded a quick meeting and indicated that she had sensational new facts regarding the Raoul Wallenberg case. "The greatest surprise that I have experienced in my entire political career occurred today at 14.00," the prime minister wrote in his journal that evening. "Nanna was apparently as shocked as we were, so she did not accept the offer to meet Wallenberg."

Tage Erlander was overwhelmed as well as convinced. Wallenberg was alive, although in poor condition, and apparently in a mental hospital. Even the normally unshakeable Undén was stunned. "Sensational," he observed as he summed up the day in his black notebook. Erlander was puzzled by the Russians. Why hadn't Khrushchev chosen the simplest path and cleared up this strange affair? Now they had to take complicated detours instead. Next, "Nanna will write to Semyonov and try to get him to arrange that Nanna be allowed to accompany Wallenberg home under another name", he wrote in his journal.

With the new information from Nanna Svartz, the Raoul Wallenberg case again acquired top priority, but under the greatest secrecy. Meetings were held daily. Tage Erlander wanted to make a new official enquiry into the case but Nanna Svartz opposed it. She first wanted to write to her colleague and meet with him again, since this was a matter of confidences shared between physicians. A worried Erlander reasoned with himself in his journal: "Wallenberg's condition may be so serious that even a day's delay may mean death. If Nanna's professor is acting on orders from the Russian government, a careful management may be misunderstood from their side. Under this assumption, the Russians know that we now know, that Wallenberg is alive."

That weekend, Ambassador Sohlman was called back to Stockholm for the deliberations. Even he was convinced that Myasnikov had lowered his guard and that the new information about Raoul Wallenberg was true. In the inner circle, the mood was almost feverish. A letter to Nikita Khrushchev from Tage Erlander was composed but, out of consideration for Nanna Svartz, it was set aside.

Tage Erlander was becoming more and more impatient. When two weeks had gone by without Nanna Svartz hearing from her colleague, he wrote about his anguish in his journal. "I again underlined that no consideration for Nanna can prevent us from springing into action. However highly I value the friendship with Nanna, we now find ourselves in a situation where our duty to Wallenberg and the country takes precedence. An unfortunate situation, but Undén was in complete agreement."

On February 17, a worried Tage Erlander went to see Professor Svartz and told her his new view of the situation. "Every day that goes by means a closed door for Wallenberg," he argued. Nanna Svartz was sympathetic but mentioned the risks associated with a formal Swedish démarche to Khrushchev. She warned Erlander that this could have the undesirable result that her medical colleagues would be forced to manage the situation by saying that Nanna had misunderstood everything.

Out of consideration for Nanna Svartz, the government waited for another week. Then Erlander gave the go-ahead and, on February 25, 1961, Sohlman delivered Erlander's letter to Nikita Khrushchev in the Kremlin. Unfortunately the timing was less than ideal. The Swedish enquiry arrived at about the same time as Erlander received a furious letter from Khrushchev via the embassy in Stockholm. Khrushchev's letter was about the ongoing crisis in the Congo and Dag Hammarskjöld, the United Nations secretary-general. The Soviet Union had long protested about both Hammarskjöld and the presence of U.N. troops in the Congo. Now their displeasure had escalated to something approaching disgust. In mid-February, Congo's former prime minister, Patrice Lumumba, had been assassinated and an irritated Soviet U.N. ambassador then held Hammarskjöld responsible for the killing.

The world situation was, in the Swedish prime minister's own words, terrible.

This was strongly impressed upon Rolf Sohlman during the Saturday meeting with Nikita Khrushchev. As the Soviet leader opened the envelope he asked Sohlman about its contents. The answer, "Raoul Wallenberg", caused him to set it to one side, unread. Irritated, Khrushchev explained that if Sweden was taking up that subject again he might as well ask why King Karl XII had attacked Peter the Great. A neutral country such as Sweden should not enter into the cold war in this way. "Sweden is now chiming in with the most reactionary choir," Khrushchev thundered and asked Sohlman not to bother him any more with such questions.

Tage Erlander had expressed himself in a gracious manner in the letter to Khrushchev. He calmly informed the Soviet leader about Professor Nanna Svartz's visit to Moscow and her new information that Raoul Wallenberg was in a mental institution. He did not mention any names, but wrote that Svartz had received this information from "an internationally renowned representative of the Soviet medical community". Erlander concluded by bringing up the question of the transportation arrangements:

> Foreign Minister Undén and I have discussed the most reasonable way to bring Wallenberg back to Sweden. We have arrived at the conclusion that it would be best if a Swedish physician could immediately travel to Moscow and help determine, with Soviet colleagues, the best mode of transport, medical care etc.

Like the prime minister, Fredrik and Maj von Dardel were patients of Nanna Svartz. They had interacted frequently during Fredrik's time as director of the Karolinska Hospital and Svartz even had a painting by Fredrik on the wall in her surgery. But the professor was bound to silence. She could not tell Raoul's parents anything of the significant news she brought home with her from Moscow, although they had asked her before the trip if she could possibly enquire about their son. At the height of the ensuing drama, on Friday, February 10, Raoul's mother and stepfather had met Tage Erlander. The prime minister also did not mention what was going on. Both Maj and Fredrik noticed that Erlander was more welcoming and open than normal, but they assumed that this was because Undén was not present.

The von Dardels' meeting with the prime minister was about a letter too. But it was only one in a succession of meetings about a promised but not yet dispatched letter to the Soviet Union. They had carried on like this for almost two years. Maj and Fredrik called it Erlander's "politics of postponement". New witnesses continued to stream in and Maj and Fredrik wanted to use them to pressure the Russians. But they had the decided impression that the Foreign Ministry preferred to doubt and thereby disregard all new witnesses: because it was easier.

Fredrik von Dardel felt the government was getting off much too lightly. After Gromyko's memo in February 1957, things had only gained any kind of momentum on a single occasion. In the autumn of 1958, a few liberated war prisoners had said that Raoul Wallenberg had been seen in a prison in the Soviet city of Vladimir. The government had sent a new official Swedish démarche to the Soviet Union and a Wallenberg campaign had flared up in the newspapers. But the only thing to come out of all this was that a fuming Khrushchev cancelled his planned visit to Sweden in 1959.

Since then, the family had not heard anything except these endless litanies about consideration for the global situation and the emotional state of the Russians. "Under a well-meaning exterior, Erlander is slippery as an eel and twists himself both physically and figuratively," Fredrik von Dardel wrote in his journal. Finally, he lost his patience:

These lazy and cowardly gentlemen in the Foreign Ministry weigh each word that is written with anxious expressions as if it matters how you articulate your wishes to a Khrushchev who screams and shouts, bangs his fist on the table and even takes off his shoe and bangs it on the rostrum when he appears at the United Nations. And if the letter – as the intention has been – is delivered under Sohlman's officious equivocations surely very little notice will be taken of it.

He wrote the latter at the end of 1960. Only a few months later, everything had changed. After Nanna Svartz's astonishing news at the end of January 1961, Erlander's politics of postponement was a thing of the past and the prime minister was filled to bursting with anticipation, concern and excitement. But of this, Maj and Fredrik von Dardel heard nothing.

It was not until the end of March 1961 that Professor Nanna Svartz could finally return to Moscow and follow up this very promising lead. During this time, her colleague, Professor Myasnikov, had been approached by the K.G.B. Or, as he put it in his memoirs, "I suddenly receive a telephone call from the 'special agency': 'What did Mrs. Svartz discuss with you in your office?'"

Myasnikov still agreed to meet with Nanna Svartz when she returned. The professor now had another colleague with him, as a chaperone of sorts. Nanna Svartz noticed that Myasnikov was nervous. This time he denied that he knew anything about Raoul Wallenberg. But Nanna Svartz still picked up the thread from January and asked if she could meet with the Swedish prisoner this time. Myasnikov replied evasively that this would have to be determined at a higher level, in the event that Wallenberg was not dead.

Once they had spent some time together, he began to relax. Myasnikov was angry, as it turned out. He was outraged that Nanna Svartz had broken her, as he put it, "collegial duty of discretion". He said that he had spoken with Semyonov about the case and been told about the Swedish enquiry.

"I cannot do any more and I cannot speak with Khrushchev, who is furious. And in any case I do not know where W[allenberg] is. Maybe he is dead," Myasnikov said, according to the summary of the conversation that Nanna Svartz wrote down the following day.

"Then he must have died recently since you said in January that he was in a mental institution and you asked me if I wanted to see him," Nanna Svartz said.

"Did I say that? It must have been a misunderstanding due to my poor German. I don't know anything about W[allenberg]."

"I find that hard to believe after our conversation in January, when you knew the case well and mentioned that W[allenberg] was mentally ill."

"I said 'vielleicht' [maybe]. Here you were, a highly esteemed colleague and we had a private conversation. It it very inappropriate of you not to have treated this conversation confidentially. There should not have been a letter to Khrushchev. It makes matters more difficult and, as I said, he was deeply offended."

Myasnikov emphasised that, in future, they should limit their conversations to questions of science, not politics.

"This is not politics, this is humanism," Nanna Svartz then replied, according to the Soviet professor's recollections of the conversation.

Afterwards Myasnikov received signals from higher up that additional meetings with Professor Svartz were not recommended. Nanna Svartz soon discovered that he was no longer reachable through the usual channels. Semyonov, who is claimed to have wanted to meet with her, was also unavailable. After ten days, Svartz gave up and went home to celebrate Easter.

There was no reaction from Moscow to Erlander's letter about the travel arrangements for Raoul Wallenberg. Through informal contacts Sohlman understood that the letter had arrived and that the Russians were wondering about the real political motive for the new Swedish demands. And what was the matter with Professor Svartz? Was she schizophrenic?

At the end of April 1961 there was suddenly a telegram from Nikita Khrushchev. Tage Erlander's heart skipped a beat until he had it translated and realised that the Soviet leader was only thanking him for the Swedish congratulations for Yuri Gagarin's space flight.

Maj and Fredrik von Dardel continued to apply pressure, ignorant of the drama that had been played out over the past months. Their son's case was relevant again for other reasons. Raoul Wallenberg had gained attention when the trial of Adolf Eichmann began in Jerusalem in April 1961. In his presentation of the case, the prosecutor called the Swedish diplomat "a man of sterling qualities". Swedish newspapers picked this up and proudly related his description of how the Swede Wallenberg had been a thorn in Eichmann's side, how he, at risk of losing his own life, undertook operations that saved the lives of thousands of Hungarian Jews.

The situation became increasingly difficult. After deliberations with his closest confidants, it was decided that Erlander should hint to the family about what had transpired. But only hint. The prime minister was to say to Maj and Fredrik von Dardel that he had earlier that year received interesting information and that he had already sent a letter to Khrushchev. He was to express regret that he could not share the details with them owing to the risk that all would be lost, and he was to ask them not to tell anyone about this.

Maj and Fredrik got the astonishing news in a letter and did not know what to think. The fact that information was being withheld from them was unpleasant. Again and again they tried to find out more and at regular intervals some small clue trickled out, as if to keep them engaged. It became a drawn-out and almost humiliating guessing game. In December 1961 they were told in great secrecy that the new lead was so important that Ambassador Sohlman had been summoned back home several times and that the matter related to Raoul having been alive in a Soviet prison as recently as a year ago. Half a year later they were told that Sohlman had said that they "had never stood so close to the mark as now" and that it was really only about locating exactly where Raoul was. During the summer of 1963 they met with Sohlman himself who, in confidence, shared with them that, at the start of 1961, Raoul was not in prison but rather had been receiving good "physical and medical" care. But when they asked if this meant that he was in a hospital they received only evasive answers.

In September 1962, the "national treasure" Östen Undén stepped down for health reasons. As the family saw it, this meant that a large government obstacle had been removed from the management of their son's case. But their hopes for more involvement in the Wallenberg affair were dashed when the previously so assured Erlander suddenly began to sound uncertain again.

It was like trying to read in darkness. They understood nothing. What were they to believe? What should they do?

In the summer of 1964, it was hoped that the blunder of 1959 could be repaired. Nikita Khrushchev had again been invited for a state visit to Sweden, which would be the first such visit by a Soviet leader. Nothing could go wrong: a second cancelled visit would be a diplomatic catastrophe.

And yet the preparations amounted to political warfare. At the centre, not surprisingly, was the unanswered question about Raoul Wallenberg and – in the best of all worlds – the form his repatriation should take. Prime Minister Erlander and his associates still felt that Nanna Svartz's information had the ring of authenticity. They were provoked by the fact that the Soviet Union had ignored the new lead for three years. Now or never, they thought.

The months before Khrushchev's Swedish trip were difficult for the Swedish diplomats in Moscow. "Why do you want to jeopardise relations between the Soviet Union and Sweden by bringing up the Wallenberg case again? What other motives lie behind this?" officials at the Foreign Ministry snidely asked outgoing Ambassador Rolf Sohlman at his final diplomatic engagements. His successor, Gunnar Jarring, heard the same mantra. The head of the Scandinavian division also reminded them that Nikita Khrushchev himself had lost a son in the war and that they did not even know where he was buried. The parties only appeared to agree on one thing: the only significant problem in Swedish–Soviet relations for the moment was the Raoul Wallenberg case.

In March, Gromyko, the foreign minister, came to Stockholm as part of the planning process for Khrushchev's five-day visit. Erlander took the occasion to emphasise that Sweden had not given up and that he was going to give the Raoul Wallenberg case the highest priority during the coming discussions with Khrushchev. "We have nothing to add," Gromyko sighed. "We have had a war and do not know what has happened to your citizen. There are millions who have died in this war. Apart from the facts that you have earlier received there are no traces of, or information about, him."

To judge from these preliminary encounters it was going to be difficult to avoid an unfortunate confrontation during the historic visit. It was probably the reason that Nanna Svartz received an unexpected letter from her colleague in Moscow at the end of April. Strangely enough he wrote in Russian this time, as if to ensure that there would be no misunderstandings. It almost appeared dictated:

> I write to you in connection with newly emerged statements in Stockholm regarding Wallenberg's fate. In these I was referred to as having provided you with information about him during your visit ... As you surely remember, I said at the time that I know nothing about Mr Wallenberg, have never heard his name and do not have the slightest idea if he is alive or not.

Myasnikov wrote that it had all been a misunderstanding and that he was not Khrushchev's physician since the Soviet leader, "as everyone knows", was completely healthy.

Nikita Khrushchev and his wife Nina arrived at Skeppsbron quay in Stockholm. Three thousand Swedish police were on hand in the town and Prime Minister Tage Erlander was at the quay to greet the couple. "Minister President! As you for the first time step onto Swedish soil I bid you a hearty welcome to our country," a deferential prime minister said after a gun salute.

It was claimed that the newly concluded trial of the Soviet spy Stig Wennerström had been hurried along in order to avoid unnecessary irritation for the guests. The only blot on the first day from a Soviet perspective were the headlines in Russian that the newspaper *Expressen* had plastered all over Stockholm: "Where is Raoul Wallenberg?" The newspaper had published a series of articles about Raoul Wallenberg leading up to Khrushchev's visit and now followed up with a front-page editorial, written both in Swedish and Russian.

> We see you step ashore on our soil. We see your associates accompany you. But the one who we would most like to see we do not; our countryman who has been swallowed up by your land. You come empty-handed to us, regardless of the gifts in your baggage. You come all too alone, despite the fifty-man entourage. Read here who you should have had with you in order to be truly welcome: Raoul Wallenberg.

Maj von Dardel had earlier been in touch with the Foreign Ministry and asked to meet with Khrushchev at some point during the five days, but she had been turned down. This rejection was an additional challenge for her in an already difficult situation. Raoul's now seventy-year-old mother had slipped in January and fallen so badly that she had broken her left thigh and left arm. She had been treated in a hospital for several months and was not yet fully recovered. It turned out that she had osteoporosis: she suffered from the pain all year.

From their vantage point, Maj and Fredrik observed the successful Soviet visit, which Fredrik called a "clownish charm offensive" in his journal. It stung to see how Nikita Khrushchev won the hearts of the Swedish people, how he – as Fredrik put it – was "constantly surrounded by a large police escort to protect his valuable life. Every day there have been opulent luncheons and dinners and long speeches that give Khrushchev the opportunity to present coarse witticisms that are received with encouraging laughter."

The analysis was not exaggerated. The Swedish media almost seemed to have fallen in love with this Soviet leader, who appeared so down-to-earth, human and jovial and who cheerfully took an oar in the prime minister's rowing boat at his residence in Harpsund. Even Tage Erlander appeared enlivened by the visit.

But behind the scenes the tone was harsh and unrelenting. Tage Erlander had brought up Raoul Wallenberg at their very private first meeting and Khrushchev had blown up, "something akin to a temper tantrum". Perhaps he should just go home? It was an attack on his honour not to believe him.

Should he have to be held accountable for everything that happened during the Stalin years, Khrushchev had asked in agitation, according to Erlander's report to the rest of the government.

This tension continued for the course of the entire visit, at a safe distance from the charmed Swedish journalists. There were abrupt changes. "A successful Harpsund evening was followed by a grim day as we have to face the Wallenberg question. Perhaps this is what will fell us?" Tage Erlander wrote in his journal as the week was almost at an end.

The government was called to a crisis meeting.

Both Erlander and Olof Palme wanted to take a hard line against the Soviet Union. If the Russians did not agree to investigate the Wallenberg case, the Swedes should boycott the expected joint communiqué, according to Erlander and Palme. But Torsten Nilsson, who had succeeded Östen Undén at the Foreign Ministry, convinced the rest of the ministers to take a more cautious approach. To refuse to endorse the communiqué was tantamount to a diplomatic declaration of war and one that Sweden could not afford, Nilsson said. Perhaps the Svartz affair was a misunderstanding?

Erlander and Palme gave way. The government preferred a "watered-down communiqué" accompanied by a sharply worded statement regarding the lack of results in the Wallenberg case. But Tage Erlander explained to the rest of the government that it did not mean that his attitude had changed. He said that he was "firmly with Nanna" and that he still believed in her information.

Thus Nikita Khrushchev, despite the confrontation, was able to travel home in what appeared to be nothing but blazing Swedish sun. At a lunch speech at Gothenburg City Hall, he was applauded as he made an allusion to Karl XII's war against Peter the Great. Peals of laughter had erupted after Khrushchev's comment, but it was perhaps not his sense of humour that inspired the Soviet leader to bring up the battle at Poltava that day: "As a guest in your country I therefore bring this question to a head and I ask Prime Minister Erlander: Do you wish to wage war on the Soviet Union or not, Mr Prime Minister?"

One year later, in July 1965, a final effort was made to attain definitive clarity regarding what had actually been said by the two eminent professors on that January day in 1961. By then Khrushchev was gone, accused of having replaced a Stalin cult with a Khrushchev cult, and deposed in favour of a less impulsive and rather lacklustre party bureaucrat, Leonid Brezhnev.

Nanna Svartz and Alexander Myasnikov met again in the same office, reluctantly brought together by the Swedish ambassador Gunnar Jarring. Misunderstanding or not, this time everything should be sorted out and the conversation transcribed in its entirety. The two stubborn professors went at it for one hour and forty-five minutes, like boxers in the tenth round. They got nowhere. Neither was able to let down their guard and admit a mistake. Neither had a strong enough argument for a knockout.

Nanna Svartz did not yield an inch: Myasnikov had told her that Wallenberg lived, but that he was in poor condition and in a mental institution. Myasnikov claimed that she had missed the qualifying statement. He had been speculating and told her that *if* Wallenberg lived *perhaps* he would be in poor condition and in a mental institution. They had reached the end of the road. To Tage Erlander it was clear that the next step had to be that the failed Nanna Svartz lead was made public. The government decided to publish a new white paper during the autumn with the most central documents that had emerged over the past few years.

For several years, Maj and Fredrik von Dardel had badgered Erlander to tell them more about his groundbreaking new lead. But, although all those involved understood the explosive power in the news about the Nanna Svartz lead, Maj and Fredrik von Dardel heard nothing until a few hours before Erlander's press conference.

Tage Erlander blamed a cold and let Olof Palme drop the bomb on Raoul's parents. They were taken completely by surprise. They understood at once why Nanna Svartz had been less present in their life over the past few years. Palme explained that the government had seriously examined Nanna Svartz's information and followed it to the end but without getting anywhere. Now the new lead would be added to the documents. The Raoul Wallenberg case would always be kept open but, after this, it would take "something substantially new" for them to take up the subject with the Russians again.

Afterwards Maj and Fredrik looked up Nanna Svartz, who confirmed everything. Fredrik von Dardel contains his emotions in his journal but, as their daughter Nina Lagergren recalls, her parents were upset at the government's withholding of information, but also positively surprised. Nanna Svartz had, after all, tried to do something. That was more than could be said about many others.

The newspapers ran dramatic headlines. Nanna Svartz was the name of the day. But although the medical professor insisted that she had not been mistaken, there was a sense of finality in many of the commentaries. This was also evident at the foreign relations committee meeting several weeks later. There the former foreign minister Östen Undén made a speech: "Never has so much effort and so much money been devoted to the search for a Swedish citizen in a foreign country. This should not be lamented. But, in the end, we must not forget that a nation's means to search for their citizens in a foreign country are limited. We cannot force our way to relevant material. We cannot call in witnesses from the Soviet Union. And, in the long run, we cannot afford to allow an unresolved case to interfere with our future relations with the Soviet Union. The Wallenberg case is ready to be closed," Undén said.

But Maj and Fredrik von Dardel had appealed to Olof Palme not to let the government make any statement that could be interpreted to mean that the Wallenberg case would be closed. Their appeal was heard. In practical terms, the Wallenberg case was nonetheless, from this point on, set aside from the political priorities.

A silence heavier than ever before descended upon the retired couple Maj and Fredrik von Dardel's life and their struggles. So many hopes, so many disappointments. And yet this was not the last. In November, Nanna Svartz told Fredrik von Dardel in confidence that her main source, the eminent Professor Myasnikov, had abruptly died of a "shock to the heart" at sixty-six years of age.

A couple of months later, the Swedish historian Hans Villius and his wife Elsa published a book about Raoul Wallenberg. In an attempt to get to the bottom of the story, they brought into question all the witnesses after the summer of 1947 and argued that Smoltsov's death certificate was authentic. Raoul Wallenberg had probably died in the Soviet Union in July of that year, they claimed. Tage Erlander criticised their conclusions but, to the von Dardels, it appeared as if the Swedish political apparatus now assumed that the Villius couple were right. In the coming years, Raoul Wallenberg's family would feel very alone in their struggle.

*

The world was changing rapidly. The remaining years of the sixties would encompass the Prague Spring, the student revolts of May 1968, the Vietnam War, Tage Erlander's resignation and the arrival of Prime Minister Olof Palme. But for Maj and Fredrik von Dardel, who now lived in an apartment in Djursholm outside Stockholm, it was as if life stood still. The twenty-fifth anniversary of their son's disappearance came and went. Soon it was thirty years since Raoul had vanished and still most of their existence centred around him. They wrote their daily letters and made their daily calls. New leads appeared regularly and people claiming to have witness accounts came and went, sat down on their sofa and demanded time and energy. One fantastic story after another was conscientiously taken down in the increasingly shaky hand of Fredrik von Dardel. The couple were starting to have trouble with their eyesight but no aches and pains in the world could stop them from listening energetically, as if every new story were the key to finding the solution.

Monastyrka, Tyumen, Suzdal and Zavidovo – in the end there were countless prison camps where Raoul Wallenberg had been seen either in forced labour or wasting away in a hospital bed. The witness accounts were also starting to take on mystical dimensions. One missionary had a vision in a dream and wrote to the von Dardels that Raoul Wallenberg was living in Jerusalem under the assumed name Sven Gustafsson. A woman told them how she had met Raoul in the spirit world, how he had sent a greeting saying that he had been freed from his body and was now at peace. Raoul's parents declined her offer of a follow-up séance. "We do not want to compromise Raoul's case with any fantasies," a despondent Fredrik von Dardel wrote in his journal. At last the family lost count of all the harrowing disappointments.

The world became radicalised and Sweden was no exception. On the streets of Stockholm, leftist protesters wearing Palestinian scarves became ever more assertive. In the 1968 elections, the Social Democrats took more than 50 per cent of the votes after an agitated campaign against the Swedish commercial banks and their directors. The Wallenberg-owned Stockholms Enskilda Bank was the central target and the lustre of Raoul's family name dimmed as the anti-capitalist chorus grew louder.

Raoul's brother Guy von Dardel had become a professor in Lund and moved home from Switzerland with his wife Matilda and his daughters Marie and Louise. Guy had intentionally shielded his children from the raw details of his brother's story. Now they learned about their relative through the partisan views of the Swedish left wing. "Raoul Wallenberg, can't you hear from the name that he is a capitalist and bourgeois? He doesn't deserve a second thought."

Marie and Louise von Dardel thought that it was unfair. Their grandmother Maj was hardly swimming in money. For them, Maj was a fighter who walked with a stick, a grandmother who broke her bones constantly, counted each krona and sewed doll's clothes that she sold at the N.K. department store; who could be funny and tough, and only a second later fall into a black hole of despair and tears. It was with pain that the grandchildren saw how socially isolated Maj and Fredrik had become. In Sweden, no-one was interested in hearing about Raoul any longer, not without moralising over Maj and Fredrik's efforts. "But don't you understand that he is dead?"

Later, during the seventies, Louise von Dardel summoned her courage. One day when Maj was again weeping, Louise asked her grandmother why she carried on when things were so hopeless. Maj answered that she could not stop hoping but that she also felt she had a responsibility to other mothers who were searching for their children. "You know, one can't accept the fact that a person just disappears."

The family was not aware of it, but there was actually one other person in Sweden who had trouble forgetting about Raoul Wallenberg's fate. An aged and frail Staffan Söderblom was living out his days in an apartment in Uppsala, considerably affected by mental illness. His diplomatic career had come to an abrupt end in the early 1950s, only a couple of years after the postings to Moscow and Bern. Six months into a sojourn in Mao's China, the then 51-year-old had suffered a nervous collapse, been forced to return home and declared incapacitated. His anxiety was so severe that he later underwent a lobotomy.

Now he was more than seventy years old, weak and emotionally remote. Relatives who visited him could find him sitting with an empty gaze, mumbling the same mantra: "Wallenberg, Wallenberg".

Later this period would be called "the quiet years" of the Wallenberg case. After the drama of Nanna Svartz's testimony, Swedish officials stepped hard on the brakes. The Soviet Union would not be troubled by a single official

Swedish word about Raoul Wallenberg for fourteen years.

After the Nanna Svartz affair, something significantly new would have to have emerged for the government to threaten Swedish–Soviet relations with any official statements about Raoul Wallenberg. In the early seventies, the foreign minister at the time happened to claim publicly that the government had "shelved" the case, though there was still an official at the Foreign Ministry's "eastern bureau" who formally counted the Raoul Wallenberg case among his assignments. For long periods nothing happened, punctuated by bursts of excitement, which quickly fizzled out: Raoul Wallenberg had been spotted in a prison camp on Wrangel Island in the Arctic Ocean. A credible source with contacts in the Eastern Bloc claimed to be conveying a proposal for an exchange between Wallenberg and the Soviet spy Stig Wennerström.

The documentation about Raoul Wallenberg now filled 20,000 pages and was stored in two large tightly guarded steel cases at the Foreign Ministry. Not even the family could request any of the contents. To officials there, Raoul Wallenberg belonged to the most secret of secret issues. It was not a case to be gossiped about with colleagues during coffee breaks. The case both did and did not exist, the leads were both there and not there.

Several times the family was advised to look beyond Sweden's borders in order to move forward. Maj had also written a letter to Henry Kissinger to say she wondered if he "could do something to cast new light on my son's fate". Her hopes cannot have been great. She had written the year before also without getting any reply.

Relations between Sweden and the United States had not completely recovered after Christmas 1972, when Olof Palme compared the U.S. bombings of Hanoi with the Nazis' mass murders at Treblinka and the massacre in Babi Yar. It was known that Henry Kissinger, who himself had fled the Nazis with his family, had been particularly offended and that it was he who, in Nixon's absence, had recalled the American ambassador from Sweden. This time Maj von Dardel received an answer from the United States stating that there was nothing Kissinger could do.

But there were other threads that could be tugged upon. During 1974, the Soviet writer Alexander Solzhenitsyn was forced into exile. In December of that same year he travelled to Sweden to receive the Nobel Prize in Literature that he had been given in 1970. Maj von Dardel had earlier been in touch with the Nobel Foundation and asked for a meeting with Solzhenitsyn. After all, the author had been taken to the Lubyanka prison in the same month as Raoul and could perhaps help them.

Unfortunately Maj von Dardel lay ill with pneumonia. But Alexander Solzhenitsyn chose to set off for the von Dardel home in Djursholm on the day after the Nobel Prize ceremony. It was, according to Fredrik von Dardel's journal, "an imposing, almost biblical figure", who strode into the apartment.

Solzhenitsyn said that the Soviet Union had many places where they could hide their prisoners and that it was very possible that Raoul Wallenberg was alive. His suggestion to the family was that they should try to awaken global interest in the question. Maj and Fredrik could, for example, write an open letter to the international Jewish organisations that worked to free imprisoned Jews in the Soviet Union. They could then send the letter to the English newspaper *The Times*, Solzhenitsyn went on. Before he left, he hugged the feverish Maj and told her that he wished she would live long enough to see her son.

Maj and Fredrik did as he said. They turned both to the *New York Times* and *Neue Zürcher Zeitung*. But, outside Sweden, hardly anyone knew who Raoul Wallenberg was. The letter never took hold in the world media in the way that Solzhenitsyn had inspired them to hope.

Maj von Dardel felt despair. "The last words that his young father said to me on his death bed was, 'Take good care of our son.' Although he [Raoul] was not yet born, his dying father sensed that the child was a boy. I have failed!" she wrote in a letter at this time.

But things were about to change.

CHAPTER 22

The Making of an American Hero

The transformation in the profile of Raoul Wallenberg's case at the end of the seventies could, on the surface, be described as a matter of chance. Suddenly the wind simply gathered strength. Suddenly everything fell into place. And in one fell swoop the hitherto internationally unknown Raoul Wallenberg turned from an individual Swedish family's tragedy to a world-renowned missing hero. Fate finally played into the hands of the battered family. The Swedish diplomat at last received his well-deserved international recognition and avoided by a hair's breadth the fate of being relegated in history to simply an irritant in Swedish–Soviet relations.

Now came the laudatory speeches, the monuments and honorary awards. Now came the books and films, the heroic epics that, in many cases, were written by foreign authors, primarily American. In the early eighties, Raoul Wallenberg was made an honorary American citizen, the first to be so recognised since Winston Churchill. Canada and Israel followed suit and schools, streets and squares in many countries were named after Raoul Wallenberg before even Stockholm got its own Raoul Wallenberg Square in 1987. The first postage stamp with Raoul Wallenberg's picture was not Swedish but Israeli.

It was as if the world wanted to take over where Sweden had failed. Lost in their diplomatic labyrinths, the Swedish politicians had missed the most important thing – to tell the world and the new generation of Swedes about Raoul Wallenberg's admirable efforts for the Hungarian Jews in the final phase of the Second World War. Most of those who attended Swedish schools in the seventies probably knew that Raoul Wallenberg was a Swedish diplomat who went missing, but they had very limited knowledge of what he had actually accomplished in Budapest. For them his name was often associated with a certain political fatigue, reflected in the tired comments of the adults: "Oh for heaven's sake, not Raoul Wallenberg again."

The international interest became a significant alarm clock for an embarrassingly sleepy Swedish public. Things did not stop with the public honours. It seemed that the world also wanted to take over responsibility for solving the mystery. Suddenly Raoul Wallenberg's case landed on the desk of the American president. The Soviet Union would once again be sternly questioned about the missing Swede, but now by American politicians in tandem with an impressive international public campaign, whose clear epicentre was in the United States.

What emerged was not purely a game of chance.

Raoul Wallenberg had become the object of a covert psychological C.I.A. operation, directed mainly against European media, but also consisting of hidden attempts to steer the Swedish government's foreign policy agenda. A parallel grassroots campaign to awaken the American public's interest in the Swede was also set in motion.

In hindsight it is easy to see that all the commotion on the political scene was not simply driven by a desire to help the despairing Swedish family. This did not matter so much as long as the strong new engine was pulling the case in the right direction. Yet, during the course of the journey, there were inevitable painful moments, when it became clear that global politics and maternal love were not the same thing.

But to understand all of this we have to go back to the beginning. What was it that actually happened?

It was not only contempt for the Swedish prime minister Olof Palme's stance on Vietnam that made Henry Kissinger dismiss Maj von Dardel's cry for help in 1974. Kissinger was a thoroughly results-oriented politician. He was the one who lay behind the de-ideologised American foreign policy under Richard Nixon. According to Kissinger's doctrine it was more important for the United States to come to an agreement about disarmament with the Soviet Union or to begin a dialogue with China, than for the nation to articulate its abhorrence of human rights abuses in communist countries. It was no coincidence that the Soviet leader Leonid Brezhnev was the only foreign dignitary to, up until the very last moment, express his unreserved support for Richard Nixon during the Watergate scandal of 1974.

The question of the missing Swedish diplomat Wallenberg sat uneasily with the Kissinger-influenced de-escalation politics pursued under Presidents Nixon and Ford. After his departure from office, Kissinger explained his position at a press conference in Berlin 1978, when a man in the audience stood up and asked what could be done for Raoul Wallenberg:

> My policy on human rights has always been to raise them privately and not make a public issue of them, on the theory that I believe it is more effective to help in human rights issues if one does not turn them into matters of state and into humiliations of the major country involved.

In the United States there were many who felt the opposite. Nixon and Kissinger's attitude was met with loud opposition from another strand in American opinion. For these opponents of realpolitik, most, but not all of whom were democrats, human rights had an unquestioned place at the top of foreign policy issues. Whatever the benefits of détente politics, they believed that the United States could not justify turning a blind eye to the ongoing repression in the Soviet Union.

In this loud-voiced American campaign around human rights, both Soviet prisoners and dissidents would play a large role. And, with the election of Democrat Jimmy Carter as president in 1976, everything changed. Carter sailed into the White House on the back of the human rights movement, which had gathered strength after the historic Helsinki agreement about security and cooperation in Europe in 1975. Even the Soviet leader Leonid Brezhnev had put his signature to the Helsinki declaration, which included a promise to respect "human rights and fundamental freedoms". With this, the Carter regime was free to pounce on any perceived Soviet transgressions. A different kind of cold war was beginning to take shape.

The Kremlin appeared taken aback by the new American tone. Ambassador Dobrynin in Washington, D.C. was ordered to point out that the criticism of the Soviet Union's treatment of its citizens was in conflict with Brezhnev and Nixon's agreement not to involve themselves in each other's domestic affairs. President Carter replied by brazenly inviting the Soviet dissident Vladimir Bukovsky to the White House. The mutual understanding of the

Brezhnev–Nixon era seemed to have evaporated.

It was in the midst of these tensions that the sudden international interest in Raoul Wallenberg blossomed at the end of the seventies. The Wallenberg case was not regarded as an unnecessary piece of gravel in the machinery of realpolitik, but as the ultimate symbol of evil in the Soviet system. Raoul Wallenberg had not only been unjustly imprisoned by communists, he was also a hero of the Second World War, one that many American Jews had to thank for their lives. And commemorating the Holocaust was another issue that the new Carter administration would place high on the list of its priorities.

The Nazi hunter Simon Wiesenthal in Vienna belonged to those European Jews who had survived the death camps of the Holocaust. He had not been saved by Raoul Wallenberg, but was deeply involved in the case. Maj von Dardel had written to him for the first time in the early seventies and Wiesenthal saw it as a matter of honour that his documentation centre, which had so successfully charted Nazi crimes, would also help the Swedish diplomat who had saved tens of thousands of Hungarian Jews from Eichmann. Maj's words echoed in his mind:

Not knowing is the worst. To know that my son may be alive, that he may be suffering, has been admitted to a mental institution, is starving in a prison or forced to perform hard labour, is much worse than if I could know with certainty that he were dead.

Maj and Fredrik von Dardel appreciated Wiesenthal's efforts. They had applied for and been given 10,000 kronor from one of the Wallenberg family's funds to help support his work. In the past few years Wiesenthal had been searching for witnesses among those Jews who had recently emigrated from the Soviet Union to Israel. And he had done what he could to try to awaken international interest in Raoul Wallenberg, by among other things contacting some of the more prominent members of the Human Rights movement. But it was not until Jimmy Carter swore the presidential oath on January 29, 1977 that things started to progress.

Simon Wiesenthal cooperated in part with the International Sakharov

Committee, an advocacy group that had been formed after the Helsinki agreement to monitor crimes against humanity in Eastern Europe. At the end of November 1977, the Sakharov Committee planned to hold a large international hearing in Rome. Maj von Dardel had been in touch beforehand, after receiving a call for financial support, and had promised to contribute if her son's case was taken up in Rome. The chairman had replied that the Sakharov Committee unfortunately did not work with "historic cases".

But, with less than a month left before the hearing in Rome, something happened. Simon Wiesenthal had spent a few weeks in the United States and now returned to Europe with renewed energy. He wrote to Maj von Dardel that he had discussed the Raoul Wallenberg case. "This case shouldn't fall into oblivion, I will see to that!" an excited Wiesenthal wrote to Maj von Dardel in November 1977. "I am planning shortly to launch a more considerable effort to solve the Wallenberg case and I will be in touch with you again at the beginning of next year." He emphasised that there was no need for Maj von Dardel to contribute financially to this venture.

The Sakharov committee hearing in Rome was extended by one day. At a press conference on November 28, Simon Wiesenthal announced the sensational news about the missing Swedish diplomat Raoul Wallenberg that had reached him "a month ago". A new witness had turned up who, as late as 1975, had seen Wallenberg at a mental institution in Irkutsk, where he had been brought from a camp on Wrangel Island in the Arctic Ocean. As expected, this news made headlines in several countries.

In the days before Christmas 1977, Wiesenthal repeated the same sensational message in *New York Magazine*. Under the headline "A Nazi Hunter takes on the Russians", it was revealed that Simon Wiesenthal had found new purpose after his hunt for Nazis: documenting the fate of Soviet political prisoners. Raoul Wallenberg was his flagship example. According to the article, Wiesenthal had, with his fresh new witness, solved the now 33-year-old mystery.

There was, however, one problem. The sensational witness in question was neither new nor particularly reliable. His name was Efim Moshinsky, he lived in Israel and claimed to be a former Soviet political prisoner. He had turned up before, in 1973, and spread information about Raoul Wallenberg that was afterwards dismissed as pure fabrication. That time, his claim was that Wallenberg had been seen in a camp on Wrangel Island. Soon it became clear that the facts about the mental hospital in Irkutsk also had to be dismissed. As early as January 1978, Wiesenthal wrote to the von Dardels and told them that the man who had figured in the headlines before Christmas unfortunately appeared to be a liar.

But the doubts surrounding the new Raoul Wallenberg witness had not as yet drawn any international media attention.

It was at this stage that the housewife and French teacher Annette Lantos strode onto the scene. She lived south of San Francisco in California and was married to the former economics professor Tom Lantos, who was a foreign policy adviser to a few Democratic senators and would soon begin a campaign for election to Congress. The Lantos couple knew the Raoul Wallenberg case well. They were both Jewish and originally from Hungary and, as they saw it, they had Wallenberg to thank for the fact that they had survived the Holocaust. They had never forgotten their saviour and were eager to do whatever they could to establish at least a wider recognition of his deeds.

The Lantos couple were close to a few of the senators who had been driving forces in the human rights campaigns. One of President Jimmy Carter's closest advisers, Stuart Eizenstat, belonged to their circle of friends. During private dinners, the Lantos couple had told Eizenstat about Raoul Wallenberg and his role in so many of Budapest's Jews being saved from the Holocaust. It was in this context that Simon Wiesenthal's unreliable December news was picked up and now transformed into a significant American investment in the Raoul Wallenberg case.

If one examines Maj von Dardel's correspondence from this time and compares it to the Swedish and American official telegrams in the same period, it is possible to identify Monday, January 9, 1978 as the starting point for the American campaign that was to come. That Monday, Annette Lantos took up her red pen and wrote her first letter to Raoul's mother in Sweden. There would be many more. During the coming year the von Dardel couple's mail increased tenfold, in large part owing to the fact that Annette Lantos' new involvement happened to coincide with almost as voluminous a correspondence from a West German human rights activist with Jewish heritage.

In her first letter, Mrs Lantos told Maj von Dardel that she had read an interview with Simon Wiesenthal in *New York Magazine* just before Christmas and had, as a result, understood that Raoul Wallenberg was still alive. Since then she had not been able to drop the case. During the three weeks over Christmas and the New Year she had worked hard to raise awareness and had gathered documentation for a special Raoul Wallenberg file. She had, for example, had some articles from the Russian émigré journal *Kontinent* translated.

Now she had good news for the von Dardels. Her work had yielded results. According to Annette Lantos, President Carter's senior adviser Eizenstat had already placed Raoul Wallenberg's name on the U.S. State Department's list of top priority political prisoners in the Soviet Union, prisoners whose cases the United States would henceforth pursue in their negotiations with the Kremlin.

It was a political sensation. If this was true, it meant that there was a decision at the highest political level to get involved in one of the most sensitive bilateral foreign policy cases in Swedish politics. And this controversial move was claimed to have been effected in record time, without first consulting either the Swedish government or Raoul Wallenberg's family. It all seemed highly unlikely.

In truth, matters were more complicated than that. The American ambassador in Stockholm described the situation like this in a letter in January 1978:

> ... diplomatically the affair is one that is between the Government of Sweden and that of the Soviet Union. There is legally and diplomatically nothing that my Government . . . is able to do . . . In a personal sense it is very frustrating for me to study about such a business and find that officially I can do nothing.

It would be wrong to say that the Swedish diplomatic actions in the Wallenberg case deserved this respect. But principles were principles, and other strategies needed. An intense private campaign to raise American awareness on the Wallenberg case, bring it to international attention and make it American could perhaps change things, and fit perfectly with President Carter's Human Rights agenda. This was later confirmed by Annette Lantos, in an interview for this book.

"That is absolutely correct. That was my part in it. I was to create such an interest, to create such a demand on the part of Americans that we do something about this outrageous injustice, public interest and public support, so that the president would be able to act."

Stuart Eizenstat later explained the deliberate strategy to the author:

> It didn't seem that the Raoul Wallenberg case was such a high priority to the Swedish government. So I wanted to elevate it on their agenda, so that they would pursue this more aggressively with the Soviets, because it was after all their citizen who was involved. I don't think the Swedish government wanted to stir the water with the Soviets, making this into an issue. But we did everything we could to keep pushing them.

For those in Sweden who cared about Raoul Wallenberg, this overnight American interest represented a sudden light in the darkness of the past fifteen years. Finally someone wanted to do something.

Annette Lantos was quick and professional. She sent several letters a month to Sweden with instructions. Soon the 87-year-old Maj von Dardel, who had broken her right arm and whose sight was failing, was asked to write to President Jimmy Carter and Stuart Eizenstat and apply to the United States for help. Lantos also wanted Maj to write to Solzhenitsyn and Amnesty International and ask them to contact Carter on the same matter. Annette Lantos emphasised in her message that such letters were needed for the special Raoul Wallenberg file that was already with Carter's chief adviser, Eizenstat. For unclear reasons, Lantos also gave Maj the name of a certain journalist at the foreign desk of the national radio station, *Sveriges Radio*, in Stockholm. She had written to him herself and now she urged Maj von Dardel to make contact and push forward.

Before the month of January was over, Annette Lantos was on a plane to Washington, D.C. to confirm support from the Swedish embassy for an American Raoul Wallenberg campaign. Because, as she pointed out, without the green light from Sweden, the matter could not be brought before President Carter. Only one month had gone by since she had read the interview with Simon Wiesenthal, but Annette Lantos could tell Maj von Dardel that she had already managed to involve the prominent American journalist Jack Anderson, columnist at the *Washington Post*, among others. Jack Anderson would be able to add publicity about Raoul Wallenberg in some 950 newspapers, assuming the Swedish embassy was on board.

At the Swedish embassy in Washington, Annette Lantos was received as the private person that she was. It was explained to her that Raoul Wallenberg was by no means a forgotten case in Sweden. She heard that her involvement was greatly appreciated but that the political responsibility to pursue Raoul Wallenberg's case lay with the Swedish government, not the United States.

Mrs Lantos was offended by this answer. The Swedish diplomats could not understand why, "unless she really means that the embassy should encourage the senators, State Department and the White House to take up the case with President Carter, which means that this becomes a link in his human rights dispute with Brezhnev. We can naturally not do anything of the sort without instructions from the government," the Swedish ambassador Wilhelm Wachtmeister wrote in a telegram to the Foreign Ministry in Stockholm.

At the Foreign Ministry, there were ongoing deliberations about Moshinsky, the dissident whose testimony had added urgency to both Simon Wiesenthal's and Annette Lantos' actions. Since the Americans had also had contact with him, the Foreign Ministry had sent over some formal questions to the U.S. State Department. They wanted the Americans' opinion of Moshinsky's credibility and also to know if the U.S. had any satellite imagery that could confirm or deny the existence of a prison camp on Wrangel Island.

But the American answer was a long time coming. In the meantime, Håkan Wilkens, the Swedish embassy representative in Tel Aviv, became completely convinced that Moshinsky was lying. The two handwritten letters that the former prisoner had presented as "evidence" were clear fabrications. Even Wiesenthal realised his mistake and made this public. When the answer from the State Department finally arrived in April 1978, it was found to be insipid. The U.S. had "incomplete" information about Moshinsky and, although there were satellite images that clearly ruled out the existence of a prison camp on Wrangel Island, these were not sent over to the Swedes. At the Foreign Ministry they complained loudly over what they regarded as the Americans' unwillingness to help.

The State Department's lack of cooperation was in part due to the C.I.A., to whom the official Swedish questions had been directed. The C.I.A. had provided an answer to the State Department, with rigid demands about the limits for its dissemination. It was as if the Americans wanted to keep the new information alive as long as possible, even though they knew that it was false.

The C.I.A. had their main headquarters some distance from the U.S. government offices, in the suburb of Langley, approximately ten kilometres north of the capital city. The C.I.A. had long shown an interest in the Raoul Wallenberg case, largely within the purview of its more psychological and propaganda-oriented operations. This had manifested itself mainly in planting news about Raoul Wallenberg by way of decoys in the mass media, in order to affront the Soviet Union and strengthen the Swedish public's disdain of communism. In 1974, for example, it was claimed that the character "Andersson" in a book by Solzhenitsyn was Wallenberg. The C.I.A. in Europe informed Langley that this was false, but that the information could still be disseminated (through their assets) to media in Sweden "to cause the local Soviet embassy some mild discomforts".

The new president's cold-war-oriented involvement in human rights had left its mark on the C.I.A.'s work too. A clear escalation of the C.I.A.'s interest in Raoul Wallenberg was now discernible in internal telegrams, especially those that came to be filed under the new programme title "Human Rights in the U.S.S.R. and Eastern Europe". The budget for propaganda activities also appears to have increased. The C.I.A. would henceforth arrange travel funds for journalists who wanted to write about Raoul Wallenberg as well as order, sponsor and direct the contents of documentary films about Raoul Wallenberg. But none of this happened openly. It is not even clear if the journalists involved had any idea who was behind this.

From these C.I.A. telegrams one can see that the intelligence agency was collaborating with an anonymous asset at the West German television channel Z.D.F.'s political documentary programme, *Z.D.F. Magazin*. This television programme came to play an absolutely decisive role when the new wave of international interest in Raoul Wallenberg gathered momentum. As if by coincidence, the West German television programme specialised in reports on oppression in communist countries.

"Invisible" media plants were part of the C.I.A.'s propaganda work on Soviet human rights abuses. It was a part of the C.I.A.'s so-called psychological operations, or "psy-ops" as they are referred to today. In a hearing at Congress on December 27, 1977 about the C.I.A.'s media relations, the former head of the C.I.A., William Colby, talked about the intelligence agency's work in influencing the political development of foreign countries. "Obvious ways to exercise influence have been through foreign newspapers and other media," said William Colby. He confessed that, on occasion, C.I.A. agents had acted under the cover of journalism, even as employed reporters.

In the hearing Colby defended the C.I.A.'s use of so-called grey and black propaganda: covert operations where information either is spread through a third source to cover the real one (grey propaganda) or fabricated, but presented as credible (black propaganda). Colby argued that these methods historically had been an effective "support of the voices of freedom in the face of the massive propaganda campaigns of the communist world".

One might add that these sorts of propaganda campaigns were implemented even more enthusiastically by the Soviet intelligence agencies.

The discrediting of Moshinsky did nothing to discourage Annette Lantos. Nor did the apparent scepticism of the Swedes about throwing the Wallenberg case in with President Carter's political campaign against the Soviet Union. "Since the Swedish ambassador for the moment appears to rule out all government actions we are trying to see if publicity in strategic newspapers . . . could help," Annette Lantos wrote to Maj von Dardel in spring 1978. Lantos said that she had again been in touch with Jack Anderson, who was waiting to begin. It was something of an understatement. Anderson appears to have participated in the shaping of the campaign strategy. "The most important paper for our purposes will be the *Washington Post*," Jack Anderson's assistant wrote to Lantos before the publication of Anderson's first article. "It has been a pleasure working with you."

Nor does Simon Wiesenthal seem to have let himself be distracted by the Moshinsky misinformation. He now planned to raise awareness among the American public and had therefore put himself in contact with the columnist Jack Anderson, he wrote to Maj in spring 1978. In the summer, Wiesenthal came to Sweden, more eager than ever. He now wanted to start an international Raoul Wallenberg committee, which would force the Russians against the wall and be given the mandate to appeal to President Carter if the Soviet Union did not answer.

In California, Annette Lantos speeded up her campaign. She and her husband Tom planned, among other things, an open letter to the *New York Times* and a slot for the television programme *60 Minutes*. But the reluctant attitude of the Swedish embassy posed a problem. It was therefore even more important that the initiatives came from Maj von Dardel, Lantos underlined. In a letter to a friend of the family she recommended strongly that the von Dardels hire a professional American PR company.

In Sweden, however, this American renaissance was invisible. Fredrik and Maj von Dardel were pleased at the unexpected actions on the other side of the Atlantic but, in general, they were more despondent than ever. During the spring, Moshinsky had the poor taste to send them a clearly fabricated letter addressed to "My dearly beloved Mother", a letter that he claimed had been dictated by Raoul Wallenberg in Irkutsk. Their trials did not end there. Fredrik and Maj had invested great hope in the Swedish royal couple's visit to the Soviet Union in June 1978. When nothing came of this visit, the von Dardels felt as if the darkness was thicker than ever, which the now 93-year-old Fredrik von Dardel confided to his journal.

Our long campaign for Raoul has not led to his liberation or any clarity about his fate. We have tried as long as our strength has lasted, but now we can no longer go on. I can't read any longer and can barely write and Maj's sight is also poor. I have to give up.

Raoul Wallenberg's stepfather had a plan. He had long been active in the debate over assisted death. Fredrik von Dardel was of the firm opinion that individuals should be allowed to decide when they wanted to end their lives.

"I have to give up," Fredrik von Dardel had written in his journal on July 10, 1978. That same day he contacted a Swedish physician who shared his views and who wanted to help. Fredrik von Dardel wrote to the doctor on behalf of himself and his wife in order to thank him for the sleeping pills he had prescribed. But the time was not yet quite right.

*

Raoul's siblings, Nina Lagergren and Guy von Dardel, now took over responsibility from their exhausted parents. It was with mixed feelings that Guy regarded the events of the recent past. The publicity in the U.S. was perhaps positive but there were also risks. "I feel it is important that our actions for Raoul do not become part of a more general anti-Soviet campaign," Guy von Dardel wrote to Annette Lantos in California at the end of 1978. He made it clear that the family did not have the finances to hire any American lobbyists and he expressed scepticism towards the value of interventions from other governments. As he saw it, the primary goal had to be changing the attitude of the Swedish government. For this, new and credible facts were needed.

In the current campaign, Guy von Dardel said, there were a few glaring errors that should be corrected. However important Simon Wiesenthal's contributions had been for the family, his new witness Moshinsky had not "solved the mystery". It was therefore unfortunate, he felt, that the claim had resurfaced in a new full-page advertisment from the Lantos campaign.

Annette Lantos replied that she knew that Moshinsky's witness account did not hold water. But outwardly she was still maintaining that Wiesenthal's statement was valid since it had attracted such attention. She wrote to the von Dardels that she could not see "that we can gain any advantage by getting hung-up on exact details".

In autumn 1978 the prospects of influencing the Swedish government in the Raoul Wallenberg case seemed better than for a long while. The Social Democrats' forty-four-year – and, in the end, quite fatigued – reign had been broken when a coalition of centre-right parties took office two years earlier. The coalition government hastily disbanded in October 1978, but it was replaced by a Liberal Party minority government, which was something of a bonus in the context. The Liberal Party contained many politicians who were interested in the Raoul Wallenberg case.

The basic problem remained, however. Something "definitively new" was required for the Swedish government to be able to approach the Russians again. It was what Nina Lagergren and Guy von Dardel were told in November when they met the new foreign minister, Hans Blix. This was the same message the Americans had been receiving from the Swedish embassy in Washington, D.C.

Fresh facts were needed, and new facts did come in, albeit from slightly unexpected sources.

At the end of November 1978, an official at the Foreign Ministry's eastern bureau, Sven Hirdman, was contacted by a Swedish television reporter who claimed to have received a tip-off from a colleague at Z.D.F. Magazin, the West German television programme. The tip was about a Polish Jew, Abraham Kalinski, who had been imprisoned in the Soviet Union for almost twenty years, but who now lived in Israel. According to the German colleague, Kalinski had not only met Raoul Wallenberg himself in the fifties, he had also heard about people who had done so as recently as five or six years ago.

The television reporter told Hirdman that the West German journalist was not interested in Wallenberg and had therefore contacted him in Stockholm. The Swedish reporter said he was prepared to wait with his scoop if the Foreign Ministry wanted to speak with Kalinski first.

Of course the Foreign Ministry wanted a head start and so Sven Hirdman sent an urgent telegram to the embassy in Tel Aviv. By way of the unexpectedly diligent and cooperative German journalist at Z.D.F. Magazin he managed to get hold of an address and telephone number for Kalinski's relatives in Haifa. Soon Wilkens at the Swedish embassy was on his way there to meet the new witness. The Z.D.F. journalist eventually received a written thank you from the Swedish government for his nimble assistance in the matter. What Sven Hirdman did not know was that the German journalist would later recount everything at one of his regular meetings with the C.I.A.

After the visit in Haifa, Wilkens reported that the hot witness Kalinski was in his sixties and appeared quite convincing. Kalinski said that he had been in the Vladimir prison in the late fifties and that he then, by way of smuggled messages, had come to know a fellow inmate by the name of Raoul, who was in a neighbouring cell. Kalinski would soon be travelling to New York "for conversations with American officials about his Soviet experiences", Wilkens wrote in his report to Stockholm. Once there, Kalinski would contact a person who he knew had met Raoul Wallenberg in the same prison in the sixties.

Kalinski's credibility would also falter with time, but his significance did not lie in what he could say about Raoul Wallenberg, but in the total change of tone that his entrance to the scene meant for the Wallenberg case. Even thirty-three years later one can sense the feverishness in the Foreign Ministry classified internal telegram exchanges. The circle of trust at the ministry was strictly limited. The Swedish consul in New York, who was prepared for Kalinski's arrival in mid-December, was under a gagging order and also required to keep all telegrams about the new lead under lock and key.

In December 1978, Cabinet Secretary Leif Leifland and Sven Hirdman happened to be going to the United States on business. They immediately added a three-hour meeting with the new witness to their agenda. Kalinski was chatty, "jumping from one association to the other" and came with at least three startling pieces of information: 1) he knew that a Jan Kaplan, an antique dealer in Moscow, had seen Wallenberg in the infirmary at Butyrka prison in 1975. 2) He had himself seen Raoul in the exercise yard in Vladimir some twenty times during the years 1956–1958. 3) He had been in tapping contact with Wallenberg in the prison.

This news was sensational and definitely deserved further investigation. Leifland and Hirdman pleaded with Kalinski to keep his story under wraps for a while so that they could move forward with their investigation. But the former prisoner maintained that "only a massive protest action" could bring resolution for Raoul Wallenberg's fate. Kalinski suggested instead that the Swedish government should, as soon as possible, hold a press conference about his witness account and put pressure on the Russians.

Leifland and Hirdman needed to hurry. The news could leak out at any time. In addition, Christmas was approaching. Their anxiety increased and, during the following days, another request for secrecy was sent to Kalinski. But it was too late. Kalinski had already been in long conversations with a reporter, he told the Swedish consul. The reporter in question was Jack Anderson. However, there was a brief respite for the Foreign Ministry: Kalinski knew that Jack Anderson would not publish his article until two weeks later – directly after the New Year's holiday.

In interviews conducted for this book, Leif Leifland has claimed that the Foreign Ministry officials tried to apply the brakes. But they were under pressure from the threat of publicity in the United States, and further momentum was provided by the fact that Sweden happened to have a new prime minister, Ola Ullsten. The Foreign Ministry officials had the impression that Ullsten was eager to make a historic contribution during his term. Faced with the new information regarding Raoul Wallenberg, the prime minister, according to Leifland, appeared "like a starved man who hasn't seen food in weeks".

The readiness to act was impressive. On January 3, 1979, the Swedish government dispatched its first diplomatic message about Raoul Wallenberg to the Soviet Union in fourteen years. For the first time since the activities associated with Nanna Svartz in the sixties, the Swedish government judged that such a credible witness account had come in that Sweden now could proceed to diplomatic action. Sweden demanded that the Soviet Union should launch an investigation and, among other things, report whether Wallenberg had been held in the Vladimir prison at the end of the 1950s, as well as the infirmary at the Butyrka prison in Moscow as late as 1975.

The threat of imminent publication turned out to be exaggerated. It was not until the first days after the Soviet answer – which was brief and arrived at the Foreign Ministry on January 24, 1979 – that the new information turned up in the world media. The Soviet Union emphasised that "there is nothing new and cannot be anything new in the question of R. Wallenberg's fate". According to this reply, the new information from Kalinski had been investigated without altering the Soviet assessment. "Claims that R. Wallenberg was in the Soviet Union as late as 1975 do not correspond to reality," the message concluded.

The Foreign Ministry found the answer "more polite than expected". But for Maj and Fredrik von Dardel, who after the sensational Swedish enquiry had started to nurture hope again, the negative reply was more than they could bear. They believed Kalinski, not the Russians. "We can't give up!" Maj von Dardel said in a telephone interview with the evening paper *Expressen*. But she was crying when she put down the receiver.

The dismissive reaction from the Soviets was drowned by the press coverage of Abraham Kalinski, the new and exciting witness. He was interviewed again and again in all Swedish media and soon his story spread across the world.

More perceptive individuals would have been able to shoot down Kalinski's witness account by early spring. Among other things, Kalinski wrongly claimed to have seen Raoul Wallenberg being transported by air from Budapest to Moscow on January 20, 1945, which did not match the many witness accounts from Raoul's fellow prisoners. He also claimed that he had contacted the Swedish embassy in Tel Aviv after having read an article on Raoul Wallenberg. This was a lie, pure and simple.

But, at the Foreign Ministry, Abraham Kalinski was regarded as a credible witness for a long time. Today Sven Hirdman has trouble pinpointing the exact moment when the realisation that Kalinski was lying struck the Foreign Ministry. But he remembers what it was that finally caused them to drop this dream witness.

In the early eighties, Kalinski turned up with a letter about Raoul Wallenberg that he claimed had come from the physician who had been head of the prison infirmary in Vladimir. Hirdman sent Kalinski's new letter to the national forensic laboratory, which was easily able to conclude that the letter was written by Kalinski himself. The same conclusion would in time be made about the handwritten letters and cards that Kalinski presented as evidence, but these revelations only came later when the glare of publicity had faded.

Today Sven Hirdman recalls that "there were a great many articles written about Kalinski and Raoul Wallenberg that year – in the *New York Times*, in French newspapers, German newspapers – it was through Kalinski's false witness account that the Raoul Wallenberg case became internationalised. Before then, the Wallenberg case was strictly Swedish and really only known in Sweden. It was not an international case. Sweden had also never tried to achieve any kind of internationalisation. But this came with Kalinski. Reluctantly."

The C.I.A. followed the developments in the Raoul Wallenberg case closely and continued to receive reports from their active contact at the West German television channel *Z.D.F.* The contact in turn was updated through the Swedish television reporter on the breakthrough in Sweden. According to the Swede, the news about Kalinski "has had effect and has turned the general public against the Soviet Union's human rights abuses in general and the country's treatment of Raoul Wallenberg in particular".

At the C.I.A. headquarters in Langley there was palpable enthusiasm over the attention surrounding Raoul Wallenberg. Shortly thereafter a telegram from the C.I.A. headquarters went back to the station in West Germany.

H.Q. strongly suggests that . . . prepare a long feature or series of slots on the Raul [*sic*] Wallenberg case. Ideally we envisage entire

"Z.D.F. Magazin" slot devoted to story, several consecutive "Magazin" features or, if this is not possible, a . . . freelance effort for "Auslandsjornal" or similar West German T.V. news magazine programme . . . We would hope that with RTACTION [code name for the C.I.A.] assistance as necessary Wallenberg feature would include filmed interviews with A) Wallenberg's mother in Sweden B) a Swedish government official.

The C.I.A. did not stop at providing general tips to the television reporter, who was to obtain all of the desired documents (as it happens, it was of course the same person who helped Sven Hirdman with the address for Kalinski). The intelligence agency also delivered supporting materials for the *Z.D.F.* reporter in question, among other things a long article that Kalinski had recently published in Russian, as well as new contact information for the former prisoner.

Kalinski was naturally included in the C.I.A.'s list of desired interviewees in the German documentary film. They also mentioned Nanna Svartz, the professor of medicine, whose home address and telephone number were cabled over from Washington, D.C. In their frequent telegram exchanges, the C.I.A. headquarters provided the station in West Germany with direct numbers and addresses to the cabinet secretary Leif Leifland and Sven Hirdman at the Foreign Ministry. The C.I.A. kept tabs on them and sent word to West Germany when it was known that Leifland was in Stockholm. "Hopefully the Z.D.F. Feature would be purchased/used by Swedish T.V.", headquarters wrote in a telegram to the West German C.I.A. station.

Later on the project with the *Z.D.F.* documentary would be given the acronym C.A. – for covert action. This meant that the project was secret and that the documentary was classified as either grey or black propaganda.

The C.I.A. would continue to provide assistance as required in the Raoul Wallenberg case but the need for this kind of far-reaching manipulation appears to have dropped off. After the magnificent international breakthrough with Kalinski's witness account, a great deal of the desired attention came automatically. The case had reached a threshold and not much more was needed. Interest was fanned across the globe. After decades of fruitless Swedish diplomacy, the Raoul Wallenberg case became a big issue even outside Sweden's borders, and not a day too early.

At last the missing Swedish amatuer diplomat would receive the great international recognition that he so well deserved. Unfortunately not all those involved were able to witness the many accolades and awards.

Maj and Fredrik von Dardel could not face another disappointment. They lived in the firm conviction that every person has the right to determine when life is no longer meaningful. Now they had reached that time.

On Monday February 12, 1979, the 93-year-old Fredrik von Dardel was found dead in his bed. He had taken the sleeping pills that the couple had been prescribed over the summer – a large enough dose to ensure he would not wake up. Two days later, Maj von Dardel followed her husband.

Raoul Wallenberg's mother and stepfather had conveyed a final wish to their children, Nina Lagergren and Guy von Dardel. Maj and Fredrik asked them not to give up the fight for their elder brother, to continue to live with the conviction that their brother was alive – if need be until the turn of the century.

It was a promise that the siblings would keep.

†

Våra älskade

**Fredrik
von Dardel**
* 28 augusti 1885
† 12 februari 1979

Maj von Dardel
* 2 maj 1891
† 14 februari 1979

RAOUL
GUY och MATTI
NINA och GUNNAR
Barnbarn
Barnbarnsbarn

*För det tappra hjärtat är
ingenting omöjligt*

Jordfästning i stillhet. Tänk
på Amnesty International
pg. 4 59 77-6.

Versailles, spring 2010

The hens have finally laid their eggs and the cock is proudly strolling around in Marie Dupuy's garden in Versailles outside Paris. Marie Dupuy is Guy von Dardel's younger daughter and I have travelled here in order to dig through her father's very private archive. It has a special history of its own and nowadays takes up an entire upper floor of her house. Marie says that she is tempted to stamp the abbreviation L.S.T.S. on the eighty-five black archival boxes: Labour, Sweat, Tears and Stubbornness.

It was a couple of years ago that she decided to drive down to the parental home in Switzerland, fetch her father's piles of paper and organise them in an archive. She regarded this as essential self-therapy. Marie had a strong need to try to understand, one that did not lessen after her father's death in 2009.

"Father never talked about Raoul when we were children. For us this Raoul Wallenberg was a mystery, something heavy that Father carried inside him but that we never heard anything about. We knew that his half-brother had saved thousands of Jews and that he was missing, but we didn't know the details. It was as if he wanted to shield us from that story," Marie Dupuy tells me.

Marie's sister, Louise von Dardel, who joins us later in the day, adds:

"Raoul was like a large dark cloud. We did not know what was in that cloud and there were no words for it. Therefore we couldn't have a dialogue with Father about it. It was heavy and silent, as in an Ingmar Bergman film."

The cloud hovered between them and their father. His mysterious half-brother was at once absent and disturbingly present. He could not be seen in a single photograph in their childhood home, but he was always in Guy's thoughts. They recalled how they could be setting off on a family excursion, but end up sitting in the car for an hour because Guy "first had to finish writing an important letter" about Raoul. Their father was always sitting at his typewriter. When they were older they sometimes expressed mild protests at the dinner table. "Father, we don't know if Raoul is alive, but we know that we are and we are here!"

"It was a daily presence, but virtual," Marie observes.

"But when we asked Father if he could tell us more about his brother, what he was like as a person, he was simply quiet. It was easier to talk to him about physics," Louise says.

They describe their father as a warm and quiet person, somewhat withdrawn socially. He preferred the simple life – his research and walking in the mountains – to cocktail parties. They say he had a wonderful sense of humour, but it disappeared over the years.

"The work for Raoul broke him. Without the support from Mother he would never have been able to carry on so long," Marie says.

"For Father there were only two camps – you were either for or against Raoul. Everyone who wanted to help him in his investigation was *for* Raoul, anyone who in any way prevented him from it was *against* Raoul."

The Foreign Ministry belonged to the latter camp. So did Raoul's relatives from the Wallenberg banking family, who no longer wanted to support the investigations and, in a humiliating manner, forbade Guy von Dardel from researching about his brother in the private Wallenberg archives.

Marie has not counted the documentation but she estimates that she dragged home some five to eight thousand letters and memos from the parental home in Switzerland. It was not without pain that she approached the unknown part of her father's life. That the dark cloud of the family should be placed in black boxes felt natural.

"I was very surprised. I knew that Father had a lot of paper, but I had not realised how much there was! Such an enormous amount of time!"

The black boxes have been placed in white bookcases. It takes us several days to go through the most essential and we have still only scraped the surface. Here we find the entire correspondence dating back to 1945. It is clear that Guy von Dardel redoubled his efforts at the end of the seventies. Just as his sister Nina Lagergren did.

Not everything is gloomy. There are also successes, some even tremendous successes. There are breakthroughs that Maj and Fredrik von Dardel would never have dreamed of. But still no answers.

On one of these days the 87-year-old Matilda von Dardel comes to Versailles. She is Guy von Dardel's widow and Marie's mother and she tries to help direct us as well as she can. She sits on a chair and follows us with her gaze as we pick our way between piles of paper and take boxes down from the shelves. Even though she has lived through it, she appears slightly shocked at the extensiveness of the collection. She mentions the sky-high telephone bills that all the work for Raoul brought with it.

"This must have occupied Guy more than even I realised. I so wish that I had understood," says Matilda von Dardel.

CHAPTER 23

"Goodbye, Mr Wallenberg"

Nina Lagergren and Guy von Dardel had, just like their parents, grown accustomed to the Foreign Ministry's tepid interest in their missing brother. Ever since Östen Undén's time, Raoul's cause had mainly consisted of struggling alone against a headwind, being met by averted gazes, pained sighs and unanswered telephone calls. They had learned to live with it. They knew that the fight for Raoul meant hard work and having to find satisfaction in the positive exceptions. After their parents' deaths this was what the two of them expected to face.

But in spring 1979 everything suddenly changed. Now the political elite of the world rolled out their red carpets for Raoul Wallenberg's family. For a while it was almost easier for Nina Lagergren and Guy von Dardel to meet American or Israeli ministers than it had been for their parents to have a call put through in the Foreign Ministry's exchange.

The Raoul Wallenberg case had become global politics. After the international breakthrough with Abraham Kalinski's testimony in January 1979, everything happened so fast that neither Nina nor Guy really had time to think it through. In April of the same year, Nina Lagergren was summoned to a press conference in London at only two days' notice. A few British politicians engaged in human rights wanted to form a committee and demand Raoul Wallenberg's liberation from the Soviet Union. Shortly thereafter there were new summons from London. The prime minister of Israel, Menachem Begin, had been there on an official visit and received questions about Raoul Wallenberg. Now Raoul's siblings were informed that they were invited to visit Begin in Israel in early June.

It was not mere politeness. Nina and Guy were greeted at Tel Aviv airport by Prime Minister Begin's white Volvo cars. The visit was covered by international press, radio and television. Raoul Wallenberg's siblings were given a quarter of an hour alone with Menachem Begin, only interrupted at first by a television team from the B.B.C. Nina Lagergren was worried that the fifteen minutes would go by without anything substantial being said. But Begin surprised them. He said that he planned to become the first member of the Raoul Wallenberg committee that would now be formed in Israel. "Then he suddenly glanced at his calendar and said, 'The summit with Carter and Brezhnev in Vienna starts in five days. Time is short. But I will ask President Carter to take up the question with Brezhnev,'" Nina and Guy related after-wards. "Never have we been given such a chance!" they exclaimed to a reporter from the *Vecko-Journalen* magazine.

They also encountered tremendous responses from the general public during the Israel visit. Raoul Wallenberg was a legend to many Israeli fam-ilies. Young people came up and thanked Nina and Guy because Raoul had saved their parents' lives. The head of Israel's radio told them how he holed up in one of Raoul Wallenberg's Swedish houses and thus managed to escape the Holocaust. At the press conference in Vienna, an Israeli reporter stood up and said that her parents had been rescued by Raoul Wallenberg from a fully loaded deportation train.

Many touched and grateful North Americans also reached out. Nina and Guy made contact with a woman living in Canada. Her name was Yvonne Maria Singer and she had come into this world in war-torn Budapest, one morning in November 1944, in one of Raoul Wallenberg's combined offices and living quarters.

It was an intense time. Nina Lagergren had barely arrived home from Israel in mid-June before Annette Lantos called from the United States. Could Nina come to Washington, D.C. right away, before the congress closed? "Of course I had to go and we went from one person to the other, anyone Annette thought was important. Then the day came when the senators formed a special Raoul Wallenberg committee. There were full-page articles in the *Washington Post* and the *New York Times* and everywhere," Nina Lagergren recalls.

Secretary of State Cyrus Vance was one of those who received Annette Lantos and Nina Lagergren. And Nina was presented with President Jimmy Carter's medal for heroic rescue actions during the Holocaust, on Raoul's behalf. "Wallenberg's incredible courage and unselfishness is one of the great examples in modern times of the good Samaritan. If he is still alive, we must do everything possible to set him free," the new Senate group said in a statement later that summer.

Nina and Guy were of course happy and grateful at the strength of the newly awakened American interest. The family had missed this kind of response. Raoul's rescue work had after all come about because of an American initiative and it felt appropriate that the United States was taking on some of the responsibility.

It was not clear for a long time if Jimmy Carter did bring up the Raoul Wallenberg case with Brezhnev at the Vienna summit. He had in fact done so, although outside the formal agenda. Afterwards the Soviet embassy in Washington had speculated about the unexpected interest in the missing Swede. Was it Begin's plea that explained the American prioritisation of Wallenberg, they asked the Americans? The answer was no. The United States had its own interests in the matter.

The news that President Carter had asked Brezhnev about Raoul Wallenberg was kept secret. It was not revealed until several months later, in a radio phone-in. The president's initiative then became big news that helped turn the Raoul Wallenberg case into a central American question. It was presented as if Carter's initiative had been disclosed by accident, after a question from a listener.

The programme was recorded in October. Those radio listeners who wanted to take part had been asked to send their names and telephone numbers on a postcard to the president, but without mentioning the topic of their question. The thought was that listeners would be randomly selected from the collection of postcards, all to give the programme spontaneity.

A housewife in California was among the lucky few who were selected from over 24,000 entries. She was given two minutes on National Public Radio and her question to the president was about his view of the Swede Raoul Wallenberg's fate. Jimmy Carter was then able to let the American radio listeners know that he was deeply involved in this case and that he had actually discussed the matter with Leonid Brezhnev in June. Cyrus Vance had also mentioned Wallenberg in his discussion with Gromyko, the Soviet foreign minister. President Carter explained to the listeners that he intended to continue to press the Russians to clarify what had happened to Raoul Wallenberg.

This naturally created headlines in the papers and the Swedish embassy in Washington reported on the radio programme in its entirety to the Foreign Ministry in Stockholm. The caller from California described her striking luck to journalists – how incredible it was that she, an unknown housewife, had by chance got two minutes with the president. "It's amazing what he had to say. That he [Carter] could share so much information off the cuff shows how much he cares about the individual person."

Her name was Annette Lantos.

The star witness Abraham Kalinski did not let go, in fact he redoubled his efforts by travelling around Sweden and telling his story in order to – as he put it – achieve "maximum publicity". He could hardly have been displeased when he went home.

Now the Polish former prisoner focused his criticism on Sweden's contributions. Kalinski claimed, for example, that Wallenberg "would have been home a long time ago" if only Sweden had stood up for itself. "I am travelling to Stockholm to tell the Swedes that their Kissinger politics, quiet diplomacy, doesn't help in the Wallenberg affair," he told one newspaper. "The only thing the Kremlin fears is publicity," he said in another. He argued that "Swedish government, press, radio, TV – ideally with broad international cooperation" should demand full information from the Soviet Union.

Kalinski managed to find a series of new witnesses and parcelled them out in various media bursts over the course of the year. Unfortunately the new testimonies were difficult to verify, the Swedish embassy in Moscow complained. Swedish diplomats would risk the security of the witnesses if they tried to investigate their claims on location.

This problem also pertained to the highly interesting letters from Moscow that appeared by way of a tip from Abraham Kalinski during the summer of 1979. It contained indirect information from a Soviet antique dealer, Jan Kaplan, whom Kalinski had mentioned earlier. Jan Kaplan was said to have seen Raoul Wallenberg at an infirmary in the Butyrka prison in Moscow as late as 1975. From this new letter it seemed that Kaplan had been imprisoned again, since he had tried to smuggle out a letter with these facts about Wallenberg.

Many years later it would be clear that not even Jan Kaplan himself had been imprisoned in Butyrka. But now all these new facts, combined with the international attention put additional pressure on the Swedish government. In country after country, national Raoul Wallenberg committees were formed. The British, Israeli, West German and American committees had all been set up before the Swedish Raoul Wallenberg association was founded in September 1979.

The information about Kaplan prompted Prime Minister Ola Ullsten to act. Ullsten now sent his second letter that year about Raoul Wallenberg to the Soviet government. In it, he demanded a new Soviet investigation and more than implied Sweden's interest in participating in the conversations with Kaplan that he anticipated the Russians would conduct.

The C.I.A.'s European office noted the increased activity in Sweden with satisfaction. In a report home to headquarters, it was observed that Ullsten's new letter, once it was made public, would become a good news hook for the planned and C.I.A.-supported television report about Wallenberg in Z.D.F. Magazin. They mentioned that the half-hour-long documentary would probably be broadcast in early October and, in the best of all worlds, the West German contact would maybe even get an interview with Ola Ullsten. To judge from the telegrams from this time, the C.I.A. were increasingly keen to smooth the way for any journalists and writers who showed an interest in reporting or writing books about Raoul Wallenberg.

If the intent of this half-concealed American interest was to propel the formerly passive Swedish government, they had succeeded beyond expectation. The first enquiry to the Soviet Union in fourteen years had been followed by another within six months. For the first time in the entire history of the Raoul Wallenberg case, the Swedish government now did almost too much. Even today the Foreign Ministry officials become slightly embarrassed at the thought of the abrupt Swedish enquiry about the spy Stig Bergling that the government drove through in the agitated atmosphere of autumn 1979.

In March of that year, the Swedish United Nations officer Stig Bergling had been exposed as a Soviet spy and apprehended. During the autumn, he awaited trial and sentencing. He had now through his lawyer contacted Raoul

Wallenberg's family. Stig Bergling was sure he would be sentenced to life in prison and had a proposal. He wanted to be exchanged for Raoul Wallenberg. "No way should be left untested in order to bring resolution to Raoul Wallenberg's fate," was the line of the Liberal Party government when it was informed of Bergling's idea.

The Swedish diplomats in Moscow were now ordered to meet with some of their informal contacts. They sighed. In order to anticipate and soften any potential ridicule, they were asked by their closest superiors to forward the proposal for the exchange between Wallenberg and Bergling "humorously" as a "personal idea". The former Wallenberg case manager Jan Lundvik was now first secretary in Moscow. The assignment fell to him. Lundvik groaned. "I invited my contact to have lunch at the Praga restaurant in Moscow, a meeting place for diplomats. He understood my meaning right away and knew exactly what 'personal idea' meant," Jan Lundvik recalls today. "As a pure gesture of politeness he promised to forward the proposal to his superiors. He came back ten days later with the message: 'The problem is that Wallenberg is dead so the exchange can't be made.'"

Guy von Dardel felt that the new international backing should be exploited so as to make real progress in the investigation. The majority of the Foreign Ministry documentation about the case was still classified, even for the family, which Guy objected to. He had already tried to stir up interest from the Foreign Ministry for the formation of a scientific Swedish–Soviet investigative commission that could examine all the documents in the Raoul Wallenberg case. Guy had also contacted the Soviet embassy and asked to be allowed to send an informal research team to Moscow in order to examine the latest Soviet materials.

All the new international press conferences and official honours had been incredibly important in moving his brother's case along. But Guy von Dardel was a relatively retiring and quiet man. He knew that he personally would have more to contribute to the research itself. More documents and fewer cocktail parties – that was what he preferred.

The Foreign Ministry had not believed in the idea of a collaborative Swedish–Soviet research team. But the government had early on given the office of the chancellor of justice the task of examining all the ministry's documents about Raoul Wallenberg, in order to declassify them. That review was now completed.

The release of the Foreign Ministry's Wallenberg documents in January 1980 became – by Swedish measures – a media bonanza, especially since it happened to occur just after the thirty-fifth anniversary of Raoul Wallenberg's disappearance. The Swedish Raoul Wallenberg association commemorated the day by leading a torch-lit procession from the City Hall to the Soviet embassy. A thousand people had assembled outside the gates of the embassy, and the association's letter to the ambassador was read aloud before a large gathering of journalists. "Remember that we will not be silent until Raoul Wallenberg is reunited with his family," Ingrid Gärde Widemar, the head of the association, read.

Swedish newspapers fanned the flames with extensive articles on Raoul's life and his actions in Budapest. Grateful colleagues and those who had been rescued told their stories from wartime Budapest, and the missing Swedish diplomat took on human contours for a new generation of Swedes. "He didn't look like a hero at all. Not how you imagine a courageous, strong-willed and free-born hero type. He actually seemed kind of dreamy and gentle," a former co-worker at the Swedish legation in Budapest said. An 82-year-old Israeli-based Hungarian who had received a Swedish protective passport from Raoul said, "[h]e was courteous and polite, like an English diplomat. Although he was very modest, quiet and soft-spoken, he was surrounded by an aura of respect. He never really promised anything, instead he acted." The American Raoul Wallenberg committee managed to ensure the thirty-fifth anniversary coincided with new and remarkable witness testimony. Now it was claimed that Wallenberg had been sighted alive in a Soviet prison camp as late as 1978.

The atmosphere was therefore substantially heightened when Cabinet Secretary Leif Leifland released almost two thousand blue-bound formerly classified Wallenberg documents on the last day of January 1980. It was the material from 1945–49. The rest would be published in batches.

It was Staffan Söderblom's statement to Stalin in June 1946, that he personally believed Raoul Wallenberg had suffered an accident, which drew the most attention. The Foreign Ministry's clumsy actions during the initial years, when Wallenberg was confirmed to be alive, upset many people. Not least the family, who had not had the entire picture until now. "It is very embittering and we despair over how little was done and how half-hearted those efforts were. The papers speak for themselves. The most depressing thing is that they assumed that Raoul was dead," Nina Lagergren said later in an interview for the radio station Sveriges Radio. For the newspaper *Svenska Dagbladet* she said: "It is a nightmare to know that Raoul was abandoned for so many years . . . But I try to tell myself that there is no point in looking back or accusing anyone. We have to look forward and continue to act with the conviction that Raoul is alive."

In the afternoon programming on the radio, the former prime minister Tage Erlander was asked if it would not have been better to stand up to the Soviet Union during those first few years, for example by demanding an exchange of Wallenberg for some Soviet prisoner in Sweden.

"I don't think that path would have been particularly intelligent," Tage Erlander replied. "I don't think it would have succeeded any better than this other method. Undén was an unusually moral person. He absolutely refused to exchange a life for a life or to mix the exchange of a person with credits, grain shipments or whatever it might be. He felt that, in that case, Sweden would have to find a new foreign minister because he for one could not agree to it."

This line of defence was absent when Erlander was asked to comment on Söderblom's meeting with Stalin in 1946.

"The entire conversation was a disaster," Erlander said, with an unexpected degree of sharpness in his voice.

The now 79-year-old Staffan Söderblom sat in an apartment in Uppsala and heard Tage Erlander throw him, and only him, to the wolves. Then his gaze went dark. "He became extremely upset but as usual he was controlled," a relative recalls who listened to the programme with Söderblom. "I don't understand it," was all he said. "Could someone else have managed it better?"

Shortly before the end of the year, Soviet troops had marched into Afghanistan. The eighties therefore began with an alarming decline in relations between the superpowers. The United States responded to the invasion by boycotting the 1980 Olympic Games in Moscow. The cold war tension increased in all spheres and the C.I.A.'s psychological operations were still central in drawing attention to the oppressive nature of the Soviet regime.

Interest in the missing Swedish diplomat had not diminished. "The Raoul Wallenberg case continues to be useful in order to highlight Soviet crimes against humanity," the C.I.A. headquarters observed in a telegram in the spring of 1980.

The message from the C.I.A. was that all journalistic initiatives about the Wallenberg case were to be supported, no matter how fruitless they appeared.

When the newly formed international Raoul Wallenberg association was planning to organise a large hearing in Stockholm about Raoul Wallenberg, the C.I.A. tried to pull strings and move the entire enterprise from Stockholm to Vienna. They felt "this would permit much better impact and significantly improved press coverage".

But there were limits to even the American intelligence agency's influence. The large international hearing on January 17, 1981 took place as planned in the hall of mirrors of the Grand Hotel in Stockholm. The Stockholm meeting's key speaker was Raoul Wallenberg's father's cousin Marcus Wallenberg who, for the first time, spoke publicly about his relative. "It is hard to understand why the Russians kept Raoul Wallenberg. A superpower that is unable to admit its mistakes must be condemned," the 81-year-old financier said in his speech. An unexpectedly large gathering of the press was also addressed by Simon Wiesenthal, as well as the author and later Nobel Prize winner, Elie Wiesel.

The Soviet news bureau T.A.S.S. called the meeting in Stockholm a provocation and wrote that "certain circles in the West now attempt to use the case for covert purposes. These forces try not only to harm the good relations between Sweden and the Soviet Union, but also to rekindle anti-Soviet sentiments in the West."

The government of the United States now actually acted openly and without reservation for Raoul Wallenberg, without any consideration for Swedish foreign policy. The involvement was in many ways welcome, but formally the situation was complicated for Swedish diplomats. "We couldn't remain passive when the Wallenberg case came up but we also couldn't be happy when the Americans wanted to pursue it as a link in the cold war," as Ambassador Jan Lundvik explains. "It was our concern but one that we absolutely didn't want pulled into the superpower political sphere."

Jan Lundvik was the Swedish representative at the large European security conference in Madrid that was held in the autumn of 1980. He remembers how the Swedish delegation were informed at a very late stage that the United States intended to bring up the Raoul Wallenberg case during the conference. Sweden had no such plans. How should the Swedes handle the American initiative? What did their neutral politics dictate?

The discussion in Madrid ended with the Swedes dutifully backing up the American Wallenberg move, but they were far from pleased.

Jan Lundvik remembers that he had met the Soviet delegates at the security conference. One of them, Sergei Kondrashov, was both adept at languages and friendly. Much later Jan Lundvik was told that it was Kondrashov who had been called in to act as interpreter at Raoul Wallenberg's last known interrogation in the Lubyanka prison in the spring of 1947. But the Russian said nothing about this to his Swedish colleagues.

With Raoul Wallenberg so high on their list of priorities, it felt like the right time for the United States to follow this to its logical conclusion and make him an American. The Republican Ronald Reagan was installed as president on Tuesday, January 20, 1981, in a cold war atmosphere so frigid that historians would refer back to the final years of the Stalin era in order to find a reasonable comparison.

The newly elected president was presented with a proposal that involved Raoul Wallenberg within his first couple of months in the White House. It came from Tom Lantos, who had just been elected to Congress. The Democrat Lantos would have a long and illustrious political career with an emphasis on fighting against oppression and supporting human rights.

The intense work that he and his wife, Annette Lantos, had undertaken to get the United States to act on behalf of Raoul Wallenberg had borne fruit. Several books were in the pipeline and Wallenberg had been honoured with a television programme that reached a large audience.

The American campaign had acquired genuine public support. The interest in Raoul Wallenberg was definitely not only supported by the political strategies of the White House. Many American citizens lived with strong memories of the Holocaust. Not everyone had liked the 1978 series *Holocaust*, but the effect of the American and later even international success of the series was that the uncomfortable silence surrounding the Nazi crimes during the Second World War was broken. That same year Jimmy Carter had decided to form "The President's Commission on the Holocaust" in order to educate the public about the Holocaust and to honour the victims of the Nazis. The American public's consciousness about the Holocaust increased and with it so had their admiration for the energetic Swedish amateur diplomat in Budapest, who had dared to stand up to the Nazis. In all the darkness surrounding the Holocaust, Raoul Wallenberg was a model of positivity. Many regarded him as a timeless humanitarian hero, and highlighted his unselfishness and courage. Few could avoid being moved by his fate.

Tom Lantos suggested to Congress that Raoul Wallenberg should be named an honorary citizen of the United States, the first since Winston Churchill. His thought was that an honorary citizenship would make it possible for the United States to act more forcefully to free the Swede. The proposal was accepted. On Monday, October 5, 1981, President Ronald Reagan signed Raoul Wallenberg's American honorary citizenship. Raoul's siblings Nina Lagergren and Guy von Dardel took part in the ceremony, which was held in the White House Rose Garden.

The American government honoured Raoul Wallenberg with a speech. "Wherever he is, his humanity burns like a torch . . . What he did, what he accomplished was of biblical proportions," Ronald Reagan said.

The new honorary citizen also had some creative and considerably more action-oriented "countrymen". Tom and Annette Lantos had already shown this.

One of these new, motivated Americans was Marvin Makinen, a professor of molecular biology at the University of Chicago. He had spent twenty months in Vladimir prison in the Soviet Union in the sixties. When he read one of the many articles about Raoul Wallenberg in the early eighties he had a sudden insight. He realised that Wallenberg must be the same as "van den Berg", the Swedish prisoner that there had been rumours about at Vladimir. Marvin Makinen contacted Guy von Dardel with the information and offered his help. They began a lasting collaboration.

Makinen had a bold idea. He suggested to Guy von Dardel that the family take a harder line. They should sue the Soviet Union in a court of law. This idea was not as ridiculous as it sounded the first time that Guy heard it. A recent American law made it possible for an individual to sue a foreign nation in an American court. A lawyer in Chicago had recently managed to get the husband of an American woman freed after having sued the Soviet Union. Since Raoul Wallenberg was an honorary citizen there was a possibility it could work for him as well. The problem was that a lawsuit cost a lot of money.

Finally, two prominent American law firms volunteered to take the case pro bono, probably calculating that the trial would generate more in goodwill and P.R. than it would cost to run it. Thus the case of *Guy von Dardel v. Union of Soviet Socialist Republics* was born. In early 1984 they filed the papers in a Washington, D.C. court. The Soviet Union was accused of being in violation of international laws and agreements for having imprisoned and retained Raoul Wallenberg.

A year later there was good news from the court, for once. Guy von Dardel had won the case, in part because the defendant was not present. The family's demands were accepted and the Soviet Union was sentenced to: 1) within sixty days present "the person Raoul Wallenberg or his remains if he is dead," 2) within thirty days furnish all documents in Soviet possession that pertain to Raoul Wallenberg, as well as 3) pay damages of thirty-nine million dollars to the family, one million for each year that Raoul Wallenberg had been missing.

It was not quite the victory it seemed, especially in such a perennially complex diplomatic environment. "Our position from the start was that we were not interested in the money, we wanted Raoul. We were actually afraid that the Soviet Union would seize on the opportunity and pay us in order to be rid of the entire excruciating story," Guy von Dardel said later in an interview.

For his part he had tried to awaken American interest to use the sentence as a basis for new political pressure tactics. But the negotiations went on, the years went by and soon global politics had taken a new turn altogether. Mikhail Gorbachev turned up as the new First Secretary of the Central Committe of the Soviet Union's Communist Party and struck a tone that softened even the most hardened cold warriors in the U.S. State Department. Now the United States wanted to approach the Soviet Union on friendlier terms, and Raoul Wallenberg no longer fitted so well into the foreign policy agenda.

The judicial developments ended around 1989 with the State Department making sure that the claim for damages against the Soviet Union in the Raoul Wallenberg case was dismissed. Not even the American government could be counted on any longer.

Mikhail Gorbachev could not himself foresee the force of the political liberalisation that he set in motion with his introduction of *glasnost* (openness) and *perestroika* (restructuring) in the Soviet Union. If one is to believe the history books, his intent was not so much to dismantle the communist social project as to, with various key tactics, return the country to what he thought was the original spirit of Marxism-Leninism. A somewhat freer public debate (*glasnost*) and a somewhat reformed economy (*perestroika*) could assist in this regard. But it would not end there.

Gorbachev's own symbolic actions did nothing to dampen expectations. In December 1986 he personally called the exiled human rights activist and peace prize recipient Andrei Sakharov and gave him permission to leave his house arrest in Gorky (now Nizhny Novgorod). Sakharov was suddenly a free man and could return to Moscow.

What would these new Soviet developments mean for the Raoul Wallenberg case? It was not long before speculation was under way in Sweden. Guy von Dardel himself experienced the difference in attitude during a trip to Moscow in 1988, amazed that the Russians had established a department for "humanitarian questions" in their Foreign Ministry.

Andrei Sakharov and Guy von Dardel were both nuclear physicists. They knew each other from international conferences during the time before Sakharov's internal exile. When Guy now started to travel to Moscow he often slept on the couch in the kitchen of Sakharov's small apartment. He did this more and more. In time, Guy von Dardel discovered to his surprise that he enjoyed the company of Russians, more so even than Swedes. The first thing he did after his retirement in 1985 was to move back to Switzerland – among other things in order to be further away from the Swedish Foreign Ministry.

Guy had not dropped his ten-year-old idea for a Swedish–Russian research team tasked with examining all the Swedish and Soviet case documents about Raoul Wallenberg. Perhaps this could now be realised. If so, Sakharov would be an obvious choice as a member.

The new Social Democratic Swedish government had a sceptical attitude to new initiatives regarding Raoul Wallenberg. This attitude was expressed in writing in an internal Foreign Ministry memo from 1985. It said that the like-lihood of Wallenberg being alive was so small that "we can no longer allow the question to burden – and sometimes poison – our relations with the Sovi-ets". At the very least, they concluded, one should not do so as long as there was no new credible evidence. Glasnost now helped the government to begin to see new possibilities.

Guy von Dardel and Nina Lagergren continued to act on their own. In March 1989, Guy went to see Anatoly Adamishin, the Soviet deputy foreign minister, who was attending a conference about human rights in Geneva. Guy then presented his idea of forming an international scientific commission to examine the Raoul Wallenberg case. Nina Lagergren did her part by sending a letter about her brother to Mikhail Gorbachev.

In hindsight it is difficult to know what it was that finally led to the break-through. A wave of liberalisation swept through Eastern Europe and made 1989 into the year that the Iron Curtain fell. Suddenly there was goodwill. Suddenly the Russians were listening. When Deputy Foreign Minister Adam-ishin received Sweden's new ambassador in Moscow, Örjan Berner, that summer, he surprised the Swede by showing a genuine interest in the Raoul Wallenberg case. Adamishin told Berner about Guy von Dardel's idea. He suggested that Berner could contact the K.G.B. to discuss the possibility of access to Soviet archives.

That summer the atmosphere was almost revolutionary in Moscow. Debate was more open than ever and the Nobel Prize-winner Andrei Sakharov, among others, stood at its centre. Soviet newspapers, tipped off by Sakharov, started to write about the Wallenberg case and, towards the end of August, Soviet television for the first time broadcast a programme about the missing Swede.

At around the same time the Soviet ambassador in Sweden, Boris Pankin, contacted the Raoul Wallenberg association. He said that he had been asked to invite Raoul Wallenberg's siblings to Moscow. There they would meet a few "senior officials within the K.G.B." According to Pankin, the K.G.B. had decided to be cooperative. Now they wanted to show the family the original of the so-called Smoltsov report, that is to say the one-page handwritten letter, located in 1957, which claimed to be Raoul Wallenberg's death certificate. The Smoltsov report was still said to be the only document bearing Raoul Wallenberg's name in the Soviet archives.

Slowly the colossus began to move. The Soviet invitation was a huge break-through, overwhelming for the family. Nina and Guy worked hard to prepare themselves, not least mentally. Would they be allowed into the archives now? Would they be allowed to visit the prisons and the infirmaries? What if Raoul was there?

Guy von Dardel tried to think of a way to get out a message or make him-self heard. He wanted his brother to understand immediately that his siblings had come, even if they were not allowed to meet him. They had to think of a signal that would reach even a sickly or senile Raoul. "I remember that Father said he would use something from childhood, because that's what you remem-ber best. He thought of the classic Swedish children's song "*Bä bä vita lamm*" (similar to "Baa baa Black Sheep"). If he were in a prison or hospital he would walk around singing "*Bä bä vita lamm*" because he knew that Raoul would react to it," Marie Dupuy, Guy von Dardel's daughter, recalled.

On Sunday, October 15, 1989, the siblings landed in Moscow and were met by a swarm of international reporters. At this point, further information on Raoul Wallenberg had been broadcast on Soviet television. A photograph of him altered to look as if he were seventy-seven years old had been provided. He was no longer completely unknown even in the Soviet Union.

Nina Lagergren and Guy von Dardel were accompanied by Raoul's col-league Per Anger and the Wallenberg Association's secretary, Sonja Sonnen-feld. They were scheduled to meet with the K.G.B. on Monday morning. The meeting was to take place in the palatial turn-of the-century mansion that the Soviet Foreign Ministry used on official occasions. The siblings were greeted on the polished marble floors by the K.G.B.'s deputy chairman Vladimir Pirozhkov and one of the Soviet deputy vice ministers and led into a room with a large conference table.

It turned out that the points of departure for the conversation diverged strongly. The siblings had come in order to free their brother. The K.G.B. gen-eral had been assigned the task of once and for all convincing the family that Wallenberg was dead.

The collision became clear from the start of the meeting. Nina and Guy had brought a list of some twenty witnesses that they said proved that Raoul had been alive after the asserted date of death in 1947. The K.G.B. official handed them the original copy of Smoltsov's handwritten report and claimed that this was proof that their brother had died on that day. This did not impress either Guy or Nina. Neither the family nor the Swedish government had ever accepted the Smoltsov report as proof.

A moment of surprise came a bit further into the conversation. Suddenly the K.G.B. general stood up and went to get a wooden box with hinges and a lock that he placed on the table in front of Nina Lagergren. According to Soviet prison protocol, the inmate's belongings should always be returned to the family after the death of the prisoner. This was the procedure that was now to take place and, according to the K.G.B.'s plan, put an end to forty-four years of discord.

Pirozhkov opened the box. Then he lifted out Raoul Wallenberg's diplomatic passport, which had been wrapped in a small plastic bag. He laid the passport in front of the box and went on to the rest of the belongings, one after the other: an address book, a diary, some rolls of banknotes in various wartime currencies and Raoul Wallenberg's Hungarian driver's licence. Pirozhkov said that staff at the K.G.B. archive had chanced upon Raoul's things. The discovery had been made only a couple of weeks earlier, on September 22, when an archival storage room in the basement of the Lubyanka was to be cleaned. There, in a plastic bag on a shelf, lay all these items. Therefore the family would now finally receive these belongings of "the deceased", as long as they first signed a receipt.

It was clear that the K.G.B. had expected tears and gratitude. Afterwards, Nina Lagergren admitted that the moment had involved "a terrible emotional journey"; in seeing Raoul's passport, his photograph and his notebooks after so many years. His handwriting. But she controlled herself and did not intend to offer up any tears. Nor a signature.

Pirozhkov handed her a pen and an itemised list of Raoul's things in Russian. Nina Lagergren gazed at the Cyrillic letters and pushed the page back unsigned, to his noticeable irritation. Angrily, Pirozhkov put all the items back in the box, closed it and carried it away. Only later, when Swedish diplomats observed that they did not feel the Russians were truly acting in accordance with *glasnost*, was the box returned to Nina.

Nina Lagergren took the wooden box of Raoul's belongings back with her on the plane. When she returned to her home in Djursholm she placed it in her Raoul chest next to the boiler in the basement.

The meeting in Moscow had raised more questions than it had answered. If Raoul Wallenberg's diplomatic passport could appear out of nowhere after so many years, perhaps there was more to be found in the Soviet archives. Soviet prison bureaucracy was notably comprehensive. A prisoner could not move cells without it being recorded and everything was collected in the well-organised archives. Periodic thinning had occurred but it was starting to appear more and more unlikely that the Smoltsov report would be the only document that the Soviet Union could produce about the political prisoner Raoul Wallenberg.

During the October trip to Moscow, Guy von Dardel had managed to arrange a visit to Vladimir prison, two hundred kilometres east of the capital. He had even had a first glance at the archive's 80,000 prison cards. Raoul Wallenberg's name had not been found but an initial search had yielded several of the witnesses who said they had encountered the Swede there. More questions hovered in the air. Now the original copy of the Smoltsov report had been taken out, surely its authenticity could be determined, for example by Sweden's forensic laboratory in Linköping? Guy certainly wanted to go back and keep researching.

Luckily the mild Soviet mood continued. In the early spring of 1990, Sweden's ambassador to Russia, Örjan Berner, had asked for and received a meeting with the head of the K.G.B., Vladimir Kryuchkov, a rare occcurence. Kryuchkov made two astonishing pronouncements. He was going to appoint a special K.G.B. officer as a contact for archival questions. And he was also going to approve the forensic examination of the Smoltsov report that the Swedes wanted performed. Kryuchkov would also show himself prepared to go further than that. Later he told the Swedish ambassador that he had also declassified all K.G.B. employees who knew something about Raoul Wallenberg. The Swedish diplomats sensed the hand of the liberal-minded minister of the interior, Vadim Bakatin, behind these unexpected developments.

Guy von Dardel had long since formed his international research team. Unfortunately Andrei Sakharov died suddenly, shortly before Christmas 1989, but the team now included Marvin Makinen, as well as a Canadian human rights lawyer, Irwin Cotler, who had also assisted in the American trial. And to establish collaboration with Soviet experts would no longer pose a problem, not in the new era of openness. There were many historians and researchers at the human rights organisation Memorial in Moscow, who worked hard to help Soviet citizens clarify the fate of their relatives in the Gulag. One of Memorial's key members was the historian and prison expert Arseny Roginsky, who had himself been a political prisoner. He joined the von Dardel group, as did the genetic researcher and dissident, Vadim Birstein.

Towards the end of the summer of 1990, Bakatin, the minister of the interior, opened up the Vladimir prison archives for a whole week. Von Dardel's group was given free access to all documents and the possibility of interviewing prisoners. The prison director of the Interior Ministry voiced the new Soviet attitude: "We will do everything to support you in finding out what happened to this great man . . . We do not want to end up on the wrong side of history."

Guy von Dardel had two points of departure for the team's work: 1) "Conclusive" findings indicated that Raoul Wallenberg had been alive in the fifties and sixties, and 2) "Credible" evidence indicated that he had been alive even during the seventies and eighties. "I fully believe that he is still alive," Guy von Dardel told the newspaper *Upsala Nya Tidning* before he travelled back to the prison in Vladimir with Marvin Makinen, Vadim Birstein and Arseny Roginsky, among others. But, according to Vadim Birstein, the Russian researchers did not share von Dardel's optimism. They did not expect to find Raoul Wallenberg living in Vladimir prison.

When the week was over, the team had sorted out all the political prisoners from the 80,000 inmates in the Vladimir records. They had not found Raoul Wallenberg's name but, on the other hand, they knew that there were sensitive cases registered with numbers. Therefore special attention had been given to numbered inmates. Guy von Dardel had brought a list of seven independent witness accounts regarding an inmate that they claimed was Wallenberg. "When we now have access to the records, we see that everything in their testimony is borne out. Everything except when we get to the cell where Wallenberg is to said have been held. For this there is no information.

It is like a complete blank," one of the optimistic researchers observed for the newspaper *Svenska Dagbladet* afterwards. It was obviously not quite so simple.

Over the next few years Guy von Dardel made additional trips back to Vladimir prison. The Russian archival researchers could not help but notice the strong emotions that drove him.

"We saw in Guy's actions and his way of speaking that he was always thinking, 'My brother could have been sitting in this cell.' He took everything very personally. When it came to Raoul Wallenberg, he would do anything that was needed, work as long as needed. His credo was to leave no stone unturned," says Memorial's Nikita Petrov, who was often at Guy von Dardel's side during these years. "Guy was a warm and honest man. His commitment was contagious and you wanted to believe with him that Raoul was alive. But in the end, that was where our opinions diverged."

The change in political climate endured. In early 1991, Memorial's researchers Arseny Roginsky and Vadim Birstein were suddenly given the chance to review material from the Soviet Union's secret Special Archives (Osoby arkhiv). Anatoly Prokopenko, then the head of the Special Archives, gave them the opportunity to study material from an archive of war prisoners, Fond number 451.

Roginsky and Birstein had a list of names of forty prisoners who had testified to the Swedish authorities about Raoul Wallenberg during the fifties. They requested their personal files and Prokopenko gave them ten to begin with.

The first discovery was quick in coming. They found a document from the Lefortovo prison dated February 1947. It was an order for the relocation of prisoners Willy Rödel and Raoul Wallenberg to cell number 7 in the Lubyanka's "Inner Prison". It would be followed by more.

The official Soviet "truth" had already been proved to be false. The Smoltsov report was not the only existing document with Raoul Wallenberg's name in the Soviet archives. Vadim Birstein published these sensational facts in an independent journal. "It did not take long before I received a call. The K.G.B. ordered me to stop the archival review immediately. And from what I know, the rest of this enormous archive has not yet been studied in depth," Anatoly Prokopenko says.

*

Guy von Dardel had fought long and hard for it, but in the end it was from the K.G.B. and the Soviet Foreign Ministry that the formal proposal came in late spring 1991: Sweden and the Soviet Union should form a collaborative working group in order to try to respond to the remaining questions from the Swedish side regarding Raoul Wallenberg. The response should not be interpreted as a Soviet desire to reopen the case. The Russians had indicated early on that they still regarded it as "an indisputable fact" that Raoul Wallenberg died in July 1947. But now they wanted to be rid of the question. For this reason, it could be beneficial to look in the archives and "bring about a definitive resolution".

With this kind of a working group, the Foreign Ministry could finally make their way into Soviet archives and find out what had happened.

The substantial Swedish–Russian investigation included six officials from the Foreign Ministry and Guy von Dardel from the Swedish side. On the Russian side there were officials from the Russian Foreign Ministry, the K.G.B. and a few other ministries. Guy's international researchers became "adjunct independent experts".

Things started well. After the attempted coup against Gorbachev in August 1991, the situation loosened up considerably. When Gorbachev returned from house arrest in Crimea, he appointed the *glasnost* advocate Vadim Bakatin as the new head of the K.G.B. The former ambassador to Sweden Boris Pankin was rewarded with the post of foreign minister for his loyalty during the coup. These appointments were a stroke of luck for the Swedes who wanted access to Soviet archives: a liberal K.G.B. chief and a foreign minister with a personal interest in resolving historic Swedish–Soviet knots.

Soon new documents were turning up one after the other. In early autumn, the Swedes were shown interrogation journals from the Lubyanka and Lefortovo where Raoul Wallenberg's name appeared. Here and there his name had been crossed out in thick felt pen, but forensic experts could restore the original text and establish that it was the K.G.B.'s way of attempting to conceal traces of the Swedish diplomat.

There was a certain amount of stress involved. Sensational material was appearing. Historic documents in the original, even from the K.G.B., were presented in various dossiers. But the Swedes were not allowed to make any copies and they did not know when they would be allowed to return. This golden opportunity to make progress in the Wallenberg case could be over at any moment. Örjan Berner, ambassador at the time, remembers how he was given approval that autumn to go to the Foreign Ministry archives himself. He brought along his deputy, Hans Magnusson. The Russians carried in selected files and they began to read, without any particular expectations.

The Swedish diplomats found a document from 1956, signed by Molotov, the foreign minister at the time. It was an internal memo intended for the Politburo as they discussed the appropriate Soviet position to take regarding the Raoul Wallenberg testimony from newly released German prisoners of war. As Berner read in the memo, Molotov argued that it was "useful to inform the Swedish government about Wallenberg's fate". The Swedish ambassador felt he had made an essential find.

"They were going to tell us what actually happened to Wallenberg! It was a strong indication that he was in fact executed. I felt it was convincing. They would of course lie about the way in which he died, but there I became convinced that he did in fact die when they said he had. You don't lie in an internal report to the Politburo. I was convinced that the document was authentic," Berner says today.

Ironically enough, Bakatin, the head of the K.G.B., had selected Molotov's grandson Vyacheslav Nikonov as the contact for the Swedes. Nikonov did not, however, like to talk about his grandfather's role in the case and did not know anything about it.

"For me he [Molotov] was primarily a wonderful grandfather. I never asked him about Wallenberg. I asked a great deal about Lenin, Stalin and Roosevelt. When all was said and done, Wallenberg was not so important that he was on that list," Nikonov later explained to the author.

In autumn 1991, Nikonov began working quickly and efficiently. The chairman of the working group, Hans Magnusson, noted a genuine personal willingness to take on the K.G.B. apparatus. They drew up a list of former employees of the security service who could have had knowledge of Raoul Wallenberg. Hans Magnusson was present in Vyacheslav Nikonov's office as he called around to individuals who had worked within the K.G.B. during his grandfather's time. He scheduled meetings with them to discuss Wallenberg.

PART III: WHAT DETERMINES A PERSON'S FATE?

But often the Swedish–Russian working group's interview team was sent out without warning. The Swedish diplomat Björn Lyrvall was a member of the interview team and was present at some forty interviews where even members of the K.G.B. were included.

"We would drive out into some Moscow suburb, to lonely widows and poor retirees who had perhaps been prison guards in the Lubyanka under Stalin. They were marked by the terror from that time. They were often terrified when we knocked on the door, but when our K.G.B. colleagues said who they were and showed their identification, they would sigh with relief. Hardly the reaction of regular Russians," Lyrvall recalls.

The most significant name of all emerged during the first perusal of the interview list in the autumn of 1991. A Daniel Kopelyansky was noted to have conducted two interrogations with Raoul Wallenberg in the summer of 1946, the first one for two and a half hours, the second not quite as long. Kopelyansky had been a rising star in the security service at that time and he was still alive. He, if anyone, should know why Wallenberg was arrested and what had happened to the Swedish diplomat.

Björn Lyrvall remembers that the aged interpreter and interrogation leader was on his guard when the interview team turned up. They had the impression that he was afraid he would be accused of something and noticed that he frequently referred to the Jewish aid organisation Joint when they asked about Raoul Wallenberg. They wondered if he was actually trying to tell them something. Daniel Kopelyansky was questioned several times but always denied that he had ever interrogated Raoul Wallenberg. He said that a superviser who had handled the interrogation must have written in his name instead. It was possible that Wallenberg could have been a prisoner that Kopelyansky had been given the task of "softening up" with tea and a sandwich beforehand.

The K.G.B. representative in the interview team tried to appeal to Kopelyansky's patriotism. He tried to elicit his loyalty to his former employer. But nothing worked. The interviewers did not manage to extract a single word about Raoul Wallenberg. It was clear that he had made up his mind. But with every meeting the working group became more and more convinced that the man had a great deal to tell. They had noted that Kopelyansky blanched when they showed him a photograph of Raoul Wallenberg's cell mate Willy Rödel.

In February 1992, Guy von Dardel and Marvin Makinen went to the shabby little apartment in central Moscow where Kopelyansky lived. Perhaps this key witness would respond differently to a plea from Wallenberg's family. Guy walked up the stairs alone. Kopelyansky, a short man, opened the door. He was said to have had a piercing gaze, although by this time one eye was blind. "I am Raoul Wallenberg's brother. Can you help me?" Guy began in German. An animated conversation ensued. It ended with Kopelyansky grabbing a cudgel and screaming that he would call the police if Guy did not leave.

Daniel Kopelyansky died in the early 2000s. What secrets he had he took with him.

The Soviet Union had collapsed and the Swedish–Soviet working group became Swedish–Russian. After a while the setbacks started as Russia slowly fell back into the authoritarian leadership of former times. The archives became increasingly closed.

But the results so far had been encouraging. With all the new documents, the working group had already reconstructed a significantly fuller picture of Raoul Wallenberg's time in Soviet prisons and the sequence of events on the Soviet side. But one could not say that they had arrived at a final understanding of the Swedish diplomat's fate. In a way, they had more questions now than they had at the beginning.

Tensions increased. The Swedish diplomats noticed that the answers from the Russians were becoming increasingly negative and they did not understand why. Was it because there were no more documents or because the Russian side did not want to show everything? A sense that they could not get any further started to spread among the Foreign Ministry representatives. After a while it was only the almost eighty-year-old Guy von Dardel and his experts who appeared to have any remaining energy. Guy took it on himself to appoint two new foreign researchers, Susanne Berger and Susan Mesinai, who were completely unknown to the Swedish diplomats.

The Wallenberg investigation was starting to split into smaller groups. Both the ambitions and the perspectives of its members were steadily drifting apart. When the Swedish–Russian working group process had been under way for four years, the chairman Hans Magnusson was working on a draft for the final report. Guy von Dardel and his experts pointed out with outrage everything that remained to be done. Wasn't it "complete clarity" about Raoul Wallenberg's fate that they were to achieve?

The decades-old mutual mistrust between the family and the Foreign Ministry remained. Relations were not improved when Guy von Dardel, in a long article with the title, "Goodbye Mr Wallenberg" accused the Foreign Ministry of a criminal – in the moral sense of the word – obfuscation of what had happened fifty years ago. "The crime is admittedly beyond the statute of limitations and almost all the players deceased. But this doesn't mean that the truth about what happened at that time is inconsequential. It will emerge at some point despite all the obstacles," von Dardel wrote in Dagens Nyheter in 1997.

After ten years of Swedish–Russian collaboration, it was finally time. A press conference in Stockholm was scheduled for the morning of Friday, January 12, 2001. The collected international media gathered early in the government building, Rosenbad's marble-clad auditorium, Bella Venezia. What had happened to Raoul Wallenberg after January 17, 1945? Raoul Wallenberg's family sat in the front row, beside representatives from the K.G.B. (now F.S.B.).

The point of departure for the large Wallenberg investigation had been that, after fifty-six years, the family should finally receive an answer. But Nina Lagergren and Guy von Dardel already knew that this would not be the case. Guy and his independent expert would hold their own press conference about the failure later, in a considerably smaller room.

Nina was having trouble digesting an experience from the night before. Prime Minister Göran Persson had called both of the siblings. He had reached Guy von Dardel in his hotel room and Nina Lagergren at home. The prime minister said that he wanted to express the government's regrets over "the lack of involvement" during the first years of the Wallenberg case. He even said that the mistakes of 1945–1947 had "prevented a happier outcome for Raoul Wallenberg and his family". The newspapers did not delay in picking up this story. Shortly thereafter a special government investigation was appointed to look into the diplomatic mistakes that had been made.

Later the Kremlinologists would interpret this action for what it was: a Social Democrat prime minister had finally broken his silence and publicly

criticised the party saint Östen Undén. Even the prime ministers Hansson
and Erlander got a dose of this medicine. Had this ever happened before?

Nina Lagergren was not as impressed. And she thought that it was poor
form, almost insulting, that, after all these years, the prime minister had
expressed his apology over the telephone. "I'm sure that the prime minister
had good intentions but an apology can't make up for the serious mistakes
that were made and that were critical for Raoul," she said to a reporter.

Guy von Dardel climbed up to the podium. He sat there together with
the Swedish and Russian chairmen of the working group, Hans Magnusson
and Vyacheslav Tuchnin. Raoul's family, Sweden and Russia – almost all the
parties in the long Wallenberg drama were present. Only the United States
was absent. And Raoul Wallenberg himself.

The Swedish–Russian working group had turned over many stones,
revealed numerous pieces of information about Raoul's prison time and about
the false claims from the Soviets over the years. But now, at the moment of
truth, they were back to square one. They did not speak the same language.
From three parties, there were three final reports.

The Russians peppered their analysis with more questions than usual but
nonetheless maintained that, for the most part, the information reiterated
what the Soviet Union had established in 1957: that Raoul Wallenberg died on
July 17, 1947. They claimed to have proved that the Smoltsov document was
authentic, although there was possibly some uncertainty as to whether the
physician had been truthful about the cause of death. At the press conference,
Tuchnin said openly that he thought Raoul Wallenberg had been murdered.
A persistent rumour indicated that he had been shot at the Lubyanka that
day.

The Swedish conclusion was different. Careful forensic analyses had not
been able to prove that the Smoltsov document was a forgery but nor could
they prove it was authentic. It was still not possible to establish with certainty
that Raoul Wallenberg had died in 1947. Therefore one could not rule out that
he might be alive. "The burden of proving that Raoul Wallenberg is dead lies
with the Russian government," were the concluding words of the Swedish
report.

The family in turn did not trust either party. Nina Lagergren and Guy von
Dardel were deeply saddened that it seemed completely impossible to reach

the only goal that they had wanted to reach all these years: the truth.

Afterwards, when the reporters had left, the family was able to observe that the most important new development had taken place on another front. Guy von Dardel had been working on this for a while and just before Christmas he received a message. The Russian commission for the rehabilitation of the victims of the terror had decided to provide redress to Raoul Wallenberg and Vilmos Langfelder. The Russian prosecutor general stated that Wallenberg and Langfelder had been arrested and imprisoned without legal grounds. Here they had it in black and white. Their brother Raoul Wallenberg was innocent of all accusations, and a victim of the political oppression in the Soviet Union.

Nina Lagergren decided that from now on she would do whatever she could so that her brother's name would live on, as a role model for new generations.

Guy and Matti von Dardel had checked in to the Hotel Esplanade with their daughters Louise and Marie. Some Russian members of the working group were also staying there. The hotel address was Strandvägen 7a and was only located a few steps from Nybrokajen Quay, with all the now frozen, docked archipelago ferries.

In the evening, when everything was over, the Russians invited Guy and his family for a drink in one of the hotel lounges. They had brought a bottle of vodka that they poured out into Swedish shot glasses. They were well informed and told Louise von Dardel and Marie Dupuy that the Hotel Esplanade was actually located in a "Wallenberg house". Guy von Dardel could fill in details. It was in this building that the Mid-European Trading Company had once had its offices. It was here that Raoul Wallenberg and Kálmán Lauer had run their goose imports in the time before Raoul's departure for Budapest. This was also where Iver Olsen and the others at the American legation had been located.

Something felt wrong, the sisters thought. The Russians were so warm and friendly, all the while still tormenting them with ambivalent signals. Over vodka, the von Dardels again heard their Russian hosts speculate that Raoul had *not* died of a heart attack on 17 July, 1947, although this was the official Russian truth. Now they apparently thought that he had been shot a couple of months later, during the autumn of 1947. They even claimed that they had received anonymous calls from witnesses who had heard the shots.

What should the family believe? Guy von Dardel sipped his vodka in irritation, trying to control his anger. Ten years of investigation and still no substantial evidence. Only more questions.

The Russians from the security service, formerly called the K.G.B., had been standing waiting in the corner. Suddenly one of them plucked up courage and walked over to the von Dardels. He had something in his hand. As he approached he pulled a large gift box of Russian chocolates out of a bag and smilingly held it out to Raoul Wallenberg's family.

Stockholm and Moscow, 2011

Vladimir Putin is in town. Helicopters thunder over downtown Stockholm and in the Rosenbad press room, Bella Venezia, a couple of hundred journalists have been assembled for over an hour. The Russian and Swedish heads of state are to hold a combined press conference. It is claimed that this has not happened for ten years. The levels of security are extraordinary.

I have an enviable place toward the front, right behind the Russian journalists. I have only a single question to pose and the former K.G.B. officer Putin should be able to provide an answer. The newspapers present him as a macho man. "He believes in force. Once can sense this when one meets him," Prime Minister Fredrik Reinfeldt says in an interview.

I repeat my question silently to myself. "What happened to Raoul Wallenberg?"

The prospects of an answer are better than for a long time. There is a more conciliatory tone between the two countries after a period of icy cold during the Georgia conflict. I have also received an informal tip that the Raoul Wallenberg case has been mentioned during the morning discussion between the two prime ministers. Fredrik Reinfeldt actually brought up Wallenberg on President Medvedev's visit in 2009 as well. It was the first time in a very long while. Something new must be in the offing.

After the Swedish–Russian working group's final report in 2001, the Raoul Wallenberg case was removed from the foreign policy agenda. It was a mutual Swedish–Russian decision. The questions that remained about Raoul Wallenberg's fate (that is to say, all of them) were henceforth deemed to be of a historical rather than political nature. But there was one condition for the de-politicisation of the case. Both Sweden and Russia promised to give future researchers freedom to continue to seek the truth.

In part it is the contradictory facts concerning "prisoner number 7" that have caused the Swedish government to resume the matter. Was Raoul Wallenberg alive and interrogated after the claimed death date of July 17, 1947? Sweden does

not think that Russia is living up to its side of the agreement. Wallenberg researchers find it increasingly difficult to search for the truth in the relevant Russian
archives. Free access has never really existed.

Finally they are standing on the podium. The one who is claimed to be strong
stands a head shorter than the Swedish prime minister. Putin actually looks pale
and weak beside the unusually tanned Reinfeldt. I feel my courage grow.

In the rows of journalists, there has been talk that the press conference is
rehearsed. Only four questions will be taken and the lucky few have already
been informed – two Swedish and two Russian journalists. And I thought that
Sweden had a free press.

Our worst fears are confirmed. The two Russian reporters sound as if even the
questions have been handed out in advance. The Swedish news bureau T.T.'s
journalist is the only one who manages to get anything of interest from the Russian leader. His question is about Putin's criticism of Sweden's participation in the
N.A.T.O.-led Libya intervention. Suddenly the Russian prime minister's voice
becomes smooth and he starts to speak about human rights.

"When I see how easily decisions are made in the world about taking other
peoples' lives I am shocked," Putin says.

Then it is over. To my dismay I see Vladimir Putin disappear through the doors.

What happened to Raoul Wallenberg? I have to get a current, official answer.
A written interview with the head of the Foreign Ministry's second European div-
ision is what the Russian officials offer me. It could be worse. For three years
Viktor Tatarintsev was the Russian chairman in the Swedish–Russian working
group on Raoul Wallenberg. I receive a long letter. In it, I can discern the official
Russian answer, current in December 2011. It seems identical to Gromyko's mem-
orandum from 1957. Raoul Wallenberg died of natural causes on July 17, 1947,
Viktor Tatarintsev explains.

"The only reliable proof of the Swedish diplomat's death remains the report
by A. L. Smoltsov . . . which states that 'prisoner Walenberg [sic],' with whom
you are familiar, 'suddenly expired in his cell, most likely as a result of a myocardial infarction [heart attack]'," he writes and I realise that bigger muscles than
mine will be required to make any headway.

*

Sweden's foreign minister, Carl Bildt, has his office in Arvfursten Palace a stone's
throw from Stockholm Palace. The painstakingly renovated rooms are supposed

to suggest the eighteenth century but under the chandeliers in the meeting room you can hear the drone of the laser printers.

Carl Bildt has the television on when I arrive. This, the corner room with a view over Stockholm Palace, has been the office of all of his predecessors, even Christian Günther and Östen Undén. I look around. Tall mirrors, gilded frames and a laptop on the antique desk. We sit down on the sofa.

"What is the government doing today to learn the truth about the Raoul Wallenberg case?

"Until we gain complete clarity, it remains a case. These days we often keep the matter at the top of our priorities. For example, I brought it up with the Russian foreign minister, Lavrov, just the other week."

What did you say on that occasion?

"That there is new information and we ask them to be helpful to researchers. They always say that they will be, so this is only to confirm it at the highest levels."

Do you think that the Russian leadership today knows more about what happened to Raoul Wallenberg than what is in the Gromyko memorandum from 1957?

"Do you mean Putin? Well, that is hard to know. I would not think it very likely."

Why did they lie for so long, do you think?

"They lied about almost everything. The Soviet Union was a state built on a lie, towards their own citizens, towards the surrounding world."

What do you believe happened to him?

"I think it is most likely that they executed him."

In that case, why did they execute him?

"There may have been a special reason for it; it may also be that it simply happened. This was a system that executed people daily in large numbers."

Shouldn't they be able to admit as much after all those years?

"Yes, I would think so."

The answer has come from the F.S.B. archives in Moscow. I am welcome back to "see some documents". The wish list I had sent contained the obvious: Raoul Wallenberg's prisoner card, the interrogation registers and the original of Smoltsov's report. It is worth an extra trip.

I arrive and am faced with the same sparsely furnished meeting rooms, the same white teacups. But wait, there is something. On the bare wooden table, behind a bowl with chocolates, I glimpse a thin, grey-yellow piece of cardboard approximately the size of an A6 envelope. It is Raoul Wallenberg's prisoner card. The original.

The velvet-eyed Khristoforov has been prevented from coming at the last moment. His replacement looks puzzled when I ask permission to hold the prison card. "Just for a little while," I say. He nods.

I run my forefinger over the rough surface. One can see that the prisoner card has been folded. The writing is nicely rounded and Raoul Wallenberg's name is written in ink, perhaps even with a hint of methyl violet. Raoul has not signed the card and the box for his fingerprint is empty. Arrested: January 19, 1945. Arrival at the Lubyanka: February 6, 1945

My throat tightens, but I pull myself together. And the prison interrogation register?

"Those you can't see, since it contains information about other prisoners," my host explains.

And the original of Smoltsov's report?

He explains that they never show anything other than copies in Russian archives, and points out the bad one published in the report from the Swedish–Russian working group.

Afterwards, I stop for a while at Lubyanka Square. I glance at some big road sweepers and a bottomless emptiness overpowers me. They keep driving around, spraying water over the roundabout, where in the middle a statue of Felix Dzerzhinsky, the K.G.B.'s founder, used to stand, before the Soviet Union fell to pieces.

In my pocket, I have two pieces of chocolate from the F.S.B. archive's glass bowl. When I unfold the glossy paper I'm startled: the F.S.B. chocolate's logo is three colourful theatre masks.

EPILOGUE

Djursholm, summer 2011

Little Raoul is in town and I am going to meet him. He has nine teeth and a light-blue dummy and his full name is Raoul Stig Lago Wernstedt. He has just turned one and is Nina Lagergren's tenth great-grandchild, the first in the family to carry the same first name as the brother that Nina never saw again.

For decades, the name Raoul has been reserved for the man who was one day to return. But slowly there has been a change. Almost imperceptibly, one conviction has been replaced by another. Now this great-grandchild is staggering around in his great-grandmother's kitchen and if one says "Raoul!" he stops and grins widely. A one-year-old charmer who loves to play with bricks is now the guarantor of the name's – and the world-famous initials "R.W." – continued survival in the family.

Ninety-one-year-old Nina Lagergren offers chilled pineapple juice. It is a cloudless early summer morning at that time of the year when Sweden shows its very best side. On this day, we won't talk about any of the sadness, about all the lies and false leads. The questions are nevertheless ever present. I know that Nina still hopes to learn the truth about what happened to her brother.

"You would think it is the least they can do. What is the harm in it? What do they have to lose?" she asked despondently when we last talked.

But now little Raoul is here and the sun is shining through the kitchen window of the apartment. He has just started daycare, his parents Fredrik and Anna Wernstedt tell me.

Raoul is wearing a yellow-and-white striped shirt and is crawling under the table, sorting his bricks into his great-grandmother's jars. When you see his smile it is hard not to think of Maj von Dardel's descriptions in letters of Raoul Wallenberg's first year in 1910: "When he laughs and looks so incredibly delighted as he does then it is quite contagious."

His father Fredrik is thirty-one. Just like his siblings, cousins and second cousins he has grown up with the case always in the background, and with the person Raoul Wallenberg as a role model. Fredrik tells me that he is now reading Maj von Dardel's letters a second time. He recognises so much in her description of her little Raoul. They share their curiosity, Fredrik observes and chases after his son who is already on his way into his great-grandmother's living room.

The rest of us follow. There is a large box on the table, filled with antique oval boxes from the toy manufacturer E. Heinrichsen in Nuremberg. Nina wants to show yet another great-grandchild the hand-painted tin soldiers that her brother Raoul once played with, the ones that he inherited from the father who died before he was born. They are more than a hundred years old.

"Look, here we are with all the soldiers!" Nina calls out in delight.

She watches Fredrik as he arranges a row of hardy Roman warriors on the table. Soon they are joined by leaf-thin Hussars in red-and-blue uniforms. Little Raoul grabs a gun carriage, crawls up into an armchair and tries to put it in his mouth. When he has investigated the piece thoroughly he holds it out to Nina and fires off another infectious smile.

"Thank you, thank you, Raoul," Nina says and gazes lovingly at him.

Outside, Sweden is waking up to another beautiful day. Families in holiday mode stream out into the sun. Seedlings are to be planted, the potatoes earthed up. Cars drive in heavy traffic from the nurseries with soil, geraniums and tomatoes. Sweden is intent on sprouting and cultivating, as it should be, as it has in all the years in the past and will in all the years of the future.

By the side of the road the lupins reach for the sky. Here and there peonies are blooming and in some gardens you can glimpse the delicate blue and yellow flower that carries the most beautiful of all Swedish names:

Förgätmigej.

Forget me not.

ACKNOWLEDGEMENTS

I would first and foremost like to extend my warmest gratitude to Raoul Wallenberg's half-sister Nina Lagergren, who ever since our first contact in the summer of 2009 has spent endless interview hours telling me about her brother Raoul, and leading me through the many twists and turns of the family's drama. My special thanks also to Guy von Dardel's widow, Matilda von Dardel, who answered many questions and gave me access to Guy von Dardel's private archive. My research would not have been possible without the help of Nina's and Guy's children, above all Mi Ankarcrona and Marie Dupuy. The Helge Ax:son Johnson Foundation, the Writer's Photocopy Fund and the Foreign Ministry Fund for Independent Research on Raoul Wallenberg have all awarded me grants and thereby enabled my trips abroad.

It was with deep respect that I approached the large cohort of existing experts on the topic. The Swedish Foreign Ministry's doyen of the Raoul Wallenberg case, Ambassador Jan Lundvik, was immediately responsive and has patiently shared his great knowledge with me, on the subject of both Wallenberg and Hungary. Jan Lundvik facilitated contact with Gábor Forgács, who by then was probably the only one still able to describe the work and atmosphere in Wallenberg's innermost circle. Now he is no longer with us. My warmest thanks to both for their invaluable contributions to this project.

I pestered a number of former Swedish Foreign Ministry officials in their retirement. Among these I particularly want to thank Leif Leifland, who died in 2015, and Sven Hirdman.

Many researchers on subjects central to the book have generously taken time out of their busy schedules to share their findings and answer my tiresome questions. A warm thanks above all to the Wallenberg experts Johan Matz, Göran Rydeberg, Susanne Berger, Gellért Kovács and Georg Sessler, as well as economics professor Håkan Lindgren and the intelligence researcher Craig McKay. My deepest collective thanks also to the great number of individuals I have subjected to lengthy interviews.

A considerable research project of this kind is not possible without helpful archivists, among whom I particularly want to single out the staff of the Swedish National Archives and the Stockholm City Archives, as well as Stephan Bergman at *Dagens Nyheter* and *Expressen*'s archive. I also owe a debt of gratitude to the Swedish Government Offices archive for the donation of the forty-nine "blue books", which contain a great deal of the documentation on the Wallenberg case.

Gloria von Berg, Anna Végh, Levente Harmatha, Richard Zwillinger and Michael Davies have all generously provided information about the various

Budapest environments where Raoul Wallenberg spent his time in the autumn of 1944. But one cannot go everywhere and so, with time, the number of co-workers and translators has grown. A warm thank you to Katalin Garam (Budapest), Maria Ludkovskaya (Moscow), Peter Andreasson (Washington), Katja Lucke (Berlin), Sam Nadonnichols (Ann Arbor), and last but not least Slavicist Mattias Ågren, journalist Fabian Sturm and translator Peter Samuelsson in Stockholm. I also want to recognise Joshua Prager (for important advice at the beginning of the project), Fredrik Laurin (for masterly Excel-assistance), Mary Anne Drew (for material from the College of Architecture, Ann Arbor), Henrik Berggren (for valuable input on various sections of the manuscript), and Lena Milton (for all last-minute requests at the National Archives).

My group of early readers should be commended for having held out until the end. I owe an enormous debt of gratitude to my parents Sonja and Per Carlberg, my brother Anders Carlberg and my friend Ewa Stenberg. Among them is also my friend Eva Apelqvist, from Wisconsin, U.S.A., whose contributions to this book have gone far beyond the call of duty: I do not have the words to express how grateful I am.

My beloved mother-in-law Margareta Nuder managed to read four chapters before she – all too soon – left us in April 2011. It pains me that she never had a chance to see the completed work.

Norstedts Publishing House provided top talents like Jenny Tenenbaum, Per Faustino, Ulla Renström, Lars Molin and above all Stefan Hilding, whose engagement and humour turned even the most demanding phases of the final spurt into a joy. I was very proud to have MacLehose Press as my English publisher and became even more enthusiastic once I had the pleasure of working with such sympathetic and professional people as Christopher MacLehose, Katharina Bielenberg and Josh Ireland. The transfer to the English language demanded a highly competent translator. I am so grateful for the great work of Ebba Segerberg.

An author who launches into an undertaking such as this one inevitably becomes unbearable to those in her immediate surroundings. At the same time, she requires the maximum amount of love and consideration in order to see it through. It should be an insoluble dilemma, but not for my wonderful family. Pär, Johanna and Sara – I could never have done this without you.

Ingrid Carlberg
Budapest and Stockholm,
March 2012 and November 2015

SOURCES AND BIBLIOGRAPHY

I have been anxious to base the central story, as much as possible, on primary sources. For the broader, more contextual material (on contemporary Sweden and Europe, the wider family story, historical background etc.) I have drawn more heavily on published sources, including contemporary news coverage. Detailed notes to the text can be found at www.maclehosepress.com/wallenbergnotes.

OVERVIEW OF PRIMARY SOURCES

PART I

The account of Raoul Wallenberg's family history and his life before Budapest is based mainly on family letters from either the huge private Raoul Wallenberg Archive in the Riksarkivet, Stockholm (the Swedish National Archives) or the private archives and photograph albums of members of the family. Interviews with family members (mainly his half-sister, Nina Lagergren) have also yielded a great deal of valuable supplementary information.

For R.W.'s time in school the archive of the Nya Elementarskolan, Stadsarkivet (the Stockholm City Archives) has been a rich source, as have notes from his schoolmates.

When it came to the years R.W. spent at the University of Michigan, Ann Arbor and his year as a trainee in South Africa and Palestine, I was able to consult private letters and telegrams, in addition to notes and letters from his fellow students, which are kept at the Bentley Historical Library. Copies of his original compositions are kept in Nina Lagergren's private archive and his architectural sketches are retained by the Architectural Museum of Stockholm.

In the depiction of the relationship between Raoul's branch of the family and the rest of the Wallenberg banking dynasty the regular primary sources have been complemented by released documents, engagement diaries, travel itineraries and private letters contained in the Wallenberg Archives in Stockholm. I was also able to interview Raoul Wallenberg's second cousin, Peter Wallenberg, who was *pater-familias* of the Wallenberg group until his death in 2015.

My research into Raoul Wallenberg's years as a businessman have been enriched by new discoveries in two important Swedish government archives: the Statens Utlänningskommission (National Foreigners' Commission) at the Riksarkivet, Stockholm, which contains detailed information about the life of R.W.'s

605   SOURCES AND BIBLIOGRAPHY

co-workers; and the archives of the Statens Hästexportberedning, Sveriges Livs-
medelskommission, Sveriges Handelskommission (the Swedish authorities
responsible for the horse trade and the import/export of food during the war),
where a huge amount of hitherto unknown business correspondence in RW's
hand has been found.

The archive of the Bolagsverket (the Swedish equivalent of Companies House)
contains useful company documents regarding the history of Mellaneuropeiska
Handelsaktiebolaget and Banan-kompaniet. My interview with R.W.'s cousin
Lennart Hagströmer yielded important insights into this phase of his life, as did
previously unreleased business correspondence with between the cousins.

Surviving invitations and short letters of thanks to R.W. from friends, found
in Guy von Dardel's archive, have been useful in understanding R.W.'s life in
the months immediately before he left for Budapest. For 1944, Raoul Wallenberg's
private diary, handed over to his family by the K.G.B. in 1989, has been an important primary source.

PART II

The primary sources for the account of R.W.'s six months in Budapest consist
largely (in addition to the private correspondence and other general sources mentioned above) of the following: Telegrams and day-to-day documentation from
the Budapest legation file in the Swedish Foreign Ministry (Utrikesdeparte-
mentet, U.D.) Archive, kept at the Riksarkivet, Stockholm, the volumnious U.D.
file on the Raoul Wallenberg case, the biggest dossier in the whole U.D. Archive,
Riksarkivet, Stockholm. (This is not to be confused with the huge private Raoul
Wallenberg archive, also kept at the Riksarkivet, Stockholm.) Raoul Wallenberg's
personal dairy and address book from 1944, Kalman Lauer's Files, at the Riksarkivet, Stockholm (in the private Raoul Wallenberg Archive), documents and
telegrams from the War Refugee Board and the U.S. Department of State, as well
as the archives of the German Foreign Ministry and the Hungarian authorities
(including documents published in the first Hungarian book about R.W. by Jenő
Lévai).

For more personal contributions I have consulted primary sources, such as
Margareta Bauer's diary and private memoirs, transcribed interviews with Per
Anger, Laszlö Pető, Kazmer Kállay, Thomas Veres, Johnny Moser, Pál Szalai and
Giorgio Perlasca, in the Raoul Wallenberg Project Archive, Uppsala Universitet.
In addition to my own interviews with some of R.W.'s surviving colleagues and
also individuals saved by his actions, the Rudolph Philipp Archive at the Riks-
arkivet, Stockholm has been important, since his research covered part of the
time R.W. spent in Budapest.

PART III

This part of the story, concerning the whole post-war drama and the Swedish diplomatic failure in relation to the Raoul Wallenberg case, covers the period 1945–2012 (when the Swedish edition of this book was published). The primary sources relating to this part worth mentioning are: the Raoul Wallenberg File (U.D. P2 Eu1) in the Swedish Foreign Ministry's archive at the Riksarkivet Stockholm, which includes relevant parts of the Moscow legation's archive (U.D. Hp 80 Ea); the private archive of Guy von Dardel (eighty-five boxes), which is currently maintained by his daughter, Marie Dupuy; Fredrik von Dardel's voluminous diary in the Raoul Wallenberg Archive (private), the Riksarkivet, Stockholm and Rudolph Philipp's rich archive in the same place.

The Soviet perspective is covered by internal Soviet documents on R.W.'s arrest, his time in the Lyubyanka and Lefortovo prisons and on the ongoing diplomatic dispute surrounding his disappearance. A great deal, but far from all, of the Soviet documents linked to the Wallenberg case were released at the end of the 1980s and the beginning of the 1990s. They were made available by the so-called Swedish–Russian Working Group, (U.D. II:52, 2000). The Soviet documentation contains, among other things, information on the times and dates for the interrogations R.W. But no interrogation transcripts have ever been released. R.W. was neither prosecuted nor sentenced by any court in the Soviet Union.

For the depiction of U.S. interest in the Wallenberg case the main primary source is the C.I.A. archive, Raoul Wallenberg Personality File (Record file 263), National Archives, Washington. The interesting political game preceding the new Swedish diplomatic note in 1979 (Chapter 22) was revealed by cross-referencing telegrams, notes and other contemporary documentation in three different archives: the Swedish Foreign Ministry's archive, the C.I.A. archive (R.W. Personality File) and Fredrik von Dardel's diary, which includes the family's incoming and outgoing correspondence.

For details on R.W.'s everyday life in prison a rich source has been the eyewitness reports from R.W.'s fellow inmates in the Lubyanka and Lefortovo contained in the first white paper published by the Swedish Foreign Ministry (1957) and in the Swedish Foreign Ministry's Raoul Wallenberg file. Contemporary reflections from Swedish Prime Minister Tage Erlander and Foreign Minister Östen Undén are based on their respective diaries.

ARCHIVES

PUBLIC ARCHIVES

The National Archives (R.A.), Stockholm
    Archive of the Ministry of Justice
    Archive of the National Commission on Foreigners
    Archive of the National Equine Export Commission
    Archive of the National Food Commission
    Archive of the Swedish Foreign Ministry
    Archive of the National Trade Commission
    Archive of the Swedish Security Service
    Raoul Wallenberg Archive (RWA) (individual archive)
    The Swedish Patent and Registration Office
Archive of Skeppsholm Congregation, Stockholm
Women's Historical Collection, Gothenburg University
Stockholm City Archive (S.A.)
    Nya Elementarskolan archive
    Archive of the Stockholm Airport Commission
Stockholm City Museum
    "Inner city inventory", "Östermalm inventory"
The Royal Library (K.B.), Stockholm
    Vardagstryck
The Museum of Architecture, Stockholm
The Army Museum, Stockholm
    Raoul Wallenberg's pocket diary, 1944 (donated by Nina Lagergren)
    Raoul Wallenberg's telephone and address book, 1944 (donated by Nina
    Lagergren)
University of Michigan, Ann Arbor
    Bentley Historical Library
College of Architecture, Ann Arbor
Archive of the Swedish Companies Registration Office
Uppsala University Library
    Archive of Uppsala University (U.U.A.)
        The Raoul Wallenberg Project (R.W.P.)
            Series F2 C/ Interview records
            Series F3 B.1/ Documents from archive in Budapest,
            The Hungarian internal and foreign ministries
Archive of the [Swedish] Foreign Ministry, Government Offices

The Raoul Wallenberg dossier (U.D. P2 Eu1, also F1a, vol. 14 and F1b, vol. 1 respectively [the Nanna Svartz case])

"The Blue Books", volumes 1–49

"Raoul Wallenberg – database of witness accounts and documents", www.wallenbergdatabase.ud.se (The documents in the Russian archives that have been made public, such as the former K.G.B. archive, archive of the former Central Committee, central archive of the Ministry of Defence, archive of the Foreign Ministry and presidential archive)

Politisches Archiv des Auswärtigen Amts (P.A. A.A.), Berlin

National Archives (N.A.), Washington D.C. and College Park, Maryland

    Central Intelligence Agency Archives (C.I.A.A.)

Library of Congress, Washington, D.C.

    Otto Fleischmann Papers

Yad Vashem Archive, Jerusalem

M.O.L., Magyar Országos Levéltár (Hungarian National Archive)

K.U.M., Külügy Minisztérium Arkiv (Hungarian Ministry of Foreign Affairs and Trade)

PRIVATE ARCHIVES

Elena Anger

Birgit Brulin

Helene Carlbäck

Guy von Dardel

Lennart Hagströmer

Nina Lagergren

Gustaf Söderlund

Nathan and Anna Söderblom's family archive (sealed deposit, Uppsala University Library, by way of special permission from Dr Staffan Runestam)

Raoul Wallenberg archive (maintained as a private archive at the Swedish National Archives)

Fredrik von Dardel's journals, 1952–1978

The Foundation for Economic History Research within Banking and Enterprise, or the Wallenberg Archive (W.A.), Stockholm (unfortunately without open access)

BIBLIOGRAPHY

BOOKS

Agrell, Wilhelm, *Stockholm som spioncentral* (Historiska media, 2006)

Agrell, Wilhelm, *Venona: spåren från ett underrättelsekrig* (Historiska media, 2003)

Ahlberg Gösta, *Stockholms befolkningstillväxt efter 1850* (Almqvist & Wiksell, 1958)

Anger, Per, *Med Raoul Wallenberg i Budapest. Minnen från krigsåren i Ungern* (Norstedts, 1979)

Arnstad Henrik, *Spelaren Christian Günther. Sverige under andra världskriget* (Wahlström & Widstrand, 2006)

Bachner, Henrik, *Judefrågan. Debatt om antisemitismen i 1930-talets Sverige* (Atlantis, 2009)

Bauer, Yehuda, *Jews for Sale? Nazi-Jewish Negotiations, 1933–1945* (Yale University Press, 1994)

Beevor, Antony, *D-Day. The Battle for Normandy* (Viking, 2009)

Berg, Lars G:son, *Boken som försvann. Vad hände i Budapest?* (new edition, Textab Förlag, 1983)

Berthon, Simon and Potts, Joanna, *Warlords*, (Da Capo Press, 2006)

Bierman, John, *Raoul Wallenberg: en hjälte i vår tid: Biografi om »mannen som räddade 100 000 judar«, hans liv, kamp och försvinnande*, (AWE/Gebers, 1982)

Birstein, Vadim, *SMERSH. Stalin's Secret Weapon*, (Biteback Publishing, 2011)

Björkman-Goldschmidt, Elsa, *Elsa Brändström* (Norstedts, 1969)

Blanck, Dag, *Sverige-Amerikastiftelsen. De första sjuttio åren. 1919–1989* (Sverige-Amerikastiftelsen, 1989)

Boheman, Erik, *På vakt. Kabinettssekreterare under andra världskriget* (Norstedts, 1964)

Bolinder, Jean, *30-tal* (Liber Läromedel, 1977)

Bondor, Vilmos, *A Mikó rejtély* (Püski, 1995)

Braham, Randolph L., "The Holocaust in Hungary: A Retrospective Analysis", in Braham, Randolph L. and Miller, Scott (eds), *The Nazis' Last Victims* (Wayne State University Press, 1998)

Braham, Randolph L., *The Politics of Genocide. The Holocaust in Hungary* (condensed edition) (Wayne State University Press, 2000)

Brandell, Ulf, *Dagbok med DN*, (Bokförlaget Trevi, 1976)

Bruchfeld, Stéphane and Levine, Paul A, ... *om detta må ni berätta ... En bok om Förintelsen i Europa 1933–1945* (revised edition), Forum för Levande Historia, 2009

Brink, Lars, *När hoten var starka. Uppkomsten av en väpnad folkrörelse*, akademisk avhandling (Text & Bild Konsult, Göteborg, 2009)

Broberg, Gunnar, *Statlig rasforskning. En historik över rasbiologiska institutet* (Lunds universitet, 1995)

Browning, Christopher R., *Ordinary men. Reserve Police Battalion 101 and the Final Solution in Poland* (HarperPerennial, 1992)

Browning, Christopher R., *The Final Solution and the German Foreign Office* (Holmes & Meier Publishers, Inc, 1978)

Carlbäck, Helene, *Sverige i ryska arkiv: Guide till ryska källor om svensk historia under 1900-talet* (The Swedish National Archives, 1999)

Carlgren, Wilhelm, *Sveriges utrikespolitik 1939–1945* (Allmänna förlaget, 1973)

Carlsson, E., *Skolgeografi uti två årskurser* (P. A. Norstedts & Söner, 1887)

Carlsson, Sten, "Sverige under första världskriget", i *Den svenska historien* (new edition Bonnier Lexikon, 1979)

Cartledge, Bryan, *The Will to Survive. A History of Hungary* (Timewell Press, 2006)

Cassel, Gustav, *Socialism eller framåtskridande* (Norstedts, 1928)

Cesarini, David, *Adolf Eichmann. Byråkrat och massmördare* (new edition Månpocket, 2006)

Khristoforov, V. S. (ed.), *Tredje rikets diplomatiska hemligheter: Tyska diplomater, chefer för utländska militära beskickningar, militär- och polisattachéer i sovjetisk fångenskap: Material ur förundersökningarna*, Internationella fonden "Demokratija", Moskva, 2011. (Tayny diplomatii Tret'ego Reykha 1944–1955: Germanskie diplomaty, rukovoditeli zarubezhnykh voennykh missiy, voennye i politseyskie attasye v sovetskom plenu: dokumenty iz sledstvennykh del 1944–1955 (Moskva: Mezhdunarodny fond "Demokratiya", 2011)

Churchill, Winston S. & Churchill, Randolph, *Att vinna freden. Tal hållna efter kriget* (Skoglunds Bokförlag, 1949)

Chuev, Felix and Albert Resis (ed.), *Molotov Remembers. Inside Kremlin Politics, Conversations with Felix Chuev*, (Ivan R. Dee Publisher, 1991)

Cornelius, Deborah S, *Hungary in World War II. Caught in the Cauldron* (Fordham University Press, 2011)

Cornwell, John, *Hitler's Pope. The Secret History of Pius XII* (Viking, 1999)

Christmas of Raoul Wallenberg 1944 (Kolor Optika Bt, 2004)

Dahlberg, Hans, *I Sverige under andra världskriget* (Bonnier Fakta, 1983)

von Dardel, Fredrik, *Raoul Wallenberg – fakta kring ett öde* (Proprius förlag, 1970)

von Dardel, Maj, *Raoul* (Rabén & Sjögren, 1984)

Denham, Henry, *Inside The Nazi Ring: A Naval Attaché in Sweden 1940–45* (John Murray Publishers Ltd, 1984)

Derogy, Jacques, *Fallet Raoul Wallenberg* (Berghs förlag, 1980)

Dolgun, Alexander, *En amerikan i Gulag* (Askild & Kärnekull, 1975)

Drangel, Louise, *Den kämpande demokratin* (Liber, 1976)

Dryselius, Mats, *Kappsta – en fristad. En inventering av historiska förutsättningar och framtida möjligheter* (Lidingö kommun, 1984)

Eby, Cecil D., *Hungary at War. Civilians and Soldiers in World War II* (The Pennsylvania State University Press, 2009)

Einhorn, Lena, *Handelsresande i liv. Om vilja och vankelmod i krigets skugga* (third edition, Norstedts, 2006)

Ekdahl, Niklas, *Per Albin Hansson* (Albert Bonniers förlag, 2010)

Ember, Mária, *Ránk akarták kenni* (Héttorony könyvkiadó, 1992)

Ember, Mária, *Wallenberg Budapesten* (Vársháza, 2000)

Englund, Terje B., *Spionen som kom for sent. Tsjekkoslovakisk efterretning i Norge* (Aschehoug, 2010)

Ericsson, Anne-Marie, *M/S Kungsholms inredning: mästerverk i art deco* (Atlantis, 2005)

Eriksson, Eva, *Den moderna stadens födelse* (Ordfronts förlag, 1990)

Eriksson, Eva, *Den moderna staden tar form. Arkitektur och debatt 1910–1935* (Ordfront, 2001)

Erlander, Tage, *Dagböcker 1945–1949* (Gidlunds förlag, 2001)

Erlander, Tage, *Dagböcker 1950–1951* (Gidlunds förlag, 2001)

Erlander, Tage, *Dagböcker 1952* (Gidlunds förlag, 2002)

Erlander, Tage, *Dagböcker 1956* (Gidlunds förlag, 2006)

Erlander, Tage, *Dagböcker 1957* (Gidlunds förlag, 2007)

Erlander, Tage, *Dagböcker 1961–1962,* (Gidlunds förlag, 2011)

Forgács, Gábor, *Emlék és valóság. Mindennapjaim Raoul Wallenberggel* (*Minnen och verklighet. Mina dagar med Raoul Wallenberg*) (Kolor Optika Nyomda és Kiadó, 2006)

Franzén, Nils-Olof, *I Sverige under första världskriget. Undan stormen* (new edition, Albert Bonniers förlag, 2001)

Friedel, Robert, *Zipper: An Exploration in Novelty* (Norton, 1995)

Friedländer, Saul, *The Years of Extermination. Nazi Germany and the Jews 1939–1945* (Phoenix, 2008)

Friman, Helena and Söderström, Göran, *Stockholm. En historia i kartor och bilder* (Bonnier Fakta, 2008)

Gersten, Alan, *A Conspiracy of Indifference. The Raoul Wallenberg Story* (Xlibris Corporation, 2001)

Gilbert, Martin, *Israel. A History* (William Morrow and Company 1998)

Grafström, Sven, *Anteckningar 1938–1944* (The Royal Society for the publication of documents related to the history of Scandinavia, 1989)

Gårdlund, Torsten, *Marcus Wallenberg 1864–1943. Hans liv och gärning* (Norstedts, 1976)

Hadenius, Stig, Molin, Björn and Wieslander, Hans, *Sverige efter 1900. En modern politisk historia*, (new edition, Bonnier Alba, 1993)

Hansson, Svante, *Flykt och överlevnad. Flyktingverksamhet i Mosaiska församlingen i Stockholm 1933–1950*, (Hillelförlaget, 2004)

Harmincad Utca 6. A Twentieth Century Story of Budapest (British Embassy, 1999)

Harriman, W. Averell and Abel, Elie, *Special Envoy to Churchill and Stalin 1941–1946* (Random House, 1975)

Hasselberg, Per-Erik, *Klippan 12 – en Strandvägsbyggnad* (Art & Auto Stockholm AB, 2004)

Henrikson, Alf, *Svensk historia* (Bonniers, 1966)

Historic Photographs of the University of Michigan (Turner Publishing, 2007)

Holm, Yngvar, *Den store boken om amerikabåtene. Nasjonens maritime stolthet* (Edvardsen forlag, 2004)

Horthy, Miklós, *Memoirs* (Andrew L. Simon, 2000)

Hägglöf, Gunnar, *Svensk krigshandelspolitik under andra världskriget* (Norstedts, 1958)

Hägglöf, Ingemar, *Berätta för Joen. Mina år med ryssarna* (Norstedts, 1984)

Höjer, Henrik, *Al Capone. Gangstern och den amerikanska drömmen* (Albert Bonniers Förlag, 2009)

Isaksson, Anders, *Per Albin. IV, Landsfadern* (Wahlström & Widstrand, 2000)

Isling, Åke, *Kampen för och mot en demokratisk skola. Samhällsstruktur och skolorganisation* (Sober Förlags AB, 1980)

Jacobi, Jutti, *Zarah Leander. Das Leben einer Diva* (Hoffmann u. Campe Vlg GmbH, 2006)

Jansson, Herbert, "Victoriaförsamlingen på Tredje rikets tid", in *Svenska Victoriaförsamlingen i Berlin 1903–2003*, (ed.) Sven Ekdahl (Svenska Victoriaförsamlingen, 2003)

Kasztner, Rezső, *Der Kasztner-Bericht über Eichmanns Menschenhandel in Ungarn* (Kindler, 1946)

Kershaw, Alex, *The Envoy* (Da Capo Press, 2010)

Kissinger, Henry, *De första åren i Vita Huset* (Norstedts, 1979)

Klee, Ernst, *Das Personenlexikon zum Dritten Reich. Wer war was vor und nach 1945* (S. Fischer Verlag GmbH, 2003)

Klein, Georg, *Jag återvänder aldrig. Essäer i Förintelsens skugga* (Albert Bonniers förlag, 2011)

Komarov, Alexey, "Khrushchev and Sweden", in *Peaceful coexistence? Soviet Union and Sweden in the Khrushchev era*, ed. Carlbäck, Helene, Komarov, Alexey and Molin, Karl, Baltic and East European Studies 10, Centre for Baltic and East European Studies (CBEES) (The Institute of Universal History, 2011)

Korányi, Erwin, *Dreams and Tears: Chronicle of a Life* (General Store Publishing House, 2006)

Korobochkin, Maxim, "Soviet views on Sweden's neutrality and foreign policy, 1945–1950", in *Peaceful coexistence? Soviet Union and Sweden in the Khrushchev era*, ed. Carlbäck, Helene, Komarov, Alexey and Molin, Karl, Baltic and East Euoropean Studies 10, Centre for Baltic and East European Studies (CBEES) (The Institute of Universal History, 2011)

Kronvall, Olof, "Rolf Sohlman", in *Svenska diplomatprofiler under 1900-talet*, ed. Artéus, Gunnar and Leifland, Leif (Probus förlag, 2001)

Krönika över 20:e århundradet, ed. Söderberg, Margareta (Bonniers, 1988)

Kvist Geverts, Karin, "'Fader Byråkratius' rädsla för antisemitism. Attityder mot judiska flyktingar inom Socialstyrelsens utlänningsbyrå", in *En problematisk relation. Flyktingpolitik och judiska flyktingar i Sverige 1920–1950*, ed. Andersson, Lars M. and Kvist Geverts, Karin (Opuscula Historica Upsaliensia 36, 2008)

Lajos, Attila, *Hjälten och offren, Raoul Wallenberg och judarna i Budapest* (Emigrantinstitutets skriftserie 15, 2004)

Langlet, Nina, *Kaos i Budapest* (Harriers, 1982)

Langlet, Valdemar, *Verk och dagar i Budapest* (Wahlström & Widstrand, 1946)

Larsson, Lennart Jr, *Ett brokigt liv som köpman i Stockholm-Budapest-Hongkong* (Stenströms, 1993)

Leijonhufvud, Christer, *Stockholm på 1940-talet. Beredskapsår och efterkrigstid i unika färger* (Trafik-Nostalgiska Förlaget, 2009)

Lester, Eleonore, *Wallenberg: The Man in the Iron Web* (Prentice-Hall, 1982)

Lévai, Jenő (ed.), *Eichmann in Hungary. Documents* (Pannonia Press, 1961)

Lévai, Jenő, *Raoul Wallenberg – hjälten i Budapest* (Saxon & Lindströms, 1948)

Lévai, Jenő, *Raoul Wallenberg* (English edition, WhiteAnt Occasional Publishing, 1989)

Levine, Paul A., *From Indifference to Activism. Swedish Diplomacy and the Holocaust 1938–1944* (Studia Historica Upsaliensia, 1998)

Levine, Paul A., *Raoul Wallenberg in Budapest. Myth, History and Holocaust* (Vallentine Mitchell, 2010)

Lindberg, Hans, *Svensk flyktingpolitik under internationellt tryck 1936–1941* (Allmänna Förlaget, 1973)

Lindgren, Håkan, *Jacob Wallenberg 1892–1980* (Atlantis, 2007)

Lindorm, Per-Erik, *Gustav V och hans tid, 1907–1918* (Wahlström & Widstrand, 1979)

Lindorm, Per-Erik, *Stockholm genom sju sekler* (Sohlman, 1951)

Lindquist, Bosse, *Förädlade svenskar* (Alfabeta, 1991)

Lindström, Ulla, *I regeringen* (Bonniers, 1969)

Lindström, Ulla, *Och regeringen satt kvar!* (Bonniers, 1970)

Lozowick, Yaacov, *Hitler's Bureaucrats. The Nazi Security Police and the Banality of Evil* (Continuum Studies in the Third Reich, Continuum, 2000)

Lundh, Christer and Ohlsson, Rolf, *Från arbetskraftsimport till flyktinginvandring* (SNS Förlag, 1994)

Magnergård, Omar, *I andra världskrigets skugga* (Svenska Dagbladet, 1985)

Magnusson, Lars, *Sveriges ekonomiska historia* (Norstedts, 2010)

Marton, Kati, *Wallenberg: Missing Hero* (Random House, 1982)

Medvedev, Roy A., *All Stalin's Men* (Basil Blackwell, 1983)

Medvedev, Zhores A. and Medvedev, Roy A., *The Unknown Stalin* (I. B. Tauris, 2010)

Myasnikov, A. L., *Ya lechil Stalina* (Eksmo, 2011)

Montefiore, Simon Sebag, *Stalin. Den röde tsaren och hans hov* (Prisma, 2003)

Müller-Tupath, Karla, *Reichsführers gehörsamster Becher. Eine deutsche Karriere* (Aufbau-Verlag, 1999)

Möller, Tommy, *Svensk politisk historia* (Studentlitteratur, 2007)

Möller, Yngve, *Östen Undén. En biografi* (Norstedts, 1986)

Nordisk familjebok (Uggleupplagan, 1921)

Nylander, Gert, *German Resistance Movement and England* (The Foundation for Economic History Research within Banking and Enterprise, 1999)

Nylander, Gert and Perlinge, Anders (eds), *Raoul Wallenberg in documents, 1927–1947* (The Foundation for Economic History Research within Banking and Enterprise, 2000)

Odelberg, Axel, *Äventyr på riktigt. Berättelsen om upptäckaren Sven Hedin* (Norstedts, 2008)

Olsson, Ulf, *Att förvalta ett pund. Marcus Wallenberg 1899–1992* (Ekerlids, 2000)

Olsson, Ulf, *Finansfursten. K A Wallenberg 1853–1938* (Atlantis, 2006)

Olsson, Ulf, *I utvecklingens centrum. Skandinaviska Enskilda Banken och dess föregångare 1856–1996* (Skandinaviska Enskilda Banken, 1997)

Olsson, Ulf, *Stockholms Enskilda Bank and the Bosch Group 1939–1950* (The Foundation for Economic History Research within Banking and Enterprise, 1998)

Palm, Thede, *Några studier till T-kontorets historia* (The Royal Society for the publication of documents related to the history of Scandinavia, volume 21, 1999)

Parvilahti, Unto, *Berias gårdar* (Natur & Kultur, 1958)

Persson, Carl and Sundelin, Anders, *Utan omsvep* (Norstedts, 1990)

Petri, Gustaf, *Mina hemvärnsår* (Kooperativa förbundets bokförlag, 1952)

Perlmutter, Amos, *FDR & Stalin. A Not So Grand Alliance, 1943–1945* (University of Missouri, 1993)

Perwe, Johan, "Hjälpnätverk och motstånd 1933–1945", in *Svenska Victoriaförsamlingen i Berlin 1903–2003*, ed. Sven Ekdahl (Svenska Victoriaförsamlingen, 2003)

Petersson, Olof, *Studentexamen* (SNS, 2010)

Petersson, Olof, *Svensk politik* (Publica, 1993)

Petri, Lennart, *Sverige i stora världen. Minnen & reflexioner från 40 års diplomattjänst* (Atlantis, 1996)

Pető, László, *Det ändlösa tåget. Requiem* (Textab Förlag, 1984)

Philipp, Rudolf, *Raoul Wallenberg* (Förlags AB Viken, 1981)

von Platen, Gustaf, *Resa till det förflutna. Lättsinne i allvarstid* (Fischer & Co, 1993)

Porter, Anna, *Kasztner's Train* (Walker & Company, 2007)

Rayfield, Donald, *Stalin and His Hangmen* (Random House, 2005)

Roseman, Mark, *The Wannsee Conference and The Final Solution* (Picador, 2002)

Rosenberg, Göran, *Det förlorade landet* (Albert Bonniers förlag, 1996)

Rosenfeld, Harvey, *Raoul Wallenberg. The Mystery Lives On* (iUniverse, 1982)

Runberg, Björn, *Valdemar Langlet. Räddaren i faran. Wallenberg var inte ensam* (Megilla-Förlaget, 2001)

Ruth, Nancy, *More Than a Handsome Box. Education in Architecture at the University of Michigan 1876–1986* (The University of Michigan College of Architecture and Urban Planning, 1995)

Räddningen. Judarna ska deporteras. De svenska hjälpinsatserna. Rapporter ur UD:s arkiv (Fischer & Co, 1997)

Rönnholm, Nils, *Tillägg till Carlssons skolgeografi första kursen* (P A Norstedts & Söner, 1919)

Salén, Sven, *Salénrederierna 1915–1965* (Salénrederierna, 1965)

af Sandeberg, Edward, *Nu kan det sägas. Sanningen om min fångenskap i Sovjet och Berlins fall* (Saxon & Lindströms, 1946)

Schellenberg, Walter, *The Schellenberg Memoirs* (Andre Deutsch, 1956)

Schiller, Bernt, *Varför ryssarna tog Raoul Wallenberg* (Natur & Kultur, 1991)

Schön, Lennart, *En modern svensk ekonomisk historia* (SNS Förlag, 2000)

Schüllerquist, Bengt, *Från kosackval till kohandel. SAP:s väg till makten* (Tiden, 1992)

Sereny, Gitta, *Albert Speer och sanningen* (Bonnier Alba, 1995)

Service, Robert, *The Penguin History of Modern Russia* (third edition, Penguin Books, 2009)

Shackman, Grace, *Ann Arbor in the 20th Century, A Photographic History* (Arcadia, 2002)

Sjöquist, Eric, *Affären Wallenberg* (Bonniers, 1974)

Sjöquist, Eric, *Dramat Raoul Wallenberg* (Norstedts, 2001)

Sjöquist, Eric, *Raoul Wallenberg. Diplomaten som försvann* (Askild & Kärnekull, 1981)

Solzhenitsyn, Alexander, *Gulagarkipelagen. Fängelseindustrin* (Wahlström & Widstrand, 1974)

Solzhenitsyn, Alexander, *I den första kretsen* (new edition, Brombergs förlag, 2010)

Stenvång, Eva, *100 år med AB Banan-Kompaniet, 1909–2009* (AB Banan-Kompaniet and Kulturhistoriska Bokförlaget, 2009)

Sudoplatov, Pavel and Anatoly, *Direktoratet. Stalins spionchef berättar*, with Jerrold L. and Leona P. Schecter (Norstedts, 1994)

Svanberg, Ingvar and Tydén, Mattias, *Sverige och Förintelsen. Debatt och dokument om Europas judar 1933–1945* (Arena, 1997)

Svartz, Nanna, *Steg för steg* (Albert Bonniers Förlag, 1968)

Szabó, Tamás, *Who Was the Man in the Leather Coat?* (e-book, 2011)

Szita, Szabolcs, *Raoul Wallenberggel Moszkváig, Langfelder Vilmos élete és családtörténete* (Aura Kiadó, 2011)

Szita, Scabolcs, *Trading in Lives? Operations of the Jewish Relief and Rescue Committee in Budapest 1944–1945* (Central European University Press, 2005)

Taubman, William, *Khrushchev. The Man and his Era* (Norton, 2003)

Tennant, Peter, *Vid sidan av kriget. Diplomat i Sverige 1939–1945* (Legenda, 1989)

The Intelligence Community 1950–1955, eds Keane, Douglas and Warner, Michael (United States Government Printing Office, 2007)

Tingsten, Herbert, *Gud och fosterlandet. Studier i hundra års skolpropaganda* (Norstedts, 1969)

Tjerneld, Staffan, *Det romantiska tjugotalet* (Norstedts, 1963)

Tjerneld, Staffan, *Hundra år på Östermalm* (Höjerings, 1984)

Tjerneld, Staffan, *Stockholmsliv. Hur vi bott, arbetat och roat oss under 100 år. Norr om Strömmen* (Norstedts, 1949)

Tschuy, Theo, *Dangerous Diplomacy. The Story of Carl Lutz, Rescuer of 62,000 Hungarian Jews* (Wm. B. Eerdmans, 2000)

Ullman, Magnus, *Seglare, redare, sångare: en bok om Sven Salén* (SNS, 1991)

Undén, Östen, *Anteckningar 1918–1952* (The Royal Society for the publication of documents related to the history of Scandinavia, 2002)

Ungváry, Krisztián, *Battle for Budapest. 100 Days in World War II* (I.B. Tauris, 2010)

Vaksberg, Arkady, *Aleksandra Kollontaj* (Norstedts, 1996)

Vaksberg, Arkady, *Giftlaboratoriet. Från Lenin till Putin – 90 år av politiska mord* (Norstedts, 2007)

Vaksberg, Arkady, *Skjut de galna hundarna* (Norstedts, 1990)

Villius, Elsa and Hans, *Fallet Raoul Wallenberg* (Gebers, 1966)

Wallenberg, Gustaf and Wallenberg, Raoul, *Älskade farfar* (Bonniers, 1987)

Wallenberg, Raoul, *Några förslag till ett friluftsbad å Riddarholmen* (Kungl. boktr., 1935)

Wallenberg, Raoul, *Letters and Dispatches 1924–1944* (Arcade Publishing, 1987)

Werbell, Frederick E and Clarke, Thurston, *Raoul Wallenberg – en försvunnen hjälte* (Wahlströms, 1985)

Wyman, David S., *The Abandonment of the Jews. America and the Holocaust, 1941–1945* (new edition, The New Press, 2007)

Wästberg, Per, *Carlssons skola 1871–1971: en minnesskrift* (Bonniers, 1971)

Zetterberg, Kent, "Staffan Söderblom", i *Svenska diplomatprofiler under 1900-talet*, ed. Artéus, Gunnar and Leifland, Leif (Probus förlag, 2001)

Zubok, Vladislav M, *Failed Empire. The Soviet Union in the Cold War from Stalin to Gorbachev* (The University of North Carolina Press, 2007)

Zwack, Anne Marshall, *If You Wear Galoshes, You're An Emigre, Peter Zwack. A Memoir* (Hungarian Ab Ovo Publishing House, 2001)

Åmark, Klas, *Att bo granne med ondskan. Sveriges förhållande till nazismen, Nazityskland och förintelsen* (Albert Bonniers förlag, 2011)

Älmeberg, Roger, *Hemliga förbindelser. DC-3:an, Sverige och Kalla kriget* (Norstedts, 2007)

SELECTED ARTICLES

Berger, Susanne, and Birstein, Vadim, "Latest Wallenberg Development", 19 March 2012, www.vadimbirstein.se

Birstein, Vadim, "The Secret of Cell Number Seven" (or) "Taina kamery nomer sem'", *Nezavisimaya gazeta*, 25 April 1991, www.vadimbirstein.com

Birstein, Vadim and Berger, Susanne, "Surprised Again – New Documentation about Raoul Wallenberg's Cellmate Surfaces", www.vadimbirstein.com

Birstein, Vadim J., "The Mystery of Raoul Wallenberg's Death", originally published in the Russian journal *Evereiskie novosti*, no. 2, July 2002, www.vadimbirstein.com

Gellértfy, Péter, "A magyar tengerészet története Trianontól a második világháborúig" ("Hungarian seafaring history from Trianon to World War Two"), www.portfiume.gportal.hu

Lindgren, Håkan, "The Long Term Viability of the Wallenberg Family Business Group. The Role of 'A Dynastic Drive'", Biographies of the Financial World. International Symposium at the Stockholm School of Economics, August 20–21, 2010.

Lindgren, Håkan, "Esse non videri. Om värderingar och självbilder i den wallenbergska familjetraditionen", Handelshögskolan, Stockholm, 2003

Löfgren, Svante, "Moder Sveas smidde guldgosse", *Allt*, May 1949

"The Manfréd Weiss–SS Deal of 1944. Excerpts from the Memoirs of George Hoff", *Legal Council Hungarian Studies* 711–2 1991/92

Matz, Johan, "Sweden, The United States and the Bureaucratic Politics of the Raoul Wallenberg Mission to Hungary in 1944", in *Journal of Cold War Studies*, vol. 14, no. 2, 2012

Ribbing, Seved, "Per Johan Wising. Minnesteckning", *Hygiea. Medicinsk och Farmaceutisk Månadsskrift*, 1913

Wallenberg, Raoul, "Sydafrikanska intryck", *Jorden Runt*, no. 8, 1936

SWEDISH NEWSPAPERS AND MAGAZINES

Aftonbladet
Aftontidningen
Arbetaren
Arbetet
Byggmästaren
Dagens Nyheter
Folkets Dagblad
Göteborgs Handels- och Sjöfarts-Tidning

Göteborgs-Posten
Helsingborgs Dagblad
Nya Dagligt Allehanda
Social-Demokraten
Stockholms-Tidningen
Svenska Dagbladet
Upsala Nya Tidning
Vecko-Journalen

PUBLIC DOCUMENTS

White paper, Swedish Foreign Ministry, 1957, U.D. II:9
The Swedish Foreign Ministry's document archive regarding Raoul Wallenberg, 1965
The Swedish Foreign Ministry's public document collection, "The Blue Books" volumes 1–49
S.O.U. 1999:20
"Raoul Wallenberg. Redovisning av den svensk-ryska arbetsgruppen", Swedish Foreign Ministry's reports, Series II:52, 2000 (also the investigations archive, Swedish Foreign Ministry)
"Ett diplomatiskt misslyckande", S.O.U. 2003:18 (also investigations archive, The National Archives)
"Rapport om verksamheten i den rysk-svenska arbetsgruppen för fastställande av Raoul Wallenbergs öde (1991–2000)", 2004

SELECTED MEMOS AND REPORTS

Berger, Susanne, "Stuck In Neutral. The Reasons behind Sweden's Passivity in the Raoul Wallenberg Case", 2005, research memo published at www.raoul-wallenberg.eu.
McKay, Craig G., "What happened in Cairo", report presented at a Foreign Ministry symposium on Raoul Wallenberg, January 28, 2011
McKay, Craig G., "Work on the Dutch Connection", report presented at a Foreign Ministry symposium on Raoul Wallenberg, January 28, 2011
McKay, Craig G., "A friend indeed. The secret service of Lolle Smit", http://www.raoul-wallenberg.eu/general/a-friend-indeed-the-secret-service-of-lolle-smit
McKay, Craig G., "Excerpts from McKay's Notes on Raoul Wallenberg", www.raoul-wallenberg.eu

Memo with excerpts from Tage Erlander's as yet unpublished journals, by Ulf Larsson, September 4, 2002, as a basis for the investigation S.O.U. 2003:18

"Raoul Wallenbergs kabinettspass och utrikesresor 1941–1942", internal memo by Sven Johansson, Swedish Foreign Ministry, 1997

"Debriefing av Jan Lundvik angående fallet Raoul Wallenberg. I samtal med Harald Hamrin, Krister Wahlbäck och Göran Rydeberg", memo, 10 February as well as March 3, 2009, Swedish Foreign Ministry

"Raoul Wallenberg: Material i Bundesarchiv, Bern", internal Swedish Foreign Ministry memo written by Jan Lundvik, October 26, 1999

"Hur kan Moskva tänkas ha uppfattat det svenska agerandet i Raoul Wallenberg-ärendet", internal memo by Jan Lundvik, June 9, 2000, U.D.

"Söderblom, Undén och Wallenberg-ärendet", internal Swedish Foreign Ministry memo by Krister Wahlbäck, January 9, 2001

"Specialberättelser" regarding events at the Swedish legation in Budapest December 1944 and February 1945, published by Per Anger, Ivan Danielsson, Lars G:son Berg, Denez Mezey . . . , May 2, 1945, U.D.

Kovács, Gellért, "Raoul Wallenberg. Forskning i hans fotspår i Budapest 1944–45. En kartläggning av Raoul Wallenbergs verksamhet och kontaktnät", Swedish Foreign Ministry report, Stockholm, 2011

Kronvall, Olof, "Östen Undens Sovjetsyn och Sovjetpolitik 1945–1962", working report n. 13, from the research programme "Sverige under kalla kriget", 2003

Rydeberg, Göran, Raoul Wallenberg. Ett öde. Historik och nya forskningsfält, book manuscript developed from Rydeberg's report for the Swedish Foreign Ministry, www.raoul-wallenberg.eu.

Sessler, Georg, "PM. En genomgång av Attila Lajos avhandling Hjälten och offren, Raoul Wallenberg och judarna i Budapest", Swedish Foreign Ministry report, Stockholm, 2011

SELECTED UNPUBLISHED SOURCES

Bauer, Margareta, Minnesanteckningar från krigsåren i Budapest 1943–1945, 1996

Margareta Bauer's journal notations, as related in a memo by Jan Lundvik, Swedish Foreign Ministry, March 19, 1997

Fredrik von Dardel's journal in the Raoul Wallenberg archive, National Archives

Maj von Dardel's private photograph album

Ember, Mária, Lundvik, Jan and Forgács, Gábor, Identifizierung von Namen in Raoul Wallenbergs Notizbüchern, internal working paper for the Swedish Foreign Ministry, 2000–2002

Excerpt from Rolf af Klintberg's journal notations, made available to the author by his son Bengt af Klintberg

Lutz, Carl, *Bericht über die Geschehnisse bei der Schweizerischen Gesandtschaft in Budapest, der Schutzmachtabteilung und den unter ihren Schutz stehenden Bureaux und Gebäuden (Oktober 1944–April 1945)*, private memoir, gift to Per Anger at the Swedish Foreign Ministry 1969. A copy made available to the author by Jan Lundvik.

OTHER

"A Tribute to The Lost Hero of the Holocaust", The Simon Wiesenthal Center remembers Raoul Wallenberg, Simon Wiesenthal Center, 1985
"FSB Headquarters, Lubyanka", www.agentura.ru.
Ljubljanka – Lefortovskaja – Vladimir. Vad vi vet och inte vet om Raoul Wallenberg, television documentary by Hans Villius, Sveriges Television, February 2, 1965, prod.nr. 4309/64
"På denna plats: en vandring genom krigets Stockholm 1933–1945", Forum för levande historia, 2008
"Vittnesmål för svensk-sovjetiska kompetenta myndigheter angående svenske diplomaten Raoul Wallenberg", nedtecknat och översatt av dåvarande doktoranden i historia, Helene Carlbäck-Isotalo, October 12, 1989, made available to the author from professor Helene Carlbäck's private archive.
"30 år i täten", brochure from AB Banan-Kompaniet 1939
"AB Banan-Kompaniet 90 år: 1909–1999", brochure from AB Banan-Kompaniet 1999
Berger, Susanne, "Jacob Wallenberg's Initiative", May 5, 2005, www.raoul-wallenberg.eu
Conway, John S, "The first report about Auschwitz", Simon Wiesenthal Center (motlc.wiesenthal.com).
"Csepel Hungaro-Swedish Shipping Co. Ltd. – Budapest – 1941–1945" or "Csepel Magyar-Svéd Hajózási RT. – Budapest – 1941–1945", an excerpt from Dr Juba Ferenc, *A magyar tengerészet nagyjai* (Great Figures From the Hungarian Navy) published at www.hajoregiszter.hu
"Direkt, Studio 13", Sveriges Radio, January 31, 1980
"Globus Produkter", marketing brochure, The Royal Library's division for ephemera, 1942
Kern, Gary, "How 'Uncle Joe' bugged FDR", Studies in Intelligence, Central Intelligence Agency, www.cia.gov
The Red Book, Stockholm telephone directory, The Royal Library

INTERVIEWS

Jan Anger	Nina Lagergren
Sverker Åström	Annette Lantos
Margareta Bauer	Leif Leifland
János Beer (via e-mail)	Håkan Lindgren
Gloria von Berg	Jan Lundvik
Susanne Berger	Björn Lyrvall
Örjan Berner	Hans Magnusson
Tomas Bertelman	Vjatjeslav Nikonov
Carl Bildt	Staffan Paues
Alice Breuer	Thage G Petersson
Birgit Brulin	Nikita Petrov
Helene Carlbäck	Attila Pók
Caroline Grinda Christensen	Anatoly Prokopenko
Louise von Dardel	Arseny Roginsky
Matilda von Dardel	Louise Schlyter
John Drakenberg	Eric Sjöquist
Marie Dupuy	Michael Sohlman
Stuart Eizenstat	Gunvor Svartz
Gábor Forgács	Szabolcs Szita
Katalin Garam	Gustaf Söderlund
Lennart Hagströmer	Viktor Tatarintsev (via e-mail)
Sven Hagströmer	Jury Trambitsky
Sven Hirdman	Frank Vajda
Ann Ighe	Marianne Vaney (via e-mail)
Gustav Kadelburger	Anna Végh
Gabriella Kassius	Kate Wacz
Vasily Khristoforov	Gitte Wallenberg
Georg Klein	Peter Wallenberg
Rolf af Klintberg	Peter Zwack (email)

PICTURE CREDITS

1–21, 24–27, 30, 36, 75 © Private archive/Nina Lagergren

31, 51, 59 © Private archive/Nina Lagergren – reproduction Karl Gabor,

39 © Private archive/Nina Lagergren – reproduction Posten Frimärke

22, 23, 83 © Private archive/Guy von Dardel

28 © Image from the Swedish Centre for Architecture and Design's collections/Arkitekturmuseet,

29 © Private archive/Caroline Jacobsen

32 © Förlaget Nordisk Konst

33 © Banan-kompaniet, Vardagtryck, KB

34, 35, 41, 52, 80, 82, 86 © Scanpix

37 © National Archives of Hungary

38 © Collection of Karl Sandel/IBL

40 © Süddeutsche Zeitung-Photo/IBL

42 © Geschichte in Chronologie

43, 81 © Roger-Viollet/IBL

44 © Riksarkivet – Passport owned by Nina Lagergren. Photographed by Riksarkivet Stockholm. Utrikesdepartementets archive for the year 1920, HP 109

45 © RiKu Public Affairs Section

46 © U.S. Embassy Stockholm

47, 48 © S.F.E.H.F. – The Foundation for Economic History Research within Banking and Enterprise, Stockholm

49, 57, 62 © Armémuseum (deposit by Nina Lagergren)

50, 56, 72, 73 © Private archive/Thomas (Tamás) Veres

53 © Private archive/Elena Anger

54 © Lutz archive, Münchenbuchsee

55, 63–66 © Swedish Foreign Ministry (Utrikesdepartementet)

58, 68, 71 © MTI Photo, Budapest

60, 67 © Museum Kiscell, Budapest

61 © Private archive/Barbara Everingham

69 © Jan Herdevall

70, 92 © Ingrid Carlberg

74 © Riksarkivet

76 © Corbis/Scanpix

77 © F.S.B. archive, Moscow (photograph by Ingrid Carlberg)

85 © Lennart Nilsson/Scanpix

87 © Expressen

88 © Aftonbladet/IBL

89 © Lars Nyberg/Scanpix

90 © Jan Collsiöö/Scanpix

91 © Posten Frimärke

93 © Thomas Karlsson/*Dagens Nyheter*/Scanpix

94 © Pete Souza/Official White House photograph

FAM

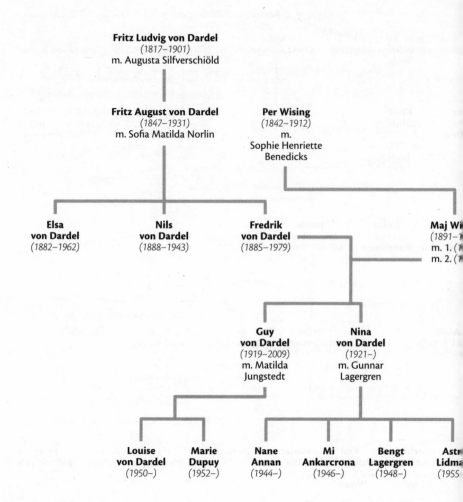

Fritz Ludvig von Dardel
(1817–1901)
m. Augusta Silfverschiöld

Fritz August von Dardel
(1847–1931)
m. Sofia Matilda Norlin

Per Wising
(1842–1912)
m.
Sophie Henriette
Benedicks

Elsa
von Dardel
(1882–1962)

Nils
von Dardel
(1888–1943)

Fredrik
von Dardel
(1885–1979)

Maj Wi
(1891–1
m. 1. *(1*
m. 2. *(1*

Guy
von Dardel
(1919–2009)
m. Matilda
Jungstedt

Nina
von Dardel
(1921–)
m. Gunnar
Lagergren

Louise
von Dardel
(1950–)

Marie
Dupuy
(1952–)

Nane
Annan
(1944–)

Mi
Ankarcrona
(1946–)

Bengt
Lagergren
(1948–)

Astr
Lidma
(1955

EE

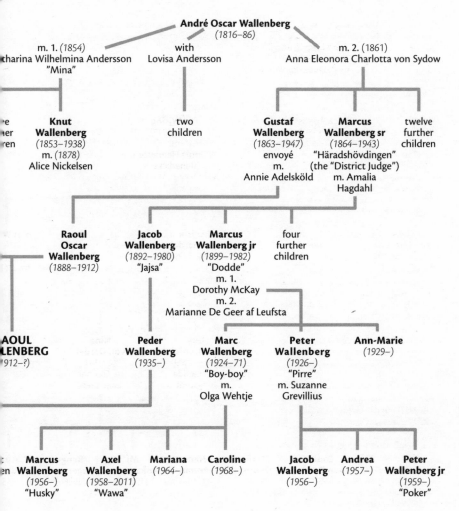

André Oscar Wallenberg
(1816–86)

m. 1. *(1854)*
harina Wilhelmina Andersson
"Mina"

with
Lovisa Andersson

m. 2. *(1861)*
Anna Eleonora Charlotta von Sydow

e
er
ren

Knut
Wallenberg
(1853–1938)
m. *(1878)*
Alice Nickelsen

two
children

Gustaf
Wallenberg
(1863–1947)
envoyé
m.
Annie Adelsköld

Marcus
Wallenberg sr
(1864–1943)
"Häradshövdingen"
(the "District Judge")
m. Amalia
Hagdahl

twelve
further
children

Raoul
Oscar
Wallenberg
(1888–1912)

Jacob
Wallenberg
(1892–1980)
"Jajsa"

Marcus
Wallenberg jr
(1899–1982)
"Dodde"
m. 1.
Dorothy McKay
m. 2.
Marianne De Geer af Leufsta

four
further
children

AOUL
LENBERG
912–?)

Peder
Wallenberg
(1935–)

Marc
Wallenberg
(1924–71)
"Boy-boy"
m.
Olga Wehtje

Peter
Wallenberg
(1926–)
"Pirre"
m. Suzanne
Grevillius

Ann-Marie
(1929–)

Marcus
en **Wallenberg**
(1956–)
"Husky"

Axel
Wallenberg
(1958–2011)
"Wawa"

Mariana
(1964–)

Caroline
(1968–)

Jacob
Wallenberg
(1956–)

Andrea
(1957–)

Peter
Wallenberg jr
(1959–)
"Poker"

INDEX

INGRID CARLBERG is a Swedish author and journalist. Her book about the life and fate of Raoul Wallenberg was awarded the prestigious August Prize for non-fiction, as also the Swedish Academy's Axel Hirsch Prize for a "biography of considerable artistic and cultural merit". Carlberg worked at the Swedish daily newspaper *Dagens Nyheter* from 1990 to 2010, as an investigative and features journalist. She has an honorary doctorate from Uppsala University, awarded for her book *The Pill: A Tale of Doctors and Depression, Freud and Researchers, People and Markets* about the history of anti-depressants. *The Pill* won four awards including the Guldspaden for the best work of investigative journalism, and was nominated for the August Prize.

EBBA SEGERBERG has translated works from Swedish by John Ajvide Lindqvist, Kjell Westö and Henning Mankell. She is Director of Communications in Arts & Sciences at Washington University in St Louis.

BUDAPEST
1944

Modern place names are in brackets where they differ from those in 1944.

0   1

kilometre

*R ó z s a -
d o m b*

Budakeszi út

Olasz fasor (Szilágyi Erzsébet fasor)

Retek   utca

Ostrom u.

Városmajor utca

S v á b h e g y

Raoul
Wallenberg's
residence (1)

German legation

Úri utca

Countess Nákó's villa an
Per Anger's secret apart

V á r h e g y

Prince Eszterh
palace

Tárnok u.

Attila út

Krisztina körút

Hum. dept.
(branch office)

Tigris u.

Dezső u.

Raoul
Wallenberg's
residence (2)

Gömbös Gyula út (Alkotás utca)